Emerging Technologies in Wireless Ad-hoc Networks:

Applications and Future Development

Raul Aquino-Santos
University of Colima, Mexico

Víctor Rangel-Licea
National Autonomous University of Mexico, Mexico

Arthur Edwards-Block
University of Colima, México

A volume in the Advances in Wireless Technologies and Telecommunication (AWTT) Book Series

Director of Editorial Content: Kristin Klinger
Director of Book Publications: Julia Mosemann
Acquisitions Editor: Lindsay Johnston
Development Editor: Joel Gamon
Typesetter: Deanna Jo Zombro
Production Editor: Jamie Snavely
Cover Design: Lisa Tosheff

Published in the United States of America by
Information Science Reference (an imprint of IGI Global)
701 E. Chocolate Avenue
Hershey PA 17033
Tel: 717-533-8845
Fax: 717-533-8661
E-mail: cust@igi-global.com
Web site: http://www.igi-global.com

Library of Congress Cataloging-in-Publication Data

Emerging technologies in wireless ad-hoc networks: applications and future development / Raul Aquino Santos, Victor Rangel Licea, and Arthur Edwards Block, editors.
p. cm.
Includes bibliographical references and index.
Summary: This book provides the rationale, state-of-the-art studies and practical applications, proof-of-concepts, experimental studies, and future development on the use of emerging technologies in wireless ad-hoc networks -- Provided by publisher.
ISBN 978-1-60960-027-3 (hardcover) -- ISBN 978-1-60960-029-7 (ebook) 1. Ad hoc networks (Computer networks) I. Aquino Santos, Raul, 1965- II. Rangel Licea, Victor, 1972- III. Block, Arthur Edwards, 1957-
TK5105.77.E44 2011
004.6'8--dc22
2010049838

This book is published in the IGI Global book series Advances in Wireless Technologies and Telecommunication (AWTT) (ISSN: 2327-3305; eISSN: 2327-3313)

British Cataloguing in Publication Data
A Cataloguing in Publication record for this book is available from the British Library.

Advances in Wireless Technologies and Telecommunication (AWTT) Book Series

Xiaoge Xu
The University of Nottingham Ningbo China

ISSN: 2327-3305
EISSN: 2327-3313

Mission

The wireless computing industry is constantly evolving, redesigning the ways in which individuals share information. Wireless technology and telecommunication remain one of the most important technologies in business organizations. The utilization of these technologies has enhanced business efficiency by enabling dynamic resources in all aspects of society.

The **Advances in Wireless Technologies and Telecommunication (AWTT) Book Series** aims to provide researchers and academic communities with quality research on the concepts and developments in the wireless technology fields. Developers, engineers, students, research strategists, and IT managers will find this series useful to gain insight into next generation wireless technologies and telecommunication.

Coverage

- Cellular Networks
- Digital Communication
- Global Telecommunications
- Grid Communications
- Mobile Technology
- Mobile Web Services
- Network Management
- Virtual Network Operations
- Wireless Broadband
- Wireless Sensor Networks

IGI Global is currently accepting manuscripts for publication within this series. To submit a proposal for a volume in this series, please contact our Acquisition Editors at Acquisitions@igi-global.com or visit: http://www.igi-global.com/publish/.

The Advances in Wireless Technologies and Telecommunication (AWTT) Book Series (ISSN 2327-3305) is published by IGI Global, 701 E. Chocolate Avenue, Hershey, PA 17033-1240, USA, www.igi-global.com. This series is composed of titles available for purchase individually; each title is edited to be contextually exclusive from any other title within the series. For pricing and ordering information please visit http://www.igi-global.com/book-series/advances-wireless-technologies-telecommunication-awtt/73684. Postmaster: Send all address changes to above address.

Titles in this Series

For a list of additional titles in this series, please visit: www.igi-global.com

Cognitive Radio Technology Applications for Wireless and Mobile Ad Hoc Networks
Natarajan Meghanathan (Jackson State University, USA) and Yenumula B. Reddy (Grambling State University, USA)
Information Science Reference • copyright 2013 • 370pp • H/C (ISBN: 9781466642218) • US $190.00 (our price)

Evolution of Cognitive Networks and Self-Adaptive Communication Systems
Thomas D. Lagkas (University of Western Macedonia, Greece) Panagiotis Sarigiannidis (University of Western Macedonia, Greece) Malamati Louta (University of Western Macedonia, Greece) and Periklis Chatzimisios (Alexander TEI of Thessaloniki, Greece)
Information Science Reference • copyright 2013 • 438pp • H/C (ISBN: 9781466641891) • US $195.00 (our price)

Tools for Mobile Multimedia Programming and Development
D. Tjondronegoro (Queensland University of Technology, Australia)
Information Science Reference • copyright 2013 • 357pp • H/C (ISBN: 9781466640542) • US $190.00 (our price)

Cognitive Radio and Interference Management: Technology and Strategy
Meng-Lin Ku (National Central University, Taiwan, R.O.C.) and Jia-Chin Lin (National Central University, Taiwan, R.O.C.)
Information Science Reference • copyright 2013 • 354pp • H/C (ISBN: 9781466620056) • US $190.00 (our price)

Wireless Radio-Frequency Standards and System Design Advanced Techniques
Gianluca Cornetta (Universidad San Pablo-CEU, Spain) David J. Santos (Universidad San Pablo-CEU, Spain) and Jose Manuel Vazquez (Universidad San Pablo-CEU, Spain)
Engineering Science Reference • copyright 2012 • 422pp • H/C (ISBN: 9781466600836) • US $195.00 (our price)

Femtocell Communications and Technologies Business Opportunities and Deployment Challenges
Rashid A. Saeed (UIA, Malaysia) Bharat S. Chaudhari (International Institute of Information Technology, India) and Rania A. Mokhtar (Sudan University of Science and Technology, Sudan)
Information Science Reference • copyright 2012 • 295pp • H/C (ISBN: 9781466600928) • US $190.00 (our price)

Advanced Communication Protocol Technologies Solutions, Methods, and Applications
Katalin Tarnay (University of Pannonia, Hungary) Gusztáv Adamis (Budapest University of Technology and Economics, Hungary) and Tibor Dulai (University of Pannonia, Hungary)
Information Science Reference • copyright 2011 • 592pp • H/C (ISBN: 9781609607326) • US $195.00 (our price)

Editorial Advisory Board

List of Reviewers

Table of Contents

Foreword xviii

Preface xix

Acknowledgment xxiv

Section 1
Wireless Sensor Networks

Chapter 1
A Survey on Localization in Wireless Sensor Networks 1
Ricardo Marcelín-Jiménez, UAM-Iztapalapa, Mexico
Miguel Ángel Ruiz-Sánchez, UAM-Iztapalapa, Mexico
Mauricio López-Villaseñor, UAM-Iztapalapa, Mexico
Victor M. Ramos-Ramos, UAM-Iztapalapa, Mexico
Carlos E. Moreno-Escobar, UAM-Iztapalapa, Mexico
Manuel E. Ruiz-Sandoval, UAM-Azcapotzalco, Mexico

Chapter 2
Low Power Design Techniques for Wireless Sensor Networks 15
José Aedo, Universidad de Antioquia, Colombia
Natalia Gaviria, Universidad de Antioquia, Colombia
Johnny Aguirre, Universidad de Antioquia, Colombia
Danny Múnera, Universidad de Antioquia, Colombia

Chapter 3
A Forward & Backward Secure Key Management in Wireless Sensor Networks for PCS/SCADA 41
Hani Alzaid, Queensland University of Technology, Australia & King Abdulaziz City for Science and Technology, Saudi Arabia
Dong Gook Park, Sunchon National University, South Korea
Juan Gonzàlez Nieto, Queensland University of Technology, Australia
Colin Boyd, Queensland University of Technology, Australia
Ernest Foo, Queensland University of Technology, Australia

Chapter 10
Key Management Protocols in Mobile Ad Hoc Networks ... 181
Mohamed Elboukhari, University Mohamed Ist, Morocco
Mostafa Azizi, University Mohamed Ist, Morocco
Abdelmalek Azizi, University Mohamed Ist, Morocco & Academy Hassan II of Sciences & Technology, Morocco

Chapter 11
Connectivity and Topology Organization in Ad-Hoc Networks for Service Delivery ... 202
Cesar Vargas-Rosales, Instituto Tecnológico y de Estudios Superiores de Monterrey, Mexico
Sergio Barrientos, Instituto Tecnológico y de Estudios Superiores de Monterrey, Mexico
David Munoz, Instituto Tecnológico y de Estudios Superiores de Monterrey, Mexico
Jose R. Rodriguez, Instituto Tecnológico y de Estudios Superiores de Monterrey, Mexico

Chapter 12
Location Acquisition and Applications in Mobile and Ad-Hoc Environments ... 229
David Muñoz Rodriguez, Instituto Tecnológico y de Estudios Superiores de Monterrey, Mexico
José Ramón Rodríguez Cruz, Instituto Tecnológico y de Estudios Superiores de Monterrey, Mexico
Cesar Vargas Rosales, Instituto Tecnológico y de Estudios Superiores de Monterrey, Mexico
Daniel Elias Muñoz Jimenez, Instituto Tecnológico y de Estudios Superiores de Monterrey, Mexico

Chapter 13
Quality of Service in Wireless Ad Hoc Networks and New Trends ... 254
Sudhir K. Routray, Eritrea Institute of Technology, Eritrea

Section 3
Hybrid Networks

Chapter 14
Challenges of Emerging Technologies in Transportation Systems ... 282
Antonio Guerrero-Ibáñez, University of Colima, México
Pedro Damián-Reyes, University of Colima, México

Chapter 15
IP Mobility Support in Hybrid Wired-Mobile Ad Hoc Networks ... 309
Luis Armando Villaseñor-González, CICESE Research Center, Mexico

Detailed Table of Contents

Foreword xviii

Preface xix

Acknowledgment xxiv

Section 1
Wireless Sensor Networks

Chapter 1
A Survey on Localization in Wireless Sensor Networks 1
Ricardo Marcelín-Jiménez, UAM-Iztapalapa, Mexico
Miguel Ángel Ruiz-Sánchez, UAM-Iztapalapa, Mexico
Mauricio López-Villaseñor, UAM-Iztapalapa, Mexico
Victor M. Ramos-Ramos, UAM-Iztapalapa, Mexico
Carlos E. Moreno-Escobar, UAM-Iztapalapa, Mexico
Manuel E. Ruiz-Sandoval, UAM-Azcapotzalco, Mexico

Localization is a fundamental challenge of wireless sensor networks in many applications because a set of nodes must be aware of individual positions, based only on their own resources, i.e. without the aid of external agents. This problem has been tackled using different approaches that provide good solutions under specific circumstances. Nevertheless, new conditions, including massive node deployment or irregular topologies, call for further study and development.

Chapter 2
Low Power Design Techniques for Wireless Sensor Networks 15
José Aedo, Universidad de Antioquia, Colombia
Natalia Gaviria, Universidad de Antioquia, Colombia
Johnny Aguirre, Universidad de Antioquia, Colombia
Danny Múnera, Universidad de Antioquia, Colombia

WSNs can be applied in several areas for the monitoring and control of variables. In the design process of a WSN, one of the most important design objectives is to minimize the energy required for sensing, signal processing and communication tasks to extend the lifetime of the network. This chapter discuss-

es a broad variety of schemes used to reduce power consumption in WSNs. The design of sensors nodes involves several core aspects, such as supported sensors, the communication interface, applications, the control system and peripherals. Strategies to preserve the energy used by each of these components are discussed. A specific scheme using digital signal processing to reduce power consumption by decreasing the number of transmissions is proposed. The chapter also considers protocol architectures, focusing on link layer, network layer, and cross-layer approaches. Finally, a comparative analysis among the main techniques is presented.

Hani Alzaid, Queensland University of Technology, Australia & King Abdulaziz City for Science and Technology, Saudi Arabia
Dong Gook Park, Sunchon National University, South Korea
Juan Gonzàlez Nieto, Queensland University of Technology, Australia
Colin Boyd, Queensland University of Technology, Australia
Ernest Foo, Queensland University of Technology, Australia

Process Control Systems (PCSs) or Supervisory Control and Data Acquisition (SCADA) systems have recently been added to the already wide collection of wireless sensor network applications. The PCS/SCADA environment is somewhat more amenable to the use of heavy cryptographic mechanisms such as public key cryptography than other sensor application environments. The sensor nodes in this environment, however, are still open to devastating attacks such as node capture, which makes the design of secure key management challenging. This chapter introduces an adversary model with which we can assess key management protocols. It also proposes a key management scheme to defeat node capture attack by offering both forward and backward secrecies. The scheme overcomes the pitfalls of a comparative scheme while being not computationally more expensive.

Leonardo Betancur Agudelo, Universidad Pontificia Bolivariana, Colombia
Andres Navarro Cadavid, Universidad ICESI, Colombia

Nowadays, wireless Body Area Networks (wBAN) have gained more relevance, in particular in the areas of health care, emergencies, ranging, location, domotics and entertainment applications. Regulations and several wireless protocols and standards have appeared in recent years. Some of them, like Bluetooth, ZigBee, Ultra Wide Band (UWB), ECMA368, WiFi, GPRS and mobile applications offer different kinds of solutions for personal area communications. In this chapter, body area network channel modelling will be described; also, a brief description of the applications and state-of-the-art of regulation and standardization processes pertaining to these kinds of networks will be presented. For each topic, the chapter shows not only the main technical characteristics, but also the technical problems and challenges in recent and future research. Finally, the chapter provides an analysis of Body Area Networks, opinions about the future and possible scenarios in the short- and medium-term for the development of standards and applications and their impacts on our daily lives.

Chapter 5
mHealth: Software Development and Wireless Technologies Applications.. 92
Juan Ivan Nieto Hipólito, Autonomous University of Baja California, México
Mabel Vázquez Briseño, Autonomous University of Baja California, México
Humberto Cervantes de Ávila, Autonomous University of Baja California, México
Miguel Enrique Martínez Rosas, Autonomous University of Baja California, México
Oleg Yu Sergiyenko, Autonomous University of Baja California, México

mHealth is a very attractive field for mobile applications developers, but it also involves new challenges that developers of programs intended for standard desktops do not usually face. Hence, the first part of this chapter is devoted to survey the development platforms and languages utilized to develop the associated applications of the mHealth system. mHealth is a communications system that consists of mobile devices for collecting and delivering clinical health data to practitioners, researchers and patients. It is also a tool used in the real-time monitoring of patient vital signs, and direct provision of care. Therefore, the second part of this chapter will focuses on the survey of wireless technologies envisioned for use in the mHealth system.

Chapter 6
Wireless Sensor Networks (WSN) Applied in Agriculture.. 115
Miguel Enrique Martínez-Rosas, Universidad Autónoma de Baja California, México
Humberto Cervantes De Ávila, Universidad Autónoma de Baja California, México
Juan Iván Nieto Hipólito, Universidad Autónoma de Baja California, México
José Rosario Gallardo López, University of Ottawa, Canada

This chapter presents an overview of recent developments, challenges and opportunities related to the application of wireless sensor networks (WSN) in agriculture. The material presented here is introductory in nature and has been designed to be useful for students starting to work in the field of WSN and for researchers looking for state-of-the-art information in general or specific details related to their practical application in agriculture.

Chapter 7
Wireless Data Acquisition System for Greenhouses... 136
Jaime Ortegón Aguilar, Universidad de Quintana Roo, México
Javier Vázquez Castillo, Universidad de Quintana Roo, México
Freddy Chan Puc, Universidad de Quintana Roo, México
Alejandro Castillo Atoche, Universidad Autónoma de Yucatán, México
Mayra Palomino Cardeña, Universidad de Quintana Roo, México
César Rosado Villanueva, Universidad de Quintana Roo, México

This chapter presents a novel wireless data acquisition system. The system has been designed to take advantage of inexpensive robotics systems like Lego NXT, which establishes a new paradigm in the wireless ad-hoc networks field. The system architecture can record data from different variables in greenhouse environments. These wireless systems employ wireless access points (WAPs) and wireless-fidelity (Wi-Fi) adapter modules for data acquisition that sample the environment. The measurements

data are transmitted to a central station or inclusive to another different node. The acquisition system was designed and adapted to be used in greenhouses located in Quintana Roo, Mexico, where the typical relevant variables are temperature, luminosity and humidity. The developed system uses virtual instrumentation to measure and record environmental variables. The proposed implementation uses commercial data acquisition boards and sensors to gather data, which are processed and visualized with the LabVIEW-based software.

Section 2
Wireless Ad Hoc Networks

Chapter 8
Power Aware Routing in Wireless Mobile Ad Hoc Networks 149
G. Varaprasad, B.M.S. College of Engineering, India

Wireless mobile ad hoc networks are gaining importance because of their flexibility, mobility, and ability to work with a limited infrastructure. If the battery of a node is drained out, then it cannot communicate with other nodes and the number of dead nodes makes the network partition. In order to overcome the network partition problem, this chapter presents different routing algorithms for wireless mobile ad hoc networks. Different routing algorithms use different metrics, namely transmission power, residual battery capacity and noncritical nodes to forward data packets from the source to destination. Minimum total transmission power routing uses the transmission power as metric to forward the packets but it cannot increase the lifetimes of the node and network. In conditional max-min battery capacity routing, it increases network lifetime and reduces power consumption over the network. Noncritical nodes with more residual battery capacity based routing models will increase the network lifetime and network throughput.

Chapter 9
Network Address Management in MANETs Using an Ant Colony Metaphor.................................. 162
Alvaro Pachón, Universidad Icesi, Colombia
Juan M. Madrid, Universidad Icesi, Colombia

Address management is a critical network process, since any node wishing to join a network must first obtain an address. Network address management in a mobile ad-hoc network (MANET) is a particular challenge due to the unique operating conditions of such networks, their dynamic topology, and the events that take place inside them. This chapter presents a proposal for solving the address management problem in a MANET by applying the self-organization and emergency principles governing the behavior of social insect colonies, particularly ant colonies.

Chapter 10
Key Management Protocols in Mobile Ad Hoc Networks 181
Mohamed Elboukhari, University Mohamed Ist, Morocco
Mostafa Azizi, University Mohamed Ist, Morocco
Abdelmalek Azizi, University Mohamed Ist, Morocco & Academy Hassan II of Sciences & Technology, Morocco

Mobile ad hoc networks (MANETs) have received tremendous attention in recent years because of their self-organization and self-maintenance capabilities. MANETs are networks that do not have an underlying fixed infrastructure. However, these networks tend to be vulnerable to a number of attacks. They don't obey a centralized network management functionality; furthermore, the network topology changes dynamically. Therefore, security has become a primary concern in MANETs. The major problem in providing security services in such networks is how to manage cryptography keys, making key management a central component in MANETs. This chapter gives an overview of security in this kind of network and presents a number of MANETs key management protocols according to recent literature.

Chapter 11
Connectivity and Topology Organization in Ad-Hoc Networks for Service Delivery 202
Cesar Vargas-Rosales, Instituto Tecnológico y de Estudios Superiores de Monterrey, Mexico
Sergio Barrientos, Instituto Tecnológico y de Estudios Superiores de Monterrey, Mexico
David Munoz, Instituto Tecnológico y de Estudios Superiores de Monterrey, Mexico
Jose R. Rodriguez, Instituto Tecnológico y de Estudios Superiores de Monterrey, Mexico

This chapter introduces the concept of connectivity and robustness of a mobile ad-hoc network as a function of the node density and coverage radius. It presents an elementary analytical model based on the spatial Poisson process to formulate the connectivity problem as the computation of the existence of wireless links forming paths obtained by Dijkstra's shortest path algorithm. It also introduces a simple clustering strategy that starts forming groups based on one-hop distance and then adjust the coverage radius of the nodes in order to decrease the interference, processing load and isolated nodes in the network. It includes results of scenarios with different robustness of origin-destination pairs and number of clusters and shows the benefits of using the introduced policies.

Chapter 12
Location Acquisition and Applications in Mobile and Ad-Hoc Environments 229
David Muñoz Rodriguez, Instituto Tecnológico y de Estudios Superiores de Monterrey, Mexico
José Ramón Rodríguez Cruz, Instituto Tecnológico y de Estudios Superiores de Monterrey, Mexico
Cesar Vargas Rosales, Instituto Tecnológico y de Estudios Superiores de Monterrey, Mexico
Daniel Elias Muñoz Jimenez, Instituto Tecnológico y de Estudios Superiores de Monterrey, Mexico

This chapter addresses the relevance of location information as an important resource that supports other applications. This information is important for better network planning, development of new location-based services, fast deployment of assistance services, and support of surveillance and safety regulations, among others. Accuracy of location acquisition processes is an important factor because the potential for multiple new location-based services depends on it. However, noise is always present at least in two forms. Measurements taken with electronic instruments are inherently noisy and estimation algorithms introduce noise of their own in the assumption process. For this reason, this chapter explores several methods and techniques. A well- balanced solution should take into account the compromise between accuracy and delay and/or complexity. Many solutions have been proposed for new needs and new applications which demand more timely and accurate position locations of users or objects.

Chapter 13
Quality of Service in Wireless Ad Hoc Networks and New Trends 254
Sudhir K. Routray, Eritrea Institute of Technology, Eritrea

This chapter introduces basic needs of quality of service (QoS) of RF ad hoc networks (mainly wireless), presents the main metrics of quality of service and the QoS effects on overall performance, and briefly discusses quality of service of wireless systems with respect to the upcoming new technologies like 3GPP LTE and the role of WLAN, while representing network QoS improvement and optimization tools and their successful applications in performance analysis. The chapter focuses on IEEE 802.11e, the main revision of the 802.11 for better QoS provisioning, as well as the coordination between planning and the performance of systems for better QoS. Additionally, it addresses the current and new trends of QoS stuff for different cellular networks and their impact on the QoS of ad-hoc networks. The chapter also explores new trends of QoS of emerging networks like the WiMAX and 4G and looks to the probable hybrid networks of the future and their QoS aspects.

Section 3
Hybrid Networks

Chapter 14
Challenges of Emerging Technologies in Transportation Systems.. 282
Antonio Guerrero-Ibáñez, University of Colima, México
Pedro Damián-Reyes, University of Colima, México

Nowadays, the number of vehicles and the need for transportation is growing quickly. There are more vehicles on the roads driving more kilometers. The road networks in major cities are not sufficient to cater for the current traffic demands due to the size of roads available. As a result, the modern society is facing more traffic jams, higher fuel bills and the increase of CO_2 emissions. It is imperative to improve the safety and efficiency of transportation. Developing a sustainable transportation system requires a better use of existing infrastructure and the application of emerging technologies. This chapter gives the readers a global vision of the traffic and transportation issues and how emerging technologies such as wireless, sensing, cellular and computing technologies contribute to the solution of transportation problems in all cities of the world.

Chapter 15
IP Mobility Support in Hybrid Wired-Mobile Ad Hoc Networks 309
Luis Armando Villaseñor-González, CICESE Research Center, Mexico

Mobile ad hoc networks (MANETs) make use of a distributed routing mechanism to support connectivity between nodes within the ad hoc network. A wireless ad hoc network can be deployed for multiple applications, such as extending the coverage of wire based networks, where interworking is achieved via wireless access routers. However, the implementation of a hybrid (i.e. wired and wireless) network is not straightforward and several issues must be solved for these types of deployments to become a reality. One concern is related to terminal mobility while preserving ongoing communication sessions

over IP networks; as a mobile node moves from one subnetwork to a new subnetwork, a mobility protocol (e.g. Mobile IP) is required for the mobile node to preserve a communication session without having to reestablish the session with a correspondent node. This issue is more complex in a hybrid network where the wireless domain is composed of a mobile ad hoc network (MANET). For instance, MANET routing protocols usually do not account for the connectivity toward a wired network, such as the Internet, via a single or multiple access routers. As a result, there are multiple routing issues that must be taken into consideration to support interconnectivity between nodes located in a hybrid network topology. The main contribution of this work is to present a review on the state of the art of IP mobility support for hybrid wired–MANETs and discuss some of the relevant issues in this area. In addition, two case studies are presented where macromobility (e.g. Mobile IP) and micromobility (Mobile-IP – HAWAII) protocols are implemented to support IP mobility on hybrid networks.

Chapter 16
Game Theory for Resource Allocation in Wireless Networks..335
Danda B. Rawat, Old Dominion University, USA
Chandra Bajracharya, Old Dominion University, USA
Gongjun Yan, Old Dominion University, USA

Wireless technologies and devices are becoming increasingly ubiquitous in modern society. Wireless resources are natural and fixed, whereas wireless technologies and devices are increasing day-by-day, resulting in spectrum scarcity. As a consequence, efficient use of limited wireless resources has become an issue of vital importance in wireless systems. As demand increases, management of limited wireless resources for optimal allocation becomes crucial. Optimal allocation of limited wireless resources results in quick and reliable dissemination of information to larger service areas. Recently, game theory has emerged as an efficient tool to help optimally allocate wireless resources. Game theory is an optimization technique based on strategic situations and decision-making, and has found its application in numerous fields. The first part of this chapter presents a review of game theory and its application in resource allocation at different layers of the protocol stack of the network model. As shown by a recent study, static assignment of frequency spectrum by governmental bodies, such as FCC (Federal Communications Commission) in the United States, is inefficient since the licensed systems do not always fully utilize their frequency bands. In such a scenario, unlicensed secondary (cognitive radio) users can identify the idle spectrum bands and use them opportunistically. In order to access the licensed spectrum dynamically and opportunistically, the dynamic spectrum access functionality needs to be incorporated in the next generation (XG) wireless networks. Different game theory approaches for dynamic spectrum access are discussed in the second part of the chapter.

Compilation of References...353

About the Contributors...377

Index...387

Foreword

This book has been written by an enthusiastic team of researchers to help those who are interested in using ad-hoc networks and their applications to organize nodes on the fly. The ideas and methods discussed are "state of the art" and well respected internationally. Ad-hoc networks promise to allow us to evolve toward communications systems that are properly compatible with the natural behavior of humans.

Billing aside, on the way to the "Global Village," there are perhaps only two serious challenges. One is power, for mobility on a wire cannot be truly nomadic. Ad-hoc helps us here for it concludes to portable, inter-vehicular and maximal life wireless sensing, all of which are tending to low power.

The second serious challenge is how to make a set of nodes self organizing, and this is the domain of ad-hoc networks. This is the work of the authors in this volume. It can be argued that in the absence of the infrastructure provided by the cellular air interface or wired, only self organizing networks using ad-hoc techniques offer the robustness and converged routing necessary to deal with mobile nodes.

For the most part, wireless communications is still very much an extension to fixed networks and most devices simply map a fixed infrastructure distorted by a little mobility. Nevertheless, the three great drivers of multimedia, global positioning and license free short range radio have the industry well motivated toward people centric applications. Ad-hoc is highly likely to enable the next "killer-app" and is therefore very popular in the research of broadband use.

Wireless sensing is also covered in this book. A swarm of bees, a flock of birds and a shoal of fish are all examples of natural ad-hoc networks with low bandwidth and all of these provide clues to the use of such protocols in the "intelligent dust" theme for wireless sensor networks.

For over twenty years I have seen communications evolving towards humans. In fact, Cellular Mobile is now so pervasive that many people are rarely more than a few centimeters away from the technology. Ad-hoc networks offer fresh possibilities on top of this most useful of our endeavors.

Rob Edwards PhD SMIEE, MIET
Centre for Mobile Communications Research
Loughborough University, UK

Preface

The need to transfer increasing amounts of data in a formidable number of environments in a flexible and reliable way has resulted in the exponential growth of wireless networks. The expanded use of wireless networks has led to significant improvements in digital and RF circuits, new large-scale circuit integration, and other miniaturization technologies that make portable radio equipment smaller, cheaper, and more reliable. Wireless Local Area Networks (WLANs) represent flexible data communications systems that can be implemented as an extension to or as an alternative for a wired LAN. Using a form of electromagnetic radiation as the network medium, most commonly in the form of radio waves, wireless LANs transmit and receive data over air, thus minimizing the need for wired connections (cables). Wireless LANs offer the advantage of combining data connectivity with user mobility. By combining mobile devices with wireless communications technologies, the vision of being connected at anytime and anywhere is quickly becoming a reality. The use of ubiquitous systems and technologies is very close on the horizon.

Whereas today's expensive wireless infrastructure depends on centrally deployed hub and one hop stations, mobile ad hoc networks consist of devices that autonomously self-organize in networks. In ad hoc networks, many individual devices must work together seamlessly to make a network function correctly. The operation of so many devices that must work collaboratively while dynamically adjusting to a quickly changing topology is what makes ad hoc wireless networking so difficult to realize.

The many physical and economic limitations of wireless networks also represent important challenges. The large degree of freedom and their self-organizing capabilities make ad-hoc networks completely different from any other networking solution. For the first time, users have the opportunity to create their own networks, which can be deployed with more ease and at less cost than convention cabled networks. In short, difficulties related to the development of technologies and their subsequent deployment pale in comparison to the potential rewards.

Ad-hoc networks represent a key step in the evolution of wireless networks. However, they inherit the traditional limitations of wireless and mobile communications, including the efficient use and allocation of bandwidth resources, energy consumption and coverage.

A Mobile Ad Hoc Network (MANET) is formed by a collection of mobile nodes which communicate using a wireless medium. Additionally, a MANET can be defined as an autonomous network with no single point of coordination. These types of networks are characterized by their dynamic topologies, limited bandwidth and restricted power. Each individual mobile node in a MANET can potentially transmit information using a direct link or a multi-hop link to propagate packets to a destination node. As a result, all the mobile nodes in a MANET must implement a single routing strategy. Consequently, the design of fast and efficient routing protocols is essential to insure the efficient performance of mobile ad hoc networks.

Mobile nodes in a MANET do not require a specific hierarchical sub-network addressing scheme, unlike wired networks that require a specific IP address for each member of a specific sub-network. As a result, MANETs and wired networks face different routing issues related to how to provide the necessary connectivity between nodes. Whereas routing in conventional networks is carried out by assigning specific IP addresses, there is no previously established routing information for nodes within a MANET. This is precisely because IP addresses function based on the premise of a set, stable and static connection. MANETS, on the other hand, must work precisely in environments that are highly dynamic and mobile, making assigning specific addresses extremely challenging. In order to provide connectivity in dynamically changing topologies, nodes within MANETs usually have to forward routing information to other nodes outside the MANET, and there is usually no implicit support for the connectivity between mobile nodes and a wired network via an access router (AR).

Recent advances in micro-electro-mechanical systems (MEMS) technology have made the deployment of wireless sensor nodes a reality, in part, because they are small, inexpensive and energy efficient. Each node of a sensor network consists of three basic subsystems: a sensor subsystem to monitor local environment parameters, a processing subsystem to provide computation support to the node, and a communication subsystem to provide wireless communications to exchange information with neighboring nodes. Because each individual sensor node can only cover a relatively limited area, it needs to be connected with other nodes in a coordinated fashion to form a sensor network (SN), which can provide large amounts of detailed information about a given geographic area.

Sensors are devices that produce a measurable response to a change in a physical condition like temperature and pressure. Basically, each sensor node is comprised of a sensing, processing, transmission and power unit. The processing unit is responsible for collecting and processing signals transmitted from sensors and forwarding them to the network. The transmission unit provides the signal transfer medium from sensors to the exterior world or computer network. It also has a communication mechanism to establish and maintain the wireless sensor network, which is usually ad-hoc. The power supply unit consists of a battery and a dc-dc converter that powers the node.

Sensor networks are generally deployed into an unplanned infrastructure where there is no a priori knowledge of their specific location. The resulting problem of estimating the spatial coordinates of the node is referred to as location. Most of the proposed localization techniques today depend on recursive trilateration/multilateration techniques.

Consequently, a wireless sensor network (WSN) can be described as a collection of intercommunicated wireless sensor nodes which coordinate to perform a specific action. Unlike traditional wireless networks, WSNs depend on dense deployment and coordination to carry out their task. Wireless sensor nodes measure conditions in the environment surrounding them and then transform these measurements into signals that can be processed to reveal specific information about phenomena located within a coverage area around these sensor nodes.

WSNs have a variety of applications. Examples include environmental monitoring –which involves monitoring air, soil and water, condition-based maintenance, habitat monitoring (determining the plant and animal species population and behavior), seismic detection, military surveillance, inventory tracking, smart spaces, and many more. Despite their many diverse applications, WSNs pose a number of unique technical challenges due to the following factors: fault tolerance (robustness), scalability, production costs, operating environment, sensor network topology, hardware constraint, transmission media and power consumption.

To date, the ZigBee Alliance has developed a communication standard for WSNs to support low-cost, low-power consumption, two-way wireless communications. Solutions adopting the ZigBee standard will be embedded in consumer electronics, home and building automation, industrial controls, PC peripherals, medical sensor applications, toys and games.

The enormous cost of providing health care to patients with chronic conditions requires new strategies to more efficiently provide monitoring and support in a remote, distributed, and noninvasive atmosphere. Wireless electromechanical sensors allow the internal biologically-controlled mega-network, governed by the central nervous system, to communicate with an external body sensor network by means of wireless communication technology. This is particularly significant because it permits internal biological functions to be communicated to a monitoring center, where a real-time diagnosis can be made and an intervention plan can be developed. The term "biologically-controlled mega-network" refers to the central nervous system and the proper execution of complex biological systems, which depends on the intricate coordination of a large number of events and their participating components.

Diverse projects around the world are trying to improve the quality of medical attention by providing remote medical monitoring. These projects are currently developing mobile monitoring systems and integrating remote monitoring into their healthcare protocols, in order to provide expanded healthcare services for persons who require monitoring and follow-up, but do not require immediate medical intervention or hospitalization.

The importance of monitoring patient health is significant in terms of prevention, particularly if the human and economic costs of early detection can reduce suffering and medical costs. The early diagnosis and treatment of a variety of diseases can radically alter healthcare alternatives or medical treatments. This is particularly true with illnesses such as cardiovascular disease or diabetes. In the case of cardiovascular disease, 4% of the population over 60 and more than 9% of persons over 80 years of age have arrhythmias, or abnormal heart rates, which require occasional diminutive electrical shocks applied to the heart. Sensors can identify at-risk patients by monitoring and transmitting their real-time cardiac rhythms to medical professionals who can subsequently determine whether or not they require a pacemaker to assist establish and maintain normal sinus rhythm.

Diabetes is an increasingly significant progressive chronic disease that affects several vital organs. The number of people diagnosed in the United States with diabetes has increased dramatically the last 40 years, mainly due to obesity. Presently, approximately 24,000 people become blind and 56,000 people suffer renal failure because of diabetes every year in the United States. Once diagnosed, patients require constant monitoring of their blood glucose levels. Type II diabetes patients often do not require insulin to effectively manage this disease. These patients rely on effective management protocols requiring periodic blood samples at specified intervals, as well as dietary restrictions, weight loss in the case of obese patients, and exercise. The management of diabetes generally requires motivation and adherence to a new lifestyle that, in large part, depends on changing habits and behaviors. Body sensor networks used to manage diabetes will one day involve implanted sensors, not only to monitor patient glucose levels, but to administer insulin in a timely fashion. In sum, the abovementioned chronic diseases exemplify the need for biochemical and physiological continuous monitoring.

Future applications in agriculture will extensively employ wireless sensor networks that function in real time in conjunction with communications systems, mechanical actuators, and even robots to monitor and intervene in crop cultivation. A WSN permits remote monitoring of many parameters, depending on the type of sensors used and the coverage area. This type of network consists of a large number of sensor nodes that are wirelessly connected to each other, to electromechanical devices, and to a communications network, all of which form a triad to monitor and control crop development. Generally, each node of a WSN consists of sensors and/or actuators. Sensors are characterized by their limited memory and computation capacities, but one advantage of sensors is that they require little power to perform their functions. Wireless sensor networks consisting of many nodes are currently being used in densely populated large scale areas. WSNs can have homogenous structures, where all nodes present similar characteristics, or heterogeneous structures, where some nodes are more powerful than others or are differentiated by physical characteristics, including the type of battery or antenna the individual nodes use, or whether specific nodes are static or dynamic.

Future developments in automobile manufacturing will also include new communication technologies. The major goals are to provide increased automotive safety, to achieve smooth traffic flow on the roads, and to improve passenger convenience by providing them with information and entertainment. In order to avoid communication costs and guarantee the low delays required for the exchange of safety related data between cars, inter-vehicle communication (IVC) systems based on wireless ad-hoc networks represent a promising solution for future road communication scenarios. IVC allows Vehicles to organize themselves locally in ad-hoc networks without any pre-installed infrastructure. Communication in future IVC systems will not be restricted to neighbored vehicles travelling within the radio transmission range, as in typical wireless scenarios, the IVC system will also provide multi-hop communication capabilities by using "relay" vehicles that are travelling between the sender and receiver. Vehicles between source-destination act as intermediates vehicles, relaying the data to the receiver. As a result, the multi-hop capability of the IVC system significantly increases the virtual communication range, as it enables communication with more distance vehicles.

Current developments in wireless ad hoc routing protocols have fuelled the development of hybrid networks which allow the integration of MANETs to the Internet. There is currently an intrinsic problem related to mobility in computer data networks which implement the IP network protocol stack. This issue is related to the fact that an IP address is commonly used as the node's identifier and locator within a sub-network. When a node changes its point of attachment to the network (e.g. the mobile node moves to a different sub-network) the assigned IP address can no longer be used as a locator for the node in the new sub-network. To address this issue, different proposals such as the Mobile IP mechanism have been developed to support macro-mobility (i.e. mobility between different administrative domains). There are presently two important proposals to provide macro-mobility support for the IPv4 and IPv6 network protocol stacks, namely mobile IPv4 (MIPv4) and mobile IPv6 (MIPv6). It should be noted that the IPv6 protocol stack supports mobility, but this mechanism is only effective in wireless networks where the mobile nodes are one-hop away from the access router.

This book is organized as follows:

- Section I describes theory and application of wireless sensor networks;
- Section II analyses the operation and application of wireless ad hoc networks
- Section III discusses how to integrate traditional wired infrastructure and ad hoc networks into hybrid networks.

In more detail:

Section 1 includes chapters titled: *A Survey on Location in Wireless Sensor Networks, Low Power Design Techniques for Wireless Sensor Networks, A Forward and Backward Secure Key Management* *in Wireless Sensor Networks for PCS/SCADA, Body Area Networks: Channels Models and Applications in Wireless Sensor Networks, m: Health Software Development and Wireless Technologies Applications, Wireless Sensor Networks (WSN) Applied in Agriculture and Wireless Data Acquisition System for Greenhouses*.

Section 2 includes: *Power Aware Routing in Wireless Mobile Ad hoc Networks, Network Address Management in MANET Using an Ant Colony Metaphor, Key Management Protocols in Mobile Ad hoc Networks, Connectivity and Topology Organization in Ad-hoc Networks for Service Delivery, Location Acquisition and Applications in Mobile Ad hoc Networks, and Quality of Service in Wireless Ad-hoc and New Trends*.

Section 3 includes: *Challenges of Emerging Technologies in Transportation Systems, IP Mobility Support in Hybrid Wired Mobile Ad hoc Networks and Game Theory for Resource Allocation in Wireless Networks*.

Raúl Aquino Santos
University of Colima, Mexico

Victor Rangel Licea
National Autonomous University of Mexico, Mexico

Arthur Edwards Block
University of Colima, Mexico

Acknowledgment

Editors would like to thank the National Council of Science and Technology in Mexico for their support of the project "Development of a technological platforms for wireless sensor networks," under the grants numbers 129250, 129656, 129351 and 140916.

This work was supported by DGAPA, National Autonomous University of Mexico (UNAM) under Grant PAPIIT IN108910, PAPIME PE 103807 and CONACYT 105279.

Raúl Aquino Santos
University of Colima, Mexico

Victor Rangel Licea
National Autonomous University of Mexico, Mexico

Arthur Edwards Block
University of Colima, Mexico

Section 1
Wireless Sensor Networks

Chapter 1
A Survey on Localization in Wireless Sensor Networks

Ricardo Marcelín-Jiménez
UAM-Iztapalapa, Mexico

Miguel Ángel Ruiz-Sánchez
UAM-Iztapalapa, Mexico

Mauricio López-Villaseñor
UAM-Iztapalapa, Mexico

Victor M. Ramos-Ramos
UAM-Iztapalapa, Mexico

Carlos E. Moreno-Escobar
UAM-Iztapalapa, Mexico

Manuel E. Ruiz-Sandoval
UAM-Azcapotzalco, Mexico

ABSTRACT

Localization is a fundamental challenge of wireless sensor networks in many applications because a set of nodes must be aware of individual positions, based only on their own resources, i.e. without the aid of external agents. This problem has been tackled using different approaches that provide good solutions under specific circumstances. Nevertheless, new conditions, including massive node deployment or irregular topologies, call for further study and development.

INTRODUCTION

A Wireless Sensor Network (WSN) is essentially a large number of small sensing self-powered nodes which gather information and communicate in a wireless fashion, with a common end goal. For a general review of the characteristics, applications and communication protocols in WSNs, see surveys in Akyildiz, Su, Sankarasubramaniam and Cayirci (2002) and Yick, Mukherjee and Ghosal (2008).

DOI: 10.4018/978-1-60960-027-3.ch001

Wireless Sensor Networks represent an emerging technology with a wide spectrum of potential applications and, at the same time, they are also a source of challenging problems. One such challenging problem is how to accurately find the location of each sensor node. Node localization is important because it can enable new WSN applications. For example, with node localization capability, monitoring systems can determine the specific source of a critical event. Node localization capability can also be used to enhance the operation of a WSN. For example, a node can forward packets to its final destination, based solely on the position of the nodes that make up its neighborhood (Marcelín-Jiménez, 2007). This routing strategy fosters local work and limits energy consumption.

To solve the node localization problem, a global positioning system (GPS) may provide a good starting point. Nevertheless, the utilization of a GPS is strongly limited by budgetary constraints and it is not recommended for indoor systems where satellite reception can be poor.

For a small set of nodes, individual positions can be programmed manually. In some other cases, a mobile node exists which is always aware of its position and performs a comprehensive tour across the underlying network in order to inform each node about its particular location. Nevertheless, when nodes are randomly placed, the number of nodes is massive, or a mobile "supervisor" is unfeasible; an automatic procedure is required. Moreover, since node localization is a fundamental operation in WSNs, the solution to the localization problem needs to comply with several attributes including accuracy, efficiency and robustness.

A set of very fine survey papers on localization is: Mao, Fidan and Anderson (2007); Pestana-Leao and Rodríguez-Peralta (2007); Langendoen and Reijers (2003); Patwari (2005). Nevertheless, recent results have arisen which justify revisiting this subject. This chapter focuses on automatic localization procedures, where the solution is built from the information each node has about its surroundings. There is not an external entity with a complete view of the landscape that can help each node know its coordinates. Instead, nodes solve the problem by themselves.

The rest of this chapter includes the following sections: Section THE PROBLEM formally states the subject. There are two main sources of addressing localization: graph theory and optimization; we present both approaches. Throughout the remaining subsections, we will see how these complementary views may be correlated in order to tackle the difficult parts of this problem. We provide a short description of distance measurement techniques. As we will see, obtaining measurements of the distance between each couple of sensor nodes is a necessary condition to find a solution to the node localization problem. Next, we classify solutions to the localization problem into two categories: centralized and distributed. Since measurements have intrinsic noise, we will describe methods that can be used to determine the errors bounds associated to the localization problem. We end this section by reviewing the necessary conditions to find a unique solution to the localization problem. When such conditions are not satisfied, the problem turns to be NP-complete. Section ALTERNATIVES gathers the most important results and new trends on the subject. We also point out some of the emerging approaches to solve the localization problem. Finally, in CONCLUSION we summarize our findings.

THE PROBLEM

Models

Sensors can be deployed on 2D or 3D spaces. For the sake of simplicity, we will limit our exposition to the former case. Nevertheless, we will indicate when a method can be extended to 3D spaces. A great deal of research has been done on the topic of localization in ad-hoc sensor networks

(Ganesan et al., 2002; Hightower & Borriello, 2001). Localization has been addressed using different tools and methods. The initial approaches came from graph theory and optimization theory. In the rest of this section, we will present these complementary views.

From a graph theory viewpoint, a network is modelled by a graph $G=(V,E)$, with an edge between any two nodes that can communicate them directly. Usually, a multi-hop radio network is modelled as a unit disk graph (UDG). In a UDG $G=(V,E)$, there is an edge $\{u,v\}\in E$ if and only if the Euclidean distance between u and v is 1.

An embedding of a graph $G=(V,E)$ in the Euclidean plane is a mapping $f: V\rightarrow\mathbb{R}^2$; that is, every vertex $v_j\in V, j=1,2,\ldots,n$ is mapped to a point $x_j\in\mathbb{R}^2$ in the plane. A realization of a unit disk graph $G=(V,E)$ in the Euclidean plane is an embedding of G such that $\{u,v\}\in E\leftrightarrow d(f(v),f(u))\leq 1$ where d is the Euclidean distance between two points. Therefore, localization consists of the realization of a unit disk graph in the Euclidean plane.

Localization is also seen as an optimization problem. Given a set of measured distances between the nodes that make up the network, we need to estimate the location of each node on a plane, up to rotation and translation, while minimizing the error between the measured distances and the distances resulting from the estimated positions. Designers introduce nodes with fixed and known locations, called *beacons* or *anchors*, in order to help the system settle the reference coordinates.

In a sensor network in R^2 there are two types of nodes: common sensors and anchors. A common sensor j is a node whose position has to be estimated, which is denoted by $x_j\in\mathbb{R}^2, j=1,2,\ldots,n$. In contrast, each anchor k, has a well-known position $a_k\in\mathbb{R}^2$, $k=1,2,\ldots,m$. Let d_{ij} be the Euclidean distance between a pair of common nodes i and j, and let d_{jk} be the Euclidean distance between a common node j and an anchor k.

In many cases, there are unknown pairs of distances, so the pairs of nodes for which mutual distances are known is denoted as $(i,j)\in N_x$ for sensor/sensor and $(j,k)\in N_a$ for sensor/anchor pairs, respectively. The localization problem in $\mathbb{R}^2$ can be stated as: given m anchor locations a_k, $k=1,2,\ldots,m$ and some distance measurements d_{ij}, $(i,j)\in N_x$, d_{jk}, $(j,k)\in N_a$, find x_j, $j=1,2,\ldots,n$, the locations of common sensors, such that (ideally)

$$\left|x_i, x_j\right|^2 = d_{ij}^{\ 2}, \forall\left(i,j\right) \in N_x \tag{1}$$

$$\left|x_j, x_k\right|^2 = d_{jk}^{\ 2}, \forall\left(j,k\right) \in N_a \tag{2}$$

In many instances of the problem, noisy measurements introduce uncertainty in the calculations. Under such conditions, the problem can be reformulated in the following way,

$$Min\{\left|x_i - x_j\right|^2 - d_{ij}^{\ 2}\} \tag{3}$$

$$Min\{\left|x_j - x_k\right|^2 - d_{jk}^{\ 2}\} \tag{4}$$

Notice that anchors help the system to fix an absolute reference. Otherwise, i.e. when there are no anchors at all, the solution shows only relative positions. In other words, the "drawing" of the original network can be rotated or translated. This is shown in Figure 1; Table 1 shows the information associated to the distances between several cities in Mexico.

Solution Methods and Benchmarking

Different techniques have been proposed to *measure the distances* that make up the input set of the localization problem. These techniques can be classified into two main categories: *range-based* and *connectivity-based* (also called range free). The former depends on a physical signal exchanged between two points whose value is a function of the length, or relative position, of the line of sight from transmitter to receiver, e.g.

Figure 1. Left, Solution without absolute references. Right, Solution where anchors are considered

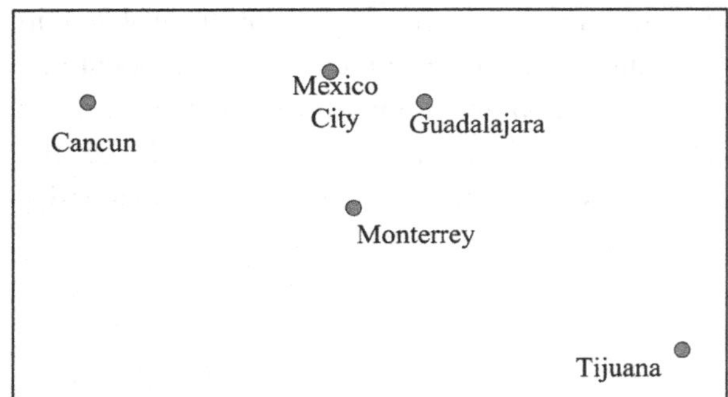

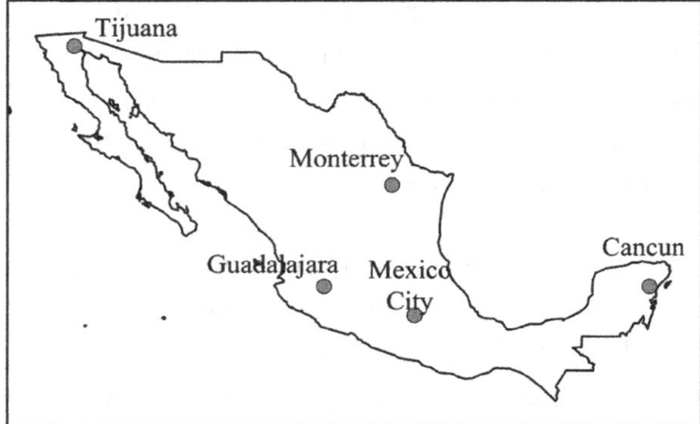

Table 1. Distances between five cities in Mexico

	Mexico City	Monterrey	Guadalajara	Cancún	Tijuana
Mexico City	0	989	480	1779	2880
Monterrey	989	0	777	2382	2388
Guadalajara	480	777	0	2360	2298
Cancún	1779	2382	2360	0	4659
Tijuana	2880	2388	2298	4659	0

Angle of Arrival (AoA), Time of Arrival (ToA), and Received Signal Strength (RSS).

- **Angle of Arrival (AoA)** is a measurement comprising the direction of propagation of a radio-frequency wave incident on an antenna array. In the time domain, techniques are classified into two main categories: those making use of amplitude response (beamforming) and those counting on phase response (phase interferometry). In both cases, accuracy is strongly limited by the antenna's directivity and environmental conditions, such as line of sight loss, shadowing and multipath (Cederval & Moses, 1997; Krim & Viberg, 1996). In order to improve performance, alternative techniques such as super-resolution have been suggested (Roy & Kailath, 1989).
- **Time of Arrival (ToA)** uses an electromagnetic wave whose propagation time is a function of the distance between two points. In one-way trip measurement, this depends on the elapsed time from the moment a given source starts broadcasting a signal to the moment it is received at some destination. In this case, the major challenge comes from the fact that both ends are required to synchronize their local clocks with a very high degree of accuracy. In some applications, a source simultaneously sends an acoustic signal and a radio signal. Knowing that the speed of sound passing through air is much slower than the speed of light (RF) passing through air, the receiver uses the time difference between receiving the RF pulse and the sonic pulse to estimate the propagation time. Alternatively, in round-trip measurements, a single clock at the source is required. Nevertheless, because the destination receives and retransmits the signal back to

the source, it is necessary to know in advance the time it takes this local processing at the "mirror" end. In both cases, unfortunately, measurements are limited by noise, bandwidth, multipath, and line of sight loss. Under these considerations, as in the AOA techniques, super-resolution methods have shown promise (Li & Pahlavan, 2004).

- **Received Signal Strength (RSS)** is a measurement based on electromagnetic signal power, which is known to decline according to a given model, depending on the distance between source and receiver. The receiver knows in advance the initial signal power and, therefore, can calculate the distance as a function of attenuation. This approach can be applied provided the analytical model and the parameters featuring decline are available. The problem with RSS is that each particular settlement or environment may require a revision of the working assumptions. When this description is incomplete, an alternative technique, called RSS profile-based, can be considered. In this context, some sources are set in operation and deployed at fixed positions inside the service region. Next, a map is built recording the received signal power at different points. Evidently, a more detailed map requires a larger number of recording points. In this case, the price to pay is the construction of a database storing the profile of the featured zone (Bahl & Padmanabhan, 2000; Nerguizian, Despins & Affes, 2006).

The down side of range-based techniques is that they require additional hardware that may impact the price of individual nodes. A further disadvantage is that they can be very sensitive to environmental conditions. In contrast, *connectivity-based techniques* depend on the number of hops separating any two nodes. In this case, we assume that two nodes sharing an edge are separated by one distance unit. For both categories, *indirect measurements may be completed using a distributed procedure such as the distance-vector algorithm (DV)*, where each node successively propagates the distances it knows to the different places in the network.

Additionally, most techniques use distance or angle measurements from a fixed set of anchor nodes (Doherty, Ghaoui & Pister, 2001; Savarese, Rabaey & Langendoen, 2002; Savvides, Han & Srivastava, 2001, 2002; Shang, Ruml, Zhang & Frormherz, 2003, 2004) or employ a grid of anchors with known positions (Bulusu, Heidemann & Estrin, 2000; Howard, Matarić & Sukhatme, 2001). Niculescu and Nath (2003) describe the "DV-Hop" and related "DV-Distance" and Euclidean approaches which are quite effective in dense and regular topologies.

Solution methods are classified according to the involved places where calculations are performed. In *centralized methods*, all measurements are gathered at one single point where a global model is built. When the model is solved, each node receives information with its estimated position. The main drawback of centralized methods is the number of exchanged messages, i.e. the communications' complexity may impact the energy budget of the whole system and, consequently, on its life-span. Therefore, centralized methods do not scale up well. In *distributed methods*, on the other side, each node exchanges its local knowledge only with its neighbours, so as to estimate its individual position.

Research on localization methods has produced very good methods that offer excellent performance when the deployed sensors make up a dense and globally uniform network. Among the most relevant works we find MultiDimensional Scaling (MDS) and SemiDefinite Programming (SDP), which are both centralized (initially). MDS is a method from linear programming, while SDP comes from convex optimization. Also, both methods exhibit polynomial complexity on the number of involved operations but, in the worst case, SDP is more expensive than MDS. On the other side, SDP is more robust and less sensitive to noise.

Shang et al. (2003) demonstrates the use of a data analysis technique called "multidimensional scaling" (MDS) in estimating positions of unknown nodes. First, using basic connectivity or distance information, a rough estimate of relative node distances is made. Then, classical MDS (which basically involves using eigenvector decomposition) is used to obtain a relative map of the node positions. Finally, an absolute map is obtained by using the known node positions. This technique works well with few anchors and provides reasonably high connectivity. For instance, for a connectivity level of 12 and 2% anchors, the error is about half the radio range.

MDS works in 2D as well as 3D. It proceeds in three complementary phases. In the first phase, the input data is arranged in a distance matrix. In the second phase, the eigenvalues and eigenvectors of the distance matrix are calculated and positions are estimated based on these results. Although these locations may be accurate relative to one another, the entire map will be arbitrarily rotated and translated relative to the true node positions. In the third phase, the relative map is linearly transformed by using scaling, rotation, and reflection. The goal is to minimize the sum of squared errors among the true locations of the anchors and their transformed positions in the MDS map. Clearly, information about anchors is not considered until the last phase. Localization via MDS has $O(N^3)$ complexity.

SemiDefinite Programming (SDP) is a subfield of convex optimization concerned with the optimization of a linear objective function over the intersection of the cone of positive semidefinite matrices with an affine space. SDP can be efficiently solved by interior point methods. Localization by means of SDP has $O(N^6)$ complexity. Besides, SDP also works in 3D.

An approach closely related to SDP is described in Doherty et. al. (2001). In this work, the proximity constraints between nodes within the 'hearing distance' are modelled as convex constraints. Then, a feasibility problem can be solved by efficient convex programming techniques.

There are also very good distributed methods that provide excellent results under similar instances.

Savarese et al. (2002) present a two-phase algorithm in which the start-up phase involves finding the rough positions of the nodes using a technique similar to the "DV-Hop" approach. The refinement phase improves the accuracy of the estimated positions by performing least squares triangulations using its own estimates and the estimates other nodes its neighbourhood. This method can accurately estimate points within one third of the radio range. the "iterative multilateration" technique proposed by Savvides et al. (2001) yields good results when the number of anchor nodes is high. Most of the nodes that are connected to three or more anchors compute their position by triangulation and upgrade themselves to anchor nodes. Now their position information can also be used by the other common nodes to estimate their positions in subsequent iterations.

Howard et. al. (2001), Priyantha, Miu and Balakrishnan (2001), and Vicaire and Stankovic (2004) have discussed using spring-based heuristics, also called mass relaxation. The mass-spring method is a distributed optimization approach where, for a given network $G(V,E)$, each edge $e=(u,v)\in E$, is regarded as a spring that links two masses placed at nodes u and v, respectively (Vicaire & Stankovic, 2004). It is assumed that the length of the spring, in steady state, equals the measured distance between u and v. If the estimated distance is shorter than the measured distance, the spring pushes both ends away. On the other hand, if the estimated distance is longer than the measured distance, the spring pulls both ends closer. Different schemes evaluate the spring strength in different ways. Nevertheless, all schemes proceed in an iterative process. In each step, nodes are re-located according to the forces acting on them. The process stops when each node reaches equilibrium, i.e. the resulting forces on each node are equal to zero.

It is important to note that when noise and uncertainty are part of the problem, there is no exact solution. Instead, practitioners often choose to solve the problem by approximation. In this context, they may profit from some techniques borrowed from heuristics such as Kannan, Mao and Vucetic (2006).

Independent of the solution, *accuracy* is a major concern and a quality attribute required of all localization methods. Since distance measurements have intrinsic noise, we must determine the error bounds for each particular case of the localization problem. The *Crámer-Rao Lower Bound* (CRLB) can be used to determine these error bounds. These error bounds do not depend on the method, but on the context of the particular case of the problem. Therefore, the CRLB is regarded as a benchmark. Different methods can be compared, based on this approach. Also, CRLB can help determine the moment when an iterative method should be stopped. Savvides, Garber, Adlakha, Moses and Srivastava (2003) derive the CRLB for network localization, expressing the expected error characteristics for an ideal algorithm, and comparing it to the actual error in an algorithm based on multilateration. They draw the important conclusion that the error introduced by the algorithm is just as important as measurement error in assessing end-to-end localization accuracy. Niculescu and Nath (2004) also apply the CRLB to a few general classes of localization algorithms. Patwari and Hero III (2003) developed a Monte-Carlo simulation tool that calculates the CRLB for different settlements. In McGuire, Plataniotis, and Venetsanopoulos (2003), authors discuss the limitations of the Crámer-Rao bound and suggest two alternative methods, developed by Weinstein and Weiss (1988) and Bell, Steinberg, Ephraim, and Van Trees (1997), respectively. They also present the corresponding Monte-Carlo simulations to estimate the Weinstein-Weiss and Ziv-Zakai bounds, as they are known.

Eren et al. (2004), provide a theoretical foundation for network localization in terms of graph rigidity theory. They show that a network has a unique localization if and only if its underlying graph is generically globally rigid. In addition, they show that a certain subclass of globally rigid graphs, trilateration graphs, can be constructed and localized in linear time. Given a set of rigid bars connected by hinges, rigidity theory studies whether these bars can be moved continuously or not. The main idea is that the more connected a graph, the less deformable it becomes. Up to rotations and translations, which are always possible, a minimum number of edges is required to make a "stiff" graph. Suppose, for instance, that four nodes a, b, c and d are connected as shown in Figure 2. In case A, nodes can move independently from each other. In case B, the graph admits only rigid transformations; that is, flips. Finally, in case C, the graph admits only translations and rotations. This is an example of global rigidity.

In graph theory, the problem of finding Euclidean positions for the nodes of a graph is known as the graph realization problem. When distance measurements between nodes have an intrinsic noise or incertitude, global rigidity is necessary, but not sufficient, to solve the problem of graph realization. Under this consideration, Moore, Leonard, Rus and Teller (2004) developed the concept of "Robust Distributed Localization," based on robust quadrilaterals. A graph of this type has four nodes, each of them connected to the others and any three of them make up a triangle. For each triangle, let b its shortest side and è its smallest angle. There is a threshold b_{min}, which is a function of the measurements variability. Based on these parameters, a new condition is defined

$$b \sin 2\theta > b_{min} \tag{5}$$

Figure 2. Condition for global rigidity

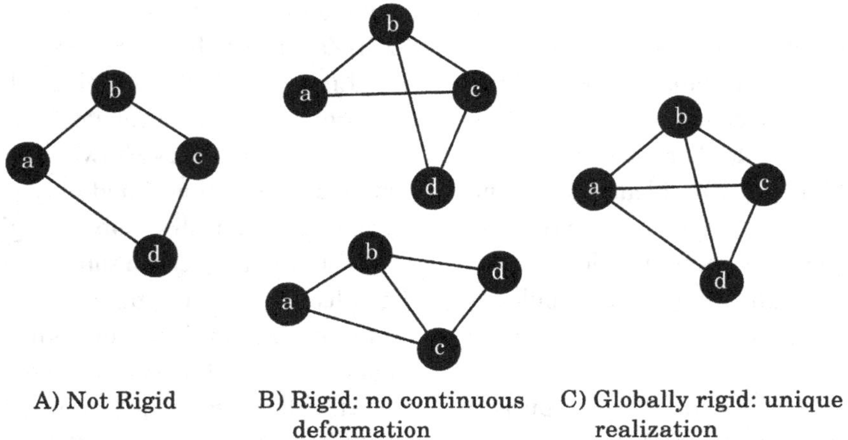

Figure 3. Conditions for a robust quadrilateral

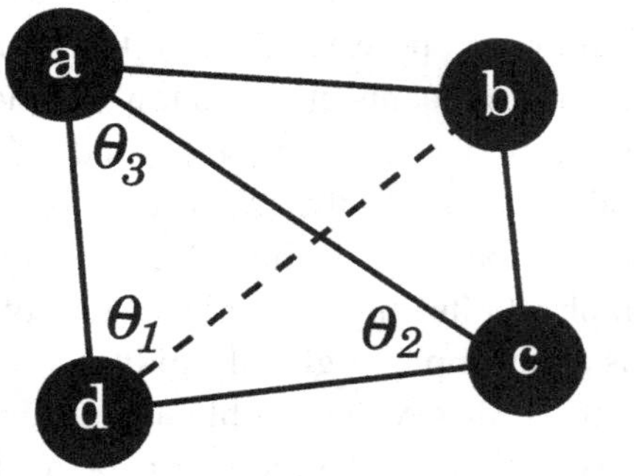

When each of the four triangles complies with this condition, the corresponding nodes form a robust quadrilateral. The idea behind this new construction is to reduce the probability of incorrect localizations due to flip ambiguities that may arise in rigid graphs with noisy measurements.

This work introduces a distributed algorithm, where each node is able to recognize its self-centered cluster, that is, all the robust quadrilaterals it belongs to. Now one cluster is chosen and one of its quadrilaterals is picked up and fixed to start the realization. The remaining quadrilaterals are found by trilateration. When all quadrilaterals have been incorporated, a new cluster sharing quads with the last cluster is chosen. The procedure continues until all clusters have been visited. This approach implies that simple measurement techniques based on hop distances are ruled out. Furthermore, even without noise, each node in the network must have approximately 10 or more degrees before 100% node localization can be attained.

All methods so far considered may show a rather poor performance when the underlying network is sparse. That is, when the network has holes or regions with lower density. There is a set of minimal conditions that guarantee UDG realization. The most important theoretical result on the subject, however, shows that localization is an NP-complete problem for sparse networks (Aspnes, Goldenberg & Yang, 2004).

ALTERNATIVES, REVISITING THE PROBLEM

New trends have been observed after the NP-completeness of the problem. Approximation techniques and heuristics are now being tested. The approach followed by several teams, where the network is seen as a set of homogeneous regions, appears to be promising. In this approach, regions are "stitched" together as in a patchwork, in order to settle each "patch" within a global context. In this new view of the problem, the key issue consists of finding the best way to partition the graph into small and homogeneous sub-graphs that later have to be articulated to render a globally consistent localization.

The idea of dividing the entire network into clusters with homogeneous properties dates back to the work of Awerbuch (1985) on network synchronization. More recently, Peleg (2000) describes different techniques that produce graph covers. All these methods place strong emphasis on the utilization of local resources supporting the cover construction. It is important to note that locally-based covers are robust because they tolerate dynamic node insertion and mobility. Figure 4 shows a WSN (on the left) which is divided into small regions or clusters using the γ-synchronizer (on the right).

Shang and Ruml (2003, 2004) developed an extension of their work on MDS, considering this distributed approach. Here, local clusters with regular topologies are solved separately using MDS, and then subsequently stitched together. This idea of local clusters was also proposed by Čapkun, Hamdi and Hubaux (2001). Similarly, Biswas, Lian, Wang and Ye (2006) divide the network into clusters solved separately using SDP and latter assembled together to produce global coordinates.

Kröller, Fekete, Pfisterer and Fischer (2006) suggest utilizing a family of combinatorial structures called "m-flowers" which can be identified within a given network. The main idea is to "grow" as many flowers as possible wherever the node layout allows these constructions. Immediately, and provided that it is possible, flowers are connected to each other by means of bridge edges. Among the most appealing properties of this method is that it makes it possible to recognize when a given node lies either at the inner or the outer face of a flower petal. Therefore, it is possible to settle the network regions and define the position of a given node with respect to the corresponding boundaries.

Paschalidis and Guo (2007) introduced statistical location. This method relies on a set of anchors, called cluster-heads. It consists of dividing the spanned region into smaller zones. Next, each cluster-head is placed in the middle of a zone. Note that it may be the case that a given zone does not receive a cluster-head. Now, these nodes perform a sequence of measurements to evaluate the RSS for a group of packets coming from a node with an unknown position. It is assumed that these measurements follow a given pdf which is already available, i.e. it has been previously determined. Finally, the method estimates the probability that the packets under study come from the different zones that make up the system. The source is considered to be attached to the zone with the highest probability. Authors show that finding the optimal number of cluster-heads and their placement is an NP-complete problem, but they

Figure 4. Left, original network; Right, clustered network

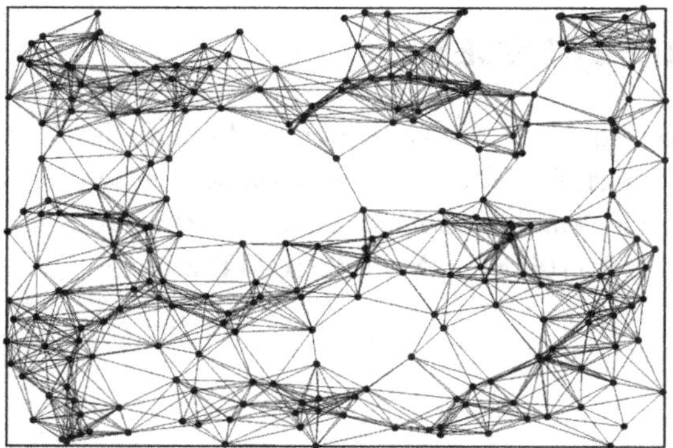

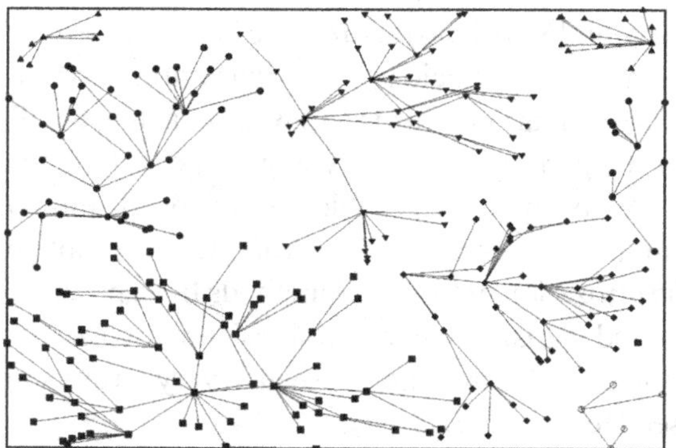

also provide alternatives. The original proposal is a centralized method, but it seems possible to develop a distributed version.

Tran and Nguyen (2006), based on their work in the AI community, offer a different but very interesting view on the subject, which is closely related to the work on statistical localization. From their perspective, localization can be regarded as a classification problem. The set of anchors turns into the training set supporting machine learning. Finally, each of the remaining nodes is supplied to the already trained device that determines the class it belongs to. That is, the zone previously defined by a given anchor. It is a centralized method that can be translated to a distributed version.

Laifenfeld and Trachtenberg (2008) developed the concept of identifying code. An identifying code is a graph where each node is labelled with the identities of nodes it shares links with, i.e. its neighbours. This label is also called codeword. An arbitrary graph may become an identifying code only if each node receives a unique and different label. A node, whose position must be fixed, can profit from this approach. The idea is that its corresponding codeword should be enough to characterize the region in lies on. Authors argue that a thorough selection of nodes where anchors are placed brings about this construction. The down-side is that not all graphs accept this treatment. Complete graphs, for instance, cannot be transformed into identifying codes. Besides, anchor placement turns out to be an NP-complete problem, for which there is a heuristic procedure only. It is a centralized method.

From a completely different perspective Srinivasan and Wu (2006) address the localization when threatened by malicious nodes transmitting ambiguous information. This is a new approach that calls for the participation of cryptographic techniques.

A closely related problem is the localization of a mobile across a sensor network. In this problem, the utilization of tools and methods from probability and statistics, such as Bayesian networks and Monte-Carlo simulation, seems very promising (see Hu & Evans, 2004).

CONCLUSION

The problem of localization requires a very complete toolbox where designers can find the most appropiate method, depending on the particular instance of the problem they are dealing with. Exact methods with polynomial complexities work well on homogeneous networks. Nevertheless, these methods have to be adapted or replaced when the input measurements are noisy. In these cases, we talk about approximation methods. Furthermore, as the problem turns into NP-complete when dealing with sparse networks, heuristic methods offer solutions with bounded errors, under reasonable complexities.

Designers need to take into account the specific application context to help them select the best suited localization procedure. That is, it is quite important to understand the key issues of the particular instance of the problem: energy, measurements techniques, network size, density, structure, topology, anchors, etc. Also, the set of attributes expected from the corresponding method, including accuracy, robustness and complexity must be considered. It might be the case, for instance, that many applications can be solved by simpler solutions, where any node is able to recognize the region or zone it belongs to.

If necessary, localization must be solved right after MAC operations, and probably before routing. Localization is not the goal in itself, but it is a fundamental service underlying most of the key operations of modern wireless networks such as naming, addressing, topology control and routing.

REFERENCES

Akyildiz, I. F., Su, W., Sankarasubramaniam, Y., & Cayirci, E. (2002). A survey on sensor networks. *IEEE Communications Magazine*, *40*(8), 102–114. doi:10.1109/MCOM.2002.1024422

Aspnes, J., Goldenberg, B., & Yang, R. Y. (2004). On the computational complexity of sensor network localization. In A. Nikoletseas & J. Rolim (Eds.), In *Proceedings of First International Workshop on Algorithmic Aspects of Wireless Sensor Networks (ALGOSENSORS 2004)* (pp. 32-44). New York: Springer-Verlag.

Awerbuch, B. (1985). Complexity of network synchronization. [JACM]. *Journal of the ACM*, *32*(4), 804–823. doi:10.1145/4221.4227

Bahl, P., & Padmanabhan, V. N. (2000). RADAR: An in-building RF-based user location and tracking system. In *Proceedings of the Nineteenth Annual Joint Conference of the IEEE Computer and Communications Societies, INFOCOMM 2000* (pp. 775-784).

Bell, K. L., Steinberg, Y., Ephraim, Y., & Van Trees, H. L. (1997). Extended Ziv-Zakai lower bound for vector parameter estimation. *IEEE Transactions on Information Theory*, *43*(2), 624–637. doi:10.1109/18.556118

Biswas, P., Lian, T., Wang, T., & Ye, Y. (2006). Semidefinite programming based algorithms for sensor network localization. [TOSN]. *ACM Transactions on Sensor Networks*, *2*(2), 188–220. doi:10.1145/1149283.1149286

Bulusu, N., Heidemann, J., & Estrin, D. (2000). GPS-less low-cost outdoor localization for very small devices. *IEEE Personal Communications*, *7*(5), 28–34. doi:10.1109/98.878533

Čapkun, S., Hamdi, M., & Hubaux, J. (2001). GPS-free positioning in mobile ad-hoc networks. In *Proceedings of the 34th Annual Hawaii International Conference on System Sciences*, (pp. 3481–3490). Washington, DC: IEEE Computer Society.

Cederval, M., & Moses, R. L. (1997). Efficient maximum likelihood DOA estimation for signal with known waveforms in the presence of multipath. *IEEE Transactions on Signal Processing*, *45*(3), 808–811. doi:10.1109/78.558512

Chong, E. K. P., & Zak, S. H. (Eds.). (2008). *An introduction to optimization*. Hoboken, NJ: John Wiley and Sons.

Cox, T., & Cox, M. (Eds.). (1994). *Monographs on Statistics and Applied Probability 59: Multidimensional Scaling*. London: Chapman and Hall.

Doherty, L., Ghaoui, L. E., & Pister, K. S. J. (2001). Convex position estimation in wireless sensor networks. [Washington, DC: IEEE Computer Society.]. *Proceedings - IEEE INFOCOM, 2001*, 1655–1663.

Eren, T., Goldenberg, D. K., Whitley, W., Yang, R. Y., Morse, A. S., Anderson, B. D. O., & Belhumer, P. N. (2004). Rigidity, computation, and randomization in network localization. [Washington, DC: IEEE Computer Society.]. *Proceedings - IEEE INFOCOM, 2004*, 2673–2684.

Ganesan, D., Krishnamachari, B., Woo, A., Culler, D., Estrin, D., & Wicker, S. (2002). *An empirical study of epidemic algorithms in large scale multihop wireless networks* (Report No. IRB-TR-02-003). Berkeley, CA: Intel Research Berkeley.

Garey, M. R., & Johnson, D. S. (1979). *Computers and intractability: A guide to the theory of NP-completeness*. New York: W. H. Freeman.

Groenen, P., & Borg, I. (Eds.). (1997). *Modern multidimensional scaling, theory and applications*. New York: Springer-Verlag.

Hightower, J., & Borriello, G. (2001). Location systems for ubiquitous computing. *Computer*, *34*(8), 57–66. doi:10.1109/2.940014

Howard, A., Matarić, M., & Sukhatme, G. (2001). Relaxation on a mesh: A formalism for generalized localization. In *Proceedings of the IEEE/RSJ International Conference on Intelligent Robots and Systems* (pp. 1055–1060). Washington, DC: IEEE Computer Society

Hu, L., & Evans, D. (2004). Localization for mobile networks. In *Proceedings of the 10th annual international conference on Mobile Computing and Networking*, Philadelphia, PA (pp 45-57). New York: ACM.

Kannan, A. A., Mao, G., & Vucetic, B. (2006). Simulated annealing based wireless sensor network localization. *Journal of Computers*, *1*(2), 15–22. doi:10.4304/jcp.1.2.15-22

Karl, H., & Willig, A. (Eds.). (2005). *Protocols and architectures for wireless sensor networks*. Chichester, UK: John Wiley & Sons. doi:10.1002/0470095121

Krim, H., & Viberg, M. (1996). Two decades of array signal processing research: The parametric approach. *IEEE Signal Processing Magazine*, *13*, 67–94. doi:10.1109/79.526899

Kröller, A., Fekete, S., Pfisterer, D., & Fischer, S. (2006). Deterministic boundary recognition and topology extraction for large sensor networks. In *Proceedings of the seventeenth annual ACM-SIAM Symposium on Discrete Algorithms (SODA)* (pp. 1000-1009). New York: ACM press.

Kruskal, J. B., & Wish, M. (1978). Multidimensional scaling. In Uslaner, E. (Ed.), *Sage university papers: Quantitative applications in the social sciences*. Newbury Park, CA: Sage Publications.

Laifenfeld, M., & Trachtenberg, A. (2008). Identifying codes and covering problems. *IEEE Transactions on Information Theory*, *54*(9), 3929–3950. doi:10.1109/TIT.2008.928263

Langendoen, K., & Reijers, N. (2003). Distributed localization in wireless sensor networks: a quantitative comparison. *Computer Networks: The International Journal of Computer and Telecommunications Networking*, *43*(4), 499–518.

Li, X., & Pahlavan, K. (2004). Super-resolution TOA estimation with diversity for indoor geolocation. *IEEE Transactions on Wireless Communications*, *3*(1), 224–234. doi:10.1109/TWC.2003.819035

Mao, G., & Fidan, B. (Eds.). (2009). *Localization algorithms and strategies for wireless sensor networks*. Hershey, PA: Information Science Reference.

Mao, G., Fidan, B., & Anderson, B. D. O. (2007). Localization. In Mahalik, N. P. (Ed.), *Sensor networks configuration: Fundamentals, standards, platforms and applications* (pp. 281–315). New York: Springer-Verlag.

Marcelín-Jiménez, R. (2007). Locally-constructed trees for ad-hoc routing. *Telecommunication Systems*, *36*(1-3), 39–48. doi:10.1007/s11235-007-9055-z

McGuire, M., Plataniotis, K. N., & Venetsanopoulos, A. N. (2003). Location of mobile terminals using time measurements and survey points. *IEEE Transactions on Vehicular Technology*, *52*(4), 999–1011. doi:10.1109/TVT.2003.814222

Moore, D., Leonard, J., Rus, D., & Teller, S. (2004). Robust distributed network localization with noisy range measurements. In J. A. Stankovic (Ed.), *Proceedings of the 2nd International Conference on Embedded Networked Sensor Systems* (pp. 50-61). New York: ACM Press.

Nerguizian, C., Despins, C., & Affes, S. (2006). Geolocation in mines with an impulse fingerprinting technique and neural networks. *IEEE Transactions on Wireless Communications*, *5*(3), 603–611. doi:10.1109/TWC.2006.1611090

Niculescu, D., & Nath, B. (2003, March). *Ad hoc positioning system using AoA*. Paper presented at the IEEE Twenty-Second Annual Joint Conference of the IEEE Computer and Communications Societies, San Francisco, CA.

Niculescu, D., & Nath, B. (2003). DV Based positioning in ad hoc networks. *Kluwer Journal of Telecommunications Systems*, *4*(1-4), 267–280. doi:10.1023/A:1023403323460

Niculescu, D., & Nath, B. (2004). Error characteristics of ad hoc positioning systems. In J. Murai (Ed.), *Proceedings of the 5th ACM International Symposium on Mobile ad hoc Networking and Computing* (pp. 20-30). New York: ACM press.

Paschalidis, I. C., & Guo, D. (2007). Robust and distributed localization in sensor networks. In *Proceedings of the 46th IEEE Conference on Decision and Control*, New Orleans, LA (pp. 933-938). New York: IEEE Computer Society.

Patwari, N. (2005). *Location estimation in sensor networks.* Unpublished doctoral dissertation, University of Michigan, Ann Arbor, MI.

Patwari, N., & Hero, A. O., III. (2003). Using proximity and quantized RSS for sensor localization in wireless networks. In C. S. Raghavendra, & K. Sivalingam (Eds.), *Proceedings of the 2nd ACM international conference on Wireless sensor networks and applications* (pp. 20-29). New York: ACM press.

Peleg, D. (Ed.). (2000). *Distributed computing: A locality-sensitive approach.* Philadelphia, PA: Society for Industrial and Applied Mathematics.

Pestana-Leao, L. M., & Rodríguez-Peralta, L. M. (2007, October). *Collaborative localization in wireless sensor networks.* Paper presented at the Conference on Sensor Technologies and Applications (SENSORCOMM 2007), Valencia, Spain.

Priyantha, N. B., Miu, A. K. L., Balakrishnan, H., & Teller, S. (2001). The cricket compass for context-aware mobile applications. In C. Rose (Ed.), *Proceedings of the 7th annual international conference on Mobile computing and networking* (pp. 1-14). New York: ACM Press.

Rendl, W. F. (2005). Semidefinite programming and integer programming. In Aardal, K., Nemhauser, G., & Weismantel, R. (Eds.), *Handbook on discrete optimization* (pp. 393–514). Amsterdam: Elsevier.

Roy, R., & Kailath, T. (1989). ESPRIT – Estimation of signal parameters via rotational invariance techniques. *IEEE Transactions on Signal Processing, 37*(7), 984–995. doi:10.1109/29.32276

Savarese, C., Rabaey, J. M., & Langendoen, K. (2002). Robust positioning algorithms for distributed ad hoc wireless sensor networks. In C. S. Schlatter (Ed.). *Proceedings of the General Track: 2002 USENIX Annual Technical Conference* (pp. 317-327). Berkeley, CA: USENIX Association

Savvides, A., Garber, W. L., Adlakha, S., Moses, R. L., & Srivastava, M. B. (2003). On the error characteristics of multihop node localization in ad-hoc sensor networks. In F. Zhao, L. J. Guibas (Eds.), *Proceedings of the Second International Workshop IPSN 2003* (pp. 317-332). New York: Springer.

Savvides, A., Han, C. C., & Srivastava, M. B. (2001). Dynamic fine-grained localization in ad hoc networks of sensors. In C. Rose (Ed.), *Proceedings of the 7th annual international conference on Mobile computing and networking* (pp. 166–179). New York: ACM press.

Savvides, A., Park, H., & Srivastava, M. B. (2002). The bits and flops of the n-hop multilateration primitive for node localization problems. In C. S. Raghavendra, & K. M. Sivalingam (Ed.), *Proceedings of the 1st ACM International Workshop on Wireless Sensor Networks and Applications* (pp. 112–121). New York: ACM Press.

Shang, Y., Ruml, W., Zhang, Y., & Fromherz, M. P. J. (2003). Localization from mere connectivity. In M. Gerla (Ed.), *Proceedings of the 4th ACM International Symposium on Mobile Ad Hoc Networking & Computing* (pp. 201-212). New York: ACM press.

Shang, Y., Ruml, W., Zhang, Y., & Fromherz, M. P. J. (2004). Localization from connectivity in sensor networks. *IEEE Transactions on Parallel and Distributed Systems, 15*(11), 961–964. doi:10.1109/TPDS.2004.67

Shao, J. (Ed.). (1998). *Mathematical statistics*. New York: Springer.

Srinivasan, A., & Wu, J. (2006). A survey on secure localization in wireless sensor networks. In Furht, B. (Ed.), *Encyclopedia of wireless and mobile communications*. Boca Raton, FL: CRC Press, Taylor and Francis Group.

Tran, D. A., & Nguyen, T. (2006). Localization in wireless sensor networks based on support vector machines. *IEEE Transactions on Parallel and Distributed Systems*, *19*(7), 981–994. doi:10.1109/TPDS.2007.70800

Vandenberghe, L., & Boyd, S. (1996). Semidefinite programming. *SIAM Review*, *38*(1), 49–95. doi:10.1137/1038003

Vicaire, P. A., & Stankovic, J. A. (2004). *Elastic localization: Improvements on distributed, range free localization for wireless sensor networks* (Report No. CS-2004-35). Charlottesville, VA: University of Virginia.

Weinstein, E., & Weiss, A. J. (1988). A general class of lower bounds in parameter estimation. *IEEE Transactions on Information Theory*, *34*(2), 338–342. doi:10.1109/18.2647

Yick, J., Mukherjee, B., & Ghosal, D. (2008). Wireless sensor network survey. *Computer Networks*, *52*(12), 2292–2330. doi:10.1016/j.comnet.2008.04.002

Zhao, F., & Guibas, L. (Eds.). (2004). *Wireless sensor networks, an information processing approach*. San Francisco: Morgan Kaufmann.

Chapter 2
Low Power Design Techniques for Wireless Sensor Networks

José Aedo
Universidad de Antioquia, Colombia

Natalia Gaviria
Universidad de Antioquia, Colombia

Johnny Aguirre
Universidad de Antioquia, Colombia

Danny Múnera
Universidad de Antioquia, Colombia

ABSTRACT

WSNs can be applied in several areas for the monitoring and control of variables. In the design process of a WSN, one of the most important design objectives is to minimize the energy required for sensing, signal processing and communication tasks to extend the lifetime of the network. This chapter discusses a broad variety of schemes used to reduce power consumption in WSNs. The design of sensors nodes involves several core aspects, such as supported sensors, the communication interface, applications, the control system and peripherals. Strategies to preserve the energy used by each of these components are discussed. A specific scheme using digital signal processing to reduce power consumption by decreasing the number of transmissions is proposed. The chapter also considers protocol architectures, focusing on link layer, network layer, and cross-layer approaches. Finally, a comparative analysis among the main techniques is presented.

INTRODUCTION

Wireless Sensor Networks (WSNs) are defined as networks that are composed by a number of spatially distributed sensor nodes equipped with radio transceivers. Each sensor node is designed to cooperatively monitor physical variables (Culler, 2004). The node itself is relatively simple, but the real power of this technology emerges from the ability of a node to perform a task in a cooperative manner with others, thanks to communication protocols. In this manner, one of the most striking aspects of this technology lies in the reliable flow

DOI: 10.4018/978-1-60960-027-3.ch002

of information through the nodes. The applications of this technology are very wide due to the large number of different sensors that can be used in a network. Some relevant examples include environmental monitoring, using temperature humidity or illumination sensors (Tors et al., 2004); healthcare applications, using Electrocardiogram/electroencephalogram (ECG/EEG) sensors (Culler 2004; Tors et al., 2004; Lo, 2005); and home automation, using activity sensors (Heidemann, 2003).

One of the main goals of WSNs is to populate areas with large numbers of nodes, probably hundreds or even thousands, in order to track a set of variables. To achieve this goal, however, the power consumption of the nodes has to be minimized to extend the lifetime of the network. This issue has become a very relevant research challenge in the field of WSNs, since it determines the performance and cost of the entire system.

The design process of both the nodes and the network includes the following design features: they must operate with very limited power resources, require little maintenance, and have a small size (Paradiso, 2005). Other requirements which should be satisfied by WSNs include ease of deployment and low cost. The set of functions performed by WSNs together with these requirements involves a high computational complexity, which translates into a high power consumption of the devices, which limits autonomy.

The problem of power consumption has been approached by researchers from different angles that can be classified into the following categories:

- Hardware and signal acquisition
- Protocol architecture

The first approach directly deals with optimizing the embedded system (hardware) and the algorithms used for signal sensing and processing at each node. Some proposed strategies proposed to reduce power consumption by modifying the nodes include developing processing units with low power modes, distributing tasks among the different nodes and implementing different network topologies (Hill, 2003; Taieb, 2007; Imad, 2005). Some studies have presented strategies to reduce power consumption in WSNs using a signal processing theory. Alippi et al. (2007) use Kalman filters to determine the sampling frequency of sensors based on the availability of the communication channel. This estimation is performed through a handshaking protocol between the node and the server, which determines whether the frequency and its new value should be changed. Römer and Santini (2006) propose a strategy to reduce transmission by network nodes based on the Least Mean Square algorithm, in which the sink assumes the estimated values of the nodes.

The second approach aims at analyzing and proposing a modification to the network protocol architecture. This can be done either by implementing a new MAC protocol (Heidemann, 2003; Shakshuki & Malik, 2007; Polastre, Hill & Culler, 2004), a new routing protocol, (Heinzelman et al., 2000; Slama et al., 2007; Shebli et al., 2007), or by using a cross-layered approach in which the topology of the network is also considered (Jurdak et al., 2007; Wang et al., 2005). The cross-layer approach has been shown to exhibit the best performance in terms of power consumption.

The goal of this chapter is to present the state-of-the-art of the schemes used to reduce power consumption in WSNs. This chapter reviews, analyzes, and compares different strategies proposed in the literature using the above mentioned approaches. It focuses on a specific scheme proposed by the authors using digital signal processing to reduce power consumption by decreasing the number of transmissions (Gaviria et al., 2009). This chapter will also present the most important research and development challenges to reduce power consumption in WSNs.

This chapter is organized as follows: The first section describes the principles of WSNs and the main challenges associated with their design. This is followed by a discussion on low power techniques, with an analysis of the hardware and signal processing issues. Next, we present a comparison of different links and network layer protocols developed for WSNs. The chapter ends with conclusions and future work.

BACKGROUND

WSN Architecture

The use of WSNs in new fields has led to great advances in related techniques and implementations. As stated before, the difference between WSNs and typical networks is becoming greater, due to the requirements imposed by both technologies. This difference is directly reflected in the protocol architecture of both types of networks. Traditional networks are defined by the OSI reference model (Bertsekas & Gallager, 1987). This model splits the functionality of the network into smaller and independent layers, which perform very well-defined tasks in an independent way without taking into consideration the status of the other layers, as illustrated in Figure 1. This model is also characterized by the communication between adjacent layers. Early WSN applications adapt this model, reducing the OSI model to only four layers: application, network, link and physical. The OSI reference model clearly defines the specific functions of each layer. In WSNs, however, new functionalities are added due to their mobility, variable topology and the easy deployment, which adds challenges to the implementation of each particular layer. It is important to keep in mind that one the main goal designs of WSNs is energy-efficient operation. The following analysis focuses on the link and the network layers, since most of the research work concerning the protocol architecture of WSNs has been devoted to these two layers.

The transceiver plays a critical role in the hardware architecture of a sensor node because it is the highest energy consuming component. Since the MAC (Medium Access Control) protocol controls the use of the radio, its design is directly related to power consumption and, consequently, a proper design can lead to a performance boost. A MAC protocol for WSNs should address the following issues:

- Idle listening: a node listens to the medium prepared to receive a message, but does not receive it.
- Overhearing: a node receives a message addressed to a different node.
- Collisions: two or more nodes try to transmit messages at the same time, which causes interference.
- Traffic fluctuations: variations in the amount of information being transmitted over the network.
- Protocol overhead: information exchanged between nodes that is related to proper protocol operation.

The network layer is responsible for the correct transmission of information from a source to a destination node. This layer is closely linked to the type of application so that different functionalities can be implemented within the routing protocol. Besides the power constraint problem of nodes, other important issues to consider in the design of a network protocol include:

- forwarding information from other nodes (Multi-hopping).

Figure 1. OSI model

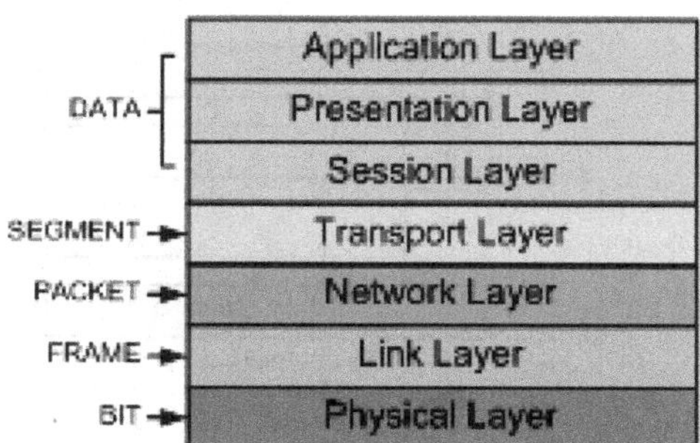

- applying application-based techniques to improve data flow (e.g. data-aggregation).
- improving the routing decisions of notes (shortest path algorithms).
- addressing changing topologies (topology control).

Traditional approaches inherited from the OSI reference model have led to the design of link and network layer protocols which try to address all of the above mentioned issues. The goal of these protocols is to optimize one or more of the layer-related parameters. This approach, however, has performed poorly WSNs because the design goals of WSNs vastly differ from those of a traditional network (Akyidiz, Su, Sankarasubramaniam, & Cayirci, 2002). Limited processing and power resources are the main factors that require the optimization of different network parameters in a simultaneous way. Bearing this in mind, an alternative model has been proposed for WSN, in which the adjacent layer communication principle of the OSI reference model has not been kept. This approach, called cross-layer (CL) design, adopts a dynamic communication strategy among the different layers, as illustrated in Figure 2.

CL tackles the design of communication protocols by actively exploiting the dependence among the different layer protocols to obtain improvements in the overall system performance, instead of focusing on the performance of a single layer. Research results have shown that this new type of protocol design improves network performance in terms of energy saving (Srivastava & Motani, 2005; Melodia, Vuran & Pompili, 2006).

Even though there is no clear consensus on the taxonomy of CL techniques, there are many implementations, and some works compiling these protocols have attempted to classify them according to their nature. Srivastava & Motani (2005) have established the basic concepts of CL design philosophy. According to their research, CL interactions can be classified into three types: direct communication among layers (adjacent or nonadjacent)

Karaca and Sokullu (2009) have developed a comparative review of different frameworks for the design of CL protocols and also collected the main evaluation and comparison criteria to analyze these systems. Below, we list the main criteria which include:

- **Adaptability:** This criterion evaluates the extent to which a framework can adapt to the changes in the requirements of different applications, hardware platforms and network topologies.
- **Power-Efficiency:** The most restricted resource in WSNs is power. This criterion refers to the reducing energy consumption by employing different strategies.
- **Instability:** The wireless channel is inherently unsteady and variable. Protocols

Figure 2. Cross-layer protocols

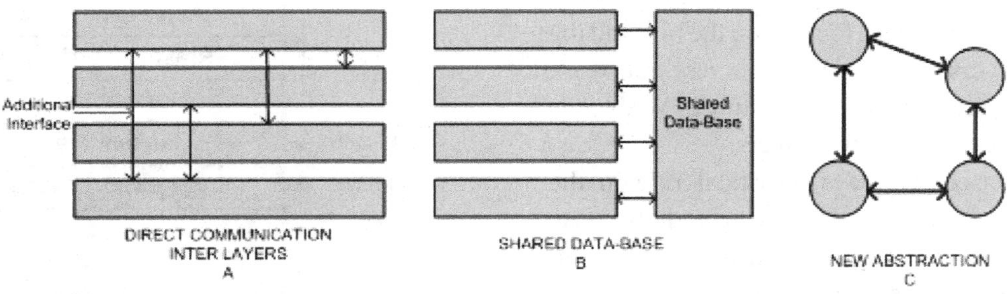

which take into consideration this feature can be classified as channel-oriented.

- **Fault tolerance**: Faults in WSNs can occur because of various reasons, including node mobility, channel fluctuations, excessive use, etc. A fault-tolerant protocol should take into account these considerations.
- **Complexity:** A CL framework can have all of the above features, but it may also have a structure that can be difficult to implement and manage. Thus, complexity is a key criterion to be considered when evaluating a CL framework.

HARDWARE ARCHITECTURE AND LOW POWER SCHEMES

The sensor node is the main component of a WSN. Its goal is to gather information from the environment and to transmit it to the collection point (also called sink). There are several challenges in designing a sensor node which are related to its processing capability and low power requirements. This section presents sensor characteristics, based on their physical architecture and processing abilities.

A Look at the Node

Nodes form the heart of a WSN. The design of the node has to consider several core aspects, which include: the supported sensors for a specific application, the communication interface, the control systems and the peripherals of the node. Node design is one of the most important factors that determine network characteristics. Consequently, it is important to understand the role of different parameters in the physical structure of the node.

As mentioned earlier, the node of a WSN is an embedded system, which is basically a collection of various simple subsystems. Although there are several implementation proposals for the architecture of a single node, it is possible to describe the typical architecture as comprised of five hardware subsystems: power, memory, sensors, control and radio, as illustrated in Figure 3 (Culler, 2004).

Control Subsystem

One of the most striking aspects of a WSN is the fact that nodes do not act as passive agents. Instead, they act as active agents with extended capabilities, providing dynamism to the network. This feature is reflected in their autonomy, which

Figure 3. Node basic architecture

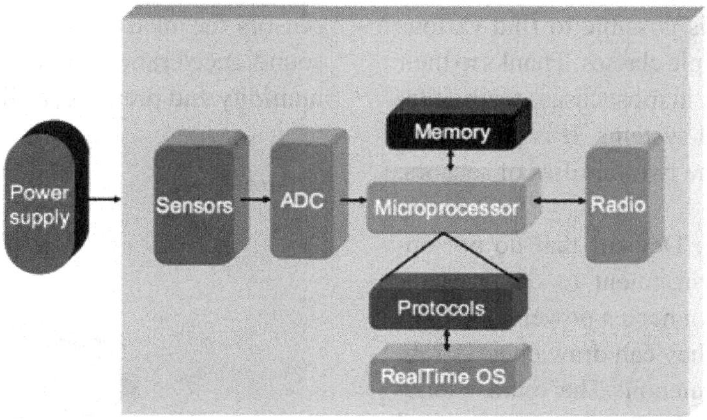

allows them to 'make decisions' and deal with certain situations that will eventually appear within their operating environment. This autonomy is possible because all nodes are equipped with data processing units. There are several ways to decide which device will be responsible for carrying out which specific task.

Because there are several families of data processing chip manufacturers in the market, node design should take into account a number of features that provide a choice between architectures or families. Some of the issues to consider when choosing a specific architecture are: power consumption, memory size, response time, clock speed, peripheral support, performance and cost.

Microcontroller units (MCUs) have the functional characteristics of microprocessors in a much more compact format. These devices have made the use of embedded systems popular because they exhibit a wide functionality integrated into a single integrated circuit and their programming is relatively simple, using high level languages. These characteristics make them a very appealing alternative for use in WSNs. There are several recognized MCU manufactures like AVR (ATMega128 microcontroller's used in mica architecture), Intel, Texas Instruments and Microchip.

Sensors

The sensors are the "senses" of a WSN. Their goal is to transform physical phenomena into electrical signals. Today, it is possible to find various chips supporting multiple classes. Thanks to their popularity, MCUs are, in most cases, easily integrated with embedded systems. It is possible to distinguish between the two families of sensors:

- **Passive sensors:** Devices that do not operate in the environment to obtain readings, which do not need a power source for transduction as they can draw energy from the same phenomenon. The extra energy required by these devices is used for signal conditioning. Typical uses for this type of sensors are devices such as thermometers, mechanical stress sensors, microphones, smoke detectors, etc.
- **Active sensors:** These are special types of devices that perform some action in the environment in order to obtain their readings. Prime examples are sonar sensors, used widely in hydro-navigation, and some types of seismic sensors.

Power

The power consumption of nodes is a subject of much discussion when discussing the type of sensor to me used in a sensor network. While it is true that the technological trend points to an increasing number of active sensors with higher complexity and precision in measurements, the disadvantage of these sensors is that they require their own power source and signal conditioning circuit, leading to increased hardware requirements within the node or sensor. Passive sensors are an inexpensive solution regarding energy consumption, since their implementation relies on a smaller amount of hardware. Recent advances in this technology have provided a new and wide range of developments in this field, related to the so-called inertial sensors based on MEMS (Micro Electro-Mechanical Systems), which have made the design of devices such as accelerometers and gyroscopes easy. WSNs have been mainly used as sensors for measuring lighting, magnetic fields, sound, acceleration, vibration, level, temperature, humidity and pressure, as illustrated in Figure 4.

Figure 4.

The radio interface, also known as a transceiver, is one of the most delicate node components in a WSN. Its task is to transmit and receive data (Tx/Rx) wirelessly. Some studies (Raghunathan et al., 2002) have shown that a transceiver is a device that has the highest power consumption when it performs tasks Tx and/or Rx compared with the power consumption of other subsystems within the node (like the sensors or the MCUs).

Commercial transceivers exhibit a standard architecture, including the stages of transmission and reception, along with signal amplifiers and mixers, as shown in Figure 5. The operation of the transceivers is performed in two states in different modes:

- **Transmission:** In this state, the circuits are activated to transmit information via the radio. The transceiver consumes a lot of power because it must transform baseband to RF. Modulation, the generation of intermediate frequency and other transmission processes, involves a large amount of hardware and consumes a lot of power when compared with the system as a whole. No other subsystems aside from the transceiver perform tasks which involve hardware operating at relatively high frequencies (more than 900 MHz).
- **Reception:** This state has two modes:
  - **Active:** The device is ready to receive data. In this mode, it uses a considerable amount of power because many active circuits are working on receiving the data.
  - **Idle:** In this mode, reception is inactive and the transceiver is consuming less power. This presents the disadvantage of requiring a prolonged period of time to switch to active mode.

Node Power Consumption

It is possible to generate a model for power consumption of a node taking standard consumption data for each of its components. Table 1 shows the typical current consumption for *mica* hardware components (Crossbow technologies, 2008).

The two models presented in the table are related to different duty cycles. In Model 1, the microcontroller unit is active 1% of the total time, whereas Model 2 assumes that this unit will be active 0.5% of the time.

SIGNAL PROCESSING STRATEGIES

Several strategies can be proposed for data sampling and packet transmission in a WSN. The simplest strategy consists of a number of nodes that sample environmental conditions using a predetermined sampling frequency and send it at the same rate to a data collection point. This approach is very easy to implement, but, from a power consumption point of view, it could be the most inefficient technique to treat data.

Figure 5. General transceiver architecture

Figure 6. Battery performance for models

Table 1. Node consumption based on components power demands

Currents			**Duty Cycles**		
	Value	**Units**	**Model 1**	**Model 2**	**Units**
Microcontroller					
current (full operation)	4	mA	1	0.5	%
current sleep	3	uA	99	99.5	%
Radio					
current in receive	7	mA	0.75	0.4	%
current xmit	10	mA	0.25	0.1	%
current sleep	2	uA	99	99.5	%
Logger					
Write	10	mA	0	0	%
Read	2	mA	0	0	%
Sleep	2	uA	100	100	%
Sensor Board					
current (full operation)	3	mA	1	0.5	%
current sleep	3	uA	99	99.5	%
Battery Specifications					
Capacity Loss/Yr	3	%			
Computed mA-hr			**Model 1**	**Model 2**	
uP			0.0430	0.0230	
Radio			0.0795	0.0400	
Flash Memory			0.0020	0.0020	
Sensor Board			0.0330	0.0180	
Total current(ma-hr) used			0.1574	0.0830	
Total power mW-hr			0.5195	0.2738	

Consequently, it is important to develop new mechanisms for nodes collecting data in WSNs. The intrinsic processing capacity of nodes (represented in the MC unit) can be exploited to implement a strategy that reduces transmission time. This hypothesis is based on the fact that the amount of energy necessary to transmit a bit of information is around 125 times larger than the energy needed to process that same bit in a conventional microcontroller.

Based on the power dissipation gain that can be obtained by using a signal processing strategy, the exploration of algorithms oriented to decrease the number of transmissions (and thus the power dissipation) in nodes has become an area of research. In order to state the signal processing problem, we will first review some of the techniques implemented and then provide, in detail, a proposed strategy based on digital filtering theory.

Related Works

In a general context, WSNs operate as a number of nodes randomly distributed in space (sometimes hundreds or thousands). Consequently, the task of keeping individual control of each node is necessary so that each node may have some autonomy in running tasks. Nodes are exploited for the processing power each node has in its control subsystem. The energy-saving techniques must cover every aspect of sensor network design and implementation, starting with the individual architecture of each node. Here, we emphasize techniques that aim to reduce the number of wireless transmissions and act on the A/D converters and sensors, in general.

Node Activity Control

Energy savings are closely related to the activity undertaken by the hardware and software components of each node. However, a higher demand for power is related to transmissions of the wireless interface. This has pushed research efforts to search for possible solutions to this problem. Table 2 lists the main methods used in the different layers of the communication architecture of this technology (Alonso, 2006).

The table shows that a significant effort needs to be made at all levels of communication within the system to try to reduce the activity of the hardware involved in the communication process. The upper layers of the architecture are not isolated from this problem. Hence, it is essential to have a good design at the application layer, since it has control over the tasks performed by the node and the efficiency with which these tasks are carried out. Studies by (Mostofi et al., 2005) and (Sinopoli et al., 2003) suggest a compromise between what is being sensed and what is subsequently transmitted. This is accomplished by analyzing the quality of radio links in sensor networks with mobile nodes. This is achieved using heuristic methods and proposing algorithms that estimate a cooperative operation, emphasizing on low power consumption by trying to reduce the activity of the hardware involved in the communication process.

Table 2. Low power efforts in communication layers

Layer	Strategy
Physical	- Low power hardware - Dynamic power control - Adaptive modulation schemes
Medium access	- Low radio duties - Channel sampling - Sleep/awake switching
Data link	- Small data correction & flow control
Network/Transport	- Not connection oriented - Simple addressing
User/OS	- Low power software design - On mote signal processing

Adaptive Sampling

Adaptive sampling can be defined as a set of strategies based on the behavior of the sampled signal in space and time (Sreenath, 2007). Some studies propose strategies to dynamically adjust the sampling rate of the sensors and/or the number of transmissions on the basis of specific characteristics of the signals or nodes. Other studies suggest techniques for developing event detection applications. The goal of these strategies is to solve the problem of finding the most likely spatial location of an event and minimizing the communication cost by considering the tradeoffs between sampling, false alarms and the radio link quality (Ermis & Saligrama, 2005). The work mentioned in Alippi et al. (2007) proposes a strategy to sample the level of snow formations using the adaptive characteristics of sensors. This approach estimates the frequency at which the signal must be sampled, based on the FFT calculated on the same samples (at the Sink), in an attempt to reduce power consumption caused by wakeup periods of the sensors and the hardware needed for signal conditioning. Sreenath (2007) discusses a strategy to control the sampling rate in mobile node applications, where conventional location algorithms could fail. This strategy involves linear regression-based models combined with localization techniques, based on Gaussian models to estimate the field of operation. A slightly different approach is suggested in Kho et al. (2007), who propose a stand-alone strategy of sampling based on the available energy characteristics of each of the nodes of a WSN. Wu (2007) proposes a routing scheme for applications that support adaptive sampling. In this strategy, each node can estimate the best path (route) to transmit its data, having information about the frequency of data reporting from the other nodes in its neighborhood. In order to achieve this, the authors modified the communication protocols so that the MAC frames in each node reports its operating frequency to its neighborhood. This allows the other nodes to have 'knowledge' of the sample being taken by the neighbors.

A different approach is adopted in the work mentioned in Rizvi and Riasat (2007), which proposes a self-adaptive approach to find the optimal number of active nodes in the network. This approach makes the WSN maintain its operation, while minimizing the number of active terminals. To achieve this goal, the strategy generates a pattern that determines the path needed to reach a given base station, activating the nodes only when it is strictly necessary to transmit a packet.

Vass et al. (2006) and Gandham et al. (2003) propose techniques to optimize energy consumption based on the assumption that there is at least one mobile base station to extract information from the network. To meet this objective, the network uses so-called rounds of time slots in which the active network nodes change, based on localization algorithms. The main idea of this strategy is to minimize the number of active nodes to those strictly necessary to transfer information to its destination.

Collaborative Schemes: Data Aggregation

In most cases, in practical applications, the spatial distribution of nodes is carried out in a random fashion, leaving some very distant from others and, conversely, others very close to each other. This feature results in certain scenarios for which it is possible to propose different strategies that focus on the treatment of information.

In event-based sensor networks, where multiple nodes are likely to notify the sink about the same event at almost the same time, the network could suffer a significant increase in energy consumption and congestion due to the propagation of redundant information. For this reason, different techniques for data aggregation have been proposed (Boulis et al., 2003; Park & Sivakumar, 2008; Jinghua et al., 2009). It has also been shown that the complexity of optimal data aggregation is an NP-hard problem in general, but this complexity could be significantly reduced in special cases (Krishnamachari et al., 2002).

There are three basic sub optimal approaches to implement aggregation between neighboring nodes in a WSN (Boulis et al., 2003; Krishnamachari et al., 2002): Center at Nearest Source schema (CNS), Shortest Paths Tree (SPT) and Greedy Incremental Tree (GIT). In CNS, the sources send their data to a destination that is geographically close to the sink. This node is then responsible for applying an aggregation function and sending the aggregated data on to the sink. In SPT, each node sends the information to the sink using the shortest path between both. An aggregation tree is formed by the combination of the overlapping paths. In the GIT schema, the trees change sequentially. Initially, the shortest path between the sink and the nearest source is determined, and then the other sources are connected to the tree sequentially, giving priority to the closest one.

Other heuristic schemes are based on special cases. Park & Sivakumar (2008) suggest a two-stage strategy for sensor to sink data delivery if there is a perfect correlation among data. In the first stage, a local aggregation of the correlated data is performed among sensors around a node in the minimum dominating set. In the second one, a global aggregation among sensors is performed. This approach has been shown to closely approximate the centralized optimal solution.

In (Jinghua et al., 2009), an Ant Colony Algorithm (ACA) is applied to solve the data aggregation problem. This heuristic has been used with success for combinatorial optimization problems. In this case, the global optimal path is determined when a group of source nodes sends data to a single sink.

Finally, when a strategy for data aggregation is adopted, it is important to consider the additional computational cost and, therefore, the additional power required. In some cases, the energy savings achieved by the aggregation strategy could be significantly reduced because of the additional power consumption required. On the other hand, the solution adopted should also avoid the loss of important data, which implies preserving data integrity. Furthermore, new strategies are required for distributed networks with multiple sink nodes. However, a detailed discussion of these topics is beyond the scope of this chapter.

Time Series

Time series are recognized worldwide as investigative techniques that perform well when constructing models to fit signal behavior. Their operation is based on the analysis of data tables, from which it is possible to produce suitable models. These methods can be related to digital filter theory, also known as predictive or adaptive filters (Hayes, 1996). The work in (Santini, 2006) proposes a strategy based on adaptive filters to estimate the behavior of a signal. To implement this strategy, an FIR filter is used as an estimator. The goal is to minimize the mean square error $E\{e(n)\}$ using the least squares technique. To ensure convergence of the algorithm, manually calibrated coefficients (or weights) $w_i(n)$ are used. The idea is to bring an acceptable model of the sensors to prevent the transmission rate from saturating the sink. A slightly different approach is proposed in (Wang et al., 2007), in which *ARMA(p, q)* models are used to decrease the rate of errors in event detection applications with WSNs. The proposed scheme depends on the collaborative work of a group node that detects a particular event in order to achieve efficient node communications. This chapter reports the development of a protocol responsible for synchronizing information between the nodes involved. The work in (Le Borgne et al., 2007) proposes a fairly aggressive strategy to bring sensed variable models of a WSN based on a time series. It proposes a series of models that can be selected based on the behavior of the sensed variable. These algorithms are executed in each sink node and report significant changes to update the model.

Theoretical Framework

Using these models, it is possible to estimate future values of a signal based on past samples. This type of processing is often known as prediction filters, filters or time-series prediction.

In an autoregressive filter, the information signal $x(n)$ can be generated through AWGN (Additive White Gaussian Noise) processing with only poles. An AR (Autoregressive) filter has the following transfer function:

Equation 1. Only poles filter, p is poles number

$$H(z)=\frac{X(z)}{V(z)}=\frac{b(0)}{1+\sum_{n=1}^{p}a_p(n)z^{-n}}$$

The corresponding discrete time representation for Equation 1 is:

Equation 2. Discrete time representation

$$x(n)+\sum_{l=1}^{p}a_p(l)x(n-1)=b(0)v(n)$$

Making use of the correlation properties, the following expression can be obtained:

Equation 3. Correlation form for an AR filter

$$r_x(k) + \sum_{l=1}^{p} a_p(l) r_x(k-1) = \sigma_v^2 \left|b(0)\right|^2 \delta(k); \quad k \geq 0$$

This expression is called the *Yule-Walker* equation. It provides the ability to calculate the response of a system when it is excited with a noise signal, through the filter coefficients $a_p(l)$. If we calculate the values $r_x(0)$, $r_x(1)$, … we will find the matrix representation of the Yule-Walker equation.

Equation 4. Matrix form of Yule-Walker

$$\begin{pmatrix} r_x(0) & r_x(1) & \cdots & r_x(p) \\ r_x(1) & r_x(0) & \cdots & r_x(p-1) \\ \vdots & \vdots & & \vdots \\ r_x(p) & r_x(p-1) & \cdots & r_x(0) \end{pmatrix} \begin{pmatrix} 1 \\ a_p(1) \\ \vdots \\ a_p(p) \end{pmatrix} = \sigma_v^2 \left|b(0)\right|^2 \begin{pmatrix} 1 \\ 0 \\ \vdots \\ 0 \end{pmatrix}$$

Hence, it is possible to model discrete time signals in the presence of noise. One of the most interesting applications, involving WSN and signal processing, would be the design of an AR filter to model the information signal. If the model is implemented in the nodes, each of them can decide whether a sample should be transmitted to the network, thus reducing the number of transmissions. This leads to a more efficient bandwidth use and to decreased power consumption during the RF transmission.

Figure 7. Signal modeling

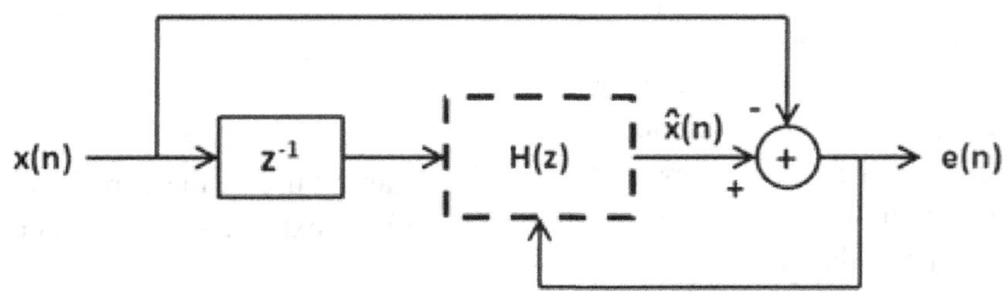

The previous approach was implemented in a WSN under controlled conditions with a reduced number of nodes, achieving the following results:

Protocol Architecture

As mentioned in the background section, there are a lot of techniques that meet many of the design goals of the WSN. We can identify three large groups of techniques which focus on link layer, network layer and cross-layer techniques. This section will perform a comparative analysis between the main techniques developed using each of these approaches.

MAC Layer Protocols

Ye, Heidemann, and Estrin (2002) developed one of the first specific MAC protocols for WSNs, namely the S-MAC (sensor-MAC). This slotted-access protocol focuses on reducing energy consumption by handling the idle-listening issue. This goal is achieved by sending the node to a sleep mode (turning off the radio transceiver) for a long time and only waking up (turning on) and listening to the channel for a short period of time (see Figure 11). The duty cycle of the node is fixed for all nodes in the network and can only be changed by the designer during the compilation cycle. S-MAC implements a synchronization mechanism in which all nodes periodically send sync messages. The goal of the sync messages is to divide the network into a virtual cluster. The nodes

Figure 8. Instant power for a typical data acquisition application. Peaks correspond to data transmission

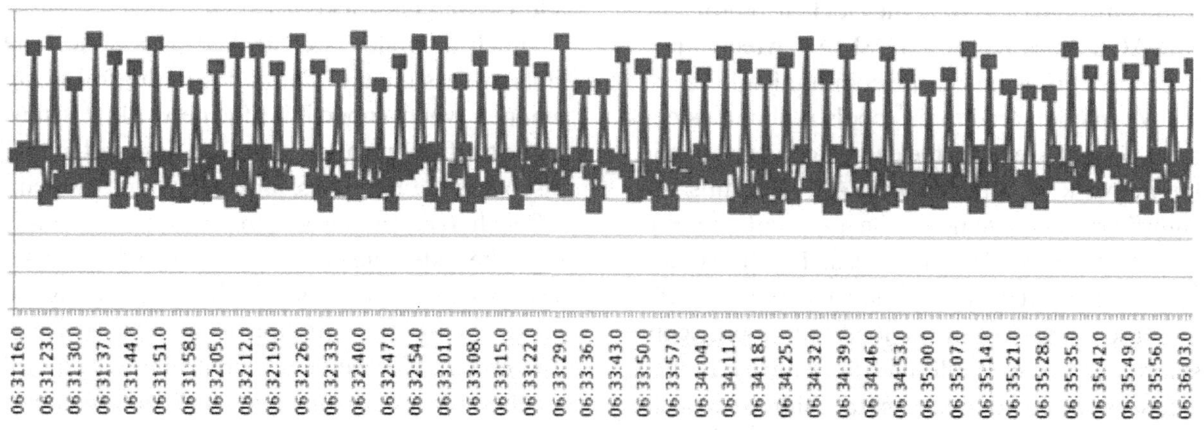

Figure 9. Instant power for an AR filter running in a node

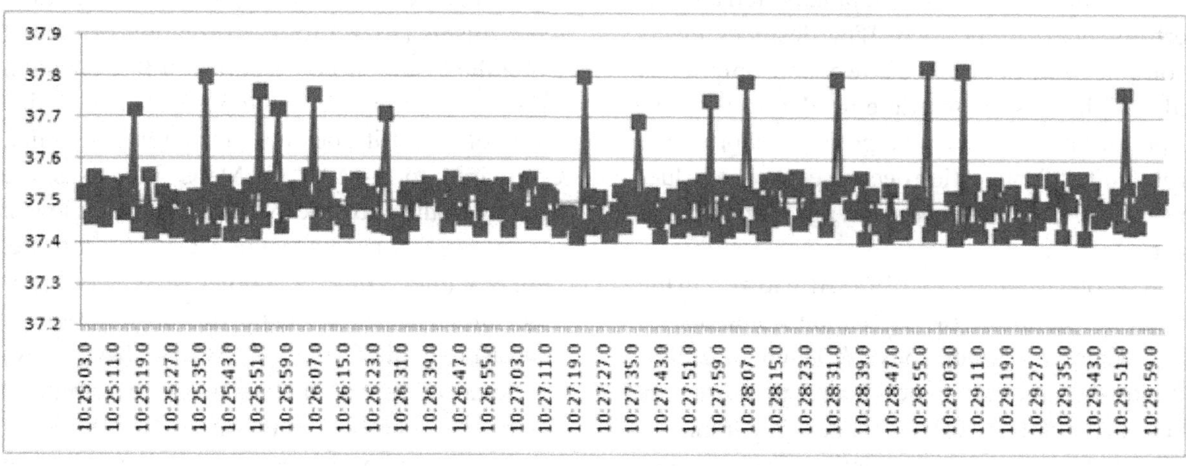

Figure 10. Power consumption for the two previous scenarios

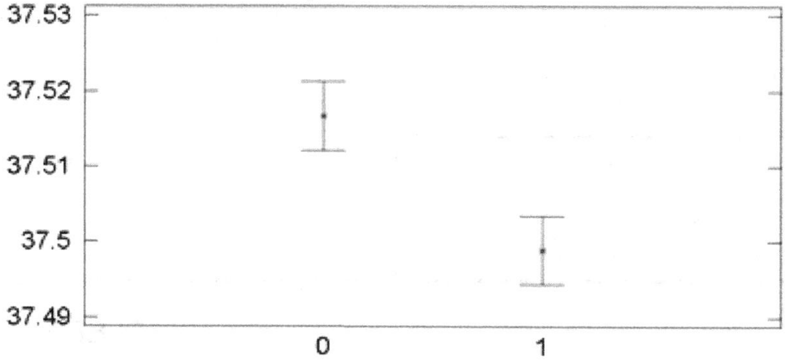

within a cluster go into the listening mode at the same time, thus avoiding the clock drift problem. S-MAC uses the RTS/CTS CSMA/CA techniques to prevent collisions in the communication.

When compared to protocols without a sleep state, S-MAC reduces the energy consumption in the network by a factor of 6. Although this is a significant achievement, the protocol presents several problems in other areas. The fixed duty cycle affects data packet latency when traffic increases. With low traffic loads, the energy consumption is acceptable and the latency is low. There are more nodes competing simultaneously for the available channel when the traffic load increases, which increases the probability of collisions, and hence the latency. There is a tradeoff between the length of the sleeping period and the performance of the protocol. If the designer selects a long sleeping period, the power consumption is reduced, but also is the time needed to transmit information. If the sleeping period is shorter, the probability of congestion decreases (hence reducing latency), but the energy saving is not significant.

A second MAC protocol aimed at lowering the power consumption of WSNs, the frame-access L-MAC protocol (van Hoesel & Havinga, 2004), divides the communication frame in short time slots. The number of slots is a design parameter, defined at the time of compilation. Each slot has two sections: traffic control and data transmission. When a node needs to transmit a data packet, it waits for its time slot to arrive and then broadcasts an information message containing the destination address and the packet size.

Each time slot is controlled by a node. The slots are assigned to the nodes in the following manner: when a node joins the network, it listens to the traffic control period of the time slot until it discovers the free ones, and claims one of them. After choosing a time slot to transmit a data message, the node enters the active state and broadcasts a control message to its neighbors, indicating the length of the transmission in number of slots. The nodes that receive this control message turn off their radios during the transmission of data if they are not the destination node and if they do not need to schedule a message. LMAC allows the transmission of unicast and broadcast messages. LMAC does not implement recognition mechanisms (ACK) for confirmation of receipt under the assumption of a collision-free channel. This assumption affects the performance of this protocol, since it does not allow for scalability. Compared to S-MAC, L-MAC increases the lifetime of the network for different traffic loads.

The random-access protocol B-MAC (Polastre, Hill, & Culler, 2004) is another MAC layer protocol aimed at decreasing power consumption. In contrast to S-MAC and L-MAC, B-MAC allows for some of its parameters to be reconfigured during the operation of the network, thus making it tolerant to changes in the network. The protocol was designed to be scalable and simple to implement. Because its an asynchronous protocol, B-MAC eliminates the overhead caused by node synchronization and cluster programming.

Figure 11. S-MAC frame

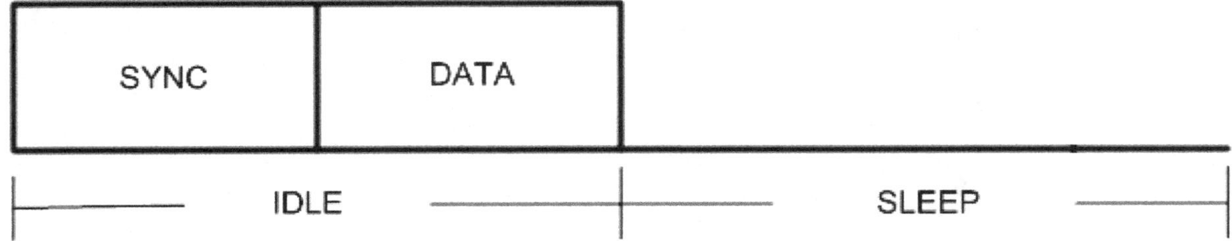

Under this protocol, nodes periodically wake up to check channel activity, a process called check interval. B-MAC defines eight check intervals, which correspond to the eight listening modes. To ensure that all packets are heard by the nodes, they are sent with a preamble whose reception time is longer than the interval of checking (See Figure 12). The protocol does not require an RTS-CTS system to coordinate the transmission of packets. It finds the optimal listening mode nodes analytically, based on the number of neighbors of each node. Compared with slotted-access protocols and frame access-protocols, B-MAC is very simple to implement, which is very important for low resource nodes like the ones in WSNs. The possibility of changing the check interval during operation is a very important feature from a cross-layer perspective. Besides, the authors say that B-MAC provides significant power savings when compared with S-MAC.

The MAC protocols mentioned here are the most relevant, although they are not the only ones. Since the S-MAC was developed, many new proposed MAC protocols for WSNs have been published. More complete information can be found in the book MAC Alphabet Soup (Langendoen, 2005), which compiles the majority of MAC protocols for WSNs.

The selection of a specific MAC protocol for a WSN is a tradeoff between different performance parameters of the network. Even though power consumption is a very important aspect, its reduction may lead to an increased latency or a higher packet loss rate. The main decision factor is the specific application and its performance requirements. Obviously, one cannot leave out of the equation the importance between the computational complexity of implementation and the reliability of algorithms.

It is clear that for every application, the goal is to have a MAC protocol that delivers very low latency with minimum power consumption. However, in practice this does not happen. As we have seen earlier, in general, network quality of service is sacrificed when reducing the active time of nodes in favor of lower power consumption.

This effect was assessed in this work through a simulation model developed on the simulation platform OMNeT++ (Varga, 2009). Figure 13 shows the latency results for a WSN under a monitoring application. As shown in the figure, the CSMA protocol performs the best in terms of packet latency for different traffic conditions. This is followed by B-MAC, which exhibits a higher latency value. The simulations show L-MAC has the highest latency, which should be expected because of its extended time penalty when delivering packets.

Figure 14 shows the results of the lifetime of the network for a specific implementation. Here, the L-MAC protocol obtains the longest network lifetime, despite performing poorly in terms of latency. The second-best performance is obtained by the BMAC protocol, which is somewhat lower. The worst performer is the CSMA protocol, which has the shortest lifetime.

Figure 12. B-MAC protocol

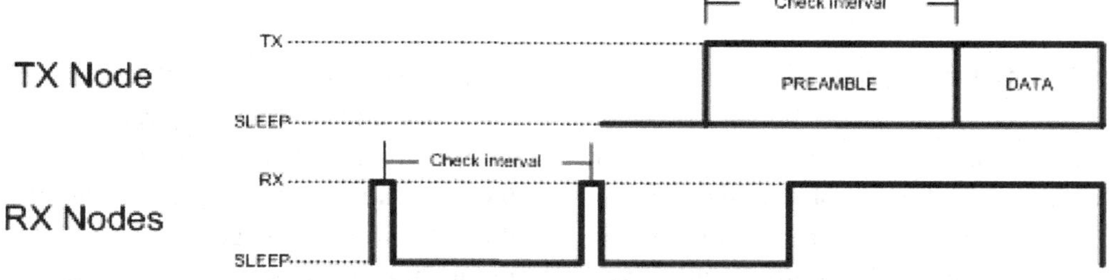

Figure 13. Latency in WSN for monitoring

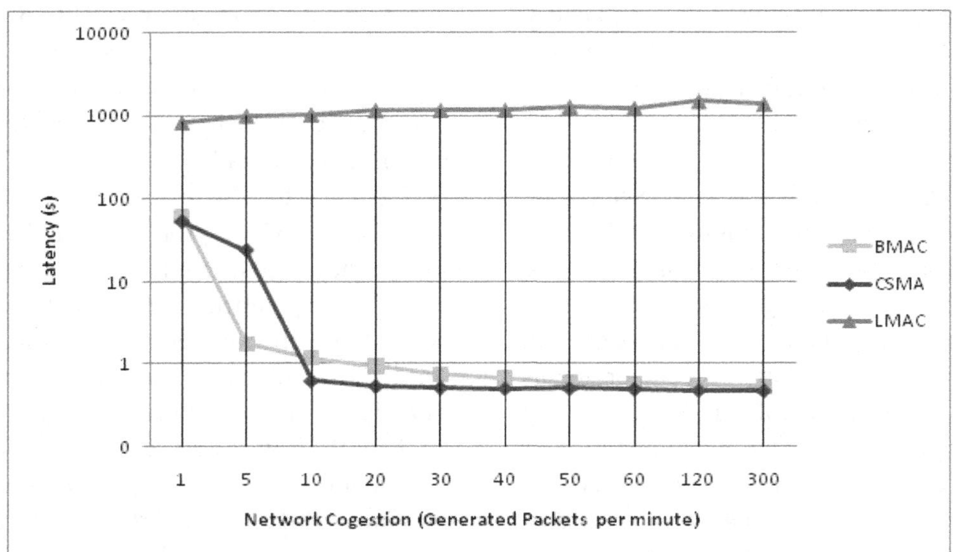

Figure 14. Network lifetime in WSN for monitoring

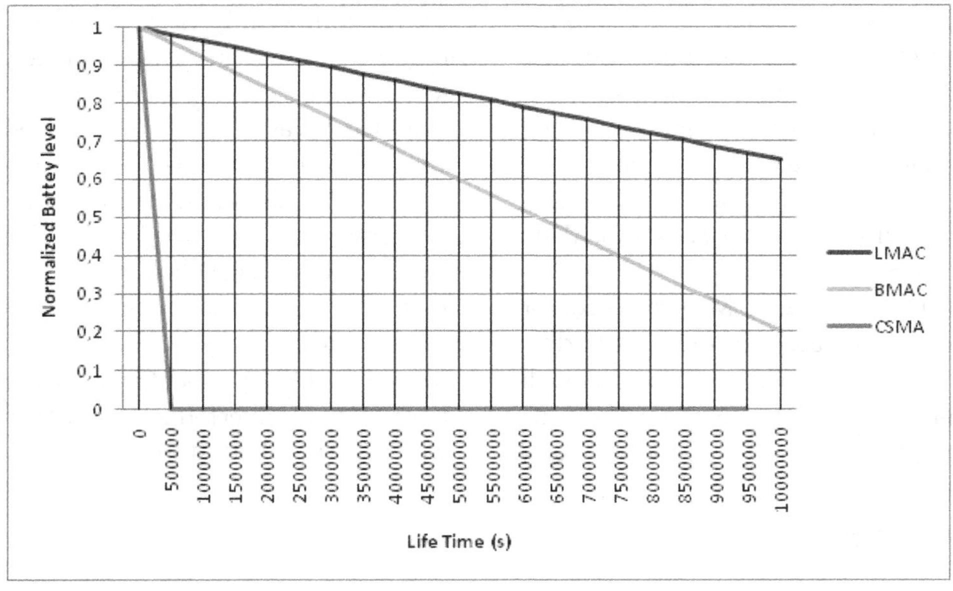

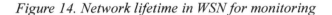

Network Layer Protocols

SPIN (Heinzelman, Kulik & Balakrishnan, 1999) is a family of flat routing protocols that disseminate the information sent from each individual node to every other network node, assuming all nodes act as base stations. This allows users to consult any node and immediately receive the required information. Since neighboring nodes frequently have redundant information, the protocol is designed to allow negotiation so that only non-redundant data is sent. This is done in SPIN by self-assignment of high level names (meta-data). Another important feature of SPIN is that it can have information about the remaining power of the node and adapt the protocol accordingly. These protocols work in a time-driven mode (periodic data information) and distribute the information throughout the network, even when the user does not request any data.

Direct Diffusion (Intanagonwiwat, Govindan & Estrin, 2000) is a data-centric routing protocol. This protocol suggests using attribute-value pairs for data and queries from the sensors, based on the concept of on-demand routing. The operation of the protocol is based on the definition of a parameter called interest, which is application dependent and defined by the network designer. To create a query, interest is defined using a list of attribute-value pairs, such as the name of objects, interval, duration, geographical area, etc. The interest is transmitted to the sink node through its neighbors. Each node receiving the interest can temporarily store it for later use. Interests in the cache are used to compare with the received data. The interest entry also contains several gradient fields. A gradient is a link from a neighbor which was received on interest (characterized by the data rate, duration and expiration date fields derived from interest received). Therefore, by using interest and gradients, paths are established between the sources and sink node. Several routes can be set so that one of them is selected (enforcement of routes). The receiver forwards the original message of interest along the selected route with a small range and thus reinforces the source node on the route to send data more frequently. Direct diffusion differs from SPIN in terms of the mechanism of formal data. In direct diffusion, sink queries are conditioned to the availability of data for tasks of dissemination (flooding). In SPIN, the sensors announce the availability of data allowing the nodes to consult stakeholders. Direct diffusion has many advantages because it uses the data-centric technique: all communication is neighbor to neighbor, without a mechanism for addressing the node. Each node can add and store its neighbors' information, in addition to its normal task of capturing the signal. Caching is a great advantage in terms of energy efficiency and latency. In addition, direct diffusion on-demand protocol has no need to maintain the topology of the entire network. However, direct diffusion cannot be implemented in all sensor network applications. Applications that require a continuous supply of data to the sink do not work efficiently with an on-demand consulting model. Therefore, direct diffusion is not a good option for environmental monitoring applications. In addition, the classification system used in direct diffusion is dependent on the application. The process of comparing data and queries may require some additional overhead in the sensor nodes.

An alternative approach to routing protocols uses a hierarchy, leading to some advantages in terms of scalability and efficiency of network communication. The most representative algorithm of this family is Low Energy Adaptive Clustering Hierarchy (LEACH) (Heinzelman, Chandrakasan, & Balakrishnan, 2000). LEACH creates clusters of sensor nodes based on received signal strength and uses a cluster head in the local cluster as a router to the sink. Data processing, such as fusion and aggregation, is performed on the local cluster. The cluster heads are randomly changed in order to balance the energy consumption of nodes. This decision is made by the nodes by randomly choosing numbers between 0 and 1. As nodes die randomly, the dynamic distribution increases the lifetime of the network. LEACH is completely distributed and requires no global knowledge of the network. The main limitation of LEACH is that it uses single-hop routing, i.e. each node can transmit directly to the cluster head and sink. Hence, it is not applicable to networks deployed in large regions. Moreover, the idea of dynamic clustering brings additional costs, including changes in the head, which can reduce the increase in energy consumption.

The last family of routing protocols is Location-Based, in which nodes are addressed with information regarding their location. One of the most representative protocols using this approach is Geographic and Energy Aware Routing (GEAR) (Yu, Estrin & Govindan, 2001). This protocol uses geographic information to make routing decisions while spreading requirements in areas which often include geographic attributes. The GEAR algorithm routes a package to a selected region, based on energy conservation and selection of the neighbor's heuristics from geographic information. The main objective of this protocol is to limit the spread of interest developed in direct diffusion, only sending this information to the regions of interest and not to the entire network. Each node computes two values: the estimated cost, which refers to a node's residual energy and the distance to the destination, and the cost of learning, which is a refined value of the estimated cost taking into account the routing gaps throughout the network. A gap occurs when a node does not have a close neighbor to reach the target region. If there are holes, the estimated cost is equal to the cost of learning. Table 3 summarizes and compares the network layer approaches discussed above.

Cross-Layer Protocols

As mentioned earlier, the goal of a CL approach is to simultaneously optimize performance parameters of different layers. This approach has proven to perform better in terms of power consumption.

One of the first attempts to develop a CL design in WSNs is the TinyCubus framework (Marrón, Lachenmann & Minder, 2005), which consists of a data management framework (DMF), a Cross-Layer Framework (CLF) and a configuration engine (EC). The DMF allows dynamic selection and tailoring of systems and data management components. The CLF supports the exchange of data and other forms of interaction between components to achieve cross-layer optimizations. The EC allows code to be distributed reliably and efficiently. The optimization is application oriented, i.e. the specific parameters to use in the optimization process depend on the specific application of the WSN. It also considers the network topology as part of the optimization process. The general goal is to optimize the network layer protocol to minimize the power consumption by using application layer and topology information.

Another CL framework based on an exchange of data between layers from a common compo-

Table 3. Network layer algorithms

Routing Protocol	Principles	Advantage	Disadvantage
SPIN	Flat network, flooding.	Data-Aggregation. Fast access to information. Time-Driven applications.	Not good power saving. Inefficient use of channels. Limited mobility.
Direct Diffusion	Flat network, optimized flooding.	Data-Aggregation. Negotiation-based. Event-Driven applications. Fault tolerant.	Not good power saving Less scalability. Limited mobility.
LEACH	Hierarchical network	Maximum Power usage. Event and Time Driven.	No multipath. Not functional in large networks. Complex implementation. Limited Data-Aggregation (only in the local cluster).
GEAR	Location-based	Geographical information, for routing path. Delimited disseminations. Fault tolerant.	Limited mobility. Not good power saving.

nent was developed by (Su & Lim, 2006). This framework is based on the principle of systematically organizing the interactions between layers through the definition of an optimization agent (Agent Based Optimization - OAB). The major contribution of OAB is to combine the internal interactions of the layers in a central repository, called an optimization agent. This framework allows for the individual optimization of each layer by obtaining critical information from the repository, and locally optimizing each layer.

A third CL framework (XLM) is based on a unified optimization scheme (Akyildiz, Vuran & Akan, 2006). This framework is developed to achieve efficient and reliable communication with minimum energy expenditure. XLM combines functionality of the common protocols of each layer in a simple CL module that functions on the limited resources of sensor nodes. The operation of the XLM is built on the basis of a new concept, initiative determination, and also implements received-based contention with the help of geographical information, local congestion control and distributed duty cycle radio operation. An outline of the structure of the protocol is shown in Figure 15.

Figure 15. XML scheme

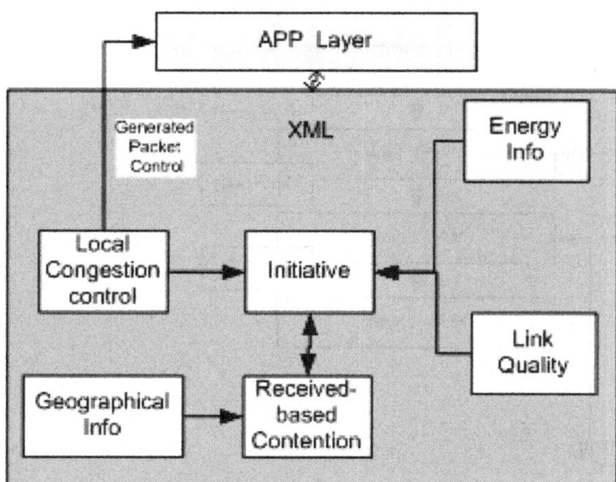

The value of initiative determination is calculated based on four variables, each representing a threshold that must be satisfied. The initiative is 1 if all four conditions are successful. The variables are related on the received signal to noise ratio, transmitted packets (forwarded and generated), buffer capacity and remaining energy of the node. Let I represent the initiative, which is computed as follows in Equation 5.

Equation 5. Initiative determination in XML

$$I = \begin{cases} 1, & if \begin{cases} \varepsilon_{RTS} \geq \varepsilon_{Th} \\ \lambda_{relay} \leq \lambda_{relay}^{Th} \\ \beta \leq \beta^{Max} \\ E_{rem} \geq E_{rem}^{\min} \end{cases} \\ 0, & othercase \end{cases}$$

The initiative determination concept is based on the principle that each node negotiates its participation in the communication process. So, if a node receives a RTS packet, it immediately evaluates the initiative equation and determines all the values needed. If all values are greater than the threshold, the initiative takes the value of 1 and the node initiates a received-based contention to compete with its neighbors by sending the CTS packet.

The first term in the Equation 1 $\varepsilon_{RTS} \geq \varepsilon_{Th}$, is the link quality. When the node receives the RTS packet, it uses the signal level to compute the signal to noise ratio ε_{RTS}. If this value is greater than the threshold (ensuring a reliable link), the condition is satisfied. The second term in the equation $\lambda_{relay} \leq \lambda_{relay}^{Th}$ is related to the capacity of the protocol to control local congestion. λ_{relay} refers to the number of packets that a node actually relays. If this value is greater than the threshold, the condition is not satisfied and the initiative is 0. The protocol can control the node packets generated by reducing the rate of generated packet due to the sensing activity. This control is executed with the factor of regulation β. When β increases, the generated packets are sent. When β is less than a β^{Max}, the node always decides not to forward packets and other neighbors take this work, thus balancing the load of the network.

At last, if the remaining energy in the node is less than a defined threshold $E_{rem} \geq E_{rem}^{min}$, this node does not participate in the communication.

The strongest point of this framework is that it takes into account a number of requirements for physical and network layers and combines them into a simple structure. Being predominantly a solution based on the network layer, this framework does not address the application layer.

Jurdak, Baldi, & Videira Lopes (2007) propose a CL optimization framework, locally and globally. Initially, the nodes are enabled to adjust their routing behavior in the MAC layer according to the local status. For the network layer, the framework extends a cost function for routing decisions. This cost function includes physical, link and application layer information and even QoS metrics such as latency and reliability. An outline of the structure of the protocol is shown in Figure 16.

The principal core of this work is the ALPL (Adaptive Low Power Listening) that controls parameters of the MAC protocol in B-MAC, ensuring the consistency of the joint optimization between the network layer and link layer. The ALPL controls the listening mode of the B-MAC protocol of each node according to the information of the local state. In this case, the states can be defined by the network designer according to the application target or the QoS requirements.

The WSN analyzed in this study uses a proactive protocol, specifically MintRoute of TinyOS (Woo, Tong & Culler, 2003). It allows the framework to exchange the node state information via periodic update routing packets. Initially, the nodes start in a listening mode *Linit*. Then, the nodes send presence and state messages. With this information, the nodes create graphs and data flows to the base station. Each node calculates the local state according to its number of descendents, and chooses its optimal listening mode. In the next update routing period, the node communicates to its neighbors its new listening mode, and they save this information in the routing table. So, if a node wants to communicate with others, it must first go to the routing table to read the optimal listening mode and send a preamble with the correct duration.

To change the network topology, the framework implements an extension in the original cost function of the MintRoute protocol. Thus, if a node wants to evaluate the cost of using a node M as parent, the node must evaluate Equation 6.

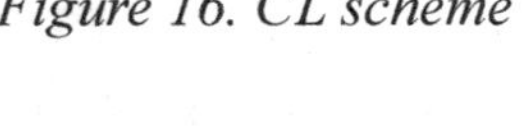
Figure 16. CL scheme

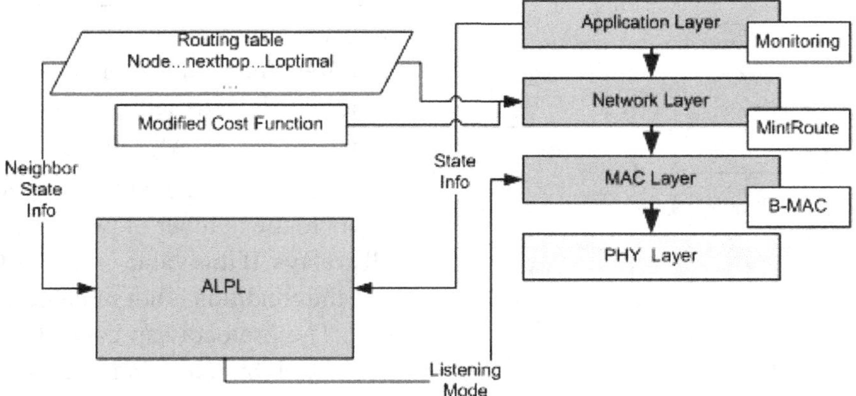

Equation 6. CL cost function

$$C(M) = \begin{cases} C_{mintRoute}(M) + \alpha C(radio) + \beta C(sensing) & H(M) \leq H(RP) \\ C_{mintRoute}(M) & H(M) > H(RP) \end{cases}$$

Where, $C_{mintRoute}(M)$ is the original cost function of the MintRoute protocol, $C(radio)$ is the cost of the radio activity, $C(sensing)$ is the cost of applying layer activity, α and β are weight constants, $H(M)$ is the hop number to reach node M and $H(RP)$ is the hop number to reach the current routing parent.

The main advantage of this framework is that it allows both local optimization at the node level and global network optimization by changing the routing topology. It also allows flexibility in deployed applications and adaptability to changes in the network. Its weakness lies in the fact that it lacks a clear mechanism to scale this solution to highly dynamic sensor networks.

CONCLUSION

WSNs have great potential for useful and practical applications. In recent years, there has been a growing interest in developing mechanisms to improve their performance in terms of maximizing network lifetime. This chapter presented a broad description of strategies for the design of nodes and protocols for WSNs. This chapter also examined a wide range of mechanisms to minimize the energy needed for node sensing and communication. The design of WSN applications that take into account these diverse alternatives is a complex task. A good simulation framework is very useful in analyzing the performance of a specific strategy prior to physically implementing the network.

At the protocol level, it is necessary to clearly define the quality of service required to apply and optimize the available hardware resources. With this information, the designer should analyze the necessary trade-offs to meet these requirements. The main goal of this work was to discuss the main features of the most widely used algorithms in order to give readers an idea about which are better suited to specific applications, based on a comprehensive analysis of the options.

The power consumption of nodes depends on the number of transmissions performed in the network. This is because the use of a radio frequency interface requires a considerable amount of energy. The impact of a signal processing strategy for a node does not represent a substantial change in its processing power. This goal is met by performing data processing tasks under low priority FIFO, thus allowing power preservation.

One of the most important features of the signal processing strategy in nodes is the lack of

Table 4. Summary and comparison of CL approaches

Cross-Layer Framework	Structure	Layers	Features
TinyTube	Interlayer communication	Application Network	Optimizes network layer. TinyOS implementation
OAB	Shared-Database	All	Optimizes each layer No global optimization
XLM	New abstraction	Network Link	Initiative determination-based Simple structure Local and global optimization
ALPL	Interlayer Communication Shared Data-base	Application Network Link Physic information	Uses B-MAC with ALPL Local and global optimization Cost function can be extended for QoS metrics.

a-priori knowledge of the statistical properties of the observed phenomena. This feature allows the technique to be applied in many practical applications. Also, this approach can be easily integrated in a variety of different approaches, including techniques like data aggregation and data fusion.

FUTURE TRENDS

Wireless sensor network technology has experimented a great development in the last few years. Today, diverse applications can be built through bare hardware and some available middleware (Crossbow, 2009; Madden et al., 2005). However, there is no mature high-level design methodology which guarantees the design of the sensor network with the QoS, latency, robustness and network lifetime requirements defined by the application domain (Campanoni & Fornaciari, 2008), (Bonivento, Fischione & Necchi, 2007). There are different priorities on what is required, depending on the application domain. Generally, network lifetime is the most important parameter for the network design. Some tradeoffs were discussed in this chapter; nevertheless QoS parameters should be taken into account so that networks can perform the sensing tasks and deliver sensory data. Important QoS measures are Sensing Coverage (Ye, Zhong, Cheng & Zhang, 2003), Data delivery Ratio (DDR), Quality of Surveillance (QoSv) (Gui & Mohapatra, 2004) and Balanced Energy Consumption among the nodes (Wang & Xiao, 2006). Therefore, it is necessary to develop a framework to permit high-level analysis and design, where quantitative models that evaluate different parameters and their interrelations should be available for different platforms and network architectures. Along with this infrastructure, simulation tools which evaluate different configuration and architectures schemes at high level should be integrated to determine the best implementation. Also, synthesis algorithms for sensor network hardware and software components should be developed. Some recent works have started to consider this problem (Sangiovanni & Vincentelli, 2008; Bonivento, Fischione & Necchi, 2007).

REFERENCES

Akyidiz, I. F., Su, W., Sankarasubramaniam, Y., & Cayirci, E. (2002). A survey on sensor networks. *IEEE Communications Magazine*, *40*(8), 102–116. doi:10.1109/MCOM.2002.1024422

Akyildiz, I. F., Vuran, M. C., & Akan, O. B. (2006). A Cross-Layer Protocol for Wireless Sensor Networks. *Conference on Information Sciences and Systems (CISS)*. Princeton, NJ.

Alippi, C., Anastasi, G., Galperti, C., Mancini, F., & Roveri, M. (2007). Adaptive sampling for energy conservation in wireless sensor networks for snow monitoring applications. In *Proceedings of the IEEE International Conference on Mobile Adhoc and Sensor Systems*, (pp. 1-6).

Bertsekas, D., & Gallager, R. (1992). *Data Networks* (2nd ed.). Prentice Hall.

Bonivento, A., Fischione, C., & Necchi, L. (2007). System Level Design for clustered wireless sensor networks. *IEEE Trans. on Industrial Informatics*, *3*(3), 204–214.

Boulis, A., Ganeriwal, S., & Srivastava, M. B. (2003). Aggregation in sensor networks: an energy-accuracy trade-off. In *Proceedings of the IEEE International Workshop on Sensor Network Protocols and Applications*, (pp. 128-138).

Campanoni, S., & Fornaciari, W. (2008). Models and tradeoffs in WSN sytem-level Design. In *Proceedings of the 11th Euromicro Conference on Digital System Design*, (pp. 676-683).

Crossbow. (2009). *Xbow*. Retrieved December from http://www.crossbow.com

Crossbow Technologies. (2008). *Crosbow techonologies*. Retrieved 2008, from http://www.xbow.com

Culler, D. (2004). *Computers*. IEEE Press.

Ermis, E., & Saligrama, V. (2005). Adaptive statistical sampling methods for decentralized estimation and detection of localized phenomena. *Paper presented at the 4th international symposium on Information processing in sensor networks.*

Gandham, S. R., Dawande, M., Prakash, R., & Venkatesan, S. (2003). Energy efficient schemes for wireless sensor networks with multiple mobile base stations. In [GLOBECOM]. *Proceedings of the IEEE Global Telecommunications Conference*, *1*, 377–381.

Gaviria, N., Aguirre, J. A., & Aedo, J. E. (2009). Data collection and Signal Processing strategy for low power consumption in Wireless Sensor Networks Nodes. In *Proceedings of the IEEE 2009 Latincom*, (pp. 1-5).

Gui, C., & Mohapatra, P. (2004). Power conservation and quality of Surveillance in target tracking sensor networks. In *Proceedings of ACM Mobile Computing and Networking Conference (MobiCom)*, (pp. 129-143).

Hayes, M. (1996). *Statistical Digital Signal Processing and Modeling*. John Wiley & Sons.

Heidemann, J. (2003). Medium Access Control in Wireless Sensor Networks. *USC/ISI Tech. Report ISI-TR-580.*

Heinzelman, W., Chandrakasan, A., & Balakrishnan, H. (2000). Energy-Efficient Communication Protocol for Wireless Microsensor Networks. *Paper presented at the 33rd Hawaii International Conference on System Sciences (HICSS).*

Heinzelman, W., Kulik, J., & Balakrishnan, H. (1999). Adaptive Protocols for Information Dissemination in Wireless Sensor Networks. In *Proceedings of the 5th ACM/IEEE Mobile Computing and Networking Conference (MobiCom)*, (pp. 174-185). Seattle.

Hill, J. L. (2003). *System architecture for wireless sensor networks*. PhD Thesis. University of California, Berkeley.

Holger, K., & Willing, A. (2005). *Protocols and Architectures for Wireless Sensor Networks*. John Wiley & Sons.

Imad, M., & Ilyas, M. (2005). *Handbook of Sensor Network: Compact Wireless and Wired Sensing Systems*. CRC Press.

Intanagonwiwat, C., Govindan, R., & Estrin, D. (2000). Directed diffusion: a scalable and robust communication paradigm for sensor networks. In *Proceedings of the ACM Mobile Computing and Networking (MobiCom)*, (pp. 56-67). Boston.

Jinghua, W., Huan, H., Bo, C., Yuanyuan, C., & Tingting, G. (2009). Data Aggregation and Routing in Wireless Sensor Networks Using Improved Ant Colony Algorithm. *International Forum on Computer Science-Technology and Applications*, *3*, 215–218. doi:10.1109/IFCSTA.2009.292

Jurdak, R., Baldi, P., & Videira Lopes, C. (2007). Adaptive Low Power Listening for Wireless Sensor Networks. *IEEE Transactions on Mobile Computing*, *6*(8), 988–1004. doi:10.1109/TMC.2007.1037

Karaca, O., & Sokullu, R. (2009). Comparative Study of Cross Layer Frameworks for Wireless Sensor Networks. In *Proceedings of the Wireless Communication Society, Vehicular Technology, Information Theory and Aerospace & Electronics Systems Technology (Wireless VITAE)*, (pp. 896-900). Denmark.

Kho, J., Rogers, A., & Jennings, N. R. (2007). Decentralised adaptive sampling of wireless sensor networks. In *Proceedings of the First International Workshop on Agent Technology for Sensor Networks, a workshop of the 6th International Joint Conference on Autonomous Agents and Multiagent Systems (AAMAS-07)*, (pp. 55-62).

Krishnamachari, B., Estrin, E., & Wicker, S. (2002). Impact of data aggregation in wireless sensor networks. *Paper presented at the 22nd International Conference on Distributed Computing Systems.*

Langendoen, K. (2005). *The MAC alphabet soup.* Retrieved October 2009, from https://apstwo.st.ewi.tudelft.nl/~koen/MACsoup

Le Borgne, Y., Santini, S., & Bontempi, G. (2007). Adaptive model selection for time series prediction in wireless sensor networks. *Signal Processing, 87*(12), 3010–3020. doi:10.1016/j.sigpro.2007.05.015

Lo, B. (2005). Body Sensor Network-Wireless Sensor Platform for Pervasive Healthcare Monitor. *Paper presented at the 3rd International conference on Pervasive Computing (PERVASIVE).*

Madden, S., Franklin, M., Hellertein, J., & Hong, W. (2005). TinyDB: and acquisitional query processing system for sensor networks. *ACM Transactions on Database Systems, 30*(1), 122–173. doi:10.1145/1061318.1061322

Marrón, P. J., Lachenmann, A., & Minder, D. (2005). TinyCubus: A Flexible and Adaptive Framework for Sensor Networks. In *Proceedings of the 2nd European Workshop on Wireless Sensor Networks*, (pp. 278-289).

Melodia, T., Vuran, M. C., & Pompili, D. (2006). The state-of-the-art in cross-layer design for wireless sensor networks. In *Proceedings of the EuroNGI Workshops on Wireless and Mobility*, Springer Lecture Notes on Computer Science (LNCS), Vol. 388, (pp. 78-92).

Mostofi, Y., Chung, T. H., Murray, R. M., & Burdick, J. W. (2005). Communication and sensing trade-offs in decentralized mobile sensor networks: a cross-layer design approach. In *Proceedings of the 4th international symposium on information processing in sensor networks*, (pp. 118 – 125).

Paradiso, J. (2005). Energy scavenging for mobile and wireless electronics. *IEEE Pervasive Computing Journal, 4*(1), 18–27. doi:10.1109/MPRV.2005.9

Park, S., & Sivakumar, R. (2008). Energy Efficient Correlated Data Aggregation for Wireless Sensor Networks. *International Journal of Distributed Sensor Networks, 4*(1), 13–27. doi:10.1080/15501320701774592

Polastre, J., Hill, J., & Culler, D. (2004). Versatile Low Power Media Access for Wireless Sensor Networks. *Paper presented at the 2nd ACM Conference on Embedded Networked Sensor Systems.* Baltimore.

Proakis, J. (2006). *Digital Signal Processing.* Prentice Hall.

Raghunathan, V., Schurgers, C., Park, S., & Srivastava, M. (2002). Energy aware wireless sensor networks. *IEEE Signal Processing Magazine, 19*(2), 40–50. doi:10.1109/79.985679

Rizvi, S., & Riasat, A. (2007). Use of self-adaptive methodology in wireless sensor networks for reducing energy consumption. In *Proceedings of the International Conference on Information and Emerging Technologies.* (pp. 1-7).

Römer, K., & Santini, S. (2006). An Adaptive Strategy for Quality-Based Data Reduction in Wireless Sensor Networks. In *Proceedings of the 3rd International Conference on Networked Sensing Systems* (INSS), (pp. 29-36).

Sangiovanni-Vincentelli, A. (2008). Is a Unified Methodology for System-Level Design Possible? Special Issue on Design in the Late and Post-Silicon Era. *IEEE Design & Test of Computers, 25*(4), 346–358. doi:10.1109/MDT.2008.104

Santini, S. (2006). Towards adaptive wireless sensor networks. *Paper presented at the 3rd European Workshop on Wireless Sensor Networks.*

Shakshuki, E., & Malik, H. (2007). Agent Based Approach to Minimize Energy Consumption for Border Nodes in Wireless Sensor Network. In *Proceedings of the 21st International Conference on Advanced Networking and Applications*. (pp. 134-141).

Shebli, F., Dayoub, I., Rouvaen, J. M., & Zaouche, A. (2007). A new optimization approach for energy consumption within wireless sensor networks. In *Proceedings of the Third Advanced International Conference on Telecommunications (AICT)*, (pp. 14-20).

Sinopoli, B., Sharp, C., Schenato, L., Schaffert, S., & Sastry, S. S. (2003). Distributed control applications within sensor networks. *IEEE Proceedings*, *91*(8), 1235–1246. doi:10.1109/JPROC.2003.814926

Slama, I. Jouaber, B., & Zeghlache, D. (2007). Optimal Power management scheme for Heterogeneous Wireless Sensor Networks: Lifetime Maximization under QoS and Energy Constraints. In *Proceedings of the Third International Conference on Networking and Services*. (pp. 66-75).

Sohraby, K., Minoli, D., & Znati, T. (2007). *Wireless Sensor Networks: Technology, Protocols, and Applications*. Wiley & Son. doi:10.1002/047011276X

Sreenath, K. (2007). *Adaptive sampling with mobile WSN.* Msc. Thesis, University Of Texas At Arlington.

Srivastava, V., & Motani, M. (2005). Cross-Layer Design: A Survey and the Road Ahead. *IEEE Communications Magazine*, *43*(12), 112–119. doi:10.1109/MCOM.2005.1561928

Su, W., & Lim, T. L. (2006). Cross-Layer Design and Optimization for Wireless Sensor Networks. *Paper presented at the Seventh ACIS International Conference on Software Engineering, Artificial Intelligence, Networking, and Parallel/Distributed Computing (SNPD).* Las Vegas.

Tors, F., Sanders, S., Winters, C., Brebels, S., & Van Hoof, C. (2004). Wireless network of autonomous environmental sensors. *Proceedings of IEEE Sensors*, *2*, 923–926. doi:10.1109/ICSENS.2004.1426322

Van Hoesel, L. F., & Havinga, P. J. (2004). A Lightweight Medium Access Protocol (LMAC) for Wireless Sensor Networks: Reducing Preamble Transmissions and Transceiver State Switches. *Paper presented at the 1st International Workshop on Networked Sensing Systems (INSS).* Tokio, Japan.

Varga, A. (2009). *OMNeT++ Community Site*. Retrieved November 2009, from http://www.omnetpp.org/

Vass, D., Vincze, Z., Vida, R., & Vidács, A. (2006). *Energy Effiency in Wireless Sensor Networks Using Mobile Base Station.* In book: EUNICE 2005: Networks and Applications Towards a Ubiquitously Connected, 196, 173-186. Boston:Springer.

Wang, L., & Xiao, Y. (2006). A survey of Energy-Efficient Scheduling Mechanism in Sensor Netwoks. *Mobile Networks and Applications*, *11*(5), 723–740. doi:10.1007/s11036-006-7798-5

Wang, Q., Fan, Y., Dong, Ya., & Duan, S. (2005). Power auto-adaptive wireless sensor network and application. In. *Proceedings of the IEEE International Symposium on Communications and Information Technology*, *1*, 391–395.

Wang, X., Ma, J., Wang, S., & Bi, D. (2007). Time series forecasting for energy-effcient organization of wireless sensor networks. *Sensors (Basel, Switzerland)*, *7*, 1766–1792. doi:10.3390/s7091766

Woo, A., Tong, T., & Culler, D. (2003). Taming the Underlying Challenges of Reliable Multihop Routing in sensors networks. In *Proceeding of ACM SenSys*, (pp. 14-27).

Ye, F., Zhong, G., Cheng, L., & Zhang, L. (2003). PEAS: A robust energy conserving protocols for long-lived sensor network. In *Proceeding of the 23rd International Conference on Distributed Computing Systems*, (pp. 28-37).

Ye, W., Heidemann, J., & Estrin, D. (2002). An energy-efficient MAC protocol for wireless sensor networks. In *Proceeding of the 21st Conference of the IEEE Computer and Communications Societies (INFOCOM)*, (pp. 1567–1576). New York.

Yu, Y., Estrin, D., & Govindan, R. (2001). *Geographical and Energy-Aware Routing: A Recursive Data Dissemination Protocol for Wireless Sensor Networks. Technical Report*. UCLA Computer Science Department.

Zhang, W., & Liang, Z. Hou., Z, & Tan., M. (2007). A Power Efficient Routing Protocol for Wireless Sensor Network. Networking, Sensing and Control. In *Proceeding of the IEEE International Conference on Networking, Sensing and Control*, (pp. 20-25).

Zhao, A., Yu, J., & Li, Z. (2009). A Data Aggregation Scheme in Wireless Sensor Networks for Structure Monitoring. In *Proceeding of the International Conference on Information Management, Innovation Management and Industrial Engineering*, Vol. 4, (pp. 623-626).

Chapter 3
A Forward & Backward Secure Key Management in Wireless Sensor Networks for PCS/SCADA

Hani Alzaid
Queensland University of Technology, Australia & King Abdulaziz City for Science and Technology, Saudi Arabia

Dong Gook Park
Sunchon National University, South Korea

Juan Gonzàlez Nieto
Queensland University of Technology, Australia

Colin Boyd
Queensland University of Technology, Australia

Ernest Foo
Queensland University of Technology, Australia

ABSTRACT

Process Control Systems (PCSs) or Supervisory Control and Data Acquisition (SCADA) systems have recently been added to the already wide collection of wireless sensor network applications. The PCS/SCADA environment is somewhat more amenable to the use of heavy cryptographic mechanisms such as public key cryptography than other sensor application environments. The sensor nodes in this environment, however, are still open to devastating attacks such as node capture, which makes the design of secure key management challenging. This chapter introduces an adversary model with which we can assess key management protocols. It also proposes a key management scheme to defeat node capture attack by offering both forward and backward secrecies. The scheme overcomes the pitfalls of a comparative scheme while being not computationally more expensive.

DOI: 10.4018/978-1-60960-027-3.ch003

INTRODUCTION

Process Control Systems (PCSs) or Supervisory Control and Data Acquisition (SCADA) systems are used to monitor and control a plant or equipment in industries such as energy, oil and gas refining, and transportation. SCADA systems enable the transfer of data between the network manager and a number of Remote Terminal Units (RTUs), sensor nodes, etc. A SCADA system gathers critical information (such as where a leak in a pipeline has occurred) and then transfers this information back to the network manager. The network manager is responsible for alerting the home station about the leak and carrying out necessary analysis such as determining whether the leak is critical or not.

Owners and operators of SCADA systems aim to increase the monitoring sensitivity of their systems and reduce the day to day running cost wherever possible. The intelligent monitoring capabilities of Wireless Sensor Networks (WSNs) mean that integration between SCADA and WSNs can be one way to achieve these aims. WSNs facilitate the monitoring process by performing specific tasks such as sensing physical phenomena at a remote field and then reporting them back to the network manager. They can form the "eyes and ears" of SCADA systems. Nodes, which are capable of performing functions such as gas detection and temperature sensing, provide information that can tell an experienced operator how well oil/gas pipelines are performing.

Roman et al. highlighted the role that WSNs can play in SCADA (2007). They argued that WSNs can aid the functionality of SCADA systems by providing monitoring, alerts, and information on demand. However, security vulnerabilities can be introduced to SCADA systems by WSNs. One of these potential vulnerabilities is the security compromise of sensor nodes, given the lack of tamper resistant packaging (Hartung, Balasalle & Han, 2005). By gaining physical access, an adversary can gain control of one or more sensor nodes and readily access sensitive information such as keys or passwords. The adversary can therefore easily get access to the plain text of encrypted messages that are routed through the compromised nodes -- compromising data confidentiality. The adversary may also inject its own commodity nodes into the network by fooling legitimate nodes into believing that the commodity node is a legitimate member of the network. Another adversary activity is to launch a selective forwarding attack. In this type of attack, the node under control of the adversary selectively drops legitimate packets in order to affect the overall performance of the system (Karlof & Wagner, 2003).

In this chapter, we focus on strengthening the security level at the weakest component of the SCADA system which exists in remote fields (Beaver, Gallup, Neumann & Torgerson, 2002). The remote field has the weakest physical security requirements and consists of substations and intelligent electronic devices such as sensors, which will be discussed in Section Scada. We introduce a new model of adversary with which we can evaluate key management protocols. We then propose a new key management protocol that updates the shared symmetric key between the network manager and a sensor node or between the network manager and a group of sensor nodes. Finally, we analyze the performance of our proposal and compare it with those of Nilsson et al.'s scheme (Nilsson, Roosta, Lindqvist & Valdes, 2008). This performance analysis covers memory overhead, communication cost, and computation cost for these schemes.

SCADA

To best understand the added value of the proposed scheme, some understanding of SCADA is in order. Today's SCADA systems (the third generation) are a combination of legacy and modern technology (McClanahan, 2003). The third generation SCADA has become an open system architecture rather than a vendor controlled architecture as in the second generation of SCADA. The third generation of SCADA uses open standards and protocols which facilitate distribution of its functionalities. We refer readers interested in the differences between these generations to the paper by McClanahan (2003).

Figure 1 shows a simplified SCADA system architecture which is composed of the following components:

Master Center

The master center component contains the network manager, human machine interaction, database storage, processing server, etc. It has the highest physical security level compared to other components. Generally speaking, it receives monitoring information from remote fields (through the communication system component), processes it, and then makes decisions.

Historian

The historian is a backup for the SCADA system data which is often located in a separate subnet different to the one where the master center component exists. The master center component is able to access the historian in order to backup the data of the SCADA system.

Remote Fields

The remote fields are composed of substations (gateways) and intelligent electronic devices (IEDs) (Beaver et al., 2002) which can be physically distant from the SCADA master center and, in many cases, are not physically secured due to the largeness or remoteness of the coverage area. The substation connects IEDs with the master center component through the communication component. The substation has a high degree of complexity and might have better physical security than IEDs. The IEDs can be sensor nodes, remote terminal units, or relays to name a few.

Figure 1. The simplified version of PCS/SCADA

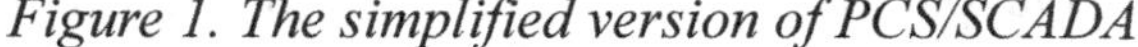

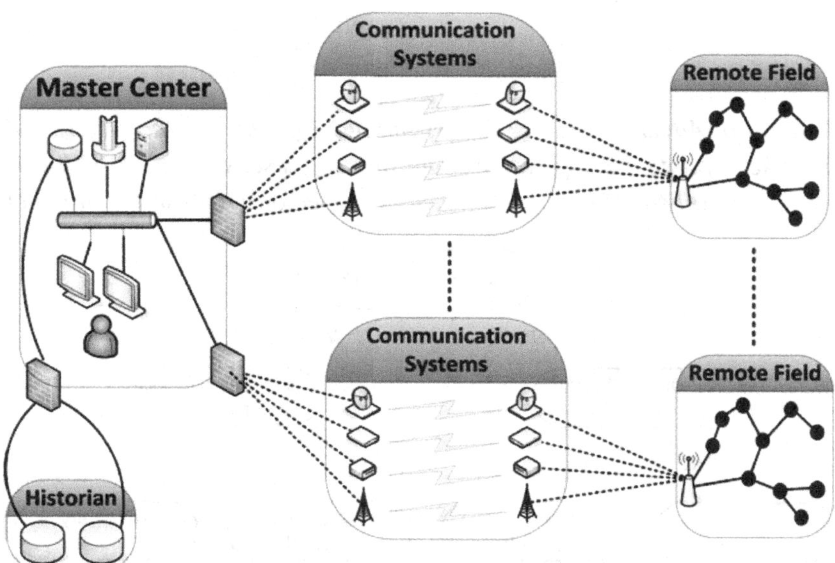

Communication Systems

The communication systems are responsible for transferring monitored data (control data) from remote field components (master center) to master center component (remote field components). This communication can be done via fiber optics, radio, satellite, etc.

According to the SCADA system architecture shown in Figure 2, the network manager, in the master center component, can communicate with the WSNs in the remote fields in two different ways as follows:

- It can broadcast information/commands to a group of sensor nodes, especially when there is no indication of a node compromise in the group.
- It can unicast information/commands to a specific sensor node, which helps move compromised sensor nodes from a particular group. In other words, this option helps the network manger eliminate the group membership from compromised nodes.

Thus, a secure key management framework is needed to establish and update the cryptographic keys (group and pairwise keys) which are used to secure the two ways of communication discussed above.

BACKGROUND

When designing a key management protocol for WSNs, the most challenging security threat would be node capture. The limited resources in sensor nodes make defending against this type of threat very hard. Node capture will translate into compromise of all the credentials stored in the sensor node. Furthermore, the adversary can compromise all software installed within the sensor node, especially random number generation functions. For example, the adversary can modify the code or replace it with his own code to mislead functions related to SCADA/PCS, use a fixed number instead of random numbers for input to security protocols, or launch a selective forwarding attack. However, the computational power of the adversary falls short of compromising the network manager and gateways which have reasonable physical security. Their physical security increases in proportion to the importance of the domain where a SCADA/PCS is deployed.

Our purpose in this chapter is to propose a key management scheme which is resilient to node capture: i.e., a scheme that enables sensor nodes

Figure 2. Classification of Adversaries: "Seamless monitoring" means the adversary keeps monitoring every subsequent key update message after compromising a sensor node; "software modification" includes alteration of any software installed in the node, especially the random number generator.

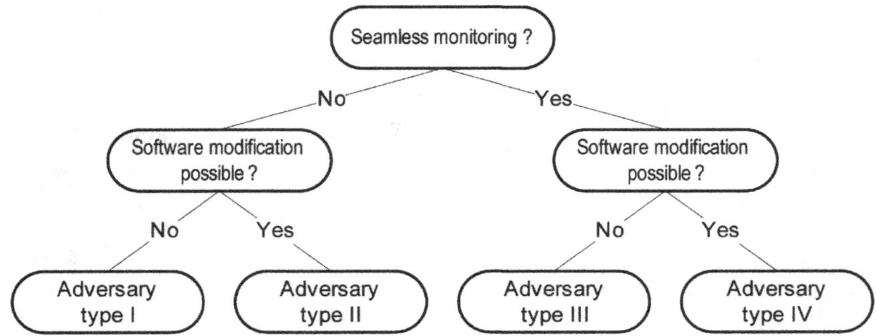

to recover their secure status even after they have been captured and then released back. Consequently, we are interested in what the adversary can do both when a node is captured, and after it is released back. Key disclosure is trivial after a sensor node has been compromised. The question is what else should be done by the adversary to keep control of the node after the node was returned to the field?

The adversary will try to ensure that the node uses values of its choice for all cryptographic keys or keying materials. For this purpose, the adversary may try to modify software components (especially the random number generation component) and monitor all or part of subsequent key update messages. In this regard, we use the following criteria to classify adversaries.

- The adversary can read and modify all the software code and configurations, including secret keys, installed in the sensor node. For example, once the adversary has succeeded in compromising a sensor node, the adversary can alter any software installed in this node, especially the random number generator.
- The adversary can carry out seamless monitoring of all the subsequent key update protocol exchanges. After compromising a sensor node, the adversary can monitor every subsequent key update message within the SCADA network.

According to the above two criteria, we divide the adversaries into four distinct types as shown in Figure 2. Type I is the weakest adversary: capable of neither seamless monitoring nor software compromise; Type IV is the strongest: capable of both seamless monitoring and software compromise. Type IV is so powerful that it is unlikely that any practical cryptographic countermeasure for WSNs against this adversary can be devised. The use of tamper-proof technology will be needed to cope with this type of adversary, but it is outside the scope of this chapter. Our goal in the chapter is to have a new key management scheme which uses cryptographic countermeasures to defend the other three types of attackers.

An interesting point here is that both software modification and software-based random number generation have similar consequences for cryptographic protocols. Software algorithm-based random number generation does not give true random numbers, which can only be obtained from a strong physical source of randomness. One consequence of this similarity is that it makes no sense to use expensive tamper-proof technologies while true random number generation is not used. Put a different way, we do not have to bother with true random number generation when software modification is assumed to be within the capabilities of the adversary.

Having identified different types of adversaries, we have the following concerns with regard to node capture and the consequent disclosure of all the internal data of the captured node:

- **Past key secrecy:** The past keys should not be compromised.
- **Future key secrecy:** The future keys should not be compromised.

The requirement of resilience to node capture rules out the use of any long-term keys; the keys must change or evolve continuously over time, with old prior keys deleted securely. In other words, we require a key evolution scheme to achieve past/future key secrecy against the threat of node capture.

Terminology: To the best of our knowledge, the terms "past/future key secrecy" have never been used in previous literature except in our initial proposal that has been recently published (Alzaid, Park, Nieto, Boyd & Foo, 2009). Similar terminology include "(perfect) forward secrecy" and "backward secrecy", which has always been quite confusing. The term "(perfect) forward secrecy" goes back to Günther (1989). The original

Table 1. Notations for the proposed scheme

M	Network manager
N	Sensor node
K_{MN}	Shared pairwise key between M and N
s_0, t_0	Pre-installed global secret data in every N
K_G^i	The i-th group key ($i \geq 0$)
r_X	Random nonce chosen by entity X
(K_M^{-1}, K_M)	Asymmetric key pair of network manager
$\{m\}_K$	Encryption of message m under the key K
$h(.)$	A cryptographic hash function
$h_K(.)$	A keyed hash function using the key K
$MAC_K(m)$	A message authentication code function on m using the key K

term assumes a long-term key and session keys established by the key, and means that the current session key is not compromised by the "future" (thus, the expression "forward") exposure of the long-term key. This terminology, somehow, seems to have got a slightly different usage in the context of group key communication; it concerns the contamination of a group key at a particular time by the compromise of an older/newer group key. The inherent ambiguity has brought a twin terminology: "backward secrecy". Some authors choose the term "backward secrecy" to mean "forward secrecy" as used by other authors, and vice versa. To avoid all this confusion, we will use a new more concrete expression: "past/future key secrecy" as defined in the previous paragraph. The notation to be used in the rest of the chapter can be found in Table 1.

RELATED WORK

There are several papers dealing with key management designs for SCADA systems such as (Dawson, Boyd, Dawson & Nieto, 2006; Pietre-Cambacedes & Sitbon, 2008). However, these designs either use heavy cryptographic mechanisms, unsuited to resource constrained devices, or do not consider the integration of WSNs within SCADA.

Protocol 1: Pairwise key update protocol by Nilsson et al. (2008)

N: generates a random number r_N

1. $M \leftarrow N: \{r_N\}_{K_M}, MAC_{K_{MN}}(\{r_N\}_{K_M})$

M, N: compute the new pairwise key $K'_{MN} = h(K_{MN}, r_N)$

Protocol 2: Group key update protocol by Nilsson et al. (2008)

M: generates a new group key K'_G and a random number r_M

1. $M \rightarrow N: \{K'_G, r_M\}_{K_{MN}}$
2. $M \leftarrow N: MAC_{K'_G}(N, r_M)$

To the best of our knowledge, the only existing key management in the wireless control environment, that considers the integration between SCADA/PCS and WSNs, has been proposed by Nilsson et al. (2008). They designed two key update protocols: the first one updates the pairwise symmetric key between the network manager M and a sensor node N (as described in Protocol 1), while the other scheme updates the global or group key among M and the whole group G of sensor nodes (as described in Protocol 2). They claim that the protocols provide both forward and backward secrecy (or in our newly defined terminology, they provide both past and future key secrecy). This, unfortunately, is not the case.

To initiate the group key update protocol, M generates a new group key K'_G randomly. It then encrypts it with another random number r_M and sends it over the network to the target group. No node in the group has any clue whether the received key is fresh or not. In other words, the freshness property, from the viewpoint of N does not hold since the two values (the new group key K'_G and the random number r_M) are random values chosen by M. It is both impractical and insecure for each sensor node to maintain a list of keys that have been used. Thus, an external adversary could record a rekeying message and then re-inject it into the network, which leads to the group key being updated with an old key. Consequently, the group enters a key mismatch phase where the key version that the group of sensors uses is different to the one that is used by M.

One good security practice is to minimize the damage caused by a compromised node. However, the authors did not consider common attacks in WSNs such as selective forwarding (Karlof & Wagner, 2003) or node compromise (Hartung et al., 2005). If a single sensor node has the ability to affect the operation of a good number of other sensor nodes, then the adversary will try to compromise that node. For example, if an adversary compromises a sensor node in a multi-hop path, then it will be able to oblige all other nodes downstream to enter the key mismatch phase. The adversary simply drops the rekeying message from M for the group key, and then uses the new group key to calculate MACs on the received nonce and the identities of nodes downstream, which results in a successful impersonation attack. We can easily fix the problem by replacing the MAC data with other data: e.g. $MAC_{K_{MN}}(K'_G, r_M)$.

Moreover, to initiate the pairwise key update protocol N generates a random number r_N and encrypts it with the network manager's public key K_M. It subsequently computes the MAC on the encryption result and sends this MAC and the encryption result over the network to M. The new pairwise key can be calculated at the sender, N and at the receiver M, by hashing r_N with the previous pairwise key. This means that the new pairwise key is always determined by N. The adversary consequently is able to know all the future keys once he has compromised N. A closer look at the protocols, Protocol 1 and Protocol 2, reveals their more serious defects.

- **Defect I.** The whole value of the new group key is directly carried by the protocol messages, encrypted under the pairwise key K_{MN}. The consequence is that compromise of the pairwise key for just one node leads to compromise of the group key for the whole group. This is a more serious problem than it might appear, because the pairwise key compromise does not necessarily require node capture.
- **Defect II.** The value of the new pairwise key K'_{MN} is only determined by the sensor node. When a Type II or IV adversary (capable of compromising the key generation codes stored in the node) captures a node, all the future pairwise keys for that node can be pre-determined by the adversary. Namely, physical compromise of the node immediately leads to compromise of all the future pairwise keys if the adversary can modify the codes installed in the node. This, in turn, leads to compromise of all future group keys as well because, as mentioned in Defect I, the group key is delivered encrypted under the pairwise key. Hence, contrary to Nilsson et al.'s claim, the scheme does not provide "future key secrecy", against node compromise, for either the pairwise key or the group key.
- **Defect III.** Although not explicitly shown in the protocol descriptions above, the key input r_N for the new pairwise key K'_{MN} is not really random in Nilsson et al.'s scheme; it is in fact a function of a pre-installed secret key and a counter value stored in the node. This means that, when the node is captured and all the installed data including keys exposed to the adversary, all the past pairwise keys as well as the future keys can immediately be computed even without recording a single key update message. In fact, this failure is due not only to Defect III, but also to Defect II.

> Note that, due to the combination of Defect III and Defect II, the adversary does not have to modify the node's software at all in order to extract all the past and future pairwise keys. Hence, Nilsson et al.'s scheme offers no minimum level of past or future key secrecy against node compromise. Moreover, the adversary can extract any group key in the past or future if he has collected the records of the corresponding group key update message. Note also that, for this, "seamless" monitoring is not needed by the adversary. What does this mean? The scheme is neither forward nor backward secure for either key type against node compromise for all types of adversary I, II, III and IV (see Figure 2).

As for past key secrecy, we note two proposed schemes in the WSN context: Klonowski et al. (2007) and Mauw et al. (2006). Both schemes use hash functions to achieve key evolution. Both schemes, however, are intended to be used not for group key update, but for updating pairwise keys for node-to-node (Klonowski et al., 2007; Ren, Das, & Zhou, 2006) or node-to-base station communication (Mauw et al., 2006).

On the other hand, as for future key secrecy, Mauw et al.'s protocol does not provide this property. The protocol is based on a hash chain scheme originally proposed for RFID security (Ohkubo, Suzuki, & Kinoshita, 2003). In RFID environments, protecting secret tag information from tampering in the future is a big concern, while it does not seem to be such a prime concern in WSNs. This is because it is more authentication and integrity than privacy that really matters in WSNs, especially SCADA/PCS. Hence, future key secrecy is more valued than past key secrecy. On the other hand, the protocol proposed by Klonowski provides future key secrecy in a "weak" sense; namely, it will be computationally hard for the adversary to compute a future key from the current compromised key if he fails to record, say ten, subsequent evolution steps (Ren et al., 2006).

THE PROPOSED SCHEME

Devising a key management scheme for WSNs is not trivial and, in particular, may not be successfully accomplished by simple adaptation of security solutions designed for wired networks. This is because of the limited resources such as energy lifetime, slow computation, small memory, and limited communication capabilities, which exist in WSNs (Vieira, Coelho, da Silva & da Mata, 2003; Walters, Liang, Shi & Chaudhary, 2006). In this section, we describe a key management scheme which secures communication between remote fields (where the WSN resides) and the master center (where the network manager resides) by considering vulnerabilities that are associated with WSNs.

Key Management Protocols

We focus on updating two types of keys, which are the *group key* and the *pairwise key*, in the wireless process control environments. A pairwise key is shared between the network manager M and each sensor node N, while the group key is shared among M and the whole group of sensor nodes.

Group Key Update Protocol

Our solution for group key rekeying also exploits the idea of key evolution using a hash chain in order to achieve past key secrecy. The protocol uses a hash chain $h^i(s_0)$, where s_0 is a pre-installed key component at the pre-deployment phase and $i \geq 0$ denotes the index for key update phases.

As for future key secrecy, we use the *reverse hash chain* technique which was first introduced by Lamport (1981). The network manager prepares in advance a hash chain of length n starting from a random seed t_{n-1} and ending with the final value t_0:

t_{n-1}, t_{n-2}:= $h(t_{n-1})$..., t_1:= $h(t_2)$, t_0:= $h(t_1)$

For reasons of convenience which will become clearer shortly, we write $h^{-i}(t_0)$ instead of t_i although h is not an invertible function and $h^{-1}(x)$ can only mean the set of all preimages of x in a strict sense. Roughly speaking, $h^{-i}(t_0)$ is the i-th preimage of t_0 in the reverse hash chain. The secret data, t_0, will be pre-installed into sensor nodes together with another key component s_0.

Now, with two secret key components s_0 and t_0 pre-installed within all sensor nodes, using Protocol 3, the group key K_G^i evolves as follows:

$$K_G^i = h^i(s_0) \oplus h^{-i}(t_0), \quad i \geq 0$$

where we define $h^0(s_0)=s_0$ and $h^0(t_0)=t_0$ (see Figure 3).

Any sensor node can easily compute the i-th hash image $h^i(s_0)$ from $h^{i-1}(s_0)$, while only the network manager knows the value of the i-th preimage $h^{-i}(t_0)$. Thus, it is only the network manager who can release the preimage into the sensor field. As a consequence, the first message in the protocol provides the sensor node with a weak form of signature from the network manager: the message could have been generated only by the network manager, not by any sensor nodes including the node itself. The check of the preimage (i.e., $h(h^{-i}(t_0))=h^{-(i-1)}(t_0)$) also ensures that the key update message is fresh.

Protocol 3: The proposed protocol for group key update

1. $M \rightarrow N:\ i, \{h^{-i}(t_0)\}_{K_{MN}}$ *# unicast* message
2. $M \leftarrow N:\ h_{K_{MN}}(K_G^i)$

M,N: increase the group key index from i-1 to i, and update the value of the group key(i.e., $K_G^i = h^i(s_0) \oplus h^{-i}(t_0)$).

After the i-th key update, the sensor node stores the index i and the secret data: $h^i(s_0)$, $h^{-i}(t_0)$ and K_G^i. Considering the highly lossy communication environment of sensor networks, the sensor node may sometimes fall behind the group key update schedule. The sensor node, however, will soon be able to catch up at the next rekeying: it can compute the correct value of the new group key simply by checking the difference of two index values – the received and the stored – and applying the corresponding number of hash operations.

Now let's assume that the adversary has somehow extracted the current value of the group key, K_G^i. However, he cannot extract from this the previous key K_G^{i-1} because he cannot compute the value of $h^{i-1}(s_0)$. Note that this holds even when the adversary has recorded all the previous key

Figure 3. Key evolution in the proposed protocol

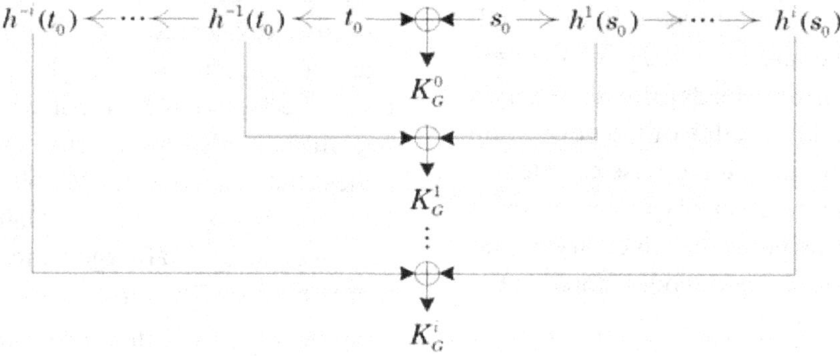

update messages, and compromised all the previous manager-to-node pairwise keys. In fact, the node capturing and extracting all the stored secret data does not surrender the past group key to the adversary. This is because the previous values for $h^i(s_0)$ were never exchanged over the air, and were deleted after group key computation. Hence the protocol provides past key secrecy for any kind of compromise: group key compromise, pairwise key compromise, and the compromise of the node itself.

The protocol also provides future key secrecy in the sense that the adversary cannot predict the next group key K_G^{i+1} just with knowledge of the current group key K_G^i. The computation of K_G^{i+1} requires knowledge of $h^{-(i+1)}(t_0)$, which has not yet been exchanged. In the next step of the key update, the adversary, without knowledge of the pairwise key K_{MN}, will not be able to obtain the value of $h^{-(i+1)}(t_0)$, from the protocol message. In fact, compromise of the pairwise key alone does not lead to the future group key compromise; it will only happen when the adversary captures a sensor node, thereby extracting the hidden component $h^i(s_0)$. Hence, the protocol satisfies future key secrecy in the face of group key and/or pairwise key compromise; simple delivery of the encrypted value of the new group key, as in (Nilsson et al., 2008), cannot provide this kind of resilience. Protocol 3 will fail to provide future key secrecy only when the node is physically captured. Even in the case of capture, the adversary should listen to the key update message to extract the future group key. Furthermore, when the pairwise key is updated, any adversary of type I, II, or III will not be able to have any knowledge of the new pairwise key. This, in turn, leads to the adversary's failure to have any knowledge of the new group key established using the new pairwise key. Hence, we achieve the future group key secrecy even after node capture, as far as the adversary has no ability to modify the software codes stored in the node.

Protocol 3 uses the pairwise key K_{MN} to encrypt the i-th preimage $h^{-i}(t_0)$ in the first message, and also to provide key confirmation by computing keyed hash of the new group key. This is in order to rule out any compromised or suspicious sensor nodes from group key update.

Our protocol, however, has one limitation: it is vulnerable to a kind of collusion attack. Assume that a sensor node was captured at a key update phase i and another node was subsequently captured again at the phase i+10. Then, the adversary can extract all the group keys for the phases i to i+10. Of course, this compromise is limited to past keys, not future keys. We call this attack a "*sandwich attack*" which will be considered in our future work.

Pairwise Key Update Protocol

Protocol 4: The proposed protocol for pairwise key update

1. $M \rightarrow N:\ i, \{h^{-i}(t_0), g^{r_M}\}_{K_G^{i-1}}$ # *broadcast* message
2. $M \leftarrow N:\ \{g^{r_N}\}_{K_{MN}}, h_{K_{MN}}(g^{r_M}, g^{r_N})$

N: keeps the hashed value of the current pairwise key: $K_{MN}^1 = h(K_{MN})$

M,N: increase the group key index from i-1 to i, and update the values of the pairwise key (i.e., to $K_{MN} := g^{r_M r_N}$) and the group key (i.e., to $K_G^i := h^i(s_0) \oplus h^{-i}(t_0)$)

Protocol 4 shows the rekeying protocol for the pairwise key shared between the network manager and the sensor node. This protocol is based on Diffie-Hellman protocol which has recently become not only feasible on resource constrained nodes, but attractive for WSNs (Szczechowiak, Oliveira, Scott, Collier & Dahab, 2008). The network manager M first generates a secret random number r_M and computes the Diffie-Hellman component g^{r_M}. It then *broadcasts* Message 1, which includes the index i of the next group key, and ciphertexts of the next group key component $h^{-i}(t_0)$ and a Diffie-Hellman component g^{r_M} encrypted under the current group key K_G^{i-1}.

The inclusion of the group key index i in the first message enables each sensor node to check if it has the current value of the group key; if not, the node can request that the network manager sends the latest key component $h^{-i}(t_0)$. Thus, the group key rekeying protocol exchange as described in Protocol 3 can be inserted between Messages 1 and 2 of the protocol in the case of a group key index mismatch.

After retrieving the plaintext of Message 1 using the group key, the node checks the preimage if $h(h^{-i}(t_0))=h^{-(i-1)}(t_0)$. This check provides the node with evidence that M has really started the pairwise key update session. Considering that Message 1 is a broadcast message encrypted using the "group" key, it would be impossible to provide this evidence without using the preimage as used here. Of course, using digital signature/verification is a different story.

Now the node constructs the second message of the protocol: it generates its own Diffie-Hellman component g^{r_N}, encrypts it, and generates the keyed hash of both Diffie-Hellman components under the current pairwise key K_{MN}. After sending the message to M, the node computes the new group key, $K_G^i = h^i(s_0) \oplus h^{-i}(t_0)$, increases the group key index from i-1 to i, and computes the Diffie-Hellman key $g^{r_M r_N}$ to be used as the new pairwise key, while keeping the hash $h(K_{MN})$ of the old pairwise key and safely deleting the old key.

On receiving Message 2, M decrypts g^{r_N} and verifies the keyed hash from N. The inclusion of g^{r_M} and g^{r_N} in the hash provides M with confidence about the freshness and authenticity, respectively, of the message.

Use of Diffie-Hellman key agreement for the pairwise key update provides both past and future pairwise key secrecy; the key inputs are temporary random, and thus no relation to either the previous or next key inputs. Even after node compromise, if the attacker is not able to modify the software codes in the node (i.e., the adversary of types I or III), or if the adversary fails to record the key update messages (i.e., the adversary of types I or II), the node will escape from the control of the adversary and recover the secure status. Thus, our scheme satisfies past pairwise key secrecy for all adversary types, and future pairwise key secrecy for any adversary type except type IV, even against node capture and its compromise.

Impersonation Attack: If the adversary is in full control of a compromised node and has installed his own malicious attacking software, then the adversary's node can still impersonate M to some other victim node. The impersonating node may succeed in causing the victim to receive a fake Diffie-Hellman component, say g^x. But this is the limit of the attack. The attacking node has only two options when receiving Message 2 from the victim node: (1) forward the message verbatim to M, or (2) cut out the message. In the first case, M will get not the expected hash of g^{r_M} and g^{r_N} but rather a strange one, which is a hash of g^x and g^{r_N}. In the second case, M will see no response from N. In both cases, M will issue Message 1 again through the unicast channel to N, which will finally lead to key agreement between M and N.

Delivery Failure Management: The delivery failure in the WSNs will lead to key mismatches of group keys and/or pairwise keys. With no long term key available in our key update protocols, key mismatch is a big concern and should be handled carefully. Simple retransmission of the protocol messages is not a solution as it may open the door to replay attacks. Moreover, the retransmission may require the sensor node to revert to the old key, even after it has successfully updated the pairwise key. Consequently, the node must keep two keys at the same time: the old key and the new updated key.

Our solution is to use key evolution once again. With no response from the node *N*, the manager *M* initiates Protocol 5 over the unicast channel to *N*.

Protocol 5: The protocol to handle delivery failure

1. $M \rightarrow N: \ i, j, \{h^{-i}(t_0), g^{r_M}\}_{K^j_{MN}}$ # *unicast* message
2. $M \leftarrow N: \ \{g^{r_N}\}_{K^j_{MN}}, h_{K^j_{MN}}(g^{r_M}, g^{t_N})$

M,N: update the values of the pairwise key (i.e., $K_{MN} := g^{r_M r_N}$)

N: increases the indice *i* and *j*, and updates the values of the group key (i.e., $K^i_G = h^i(s_0) \oplus h^{-i}(t_0)$), and then keeps the hashed value of the old key (i.e., $K^{j+1}_{MN} = h(K^j_{MN})$).

Here, $K^j_{MN} = h^j(K_{MN})$ is a hashed copy of the current key from *M*'s viewpoint. For the first protocol run, the index *j* is set to 1; it will be increased by one whenever the protocol is retried. On receipt of Message 1 over the unicast channel, the sensor node *N* compares the received group key indices *i,j* with the stored indices i', j', and executes the required action as follows:

Case 1: $i = i'$ and $j \geq j'$. For simplicity, consider the case $j = j' = 1$. The pairwise key update protocol 4 has just been run, but the reply message of the protocol failed to arrive at *M*. The node *N* has been keeping the hashed copy $K^1_{MN} = h(K_{MN})$ of the old pairwise key, which is applied to the ciphertext for Message 1 of Protocol 5. The retrieved value of $h^{-i}(t_0)$ ensures the authenticity of the message; the entity other than *N*, in possession of $h^{-i}(t_0)$ and K^1_{MN}, should be *M*. The node decrypts the encrypted part of Message 1 using K^1_{MN}. Then, *N* follows exactly the same step as in Protocol 4, except that it uses the hash of the old pairwise key instead of the current pairwise key. At the end of the protocol run, *N* will end up with a new pairwise key, and the hash of K^1_{MN}, i.e., K^2_{MN}; now *j*=2. The current pairwise key is simply deleted. One or more failure again will be followed by reinitiation of the protocol by *M* with *j* increased. It could also happen that Message 1 itself fails to arrive at *N*, and subsequently *M* retries the protocol. This will lead to the case $j > j'$.

Case 2: $i = i'$ and $j < j'$. This cannot happen and must be a bogus message from another sensor node. *N* should ignore Message 1.

Case 3: $i > i'$. This happens when the node *N* has never been involved in the pairwise key update protocol due to delivery failure of Message 1 of Protocol 4. In this case, *N* applies the hash to the current pairwise key *j* times, and uses the resulting value as the decryption key for Message 1.

Case 4: $i < i'$. This is another case of a replay attack. *N* should ignore Message 1.

Now, the old key does not need to be kept to handle the key mismatch, instead a hashed copy of the key is kept. Thus, Protocol 5 is as secure as Protocol 4 because it inherits all the strong features from Protocol 4.

Putting It All Together

In our scheme, the pairwise key is used to secure delivery of the group key update information in Protocol 3. The group key, in turn, encrypts the Diffie-Hellman components to establish a new pairwise key in Protocol 4. This combination helps the sensor network recover its security quickly after the capture of some sensor nodes and the compromise of their keys.

Figure 4 illustrates how all the keys and keying data are related to each other as they evolve over time. Note that the whole key is not delivered over the air. The reverse hash component ($h^{-i}(t_0)$) is exchanged wirelessly, but not the forward hash chain component ($h^i(s_0)$). Thus, unlike the scheme of Nilsson et al. (see Defect I in Section Related

Figure 4. Relations between keys and keying materials and the significance of node compromise

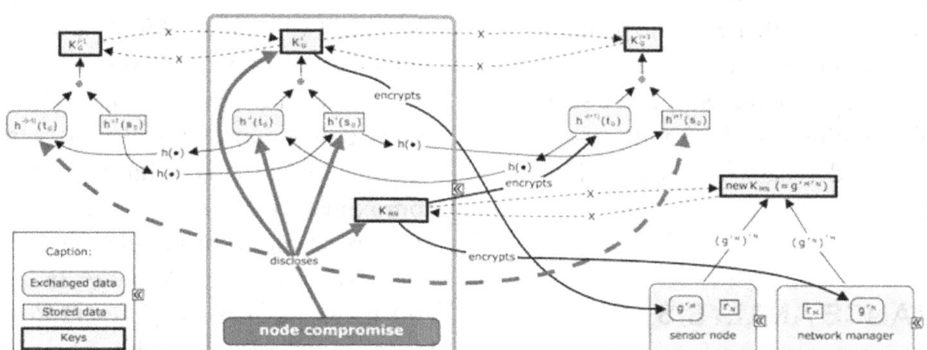

Work), pairwise key compromise alone does not lead to group key compromise, and vice versa.

Using the inverse hash chain as well as the hash chain, we achieve both past and future group key secrecy simultaneously. Furthermore, the group key update message provides inherent message authenticity.

Both *M* and *N* contribute their Diffie-Hellman inputs to the computation of the new pairwise key, and thus the adversary cannot determine the future values of the pairwise key, even after node capture and the resulting compromise of the built-in software, which is not the case in the scheme of Nilsson et al. (see Defect II in Section Related Work).

Carefully designed with node capture in mind, our scheme does not surrender all the key components required to retrieve the past/future group/pairwise keys. Only an adversary equipped with both seamless monitoring and software compromise (i.e., the type IV adversary) can keep the control of a sensor node if it is captured.

Figure 5 shows how the node recovers its secure state with the help of the key update protocols, after it has been captured and all the keys in it are compromised. Without seamless monitoring (i.e., adversary types I and II), the adversary will soon lose all the control of the keys. Even with adversary type III (i.e., seamless monitoring but no software compromise), the node will eventu-

Figure 5. State diagram of key disclosure

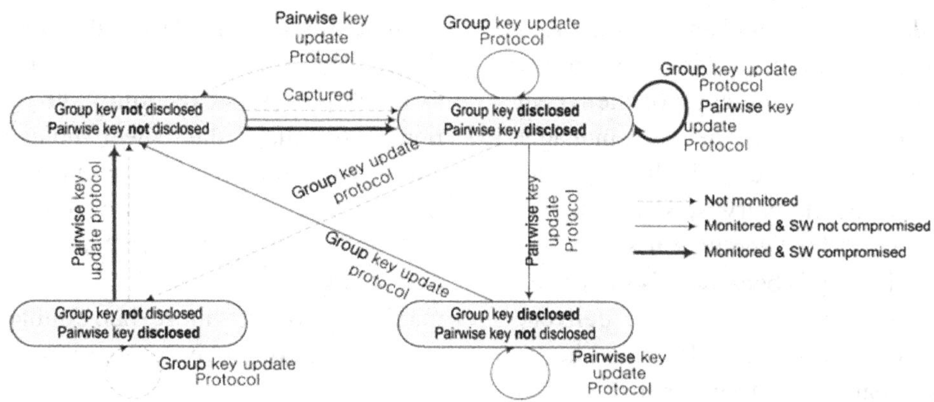

ally recover the secrecy of both keys. Only for adversary type IV (i.e., both seamless monitoring and software compromise), there is no path available back to the original secure state. We argue that a non cryptographic countermeasure such as tamper-proof technology is additionally required to fight against an adversary of type IV, which is the strongest type.

PERFORMANCE ANALYSIS

Due to the resource constraints in WSNs (Crossbow Technology Inc., 2006), new metrics such as energy efficiency have been introduced in validate the performance of new proposals. In this section, we analyze the performance of our proposal and then compare it with the performance analysis of the similar scheme proposed by Nilsson et al. (2008). Our performance analysis covers memory overhead, communication cost, and computation cost for these schemes. To the best of our knowledge, the performance analysis for these schemes does not exist in the current literature.

Memory Overhead

In this section, we discuss the amount of memory required by our proposal. Each sensor node in our proposal, prior to the deployment phase, stores four pieces of information: the secret data (a reverse hash chain component ($h^{-i}(t_0)$) and a forward hash chain component ($h^i(s_0)$), two indexes: one for the group key update phase (i) and another one (j) to handle the delivery failure problems. Then, the sensor node needs to keep a copy of the recent pairwise key shared with the network manager (which is K_{MN}), the group key (which is K_G), and a hashed copy of the old pairwise key (which is $h^j(K_{MN})$). The reason for keeping a hashed copy of the old pairwise key is because it is to be used when the network manager runs the delivery failure protocol (Protocol 5) as described in the Delivery failure management paragraph in Section The Proposed Scheme. In other words, a sensor node needs to store two symmetric keys (K_{MN}, K_G), two secret values ($h^i(s_0)$,$h^{-i}(t_0)$), two indexes (i,j), and a hashed copy of the previous pairwise key.

Consequently, each sensor node in our proposal needs to store approximately 100 bytes to achieve 128 bit security. This memory overhead occupies approximately 0.078% of the total program flash memory at the most popular sensor end device mica2 (Crossbow Technology Inc., 2006). The 100 bytes include two keys (256 bit and 128 bit long each), two 128 bit secret data, two 16 bit indexes, and one 128 bit hashed value of the previous pairwise key (see Table 2).

On the other hand, Nilsson et al.'s scheme occupies approximately 128 bytes, which is equivalent to 0.1% of the total program memory to achieve the same level of security. This memory overhead includes two 256 bit pairwise keys between the network manager and the sensor node (one is the current pairwise key and the other is a copy of the previous key to handle the key delivery failure), one pre-installed 128 bit secret key that is used to generate the random number, one 256 bit public key for the network manager, and one 128 bit group key (see Table 2).

Communication Overhead

The communication between sensor nodes is considered the biggest factor that depletes the sensor's battery since it consumes most of the available power. It consumes much more than sensing and computation activities. Hill et al. (2000) concluded that each bit transmitted in WSNs consumes about as much power as executing 800-1000 instructions. The mica2 data sheet indicates that the energy consumption of communication, which is the focus of this section, is unequal for sending and receiving (Crossbow Technology Inc., 2006). The energy consumption of transmitting with maximum power is more than double the energy consumption of receiving activities.

Table 2. Memory overhead comparison

Stored information per sensor	Nilsson et al. (2008)		Alzaid et al. (2009)	
	Qty	*Size (bits)*	*Qty*	*Size (bits)*
Pairwise key shared with M (K_{MN}).	2	256	1	256
Key used for random number generation.	1	128	-	-
M's public key.	1	256	-	-
Group key (K_G).	1	128	1	128
Secret data.	-	-	2	128
Indexes.	-	-	2	16
Hashed value of the old pairwise key.	-	-	1	128
Total		**1024**		**800**

On one hand, the energy consumption for transmitting m bits over a distance r, according to (Ahmed et al., 2005; Heinzelman et al., 2002) can be calculated as follows:

$$E_{tx}(m,r)=mE_c+mer^s,$$

where

$$e=\begin{cases}e_1 s=2 & r<r_{cr}\\ e_2 s=4 & r>r_{cr}\end{cases}$$

Here, E_c represents the minimum energy required to operate the radio circuit, e denotes the unit energy required for the transmitter amplifier, and r_{cr} is the crossover distance. The typical values for E_c, e_1 and r_{cr} are 50nJ/bit for a 1Mbps transceiver, 10pJ/bit m^2, and 86.2m, respectively.

On the other hand, the energy consumption that results from the receiving activities can be calculated as follows:

$$E_{rx}(m,r)=mE_c$$

Assuming that $r=50<r_{cr}$, Table 3 lists the number of bits that is required to be transmitted in order to accomplish the renewal of the pairwise and group keys.

The network manager M, in our proposal, initiates the pairwise key rekeying mechanism (Protocol 4), while the sensor node itself initiates the mechanism in Nilsson et al.'s scheme (Protocol 1). The initiation that is done by N leads to immediate compromise of all future keys as soon as N has been physically compromised. Our proposal, instead, requires M and N to swap the

Table 3. Number of bits transmitted/received by a sensor node

Protocol	Step	Nilsson et al. (2008)		Alzaid et al. (2009)	
		# of bits	*Consumed energy* (μJ)	*# of bits*	*Consumedenergy* (μJ)
Pairwise key	1. $M \rightarrow N$	-	-	272	13.6
		256	19.2	256	19.2
	Total	256	**19.2**	**528**	**32.8**
Group key	1. $M \rightarrow N$	256	12.8	144	7.2
		128	9.6	128	9.6
	Total	**384**	**22.4**	**272**	**16.8**

Diffie-Hellman components g^{r_M} and g^{r_N}. This increases the length of the information received by a sensor node by 34 bytes in comparison with Nilsson et al.'s scheme. Although this increase affects energy consumption, it is a must to solve the security weaknesses in Nilsson et al.'s scheme. We refer interested readers in these weaknesses to Section Related Work. Importantly, this increase in the number of transmitted bits affects the energy consumption of receiving activities (E_{rx}), but not the energy consumption of transmitting activities (E_{tx}).

Notably, the pairwise key rekeying mechanism (Protocol 4) is able to update the pairwise and group keys at the same time, especially if there is no indication of any node compromise attack or there is no need to eliminate some group members from a specific group. Table 3 shows that the communication energy consumption (E_{rx}+E_{tx}) that results from updating these two keys is 32.8μ*J* in our proposal, while it is 41.6μ*J* in Nilsson et al.'s scheme.

Although *M*, in our proposal, can update the group and the pairwise keys at the same time by running Protocol 4, *M* sometimes may need to remove specific nodes from a particular group, especially when they behave maliciously. In this case, *M* can run Protocol 3. In comparison with the group key update protocol in Nilsson et al.'s scheme (Protocol 2), the new group key in our proposal is not exchanged between the network manager and sensor nodes. Instead, only half of the group key, which is the reverse hash component ($h^{l-i}(t_0)$) is transmitted. The knowledge of only this component is not enough to construct the group key since the group is composed of two components: the reverse hash chain component ($h^{l-i}(t_0)$) and the forward hash chain component ($h^i(s_0)$).

In the first message of the group key update protocol, our proposal (Protocol 3) requires *N* to receive 14 bytes less than Nilsson et al.'s scheme (Protocol 2). This reduction in the number of bits received by *N* leads to less energy consumption. However, our proposal in the second message sends the same number of bits as Nilsson et al.'s scheme. Table 3 shows that our proposal consumes 5.6μ*J* less than Nilsson et al.'s scheme in order to update the group key. This is calculated per group key update at each sensor node.

Computation Cost

We assess, in this section, the energy consumption that results from applying cryptographic operations in our proposal, and then compare this consumption with those of Nilsson et al.'s schemes as in Table 4.

For concreteness, we assume that *RC5* is used for symmetric encryption/decryption activities, *SHA*-1 is used for hash operations, and *ECDSA* is used for public key encryption. We estimate the cost of the cryptographic operations based on the results from some analysis studies presented in (Chang et al., 2007; Meulenaer et al., 2008; Venugopalan et al., 2003; Wander et al., 2005).

To update the pairwise key, our proposal consumes 274μ*J* more energy in comparison with Nilsson et al.'s scheme. This is because *M* and *N* need to exchange Diffie-Hellman components (g^{r_M} and g^{r_N}). In the first message of Protocol 4, *N* needs to decrypt longer encrypted message because of the addition of g^{r_M}. In the second message of the protocol, *N* needs to encrypt its

Table 4. Computation cost

Protocol	Step	Consumed energy (μJ)	
		Nilsson et al.(2008)	*Alzaid et al.(2009)*
Pairwise key	1. *M*→*N*	-	304
		154	52000
		52154	278
	Total	**52308**	**52582**
Group key	1. *M*→*N*	150	278
		-	154
		154	154
	Total	**304**	**586**

Diffie-Hellman component (g^{r_N}) and hash it with the Diffie-Hellman component of *M*, which is g^{r_M} . Interestingly, this protocol can update the pairwise and group keys at the same time, especially if there is no need to eliminate some group members from the group.

Table 4 shows that the estimated computation energy consumption to run the pairwise key update protocol in our proposal is 52582μ*J*, which is sufficient to update the pairwise and the group keys at the same time. To do so in Nilsson et al.'s scheme, both protocols (the pairwise key update and the group key update) should be executed to update pairwise and group keys with a total computation cost of 52612μ*J*.

In situations where eliminating some group members from a specific group is needed, the network manager in our proposal can run Protocol 3. Table 4 shows that our group key update protocol consumes 282μ*J* more than Nilsson et al.'s scheme. This extra energy consumption comes as a result of performing three hash operations: one to verify the reverse hash component ($h^{-i}(t_0)$), another one to calculate the forward hash chain component ($h^i(s_0)$), and the last one to hash the new group key ($h_{K_{MN}}(K_G^i)$) before sending it to *M*. On the other hand, Nilsson et al.'s scheme in Protocol 2 requires *N* perform a decryption operation followed by a hash operation as discussed in Section Related Work. It is worth mentioning that this extra consumption comes as a result of mitigating some weaknesses that exist in Nilsson et al.'s scheme, as discussed in Sections Related Work and The Proposed Scheme.

CONCLUSION

Wireless sensor networks (WSNs) have a devastating security threat: node capture. The threat is so powerful that almost all existing key management protocols are helpless as node capture overthrows the fundamental assumption for cryptographic system design: secure storage of long term secret keys. This is why so-called forward secrecy and backward secrecy are required in cryptographic key management protocols for WSNs. Both terminologies are rather misleading and confusing, and so we propose what we believe are better ones: future key secrecy and past key secrecy.

Nilsson et al. (2008) recently proposed a key management scheme for WSN applications in PCS/SCADA environments, which incorrectly claimed to provide future and past key secrecies. Other proposals (only for pairwise key update) provide past key secrecy, but not future key secrecy (Klonowski et al., 2007; Mauw et al., 2006).

We noticed that any cryptographic countermeasure alone cannot prevent the most powerful adversary in the WSN context. The adversary can capture a node to extract all the confidential information, modify any built-in codes, and seamlessly monitor in order to keep control of the node. This kind of attacker can only be fought by using tamper-proof technologies as well as cryptographic ones. Seamless monitoring requires the adversary to not lose even a single session for group key or pairwise key update. The task of modifying the random number generation code will add another burden to that of seamless monitoring.

In order to measure the resilience of key management protocols, we derived four different types of adversaries varying in their capability with regard to seamless monitoring and software manipulation. As shown in Section Related Work, Nilsson et al.'s scheme, contrary to their claims, turned out to provide neither past key secrecy nor future key secrecy against node compromise by any type of adversary.

We applied Lamport's reverse hash chain as well as the usual hash chain to provide both past and future key secrecy. Our scheme avoids the delivery of the whole value of a new group key for group key update; instead only half of the value is transmitted from the network manager to the sensor nodes. This way, the compromise of a pairwise key alone does not lead to the compromise of the group key, which was not the case in the scheme by Nilsson et al. The new pairwise key in our scheme is determined by Diffie-Hellman based key agreement. However, Nilsson et al.'s scheme uses key transport, not key agreement, where the new pairwise key is determined by the sensor node and then delivered to the network manager using public key encryption. This is a vital flaw to their scheme.

Our performance analysis shows that the sensor node in our proposal consumes approximately 52614.8μJ and 602.8μJ in order to update the pairwise key and the group key, respectively. This energy consumption includes the communication cost and the computation cost as listed in Tables 3 and 4. Our proposal's energy consumption for the pairwise key update is 287.6μJ more than Nilsson et al.'s scheme. This difference is due to the security enhancements that are required to overcome the weaknesses in Nilsson et al.'s scheme, as discussed in Sections Related Work and The Proposed Scheme. To update the group key, our proposal consumes 276.4μJ more energy than Nilsson et al.'s scheme, but this additional cost is required to overcome the weaknesses of Nilsson et al.'s scheme.

In short, our scheme provides very strong resilience; both past and future key secrecy against node capture by all adversary types except Type IV. A sensor node attacked by an adversary of Type IV, in theory, cannot be protected by a cryptographic method alone and requires a non-cryptographic countermeasure such as tamper-proof protection.

ACKNOWLEDGMENT

The authors would like to acknowledge Mark Branagan and Jason Smith at Information Security Institute, Queensland University of Technology for their valuable comments.

REFERENCES

Ahmed, A. A., Shi, H., & Shang, Y. (2003). A survey on network protocols for wireless sensor. In *Proceedings of the International Conference on Information Technology: Research and Education (ITRE'03)* (pp. 301-305). New York: IEEE Computer Society.

Alzaid, H., Park, D., Nieto, J. G., Boyd, C., & Foo, E. (2009). A forward and backward secure key management in wireless sensor networks for PCS/SCADA. In *Proceedings of the first ICST International Conference on Sensor Systems and Software (SCUBE)* (Vol. 24, pp. 66-82).

Beaver, C., Gallup, D., Neumann, W., & Torgerson, M. (2002). *Key management for SCADA* (Report No. SAND2001-3252). Albuquerque, NM: Sandia National Laboratories, the Center for SCADA Security, Cryptography and Information Systems Surety Department. Retrieved October 13, 2009, from http://www.sandia.gov/scada/documents/013252.pdf

Chang, C. C., Muftic, S., & Nagel, D. J. (2007). Measurement of energy costs of security in wireless sensor nodes. In *Proceedings of the Sixteenth International Conference on Computer Communications and Networks (ICCCN'07)* (pp. 95-102). New York: IEEE Computer Society.

Crossbow Technology Inc. (2006). Mica2 datasheet. San Jose, CA: Crossbow Technology Inc. Retrieved October 13, 2009, from http://www.xbow.com/Products/Product_pdf_files/Wireless_pdf/MICA2_Datasheet.pdf

Dawson, R., Boyd, C., Dawson, E., & Nieto, J. M. G. A. L. (2006). SKMA: A key management architecture for SCADA systems. In R. Buyya, T. Ma, R. Safavi-Naini, C. Steketee & W. Susilo (Eds.), *Proceedings of the Fourth Australasian Symposium on Grid Computing and e-Research (AusGrid'06) and the Fourth Australasian Information Security Workshop (Network Security) (AISW'06),* (Vol. 54, pp. 183-192). ACT, Australia: Australian Computer Society.

Günther, C. G. (1989). An identity-based key-exchange protocol. In J. J. Quisquater & J. Vandewalle (Eds.), *Proceedings of the Workshop on the Theory and Application of Cryptographic Techniques on Advances in cryptology* (Lecture Notes in Computer Science, pp. 29-37). Berlin: Springer.

Hartung, C., Balasalle, J., & Han, R. (2005). *Node compromise in sensor networks: The need for secure systems* (Technical Report No. CU-CS-990-05). Boulder, CO: University ofColorado at Boulder, Department of Computer Science. Retrieved October 13, 2009, from http://www.cs.colorado.edu/department/publications/reports/docs/CU-CS-990-05.pdf

Heinzelman, W. B., Chandrakasan, A. P., & Balakrishnan, H. (2002). An application-specific protocol architecture for wireless microsensor networks. *IEEE Transactions on Wireless Communications*, *1*(4), 660–670. doi:10.1109/TWC.2002.804190

Hill, J. L., Szewczyk, R., Woo, A., Hollar, S., Culler, D. E., & Pister, K. S. J. (2000). System architecture directions for networked sensors. In *Proceedings of the Ninth International Conference on Architectural Support for Programming Languages and Operating Systems, (ASPLOS '00)* (pp. 93-104).

Karlof, C., & Wagner, D. (2003). Secure routing in wireless sensor networks: Attacks and countermeasures. *Ad Hoc Networks*, *1*(2-3), 293–315. doi:10.1016/S1570-8705(03)00008-8

Klonowski, M., Kutylowski, M., Ren, M., & Rybarczyk, K. (2007). *Forward-secure key evolution in wireless sensor networks.* In F. Bao, S. Ling, T. Okamoto, H. Wang & C. Xing (Eds.), *Proceedings of the Sixth International Conference on Cryptology and Network Security (CANS '07)* (Lecture Notes in Computer Science, Vol. 4856, pp. 102-120). Berlin: Springer.

Lamport, L. (1981). Password authentification with insecure communication. *Communications of the ACM*, *24*(11), 770–772. doi:10.1145/358790.358797

Lecture Notes of the Institute for Computer Sciences. Social Informatics and Telecommunications Engineering, Springer. Retrieved October 13, 2009, from http://eprints.qut.edu.au/27605/1/c27605.pdf

Mauw, S., van Vessem, I., & Bos, B. (2006). Forward secure communication in wireless sensor networks. In J. A. Clark, R. F. Paige, F. Polack & P. J. Brooke (Eds.), *Proceedings of the Third International Conference on Security in Pervasive Computing (SPC '06)* (Lecture Notes in Computer Science, Vol. 3934, pp. 32-42). Berlin: Springer.

McClanahan, R. (2003). SCADA and IP: Is network convergence really here? *Industry Applications Magazine, IEEE*, *9*(2), 29–36. doi:10.1109/MIA.2003.1180947

Meulenaer, G. D., Gosset, F., Standaert, F. X., & Pereira, O. (2008). On the energy cost of communication and cryptography in wireless sensor networks. In *Proceedings of the Fourth IEEE International Conference on Wireless & Mobile Computing, Networking & Communication, (WIMOB '08)* (pp. 580-585). New York: IEEE Computer Society.

Nilsson, D. K., Roosta, T., Lindqvist, U., & Valdes, A. (2008). Key management and secure software updates in wireless process control environments. In V. D. Gligor, J. P. Hubaux, & R. Poovendran (Eds.), *Proceedings of the first ACM conference on Wireless Network Security (WISEC '08)* (pp. 100-108). New York: ACM.

Ohkubo, M., Suzuki, K., & Kinoshita, S. (2003). Cryptographic approach to privacy-friendly tags. In *Proceedings of the Workshop on RFID Privacy.* Cambridge, MA: MIT Press.

Pietre-Cambacedes, L., & Sitbon, P. (2008). Cryptographic key management for SCADA systems-issues and perspectives. *International Journal of Security and its Applications, 2*(3), 31-40.

Ren, M., Das, T. K., & Zhou, J. (2006). Diverging keys in wireless sensor networks. In S. K. Katsikas, J. Lopez, M. Backes, S. Gritzalis, & B. Preneel (Eds.), *Proceedings of the Ninth conference on Information Security (ISC'06)* (Lecture Notes in Computer Science, Vol. 4176, pp. 257-269). Berlin: Springer.

Roman, R., Alcaraz, C., & Lopez, J. (2007). The role of wireless sensor networks in the area of critical information infrastructure protection. *Information Security Technical Report, 12*(1), 24–31. doi:10.1016/j.istr.2007.02.003

Szczechowiak, P., Oliveira, L. B., Scott, M., Collier, M., & Dahab, R. (2008). NanoECC: Testing the limits of elliptic curve cryptography in sensor networks. In *Proceedings of the Fifth European Conference (EWSN'08)* ([]). Berlin: Springer.]. *Lecture Notes in Computer Science, 4913*, 305–320. doi:10.1007/978-3-540-77690-1_19

Venugopalan, R., Ganesan, P., Peddabachagari, P., Dean, A., Mueller, F., & Sichitiu, M. (2003). Encryption overhead in embedded systems and sensor network nodes: Modeling and analysis. In J. H. Moreno, P. K. Murthy, T. M. Conte & P. Faraboschi (Eds.), *Proceedings of the International Conference on Compilers, architecture, and synthesis for embedded systems (CASES'03)* (pp. 188-197). New York: ACM.

Vieira, M. A. M., Coelho, C. N., Jr., da Silva, D. C., Jr., & da Mata, J. M. (2003). Survey on wireless sensor network devices. In *Proceedings of the Ninth IEEE International conference on Emerging Technologies and Factory Automation (ETFA'03)* (Vol. 1, pp. 537-544). New York: IEEE Computer Society.

Walters, J. P., Liang, Z., Shi, W., & Chaudhary, V. (2006). Wireless sensor network security: A survey. In Y. Xiao (Ed.), *Security in distributed, grid, and pervasive computing* (pp. 367-410). Boca Raton, FL: Auerbach Publications, CRC Press.

Wander, A., Gura, N., Eberle, H., Gupta, V., & Shantz, S. C. (2005). Energy analysis of public key cryptography for wireless sensor networks. In *Proceedings of the Third IEEE International Conference on Pervasive Computing and Communications (PerCom'05)* (pp.324-328). New York: IEEE Computer Society.

Chapter 4
Body Area Networks: Channel Models and Applications in Wireless Sensor Networks

Leonardo Betancur Agudelo
Universidad Pontificia Bolivariana, Colombia

Andres Navarro Cadavid
Universidad ICESI, Colombia

ABSTRACT

Nowadays, wireless Body Area Networks (wBAN) have gained more relevance, in particular in the areas of health care, emergencies, ranging, location, domotics and entertainment applications. Regulations and several wireless protocols and standards have appeared in recent years. Some of them, like Bluetooth, ZigBee, Ultra Wide Band (UWB), ECMA368, WiFi, GPRS and mobile applications offer different kinds of solutions for personal area communications. In this chapter, body area network channel modelling will be described; also, a brief description of the applications and state-of-the-art of regulation and standardization processes pertaining to these kinds of networks will be presented. For each topic, the chapter shows not only the main technical characteristics, but also the technical problems and challenges in recent and future research. Finally, the chapter provides an analysis of Body Area Networks, opinions about the future and possible scenarios in the short- and medium-term for the development of standards and applications and their impacts on our daily lives.

1. INTRODUCTION

In recent years, wireless communications have gained greater relevance. They presently play an important role in our lifestyle and quality of home and work life. Ubiquity allows a person to seamlessly connect with anybody who is connected in the world. The expanded uses of wireless technologies have increased and new applications have been developed. Wireless networks have been classified according to their level of coverage. Consequently, there are wide area networks, metropolitan area networks, local area networks and personal area networks. In personal area networks, there is a lot of interest in body area networks, which are communication networks that are within, near and around a person. Body area networks are the subject of a new research

DOI: 10.4018/978-1-60960-027-3.ch004

field in communications. However, there are some existing technologies that are perfectly adapted to the requirements of body area networks, such as Bluetooth, ZigBee, Ultra Wide Band, etc.

Body area networks (BANs) are small-scale communication systems whose transmissions are performed inside, around or on the human body. Consequently, transmissions of BANs have very specific characteristics. A first characteristic is that coverage is confined to distances of no more than 2 or 3 meters and, secondly, the power transmission levels are very low. Low power contributes to long battery life and reduces the levels of interference with other technologies. Equally important, operating with low power levels reduces health risks.

Body area networks are likely to be used primarily for medicine and entertainment. Medical applications focus on monitoring the human body for disease diagnosis, management and control, intelligent prostheses, surgical assistance, artificial organs, etc. Meanwhile, applications for entertainment and information exchange focus on multimedia, audio, video, and data transfer between two or more users, as well as applications for office, industry and home automation. Positioning and Internet connectivity are also offered by BANs.

Body area networks are classified into two areas according to the characteristics of the propagation medium. The first classification is called 'in body' communication, where information transfers are made through human tissue. Consequently, the signals must go through muscle, skin and some other transmission media under special conditions. Clearly, devices that support these applications are often called "invasive." On the other hand, body area networks can be for 'non invasive' or 'on body' communications, where all transmissions are made on the surface of the human body, either over the skin or clothing that we wear, or around it. Sometimes, these types of devices can be "worn."

In this chapter, we present the typical characteristics and trends of body channel models, with an analysis of the main aspects and challenges of the propagation channel. Then, we present short-term trends in research on body area networks, followed by a brief review of the state-of-the-art of regulatory and technological standards associated with this type of communication system. Next, some applications and operating scenarios for body area networks will be presented. Finally, some findings of the authors are discussed.

2. CHANNEL MODELS

One of the main challenges for new radio technologies is the modelling of the radio channel according to physical parameters like propagation media, frequency, bandwidth, etc. The main challenge is to obtain the impulse response of the channel. Body Area Networks are not an exception to this challenge, especially if we deal with in body systems. However, we will see that on body systems also present interesting challenges for channel modelling, related to the behaviour of the human body and common functions such as breathing, that affect the behaviour of radio waves.

There are two types of models: large-scale and small-scale. Large-scale models estimate the power losses due to propagation in free space, absorption and penetration into the human body. The vast majority of large-scale models are developed using statistical approaches based on measurement campaigns.

In small-scale models, we determine the channel impulse response. With this, we can determine channel distortion, frequency-selective channel fading and stability parameters. This information allows the most appropriate modulation techniques to be designed, finding the optimal transmission rates and equalization schemes in broadband. It is common to find models based on statistical approaches, but deterministic models are also a good option for modelling the channel impulse response.

In this section, we explore models of large- and small-scale technologies used in communication networks for in body and on body applications.

2.1 Channel Measurement Procedures

The most common technique to measure the channel impulse response is to use a channel sounder technique, which can be based on time domain or frequency domain measurements.

Time domain measurements in sounding are more suited for obtaining the impulse response of the channel, with some time domains capable of measuring channels in the presence of movement. This makes it ideal for measuring the channel impulse response of body area networks in the presence of breathing and constant movements of the human body. The transmitter generates very short impulses that are read at the receiver by a digital sampling oscilloscope that constructs the channel impulse response. Another technique widely used in time domain channel sounding is to send a direct sequence pulse, where the receiver uses a correlation technique to calculate the channel impulse response. For more details on the theory and procedures for operating this kind of equipment, refer to (Opperman et al., 2004).

Frequency domain measurements in channel sounding use a technique called sweeping, in which a wide frequency band is measured with a series of narrowband signals delivered via the channel and a network vector analyzer is used to record the channel impulse response. The swept time is the period of time during which the transmitter sends the whole set of narrowband signals from the start frequency to the end frequency. The number of narrowband signals defines the resolution of the measurement and the parameter measured is the S21 parameter.

Once the S21 parameter is measured, it is necessary to perform some post-processing in order to derive the channel impulse response; the most common of which is Hermite post-processing. The measurement of the signal parameter H_{S21} from F_i to $F_{Fs/2}$ is a truncated set of complex frequency information, so the missing information from 0 Hz to F_i is completed by a zero padding sequence. Later, symmetric conjugate information is added to obtain the complete signal parameter from $-F_{Fs/2}$ to $F_{Fs/2}$. At this moment, the real channel impulse response in the time domain is obtained using an inverse Fourier transform. More detailed information on the equipment set-up and post-processing techniques can be obtained in (Opperman et al., 2004).

Measurements in body area networks have particular characteristics that are different from traditional channel measurements. According to the different parameters of interest, we propose dividing the set of measurements into two different groups. The first group is made up of so-called spatial points and is used to extract the large-scale parameters. These points (see Figure 1a) are located on the body of the test subject. The second group of points are the local points, which are distributed around the human body on a grid (see Figure 1b). These points are used to extract small-scale parameters. As many test subjects as possible should be used to obtain a generalized model for any transmission condition.

2.1 On Body Channel Models

2.1.1 Large-Scale Models

Propagation losses in the channels of a body area network can be described by three main phenomena: propagation, diffraction and penetration. Diffraction is the dominant phenomenon in this type of environment. Considering the statistical path loss model, the general form of path losses is represented by:

$$PL = PL_0 + 10\eta \log_{10}\left(\frac{d}{d_0}\right) + s_{\mu,\sigma} \tag{1}$$

Figure 1. Measurement set-up for body area networks. a) large scale b) small scale

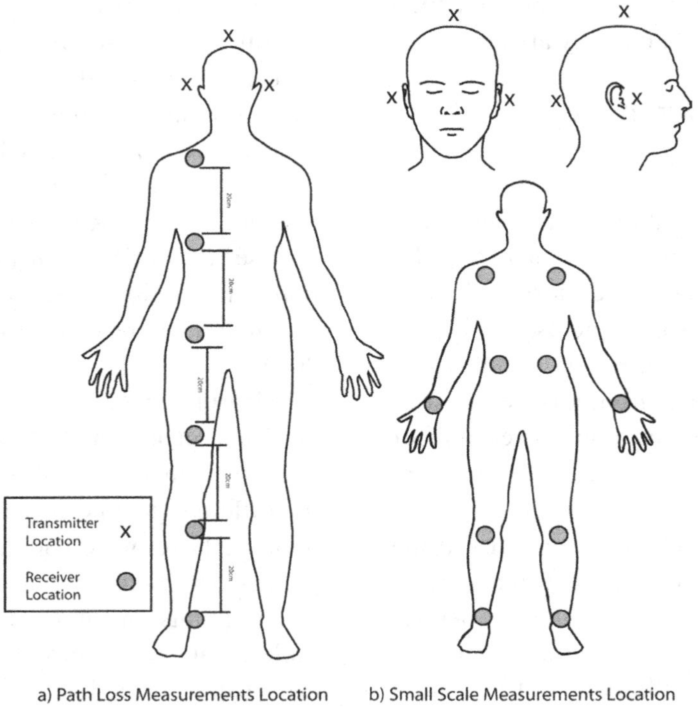

Transmitter Location X

Receiver Location

a) Path Loss Measurements Location b) Small Scale Measurements Location

Figure 2. Path loss model example for BAN

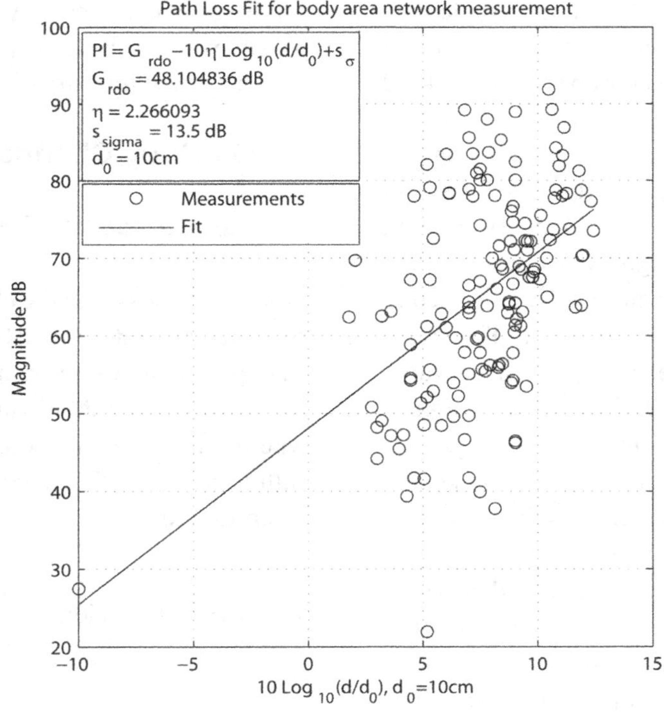

where PL are the losses for propagation in free space in dB, $10\eta\log_{10}(d/d_o)$ is the loss factor that depends on distance d, and η is the propagation index according to the environment. $PL_o=10\rho\log_{10}(f)$ is the path loss constant at a reference distance d_0 that depends on the frequency band. The term $s_{\mu,\sigma}$ is the shadowing parameter, which is modelled as a statistical variable that follows a specific distribution with mean zero and constant variance.

Typically, the propagation index is more than 3 for indoor environments. Works like (Fort, 2006; Jiangi, 2007) obtain a factor close to 6, while others (Thompson et al., 2008; Takada et al., 2008; Tayamachi et al., 2007) obtain almost the same range of factors between 3 and 5. Zasowski et al. (2009) propose a factor of 2.4. Also, in these studies, the value of PL_o is constant (constant central frequency) and fluctuates from 30 dB to 60 dB.

Our review of literature shows that path loss models for on body communications vary by up to +/- 30 dB over the same distance. So, we conclude that there is no consensus on characterizing the propagation losses around the human body.

Some other authors take a more specific approach to the path loss model. Chen et al. (2009) split the path loss model into two sections with linear slopes, raising the possibility that electromagnetic propagation can be modelled as Line of Sight (about 20 cm or less – free space) and Non Line of Sight (more than 20 cm – diffraction).

Katamay et al. (2008) provides an approximation for unlicensed bands in narrow-band applications at 400 MHz, 900 MHz, 1400 MHz and 2.4 GHz. They take all the results and interpolate a 3D function that shows clear frequency dependence for the path loss model.

The main reason for the high variability of path loss models is that changes in the channel – respiration, temperature and body movements – affect the measurement campaigns as confirmed by Thompson et al. (2008). It is necessary to establish how to improve the accuracy of models based on measurement campaigns regarding breathing, temperature and other variables of the human body.

In deterministic models, two basic techniques are used to find the human body channel model. The main technique is to analyze the signal propagation equations using surface wave propagation (wave fronts) or solutions to Maxwell's equations using FDTD or DG techniques (numerical methods) that are applied to a model of the human body. Usually, the model of the human body corresponds to a set of dielectric cylinders that represent the torso, limbs and head. Authors, including Liu et al. (2008), Gupta et al. (2008) and Tayamachi et al. (2007) have made analytical approximations to the human body, usually assuming that the human body acts as a dielectric material. Such models require high levels of processing and some of these simulation results cannot guarantee accuracy in the real world because the simulated human body model does not consider the effects produced by breathing, body temperature and dynamics.

The second technique for modelling the human body is to reduce the human body to an equivalent circuit. The human body has capacitive characteristics so it can be modelled as a series of RC circuits connected in cascade. Following the procedure of Zimmerman et al. (1995), the equivalent circuits of the human body are summarized in Figure 3. With this model, modulation techniques can be designed for communication applications where the body and skin transmit the electromagnetic signal. The only condition for this model is that the receiver and transmitter must remain in contact with the skin. This model has been used for entertainment applications as shown by Yoo et al. (2008).

2.1.2 Small-Scale Models

Small-scale models describe the shape of the impulse response of a channel (Figure 4). Through these parameters, the stability characteristic can

Figure 3. Equivalent circuit model of the human body

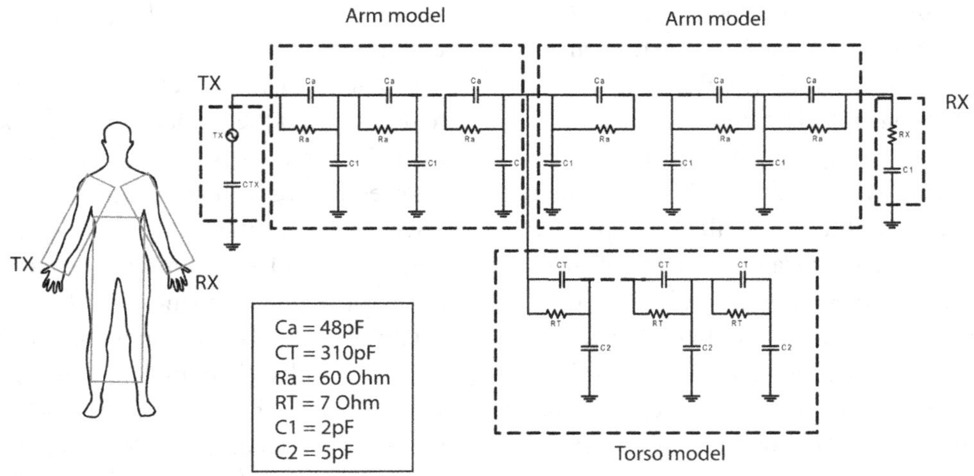

Figure 4. Channel impulse response in BAN

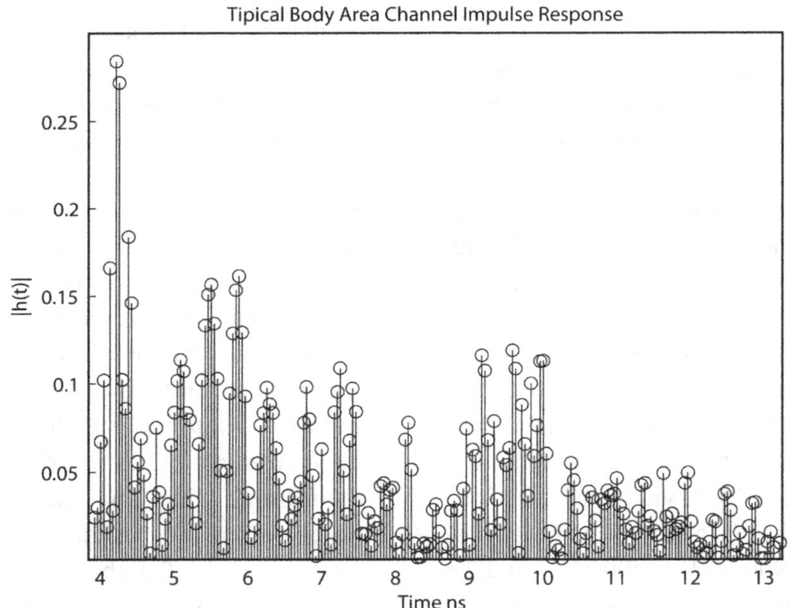

be calculated and the modulation, coding and equalization schemes can be tuned to make them suitable for communications at the lowest possible error rate.

Small-scale models can be statistical or deterministic. In a deterministic model, each of the multipath components is estimated using a ray tracing algorithm. In a statistical model, a set of probability distributions describes the shape and occurrence of the parameters of the impulse response by calculating the amplitude, delay and phase of the individual multipath components. The general model for the impulse response in a body area network channel is described as follows:

$$h(t,\tau) = \sum_{k=0}^{N} \Omega(t)\chi(t)\delta(t - \tau_k) \qquad (2)$$

where $h(t,\tau)$ is the general impulse response, $\Omega(t)$ are the amplitudes of each multipath component, $\chi(t)$ is the function that represents the variability of the channel in the time domain and τ_k is the delay index for each of the N significant multipath components. This is a general model that describes a set of multipath components without internal relationships that is widely used in narrow-band communications. However, if wideband and ultra wideband communications are considered, in particular, if these communications are performed in an indoor environment, the model used is a modified Saleh-Valenzuela channel model (Saleh et al., 1987) as follows:

$$h(t,\tau) = \sum_{k=0}^{N} \sum_{l=0}^{L} \Omega_{k,l}(t)\chi(t)\delta(t - T_l - \tau_{k,l}) \qquad (3)$$

This model assumes that the multipath components arrive in a group of rays called clusters, where the rays that belong to the same cluster are produced by the same scatter. In Figure 5, we can see the behaviour of this channel in more detail.

For simplicity, the majority of the models consider constant channels with deep fading in the frequency domain and constant behaviour in the time domain. The time window observation of the channel is the period of time during which the channel remains almost constant, so $\chi(t)$ remains constant. Statistical channels are the most common models found in the literature. In body area networks, the parameters of amplitude, arrival time and phase are calculated as follows:

Amplitude

The amplitude of each multipath component requires us to define two basic parameters, first the magnitude of each amplitude must be described, which means the value of $\Omega(t)$ is calculated only for N multipath components.

The time delay spread over a body area network channel varies from 20 ns to 80 ns according to Kovacs (2004). In fact, measurements confirm this claim. According to this time delay, the number of multipath components is not large (around 30 to 40 components) and the number of components depends on the bandwidth and frequency band. In narrow-band transmissions, the number of multipath components has an exponential distribution and arrives in the first 10 ns. In broadband

Figure 5. Channel impulse response model

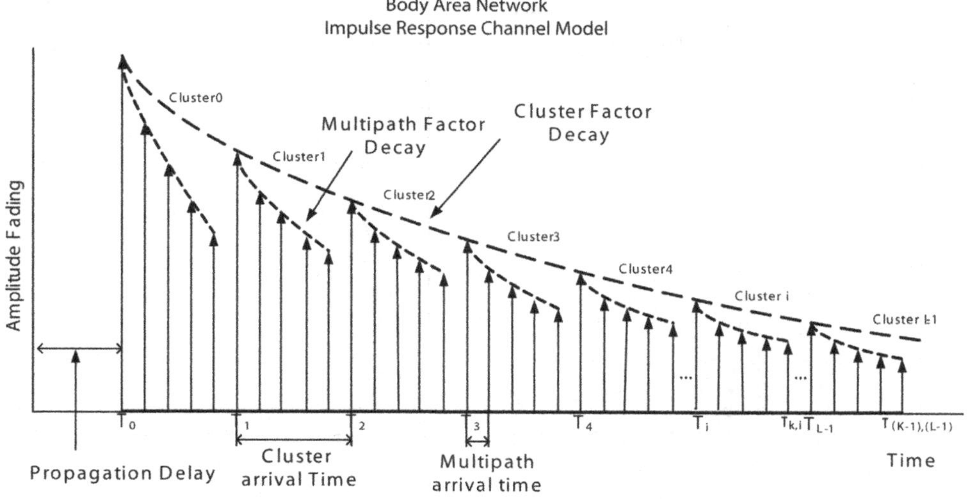

and ultra wideband systems, it is clear that the components are grouped in clusters. The number of clusters and multipath components within a network are exponentially distributed. In Figure 6, we present a histogram of the number of clusters in ultra wideband systems. The average number of clusters is 2. Figure 6b shows the cumulative distribution for the number of multipath components by cluster, where we found that the mean value is close to 40.

The magnitude of each multipath component is calculated by a probability distribution. For this purpose, all the contributions measured in each impulse response at local points are normalized and analyzed together, so we obtain a histogram and the cumulative distribution for these amplitudes. Then we apply an algorithm (e.g. linear least squares with Bisquare method) using several types of distribution. Zasowoski (2009) states that amplitude has a lognormal distribution. Chen (2009) approximates various distributions that pass the criterion of goodness of fit to the probabilistic model and found that the amplitudes follow lognormal and exponential distributions. In Katamay (2008), the amplitudes approach a lognormal distribution. Fort (2006) indicates that the contributions come in groups of clusters and states that the distribution of amplitudes follows a lognormal distribution.

In conclusion, there is a consensus that amplitude fading follows a lognormal distribution in body area networks. The use of a lognormal distribution makes sense as initial amplitudes have larger amplitudes that usually correspond to shorter distances (less than 20 cm). Consequently, it is possible that these components are along a line of sight and propagate without reflection or diffraction, while the multipath components are delayed more and have lower amplitudes because they are produced by diffraction. As a consequence, the contributions are delayed significantly and reach the receiver with less energy. The lognormal distribution is modelled in (4):

$$L\left\{ x \middle/ \mu,\sigma \right\} = pdf\left(x\right) = \frac{1}{x\sigma\sqrt{2\pi}} e^{-\frac{\left(Ln\left(x\right)-\mu\right)^2}{2\sigma^2}} \tag{4}$$

where x is the magnitude of amplitude fading and μ,σ are the mean and standard deviation, respectively.

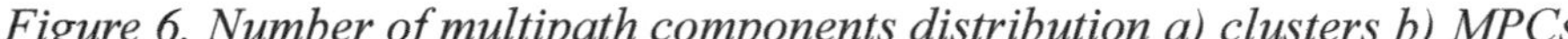
Figure 6. Number of multipath components distribution a) clusters b) MPCs

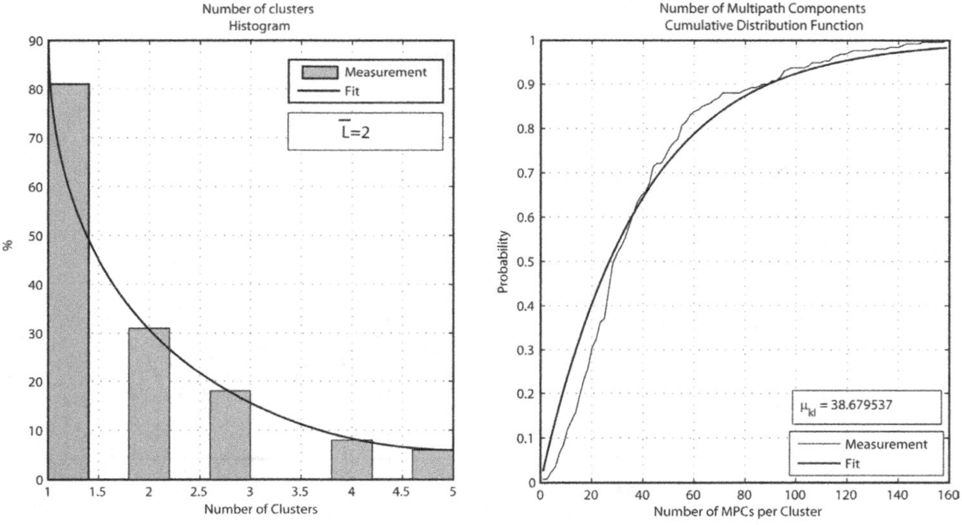

Figure 7. Distribution fading fit

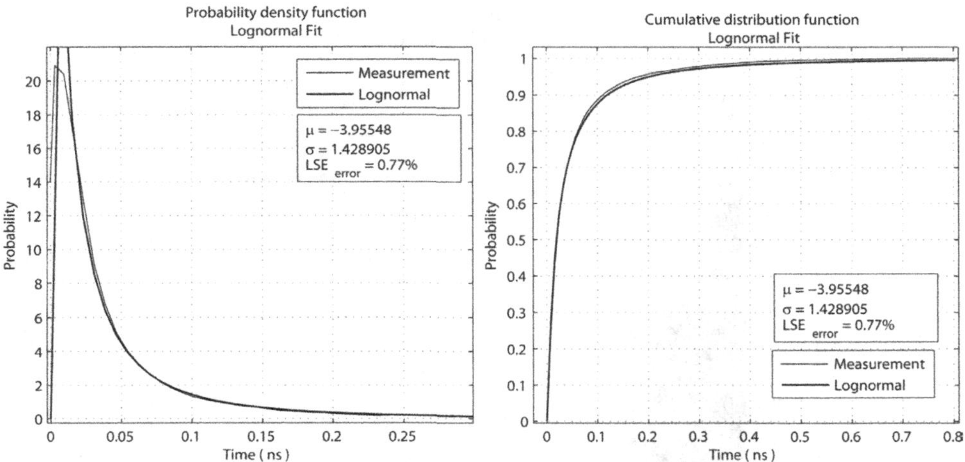

When body area network environments are considered, we have found in measurements that the fading of channel models around the human body has particular characteristics:

- In narrowband transmissions with line of sight in frequency bands below 4 GHz, amplitude fading tends to a Rayleigh distribution.
- In narrowband transmissions with no line of sight and high density of reflections, amplitude fading tries to follows a Rice distribution.
- In wideband transmissions with line of sight, amplitude fading can be fitted to a Rayleigh or Weibull distribution (Betancur, 2009).
- In ultra wideband communications with no line of sight, amplitude fading can be described by Nakagami-m and lognormal distributions (Fort, 2006; Molisch, 2004).

In addition, amplitude fading distribution alone cannot represent the magnitude behaviour of the channel impulse response. The amplitude of the multipath components also follows a shaped reduction in decay. This means that the energy of the components at the beginning of the impulse response has a larger amplitude and the following components have less energy. To model this decay factor, it is important to establish a difference between the decay factor of the multipath components within a cluster and the decay factor of the first component of the cluster. Figure 8 presents the decay factor of the first component of a cluster as an independent function that follows an envelope. The inner components of a cluster follow another decay factor function.

In order to extract these parameters, we must model the decay factor of the inner elements of a cluster. For this approach, we have to take the impulse response measurements, normalize them, and center all the clusters at t=0 for all local point measurements. In Figure 8, we can see an example of this procedure.

The next step is to fit the best envelope possible using numerical methods for function fitting. Equation 5 defines an exponential decay factor for all multipath components considering cluster structures or a simple narrowband channel model.

$$\overline{\alpha^2_{\ k}} = \overline{\alpha^2_{\ 0,0}} e^{(-\tau_k/\gamma)} \quad (5)$$

where $\overline{\alpha^2_{\ k}}$ is the amplitude for each multipath component after the first contribution $\overline{\alpha^2_{\ 0,0}}$, and γ is the decay factor of the exponential function.

Figure 8. Decay factor for multipath components

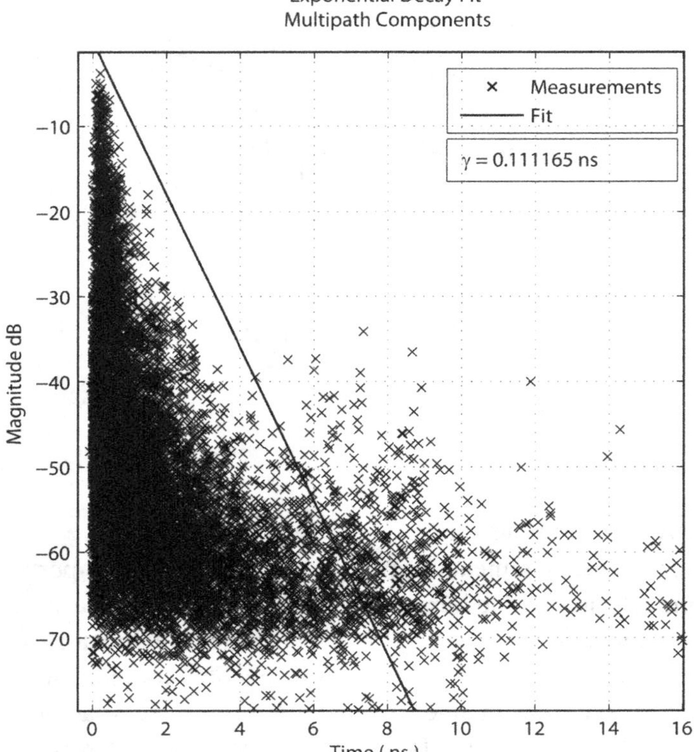

The decay factor for the first component clusters can be extracted by locating all the first components of each cluster in all local point measurements. We also recommend using a decay factor like Equation 6. In Figure 9, the fitting process is presented.

$$\overline{\alpha^2_{k,l}} = \overline{\alpha^2_{0,0}} e^{\left(-T_l/\Gamma\right)} e^{\left(-\tau_{k,l}/\gamma\right)} \tag{6}$$

where Γ is the decay factor for the first component of each cluster, and γ is the decay factor for each multipath component inside each cluster.

Other decay factor functions can be implemented. The use of exponential decay functions is considered because of the easy mathematical treatment and small fitting error.

The polarity parameter (amplitude sign + or -) depends on the phase of each multipath component. Traditionally, the phase parameter has been modelled as a uniform distribution, which means that the phase of a multipath component has the same probability of occurrence in the interval 0 to 2π and the polarity depends on the function sign applied to this parameter. Measurements confirm this fit (Betancur et al., 2009).

Time of Arrival

When the time of arrival is modelled, it is important to establish the nature of the multipath components. In those contributions which appear in clusters, we must model the cluster arrival time and multipath component arrival times (Takada, 2008; Fort, 2006).

Previous works (Chong et al., 2005; Rappaport, 1996) assume that the arrival time of the Clusters is a Poisson process; based on this assumption, we use the relationship between a Poisson and Expo-

Figure 9. Decay factor for clusters

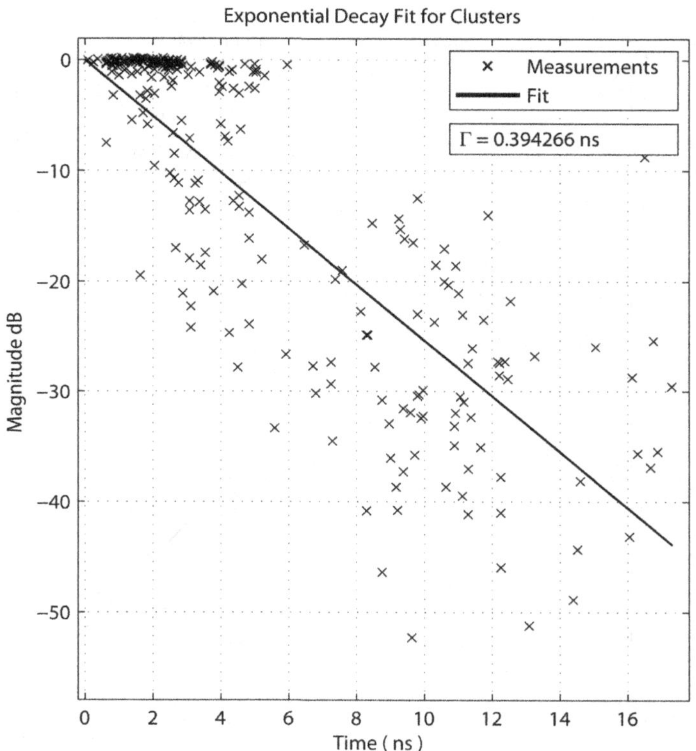

nential process. Between two Poisson events, the time follows an exponential distribution (Hardle, 2003; Gray, 2005). Hence, the inter arrival time between clusters can be described as follows:

$$p\left(T_k \mid T_{k-1}\right) = \Lambda e^{-\Lambda\left(T_k \mid T_{k-1}\right)}, k > 0 \tag{7}$$

where Λ is the inter-arrival mean time between Clusters k and $k+1$, and $p(T_k|T_{k-1})$ is the conditional probability of cluster arrival. The chart in Figure 10 plots the process fitted to an exponential distribution according to measurements.

To extract and calculate this parameter from a group of measurements and simplify the numerical methods, we recommend using the complementary cumulative distribution function of arrival times of components $CCDF_{exp}$=exp($-\Lambda x$), then using a logarithmic scale we have 1n($CCDF_{exp}$)=$-\Lambda x$, With this transformation, it is more straightforward to extract the parameter Λ by employing fitting algorithms.

Moreover, to calculate the inter-arrival times within a cluster, especially when there are overlaps between them, the authors model a mixed exponential distribution. This means that more than one source of reflection (scatter) contributes to the arrival of components in a single cluster (Molish, 2004; Chong, 2005; Betancur, 2009). The distribution is modelled according to:

$$p\left(T_l / T_{l-1}\right) = \beta\lambda_1 e^{-\lambda_1\left(T_l / T_{l-1}\right)} + \left(1-\beta\right)\lambda_2 e^{-\lambda_2\left(T_l / T_{l-1}\right)} \tag{8}$$

where β is the mixture index and λ_1 and λ_2 are the inter-arrival mean times of two exponential processes inside the same cluster. In Figure 11, the fitting process for a mixed Poisson distribution is presented.

Figure 10. Cluster time arrival

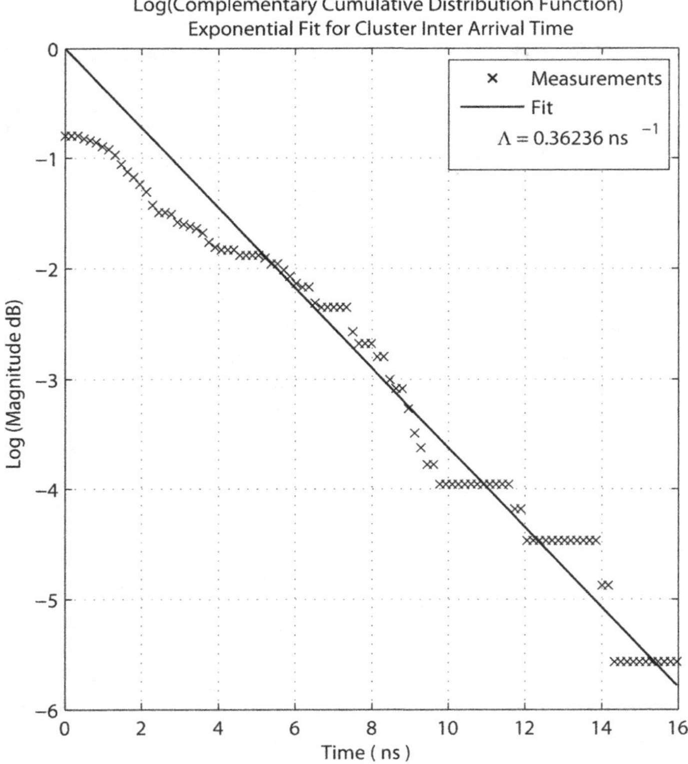

In a similar manner, the parameter of inter-arrival time for multipath components was isolated using the complementary cumulative distribution function to make the fitting algorithm perform better.

Other arrival rate models have been considered for body area networks. In Goulianos (2007), a Δ-*K* distribution process is proposed based on a model in which a conditional probabilistic process is presented. The advantage of using this model is that the adjustment performance of measures is better than for traditional Poisson models.

2.2 In Body Channel Models

In body channel models, we describe the penetration of electromagnetic waves into a material that causes losses due to absorption. The material to which we refer is the human body, which is traditionally modelled as a capacitive element, i.e. tissue such as muscle, fat and skin are propagation environments that can be reduced to a dielectric element with a fixed dielectric constant depending solely on temperature and material thickness (see Figure 12).

In this vein, a dielectric material that it is crossed by an electromagnetic wave generates reflection and penetration with a constant loss per unit distance, with the process depending on frequency. It can be said that:

- The reflection and transmission coefficients are parameters that depend on frequency
- Transmission through a dielectric material is described by the equation (Heavens, 1965; Molish, 2005):

Figure 11. Time of arrival of multipath components

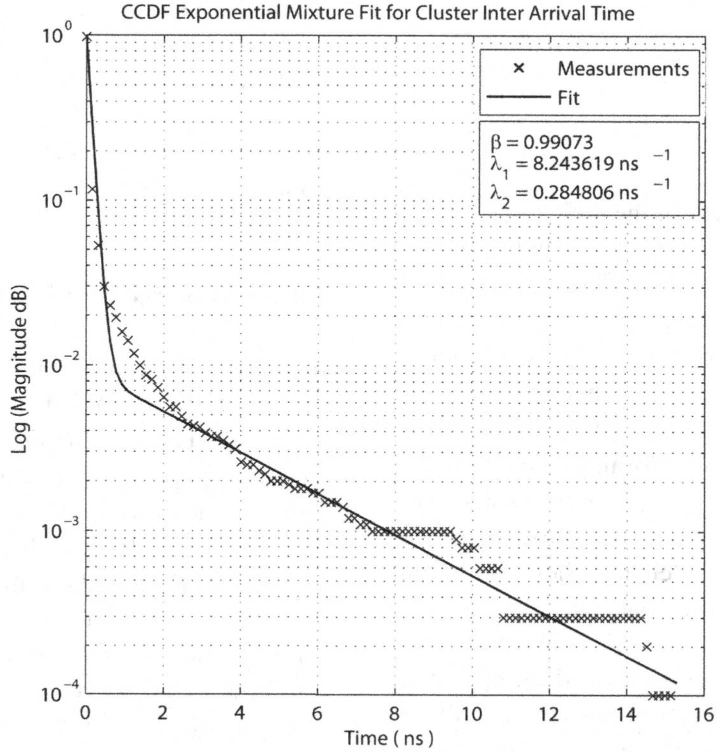

$$T = \frac{T_k T_{k+1} e^{-j\alpha(f)}}{1 + \rho_k \rho_{k+1} e^{-2j\alpha(f)}} \qquad (9)$$

where T_k is the transmission coefficient, ρ_k is the reflection coefficient and index k represents the propagation environment (two different means of propagation). $\alpha(f)$ is a frequency-dependent

Figure 12. In body electromagnetic penetration

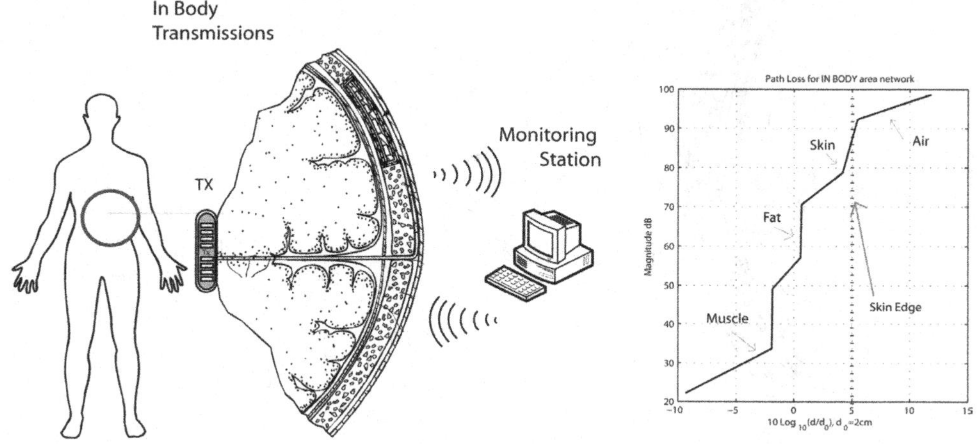

parameter that is a function of incident angle as follows:

$$\alpha = \frac{2\pi}{C_o} f\sqrt{\varepsilon_r}\, d\cos(\theta) \qquad (10)$$

where d is the thickness of the dielectric, θ is the incident angle, Co is the speed of light, f is the frequency and ε_r is the material dielectric constant.

It is still premature to develop a real and accurate channel model for in body transmission. In fact, the process of characterizing the dielectric constants of the living human is not an easy experiment to perform, especially if we consider that this value does not remain constant in the time domain. For example, muscles stretch and contract; when they change their width, the dielectric parameter also changes.

If we also consider that each propagation medium produces a different delay in the propagated signal, the originally transmitted signal will be subjected to spreading in time. So the channel model impulse response will consist of several pulses spaced by a few nanoseconds with a step factor decay. See Figure 13.

This area of research is still at an early stage and path loss and impulse response models need to be developed that allow the channel to be modelled more accurately. Preliminary results are still uncertain, so this area needs further academic research and development (Ruiz et al., 2006).

3 FUTURE RESEARCH DIRECTIONS

In previous sections, we have looked at the state-of-the-art in channel modelling of body area networks. The OSI model still presents many technical problems that must be overcome in order to implement BAN network technologies. Two major problems include the coexistence of BAN networks and their impact on the health of the human body. On the signal processing side, it is necessary to ascertain what kind of modulation, coding, channel estimation and equalization must be used to maintain wireless communications with ideal performance in spite of channel fading. This involves improving the performance of antennas and solving the problems of coverage and directive patterns.

Figure 13. Pulse transmitted through dielectric environment

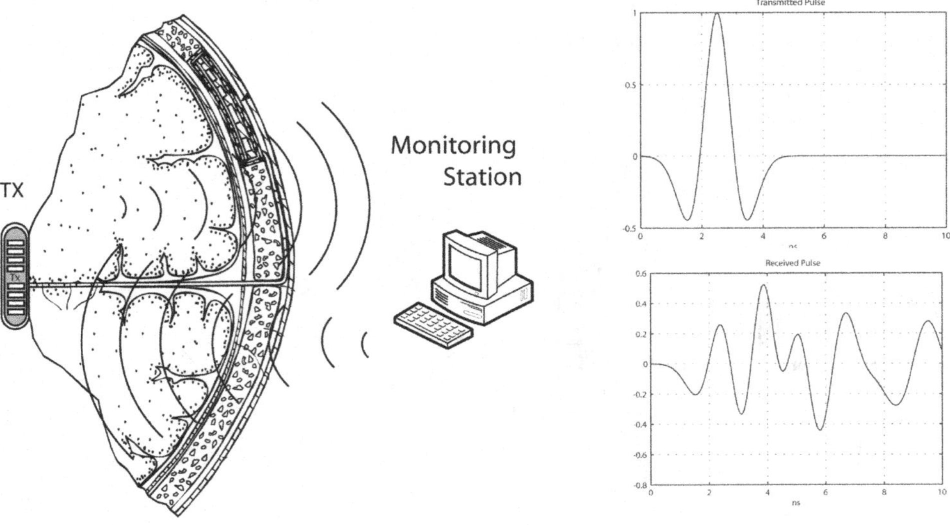

To simplify these problems, we have decided to group the open problems of research into five main areas:

3.1 Body Area Networks Channel Modelling

Channel models for body area networks have been explored previously for on body communications (Chen et al., 2009, Betancur et al., 2009; D'Errico et al., 2009; Fort et al., 2006; Gupta et al., 2008; Jianqi et al., 2007; Katayama et al., 2008; Kovacs et al., 2004; Motani et al., 2007; Roy et al., 2007, Takada et al., 2008; Yoo et al., 2008), among others. However, there are some unresolved issues with the channel models that require solutions, which are summarized as follows:

- It is necessary to find a mathematical model that considers broadband and ultra wideband channels with cluster overlapping. Also, the impact of such models on the arrival time of the various contributions in a multipath environment still has no accurate mathematical model.
- The present path loss models have large variations in the shadowing parameter. This variation must be reduced because the uncertainty of these models does not allow the receiver power to be predicted in link budget calculations. In other words, it is necessary to find a path loss model that is more credible and accurate, and takes into account the respiration process and human movement.
- There is no accurate channel model for invasive devices in body area networks. The channel models that represent transmissions from inside the human body are unclear, as far as we know there are no measurement campaigns that support the theoretical models.
- The body area network features channel fading in the frequency domain and the channel changes very fast in the time domain, so the instability of the channel is a big issue. The solution is not obviously a small-scale channel model that takes into account the movement of the human body (fading in time and frequency). Moreover, the measurement campaigns that account for this kind of situation are not clear. Hence, it is important to design this type of channel model and measurement set-up.

3.2 Antenna Design

From the works explored in the development of antennas for BAN applications, it is clear that there are two important trends:

- Invasive antenna design: a clear trend in medical applications (Yoo et al., 2008; Yazdandoost et al., 2009) is towards an antenna designed for transmission inside the human body. The most important challenge in this field is to design an antenna that compensates for all the dynamic changes and distortions introduced by the body and layers of different tissue. According to the IEEE 802.15.3 TG6 Working Group, this topic will require a lot of attention in the next few years.
- Body antenna design with constant radiation patterns: an antenna that remains in contact with the human body changes its radiation pattern, drastically, in the far and near field. Since transmission and reception antennas for BAN networks will be in contact with the body, it is necessary to explore alternative antenna designs with almost constant radiation patterns. For example, the textile antenna (Thompson et al., 2008) may provide a solution to this issue.

3.3 Receiver Designs

Due to the operating environment, devices that must operate in body area networks should be small, run with battery power for long periods of time, and must have enough processing power to control the transmission and measure the environment. Hence, the process of miniaturization is one of the challenges in receiver design.

It is not clear what type of structure a BAN receiver should have. In recent years, OFDM (Orthogonal Frequency Division Multiplexing) has gained popularity, it has been widely explored and there are many practical implementations. OFDM is, therefore, one of the candidates for wideband transmission on channels with deep fading. However, in body area networks, the BAN channel has instabilities. The channel has deep fading in the frequency domain and changes very fast in the time domain, making equalization a critical issue for OFDM technology. OFDM uses coherent demodulation, so it uses pilot carriers and training sequences to estimate the channel. When OFDM is used in a BAN environment for wideband and ultra wideband applications, equalization is insufficient to compensate for errors produced by the fast changes in the time domain. Consequently, it is necessary to develop more robust techniques to equalize OFDM in BAN channels.

On the other hand, there are receivers that use other kinds of modulation. It is common, for example, to see correlation receivers and receivers based on Rake structures. Rake receivers use several versions of the received signal delayed according to the arrival time of each multipath component. In the final stage, these receivers combine all these signals with an integrator and/or correlator. This type of receiver works well for sparse channels; however, when bandwidth and operating frequency increase, the construction of integrated circuits and scalability are significantly complicated. There have been several proposals to address these issues, including transmitted-reference receivers (Chao et al., 2005) which improve the complex process through a phase correlation, and frequency-shifted receivers (Goeckel et al., 2007) which reduce the complexity of the receiver by using mixed-stage transmission in the frequency domain and orthogonal tones.

In addition, issues remain to be solved with broadband communications in body area networks when very wide bandwidths (ultra wideband applications) or high frequency bands (60 GHz band) are considered. Sampling problems become more relevant as the number and complexity of receivers increases dramatically because of an excessive number of signal samples. Therefore, it is important to develop new techniques that reduce the number of samples. This means that new algorithms for signal processing and channel estimation below the Nyquist criterion must be implemented.

Adaptive modulation schemes are used to improve the performance of communication systems when the transmission environment is variable. Adaptive modulation attempts to use the best modulation and coding scheme according to the signal-to-noise ratio and bit error rate in the channel. CSI (Channel State Information) is a technique that allows the receiver to pick out instantaneous information from the channel in order to take decisions for adaptive modulation and equalization. CSI is obtained by processing *a priori* information in the received signal, e.g. training sequences, pilot carriers, or any element that helps to determine parameters such as noise power, noise variance, average power, signal-to-noise ratio, channel dispersion, etc. The veracity and accuracy of the information in CSI depends on the number of samples that are available. A greater number of samples provides more accurate information but requires more signal processing. If a smaller number of samples and less signal processing is used, however, accuracy decreases. Manzoor (2007), Socheleau et al. (2008), and Chen et al. (2007) show that accurate CSI requires a large number of samples and long computation times. The challenge is to explore channel state information algorithms that give accurate results with less signal processing and short processing times.

3.4 MIMO in Body Area Networks

Multiple Input Multiple Output (MIMO) applications in body area networks have several restrictions. The use of MIMO below 10 GHz makes little sense at very short distances, because interference increases and the antenna array distances are too large for practical implementations. However, in the 60 GHz band, the wavelength is small enough so that MIMO applications can use antenna arrays of a size that could be employed in BAN applications. In addition, electromagnetic wave penetration is minimal, so reflection and diffraction are the dominant phenomena. Consequently, MIMO represents an alternative that is just starting to be explored and is an open research issue (Smulders, 2009).

3.5 Cooperative Networks

The performance of communication protocols for body area networks reduces dramatically because channel variations in the time domain are severe. In fact, channel temporal variations have an impact on the performance of mesh and star type networks, increasing packet losses. One way to avoid this problem is to implement a cooperative mechanism between the elements of BAN networks, as proposed by Gorce et al. (2009), where the benefits of cooperative networks represent a solution for communication networks in hostile transmission environments is highlighted.

4. REGULATION AND STANDARDS

The communication technologies used for body area networks require low emission powers. The main reason for using low power levels is to guarantee emission levels below the threshold that can affect human health. Also, low power guarantees coexistence with other technologies. Finally, this technology uses short transmission distances (no more than 2 meters).

In recent years, several wireless regulations and standards have appeared, some of which could be used in body area communication systems. To be explicit, the IEEE, in November, 2007, formed the IEEE 802.15 Working Group TG6: Body Area Networks. The goal of this group is to develop a communication standard for optimal transmission inside, over and around the human body (IEEE Standardisation Working Group, 2007).

This working group has proposed a series of research topics that address the need to obtain an appropriate channel model to represent the human body --- not only for internal communications, but for transmission along the surface and around it. Other topics include finding suitable operating bands, modulation schemes and media access techniques that perform the best, based on technical and economic issues. To the best of our knowledge, there is no final draft establishing the precise direction of the standard, which has become a topic of great interest within the IEEE 802.15 Working Group. This working group over the next few years will chart the guidelines body area networks must follow.

There are also regulatory and standardization issues that are not strictly confined to body area networks, however the following technologies can be used in personal area networks. The most common technologies today include Bluetooth (IEEE 802.15.1), ZigBee (IEEE 802.15.4), Ultra Wide Band proposals (IEEE 802.15.4a), ECMA 368 - ISO/IEC 26907 and the regulation recommendations of the FCC made in 2002 on Ultra Wide Band networks.

Next, we provide a short description of technologies that can be used in body area networks:

Bluetooth: This is a technology (IEEE 802.15.1) that operates in the unlicensed ISM band at 2.4 GHz. It uses a Frequency Hopping Spread Spectrum over 79 different frequencies, a GFSK modulation scheme and reaches speeds up to 1 Mpbs in the first version. It also has a capacity of up to 3 Mbps in the enhanced version and a transmission power of 0 dBm, 4 dBm and 20 dBm.

Advantages:

- Global acceptance
- Low cost
- Regulation free (ISM)
- High data transmission rate (up to 3 Mbps in point-to-point connections)
- Long battery life (low power consumption)

Disadvantages:

- Unknown delay and latency in mesh mode (the precise values of these characteristics are topology-dependent)
- Limited connectivity (no more than 8 devices can be connected to the scatter net)
- Inadequate penetration (the frequency band is inadequate for penetration and through-wall applications)

Bluetooth is ideal for point-to-point applications in body area networks. In a mesh network application, performance varies because it depends on network topology, along with the specific application and data characteristics.

The device sizes are appropriate for on body communications, which means that applications for health care monitoring and data exchange can be delivered using Bluetooth networks. Bluetooth is not recommended for invasive applications because the frequency band (2.4 GHz) has strong penetration losses in the human body.

ZigBEE: (IEEE 802.15.4, 2004) This works in the 868 MHz band in Europe, 915 MHz in USA and Australia and 2.4 GHz in the rest of the world. ZigBee radios use Direct Sequence Spread Spectrum at 868 MHz, BPSK at 20 Kbps per channel and at 915 MHz and BPSK reaching speeds of up to 40 Kbps. At 2.4 GHz, the ISM band uses QPSK and can reach speeds of up to 250 Kbps per channel. The maximum radiation power does not exceed 0 dBm (1 mW).

Advantages:

- Widespread acceptance
- Low cost
- Regulation free (ISM)
- Long battery life (low power consumption)
- More adequate penetration (the 868 MHz and 915 MHz bands are, to some extent, adequate for penetrating human tissue)

Disadvantages:

- Transmission rate (the data transmission rate can reach up to 40 Kbps)
- Unknown delay and latency in mesh mode (the precise values of these characteristics are topology-dependent)
- Inadequate penetration (the 2.4 GHz frequency band is inadequate for through-wall applications)

ZigBee is adequate for on body communications, especially if information from low rate bio-signals is required. A ZigBee mesh network is not recommended for streaming data information transmissions. The current size of ZigBee devices makes it difficult to develop an in body solution. However, ZigBee can be a useful option for exchanging information in invasive devices (medical applications).

ECMA368 - MB OFDM: (ECMA368, 2007) ECMA 368 is the evolution of ultra wideband for OFDM in Europe. The first version was defined in December 2005, and the final version in December 2007. MB OFDM works from between 3.1 GHz to 10.6 GHz and its bandwidth is divided into 5 groups with internal sub-bands. It has three 528 MHz sub-bands for the first four groups and two sub-bands for the fifth. MB OFDM employs two modulation schemes: QPSK and DCM. Importantly, MB OFDM reaches speeds up to 480 Mbps. The definition of this standard uses OFDM to transmit over 128 orthogonal carriers and, for each of the groups, uses internal frequency hopping. The maximum transmitting power is -43 dBm.

Advantages:

- High data rate (up to 480 Mbps)
- Long battery life (low power consumption)
- Low interference operation

Disadvantages:

- Low commercial acceptance and deployment
- Unknown delay and latency in mesh mode (the precise values of these characteristics are topology-dependent)
- Inadequate penetration (the frequency bands are inadequate for penetration and through-wall applications.

MB OFDM is an option for high speed transmissions and is recommended for point-to-point applications, in particular for video monitoring, data exchange and high data rate transmission (bio-signals) with wide bandwidth. According to the state-of-the-art and deployment of MB OFDM devices, the applications have several complications, there are only a few manufacturers and the physical implementation is still at an early stage and more development is required. The device size is presently still too large for invasive use, so it can provide an alternative for on body applications.

FCC - UWB IR: (FCC, 2002) The FCC established a set of definitions for UWB technology in 2002, which specify spectral radiation masks and ultra wideband signals (a signal is considered to be ultra wideband when the bandwidth is more than 500 MHz or its fractional bandwidth is more than 20%). The FCC does not clarify or define the modulation schemes and media access techniques to be employed. It only defines the usage and power transmission levels and each manufacturer chooses the standard or technology required when implementing an ultra wideband solution.

Advantages:

- High data rate (700 Mbps average)
- Long battery life (low power consumption)
- Low interference operation
- Radar and imaging capabilities
- High penetration performance
- Positioning capabilities

Disadvantages:

- Lack of standardization
- Low commercial acceptance and deployment
- Mesh capabilities unknown (they depend on proprietary solutions)

Impulse radio applications are still without detailed regulation or standardization guidance on physical hardware or access to media. The particular solutions that have been explored show that this kind of technology is adequate for in body communications. The signal profile and spectral characteristics allow penetration and even imaging and radar solutions. Medicine, health care and data exchange are the most promising fields for future developments in this area. This technological solution is still at an early stage.

Other Applications without Regulation: SLLR (Specific Low Level Radio) is a proprietary technology that uses the 430 MHz band, reaches speeds up to 2400 bps and has civilian use.

Advantages:

- High human tissue penetration
- Long battery life (low power consumption)
- Low interference operation

Disadvantages:

- Low commercial acceptance and deployment
- Low data rate
- Limited connectivity (it only performs point-to-point connections)

SLLR is a proprietary solution and it is difficult to extend this technology for general use and the low bit data rate only allows signals to be transmitted with narrow bandwidth or low data transmission information. Streaming information like audio or signal monitoring are not recommended. For in body communications, SLLR can transmit through tissues of the human body. Thus, the use of this technology makes sense when intelligent implants have to exchange device configurations and historical patient information.

5. APPLICATIONS

5.1 Medical Applications

Body area networks have enormous potential in medicine because they have the potential to revolutionize many of the ways in which medicine performs fundamental processes such as diagnosis, monitoring, surgery and medical treatment. In this section, we classify the applications and operating scenarios according to network topology and characteristics of network elements as follows: Point to multi-point (diagnosis and medical monitoring), point-to-point (implants) and mesh networks (surgery and cooperative networks).

5.1.1 Medical Monitoring (Point to Multi-Point Topology)

Medical monitoring in a point to multi-point topology requires a network where a central node coordinator performs routing and network management (Wen, 2008). It is quite possible for the node coordinator to be a workstation where the doctor makes the diagnosis. The diagnosis results from the doctor's interpretation of information received from a number of peripheral nodes that depend on the central station.

For such applications, we consider two cases (see Figure 14). In the first scenario, a doctor takes the information needed to make a diagnosis from sensors placed in the patient's body; the transmission may be unidirectional from the sensors to the central station or node coordinator, and the captured information is processed by an applica-

Figure 14. Medical monitoring

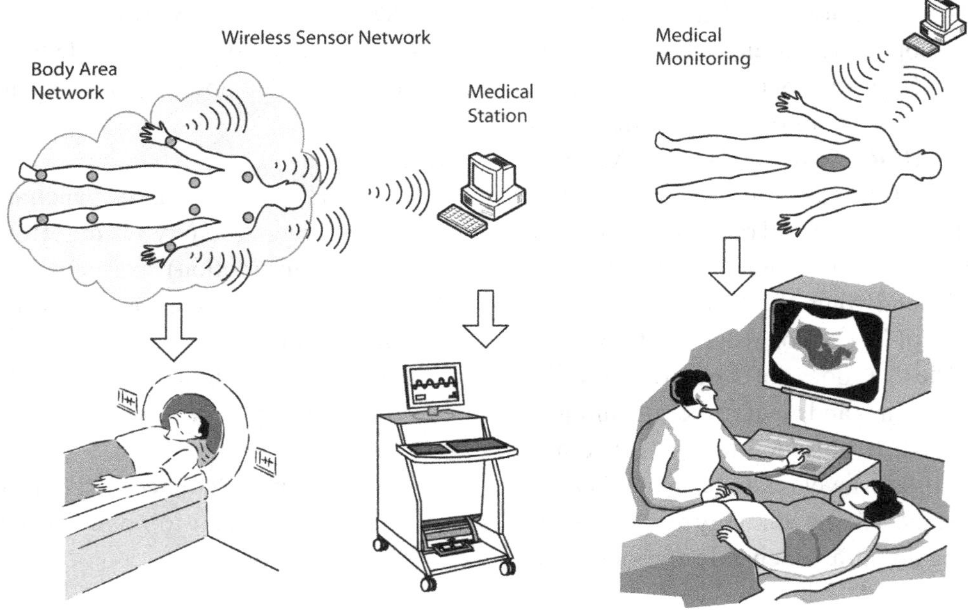

tion and/or information system, which displays the image, signals or statistical information on the workstation.

In the second case, we have the same network topology but we have several patients who are in an intensive care unit or recovery room (Wu, 2007, 2008). A centralized unit receives patient vital signs and an information system or application is responsible for keeping track of when medications need to be administered and what care needs to be provided, as well as monitor patients in real-time, generating notifications, warnings and alarms as needed.

For this type of application, the following information can be deduced:

- There is a central processing unit which becomes the coordinator or master of the network. This network element reports directly to medical staff and, in most situations, is associated with a computer, applications and databases. Also, this central node has information systems and signal processing for data, statistics and/or images.
- The peripheral elements of the network are sensors that usually operate on battery power. These sensors have low levels of complexity, are structurally simple and as small as possible. The sensors can be placed on the patient's skin (on body) or inside the body (in body).
- The sensors measure vital signs, including heart rate, pressure, temperature and density counts, as well as many other parameters. In this context, these signals require low bandwidth. Table 1 presents the bandwidths and data rates required to transmit certain parameters of the human body (Li et al., 2007).
- Time division multiplexing access is recommended when information sensors demand narrow bands and low data rates. However, frequency division multiplexing access is preferable when dedicated and critical information is required.
- In patient monitoring applications, the information transmitted is delay-sensitive. In a medical emergency, it is essential to respond as fast as possible, so frame segments should be designed to be transmitted in burst or streaming frames.
- In diagnostic applications, retransmission and error correction techniques can be deployed and the information is not delay-sensitive (delays do not impact diagnoses).
- Invasive sensors demand special antenna designs, the transmission must cross human tissue and overcome losses from reflection, refraction and free space propagation.
- The maximum distance that these networks can reach is 4 meters in diagnostic systems (with invasive and non-invasive sensors) and 8 meters for patient monitoring systems.
- The number of elements that are part of a BAN network must be no more than a dozen devices (sensors coordinated by a central node).
- The sensors should be as simple as possible and small, so that batteries can last longer.
- Frequency bands below 1 GHz are recommended for invasive monitoring. For on body communications, the frequency band depends on the standard and technology.

Table 1. Some body signal bandwidths

Signal	Bandwidth	Bit rate
Temperature	4 Hz	100 Bps
ECG	0.1 – 250 Hz	2500 Bps
EMG	15 – 200 Hz	2500 Bps
EOG	0.001 – 90 Hz	540 Bps
EEG	0.001 – 90 Hz	540 Bps
Blood pressure	4 Hz	100 Bps
Sugar rate	4 Hz	100 Bps
Max. Value	250 Hz	2500 Bps

The important issues are coexistence and interference.

Body area network applications can be extended in coverage over the last mile with a third technology like ADSL, WiMAX, WiFi, etc. This allows medical monitoring in home environments (remote patient monitoring) (Wu, 2007).

5.1.2 Medical Implants and Monitoring (Point-to-Point Topologies)

Medical implants and monitoring technology constitute a field of special interest in body area networks. In fact, some applications have already been implemented. In these applications, the topology of the network is carried out point-to-point and the network members have high signal processing capacity. They are complex and they usually transmit in wide bandwidths. Also, these kinds of devices must manage a protocol stack and transmission of information in a bi-directional way.

Endoscopy is a diagnostic procedure that can benefit from BAN technologies (Park, 2005; Chi, 2007; Xie, 2006). Referring to Figure 15, the patient swallows a pill that contains a video camera which transmits information during its journey through the patient, allowing the doctor to receive video data in real-time. In this scenario, the doctor can make a diagnosis and, in some special cases, can control the movement, focus, illumination and even perform some minor surgical procedures. This development makes it unnecessary for the patient to suffer and reduces the complexity of examinations (no anaesthesia is required and qualified staff are not required).

In this type of application, patient swallows a sensor that generates a video signal with a bandwidth of about 6 MHz because the transmitter must penetrate several inches of human tissue and several centimetres of clothing and space to reach the video receiver. It is clear that the propagation channel in this example is dynamic, variable and produces multiple effects caused by absorption, scattering and reflection during the propagation of the electromagnetic signal.

Body area networks attempt to eliminate implant cables as much as possible. The goal is to establish a wireless connection between the control signal and the electro-mechanical actuator. For

Figure 15. Intelligent implant applications

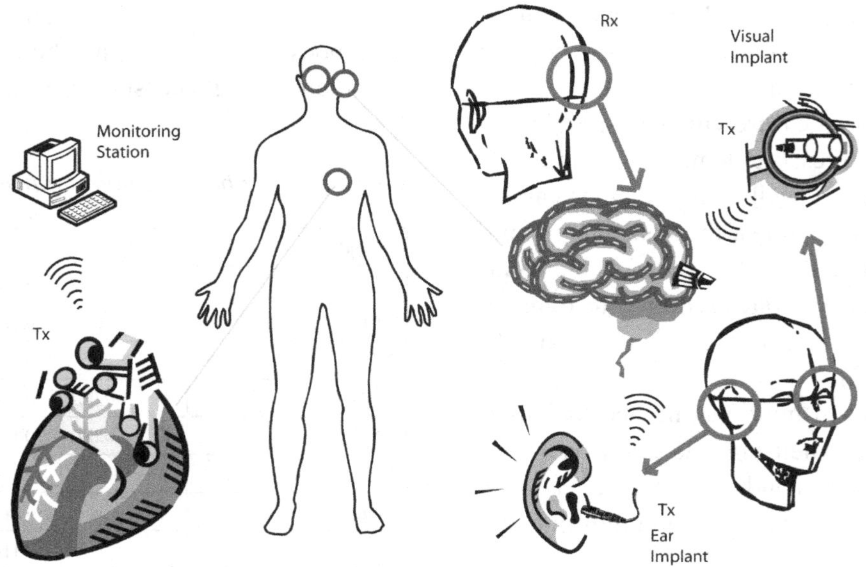

example, a quadriplegic person could control a robotic arm or an exoskeleton machine by nerve impulses relayed wirelessly from the spine (see Figure 15). In such networks, we can deduce that the elements that establish the connection are highly complex, with high levels of miniaturization and complex signal processing and control. Another example is that of an artificial eye which can transmit information directly to the cerebral cortex that processes visual information. Clearly, these are emerging applications that still need to be explored and there is a huge gap before nerve electro-interfaces can be deployed.

Another type of invasive application consists of a series of implants and/or sensors which monitor and collect information. This information can be downloaded to a computer every time a diagnosis is requested. For example, in the case of a pacemaker, the device could store historical information about the heart behaviour for weeks and even months. This information can then be downloaded to the medical network so that an accurate diagnosis can be performed (Cho, 2010).

Another current application in the BAN field is RFID. RFID can be implanted under the skin where a person's identification information can be stored in a device that is energized by electromagnetic induction to a coil using the magnetic fields of a reading device. This type of implant may extend its range of application and reach out to make measurements in the human body with low complexity.

From these types of applications, the following information can be deduced:

- The communication scheme is bi-directional at short distances from the human body and travels no further than 2 meters.
- The elements of the network are very complex devices and/or sensors which have complex digital-to-analogue interfaces and signal processing capabilities that usually transmit over wide bandwidths.
- The elements that are invasive transmit from inside the human body and require a method of channel estimation and equalization lasting a short period of time. This is necessary because human body parameters vary dynamically from moment to moment.
- In this type of application (point-to-point), there is no need to share the propagation medium with other elements. The only requirement is to ensure coexistence and decrease interference with other technologies that exist in the area.

In most of these applications, wide bandwidths are demanded and the information to be transmitted is delay-sensitive. Consequently, it is important to find what kind of modulation and coding schemes are the most appropriate.

5.1.3 Nano-Surgery and Cooperative Networks (Mesh Topologies)

In the not so far distant future, nanotechnology will have an impact on multiple disciplines; medicine is not an exception. We will focus on the type of network which is formed by a group of nanobots used for surgery (Lai, 2003). In such applications, nanobots in a network will coordinate their actions to perform surgery inside a patient's body without the need for conventional surgery and its potential risks (Cho, 2010). Nanobots, in the future, will be programmed to break down tumours, repair human tissue, remove blood clots, etc. (Lam, 2003).

The first generation of this technology is rudimentary: a range of nanomachines with very basic and limited functionality, such as moving forward, moving backward and making cuts, will be provided by mechatronic devices responding to electromagnetic signals induced to fulfil their functions. Such signals will be emitted by a network coordinator outside the patient and operated under the supervision of a doctor.

Figure 16. Nanobots for surgery applications in cooperative networks

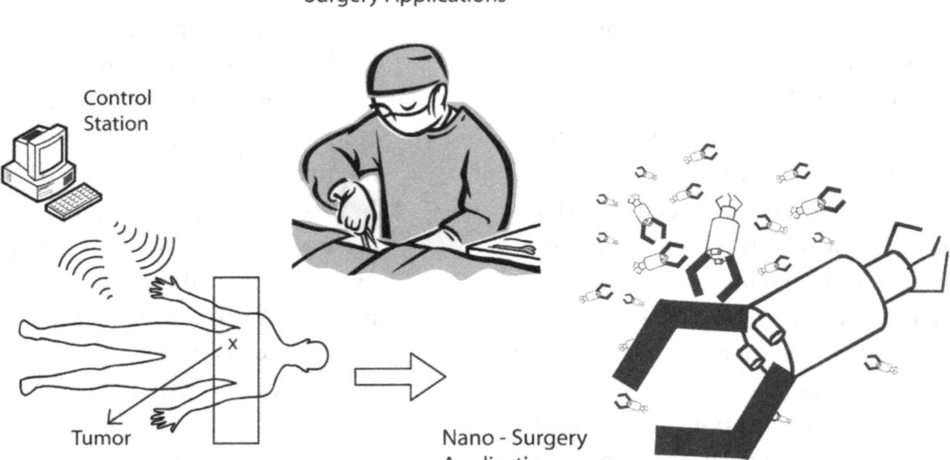

The second generation of this technology will evolve to the point where nanobots can establish mesh networks to implement and coordinate activities within the patient's body without the need for a network coordinator. This implies a higher level of miniaturization and a greater capacity of the nanobots. The nanobots will not be necessarily electronic. They could be complex chains of molecules, molecular motors or chemical actuators. They could eventually replace the functions of the human immune system against some diseases and infections.

In the beginning, the communication between these machines will use the electromagnetic spectrum and the nanobots will form cooperative networks in mesh topologies, in which any individual can share information, instructions and operating decisions with any other module within the network. Subsequently, as nano-technology advances, the nanobots may become organic molecules and their communication may be possible through chemical or electrochemical impulses like hormones.

The main challenge in such networks is to establish communication links between members of the mesh network (swarm behaviour of nanobots). In the early stages of this type of network, the logical network topology will be a point to multi-point connection with unidirectional flow of information, where nanobots execute orders that they receive from the network coordinator (with the network coordinator broadcasting instructions). In the second generation, communication will be done in an *ad hoc* network, where processing and activities will be performed by a cooperative network. In the third generation, the members of the swarm will exhibit 'intelligent' collective behaviour and they will make decisions according to the environment in which they reside. In this kind of communication, transmissions are characterized by short control messages and instructions that propagate over short distances (of the order of millimetres or centimetres) and the transmission channel is nearly constant, so communications will be easier to implement than in other wireless scenarios.

5.2 Entertainment and Information Exchange Applications

When entertainment and information applications are considered, we put special emphasis on multimedia transmissions over wireless connections, internet access and the synchronization of devices around the human body. In addition, several assumptions can be made: we assume that network topology has a star configuration and a point-to-point set-up. We notice that transmissions in these kinds of applications are performed around the human body (on body communications). Finally, the devices considered in these applications will be worn by people, e.g. watches, PDAs, MP4, mobile phones, etc. Several of these applications are presented in Figure 17 (Konstantas, 2003).

5.2.1 Multimedia Entertainment

Multimedia entertainment transmits audio and/or video streams using wireless connections between the information source and the target device that delivers the information to the sense organ by means of a delivery device (headphones, microphones, displays, etc.). Depending on the quality and amount of information to be transmitted, the application can demand wide bandwidth. Transmissions can be performed in one direction only using the downlink channel, but an uplink channel is required if flow control or additional multimedia transmission services are required. It is possible to consider multicasting applications, particularly if persons wishe to share their music, data and/or video information.

The propagation mode being considered is on body communication and the transmission medium is the human skin or proximity to the human body. The human body does not remain static, so the channel fades and changes according to the activity and movement of the person.

The network topology may vary according to the situation. It can be a point-to-point communication topology if only two devices demand multimedia transmissions, or it can be a point to multi-point transmission if a broadcasting transmission is required (more than one receiver device). Media access is not a critical issue, but the coverage area required by the receiver terminals is.

5.2.2 Information Exchange

Information exchange is the process of sending information in a bi-directional way. Bi-directional information exchange includes file sharing, music

Figure 17. Entertainment applications of body area networks

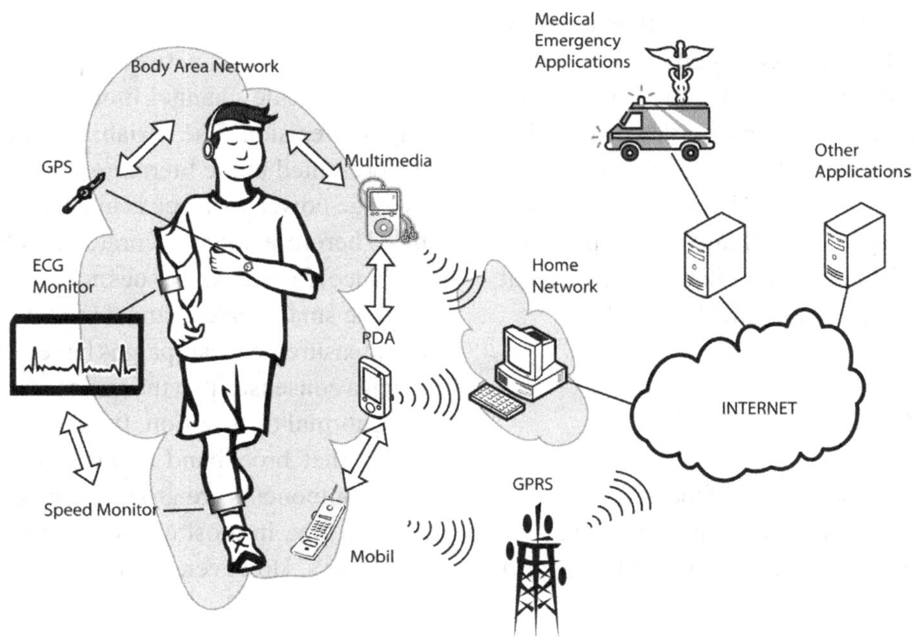

and videos between two or more devices, with the transfer made directly without using a third network element. For example, we can synchronize a digital camera or video camera with another person or with a desktop computer in the office or home without the need for cables (wireless). There may also be information exchange in the home, office, industry, or custom services in digital cities.

The propagation channel remains around the human body and variability of the channel in the time domain depends on the movement and activity of the human body at the time of information exchange. A typical topology is point-to-point and the communication is bi-directional. In some special cases, there will be an *ad hoc* wireless mesh network with no more than a dozen members. In this situation, users can share their information using multicast and broadcasting transmissions.

5.2.3 Positioning

In these types of applications, the transmission goes beyond body area networks and the distance coverage may be in the range of 8 meters. The star topology is the most common set-up, where the central station locates users by triangulating their position with the help of two other nodes, or by calculating the received signal strength over a sectored antenna. The sequence pilot estimation, beacon interval and most appropriate positioning technique can be deduced from the stability parameters of the channel model. The communication is bi-directional, symmetrical and the propagation delay time and channel equalization are relevant (O'Donovan, 2009; Domenicali, 2007).

6. CONCLUSION

Body Area Networks are one of the new emerging technologies that will give people a wide variety of new benefits, improve quality of life, support the advance of medicine and domotics, and open new horizons in the entertainment industry.

Medical applications provide the current focus of research, particularly in body area networks. The ability to interact with the central nervous system of human beings is not far away and BANs bring many benefits, including providing improved access to information and real-time monitoring. BANs also improve the quality of life of patients. For example, they can help replace prostheses and they can be used to help create artificial sense organs that will help handicapped people. In the field of medical diagnosis, BANs should improve the precision of tests and significantly increase the effectiveness of surgical and medical treatment by reducing side effects.

The greatest challenge that presently exists with body area networks is how to compensate for the dynamic effects of the rapidly changing channel (deep fading in frequency and time). It is a fact that the human body is a dynamic environment and constant motion makes it very difficult to design a channel model that can cope. It is quite probable that in the near future there will be a large number of channel models, most of them of statistical nature, and each will provide a specific solution. It is unlikely that a unified channel model will be found that provides all the features required by wireless body area network applications.

Large-scale channel models leave a serious gap in precision. The variability of current models presented in the literature is too large and the average power variance is in the order 8 dB to 14 dB. Therefore, more accurate models (minimum variance) for path loss issues need to be developed.

The small-scale channel models evaluated in our measurement campaigns have permitted us to reach a consensus that the fading channel follows a lognormal distribution. In addition, it has been found that broadband applications with multipath components are grouped into clusters and it is clear that, in most cases, there is overlapping of clusters. However, as far as we know, there is no mathematical model that characterizes this phenomenon. Today, the best approach to this type of channel model is a modified Saleh-Valenzuela channel model.

The trend in receiving devices is to reduce the structural and functional complexity circuits require to establish communications and the development of versatile antennas for invasive BAN network environments (such as prostheses and other similar types of elements inside the human body). In the near future, mesh networks in BANs will contain no more than a dozen elements because networks operating hundreds of devices will not make sense if operability, scalability and network performance are considered. The peripheral elements of BANs will be closer to the distributed sensor networks that operate with a smart central node or common sink device. Another important trend is to make the central node of the network the universal hub for several services like WAN, LAN and mobile applications. The most likely outcome is that this device will be a mobile phone.

Broadband transmissions in BAN networks concentrate on two main applications, the first application is for medical diagnosis and the second is for entertainment and information exchange. In these applications, the communication devices will be complex and expensive. On the other hand, narrow band transmissions are used for applications like monitoring vital signs, location and information transfer in sensor networks and domotics. Manufacturing will demand low cost and mass-production.

The frequency bands for BAN networks are basically the unlicensed bands (ISP), 450 MHz, 2.4 GHz and 5.2 GHz Bands and Ultra Wide Band frequency ranges (3.1 GHz to 10.6 GHz). The most probable candidates for BAN deployment are the IEEE 802.15.4a ZigBee, UWB, and MB OFDM by ECMA 368. The use of MIMO is not advisable because the short distance of BAN coverage (a few meters) will introduce interference. MIMO is only applicable to very high frequency bands (60 GHz applications) where the level of penetration is very low and high directivity can be achieved despite the short distances.

8. ACKNOWLEDGMENT

The authors are grateful to the ENSTA (Prof. Alain Sibille) and iTEAM (Prof. Narcís Cardona) research groups for the measurement campaigns of the presented channel model parameters.

9. REFERENCES

Betancur, L., Cardona, N., Navarro, A., & Traver, L. (2009). A statistical channel model for on body area networks in ultra wide band communications. In *Proceedings of the IEEE Latin-American Conference on Communications, LATINCOM* (pp. 1-6).

Cassidy, A., Zhang, Z., & Andreou, A. (2008). Impulse radio address event interconnects for body area networks and neural prostheses. In *Argentine School of Micro-Nanoelectronics: Technology and Applications* (pp. 87–92). New York: IEEE.

Chang, W., Tarng, J., & Peng, S. (2008). Frequency-space-polarization on UWB MIMO performance for body area network applications. *IEEE Antennas and Wireless Propagation Letters*, *7*, 577–580. doi:10.1109/LAWP.2008.2000640

Chao, Y., & Scholtz, R. A. (2005). Ultra-wideband transmitted reference systems. *IEEE Transactions on Vehicular Technology*, *54*(5), 1556–1569. doi:10.1109/TVT.2005.855700

Chen, Y., & Beaulieu, N. (2007). SNR estimation methods for UWB systems. *IEEE Transactions on Wireless Communications*, *6*(10), 3836–3845. doi:10.1109/TWC.2007.060141

Chen, Y., Teo, J., Lai, J., Gunawan, E., Low, K. S., Soh, C. B., & Rapajic, P. (2009). Cooperative communications in ultra-wideband wireless body area networks: Channel modeling and system diversity analysis. *IEEE Journal on Selected Areas in Communications*, *27*(1), 5–16. doi:10.1109/JSAC.2009.090102

Chi, B., Yao, J., Han, S., Xie, X., Li, G., & Wang, Z. (2007). Low-power transceiver analog front-end circuits for bidirectional high data rate wireless telemetry in medical endoscopy applications. *IEEE Transactions on Bio-Medical Engineering*, *54*(7), 1291–1299. doi:10.1109/TBME.2006.889768

Chong, C. C., & Yong, S. (2005). A generic statistical-based UWB channel model for high-rise apartments. *IEEE Transactions on Antennas and Propagation*, *53*(8), 2389–2399. doi:10.1109/TAP.2005.852505

Chow, E., Chlebowski, A., Chakraborty, S., Chappell, W., & Irazoqui, P. (2010). Fully wireless implantable cardiovascular pressure monitor integrated with a medical stent. *IEEE Transactions on Bio-Medical Engineering*, *57*(6), 1487–1496. doi:10.1109/TBME.2010.2041058

D'Errico, R., & Ouvry, L. (2009). Time-variant BAN channel characterization. *COST2100. CEA-LETI.* TD(09)879.

Domenicali, D., & Benedetto, M. D. (2007). Performance analysis for a body area network composed of IEEE 802.15.4a devices. In *Proceedings of the 4th Workshop on Positioning, Navigation and Communication (WPNC)* (pp. 273-276).

Federal Communications Commission. (2002). *Revision of Part 15 of the commission's rules regarding ultra-wideband transmission systems, first report and order*. Technical Report, Federal Communications Commission.

Fort, A., Ryckaert, J., Desset, C., Doncker, P. D., Wambacq, P., & Biesen, L. V. (2006). Ultra-wideband channel model for communication around the human body. *IEEE Journal on Selected Areas in Communications*, *24*(4), 927–933. doi:10.1109/JSAC.2005.863885

Goeckel, D., & Zhang, Q. (2007). Slightly frequency-shifted reference ultra-wideband (UWB) radio. *IEEE Transactions on Communications*, *55*(3), 508–519. doi:10.1109/TCOMM.2007.892452

Gorce, J. M., Goursaud, C., Savigny, C., & Villemaud, G. (2009). Cooperation mechanisms in BANs *COST2100. University of Lyon,* TD(09)862.

Goulianos, A. A., & Stavrou, S. (2007). UWB path arrival times in body area networks. *IEEE Antennas and Wireless Propagation Letters*, *6*, 223–226. doi:10.1109/LAWP.2007.895294

Gray, R. M., & Davisson, L. D. (2005). *An introduction to statistical signal processing*. Cambridge, UK: Cambridge University Press.

Gupta, A., & Abhayapala, T. D. (2008). Body area networks: Radio channel modelling and propagation characteristics. *In Proceedings of the Australian Communications Theory Workshop (AusCTW)* (pp. 58-63).

Hardle, W., & Simar, L. (2003). *Applied multivariate statistical analysis*. Metrika.

Heavens, O. S. (1965). *Optical properties of thin film solids*. New York: Dover.

IEEE Standarization Working Group. (2009). IEEE 802.15 WPAN Task Group 6 (TG6): Body Area Networks. Retrieved from http://www.ieee802.org/15/pub/TG6.html

Jianqi, T., Chan, S. W., Chen, Y., Gunawan, E., Low, K. S., & Soh, C. B. (2007). Time domain measurements for UWB on-body radio propagation. In *Proceedings of the IEEE Antennas and Propagation Society International Symposium* (pp. 325-328). New York: IEEE.

Jurik, A. D., & Weaver, A. C. (2008). Remote medical monitoring. *IEEE Computer*, *41*(4), 96–99.

Katayama, N., Takizawa, K., Aoyagi, T., Takada, J., Li, H., & Kohno, R. (2008). Channel model on various frequency bands for wearable body area network. In *Proceedings of the First International Symposium on Applied Sciences on Biomedical and Communication Technologies (ISABEL)* (pp. 1-5).

Konstantas, D., & Herzog, R. (2003). Continuous monitoring of vital constants for mobile users: The MobiHealth approach. In *Proceedings of the 25th Annual International Conference of the IEEE Engineering in Medicine and Biology Society* (vol. 4, pp. 3728-3731). New York: IEEE.

Kovacs, I., Pedersen, G., Eggers, P., & Olesen, K. (2004). Ultra wideband radio propagation in body area network scenarios. In *Proceedings of the IEEE Eighth International Symposium on Spread Spectrum Techniques and Applications* (pp. 102-106). New York: IEEE.

Lai, K. W. C., Kwong, C. C. H., & Li, W. J. (2003). KL probes for robotic-based cellular nano-surgery. In *Proceedings of the Third IEEE Conference on Nanotechnology* (Vol. 2, pp. 152-155). New York: IEEE.

Lam, R. H. W., Li, W. J., & Ning, X. (2003). A wireless temperature measurement guide rod for internal bone fixation surgery. In [). New York: IEEE.]. *Proceedings of the IEEE International Conference on Robotics and Automation*, *2*, 1768–1773.

Li, H., Takizawa, K. I., Zheri, B., & Kohno, R. (2007). Body area network and its standardization at IEEE 802.15.MBAN. In *Proceedings of the 16th IST Mobile and Wireless Communications Summit* (Vol. 1, pp. 1-5).

Liu, L., Doncker, P. D., & Oestges, C. (2008). Fading correlation measurement and modelling on the front and back side of a human body. *COST 2100, UCL and UBL, TD(08)642*

Manzoor, R., Majavu, W., Jeoti, V., Kamel, N., & Asif, M. (2007). Front-end estimation of noise power and SNR in OFDM systems. In *Proceedings of the International Conference on Intelligent and Advanced Systems (ICIAS)* (pp. 435-439).

Molisch, A. (2005). Ultrawideband propagation channels – Theory, measurement, and modeling. *IEEE Transactions on Vehicular Technology*, *54*(5), 1528–1545. doi:10.1109/TVT.2005.856194

Molisch, A. F., Balakrishnan, K., Cassioli, D., Chong, C. C., Emami, S., Fort, A., Karedal, J., Kunisch, J., Schantz, H., & Siwiak, U. S. K. (2004). IEEE 802.15.4a channel model- final report..

Monton, E., Hernandez, J. F., Blasco, J. M., Herve, T., Micallef, J., & Grech, I. (2008). Body area network for wireless patient monitoring. *IET Communications*, *2*(2), 215–222. doi:10.1049/iet-com:20070046

Motani, M., Yap, K., Natarajan, A., de Silva, B., Hu, S., & Chua, K. C. (2007). Network characteristics of urban environments for wireless BAN. In *Proceedings of the IEEE Biomedical Circuits and Systems Conference, (BIOCAS)* (Vol. 1, pp. 179-182). New York: IEEE.

O'Donovan, T., O'Donoghue, J., Sreenan, C., Sammon, D., O'Reilly, P., & O'Connor, K. A. (2009). A context aware wireless body area network (BAN). In *Proceedings of the International Conference on Pervasive Computing Technologies for Healthcare* (pp. 1-8).

Ohno, K., Watanabe, K., Yamada, T., Kobayashi, T., Matsuda, H., Yamazaki, N., & Ikegami, T. (2008). Wideband measurement for body effect of BAN channel. In *Proceedings of the IEEE 10th International Symposium on Spread Spectrum Techniques and Applications (ISSSTA)* (pp. 292-296).

Oliveira, C., Pedrosa, L., & Rocha, R. M. (2008). Characterizing on-body wireless sensor networks. In *Proceedings of New Technologies, Mobility and Security (NTMS)* (pp. 1-6).

Olugbara, O., Adigun, M., Ojo, S., & Mudali, P. (2007). Utility grid computing and body area network as enabler for ubiquitous rural e-healthcare service provisioning. In *Proceedings of the 9th International Conference on e-Health Networking, Application and Services* (pp. 202-207).

Opperman, I., Hamalainen, M., & Linatti, J. (2004). *UWB theory and applications*. New York: John Wiley & Sons. doi:10.1002/0470869194

Park, S., Kim, W., Lee, J., Chung, Y. S., & Cheon, C. (2008). A new receiver antenna with buffer layer for wireless capsule endoscopy in human body. In *Proceedings of the IEEE Antennas and Propagation Society International Symposium* (pp. 1-4). New York: IEEE.

Rappaport, T. (1996). *Wireless Communications: Principles and Practice* (1st ed.). New York: Prentice Hall.

Reddy, P., & Ganapathy, V. (2008). Performance of multi user detector based receivers for UWB body area networks. In *Proceedings of the 10th International Conference on e-health Networking, Applications and Services (HealthCom)* (pp. 227-231).

Roy, S. V., Oestges, C., Horlin, F., & Doncker, P. D. (2007). Ultra-wideband spatial channel characterization for body area networks. *The Second European Conference on Antennas and Propagation, EuCAP* (pp. 1-5).

Ruiz, J., Xu, J., & Shimamoto, S. (2006). Propagation characteristics of intra-body communications for body area networks. In *Proceedings of the 3rd IEEE Consumer Communications and Networking Conference (CCNC)* (Vol. 1, pp. 509-513). New York: IEEE.

Saleh, A., & Valenzuela, R. (1987). A statistical model for indoor multipath propagation. *IEEE Journal on Selected Areas in Communications*, *5*(2), 128–137. doi:10.1109/JSAC.1987.1146527

Simic, D., Jordan, A., Tao, R., Gungl, N., Simic, J., & Lang, M. (2007). *Impulse UWB radio system architecture for body area networks. 16th IST Mobile and Wireless Communications Summit* (pp. 1–5). Berlin: Springer.

Smulders, P. (2009). Statistical characterization of 60-GHz indoor radio channels. *IEEE Transactions on Antennas and Propagation*, *57*(10), 2820–2829. doi:10.1109/TAP.2009.2030524

Socheleau, F.-X., Aissa-El-Bey, A., & Houcke, S. (2008). Non data-aided SNR estimation of OFDM signals. *IEEE Communications Letters*, *12*(11), 813–815. doi:10.1109/LCOMM.2008.081134

Takada, J., Aoyagi, T., Takizawa, K., Katayama, N., Kobayashi, T., Yazdandoost, K. Y., Li, H., & Kohno, R. (2008). Static propagation and channel models in body area. *COST 2100, University of Tokyo, TD(08)639*

Tayamachi, T., Wang, Q., & Wang, J. (2007). Transmission characteristic analysis for UWB body area communications. In *Proceedings of the International Symposium on Electromagnetic Compatibility (EMC), (*pp. 75-78). New York: IEEE.

Tesi, R., Taparugssanagorn, A., Hämäläinen, M., & Iinatti, J. (2008). UWB channel measurements for wireless body area networks. *COST 2100, Oulu Finland, TD(08)649*

Thompson, W., Walker, K., Cepeda, R., Beach, M. A., & Armour, S. (2008). Ultra-wideband body area network channel measurement and analysis using textile antennas. *COST 2100, Bristol Toshiba, TD(08)629*

Timmons, N., & Scanlon, W. (2004). Analysis of the performance of IEEE 802.15.4 for medical sensor body area networking. In *Proceedings of the First Annual IEEE Communications Society Conference on Sensor and Ad Hoc Communications and Networks (SECON)* (pp. 16-24). New York: IEEE.

Watanabe, K., Hari, S., Ohnol, K., & Ikegami, T. (2008). Experiments on shadow effects of body and effective paths for UWB transmission in BAN. In *Proceedings of the International Symposium on Communications and Information Technologies (ISCIT)* (pp. 232-237). New York: IEEE.

Wen, X. (2008). Design of medical infusion monitor and protection system based on wireless communication technology. In *Proceedings of the Second International Symposium on Intelligent Information Technology Application (IITA)* (Vol. 2, pp. 755-759). New York: IEEE.

Wu, K., & Wu, X. (2007). A wireless mobile monitoring system for home healthcare and community medical services. In *Proceedings of the International Conference on Bioinformatics and Biomedical Engineering (ICBBE)*, (pp. 119-1193). New York: IEEE.

Xie, X., Li, G., & Wang, Z. (2006). ARQ scheme with adaptive block size for bidirectional wireless endoscopy system. *IEEE Proceedings on Communications*, *153*(5), 611–618. doi:10.1049/ip-com:20050338

Xu, H., & Yang, L. (2008). Ultra-wideband technology: Yesterday, today, and tomorrow. In *Proceedings of the IEEE Radio and Wireless Symposium*, (pp. 715-718). New York: IEEE.

Yazdandoost, K. Y., & Kohno, R. (2009). An antenna for medical implant communications system. *COST 2100. Medical ICT Institute, National Institute of Information and Communications Technology, New Generation Wireless Communications Research Center*. TD(09)808.

Yoo, H., & Cho, N. (2008). Body channel communication for low energy BSN/BAN. In *Proceedings of the IEEE Asia Pacific Conference on Circuits and Systems (APCCAS)*, (pp. 7-11). New York: IEEE.

Zasowski, T., Althaus, F., Stager, M., Wittneben, A., & Troster, G. (2003). UWB for noninvasive wireless body area networks: Channel measurements and results. In. *Proceedings of the IEEE Conference on Ultra Wideband Systems and Technologies*, *1*, 285–289. doi:10.1109/UWBST.2003.1267849

Zasowski, T., Meyer, G., Althaus, F., & Wittneben, A. (2006). UWB signal propagation at the human head. *IEEE Transactions on Microwave Theory and Techniques*, *54*(4), 1836–1845. doi:10.1109/TMTT.2006.871989

Zasowski, T., & Wittneben, A. (2009). Performance of UWB receivers with partial CSI using a simple body area network channel model. *IEEE Journal on Selected Areas in Communications*, *27*(1), 17–26. doi:10.1109/JSAC.2009.090103

Zimmerman, T. G. (1995). Personal Area Networks (PAN): Near-field intra body communication. Unpublished master's thesis. Boston: Media Laboratory, MIT.

Chapter 5
mHealth:
Software Development and Wireless Technologies Applications

Juan Ivan Nieto Hipólito
Autonomous University of Baja California, México

Mabel Vázquez Briseño
Autonomous University of Baja California, México

Humberto Cervantes de Ávila
Autonomous University of Baja California, México

Miguel Enrique Martínez Rosas
Autonomous University of Baja California, México

Oleg Yu Sergiyenko
Autonomous University of Baja California, México

ABSTRACT

mHealth is a very attractive field for mobile applications developers, but it also involves new challenges that developers of programs intended for standard desktops do not usually face. Hence, the first part of this chapter is devoted to survey the development platforms and languages utilized to develop the associated applications of the mHealth system. mHealth is a communications system that consists of mobile devices for collecting and delivering clinical health data to practitioners, researchers and patients. It is also a tool used in the real-time monitoring of patient vital signs, and direct provision of care. Therefore, the second part of this chapter will focuses on the survey of wireless technologies envisioned for use in the mHealth system.

INTRODUCTION

Many applications are presently being applied to mobile wireless ad-hoc networks (MANETs). These include mobile applications used for public health practice, including mobile health systems (*mHealth). mHealth* consists of mobile devices for collecting and delivering clinical health data to practitioners, researchers and patients. It is also a

DOI: 10.4018/978-1-60960-027-3.ch005

system used in the real-time monitoring of patient vital signs, and direct provision of care.

mHealth is a very attractive field for mobile applications developers, but it also involves new challenges that developers of programs intended for standard desktops do not often face. First, mobile devices have generally constrained resources; they tend to be limited in screen size, processor memory, storage capacity and energy. This severely restricts the resources that an application can use. Second, the way users interact with mobile devices is different from standard desktops. Therefore, developers need to create applications with appropriate user interfaces for mobile devices. Another important challenge of the mHealth system is the communication medium in its majority is wireless; therefore, nodes tend to be highly mobile. The main challenge, however, is that current mobile devices are very diverse, especially with regards to operating systems and runtimes. This heterogeneity causes problems for developers, because they must fit applications to as many devices as possible, including multiple versions of the same device that are still in use. While desktop application developers have three OS platforms to choose from: Windows, Linux and Mac OS X; mobile developers must choose among different development platforms and languages, each one incompatible with the others. Moreover, choosing a platform or language directly impacts the range of devices in which applications can run. At present, *Symbian* OS has the largest number of users, followed by Microsoft's Windows CE, Windows Mobile, Palm OS and Linux. Symbian OS native programming application is C ++, but it also supports applications written in Java.

The objective of this section is to describe the main mobile applications development platforms and runtimes available for developers to provide keys for choosing the appropriate one.

MOBILE SOFTWARE DEVELOPMENT PLATFORMS

As mentioned before, m-health relies on the development of mobile applications. In this context, an application is *mobile* if it runs on a mobile device and may be either, always or occasionally connected to a network. This definition includes applications that run on personal digital assistants (PDAs) and mobile phones, among other possible mobile devices. *mHealth* applications may include data storage, data processing and viewing or transmitting data to another application. The use of mobile applications, however, is more related to the providing mobile services. A mobile service can be described as an electronic service that consists of three main components: a mobile application as a client, wireless networking and a server implementation to provide the needed functionality or information (*Content*) to the user. In other words, application is a more technical term referring to the solution itself, whereas service is better associated with third parties (e.g. content provider or network based server) who provide value-added service at the end-customer. Applications can be seen either as network applications implementing the service as interfaces to these services, or as stand-alone applications in a handset that requires no network/ service connectivity (Verkasalo, 2006).

The key applications and mobile services related with *mHealth* include:

- Remote data collection
- Remote monitoring
- Communication with healthcare workers
- Diagnostic and treatment support

The implementation of such applications requires a programming platform specifically designed to run on mobile devices.

GENERIC MOBILE DEVELOPMENT APPLICATIONS PLATFORMS

There are several platforms available for mobile applications programming, among the most popular are: BREW,.Net Compact Framework, Java Micro Edition (Java Me) and more recently Android, developed by the Open HandsetAlliance. These platforms are useful for developing generic mobile applications that can be adapted to work using MANETs. They are described in the following sections, including their main characteristics and mobile devices support.

Binary Runtime Environment for Wireless (BREW)

BREW is an application execution environment that was released by Qualcomm in February 2001. Qualcomm was the first company to commercialize CDMA (Code Division Multiple Access) technology, which was originally developed for military use. Brew is a mobile platform intended to be used by network operators or service providers; it can integrate network management, billing and a program development system as an end-to-end solution for mobile telecommunication services (Wen-Tzu & Chih-Nan, 2008). Qualcomm has designed its own mobile phone operating system (OS), also named BREW, which is completely compatible with this mobile platform. The BREW environment however, can be used with other mobile operating systems such as Palm OS, Windows CE, and Symbian OS. Initially, BREW was restricted to work only on CDMA networks, but now it is capable of running on any network and can be ported to a wide range of BREW-enabled devices because it is a development platform that runs above the hardware. There are two essential components to the platform: The first one is the BREW Software Development Kit (SDK), which is used by developers to create applications; the second one, for the end user, is a piece of software or firmware required by a handset to run BREW applications on it.

Currently, there are several versions of BREW's SDK available, going from versions 1.0 to 4.0.4. Each SDK version is paired with a corresponding Application Execution Environment (AEE) on the phone. Applications written using the 1.0 SDK will run on phones equipped with later versions of the AEE. The converse is not necessarily true since each successive version incorporates new capabilities. Natively, it only supports C and C++ programming languages, but it is also possible to add Java functionality by selecting IBM's Java Virtual Machine (JVM).The JVM runs in a layer top of the BREW platform and provides standardized Java APIs for the application developer. The SDK includes the BREW Application Wizard, which is an add-in to Microsoft Visual Studio; it can be used to construct projects and provides the basic source files required to construct BREW applications. It also provides a library of functions, Application Programming Interfaces (APIs), and a set of extensions, which are reusable components or modules.

Extensions are written by developers and can be created containing one or more BREW classes. These extensions can be private to one application, or public for other applications to use, which means that they can be shared with others developers. The SDK also includes a simulator known as the BREW Emulator. It is a Windows-based program that simulates the AEE on a phone. An application runs on the emulator as a Windows.dll. As usual, there are significant differences between the emulator environment and the phone itself, but it is a good tool for learning the APIs and testing an application throughout the development process.

All BREW components are available at no cost for developers; however, running software on real mobile hardware requires a digital signature which can only be generated with tools issued by mobile content providers and Qualcomm. These extra tools are currently not free of charge. In addition, developers must be registered with Qualcomm, which also is at additional cost. In general, when choosing BREW as a development platform, it is important to consider the following costs:

1. Certification and testing: All services provided by content developers must be Qualcomm certified. For this, Qualcomm receives certification and testing fees.
2. BREW platform equipment: Operators must buy BREW platform-related software and hardware.
3. Platform fees: Qualcomm takes a fixed percentage of each service fee paid by mobile users.
4. There is also a fee to become an *Authenticated BREW Developer*.

It is important to clarify that these costs are part of the BREW Distribution System (BDS), which is intended to provide a means of selling and delivering applications to end-users and helping developers commercialize their applications. This means that these fees are not mandatory when creating non-profit applications; for example, when developing applications for research or education.

.NET Compact Framework (.NET CF)

The.NET CF is the latest initiative from Microsoft to compete with Java and BREW. The Compact Framework is a limited version of the complete. NET Framework and only requires 1.5 Megabytes, while the complete.NET CF is 30 MB in size. However, it also contains features that were exclusively designed for it to obtain optimal performance under the constraints of limited device resources. This means that code compiled under the.NET Framework may run under the. NET Compact Framework, but the opposite is not possible. As mentioned, several methods and functionalities have been remove from the original, but.NET CF still implements a compatible subset of the functionalities of the full.NET Framework. Because of this,.NET CF allow developers to use some of the same techniques to achieve similar tasks when programming for desktop PCs and servers. In the same way, it is also possible to use the same developer tools, such as Visual Studio.NET that provide, for example, The Form Designer that allows developers to design their application's user interface visually by dragging controls onto a design-time representation of the application. It also includes emulators for Pocket PC and Windows CE OS.

.NET CF provides as well its Software Development Kit (SDK) that contains all the required tools to build and compile applications. It comprises a runtime, the programming libraries and the development tools to create and execute applications on mobile phones running the.NET CF.

.NET CF has two main components: The Common Language Runtime (CLR) and the.NET CF class library.

The CLR provides a code-execution environment that manages code targeting the.NET Framework; this code is known as *managed code*. Currently, the framework supports two development languages: C#.NET and VB.NET. The CLR is designed to run on limited memory and to use battery power efficiently. It makes use of Just-In-Time (JIT) compiling to enable *managed* code to run in the native machine language of the platform on which an application is running. The JIT is responsible for translating this code into native code so that a managed program can be executed. This allows developers to create applications that can target a variety of platforms with different CPUs, without requiring recompilation. *Managed* code is also considered *safe code* because the CLR provides core services such as memory management and thread management that help avoid problems like memory leaks and memory overwrites. On the other hand, code that does not target the runtime, as is the case with C and C++, is known as *unmanaged,* or *native,* code.

The.NET CF class library is a collection of DLL files. It contains many reusable classes that provide a range of common programming tasks, including interface designs, database access, networking and input/output operations, among others. They represent the core of the platform, since all applications are built using these classes. The DLL files are written in mostly *managed* code, but some of them interact through native code directly with the operating system.

.NET CF is designed to run on Windows CE-based mobile devices such as PDAs, mobile phones, factory controllers, set-top boxes, etc. It is available as an operating system component in all Microsoft smart devices, including Pocket PC devices, Pocket PC Phone Edition, Smartphone devices, and other Windows Embedded CE-powered devices. Currently, the latest version is Microsoft.NET Compact Framework 3.5. There is also a version available for the Xbox 360 console.

Java Micro Edition (Java ME)

Java ME, previously known as J2ME, is currently the most popular platform for developing applications for mobile devices. Sixty-six percent of wireless developers target Java in some way or another. According to the Evans report, *Wireless Developers Lament Current State of Important Development Tools (2006)*, Java ME is targeted by 56% of mobile applications developers. Companies like Nokia, Sony Ericsson and Motorola have already based their platforms on Java ME specifications.

Java ME is a smaller version of Java 2 Standard Edition and includes some features targeted towards small devices. It is standardized through the Java Community Process (JCP), which consists of participants from the industry and specified in Java Specification Request (JSR).

Java ME supports platform independence and security. The overall architecture can be viewed as follows:

- A Java virtual machine (JVM) targeted to the consumer end user device. For mobile devices, the virtual machine is called KVM. K stands for Kilo, indicating the small memory footprint.
- A group of libraries and Application Programming Interfaces (APIs) in order to use the device's capabilities and other functionalities. These libraries and APIs are grouped separately according to device type. They are known as *Profiles* and *Configurations.*
- Several tools to accompany development, deployment and device configuration.

The first two components constitute the runtime, which are installed on the end user's mobile device to execute Java ME-based applications.

The *configuration* layer defines a minimum set of JVM features and core Java class libraries available on a particular category of devices. The configuration that defines small mobile devices is called the Connected Limited Device Configuration (CLDC). The *profile* layer defines the minimum set of APIs on a particular group of devices.

A *Profile* serves two main purposes: Device specialization and device portability. The first term refers to APIs that capture or exploit particularities of the device interface and capability. The second term means that applications written for a particular profile should port to any device that conforms to that profile. The Mobile Information Device Profile (MIDP) is specifically designed for cell phones. It provides the user interface, network connectivity, local data storage, and application management needed by these devices. It adds APIs in the following areas (Guiguere, 2000):

- Defining and controlling applications. Applications written to the MIDP specification are called *MIDlets* and are similar to *Applets*. A *MIDlet* defines methods that the system calls in order to start, stop (pause), and destroy the application.
- Displaying text and graphics and responding to user events. It provides the necessary classes to build user interfaces.

- Storing data. It provides a simple, record-based, persistent storage mechanism for storing data in-between application invocations.
- Network connectivity. Defines the classes to establish network connections.
- Timer notifications. Applications can schedule tasks to be executed at various intervals.

Figure 1 depicts the architectural view of the relationships between the KVM, CLDC and MIDP layers. On top of a *Configuration*, a *Profile* is added to provide further functionality to the user applications. Other different configurations and profiles have been defined, but the pair best suited for most mobile terminals is the CLDC with the MIDP on top. This combination results in minimal memory and processing requirements on the device and still provides much functionality. Another combination of *Configuration* and *Profile* is the Connected Device Configuration (CDC), together with the Personal Profile (PP). This combination is resource demanding for current cellular phones, but applications developed for the CLDC/MIDP environment should, in theory, run without modifications in a CDC/PP environment.

CLDC requires implementations to support the distribution of Java applications using compressed Java Archive files. Whenever a Java application intended for a CLDC device is created, it must be formatted into a JAR file and class files within a JAR file must contain the application attributes. As mentioned, applications that use the APIs defined by MIDP and CLDC are referred as *MIDlets*. MIDlets are developed on regular desktop computers, but the *MIDlet* itself is designed to run on a small device. To enable distribution of *MIDlets*, developers must generate a metadata file and generate a Java Application Descriptor (JAD) along with the JAR file.

The JAD file provides information to the application manager about the contents of a JAR file, including its size and location. With this information, decisions can be made as to whether or not a *MIDlet* is suitable for running on the device.

MIDlets that need to share code or data are packaged together as *MIDlet suites*. MIDlets within the same suite can share the classes and resources contained in the JAR file. MIDlets from different suites cannot interact directly.

Figure 1. Java platform micro edition architecture

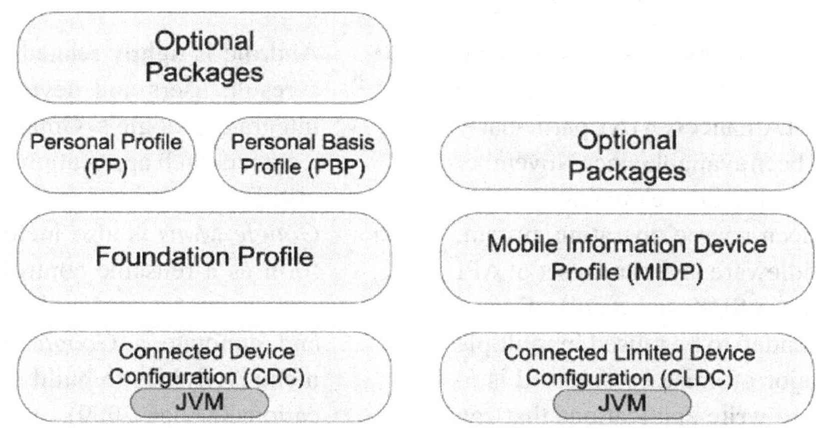

There are two ways to install a Java ME application on a mobile device:

- The direct method: Download the Java ME application from the Web onto a PC, and then upload it onto the mobile device using an USB cable, InfraRed (IR) or Bluetooth connection.
- The Over-The-Air (OTA) method: The Java application is downloaded onto the mobile device using the WAP or Web browser built into the device.

The current specification of CLCD is version 1.1 and for MIDP it is version 2.1. Many valuable functions are left as optional packages, which are not included in the MIDP profile, some of them are: Wireless messaging API, Web Services API, security and trust service API and Mobile Media API (MMAPI) that extends the functionality of the Java ME platform by providing audio, video and other time-based multimedia support to resource-constrained devices. The Java ME SDK, previously known as SUN Java Wireless ToolKit (WTK), provides a set of useful tools for the rapid development of mobile applications, allowing developers to include additional APIs for extra functions. It also provides emulators for several mobile phones. The latest version is the Java Me SDK 3.0

Android

Android is the newest platform for mobile applications development, it was released and developed by the Open Handset Alliance (OHA), particularly by Google, and has been available since November 2007. Android is a complete development platform that provides an open source operating system, an application middleware layer and a set of API libraries, along with a SDK and a collection of useful libraries intended to be reused in multiple applications. A major promise by Android is to permit developers to write applications that can take full advantage of mobile hardware. This is usually not possible when using proprietary operating systems since these systems tend to restrict resources to third-party applications. This is not the case in Android, which is built on the open Linux Kernel as it utilizes a custom virtual machine that was designed to optimize memory and hardware resources in a mobile environment. Another main difference with other available platforms is that Android is open source, thus it can be extended and improved by users and developers.

The Android SDK is freely available and provides the tools and APIs necessary to start developing mobile applications using the Java programming language. Java is a widely known language, whose use facilitates the adoption of this new platform by experimented programmers and even developers who have never programmed for mobile devices. Android utilizes its own virtual machine developed by Google, known as *Dalvik*, which is different from the one used in Java Me (KVM). The main advantage of *Dalvik* is that it has been developed to allow multiple VMs running efficiently in the same device. In this way, threading and low-level memory management is carried out by the Linux Kernel. The use of the Linux Kernel also provides the possibility to write C/C++ applications that will run directly over the OS.

Android offers some unique features that facilitate the development of innovative applications, including the following:

- Android is tightly related with *Google*. As a result, users and developers can easily integrate Google's Gmail, Calendar, and Contacts Web applications with the system utilities.
- *Google Maps* is also included in the platform as a reusable control. The *MapView* widget can be used to display, manipulate, and annotate a *Google Map* within the menu Activities to build map-based applications (Meier, 2009).

- All Applications are Created Equal. This concept is based on the fact that Android does not differentiate between the phone's core applications and third-party applications. They can all be built to have equal access to a phone's capabilities providing users with a broad spectrum of applications and services.
- Android supports applications and services that can be designed to run invisible in the background, thus making it possible to have event-driven applications running silently without requiring many device resources until they are activated.

Android's architecture is shown in Figure 2. This architecture promotes the concept of component reuse, helping developers to concentrate efforts on developing innovative applications instead of re-creating basic system functionalities that are already provided with the platform. Furthermore, any application can publish its capabilities and any other application may then make use of these capabilities subject to the security constraints of the Android framework.

The first layer in Android's architecture is the Application Layer; all applications, including native and third-party are built on this layer and make use of the same set of API libraries.

The second layer is the Application Framework layer; it provides a set of application services to create the basic building blocks of an application. The main services in this layer are:

- **Activity Manager**: An *Activity* is the part of an application that handles the graphic user interface. It is the most common part of any application since all them require user interfaces. The Activity Manager manages the life cycle of applications and provides a common navigation tool, using the history stack maintained for a set of activities.
- **Views**: It provides the controls that can be used to implement user interfaces like lists, grids, textboxes, buttons, etc.

Figure 2. Android's architecture

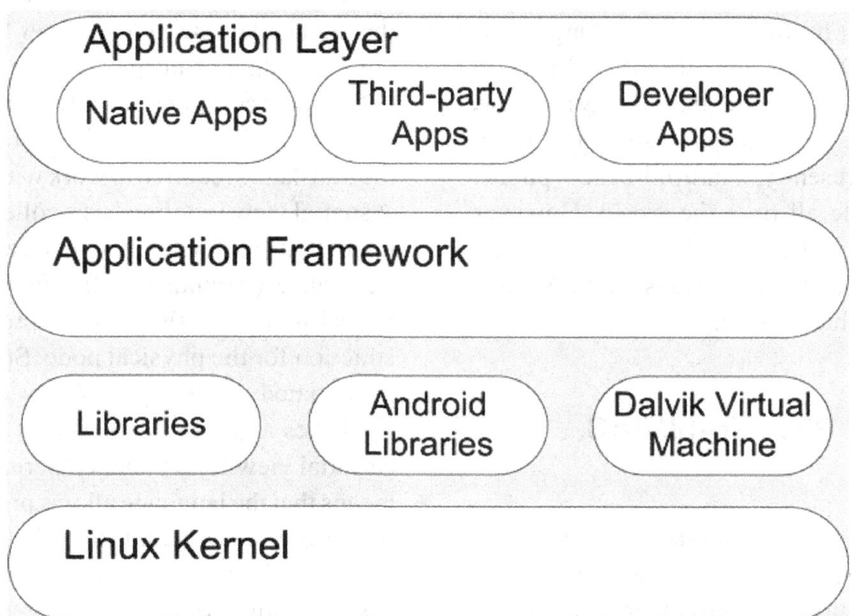

- **Resource Manager**: It allows working with files that do not contain code, such as icons, graphics, and layouts.
- **Content Provider:** A content provider allows an application to share information with other applications. It can be used to store and retrieve data instead of using files or databases.
- **Notification Manager:** It provides the mechanisms that enable all applications to display custom alerts in the status bar, like alerting the user when an e-mail arrives, among others.

The next element in the stack is the Library and Runtime layer; it includes all the libraries, including Google Java libraries, and the *Dalvik* virtual machine.

The final layer is the Kernel layer, where Linux version 2.6 communicates with the hardware and the remainder of the stack.

Although the Android SDK has been available since late 2007, the first Android-based phone was released in the US and Europe in November 2008 by HTC. Since then, the company has introduced its third Android-based device, called the HTC Hero. Industry insiders expect public adoption to increase steeply this year (Enck, Ongtang & McDaniel, 2009). Samsung has also released its first android-based phone called Galaxy and other manufactures have promised to support it in the near future. Presently, Android-based phones are not available all over the world. However, according to Google, by the end of 2009, there will be at least 18 phone models using Android worldwide (Richtel, 2009).

TOOLS FOR PROGRAMMING IN MANETS

This section includes two language-based projects intended for MANETs: *SpatialViews*, and *AmbientTalk*. These languages provide special features required in a MANET environment, where the distinctive characteristic is the ad hoc communication between devices. These languages can be particularly useful when developing mhealth applications in this type of network.

SpatialViews

SpatialViews, developed at Rutgers University, is a prototype language for the development of applications for mobile ad-hoc networks. This development considers that a programming model for ad-hoc networks must be able to describe spaces and desired services within such spaces. The goal of *SpatialViews* is to provide a high-level programming model, which allows application programmers to develop and maintain their ad-hoc network applications easily (Ni, Kremer, Stere, & Iftode, 2005). *SpatialViews* targets mobile devices such as smart phones and PDA's with communication capabilities, meaning that the language requires devices with a processor, some memory, and a network connection; it is not suitable for very resource-constrained networks. The language itself is an extension to Java ME. The implementation includes a compiler, a virtual machine and a runtime system that can be freely downloaded at the *SpatialViews* Website (http://www.cs.rutgers.edu/spatialviews). The compiler extends the compiler provided with the Java Development Kit (JDK) 1.3.1 known as *javac*, adding the translators required to work with the prototype. A spatial view is defined as a collection of virtual nodes that provides a set of services within certain geometrical boundaries. In the same context, a virtual node is defined as the programming abstraction for the physical node. Spatial views are instantiated using a *spatial view iterator*, which replicates a piece of code across all members of a spatial view for a bounded period of time. This means that the language allows programs to work over groups of devices in a kind of loop. The code inside the loop is executed on the initial device and then migrates to the next, eventually returning to the initial node. This iteration is generally done according to a physical location.

The *SpatialViews* development environment also contains a component for debugging, simulating and visualizing. It can be used for testing the code on an emulated mobile ad-hoc network. Mobility in this component is emulated by providing location and topology information, generated dynamically, to a collection of KVM processes running on the same PC. The debugger can be used to analyze the code behavior; it provides a graphical user interface consisting of a Java Applet.

AmbientTalk

AmbientTalk is a prototype language designed to serve as an experimentation platform to develop software for MANETs. It uses a completely different approach from SpatialViews. *AmbientTalk* is a complete object-oriented programming language developed by the Programming Technology Laboratory at the *Vrije Universiteit Brussels*, Belgium, in 2005. It is intended to be used in mobile ad-hoc networks and is considered an ambient-oriented language. The goal of an ambient-oriented language is to facilitate the implementation of applications deployed in a mobile ad hoc network, dealing mainly with two aspects closely related with these networks: volatile connections and zero infrastructures. The first one occurs because mobile devices only have a limited communications range that causes disconnections to occur when two communicating devices move out of this range. They will need to establish communications again, and applications will need to handle this transient disconnection to avoid failures. The second aspect is related to the lack of infrastructure in mobile ad hoc networks. To deal with this issue, applications have to find their required services dynamically in the environment. Services have to be discovered on proximate devices, possibly without the help of shared infrastructure. As an ambient-oriented language *AmbientTalk* has the following characteristics (Van Cutsem, Mostinckx, Boix, Dedecker & De Meuter, 2007):

a. It offers non-blocking communication primitives. This ensures that objects will not block waiting for communication partners for large periods of time.
b. It needs to offer primitives to both publish services or objects to the external environment and to discover them. This characteristic is known as Ambient Acquaintance Management.

AmbientTalk was developed taking characteristics of other languages, including Self Scheme and Smalltalk. As an object-based language, it relies on using objects to construct applications. Moreover, these objects are able to send messages to others. Using some predefined objects, this language implements a higher-level abstraction of resource discovery and disconnection handling. It also includes object handles and remote method invocations. All remote events are handled asynchronously. The language provides the possibility to register a block of code to be invoked when discovering a certain resource type. It also adds the ability to receive values from method invocations on remote objects.

An interpreter for the AmbientTalk language has been implemented in Java. Currently, the implementation can run on the Java ME platform, under the CDC configuration. More information about AmbientTalk, including papers, tutorials and examples can be found at its Website (http://prog.vub.ac.be/amop).

CONVERGENCE OF MOBILE DEVICES AND WIRELESS TECNOLOGIES

Nowadays *mHealth* can be seen as the future of healthcare and it is a system already changing the way healthcare is delivered. The main idea of *mHealth* is to use mobile devices everywhere and by everybody in the medical sector, including patients and health providers. Mobile devices are used as the main user interfaces, but communication between users and data retrieving relies on wireless technologies. The wireless technologies used in *mHealth* can be categorized as portable by the user and access technologies. The former are portable or wearable by the user; their sensors are responsible for obtaining raw data from the human body. Access technologies allow the access to a remote computer that may be located within a Wireless Local Area Network (mainly Wi-Fi) or on the Internet.

We review wireless technologies because when comparing them with wired networks (Ethernet, Adsl), wireless networks provide advantages, including installation (mainly), cost, and size. Wireless technology not only enables users to set up a network quickly, but also enables them to set up a network where it is inconvenient or impossible to wire cables.

Portable Wireless Technologies

Body Area Networks (BANs) and Personal Area Networks (PANs) are communication technologies wearable or closely connected to users, and can follow them wherever they go. BANs are used to interconnect devices and sensors that can be worn on clothes or implanted into the body of the patient.

BANs are currently being standardized by the IEEE802.15.6 Task Group. This Task Group was launched in November 2007, and defines BANs as "low power devices operating on, in or around the human body (but not limited to humans) to serve a variety of applications including medical, consumer electronics / personal entertainment and others" (IEEE 802.15.6, 2009).

BANs operational range is less than 10 meters with ultra low power consumption (around 100μW) and low data rate (less than 256kbps).

As it was mentioned early, BANs are under standardization and therefore there is not a definitive specification at the time of this writing. However, there are many proposals for specification to the Physical (PHY) and MAC (Medium Access Control) layers as it could be verified in (IEEE 802.15.6, 2009). Also, this web site shows BANs current and future applications.

PANs networks are two types: Bluetooth (BT) and Wireless Sensor Networks (WSN).

Bluetooth

BT is a wireless telecommunications technology designed to eliminate cables in the connections among electronic devices (BT 2009). A Special interest Group (SIG) was founded in 1998 in order to promote and to develop this technology. Actually, this SIG consists of more than 11,000 members and several business property development companies. At present BT is regulated under the standard IEEE 802.15.1 BT's most general characteristics are:

- Short operational range of less than 100 meters.
- Operates in star topology or peer-to-peer.
- Transfer rate from 1 Mbps in BT version 1.2 up to 54 Mbps in version 3.0 +HS (High Speed).
- Transmits in the ISM frequency band from 2400 to 2483.5 MHz.
- Transmitting power from 1 mW to 100 mW.

BT allows instantaneous connection among devices found in the same operational area. BT's protocol establishes a session in a transparent way to the user. The devices found in this operational area form a network known as a Piconet. A Piconet is formed with up to 8 BT devices; it has a master node and up to 7 slave nodes. The union of two or more Piconets is known as a Scatternet; the biggest Scatternet can link up to 10 Piconets.

BT, Wireless Sensor Networks and Wi-Fi (IEEE 802.11b) share the same frequency band of 2400 to 2483.5 MHz (Ferro & Potorti 2005). For this reason BT is levered on frequency hopping spread spectrum technology. The signal jumps among 79 frequencies in intervals of 1 MHz to have a high degree of tolerance to interferences.

From 1998 to now BT's evolution is v1.0 --> v1.2 --> v2.0+EDR (Enhanced Data Rate) --> v2.1+EDR and v3.0+HS (High Speed, ratified in April 2009). Versions v1.0 and v.1.2 are completely compatible. The main differences among BTs' version are in modulation technique used, as is shown in Table I.

As is listed in Table 1, BT v2.0 + EDR was ratified in November of 2004. This BT version increases the bit rate without affecting the upper layers. Effective throughput of 2.1 Mbps (without considering overhead) is achieved, while the previous versions achieved an effective throughput of 723 kbps. The difference between BT version 1.2 and 2.0+EDR is the modulation technique, as is shown in Table 1. To keep compatibility, BT v2.0 + EDR packet incorporates two additional fields: a guard band field and a synchrony word field, as is shown in the figure 3. These fields are used to indicate whether or not modulation pi/4-DQPSK or DPSK is used to transmit the data payload. The access code field and header field are transmitted using GFSK modulation, as in BT v1.2, where all the packet fields are transmitted using GFSK modulation technique.

BT v2.0 +EDR and BT v2.1 +EDR are compatible, but the latter adds new features:

- Encryption Pause Resume. The BT master device may change the connection link key. A new link key will be generated, and the hosts will be notified of this new link key. Encryption will then be paused and

Table 1. BT evolution and main parameters

	BT v1.2	BT 2.0+EDR	BT 2.1+EDR	BT 3.0 +HS
Rate(Mbps)	1Mbps	2-3Mbps	2-3Mbps	54 Mbps
Modulation	GFSK	π/4DQPSK for transmission at 2 Mpbs	π/4DQPSK for transmission at 2 Mpbs	802.11 2007 specifications
	QPSK	8DQPSK for transmission at 3 Mpbs	8DQPSK for transmission at 3 Mpbs	
Release Date	November 2003	October 2004	July 2007	April 2009

Figure 3. BT v1.2 versus BT v2.0 +EDR and BT v2.1 +EDR packets

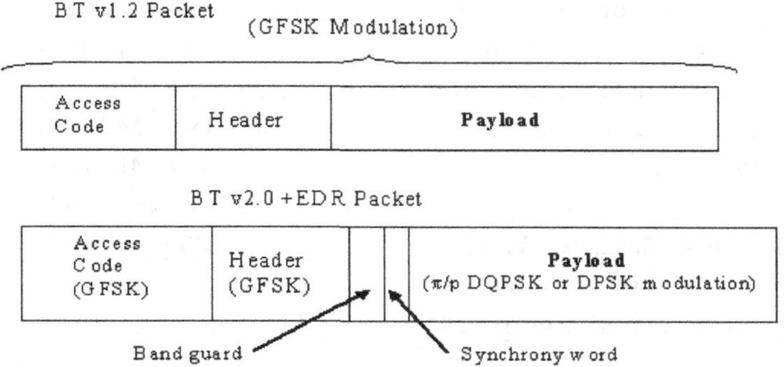

resumed immediately using this new link key to generate a new encryption key.

- Erroneous Data Reporting. This feature may be enabled for Synchronous Connection Orientated Links (SCO Links) and extended Synchronous Connection Orientated Links (eSCO Links). Synchronous links are a circuit-switching connection and provide a method of associating the Bluetooth Piconet clock with the transported data. This is achieved by reserving regular slots on the physical channel and transmitting fixed size packets at regular intervals. Such links are suitable for constant rate isochronous data, like voice or video.
- Extended Inquiry Response. It provides information about the local device in response to inquiry from remote devices.
- Link Supervision Timeout Event (LSTO). This is a command to configure a physical link.
- Packet Boundary Flag. The device supports the capability of correctly handling Host Controller Interface Asynchronous Connectionless Link Data Packets (HCI ACL Data Packets). HCI ACL Data Packets are used to pass both data and voice between BT devices.
- Secure Simple Pairing. This is a process used when two devices do not have a common link key, and an initialization key will be created using either the pairing or Secure Simple Pairing procedures.
- Sniff Subrating. This is a mode that defines the anchor points at which the master transmits to the slave. This mode allows a Host to create a guaranteed access-like connection by specifying maximum transmit and receive latencies.

The material presented to describe BT v2.1 +EDR is available in (BT Core v2.1, 2009), and it is presented here just for comparative purposes.

BT v3.0+HS is the newer BT version. It gets its speed from the IEEE 802.11 radio protocol. The inclusion of the 802.11 Protocol Adaptation Layer (PAL) provides increased throughput of data transfers at the approximate rate of 24 Mbps. This high speed will send large amounts of video, music, and photos between devices wirelessly at speeds consumers expect. Moreover, it is compatible with its earlier version due to the inclusion of Generic Alternate MAC/PHY (Generic AMP or AMP) feature. Generic AMP allows BT v3.0 +HS to alternate among radio technologies and their respective speeds (1, 2, 3 or 54 Mbps). BT v3.0 +HS Generic AMP explicitly supports standards IEEE 802.11b and IEEE 802.11g (IEEE 802.11-2007).

802.11 PAL supported operations include:

- Physical link creation and acceptance.
- Deletion of physical links.
- Physical channel selection
- Security establishment and maintenance.

In addition, Generic AMP feature may be enabled or disabled as needed in order to minimize power consumption in the system.

To allow interoperability with earlier versions, BT v3.0+HS defines two types of Controllers:

- Basic Rate (BR) / Enhanced Data Rate (EDR) Controller. It includes the Radio, Baseband, Link Manager and, optionally, HCI (Host Controller Interface). BR is for BT v1.2 and earlier versions at speeds of up to 1Mbps. EDR is for BT v2.0 and BT v2.1 at speeds of up to 3Mbps.
- Alternate MAC/PHY (AMP) Controller. It includes AMP PAL (Protocol Adaptation Layer), AMP MAC, Protocol Adaptation Layer (PAL), and, optionally, HCI. This controller is only for BT v3.0+HS.

Alternate MAC/PHY (AMP) is a secondary Controller in BT v3.0+HS. The BR/EDR radio (the primary radio) is used to perform discovery, association, connection establishment, and connection maintenance. Once a connection has been established between two devices over the BR/ EDR radio, the AMP Managers can discover the AMPs that are available on the other device. When an AMP is shared by the two devices, the Core system provides mechanisms for moving data traffic from BR/EDR Controller to an AMP Controller.

In (BT Core v3.0, 2009) the complete core specification of BT v3.0+HS can be downloaded.

The importance of including BT technology in *mHealth* applications is that it is currently installed in more than 3000 million devices, (BT 2009).

Wireless Sensor Networks

Today, WSN technology covers a wide variety of applications: e-health, demotic, military, agriculture, etc. A WSN is comprised of one or more nodes (sensors) working together to carry out a specific task (an application). WSN nodes are small nodes with limited memory and capacity that are characterized by their low power consumption. Due to these limitations, the applications running on a WSN must be of low memory consumption because the viability of memory in the sensor node is less than 64 Kbytes. Recently, some new nodes double this capacity. Hence, the implementation of applications of WSN is more challenging than in traditional networks like Wi-Fi or Ethernet.

WSN is defined under the standard IEEE 802.15.4 (IEEE 802.15.4, 2003 and IEEE 802.15.4, 2007). This standard defines specifications for the two lower levels or layers of the OSI Model: Physical (PHY) and MAC (Medium Access Control) layers. Some functions of the physical layer are to establish the physical connection, modulate channels and select channels. The MAC layer determines the channel access method, adds source and destination addresses to the packets, and detects and corrects errors, among other functions. Layers 3 and 4 (routing and transport) are not defined under this standard. The lack of specifications for layers 3 and 4 has motivated the alliance of some companies to propose routing and transport capacities in WSN. For example, ZigBee Alliance (ZigBee Alliance) has defined the Ad-hoc On-demand Distance Vector (AODV) routing protocol for layer 3. For upper layers ZigBee Alliance has defined a complete Application Framework. The IEEE 802.15.4 standard and ZigBee protocols stack are fully compatible.

WSN and ZigBee networks are also referred to as Low-Rate Wireless Personal Area Networks (LW-WPAN) because they can reach transmission speeds of up to 256 kbps and cover an area of less than 100 meters (similar to BT). Both operate in three frequency bands (ISM frequencies): 868 MHz (868-868.6), 916 MHz (902-928), and 2.4 GHz (2.4 – 2.4835). The last frequency is also used by BT and Wi-Fi IEEE 802.11g. As a consequence, extensive interference analysis among these technologies is being carried out by the research community. These interference (connivance) results are important because it is foreseen that these technologies may have to share the same operational area.

IEEE 802.15.4 and IEEE 802.11 networks employ the carrier sense multiple access with collision avoidance (CSMA-CA) mechanism for channel access. However, IEEE 802.15.4 networks do not include a request-to-send (RTS) and clear-to-send (CTS) mechanism. This is due to their low data rate.

The IEEE 802.15.4 standard (2003 version) specifies DBPSK (Differential Biphase Shift Keying) modulation for the 868 MHz and the 915 MHz Physical Layers. OQPSK (Offset Quadrature Phase Shift Keying) modulation is the method for the 2.4 GHz Physical Layer.

In August 2007, the IEEE released an addendum to the IEEE 802.15.4 2003 version. This newest IEEE 802.15.4 2007 version of WSN is based on Ultra Wide Band (UWB) technology and aims to provide an alternate PHY layer with an ultra-low complexity, ultra-low cost and ultra-low power consumption (IEEE 802.15.4a, 2007). IEEE 802.15.4 2007 WSN version is based on UWB, also known as UWB LR-PAN.

This new version allows over-the-air data rates of 851 kb/s, 250 kb/s, 110 kb/s, 40 kb/s, and 20 kb/s. In addition, it adds a new operational frequency band of 3100–10600 MHz (which varies by region: Europe, North America and worldwide).

An 802.15.4 network (in version 2003 and 2007) can be configured as one-hop star topology. In this configuration, two different types of devices are defined: a full function device (FFD) and a reduced function device (RFD). An FFD can talk to RFDs and other FFDs, and operate in three modes serving as a network coordinator, a coordinator, or like a RFD. An RFD can only talk to an FFD and is intended for extremely simple applications.

From the m-health perspective, RFDs devices will be responsible for collecting and monitoring real-time physiological variables (temperature, level of oxygen in blood, blood pressure, ECG, levels of sugar in blood, etc.) of patients under supervision. FFD devices will forward these data either to another FFD device or an access technology like Wi-Fi.

Also, WSN can be self-configuring and operate as a multi-hop network. In this configuration the presence of more than one FFD device is necessary and any of the FFD devices present in the operational area may act as coordinator of one star network and provide synchronization to other FFD coordinators.

In any topology, a device in a 802.15.4 network can use either a 64-bit IEEE address or a 16-bit short address assigned during the association procedure. A single 802.15.4 network can accommodate up to 64k (2^{16}) devices.

A valuable reason for choosing IEEE 802.15.4 networks to implement m-health application is that they employ a handshake protocol for data transfer reliability and use the Advanced Encryption Standard (AES) for secure data transfer. Moreover, its BER (bit error rate) is better than 802.15.1 and 802.11 (Timmons and Scanlon, 2004). This low value of BER is an opportunity to use WSN in medical applications.

In concordance with the above mentioned, WSN meet the requirements for *m-health* solutions. It involves real-time services, continuous data source sensing, mobility, low-maintenance and low-cost devices.

Therefore, Bluetooh/Zigbee/IEEE 802.15.4 networks provide excellent capabilities to retrieve vital information like temperature, heart rate, blood pressure, sugar levels and even fall detection. Most important, they will be the portable wireless technologies. Then, data collected with their sensors will be transmitted to a gateway or a computer with more resources (memory, hard disk, computation, etc). This gateway could be a combination of these WPAN technologies with a Wi-Fi or WAN (Wide Area Network), as is shown in Figure 4. The use of WAN technology will allow the data of the patient to be widely accessible to previously authorized medical personal.

Wireless Access Technologies (Wi-Fi)

Wi-Fi

Wireless Local Area Network (WLAN or Wi-Fi) is a mature technology, widely deployed in offices, houses, universities, etc. The first release of this standard IEEE 802.11 was in 1997 and today there are four versions of it: 802.11a, 802.11b, 802.11g and the newest, 802.11n, which was published in October 2009.

IEEE 802.11a networks operate in the frequency band of 5 GHz with data rates up to 54Mbps. IEEE 802.11b standard operates in the frequency band of 2.4 GHz with data rates up to 11Mbps. This frequency band is the same for both BT and WSN.

IEEE 802.11g wireless networks operate in the frequency band of 2.4 GHz Wi-Fi with data

Figure 4. Architecture envisioned to be used in m-health applications

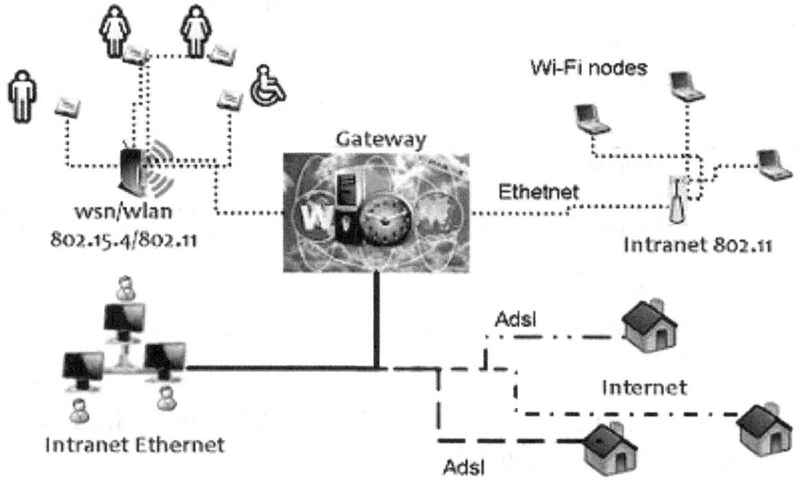

rates of up to 54Mbps (same frequency band as 802.11b, BT and WSN).

IEEE 802.11n networks, the most current generation of Wi-Fi technology, support Multiple-Input-Multiple-Output (MIMO) technology, using multiple receivers and multiple transmitters in both the client and access points to achieve improved performance. Products designated as Wi-Fi IEEE 802.11n CERTIFIED can operate in either the 2.4 or 5 GHz frequency bands and are backward compatible with 802.11 a/b/g networks. 802.11n technology can deliver data rates of up to 600 Mbps. The Wi-Fi Alliance began testing and certifying 802.11n draft 2.0 products in June 2007.

Wi-Fi networks, in its four versions, are the most visible wireless technology in the consumer market. Most portable computers, smart phones, printers, and Personal Digital Assistants (PDAs) support at least one of the IEEE 802.11 network variations. In homes and offices, Wi-Fi is widely deployed in the form of a Wireless Access Point (WAP). A WAP is a device that allows Wi-Fi nodes to conform to a wireless local network and allows connecting this Wi-Fi network to a wired network, mainly Ethernet or a phone network via Asymmetric Digital Subscriber Line (ADSL). Hence, a WAP can relay data between the Wi-Fi devices and wired devices on a local or wide area network and with this enable access to the Internet.

Wi-Fi networks can operate in two distinct modes: Ad hoc and Infrastructured. In the Infrastructured mode it operates via a WAP device, which acts as a central node that connects the wireless terminals. The WAP is usually provided in order to enable access to the Internet,

an intranet, or other wireless network. Ad hoc networks can be formed "on the fly" without the help of a WAP. In ad hoc networks, the Wi-Fi nodes may communicate directly with each other, but in a local way. Therefore, ad hoc networks have the disadvantage of lacking of a device with the capacity to enable access to the Internet. Hence, Wi-Fi networks in *m-health* applications will mainly operate in the infrastructured mode. The role of WAP will be to share data between wireless nodes (mobile nodes) and wired networks, mainly to enable access to the Internet, as shown in Figure 4. The disadvantage of Infrastructured networks over Ad hoc networks is that the WAP is a central point of failure. If it stops working, none of the wireless terminals can communicate with each other.

Table 2. Comparison of wireless technologies surveyed

Standard/Wireless Technology	Used by the user as	Operation Band	Range in meters
IEEE 802.15.6/ Body Area Network	Portable or Into	Not specified yet	10 <
IEEE 802.15.4/ Wireless Sensor Networks	Portable	868(Europe)/915(US)/2.4 GHz	100 <
IEEE 802.15.4a/ Wireless Sensor Networks UWB	Portable	250–750 KHz/3.1–5 GHz/6–10.6 GHz	100 <
IEEE 802.15.1/ Bluetooth	Portable	2.4 GHz	100 <
IEEE 802.11 a/b/g/n/ Wi-Fi	Access	5 /2.4 /2.4 /2.4 or 5 GHz	120/140/140/250 <

Table 2 shows a comparison of the wireless technologies surveyed and their role (column two) in *m-health* applications.

However, portable technologies (BANs and PANs) in which the sensor devices will be embedded still lack adequate interfaces for human interaction. For this reason, the information they sense (get from the patient or the environment) needs to be delivered to a device providing an adequate human interface and the correct application to process the information, most probably to a remote computer. A solution could be the use of mobile devices, like smart phones and PDAs, which offer appropriate display and audio output that can be used to show graphics or alarms easily understandable by patients and health providers. Moreover, this information could be sent from the mobile device to a centralized server, since most mobile devices (smart phones) have a network interface connected to the cellular network and can use services like Short Message Service (SMS) and Multimedia Messaging System (MMS). Moreover, some devices also provide other network interfaces like Wi-Fi and Bluetooth that can be used to interact with other users. In this way, patient data can be further processed at a hospital or medical facility, and even share the information with other remote locations in order to provide an adequate diagnosis. It can also help to rapidly prepare the required facilities in case of an emergency, as is shown in Figure 4.

E-HEALTH PROJECTS

This section surveys relevant examples of e-health projects, finalizing with a comparison of their characteristics.

MobiHealth

MobiHealth is a European project developed to monitor vital signals, based on a Body Area Network and an m-health service platform. MobiHealth makes use of Universal Mobile Telecommunications System (UMTS) and General Packet Radio Service (GPRS) networks. The prototype includes Bluetooth for communication between the sensors worn by the user and the central device, a PDA. The patients wear a lightweight monitoring system: the MobiHealth BAN, which is customized to their individual health needs. The MobiHealth Service Platform manages a population of BANs deployed in different locations and handles the external communication among the BANs and a remote healthcare location (Jones, 2006).

AID-N

AID-N was developed at the Johns Hopkins University Applied Physics Laboratory to explore and show how advances in technology can be employed to assist victims and responders in times of emergency. AID-N is a real-time patient monitoring system that integrates vital sign sensors, location sensors, ad-hoc networking, electronic patient records, and web portal technology to allow remote monitoring of patient status. The system aims to facilitate communication between providers at a disaster scene, medical professionals at local hospitals, and specialists available for consultation from distant facilities (Gao, 2005). The sensors are connected to IEEE 802.15.4 devices, forming an ad hoc wireless network with a portable tablet Personal Computer (PC). The tablet PC uses a wireless wideband card (EVDO) that provides high-speed network connectivity from almost anywhere.

CustoMed

Its architecture is a network enabled system that supports various wearable sensors and contains on-board general computing capabilities for executing individually tailored event detection, alerts, and network communication with various medical information services. CustoMed claims it "Can be easily custom-built for patients by non engineering staff" and that "The system will be quickly assembled from basic parts and configured for use" (Jafari & Andre, 2005). The authors of CustoMed developed a wide range of code to download onto the devices through a tool which enables physicians to pick a specific variation of code for a particular application and download it to the system components of CustoMed.

AlarmNet

AlarmNet was developed at the Department of Computer Science at the University of Virginia. It is an assisted-living and residential monitoring network for smart healthcare research that permit continuous monitoring of elders or those in need of medical assistance. It consists of an unobtrusive environment and area sensors combined with wearable interactive devices to evaluate the health of people who inhabit spaces. The network creates a continuous medical history and authorized care providers can monitor resident health and activity patterns, such as daily activity changes, which may signify changes in healthcare needs. The ALARM-NET system has been implemented with a WSN and gateways (PDAs and PCs). Customized infrared motion and dust sensors, and integrated temperature, light, pulse, and blood oxygenation sensors are employed (Wood, 2006).

CodeBlue

The University of Harvard in the USA is carrying out the CodeBlue project. This project explores the applications of WSN technology to a range of medical applications, including: pre-hospital, in-hospital emergency care, disaster response, stroke patient rehabilitation, and localization with RF (Malan et al., 2004). They have developed a range of wireless medical sensors based on TinyOS "mote" hardware platforms (IEEE 802.15.4 devices). A wireless pulse oximeter and a wireless two-lead electrocardiogram (ECG or EKG) device collect heart rate (HR), oxygen saturation (SpO2), and EKG data and relay them over a short-range (100m) wireless network to any number of receiving devices, including PDAs, laptops, or ambulance-based terminals. The data can be displayed in real time and integrated into the development of patient care records.

Wearable Health Monitoring Systems (WHMS)

WHMS is the architecture of a working wireless sensor network system for ambulatory health status monitoring. The system uses a BAN that consists of a personal server, implemented on a PDA or PC, physiological sensors, and custom-built sensor boards. The BAN includes several motion sensors that monitor the user's overall activity and an ECG sensor to monitor heart activity. The system spans a network comprised of individual health monitoring systems that connect through the Internet to a medical server tier that resides at the top of this hierarchy (Otto et al., 2006).

Ubiquitous Monitoring Environment for Wearable and Implantable Sensors (UbiMon)

UbiMon (developed at Imperial College London) is designed to address general issues related to using wearable and implantable sensors for distributed mobile monitoring. For example, the value of the research is to be demonstrated in the management of patients with arrhythmic heart disease. The UbiMon system consists of five major components: BAN node, the local processing unit, the central server, the patient database, and the workstation (WS) (Ng et al. 2004).

Advanced Care and Alert Portable Telemedical Monitor (AMON)

AMON is a wearable medical monitoring and alert system targeting high-risk cardiac/respiratory patients. The system includes continuous collection and evaluation of multiple vital signs, intelligent multi-parameter medical emergency detection, and a cellular phone connection to a medical center (Urs, 2004).

In Table 3 we summarize this section emphasizing the current status of the m-health projects. From Table 3, it is important to note:

- Battery life is a major concern.
- Only AID-N project is already in a commercial status.
- The projects analyzed require more work to be done, to be an economical option of easy deployment for the end user.

FUTURE RESEARCH DIRECTIONS

mHealth can be used to retrieve and transmit data in real-time between end-users and healthcare providers, thus helping considerably improve patient quality of care. The possibility of transmitting vital information in real time can be crucial to saving the patient's life. Moreover, the use of mobile devices can help eliminate common errors that may occur when using paper-based communication. However, there are still many issues that need to be improved in order to provide effective services of *mHealth*. Concerning mobile applications development, the existence of several non-compatible platforms and languages represents a difficulty when working with different devices. Increased efforts need to be made in order to provide a single environment for all devices. For example, a common virtual machine could be useful, allowing the execution of an application regardless of the platform for which it was implemented. This is still an open research field that can help to motivate the adoption of m-health services.

CONCLUSION

This chapter reviews wireless technologies and mobile applications frameworks useful for implementing *mHealth* services and applications. *mHealth* is already in use in hospitals and emergency settings (but still their use in homes is rare).

mHealth is a very attractive field that has been evolving in recent years thanks to the rapid advances in wireless communications linked to advances in mobile computing. *mHealth* provides a number of services to the healthcare sector, covering several fields like patient monitoring and remote data collection, among others. *mHealth* has been shown to be particularly useful in emergency telemedicine services, where the use of ambulance transport can be reduced thanks to this technology.

On the other hand, developing *mHealth* applications and services requires new efforts, since developing applications for mobile devices is still a very challenging task. In this case, besides dealing with designing and implementing the required

Table 3. Comparison of m-health projects surveyed

	MobiHealth	AID-N	CustoMed	Alarm-Net	CodeBlue	WHMS	UbiMon	AMON
Network technology/ Protocols	Bluetooth	IEEE 802.15.4	IEEE 802.15.4	IEEE 802.15.4 and Blue-tooth	IEEE 802.15.4	Zigbee	IEEE 802.15.4	NA
Hardware	PDA	MicaZ and TabletPC	Mica2dot, Pocket PC and Server	MicaZ, stargate gateways, PDAs, and PCs	MicaZ and Telos	Tmote sky and Pocket-PC.	Mica2dot, PDA and mobile Phone	Custom-built
Software	Pocket PC and Java	TinyOS and Michaels	TinyOS, Em-bedded Visual C++	TinyOS and Java	TinyOS, Windows CE and. NET	TinyOS and Windows CE	TinyOS	JAVA server
LAN/WAN technology	GPRS and UMTS	EVDO (CDMA)	Wi-Fi	*IP Network*	Ad-hoc Wi-Fi	Wi-Fi	Wi-Fi o GPRS	GSM/ UMTS
Data Rate	115 Kbps	76.8 kbps	38.4 Kbaud	NA	80 Kbps	250 Kbps	250 Kbps	NA
Frequency	2,4 GHz	2,4 GHz	433MHz.	2,4 GHz	2,4 GHz	2,4 GHz	2,4 GHz	NA
Batteries	NA	2 AA	DL2450	2 AA	2 AA	2 AA	NA	NA
Battery life	<2 hours	5–6 days	9 hours	NA	5–6 days	30 days	NA	2 days
Sensing Ca-pabilities*	ECG, SaO_2, NIBP and motion	HR, SpO_2, blood pres-sure and GPS	Pressure, GSR, flex and temperature.	HR, heart-rhythm, temperatu-re, SpO_2, GPS, accelero-meter	HR, SpO2 and ECG	ECG and accelero-meter	ECG	HR, heart rhythm, ECG, blood pres-sure, SpO_2, skin perspira-tion and temperature
Current deployment state	Prototype	Commer-cialization	Prototype	Develop-ment	Develop-ment	Prototype	Prototype	Prototype

* GSR – Galvanic skin response, ECG – Electrocardiogram, SaO2 – Blood oxygenation level, NIBP – Non invasive blood pressure, HR – Heart rate, GPS Global positioning system.

software, developers must first face the challenge of choosing the appropriate language and development platform. This choice will directly affect the range of devices that will support the application, thus the importance of making the right decision. In this chapter, valuable information related to the most popular development platform for mobile applications, as well as languages used to work directly with MANETs, has been provided. The platforms and languages introduced in this chapter can be used to implement *mHealth* services and applications, since they provide the basic required functionalities for these applications, like remote communication, persistent storage, and graphics management. The information presented in this chapter is intended to provide useful design and implementation suggestions for *mHealth* application developers as well as service providers.

The enormous potential of wireless sensor networks opens the door to entirely new applications. In this chapter, we described some examples of e-health systems. This new application of the technology has the potential to offer a wide range of benefits to patients, medical personnel, and society through continuous monitoring in the ambulatory setting, early detection of abnormal conditions, supervised rehabilitation, among others. However, we can see that these systems are mainly prototypes; today, we cannot buy and use these systems. In order for the deployment of these systems to become a reality, some actions must be taken, including: (a) high-level political and managerial decisions (including Government and private sector) to promote and apply wireless health systems in hospital and rural areas, and (b) clarification of legal and ethical issues.

REFERENCES

Anliker, U., Ward, J. A., Lukowicz, P., Tröster, G., Dolveck, F., & Baer, M. (2004, December). AMON: A Wearable Multiparameter Medical Monitoring and Alert System. *IEEE Transactions on Information Technology in Biomedicine*, *8*(4), 415–427. doi:10.1109/TITB.2004.837888

Enck, W., Ongtang, M., & McDaniel, P. (2009). Understanding android security. *IEEE Security & Privacy*, *7*(1), 50–57. doi:10.1109/MSP.2009.26

Ferro, E., & Potorti, F. (2005). Bluetooth and wi-fi wireless protocols: A survey and a comparison. *IEEE Wireless Communications Magazine*, *12*(1), 12–23. doi:10.1109/MWC.2005.1404569

Gao, T., Greenspan, D., Welsh, M., Juang, R., & Alm, A. (2005). Vital signs monitoring and patient tracking over a wireless network. In *Proceedings of the 27th Annual International Conference of the IEEE EMBS* (pp. 102-105). New York: IEEE.

Guiguere, E. (2000). *Java 2 micro edition*. Chichester, UK: John and Wiley Sons.

IEEE 802.15.4. (2003, October). IEEE 802.15.4, Wireless Medium Access Control (MAC) and Physical Layer (PHY) Specications for Low-Rate Wireless Personalworks (LRWPANS) [Technical report]. New York: IEEE.

IEEE 802.15.4a. (2007, January). IEEE p802.15.4a/d7, Part 15.4: Wireless Medium Access Control (MAC) and Physical Layer (PHY) Specifications for Low-Rate Wireless Personal Area Networks (LR-WPANS): Amendment to add alternate PHY [Technical report]. New York: IEEE.

IEEE. 802.11-2007. (2007). Standard and Amendment 1 (Radio Resource Measurement). New York: IEEE.

IEEE. 802.15.6. (2009). IEEE 802.15 WPAN™ Task Group 6 (TG6) Body Area Networks. Retrieved from http://www.ieee802.org/15/pub/TG6.html

Jafari, R., & Andre, A. E. (2005). Wireless sensor networks for health monitoring. In *Proceedings of the Second Annual International Conference on Mobile and Ubiquitous Systems (MobiQuitous)* (pp. 479-481).

Jones, V. Halteren van, A., Widya, I., Dokovski, N., Koprinkov, G., Bults, R., Konstantas, D., & Herzog, R. (2006). MobiHealth: Mobile health services based on body area networks. In S. L. Robert & H. Istepanian, *M-Health: Emerging mobile health systems* (p. 624). Berlin: Springer.

Jorstad, I., Dustdar, S., & Van Do, T. (2005). An analysis of current mobile services and enabling technologies. *International Journal of Ad Hoc and Ubiquitous Computing*, *1*(1-2).

Malan, D., Fulford-jones, T., Welsh, M., & Moulton, S. (2004). CodeBlue: An ad hoc sensor network infrastructure for emergency medical care. Paper presented in *MobiSys Workshop on Applications of Mobile Embedded Systems (WAMES 2004).*

Meier, R. (2009). *Professional Android application development*. Indianapolis, IN: Wiley Publishing, Inc.

National Institute of Standards and Technology. (2001). *FISP 197: Advanced Encryption Standard (AES), Federal Information Processing Standards Publication 197*. Gaithersburg, MD: U.S. Department of Commerce/NIST.

Ng, J. W. P., Lo, B. P., Wells, O., Sloman, M., Peters, N., Darzi, A.,...Yang, G. Z. (2004). Ubiquitous monitoring environment for wearable and implantable sensors. Paper presented at *International Conference on Ubiquitous Computing (Ubicomp).*

Ni, Y., Kremer, U., Stere, A., & Iftode, L. (2005). Programming ad-hoc networks of mobile and resource-constrained devices. In *Proceedings of the 2005 ACM SIGPLAN Conference on Programming Language Desing and Implementation* (pp. 249-260). New York: ACM.

Otto, C., Milenković, A., Sanders, C., & Jovanow, E. (2006). System architecture of a wireless body area sensor network for ubiquitous health monitoring. *Journal of Mobile Multimedia, 1*(4), 307–326.

Richtel, M. (2009, May 27). Google: Expect 18 Android phones by year's end. *The New York Times*.

The Bluetooth Special Interest Group. (2009). BT. Retrieved from http://www.bluetooth.com

The Bluetooth Special Interest Group. (2009). BT Core v2.1. Retrieved from http://www.bluetooth.com

The Bluetooth Special Interest Group. (2009). BT Core v3.0. Retrieved from http://www.bluetooth.com

Timmons, W., & Scanlon, N. F. (2004). *Analysis of the performance of IEEE 802.15.4 for medical sensor body area networking. Paper presented in*. IEEE Sensor and Ad Hoc Communications and Networks.

Van Cutsem, T., Mostinckx, S., Boix, E., Dedecker, J., & De Meuter, W. (2007). AmbientTalk: Objetc-oriented Event-driven Programming in Mobile Ad hoc Networks. In *Proceedings of the XXVI International Conference of the Chilean Society of Computer Sciencie* (pp. 3-12). Washington, DC: IEEE.

Verkasalo, H. (2006). Empirical observations on the emergence of mobile multimedia services an applications in the U.S. and Europe. In *Proceedings of the 5th International Conference on Mobile and Ubiquitous Multimedia,* Stanford, CA.

Wen-Tzu, C., & Chih-Nan, H. (2008). Entering the mobile service market via mobile platforms: Qualcomm's Brew Platform and Nokia's Preminent Platform. *Telecommunications Policy, 32*(6), 399–411. doi:10.1016/j.telpol.2008.04.004

Wood, G. V. (2006). *ALARM-NET: Wireless sensor networks for assisted-living and residential monitoring* [Technical Report CS-2006-11]. Charlottesville, VA: Department of Computer Science, University of Virginia.

ZigBee Alliance. (n.d.). Retrieved from www.zigbee.org

KEY TERMS AND DEFINITIONS

Mobile Application: An application that runs on a mobile device and is either, always or occasionally connected to a network.

Mobile Device: Small computing devices, usually consisting of a diminutive display screen for user output and a miniature keyboard or touch screen for user input. It may contain many typical computer components, including a CPU, operating system (OS), memory, disk, batteries and connections ports. However, their resources are limited when compared to a desktop or server computer. A particular characteristic is that they have limited processor speed and/ or available memory.

Mobile Operating System: Is the interface between hardware and user in a mobile device. It is in charge of managing the mobile applications that run on the device. Examples: Symbian OS, Palm OS, Windows Mobile and Android OS.

Software Development Kit (SDK): A set of development tools that help developers to create an application.

Virtual Machine: A program that is in charge of executing an application and it is used instead of using the physical machine defined by the operating system.

Wireless Local Area Network (WLAN): Wireless data network whose operation radio is about 100 meters. In m-health projects; WLANs most probably will be used in conjunction with WPAN.

Wireless Personal Area Network (WPAN): Wireless data network whose operation radio is about 10 meters or inside the POS, personal operation space.

Chapter 6
Wireless Sensor Networks (WSN) Applied in Agriculture

Miguel Enrique Martínez-Rosas
Universidad Autónoma de Baja California, México

Humberto Cervantes De Ávila
Universidad Autónoma de Baja California, México

Juan Iván Nieto Hipólito
Universidad Autónoma de Baja California, México

José Rosario Gallardo López
University of Ottawa, Canada

ABSTRACT

This chapter presents an overview of recent developments, challenges and opportunities related to the application of wireless sensor networks (WSN) in agriculture. The material presented here is introductory in nature and has been designed to be useful for students starting to work in the field of WSN and for researchers looking for state-of-the-art information in general or specific details related to their practical application in agriculture.

INTRODUCTION

In the 1950's, computers were so bulky that a person could literally walk inside of them. These days, some computers are still large enough to fill an entire building, but the big difference is that the modern ones are actually clusters composed by millions of processors interconnected to work collaboratively, achieving a processing power unimaginable for most people. Microprocessors have become so small and powerful that, in contrast to the old days, computers are beginning to "walk" inside of us. For instance, one application that is being explored for medical purposes is to insert a complex electronic device into a plastic bubble that can be swallowed by a person; this device will travel through the digestive system gathering images that can be analyzed by a physician in real time. This futuristic technology is not the only one of its kind. Combining in a single device a microprocessor, a link to the real world in the form of a sensor (e.g. to detect temperature, humidity or light, or to capture images) and a wireless com-

DOI: 10.4018/978-1-60960-027-3.ch006

munication interface, has been a common practice during the last decade or so. Other applications include automatic control of sunlight, temperature and humidity in greenhouses, automation of lighting, climate control, intrusion detection and security at home, in hotels or in office buildings, wildlife tracking, automatic inventory of containers on transoceanic carriers, etc. Usually, many such devices are deployed in the geographic area of interest and they are interconnected using the integrated wireless interface, thus creating what is referred to as a wireless sensor network (WSN).

WSN are becoming so commonplace that a standardization effort is underway. The IEEE 802.15.4 standard has been adopted as the best candidate for these types of networks. The Zigbee alliance, which is a group of companies that have joined efforts to promote the rapid development of this type of technologies, in addition to adopting the protocols described in the IEEE 802.15.4 standard for the signals to be used over the wireless medium (physical layer) and the mechanism to achieve an orderly access to the transmission capacity (medium access control), have taken on the task of creating a de-facto standard for the way the information will flow from the sensing nodes to the central repository of such data (routing), as well as for the techniques that the different types of application software will use to interact with the rest of the protocols (middleware, security, etc.). Other competing standards are IEEE 802.11 (Wi-Fi) and IEEE 802.15.1 (Bluetooth), but their use is far less widespread.

As mentioned above, researchers in companies and universities all over the world are working on applying the sensor network concept in many different areas, including agriculture, home automation and medicine. However, the true success of WSN will happen when commercial products are widely available and consumed. Its success will bring about the growth of other compatible technologies. For instance, when keeping track of a person's health signs (e.g. weight, blood pressure, temperature) and home status (e.g. energy consumed by appliances and lighting fixtures, available food in fridge and pantry, home temperature and humidity) becomes an everyday necessity, smart appliances will be needed as well as servers to concentrate and process all that information and to take the necessary actions. Stores will also need devices able to communicate with the smart appliances in the customers' homes to take orders and deliver goods. A fast and reliable network will have to be available to allow communication among such numerous and diverse devices. To give an idea of the potential growth, it has been predicted that just as billions of clients need millions of servers in the current Internet, the expected trillion wireless sensing devices to be deployed in the near future will have to be coupled to a billion other computers (Bell, 2007).

The February 2003 issue of *Technology Review* (MIT's magazine of innovation) listed 10 emerging areas of technology that will have a profound impact on the world's economy and on how we live and work (Van der Werff, 2003). The corresponding leading researchers and projects in each area are also highlighted. The first one on the list was *Brain-Wireless Sensor Networks*, which is nothing but the WSN concept we have described above. That was just the beginning of what has continued to be a sequence of successes and improvements for this technology.

Wireless technologies, in general, have been under rapid development during recent years. The types of wireless technologies being developed range from simple point-to-point two-node networks, to local-area networks covering short, medium or long distances. Examples are IrDA (Infrared Data Association), which uses infrared light for short-range, point-to-point, low-speed communications; body-area networks (WBAN), aimed at monitoring health signs or for gaming purposes; wireless personal area networks (WPAN) for short range, point-to-multi-point communications, such as Bluetooth and ZigBee; mid-range, multi-hop wireless local area network (WLAN), such as Wi-Fi; long-distance cellular phone systems, such as 3G, LTE (Long Term Evolution) and WiMAX. Most people feel the strong impact of wireless technology mainly due to the astonishing growth of the cell-phone market. However, not many people have realized that the bandwidth demand for wireless, interpersonal communications, such as cellular phones, will soon become a small share of the total available bandwidth (Vellidis et al., 2007). A far greater potential exists for development and application of other types of wireless technologies, especially wireless sensor networks, starting from military and environmental monitoring, moving towards machine-to-machine communications (M2M), and eventually reaching all aspects of our lives. Wireless sensor networks with self-organizing, self-configuring, self-diagnosing and self-healing capabilities are being developed to solve problems or to enable applications that traditional technologies could not address. Once available, these technologies will allow us to find many new applications that could not have been considered possible before (Wang, Zhang & Wang, 2006). In addition to the innovative uses of wireless technologies, even traditional applications will benefit from the advantages offered by wireless networks as compared to the existing wired solutions. A wireless approach can support mobility and increased flexibility, especially in multi-hop networks, including of course WSN (Choi, Kim, Park, Kang & Eom, 2004).

A common definition of a Wireless Sensor Networks is that they are novel wireless ad-hoc networks consisting of many self-organized embedded sensor nodes, deployed in the field of interest, that perform a specific task in a coordinate way that allows for the emergence of data-centric applications (Castillo Luzón, 2007). The term ad-hoc refers to the fact that WSN are multi-hop in nature, requiring nodes to perform tasks related to both the generation of information and its processing and/or forwarding until it reaches its intended destination; in other words, nodes act as both end-devices and routers. The final destination of all of the information collected by the sensing nodes is usually a single device, known as the sink. Some applications require the presence of more than one sink to increase reliability and security. The term self-organization is used to define the presence of a system-wide adaptive structure and functionality created from simple local interactions between individual entities. To clarify this concept, let us recall that, in a WSN, nodes are usually scattered in the field of interest without a prior knowledge of what the network size or topology are going to be. So, before nodes are able to start transmitting their collected data and forwarding data collected by other nodes, they have to discover who their neighbors are and, through them, they need to find multi-hop paths towards the sink (Edordu & Sacks, 2006). They are referred to as embedded sensor nodes because, as mentioned before, sensing, processing and communication capabilities are all incorporated into a single device. WSN nodes have a small size, are battery-powered and function autonomously. In traditional communication systems, such as the Internet, it is important to know who is at the other end of the connection. In WSN, in contrast, what matters is the information itself, associated perhaps to location and time stamps; the ID of the node that generated such information is not necessarily relevant. In that sense, it is said that WSN are data-centric, as opposed to address-centric. WSN are used for high-precision data gathering in cases for which setting up a wired infrastructure is too difficult (e.g. search-and-rescue operations in disaster areas, tactical communications in the battlefield), too expensive (e.g. environmental or habitat monitoring, controlled irrigation of large agricultural fields) or it is simply inconvenient to handle the extra wires (e.g. monitoring of an elderly person's health).

As mentioned above, WSN nodes are small, battery-operated devices. Their wireless communication range is usually small to allow them to operate during a reasonable amount of time before depleting their energy reserves. These features make each device relatively cheap. For these reasons, WSN applications that require a large number of nodes, located close to each other creating high-density deployments, are still feasible. Dense deployments generate a high degree of interaction among nodes, which in turn creates special needs for the protocols to be used. More specifically, sensor network protocols need to be scalable and energy efficient, especially because nodes may be in inhospitable or inaccessible sites (Naumowicz, 2007; Tang, Yang, Giannakis & Qin, 2007; Naushad, 2006). For the same reason, sensor networks must be robust and adaptable to be able to operate in very different environments and to adapt to changes in their surroundings (Culler, Estrin & Srivastava, 2004; Edordu & Sacks, 2006).

The design of a wireless sensor network involves challenges in the following areas: topology discovery and control, routing, medium access control, optimum localization of network nodes, and energy efficiency (Avilés García, 2008).

The notion of wireless sensor and actor networks (WSAN) has been recently coined to indicate those WSN that, in addition to the sensing nodes and the sink, also include nodes that can take actions in response to the information being collected (Ruíz Ibarra, 2006; Akyildiz & Kasimoglu, 2004). Depending on the specific application, these actor nodes may be mobile or fixed, and may coordinate among themselves to decide what the appropriate actions are and who will perform them, or may depend on the sink to make the important decisions.

An example of a WSAN application may be one that controls the color and intensity of the lighting at home depending on the time of day and the activity that the home resident is engaged in (Kim, Lee, Hwang, Won & Chung, 2006). The system creates a pre-defined profile with the person's preferences and constantly senses the person's location (at the table, on his desk, on the couch, in bed), degree of activity (still, cooking, walking), and his/her biological signs. Based on that, the system tries to identify when the person is working, ready to start eating, trying to relax or sleep. Equipped with all that information, the system makes decisions and provides, for instance, a moderate intensity and low-temperature color resembling a sunset to help the user relax, or a moderate intensity and high-temperature color to reinforce the person's concentration if he/she is working.

Regarding the main application that we are interested in, the use of computers and sensors for real-time decisions in cropping systems is increasing rapidly. People advocate the deployment of wireless sensor networks in agriculture because of their many advantages: small node size, low cost and simplicity of deployment (Wang, Zhang & Wang, 2006). Yet, the value of technology can be best realized when it is integrated with agronomic knowledge, resulting in a seamless process of information collection and interpretation, assessment of the state and needs of crops, and decisions as to the most appropriate actions. Sharing success stories can help promote this new way of agricultural management (Kitchen, 2008). There exist some other methods to measure environmental variables directly, such as meteorology stations or portable instruments attached to agricultural machinery. However, such mechanisms provide information for a specific place at a specific time. WSN, on the other hand, permits one to acquire data at a periodic rate or even in real time to more accurately track crop conditions, which can result in more productivity and better quality (Ruiz-Garcia, Lunadei, Barreiro & Robla, 2009).

HARDWARE AND SOFTWARE REQUIREMENTS FOR WIRELESS SENSORS

An obvious advantage of wireless transmission is a significant reduction and simplification in wiring and harness. It has been estimated that typical wiring cost in industrial installations is

US$ 130–650 per meter and adopting wireless technology would eliminate 20–80% of this cost. Additional savings in overall cost can be obtained by more efficient control of the equipment through effective monitoring of the environment. WSNs allow otherwise impossible sensor applications, such as monitoring dangerous, hazardous, unwired or remote areas and locations. This technology provides nearly unlimited installation flexibility for sensors and increased network robustness. Furthermore, wireless technology reduces maintenance complexity and costs. WSN allow faster deployment and installation of various types of sensors because many of these networks provide self-organizing, self-configuring, self-diagnosing and self-healing capabilities to the sensor nodes. Some of them also allow flexible extension of the network. Wireless sensor technology allows MEMS (Micro-Electro-Mechanical Systems) sensors to be integrated with signal-conditioning and radio units to form "motes" (common name given to nodes) with extremely low cost, small size and low power requirement. MEMS inertial sensors, pressure sensors, temperature sensors, humidity sensors, strain-gage sensors and various piezo- and capacitive sensors for proximity, position, velocity, acceleration, and vibration measurement have been integrated to WSN nodes and have become available on the market. Another advantage of WSN is their mobility. These sensors can be placed in transporting vehicles to monitor the "on-the-go" environment. They also can be placed on rotating equipment, such as a shaft to measure critical parameters. Most wireless sensors have signal conditioning and processing units installed at the location of the sensors and transmit signals digitally. As a result, noise pick-up becomes a less significant problem. Moreover, since wires are deleted from the transmission, reliability of signal transmission is enhanced (Wang, Zhang & Wang, 2006).

Typical hardware and software requirements for wireless sensors networks are listed in Table 1 (Stockwell, 2007). In a wireless sensor network setting, a node in the network can be formed by a sensor/data acquisition board and a mote (processor/radio board). These nodes can communicate with a gateway unit, which has the capability of communicating with other computers via other networks, such as a LAN, a WLAN, a WPAN and the Internet. Wireless sensor boards available on the market include accelerometers, barometric pressure sensors, light sensors, GPS modules, temperature sensors, humidity sensors, acoustic sensors, magnetic sensors, magnetometers, pyroelectric IR occupancy detectors, solar radiation sensors, soil moisture sensors, soil temperature sensors, wind speed sensors, rainfall meters and seismic sensors (Stockwell, 2007).

Energy constraints have a significant impact on the design and operation of wireless sensor networks. With more than one hundred million WSN nodes to be deployed over the next five years, the quest for improved power sources is already intensifying. The power needs of these wireless sensors is currently the biggest impediment keeping them from becoming completely autonomous, forcing them to be either tethered to an external power source or having lifecycles that are curtailed by batteries. Perpetual power solutions such as energy harvesting (Adee, 2010), super capacitors and rechargeable thin-film batteries promise to reduce labor costs and the environmental impact caused by disposing of millions of batteries. It is estimated that the labor cost from

Table 1. Typical requirements of wireless sensor networks

Hardware	Software
Robust radio technology	Small footprint to run on small processors
Low cost, energy-efficient processor	Efficient energy use
Flexible I/O for various sensors	Capability of fine grained concurrency
Long-lifetime energy source	High modularity
Flexible, open source development platform	Robust and low power ad hoc mesh networking

changing batteries for wireless sensors deployed worldwide in the top six markets between 2006 and 2015 (assuming no harvested energy is used) will be approximately $1.1 billion (Hatler, Gurganious & Ritter, 2008).

Recent technological advances have lead to the emergence of distributed wireless sensor and actor networks (WSANs) which are capable of observing the physical world, processing the data, making decisions based on the observations and performing appropriate actions. These networks can be an integral part of systems such as battlefield surveillance and microclimate control in buildings, nuclear, biological and chemical attack detection, home automation and environmental monitoring. In WSANs, sensor and actor nodes perform sensing and acting, respectively. Several differences between WSN and WSAN are shown in Table 2 (Akyildiz & Kasimoglu, 2004).

WIRELESS STANDARDS AND PROPRIETARY WIRELESS SENSOR TECHNOLOGIES

As nonrenewable batteries typically power sensor nodes, power efficiency becomes one of the most significant criteria for the hardware and networking protocols of WSNs, it is known that the RF transceiver is one of the biggest power consumers in the sensor or actor device. Even when the RF transceiver stays in receive mode waiting for possible incoming packets, the battery will be exhausted within a few days because the power consumption of idle listening is normally not much lower than that of transmitting (Hong & Scaglione, 2006).

Major sources of energy waste that have been identified are: collision, idle listening, overhearing, and control packet overhead. Collision is when two packets are transmitted at the same time and they collide. This results in packet loss and retransmission is required, which wastes energy. Idle listening is listening to receive possible traffic that is not sent. Overhearing means that a node picks up packets destined for other nodes, this wastes energy. Control packet overhead is the sending and receiving of less useful data packets, another source of energy waste. A fundamental task of medium access control (MAC) protocol in wireless sensor networks is to avoid collisions so that nodes can transmit packets efficiently without wasting energy. MAC protocols can be broadly divided into two types: scheduled-based and contention- based protocols. In schedule-based protocols, time slots are pre-allocated on

Table 2. Differences between WSN and WSAN

WSN	WSAN
Priority: Efficient power consumption to maximize lifetime of the network	Priority: QoS (Quality of Service) and bandwidth optimization
Low latency from the nodes to the base station	Real-time communications between nodes
Central entity performs the functions of data collection and coordination	Sensor-actor and actor-actor coordinator may occur
Many protocols and algorithms proposed	Those protocols may not be well suited for the unique features and application requirements
Low-cost, low-power sensors with limited sensing, computation, and wireless communication capabilities	Actors are resource rich nodes equipped with better processing capabilities, higher transmission powers and longer battery life
Number of sensor nodes deployed may be in the order of hundreds or thousands	Usually not necessary such a dense deployment for actor nodes
Single-hop communication is inefficient due to the long distance between sensors and the sink	Type of transmission (single-hop or multi-hop) efficiency depends on the deployment and location of actor nodes to which sensor data will be sent

the bases of time, code or frequency to individual nodes. Energy conservation is achieved because they are collision free, perform low duty cycle operations and avoid overhearing. Among their disadvantages we can point out that they are not flexible to changes, waste time slots and lack peer-to-peer communication. Examples are: Low Energy Adaptive Clustering Hierarchy (LEACH), Traffic adaptive medium access protocol (TRAMA) and Bluetooth. Contention-based protocols share a common channel between nodes. Their disadvantages are idle listening and collision. Examples of contention-based protocols are: Self-Organizing Medium Access Control (SMAC), carrier sense multiple access (CSMA), Timeout-MAC (TMAC) and 802.11 Distributed coordination function (DCF) (Van Dam & Langendoen, 2003; Naushad, 2006).

Several energy-efficient approaches have been investigated (see Table 3), including network protocols as well as cross-layer designs. At the physical layer, modulation, coding, adaptive resource allocation, and cooperative relays have been pursued to effect energy efficiency in the overall system performance (Naushad, 2006). However, all are built on the premise that the power-supplying batteries are ideal and linear. This implies that the battery power consumption equals the total power required by all energy-consuming modules, including signal processing, hardware circuitry and transmitter modules. In fact, part of the battery's capacity (stored energy) may be wasted during its discharge process. For this reason, the lifetime of battery-driven sensor nodes depends not only on the power required by energy-consuming modules, but also on the unique nonlinear characteristics of batteries (Tang, Yang, Giannakis & Qin, 2007).

In general, a lower frequency allows a longer transmission range and a stronger capability to penetrate through walls and glass. However, because radio waves with lower frequencies are easily absorbed by various materials, such as water and trees, and that radio waves with higher frequencies are easily scattered, effective transmission distance for signals carried by a high frequency radio wave may not necessarily be shorter than that reached by a lower frequency carrier at the same power rating. The 2.4 GHz band has a wider bandwidth that allows more

Table 3.Energy-efficient protocols for WSN

SMAC (Self-Organizing Medium Access Control for Sensor nets)	• Nodes periodically sleep to reduce energy consumption when listening to an idle channel • Neighboring nodes form virtual clusters to auto-synchronize on sleep schedules • Sets its radio to sleep during transmissions of other nodes and uses in channel signaling • Applies message passing to reduce latency SMAC
TRAMA (Traffic adaptive medium access protocol)	• Reduces energy consumption by ensuring that unicast, multicast, and broadcast transmissions have no collisions and by allowing nodes to switch to low power, idle state whenever they are not transmitting or receiving • Avoids the assignment of time slots to nodes when there is no traffic to send and also allows nodes to determine when they can become idle. • Influence its schedule based on traffic information to achieve energy efficiency, whether it is an event tracking application, or a monitoring application.
LEACH (Low Energy Adaptive Clustering Hierarchy)	• Protocol for microsensor networks that combines the energy-efficient cluster-based routing and media access ideas along with application specific data aggregation to achieve prolonged system lifetime • Distributed cluster formation technique that self-organizes nodes, algorithms to rotate cluster heads to distribute energy load among nodes and techniques for signal processing to save communication resources
Cluster Based Energy Efficient Scheme:	• Modified LEACH algorithm used to choose a cluster head dynamically • Route selection and setup is combined with schedule in the MAC layer to prolong lifetime of sensors

channels and frequency hopping and permits compact antennas.

The wireless standards also address the network issues for wireless sensors. Star, hybrid and mesh networks have been developed and standardized. The Bluetooth technology uses star networks, which are composed of piconets and scatternets. Each piconet connects one master node with up to seven slave nodes, whereas each scatternet connects multiple piconets, to form an ad hoc network. The ZigBee technology uses hybrid star networks, which uses multiple master nodes with routing capabilities to connect slave nodes, which have no routing capability. The most efficient networking technology uses peer-to-peer, mesh networks, which allow all the nodes in the network to have routing capability. Mesh networks allow autonomous nodes to self-assemble into the network. It also allows sensor information to propagate across the network with a high reliability and over an extended range. In addition, it allows time synchronization and low power consumption for the "listeners" in the network and thus extends battery life (Stockwell, 2007).

On the other hand, ZigBee is supported by more than 70 member companies. It adds network, security and application software to the IEEE 802.15.4 standard. Owing to its low power consumption and simple networking configuration, ZigBee is considered the most promising technology for wireless sensors. The ZigBee Alliance is not pushing a technology; rather it is providing a standardized base set of solutions for sensor and control systems. The physical layer was designed to fulfill the need for a low cost yet allowing for high levels of integration. The use of direct sequence allows the analog circuitry to be very simple and very tolerant towards inexpensive implementations. The media access control layer was designed to allow multiple topologies without complexity. The power management operation does not require multiple modes of operation. The MAC allows a reduced functionality device (RFD) that does not have flash nor large amounts of Read Only Memory (ROM) or Random-Access Memory (RAM). The MAC was designed to handle large numbers of devices without requiring them to be "parked." The network layer has been designed to allow the network to spatially grow without requiring high power transmitters. The network layer also can handle large amounts of nodes with relatively low latencies (Kinney, 2003).

When a large number of wireless sensors need to be networked, several levels of networking may be combined. For example, an 802.11 (Wi-Fi) mesh network, comprised of high-end nodes, such as gateway units, can be overlaid on a ZigBee sensor network to maintain a high level of network performance. A remote application server (RAS) can also be deployed in the field, close to a localized sensor network to: manage the network, collect localized data, host web-based applications, remotely access the cellular network via a GSM/GPRS or a CDMA-based modem and in turn, to access the Internet and remote users (Stockwell, 2007).

While the sizes of sensor devices are rapidly decreasing, the slow improvement of the energy density in batteries aggravates the problem of energy limitations in wireless sensor networks. These constraints increase the importance of energy-efficient designs in all aspects of the wireless sensor network, ranging from hardware devices to information processing schemes to networking protocols, all of which are mutually coupled.

PRECISION AGRICULTURE

Wireless sensors have been used in precision agriculture to assist in: spatial data collection, precision irrigation, variable-rate technology and supplying data to farmers (Zhang, 2004). Precision farming or precision agriculture is an agricultural concept relying on the existence of *in-field variability*. It is related to the idea of "doing the right thing, in the right place, in the right way, at the right time." It requires the use of new technologies, such as global positioning systems (GPS), sensors, satellites or aerial images and geographic information systems (GIS) to assess and understand variations. Collected information may be used to evaluate precisely optimum sowing density, estimate fertilizers and other inputs needs as well as to accurately predict crop yields. These techniques avoid applying inflexible practices to a crop, regardless of local soil/climate conditions, and may help to assess local disease or lodging (to flatten a standing crop) situations more effectively (Malvick, 1995; Sims, 2009). The idea is to know the soil and crop characteristics unique to each part of the field, and to optimize the production inputs within small portions of the field. The philosophy behind precision agriculture is that production inputs (seed, fertilizer, chemicals, etc.) should be applied only as needed and where needed for the most economic production (Gold, 2007).

With the determination of soil conditions and plant development, these technologies can lower the production costs by fine-tuning seeding, fertilizer, chemical and water use, potentially increasing production and lowering costs. These can be achieved through the approach of agricultural control and management, based on direct chemical, biological and environmental sensing. Sensor networks play a major role in that approach. In order to maximize the quantity, diversity and accuracy of information extracted from a precision agriculture WSN deployment, a variety of reliable, high-performance and cost-effective sensor technologies are needed. An important issue that arises in precision agriculture is the type of parameters to be sensed, which, except for regular environmental parameters like temperature, humidity and solar radiation, may include soil moisture, dissolved inorganics such as nitrogen and phosphorous species, as well as herbicides and pesticides (Ferentinos & Tsiligiridis, 2005; Cowan, 2000). In recent years, the idea has been forwarded that a precision agricultural system should include conservation measures that provide environmental benefits. In precision agriculture, the 1990s fascination with harvesting data has been tempered in more recent years by the realization that better decisions were often not taken. Many have actually found that with more and more information collected, their motivation to do something with it had diminished. In many cases, the ability to apply meaningful information gathered in order to obtain benefits just has not materialized. From this situation, an obvious but blatantly truthful perspective arose, "It is not good to know more unless we do more with what we know." (Kitchen, 2008)

The following premise has thus emerged: precision agriculture information increases in value when data collection, data processing, and management actions are integrated. Furthermore, precision agriculture research and development will only succeed if an integration of multiple disciplines is already forwarded (Bullock, Kitchen & Bullock, 2007). End users want to know the science and technology employed, but not necessarily the details of how or why that information is needed for an action. This phenomenon is typical of all consumers of new applications of science or technology. For precision agriculture, seamless and automated applications is captured in what Griffin et al. (Griffin et al., 2004) described as "embodied knowledge," that is, information needs to be purchased in the form of an input (e.g., hybrid corn). Since modern farming enterprises are already complicated and time-demanding, producers seeking improvements want science and technology delivered, but without increased complexity.

As a potential user group, agriculturalists are distinct from scientists doing habitat research. They focus on production rather than exploratory research, so they are not interested in spending time interpreting data. They want data that recommends a course of action, something that will save them time rather than create additional work. In addition, agriculturalists are not working in remote or fragile environments. They interact closely and physically with crops, touching and examining them each day. They know they cannot do it remotely.

Once a WSN is installed and operative, the question becomes what kind of computational interpretation is needed and what should be done once the data is interpreted. If data is simply delivered raw, it might not suggest any course of action, or it might require significant effort to draw useful conclusions. In a production environment, this extra interpretive work could be a significant waste of time (Burrell, Brooke & Beckwith, 2004).

In order to successfully implement information-driven agricultural systems such as precision agriculture, the basic principles of resource management cannot be ignored. Time and capital resources spent to collect intensive information from production fields, followed by how to process the information to provide guidance, needs to be accomplished by some type of improvement. If this is not done, negative feedback to the investor (the producer) will result in a retreat to former ways. The paramount test of improvement in an open market-based economy is profitability, since financial matters have the greatest effect on a crop producer's decision of whether to adopt practices long-term or not (Griffin et al., 2004) (Kitchen, 2008). Based on the previous observations, the information-to-action decision process of viable precision agriculture systems must be:

a) In situ sensor-based
b) Automated for real-time (or near real-time) computer processing into decisions
c) Packaged so that sensing and processing of information is a part of the equipment used to accomplish the required management action
d) Transparent to the operator/manager for decision confirmation

The last point is important for two reasons. First, producers want to maintain control, described as the "human touch" (Griffin et al., 2004), since management is still viewed as much as an "art" as it is an application of "science." Second, since technology is not fail-proof, the operator needs to have over-ride control based upon his/her own experience of what is right (Kitchen, 2008).

Precision agriculture focuses on getting the maximum production efficiency with minimum environmental impact. However, one of the major concerns of intensive agriculture is land over-exploitation, which leads to problems such as soil compaction, erosion, salinity and declining water quality. In order to prevent land over-exploitation, WSNs provide a way of measuring and monitoring the health of the soil and water quality at all stages of production. In the field of animal tracking, WSN could be used to control the movement of herds, their health and the state of the pasture (see Table 4). Currently, many WSN systems have been developed and trials and field experiments are under way. However, concrete applications are at an early stage. Applications of WSN in precision agriculture could be divided into the following reduced categories: Plant/crop monitoring, soil monitoring, climate monitoring, and insect-disease-weed monitoring (Weber, 2009).

A basic deployment of a WSN used in the agriculture sector is shown in Figure 1.

Referring to plant/crop monitoring, WSNs have been used to gather, for example, data on leaf temperature, chlorophyll content and plant water status. Based on these data, farmers have been able to detect problems at their early stages and have implemented real-time solutions.

The health and moisture of soil is a basic prerequisite for efficient plant and crop cultivation. WSNs are well suited to achieve real-time monitoring of variables such as soil fertility, soil water availability and soil compaction. On the other hand, WSN nodes can communicate with radio or mobile network weather stations to provide climate and microclimate data.

There are several environmental parameters that promote the growth and propagation of pests

Table 4. Some pasture-related activities improved by using WSN

Health of pastures evaluation	Evaluation through high-resolution remote sensing tools
Location of persistent vegetation cover	Conditions of pastures can be measured and problematic areas detected using satellite maps to build a three dimensional shape of the landscape containing leakiness values and their changes over time.
Precision irrigation and systems developed for remotely controlled, automatic irrigation.	Irrigation scheduling using sensed data together with additional information, e.g. weather data
Precision fertilization	Decision support systems (DSS) calculate the "optimal quantity and spread pattern for a fertilizer"
Behavior of cattle	Grazing habits, herd behavior and interaction with the surrounding environment
Pasture and environmental resources	The information provided by WSN helps famers to understand the state of the pasture and to find optimal ways to use the resources.

and diseases in plants that can potentially cause heavy losses in production quality and quantity each year. By estimating the probability of occurrence of pests or diseases, based on the evolution of climatic parameters (temperature, humidity, and soil moisture), farmers can more efficiently schedule the application of pesticides and fungicides. The major goal of WSN including sensors for monitoring temperature and humidity of the surrounding environment, as well as leaf wetness, is to minimize the number of sprays, employing them only when the crop is at risk. Because of the costs related to frequent applications of agrochemicals and the desire to reduce pesticide levels in the environment, farmers should be really interested on this economic and environmental friendly WSN approach (O'Reilly & Connolly, 2005; WSNIndia, 2009).

Precision agriculture that focuses on the tailored management of a crop not only involves monitoring soil, crop and climate conditions in a field, but also involves using a Decision Support

Figure 1. Typical deployment of WSN in agriculture. Data gathered from sensor nodes is collected at the base station, where it gains access to the public network.

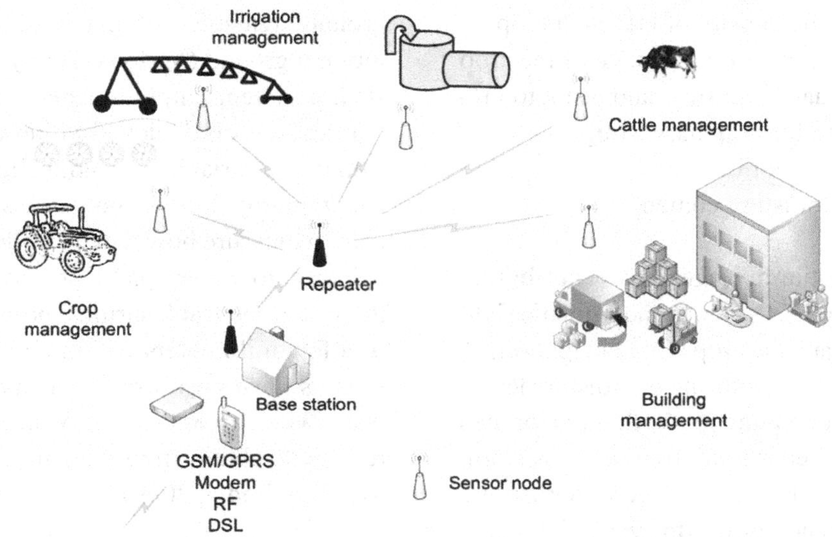

System (DSS) in order to control the treatments or to take differential actions such as the real-time variation of fertilizer or pesticide application (Edordu & Sacks, 2006).

The environmental impact of precision agriculture and animal tracking by monitoring the soil, climate and plants provides information to set a precise irrigation rate, which may lead to a reduction of water consumption. Usually, fields are irrigated with uniform amounts of water. However, the variability in a field requires different amounts for different areas due to the combination of different crops and soil types. Numerous researchers and manufacturers have attempted to develop on-the-go soil sensors to measure mechanical, physical and chemical soil properties. Most of the soil sensors belong to one of the following categories: electrical and electromagnetic, optical and radiometric, mechanical, acoustic, pneumatic and electrochemical (Adamchuk, Hummel, Morgan & Upadhyaya, 2004).

Moreover, greenhouse crops require extensive management that can be accomplished using WSNs along with the actuators. Some of the tasks to be performed include (Vertoda, 2009):

- Setting and monitoring the correct levels of carbon dioxide, temperature and humidity
- Managing nutrient supply for crops
- Measuring the density of leaves in crops
- Determining the growing stage of the crop
- Recording data over time and use it to predict the time for crop harvesting
- Reading the color of crops
- Recording moisture content

Efficient irrigation management is vital for successful crop growing. Current typical practice is to periodically irrigate the crops (time irrigation). A WSN can facilitate monitoring of moisture levels for crops and, in conjunction with an actor, can "decide" as to when it is appropriate to perform irrigation. This method can reduce water use and prevent nutrient leaching due to over-irrigation of crops. For the specific case of a vineyard, irrigation based on WSN can be used as a vine management tool. Young vines should be irrigated to optimize vine growth. Established vines can be irrigated to manage vine growth and to manipulate fruit quality and yield. Two irrigation techniques that can be adopted on established vines are regulated deficit irrigation (RDI) and partial root zone drying (PRD) (Campbell-Clause & Fisher, 2005). The water supply could be managed to produce high-quality grapes with less total water usage per grape. The yield could be improved while maintaining quality. On the other hand, health/effectiveness of irrigation hardware could be monitored and managed by remote access, allowing the owner to work from home (Holler, 2009). Different areas of an agricultural plot will often have different irrigation requirements. WSNs, therefore, can facilitate the irrigation of a subsection of the agricultural area rather than a blanket irrigation policy for the entire field. WSNs can also be used to monitor water levels in collectors of rainwater or melted snow (water catchment areas) (Vertoda, 2009).

In order to accomplish the principles of ecologically sustainable development and customer expectations, environmental monitoring has become a critical part of the agricultural operation. WSNs can be used to monitor water, air pollution and hazardous water disposal and to measure ground dynamics of glaciers, avalanches and moving ground (Vertoda, 2009). An example of such a system employs a network of miniature wireless sensors deployed within a redwood grove to measure variables, including light, temperature and humidity, Furthermore, the system has been able to measure how a tree swells and shrinks in response to water uptake or loss. As a tree uses the water, the trunk shrinks, producing a change of a few millimeters within an hour. Additional sensors have been used to measure the flow of water within trees to quantify the amount of water redwoods obtain from the soil and absorb from fog (WSNIndia, 2009).

Soil moisture tension (how dry the soil is) is another important soil property that has to be measured (usually by a tensiometer) to ensure good irrigation management. As soil dries, its tension increases, and it becomes harder for the plants to extract water from it. The amount of energy a plant must spend to extract water from the soil is directly linked to soil tension. When soil tension becomes too great, plants can no longer extract water from the soil, even if water is present in it. This means that the water is simply not available to the plants, which react by slowing or ceasing their growth. For crop production, this can be costly, since the gradual daily accumulation of small growth losses can have a significant impact on crop yield at harvest time. WSNs can provide soil moisture tension data records to ensure that plants and crops can access the water they need (Vertoda, 2009).

WSNs can play an important role in animal management and animal health applications. For example, sensors can be used to determine the estrous cycle (when female cattle are in heat). The real-time detection of when cattle are in heat would be very valuable for determining appropriate times for artificial insemination. The detection of diseases, such as mastitis and other infections, is another useful service that WSNs could provide to the farming sector (Vertoda, 2009). Experimental work of WSN for tagging farm animals has been performed using attached sensor nodes to cattle collars. Cattle collars ping each other sending their GPS position and time of each ping transmission. Based on the positioning data of each node and inertial information, the cattle's individual and herd behavior can be modeled, and new general models can be developed. As a result, farmers are able to optimally manage environmental resources and plan grazing areas to prevent environmental problems such as overgrazing and land erosion (Weber, 2009).

Supply chain management is an application area where WSNs can improve process efficiency. As an example, the use of WSN in the wine industry is mostly focused on vine growing, but this is only one stage of the wine production process. WSNs can be used to monitor temperature during vinification (the conversion of grape juice into wine), to control the addition of sulphur dioxide during fermentation (which must be strictly controlled) also, they can be used to detect the presence of acids and tannins. To complete the process, cellars must be kept at a strict temperature and humidity so WSNs can also be used during storage for that purpose (O'Reilly & Connolly, 2005).

Management and transportation of agricultural products often have stringent requirements. In order to meet these requirements, WSNs can be used as shown in Table 5.

Building management is a distinct field of application for WSNs, where farmers can not only get help to perform daily tasks (see Table 6) but can also get a reduction on costs (Vertoda, 2009).

CASES OF STUDY

WSN Used to Monitor Water-Weather Conditions on Large Areas

There is a huge WSN established in Southern Finland that covers the entire 2,000 km^{2}of the Karjaanjoki River. It is called SoilWeather and is an operational river basin scale *in-situ* WSN that provides spatially accurate, near real-time information on weather conditions, soil moisture

Table 5. Requirements for WSN applied to agricultural products

Requirement	WSN action
Conservation	Monitoring temperature on frozen and chilled food chill chain
Transportation	Monitoring vehicle speed and location using GPS
Packaging	Measuring and controlling Modified Atmosphere Packaging (MAP)
Food quality	Tracking foodstuffs at every stage of the production process

Table 6. Application areas for WSN in building management

Security	Monitoring	Management	Cost savings
Motion and video sensors Access control	Presence and health of animals Climatic conditions	Indoor environment Lighting system Energy consumption	Energy efficiency Usage of light and heath

and water quality with a high temporal resolution all-year round.

The Soil Weather WSN hosts:

- 70 sensor nodes
- 55 compact weather stations
- 4 nutrient measurement stations
- 11 turbidity measurement stations
    - Six of the turbidity stations have water level pressure sensors as well.

The typical setup of a weather station includes a weather station core and sensors for air temperature, air humidity, precipitation, wind speed and wind direction. Connected to the weather station cores there are also sensors for soil moisture and water turbidity

The network can measure soil moisture, turbidity and water level in many sites. As the SoilWeather WSN functions all year round, it has faced extreme conditions during cold winters and the measurements have been less accurate due to the freezing of sensors. Additionally, to prevent damage to sensor probes located in rivers, they in some cases have been temporally removed during winter.

The weather stations consist of easy to deploy compact devices (programmed to connect to the server automatically) that include all the sensors installed. However, in the case of water turbidity and nutrient measurements, the ease of deployment is too dependent on environmental conditions. On the other hand, the network does not need reprogramming or updating of the existing nodes when a new node or sensor is added. The SoilWeather WSN is used to monitor the water quality of the inflow and outflow of Lake Hiidenvesi (one of the largest lakes in Southern Finland) using two nutrient measurement stations and one turbidity sensor. The SoilWeather network has been functioning in a relatively reliable way, but the maintenance and data quality assurance by automatic algorithms and calibration samples requires a lot of effort, especially in continuous water monitoring over large areas (Kotamäki et al., 2009).

WSNs on Vineyards

The goal for a vineyard owner is to get the best value from the vineyard considering that water is an expensive resource and that grape quality is improved by proper irrigation (Stockwell, 2007). To achieve this goal, the owners must optimize the quality and yield of grapes, while reducing water consumption and electricity used for pumping. By using WSN to meet the above requirements, owners can not only reduce production costs but also can reduce the risk of frost and faulty irrigation systems (Vertoda, 2009; Holler, 2009). On the other hand, although many environments have a seemingly infinite variety of measurable characteristics, users needs to provide limits on what actually should be measured and how often (Burrell, Brooke & Beckwith, 2004).

While remote sensing (satellite and aerial photograph) provides an effective method to mapping surface moisture content over large areas, it averages within-pixel variability, which masks the underlying heterogeneity observed at the land surface. This problem has been solved by using a WSN to enhance the utility of the larger-scale remotely sensed averages by quantifying the underlying variability that remote sensing cannot record explicitly.

The research on WSN applications on vineyards has frequently focused on sensing the soil moisture in order to reduce the amount of water used for irrigation (López Riquelme, Soto, Suardíaz & Iborra, 2004; Ruiz-Garcia, Lunadei, Barreiro & Robla, 2009; Montero, Brasa, Montero-Garcia & Orozco, 2007). The use of WSN has helped researchers to precisely understand how water moves through a field and to develop better models to predict crop growth and yield. Such sensors could help farmers manage their nutrient and water resources. (Elbert, 2008)

In order to make a good wine, it is necessary to measure vine water status (Bogart, 2006). Usually, this is done using a pressure chamber (Turner, 1988). However, the data changes depending on the time of day, so it is difficult to monitor the data manually, which leads to loss of foliage. Because surface soil moisture content is highly variable in both space and t the plant have been used. The results were correlated with the measurements of temperature, humidity, wind speed and solar radiation to estimate evapo-transpiration rates and root-zone soil moisture (WSNIndia, 2009; Ramos Pascual, 2009).

The effects of different levels of water application during post-setting and post-veraison (change of color of the grape berries) on wine quality have been evaluated. The results showed that the best combination for wine quality is obtained by restricting water applications to 40% evapotranspiration (ETreal) during post-setting and 70% ETreal during post-veraison, with significant improvement in the global quality and wine sensory attributes. On the contrary, the worst wine quality was obtained with a water application of 100% of the ETreal during the whole growing period (Acevedo, Ortega-Farías, Hidalgo, Moreno, & Cordova, 2005).

The implementation of a WSN in vineyards has allowed farmers to not only monitor data on a web interface that displays a map of vineyard with the stress levels of the grapevines, but also to predict the pH and berry weight. In one case, sensors were able to determine a 6-hours threshold after the onset of frost, when a wine maker would need to take action to deal with the weather problem (Beckwith, Teibel & Bowen, 2004; Edordu & Sacks, 2006).

Many environments have a seemingly infinite variety of measurable characteristics, so there is a wide range of WSNs deployments used by farmers. In the specific case of vineyards, the WSNs have been mainly used to monitor environmental conditions such as: soil moisture, rainfall, wind velocity and direction, as well as air and soil temperature, in order to make decisions on a vine-by-vine basis to assess water needs and to detect pests in a timely fashion (O'Reilly & Connolly, 2005; Vertoda, 2009).WSNs have also been used as a part of custom irrigation monitoring systems to provide measurements of water pressures, storage temperatures and environmental monitoring over specific areas (Holler, 2009). In other cases, WSNs have been deployed to collect temperature, humidity and radiation data in order to obtain the spatial variability of grapes and their relation with the wine produced. Since the behavior of WSNs is a parameter of interest to farmers, their performance has also been evaluated in extreme operating conditions (Montero, Brasa, Montero-Garcia & Orozco, 2007). From the considerations mentioned above, it is clear that WSNs can play a critical role in vineyard cost management.

Early Detection of Forest Fires

The term wildfire refers to all uncontrolled fires that burn surface vegetation (grass, weeds, grainfields, brush, chaparral, tundra, forest and woodland) (Cambridge, 2009; McGraw-Hill, 2005). An average of 5–15 million hectares burn annually in boreal forests, primarily in Siberia, Canada and Alaska, and there is a growing global awareness of the importance, and vulnerability, of this region with respect to future climate change. Fire activity is strongly influenced by weather, fuels, ignition agents and human activities (Flannigan, Amiro, Logan, Stocks & Wotton, 2006). Heat waves, droughts, cyclical climate changes such as El Niño, and other weather patterns can also increase the risk and alter the behavior of wildfires dramatically. Years of precipitation followed by warm periods have encouraged more widespread fires and longer fire seasons.

Current forest surveillance systems, based on cameras, infrared sensor systems and satellite systems, cannot support real-time surveillance, monitoring and activate an automatic alarm. A WSN can detect and predict forest fires more promptly than the traditional satellite-based approaches (Ruiz-Garcia, Lunadei, Barreiro & Robla, 2009).

Burn rates of smoldering logs are up to five times greater during the day due to lower humidity, increased temperatures, and higher wind speeds. Sunlight warms the ground during the day and causes air currents to travel uphill, and downhill during the night as the land cools. Wildfires are fueled by these winds and often follow the air currents over hills and through valleys. The four major natural causes of wildfires are lightning, volcanic eruptions, sparks from rock falls and spontaneous combustion. Thus, WSN can help sense the cyclical climate changes and spontaneous combustion that can help predict fire condition (WSNIndia, 2009).

The key aspects in modeling forest fires can be obtained by analyzing the Fire Weather Index (FWI) System. This information can then be used to design efficient fire detection systems. The FWI System is one of the most comprehensive forest fire danger rating systems in North America, backed by several decades of forestry research. The analysis of FWI could be of interest for researchers working on WSNs and for sensor manufacturers who can optimize the communication and sensing modules of their products to better fit forest fire detection systems (Culler, Estrin & Srivastava, 2004; Hefeeda & Bagheri, 2007; Navarro, Azevedo & Vera, 2006).

DISCUSSION

WSNs have been used at every stage of the crop growing cycle. The optimal time for planting can be determined by monitoring climate and soil conditions while moisture concentration can be monitored during harvesting. However, the implementation of remote sensing and control capabilities based on WSN has not been widely adopted in most of the farms.

Competitive pressures and economies of scale are forcing farms to become larger. In many cases, this means that farms are becoming more dispersed because farmers have to purchase or rent properties that are not contiguous. Consequently, farmers are spending more time and energy traveling from one place to another, as they monitor the course of activities, such as irrigation, planting, harvesting and drying of grain, or check the status of livestock. Also, they must gather information from rain gauges, soil moisture sensors and other devices as well as control equipment (start pumps, closing gates, etc.) and communicate with employees. Even if farmers do not like wasting time and money doing daily tasks, these are not done remotely because current WSNs are too expensive, too unreliable or too complicated (or any combination of the above) for the farm. In order to establish a multipurpose network requires expertise to develop a wide range of potential applications. The network also needs to be developed in collaboration with private enterprises, including sensor vendors, data users and service developers. Furthermore, low-cost weather stations would make it possible for individuals, such as farmers, and small organizations to participate in the sensor networks of the future.

A key attraction for farmers to use WSNs would be to achieve a reduction in the amount of water used for irrigation. Several projects have been conducted to measure the extent of water savings using WSNs. However, water savings results range from 30-60% to cases that do not report any significant savings; therefore, a systemic approach that takes into account all known factors affecting yield is necessary.

DRAWBACKS

The distribution of crops and foliage can impose unique barriers to wireless technology, which is among the challenges faced by WSNs in agricultural applications. Wave propagation can vary in fallow fields compared with cropped fields and severe weather can cause a dramatic loss in signal strength. Reflection from farm machinery and interference from other networks also have the potential to attenuate signals. It has been reported that after deploying a WSN consisting of humidity and temperature sensors on a potato crop, radio propagation was influenced by canopy development and distance from the base modem. WSNs can experience more frequent issues (included powering down of all the sensor nodes) when:

1. Sensors are deployed in the field for the first time
2. New sensor modules are added to the network
3. The network is checked to resolve connectivity issues

There is also a limitation on the number of nodes that can be implemented on a single network and still maintain a high level of reliability.

For generations, farmers with large farms have used 2-way radios to communicate with employees. Farmers already understand the benefits of wireless communications, because they were some of the earliest adopters of cell phone technology, especially "push-to-talk" cell phones. In addition to being cheap, reliable and simple to use, cell phones have one more important attribute: compatibility. In contrast, in the case of WSN and WSNA, practically all technologies work differently, they use proprietary software, require expensive components, and are frequently cumbersome to use. Therefore, the adoption of WSN depends largely on establishing a standard that provides support and ease of use to farmers.

Finally, the inability to obtain soil characteristics rapidly and inexpensively remains a major constraint to deploying WSN in agriculture.

FUTURE TRENDS

A significant contribution to a more sustainable use of natural resources will be addressed through WSN. However, development of sensors and WSN for precision agriculture is still in its early stages and sensor applications still tend to be expensive. As farmers tend to only consider economic benefits when deciding on whether they should rely on precision agriculture or not, there is a trend from governments to help farmers recognize the environmental dimension by pointing out the economic benefits of improved soil and pasture quality, as well as the reduced applications of fertilizers and pesticides. In addition, in the future, precision agriculture will be encouraged through technical assistance and conservation programs. WSN will become easier to establish in the agricultural industry as RF technology advances. In the near future, wireless sensor networks are expected to provide new economic opportunities for agriculture through their application in remote, real-time monitoring and the control of important aspects of high quality food production and processing systems.

Collaboration will make it possible to achieve cost-effective monitoring systems to cover wide areas, which will provide good quality data from different types of sensors and will encourage joint use of data. Maintenance costs will decrease if the work is done close to the sensor location. Synergy will be obtained if data quality procedures and algorithms are defined and developed. As a result, the whole group of data providers would become beneficiaries.

Considering that in many cases soil sensors are critical to obtain usable data from WSNs, it is important to point out that while only electric and electromagnetic sensors are widely used in the present time, other technologies will also be suitable to improve the quality of soil-related information in the near future.

CONCLUSION

It is clear that WSNs are well suited to improve many applications in agriculture. Crop and irrigation management based on WSNs have led to improvements in yield and cost reduction. Moreover, WSNs can also play a key role in the supply chain, quality and building management functions. Despite the technological barriers such as incomplete standardization of technologies and energy consumption constraints, the implementation of WSNs in agriculture has the potential to be an economically viable replacement for wired networks. Currently, it is also possible to deploy cheaper versions of WSNs with reduced functionality (using limited protocols, such as SMAC along with a small number of sensors) that could be attractive to farmers, in addition to making WSNs more popular. Finally, the ubiquitous computing can be applied to agriculture and food industry in order to share resources and costs. WSN have just entered into the farms and food plants with a bright and promising future.

REFERENCES

Acevedo, O. C., Ortega-Farías, S., Hidalgo, A. C., Moreno, S. Y., & Cordova, A. F. (2005). Efecto de Diferentes Niveles de Agua Aplicada en Post-Cuaja y en Post-Pinta Sobre la Calidad del Vino cv. Cabernet Sauvignon. *Agricultura Técnica, 65*(4). doi:.doi:10.4067/S0365-28072005000400006

Adamchuk, V. I., Hummel, J. W., Morgan, M. T., & Upadhyaya, S. K. (2004). On-the-go soil sensors for precision agriculture. *Computers and Electronics in Agriculture, 44*(1), 71–91. .doi:10.1016/j.compag.2004.03.002

Adee, S. (2010, February). Wireless sensors that live forever. *IEEE Spectrum*, 14. doi:10.1109/MSPEC.2010.5397767

Akyildiz, I., & Kasimoglu, I. (2004). Wireless sensor and actor networks: Research challenges. *Ad Hoc Networks, 2*(4), 351–367. .doi:10.1016/j.adhoc.2004.04.003

Aviles Garcia, J. A. (2008). Una técnica para la caracterización de nodos en Redes de Sensores Inalámbricas. Unpublsihed doctoral thesis (pp. 1-146). Cartagena, Spain: Universidad Politécnica de Cartagena.

Beckwith, R., Teibel, D., & Bowen, P. (2004). Report from the field: Results from an agricultural wireless sensor network. In *Proceedings of the 29th Annual IEEE International Conference on Local Computer Networks (LCN)* (pp. 471-478). New York: IEEE.

Bell, G. (2007). *Bell's Law for the birth and death of computer classes: A theory of the computer's evolution* [Technical report MSR-TR-2007-146]. San Francisco, CA: Microsoft Research, Silicon Valley, Microsoft Corporation.

Bogart, K. (2006). *Three most common methods - Measuring vine water status*. Practical Winery & Vineyard Magazine.

Bullock, D. S., Kitchen, N., & Bullock, D. G. (2007, October). Multidisciplinary teams: A necessity for research in precision agriculture systems. *Crop Science*, *47*, 1765–1769. .doi:10.2135/cropsci2007.05.0280

Burrell, J., Brooke, T., & Beckwith, R. (2004). Vineyard computing: Sensor networks in agricultural production. *IEEE Pervasive Computing / IEEE Computer Society [and] IEEE Communications Society*, *3*(1), 38–45. doi:10.1109/MPRV.2004.1269130

Cambridge. (2009). *Cambridge advanced learner's dictionary* (3rd ed.). Cambridge, UK: Cambridge. Retrieved from http://dictionary.cambridge.org/dictionary

Campbell-Clause, J., & Fisher, D. (2005). *Irrigation techniques for winegrapes. Farmnote*. South Perth, Australia: Western Australian Department of Agriculture.

Castillo Luzón, C. A. (2007). *Implementación de un prototipo de red de sensores inalámbricos para invernaderos* (pp. 1–110). Quito, Ecuador: Escuela Politécnica Nacional.

Choi, S., Kim, B., Park, J., Kang, C., & Eom, D. (2004). An implementation of wireless sensor network for security system using Bluetooth. *IEEE Transactions on Consumer Electronics*, *50*(1), 236–244.

Cowan, T. (2000). Precision agriculture and site-specific management: Current status and emerging policy issues. *CRS Report for Congress*, 1-26.

Culler, D., Estrin, D., & Srivastava, M. (2004). Guest editors' introduction: Overview of sensor networks. *Computer*, *37*(8), 41–49. .doi:10.1109/MC.2004.93

Edordu, C., & Sacks, L. (2006). Self organising wireless sensor networks as a land management tool in developing countries: A preliminary survey. In *London Communications Symposium* (pp. 4-7). London: University College London.

Elbert, B. (2008). Wireless soil sensors to help farming, improve understanding of carbon, nitrogen cycles. *Biopact*. Heverlee, Belgium: Biopact. Retrieved from http://news.mongabay.com/bioenergy/

Eroski, F. (2008). Diseñan una red de sensores inalámbricos aplicables en la agricultura de precisión. Retrieved from http://www.consumer.es/seguridad-alimentaria/2008/08/12/179220.php

Ferentinos, K. P., & Tsiligiridis, T. A. (2005). Heuristic design and energy conservation of wireless sensor networks for precision agriculture. Paper presented at *International Congress on Information Technologies in Agriculture, Food and Environment (ITAFE'05)*, Adana, Turkey.

Flannigan, M. D., Amiro, B. D., Logan, K. A., Stocks, B. J., & Wotton, B. M. (2006). Forest fires and climate change in the 21st century. *Mitigation and Adaptation Strategies for Global Change*, *11*(4), 847–859. .doi:10.1007/s11027-005-9020-7

Gold, M. V. (2007). *Sustainable agriculture: Definitions and terms. Alternative Farming Systems Information Center*. Beltsville, MD: United States Department of Agriculture.

Griffin, T. W., Lowenberg-DeBoer, J., Lambert, D. M., Peone, J., Payne, T., & Daberkow, S. G. (2004). *Adoption, profitability, and making better use of precision farming data* [Staff paper]. West Lafayette, IN: Purdue University.

Hatler, M., Gurganious, D., & Ritter, M. (2008). *Perpetual power solutions for WSN*. San Diego, CA: ON World.

Hefeeda, M., & Bagheri, M. (2007). Wireless sensor networks for early detection of forest fires. In *IEEE Internatonal Conference on Mobile Adhoc and Sensor Systems*, Pisa, Italy (pp. 1-6). New York: IEEE. doi: 10.1109/MOBHOC.2007.4428702

Holler, M. (2009). Camalie cineyards. Retrieved from http://www.camalie.com/

Hong, Y., & Scaglione, A. (2006). Energy-efficient broadcasting with cooperative transmissions in wireless sensor networks. *IEEE Transactions on Wireless Communications*, *5*(10), 2844–2855. doi:10.1109/TWC.2006.04608

Kim, D., Lee, S., Hwang, T., Won, K., & Chung, D. (2006). A wireless sensor node processor with digital baseband based on adaptive threshold adjustment for emotional lighting system. *IEEE Transactions on Consumer Electronics*, *52*(4), 1362–1367. doi:10.1109/TCE.2006.273157

Kinney, P. (2003). ZigBee technology: Wireless control that simply works. In *Communications Design Conference*, San Jose, CA (pp. 1-20).

Kitchen, N. R. (2008). Emerging technologies for real-time and integrated agriculture decisions. *Computers and Electronics in Agriculture*, *61*(1), 1–3. .doi:10.1016/j.compag.2007.06.007

Kotamäki, N., Thessler, S., Koskiaho, J., Hannukkala, A. O., Huitu, H., & Huttula, T. (2009). Wireless in-situ Sensor Network for Agriculture and Water Monitoring on a River Basin Scale in Southern Finland: Evaluation from a Data User's Perspective. *Sensors (Basel, Switzerland)*, *9*(4), 2862–2883. .doi:10.3390/s90402862

López Riquelme, J., Soto, F., Suardíaz, J., & Iborra, A. (2004). Red de Sensores Inalámbrica para Agricultura de Precisión. In *II Teleco-Forum* (pp. 3–4). Cartagena, Spain: Universidad Politécnica de Cartagena.

Malvick, K. (1995). Corn stalk rots. [Department of Crop Sciences, University of Illinois at Urbana-Champaign.]. *Urbana (Caracas, Venezuela)*, IL.

McGraw-Hill. (2005). Forest fire. In *Encyclopedia of science and technology*. New York: McGraw-Hill Professional Publishing.

Montero, F., Brasa, A., Montero-Garcia, F., & Orozco, L. (2007). Redes de Sensores Inalámbricas para Viticultura de Precisión en Castilla-La Mancha. In *Proceedings of the XI Congreso SECH. Actas de Horticultura, 48*(1), 158-160. Albacete, Spain: Sociedad Española de Ciencias Hortícolas.

Naumowicz, T. (2007). Enabling wireless sensor networks: Integration of WSNs into development environments. Paper presented at *Microsoft Research Summer School 2007*, Cambridge, UK.

Naushad, H. (2006). *A survey on energy-efficient MAC protocols for wireless sensor networks* [Mid-term project report]. Lahore, Pakistan: Lahore University of Management Sciences, Wireless Communications and Computer Networks.

Navarro, J. L., Azevedo, A., & Vera, J. (2006). *Redes inalámbricas de sensores para la vigilancia no invasiva de espacios naturales*. VECTOR PLUS.

O'Reilly, F., & Connolly, M. (2005). Sensor networks and the food industry. In *Workshop on Real-World Wireless Sensor Networks (REAL-WSN'05)*, Stockholm, Sweden (pp. 1-23). Kista, Sweden: SICS.

Ramos Pascual, F. (2009). Redes de sensores inalámbricos. Retrieved from http://www.radioptica.com/sensores/

Ruiz-Garcia, L., Lunadei, L., Barreiro, P., & Robla, J. I. (2009). A review of wireless sensor technologies and applications in agriculture and food industry: State of the art and current trends. *Sensors (Basel, Switzerland)*, *9*(6), 4728–4750. .doi:10.3390/s90604728

Ruíz Ibarra, E. C. (2006). *Protocolo de enrutamiento para redes de sensores y actuadores inalámbricos*. Ensenada, México: CICESE.

Sims, J. (2009). Rapidly serving imagery. *Imaging Notes*, *24*(1), 30–33.

Stockwell, W. (2007). Wireless sensor networks for precision agriculture. In *EU-US Workshop on Wirelessly Networked Embedded Systems*. Edinburgh, Scotland: University of Edinburgh.

Tang, Q., Yang, L., Giannakis, G. B., & Qin, T. (2007). Battery power efficiency of PPM and FSK in wireless sensor networks. *IEEE Transactions on Wireless Communications*, *6*(4), 1308–1319. doi:10.1109/TWC.2007.348327

Turner, N. C. (1988). Measurement of plant water status by the pressure chamber technique. *Irrigation Science*, *9*(4), 289–308. .doi:10.1007/BF00296704

Van Dam, T., & Langendoen, K. (2003). An adaptive energy-efficient MAC protocol for wireless sensor networks. In *Proceedings of the first international conference on Embedded networked sensor systems – (SenSys '03)* (pp. 171-180). New York: ACM Press. doi: 10.1145/958491.958512

Van der Werff, T. J. (2003, February). 10 emerging technologies that will change the world. *MIT's Technology Review*.

Vellidis, G., Garrick, V., Pocknee, S., Perry, C., Kvien, C., & Tucker, M. (2007). How wireless will change agriculture. In J. Stafford, *Precision Agriculture*, Skiathos, Greece (pp. 57-67). Wageningen, The Netherlands: Wageningen Academic Publishers.

Vertoda. (2009). *Wireless sensor networks & agriculture* (pp. 1-16). Ballincolling, Ireland: Sykoinia Limited.

Wang, N., Zhang, N., & Wang, M. (2006). Wireless sensors in agriculture and food industry: Recent development and future perspective. *Computers and Electronics in Agriculture*, *50*(1), 1–14. doi:10.1016/j.compag.2005.09.003

Weber, V. (2009). Smart sensor networks: Technologies and applications for green growth. In *ICTs, the environment and climate change*, Helsingør, Denmark (pp. 1-48). Paris: Organisation for Economic Co-operation and Development.

WSNIndia. (2009). Agriculture and environmental applications. *Search*. Retrieved from http://www.wsnindia.com

Zhang, Z. (2004). Investigation of wireless sensor networks for precision agriculture. In *ASABE Annual Meeting*. St. Joseph, MI: American Society of Agricultural and Biological Engineers.

KEY TERMS AND DEFINITIONS

Crop Yield: Amount of plant crops obtained for a given area.

Irrigation Management: Refers to the scheduling of irrigation employed in order to provide only the required amount of water for a crop.

Pest: Destructive animal that attacks crops.

Precision Agriculture: For a specific field deals with using new technologies to do: the right thing, in the right place, in the right way at the right time, in order to get a desired crop yield.

Sensor: Device that "emulates" one of the human senses in order to measure a physical variable.

Soil Moisture: Property of soil regarding to the amount of water contained in it.

Wireless Sensor Network (WSN): Group of self-organized sensor nodes deployed in a field to gather required data.

Chapter 7
Wireless Data Acquisition System for Greenhouses

Jaime Ortegón Aguilar
Universidad de Quintana Roo, México

Javier Vázquez Castillo
Universidad de Quintana Roo, México

Freddy Chan Puc
Universidad de Quintana Roo, México

Alejandro Castillo Atoche
Universidad Autónoma de Yucatán, México

Mayra Palomino Cardeña
Universidad de Quintana Roo, México

César Rosado Villanueva
Universidad de Quintana Roo, México

ABSTRACT

This chapter presents a novel wireless data acquisition system. The system has been designed to take advantage of inexpensive robotics systems like Lego NXT, which establishes a new paradigm in the wireless ad-hoc networks field. The system architecture can record data from different variables in greenhouse environments. These wireless systems employ wireless access points (WAPs) and wireless-fidelity (Wi-Fi) adapter modules for data acquisition that sample the environment. The measurements data are transmitted to a central station or inclusive to another different node. The acquisition system was designed and adapted to be used in greenhouses located in Quintana Roo, Mexico, where the typical relevant variables are temperature, luminosity and humidity. The developed system uses virtual instrumentation to measure and record environmental variables. The proposed implementation uses commercial data acquisition boards and sensors to gather data, which are processed and visualized with the LabVIEW-based software.

DOI: 10.4018/978-1-60960-027-3.ch007

INTRODUCTION

Plants' growing in greenhouses is increasing economic activity at the Mexican state of Quintana Roo. There are greenhouses in two counties of Quintana Roo, Felipe Carrillo Puerto and José Maria Morelos. These greenhouses grow flowers and fruits for export. Figure 1 presents a public greenhouse located in José Maria Morelos county.

Greenhouses reproduce the optimal natural conditions for a given vegetal. The relevant variables in Quintana Roo are temperature, luminosity and humidity, which need to be carefully regulated. The state is located on the Caribbean coast in the Yucatan peninsula of Mexico. Consequently, it is warm, sunny and very humid during the entire year.

Vegetable production in greenhouses represents a major technological challenge because of the very specific interior climate control necessary for optimal production. Currently, foreign control technology is used in Quintana Roo's greenhouses, with the consequent technological dependence, lack of training and high cost of installation and maintenance.

The cost of mobile and sensor technologies has been decreasing. Moreover, sensing remote data is becoming easier and cheaper. The demand for customized products and services for data acquisition is high; however solutions must optimally integrate new generation sensors and technologies.

Virtual instrumentation uses software modules, instead of hardware, to control actuators or sensors. Such virtual instrumentation has many benefits: functionality, connectivity, low maintenance cost, reusability, open architecture, portability, flexibility, fast integration of new technologies, and information exchange with other applications. Furthermore, in recent years, virtual instrumentation has become very reliable. For this reason, many industries are turning to it to replace dedicated instruments.

The novel contribution of this chapter consists in the proposed architecture for a wireless data acquisition system. The system has been designed to take advantage of small and inexpensive robotics systems, Lego NXT (Gasperi, 2008), but can record variable greenhouse data. Also, we use WAP (wireless access point) and Wi-Fi adapters for data acquisition modules (Garcia et al., 2007; National Instruments, 2009). We exclusively measure environmental variables. Each module adapter node has one or more sensors attached to it. These nodes sample the environment by logging in and transmitting readings to a central station or to another node. Figure 2 shows an example of the Wi-Fi adapter and WAP.

The proposed application presented will reduce the complexity and number of sensors used to measure the environmental variables within greenhouses. Lego's NXT units, with sensors attached to them, move across the greenhouse

Figure 1. Two views of social greenhouse in Jose Maria Morelos, Quintana Roo

(a)

(b)

Figure 2. National instruments wireless modules. a) WAP, b) Wi-Fi data acquisition modules

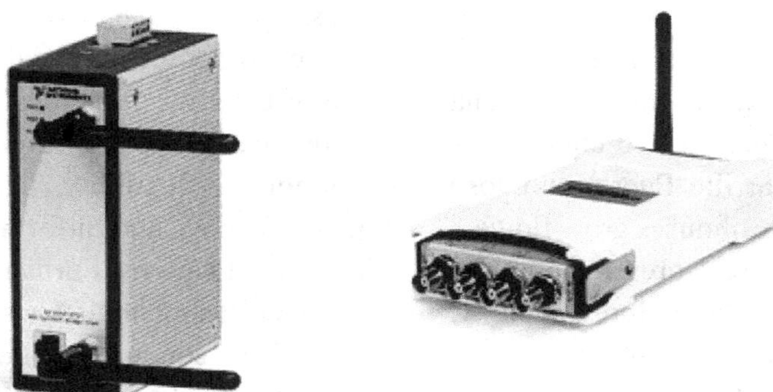

measuring variables and then record them. The NXT units transmit their records by Bluetooth messages to other NXTs, or to a central station. Finally, the central station computes statistics and controls the environment of the greenhouse.

Also, Wi-Fi adapters for data acquisition are installed to send the measurements to a central station. The latter employs a WAP-module attached to provide Wi-Fi connectivity.

BACKGROUND

Recent years have witnessed the increased use of technology in greenhouses. This is mainly due to the increasing demand for organic products and ornamental plants. If products are of high quality, they have the potential to be exported. A greenhouse is a closed structure that seeks to improve the growing process in quantity and quality of products. Being a closed structure, the key challenge is to control the variables that affect the growing process, such as humidity and temperature, among others.

Some greenhouse tasks, because of pesticides, high temperatures or humidity, may be harmful to humans. That is why mobile robotics systems have been used in the past to carry out such tasks. It should be noted that CO2 can be easily expanded into a greenhouse, with the consequent risk to humans. Furthermore, greenhouse temperatures during the day may become dangerously high for persons burdened by protective equipment when performing work-related duties (Sammons & Furukawa, 2005). Greenhouse conditions may expose workers to risks such as dehydration and pesticide exposure, which can cause damage to lung tissue and skin, in general, or even be fatal. It has been found that the genital area absorbs pesticides, even when clothed, with a dermal absorption rate of 11.8, compared with the forearm, which is 1.0 (Riley, 2003). In this study, we propose using mobile robots inside greenhouses to measure and record relevant variables. These variables directly impact the growing process of plants; knowing the values and controlling some of these variables will help improve production and safety.

A wireless sensor network (WSN) is a group of devices capable of gathering information (sensing) and exchanging information between two or more of the same devices within the same network (Karl & Willig, 2007). Various definitions exist, however, Akyildiz et al. (2002) define a wireless sensor network as a large number of small wireless devices with limited computing power, but capable of sensing and transmitting data. This definition shows the versatility of WSNs for use in various applications, including agriculture and greenhouses.

Wireless sensor networks offer advantages over wired systems because of their rapid installation and operation. Furthermore, when used in environments where the physical variables measured do not vary rapidly, system performance is increased, which allows a greater number of nodes to be connected simultaneously to the sensor network.

Recently, various proposals have been presented for sensor network applications and, more specifically, for greenhouse use. Alvarado et al. (2009) propose implementing sensor networks to model both outdoor and indoor conditions. This proposal describes the overall system architecture and the sensor array that can interact with the appropriate hardware to monitor real-time variables. This proposal has not yet been implemented; however the modules of the architecture are described in detail.

The use of wireless technologies has favored rural agriculture. Walker et al. (2008) implement and integrate various technologies to provide monitoring in rural Kenyan farms. In this work, the authors mix technologies, such as ZigBee and GPRS, to collect data and send information over long distances.

Furthermore, Wang et al. (2006) present a review of wireless communication technologies for integration in the agriculture and food industry. Also, they present a comparison of wireless standards such as Wi-Fi, Bluetooth and ZigBee. They go on to propose how technology can be incorporated to improve each of the agricultural processes, from measuring specific variable to the manipulation of control equipment. Moreover, due the degree of automation and use of new technologies, Hirakawa et al. (2002) devised a system for wireless control of a robot for use in agriculture.

Another important study is presented by Acaccia et al. (2003), who design mobile robots to be used in greenhouses. The mobile robots employ recognition capabilities for agricultural processes. Cameras have been integrated for pattern recognition to identify the degree of maturity and a robotic arm to collect the crop. A detailed study of robots and their use in greenhouses is presented by Garcia et al. (2007). Rodriguez and Berenguel (2004) (Rodríguez & Berenguel, 2004) also did some thorough work on the modeling and simulation of agricultural processes, mobile robotics and machine vision, applied to agriculture.

Virtual instrumentation is a software layer that allows users to interact with the computer as if they were interacting with the physical instrument itself. This is done through software, computers, data acquisition boards, sensors and actuators. On the other hand, virtual instrumentation has several advantages over traditional data acquisition systems: unlimited functionality, application-oriented, comprehensive connectivity, low maintenance cost, reusable, open architecture, rapid incorporation of new technologies and information exchange with other applications. Virtual instrumentation is also more portable and flexible.

Today, many applications have been developed to monitor variables using virtual instrumentation in conjunction with sensor networks. Ponce (2008) uses these technologies to perform complex control schemes to manage the dosage of nutrients in greenhouses. Kaiser and Rundel (2008) carry out a wide range of wireless environmental measurements using a single device that provides robotic control, remote configuration and data sharing over the Web. This device belongs to a measurement system that researchers use to characterize the forest understory microclimate and fluxes of carbon between the rain forest floor and the atmosphere in Costa Rica.

In this review, we analyzed advantages and disadvantages of different technologies and their feasibility for implementation in our region. In conclusion, one can deduce that the application of technology in agriculture allows optimal management in many areas of plant cultivation. Analyzing and controlling the various production inputs in a sound and efficient manner increases the profitability of production and conserves natural resources and the environment.

ARCHITECTURE DESIGNS

Solution

The state of Quintana Roo is located in the easternmost part of the Yucatan Peninsula, bordering on Belize (see Figure 3). Quintana Roo has a mean maximum temperature of 33° C and the state averages 80% relative humidity.

Nowadays, there are public and private greenhouses distributed in the geographic area of Quintana Roo, with Habanero peppers and cucumbers the main products. In most cases, the greenhouses are not automated. However, when the greenhouses are automated, this automation comes with significant technological dependence because the architectures are foreign and fixed. Because of this, the University of Quintana Roo is developing a wireless data acquisition system to collect data in greenhouse environments. The information collected can be used to decide what nutrient mix plants require as well as the amount of irrigation needed. This solution can serve as an alternative for automation of greenhouses. The relevant variables in Quintana Roo are temperature, luminosity and humidity because the state is located in the Caribbean, where it is warm, sunny and very humid all year long.

Figure 3.Map of the state of Quintana Roo

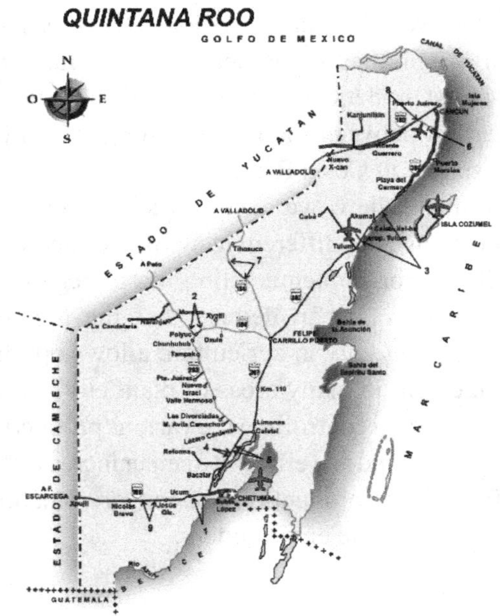

WSN technologies are widely used for modern precision agriculture monitoring. These technologies offer significant advantages over wired sensors, including their lower cost and ease of installation, as well as their simple relocation and their maximization of sensing coverage. Moreover, greenhouses typically create various microclimate layers (Teemu Ahonen, 2008). The use of mobile robots helps figure out microclimatic differences, thus providing useful information about the most convenient locations to place the sensor nodes.

LEGO's NXT are inexpensive robots that are commercially available in Mexico and several other countries. The internal hardware architecture of LEGO's NXT is very interesting; it has a microcontroller ARM7 and an Atmel's AVR coprocessor. It also has 4 input ports and 3 output ports, an A/D converter (ADC), 4 buttons and a LCD display, which permits human-computer interaction. Additionally, it has Bluetooth capability with a Bluecore 4 chip to perform wireless communications. The robot's architecture can be configured and used with National Instruments (NI) LabVIEW through the LEGO NXT Toolkit. In this way, it is possible to handle the input and output ports and acquire data using the ADC. NXT is easily expandable using retail and custom sensors. For our application, we use the LM35-AH integrated circuit for temperature readings and the HIH-3610 to measure the relative humidity. The LM35-AH has a precision of 0.5 °C and its working range temperature is from -55 to +150 °C. The HIH-3610 has a precision of 2% RH with a working range from 0 to 100% RH. The luminosity or solar radiation is measured with a SP Lite pyranometer, which has a sensibility of 80 mV/Wm2. The readings from the temperature and humidity sensors were conditioned so that NXT could use them.

The interface was developed with NI LabVIEW, which enables users to quickly develop applications. Besides the ease of programming, the natural parallel processing of LabVIEW uses the LabVIEW NXT toolkit. The NXT toolkit contains several virtual instruments to program the Lego NXT. Some of the modules are especially made to program the Bluetooth device of the NXT. Figure 4 presents the PC program to pair with NXT Bluetooth to receive data sent by the robot.

The modules presented in Figure 4 are used to scan or to find a Bluetooth device, to create the object reference or to destroy it, to check if the Bluetooth device is paired, to pair it or unpair it. There are software modules to read and write Bluetooth messages. Also, it is possible to write custom software modules for the NXT.

The NXT hardware units can have one or more sensors attached to it. The function of the NXT software module is to log the measurements and to transmit them by a Bluetooth radio to a central station or to another NXT. The central station could be a PC, a laptop or an appliance with Bluetooth capability. The whole process is presented below:

First, the robot moves along pre-defined path (see Figure 5). As it moves, it samples the environment and sends measurements to the control unit to storage and process. The data collection time can be reduced and there can be two or more robots.

Second, the participating robots share the journey through the greenhouse, sending messages between the each robot and the central unit. Having several robots using an efficient and effective communication protocol can extend coverage area.

Another advantage of wireless technology is that it minimizes the risks associated with having many cables in walkways. Finally, a real-time reconfiguration and extension to other computer/robotic systems is possible using an interface developed with LabVIEW (Palomino, Ortegón, Vázquez, & Chan, 2009).Some disadvantages related to using WSN and robots in the state's greenhouses are directly related to the high local temperatures and relative humidity. The latter has a significant impact on electronic devices where (thermal) noise increases with temperature. Greenhouses are more hostile for electronic devices because they usually increase temperature, humidity and dustiness, all of which directly affect the performance of WSN nodes and robots.

The data received by the central unit can be processed and used to generate a series of statistics. These statistics help persons make decisions about processes and correct the greenhouse management strategy. Another important control issue corresponds to monitoring data and fault-detection. For example, it is possible to sound an alarm if a

Figure 4. Use of bluetooth messages through the LabVIEW NXT toolkit

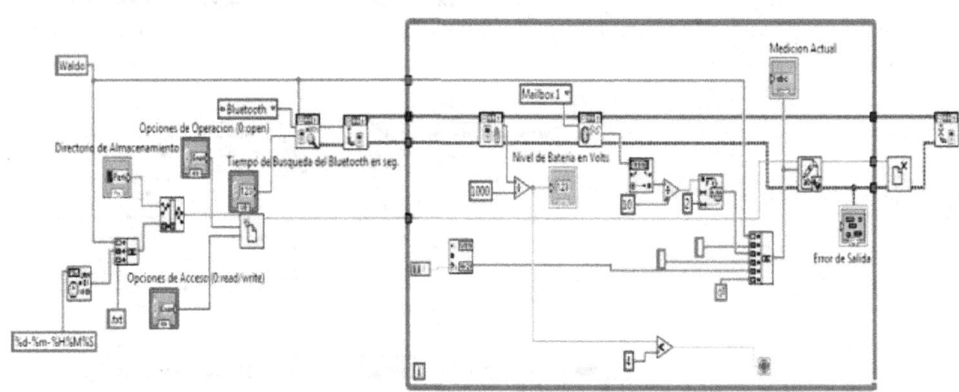

Figure 5. Robot programmable path

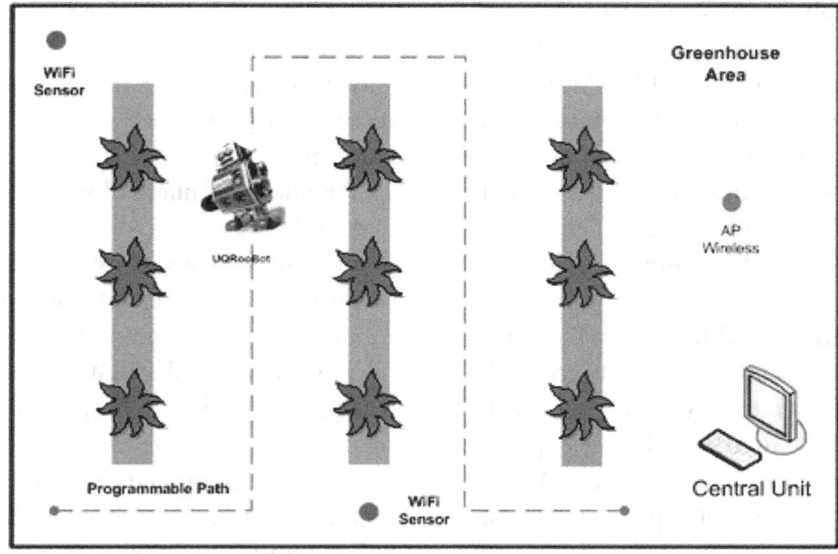

severe abnormality presents itself. The interface is designed to display data for its analysis as illustrated in Figure 6.

RESULTS

Besides the modifications made to NXT for the temperature sensor; it was implemented an in-

Figure 6. Data acquisition system interface: a) measurements module, b) graphics module, c) statistical module

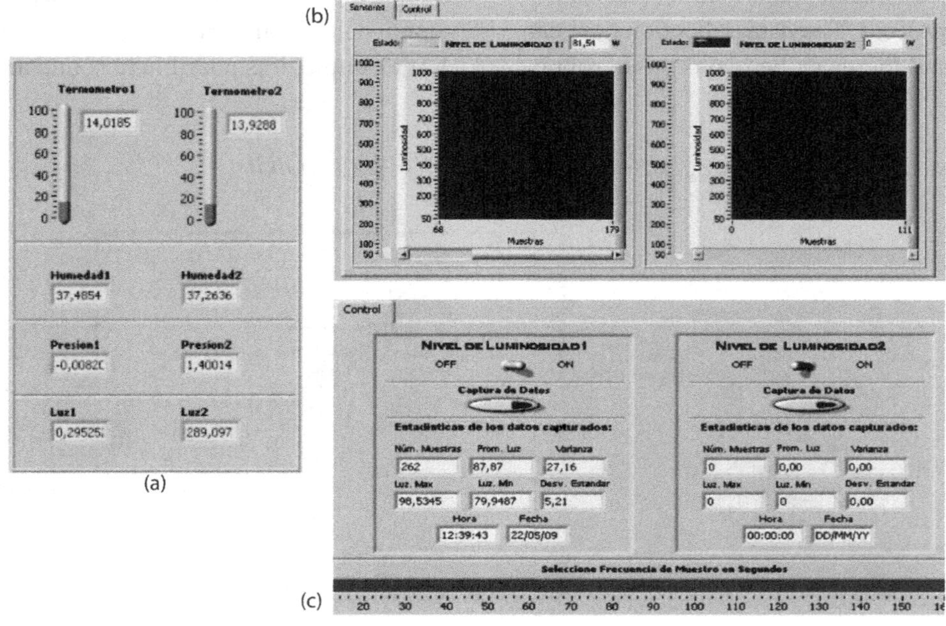

terface to configure the data acquisition system, but also capable of collect data sent by robots. During the test phase, two robots moved along a predefined trajectory collecting data and storing it in files. Figure 7 shows the configuration program for a robot named 'Waldo.' It is possible to configure the sample period, file name, and even monitor the battery level in real time. An alarm is triggered if the robot's battery level impairs data collection. Figure 8 presents data file contents. The columns correspond to the battery level, robot name, temperature and time of the sample. The sample date is included in the filename.

FUTURE RESEARCH DIRECTIONS

The implemented scheme centralizes data in a central unit at the greenhouse, where skilled people and advisors analyze the stored data regu-

Figure 7. Configuration interface

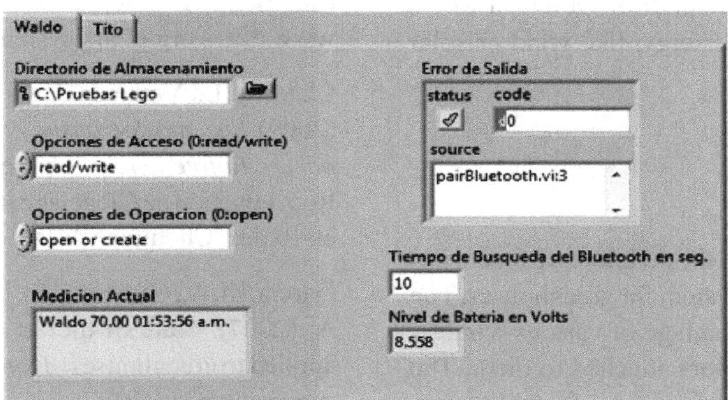

Figure 8. Data file columns correspond to battery level, robot, temperature, and time respectively

Waldo16-02-130415.txt: Bloc de notas

Archivo Edición Formato Ver Ayuda

```
8.47 waldo 27.90 01:04:42 p.m.
8.47 waldo 27.70 01:04:58 p.m.
8.49 waldo 27.90 01:05:10 p.m.
8.50 waldo 27.70 01:05:27 p.m.
8.49 waldo 27.70 01:05:39 p.m.
8.50 waldo 27.70 01:05:56 p.m.
8.49 waldo 27.70 01:06:09 p.m.
8.45 waldo 27.70 01:06:25 p.m.
8.49 waldo 27.70 01:06:38 p.m.
8.50 waldo 27.70 01:06:52 p.m.
8.49 waldo 27.70 01:07:07 p.m.
8.46 waldo 27.70 01:07:21 p.m.
8.47 waldo 27.70 01:07:35 p.m.
8.46 waldo 27.70 01:07:48 p.m.
8.43 waldo 27.70 01:08:03 p.m.
8.46 waldo 27.70 01:08:16 p.m.
8.45 waldo 27.70 01:08:31 p.m.
8.46 waldo 27.70 01:08:43 p.m.
8.47 waldo 27.90 01:08:59 p.m.
```

larly. Another alternative is to implement a large data center for many greenhouses, which can be achieved if communication is carried over long distances. The authors conducted tests to transmit data, achieving transfer rates up to 85 kbps over a distance of more than 20 km (15 miles). Because greenhouse physical variables change slowly, the transmission bandwidth is not affected significantly. Moreover, the system benefits from the state's topography, which is very flat. This very regular topography permits transmission over greater distances (Chargoy, Vázquez, Ortegón, & Chan, 2009). Similar systems can be used to determine the true potential of Quintana Roo's coasts for renewable energy, like wind or solar energy.

CONCLUSION

This chapter presented the architecture for a wireless data acquisition system for greenhouses. The architecture takes advantage of various wireless devices that have sensors attached to them. The sensors measured environmental variables such as temperature, humidity and solar radiation. These variables impact plant growth in greenhouses. Samples can be stored and processed to compute statistics, allowing greenhouse workers and advisors access to complete and timely information. The system consists of Wi-Fi modules, Lego NXT robots with Bluetooth capacities and a central unit. The robots travel around the greenhouse collecting data. As they approach other robots, they exchange data and finally send it to a central unit. This kind of system is useful as it provides the information needed for persons to make informed decisions regarding greenhouse conditions. Additionally, this system can be used to fully automate irrigation, shading, cooling and other actions that impact greenhouse production. Monitoring and automation are research fields that benefit from WSNs.

REFERENCES

Acaccia, G., Michelini, R., Molfino, R., & Razzoli, R. (2003). Mobile robots in greenhouse cultivation: Inspection and treatment of plants. Paper presented at the *1st International Workshop on Advances in Service Robotics,* Bardolino, Italia.

Akyildiz, I., Su, W., Sankarasubramaniam, Y., & Cayirci, E. (2002). Wireless sensor networks: A survey. *Computer Networks*, *38*(4), 393–422. doi:10.1016/S1389-1286(01)00302-4

Alvarado, P., González, A., & Villaseñor, L. (2009). *D2ARS*. Retrieved September 2009, from www.d2ars.org/d2ars/system/files/paper2.pdf

Chargoy, L., Vázquez, J., Ortegón, J., & Chan, F. (2009). *Sistema de transmisión a largas distancias por radiofrecuencia.* Universidad de Quintana Roo, División de Ciencias e Ingeniería, Ingeniería en Redes. Chetumal, México: UQRoo.

García, M. A., Gutiérrez, S., López, H. C., & Ruiz, A. (2007). State of the art of robot technology applied to greenhouses. *Avances en Investigación Agropecuaria, 11*(9).

Gasperi, M. (2008). *LabVIEW for LEGO MINDSTORMS NXT*. Allendale, NJ: NTS Press.

Hirakawa, A., Saraiva, A., & Cugnasca, C. (2002). Wireless robust robot for agricultural applications. In *Proceedings of the World Congress of Computers in Agriculture and Natural Resources* (pp. 13-15).

Johnson, T., & Margalho, M. (2006). Wireless sensor networks for agroclimatology monitoring in the Brazilian Amazon. In *Proceedings of the International Conference on Communication Technology,* Guilin, China (pp. 1-4).

Kaiser, W., & Rundel, P. (2008). *Researchers use NI LabVIEW and NI CompactRIO to perform environmental monitoring in the Costa Rican rain orest.* Austin, TX: National Instruments. Retrieved September 2009, from http://sine.ni.com/cs/app/doc/p/id/cs-11143

Karl, H., & Willig, A. (2007). *Protocols and architectures for wireless sensor networks*. Chichester, UK: Wiley.

National Instruments. (2009). *NI Wi-Fi Data Acquisition*. Austin, TX: National Instruments. Retrieved September 2009, from http://www.ni.com/dataacquisition/wifi/

Palomino, M., Ortegón, J., Vázquez, J., & Chan, F. (2009). Sistemas de adquisición de datos para el estado de Quintana Roo. In *Congreso Nacional de Ingeniería Eléctrica y Electrónica del Mayab,* Instituto Tecnológico de Mérida, Mexico (pp. 325-333).

Ponce, P. (2008). *Developing a novel, portable intelligent greenhouse using graphical system design.* Austin, TX: National Instruments. Retrieved September 2009, from http://sine.ni.com/cs/app/doc/p/id/cs-12081

Rodríguez, F., & Berenguel, M. (2004). *Control y Robótica en Agricultura.* España: Universidad de Almería.

Sammons, P. J., & Furukawa, T. A. (2005). Autonomous pesticide spraying robot for use in a greenhouse. In *Proceedings of the Australasian Conference on Robotics and Automation* (pp. 1-9). Sydney, Australia: ACRA.

Teemu Ahonen, R. V. (2008). Network, greenhouse monitoring with wireless sensor netword. In *Proceedings of the IEEE/ASME International Conference on Mechatronic and Embedded Systems and Applications,* Beijing (pp. 403-408). New York: IEEE.

Walker, K., Kabashi, A., Abdelnour, J., Ngugi, K., Underwood, J., Elmirghani, J., & Prodanovic, M. (2008). Interaction design for rural agricultural sensor networks. Paper presented at the *International Congress on Environmental Modelling and Software,* Catalonia, Barcelona.

Wang, N., Zhang, N., & Wang, M. (2006). Wireless sensors in agriculture and food industry: Recent development and future perspective. *Computers and Electronics in Agriculture, 50*(1), 1–14. doi:10.1016/j.compag.2005.09.003

ADDITIONAL READING

Avilés, E., & García, A. (2009). TinySOA: A service-oriented architecture for wireless sensor networks. *Service Oriented Computing and Applications, 3*(2), 99–108. doi:10.1007/s11761-009-0043-x

Bitter, R., Mohiuddin, T., & Nawrocki, M. (2006). *LabView: Advanced programming techniques.* Boca Raton, FL: CRC.

Boon, L., Toong, C., & Palaniappan, S. (2009). Monitoring of an aeroponic greenhouse with a sensor network. *International Journal of Computer Science and Network Security, 9*(3), 240–246.

Burrell, J., Brooke, T., & Beckwith, R. (2004). Vineyard computing: Sensor networks in agricultural production. *IEEE Pervasive Computing / IEEE Computer Society [and] IEEE Communications Society, 3*(1), 38–45. doi:10.1109/MPRV.2004.1269130

Carcelle, X., Heile, B., Chatellier, C., & Pailler, P. (2008). Next WSN applications using ZigBee. *Home Networking, 256*, 239-254. Boston: Springer.

Chen, L., Sun, T., & Liang, N. (2008). An evaluation study of mobility support in ZigBee networks. [New York: Springer.]. *Journal of Signal Processing Systems*, *59*(1), 111–122. doi:10.1007/s11265-008-0271-x

Culler, D., Estrind, D., & Srivastava, M. (2004). Overview of sensor networks. *IEEE Computer*, *37*(8), 41–49.

Giacomin, J. C., & Vasconcelos, F. H. (2006). Wireless sensor networks as a measurement tool in precision agriculture. Paper presented at *XVIII Imeko World Congress,* Rio de Janeiro, Brazil.

Johnson, T., & Margalho, M. (2007). Performance evaluation of wireless transmissions in an Amazonian climate. In *Procedings of Wireless Communications and Networking Conference,* Kowloon, Hong Kong (pp. 2752-2756). New York: IEEE.

Kim, Y., Evans, R., & Iversen, W. (2008). Remote sensing and control of an irrigation system using a distributed wireless sensor network. *IEEE Transactions on Instrumentation and Measurement*, *57*(7), 1379–1387. doi:10.1109/TIM.2008.917198

Kondo, N., & Ting, K. (1988). *Robotics for bioproduction systems*. St. Joseph, MI: American Society of Agricultural Engineering.

Liu, G., & Ying, Y. (2003). Application of Bluetooth technology in greenhouse environment, monitor and control. *Journal of Zhejiang University (Agriculture & Life Sciences), 29*, 329–334.

McKinion, J., Jenkins, J., Willers, J., & Read, J. (2003). Developing a wireless LAN for high-speed transfer of precision agriculture information. In *Proceedings of the 4th European Conference on Precision Agriculture,* Berlin, Germany (pp. 399-404).

McKinion, J., Turner, S., Willers, J., Read, J., Jenkins, J., & McDade, J. (2004). Wireless technology and satellite Internet access for high-speed whole farm connectivity in precision agriculture. *Agricultural Systems*, *81*(3), 201–212. doi:10.1016/j.agsy.2003.11.002

Montoya, A., Aristizábal, D., Atencio, J., Correa, C., & Montoya, N. (2008). Design and implementation of wireless sensor network using virtual instruments and ZigBee communication protocol. In *Novel algorithms and techniques in telecommunications, automation and industrial electronics* (pp. 16–21). Dordrecht, The Netherlands: Springer. doi:10.1007/978-1-4020-8737-0_4

National Instruments. (n.d.). *Introduction to the LabVIEW Wireless Sensor Network (WSN) Module Pioneer*. Austin, TX: National Instruments. Retrieved October 10, 2009, from http://zone.ni.com/devzone/cda/tut/p/id/8981

Pawlowski, A., Guzman, J., Rodríguez, F., Berenguel, M., Sánchez, J., & Dormido, S. (2009). Simulation of greenhouse climate monitoring and control with wireless sensor network and event-based control. *Sensors (Basel, Switzerland)*, *9*, 232–252. doi:10.3390/s90100232

Postolache, O., Girão, P., & Pereira, M. (2008). Virtual instrumentation. In Boston, B. (Ed.), *Data modeling for metrology and testing in measurement science* (pp. 1–39). Berlin: Springer.

Serodio, C., Cunha, J., Morais, R., Couto, C., & Monteiro, J. (2001). A networked platform for agricultural management systems. *Computers and Electronics in Agriculture*, *31*(1), 75–90. doi:10.1016/S0168-1699(00)00175-7

Sidek, O., Qayum, M., Edin, H., Mohamed, K., & Azman, M. (2009). Preliminary infrastructure development for greenhouse accounting of Malaysian rainforest using wireless sensor network. *European Journal of Scientific Research*, *33*(2), 249–260.

Torres, F., Pomares, J., Gil, P., Puente, S., & Aracil, R. (2002). *Robots y sistemas sensoriales.* Madrid, España: Prentice Hall.

Tsui, C., Carnegie, D., & Wei, P. (2009). USAR robot communication using ZigBee technology. *Progress in Robotics, 44*, 380-390. Berlin: Springer.

Yang, J., Zhang, C., Li, X., Huang, Y., Fu, S., & Acevedo, M. (2009). Integration of wireless sensor networks in environmental monitoring cyber infrastructure. [Dordrecht, The Netherlands: Springer.]. *Wireless Networks*, *16*(4), 1091–1108. doi:10.1007/s11276-009-0190-1

Zhang, W., Kantor, G., & Singh, S. (2004). Integrated wireless sensor/actuator networks in an agricultural application. Paper presented at the *Second ACM International Conference on Embedded Networked Sensor Systems,* Baltimore, MD. New York: ACM.

KEY TERMS AND DEFINITIONS

Automation: The technique of making an apparatus, a process, or a system operate automatically

Bluetooth: It is a wireless protocol for exchanging data over short distances, it is very common on mobile devices like cell phones. It creates WPANs.

General Packet Radio Service (GPRS): General Packet Radio Service. It is a standard for packet transmission available to users of cellular systems.

Greenhouse: Closed structure for plant growing or cultivation, often used for vegetables or ornamental plants.

LabVIEW: It is a platform and development environment for a visual programming language from National Instruments.

Lego NXT: Lego Mindstorms NXT is a programmable robotics kit released by Lego. It has different sensors included like light and sound. The kit can be extended with custom sensors.

Virtual Instrumentation: It is a software layer that allows users to interact with the computer as if you were interacting with the physical instrument itself.

Wi-Fi: The IEEE 802.11 b/g/n standard, it refers to Wireless Fidelity. It is an industry term to indicate that a product is certified to work with 802.11 family standards.

Wireless Personal Area Networks (WPAN): It is a network used for communication among devices close to one person. The WPAN network may extend a few meters.

Wireless Sensor Networks (WSN): Wireless Sensor Networks. It is a network of distributed sensors that may interact between them to monitor variables like temperature or humidity.

ZigBee: The IEEE 802.15.4 standard, it is designed for WPANs. ZigBee is designed to have low power consumption and low data rate but being a secure network.

Section 2
Wireless Ad Hoc Networks

Chapter 8
Power Aware Routing in Wireless Mobile Ad Hoc Networks

G. Varaprasad
B.M.S. College of Engineering, India

ABSTRACT

Wireless mobile ad hoc networks are gaining importance because of their flexibility, mobility, and ability to work with a limited infrastructure. If the battery of a node is drained out, then it cannot communicate with other nodes and the number of dead nodes makes the network partition. In order to overcome the network partition problem, this chapter presents different routing algorithms for wireless mobile ad hoc networks. Different routing algorithms use different metrics, namely transmission power, residual battery capacity and noncritical nodes to forward data packets from the source to destination. Minimum total transmission power routing uses the transmission power as metric to forward the packets but it cannot increase the lifetimes of the node and network. In conditional max-min battery capacity routing, it increases network lifetime and reduces power consumption over the network. Noncritical nodes with more residual battery capacity based routing models will increase the network lifetime and network throughput.

1. INTRODUCTION

A Mobile Ad hoc Network (MANET) is a wireless network that does not have a fixed infrastructure that is formed by an autonomous collection of mobile nodes, and communicates over wireless links. Because of node mobility, the topology will change rapidly and unpredictably over short periods of time. In the MANET, each mobile node acts as a router as well as host. This means that all the nodes participating in the network have to send and receive the data packets. Depending on the transmission range and current location of the node, the node can get in and out, forming a network in an arbitrary fashion. The network partition is a problem in MANET environments and inconsistency can prove to be very costly in mobile computation scenarios (De Moraes, Sadjadpour & Garcia-Luna-Aceves, 2006). Mobile nodes interact with other over wide spaces.

DOI: 10.4018/978-1-60960-027-3.ch008

Therefore, inconsistency can be propagated indefinitely, causing unrecoverable damage in all of the critical applications. Nodes with higher mobility have more link failures than more slowly moving nodes. It leads to the communication failures/disconnections caused by the nodes moving out of the coverage area (Chao, Sheu & Chou, 2006). The conventional routing protocols of MANETs do not consider transmission power as a design constraint. Hence, these routing protocols work towards optimizing paths in terms of delay and host, which usually results in the shortest path. A higher degree of nodes die soon since they are being used in most of the cases. The problem of routing in MANETs is complicated by node mobility, which results in the transmission of frequent topology updates that are required to optimize the paths. The regular updates need greater bandwidth and power and take more message overhead. The basic structure of a MANET environment is shown in Figure 1. The types of mobile devices and their applications range from laptops, PDAs and notebooks to cell phones. Most of these devices currently perform all the tasks of traditional PCs with the advantage of portability. The MANET is a good alternative network in rural areas, where installing basic communication infrastructure is not feasible. Another interesting application of the MANET is ubiquitous computing. Here, the intelligent nodes are used for communications (Ma & Yang, 2005).

The difference between ad hoc networks and traditional wireless networks is the absence of a centralized base station. In the MANET, there are many routing protocols used to determine an optimal path from the source to the destination. The hop-count is used in various routing algorithms like Dynamic Source Routing (DSR), Destination Sequenced Distance Vector (DSDV), Temporally Ordered Routing(TORA), etc. The conventional models use delay and throughput as metrics to forward the packets from one node to another. The DSR protocol outperforms the AODV model in less stressful situations that have a reduced number of nodes, low load and low mobility. The AODV protocol outperforms the DSR model in more stressful situations by widening performance gaps and by increasing stress in the

Figure 1. Structure of MANET

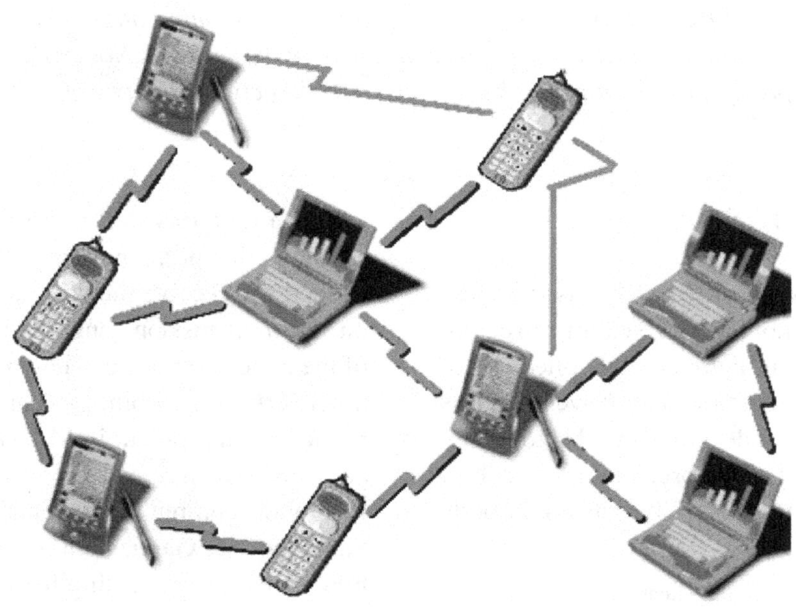

forms of increased load and high mobility. The proactive and reactive models have failed to increase the node lifetime or the network lifetime

In mobile ad hoc networks, all tasks are performed by the nodes themselves, in addition to their normal tasks. This causes an additional drain on the batteries which leads to diminishing the lifetime of nodes. One of the main design constraints in MANETs is that the nodes suffer from power constraints. Hence, every effort needs to be channeled towards reducing power consumption. More precisely, the lifetime of the network is a key design metric in MANETs. If some nodes die early due to a lack of energy, other notes will not be able to communicate with each other. Hence, the network will disconnect and the lifetime of the network will be adversely affected. Mobile devices consume power even when they are in sleep mode. For example, mobile phones constantly use power. Even if they are not actually in use, there is a constant amount of power being drained because the receiver is constantly hearing signals. In the sleep mode, power consumption (Wavelan Metricom and IR) ranges from 150mw to 170mW, while in the idle state, power consumption goes up by one order of magnitude (Kumar & Singh, n.d.). In the transmitting mode, energy consumption almost doubles. In power aware routing, transmission power depends on the distance between the source and destination, whereas in cost aware routing; the routing decision is based on the remaining lifetime of the node. Routing depends on the power control, since the power level dictates what links are available to forward the data packets (Sánchez & Ruiz, 2006).

1.1. Some of the Applications in Mobile Ad Hoc Network

a. The main aim of the MANET is to provide communication for end-users anywhere and anytime. Typical applications include disaster recovery and army operations. The MANET is not bound it specific conditions. The networks may equally show better performance in other places. For example, we can imagine a group of people with laptops at a company meeting where no network service is present or in emergency disaster relief situations coordinating efforts after a cyclone.
b. The MANET supports real time application and streaming video and audio deliverance as well as remote monitoring using micro-sensors.
c. The MANET can also monitor health and provide home networking for everyday appliances.
d. Wireless mesh networks are ad hoc wireless networks that are designed to provide communication infrastructure using mobile devices.
e. The MANET provides alternative paths to transmit data from the source to the destination. It is also provides quick reconfiguration of the link when a path fails.
f. In emergency situations, such as cyclones, the wired network could be obliterated. In this type of situation, the MANET can be used to transmit data from one node to another.

2. BACKGROUND

This section discusses some existing algorithms regarding power aware information in MANET. In the MANET, mobile nodes operate with limited battery power that require frequent recharging and replacement, which is undesirable or even impossible. When a node suffers a power failure, it will affect the node's ability to forward data packets to others. For this reason, many researchers have devoted great energy to design an energy aware routing protocol (Sánchez & Ruiz, 2006). Several recent studies have tried to increase the lifetimes of nodes and networks by using power aware metrics at different layers.

2.1. Power Controlled MAC Protocol

Power Controlled MAC Protocol (PCMA) model was proposed for MANETs, where a sender uses an appropriate transmission power level to transmit the data packets so as to increase the channel utilization and save battery power. In the PCMA model, utilization of a channel can be significantly increased because signal overlapping is reduced. The focus of PCMA model is to provide effective utilization of the channel by using the transmission power control model. The drawback of PCMA model is that it does not address the issues like how to update the topology and how to use reactive routing protocols with the help of power control models (Wu, Tseng & Sheu, 2000).

2.2. Power Aware Multi Access Protocol with Signaling

Power Aware Multi Access Protocol with Signaling (PAMAS) model is an energy efficient media access control protocol for the MANETs (Singh & Raghavendra, 1998). It uses the separate signaling channel protocol apart from the channel to transmit the data. The request-to-send and clear-to-send packets are forwarded before the packets are transmitted. The PAMAS model achieves its goal by keeping nodes in sleeping mode. The PAMAS protocol is tested in a random network, a line topology, and a fully connected network. The PAMAS protocol exhibits the best performance under a light load as well as a smaller number of nodes.

2.3. Minimum Total Transmission Power Routing

Minimum Total Transmission Power Routing (MTPR) model tries to minimize the total transmission power consumption of the nodes participating in a path (Scott & Bambos, 1996). In a dynamic environment, the MTPR model does not distribute energy consumption among all the nodes equally, while other models can efficiently balance the usage of the residual energy capacity of all the nodes. If we consider a common link $L_d = n_0, n_2, \ldots, n_D$, here, n_0 is the source and n_D is the destination and a task is $T(n_i, n_{i+1})$. The total transmission-power for all the paths is measured as follows (Singh & Raghavendra, 1998):

$$P(L_d) = \sum_{i=0}^{D-1} T(n_i, n_{i+1}) \qquad (1)$$

The optimal path (L_o) is the path that best satisfies the following:

$$P(L_o) = \underset{L_k \in L_*}{Min}\, P(L_k) \qquad (2)$$

The required transmission power is proportional to $d^{ä}$, where d is the distance between two nodes and $ä$ lies in between 2 and 4. The L_* contains all feasible paths. The drawback of this model is that the MTPR model selects a path containing more number of hops as intermediate nodes. The MTPR model allows more number of nodes participating in the network while forwarding the data packets. It also increases the end-to-end delay. The MTPR model fails to consider the remaining battery capacity of the nodes so that it may not be succeed in extending the lifetime of each node in the network (Rappaport, 1999).

2.4. Minimum Battery Cost Routing

In Minimum Battery Cost Routing (MBCR), the total transmission power is a significant parameter as it concerns the lifetime of the nodes (Singh, Woo & Raghavendra, 1998). This parameter can decrease the consumption of total transmission power over the network, but it has a dangerous drawback. The MBCR model does not consider the usage of node lifetime effectively. If the minimum total transmission power paths run through a particular node, the battery of the node will be drained rapidly and this node will die quickly. Therefore, the remaining battery capacity of each node is a more perfect parameter to express the lifetime of the node.

Let us assume that $B_i(t)$ is the battery capacity of node i and battery cost of node i is measured as follow:

$$C_i(t)=1/B_i(t) \tag{3}$$

If the battery capacity of the node is low, then the cost of node i will be increased. The battery cost of path(L_e) consists of node D and is measured as follows:

$$R(L_e) = \sum_{i=0}^{D-1} C_i(t) \tag{4}$$

Here, we should select a path i that has the minimum battery cost and which has the maximum remaining battery capacity of the nodes.

$$R(L_o) = \underset{L_e \in L_*}{Min}\, R(L_e) \tag{5}$$

In the MBCR model, the remaining battery capacity is directly applied to the routing process. It voids the usage of overused nodes, thereby increasing the lifetime of the nodes. If all the nodes contain equal battery capacity, then it will select a path having the fewest number of nodes. In path selection, it considers the sum of battery cost of all the nodes. The drawback of this model is that a path using nodes with little remaining battery capacity may be still used (Gobriel, Mosse & Melhem, 2006).

2.5. Min-Max Battery Cost Routing

Here, Min-Max Battery Cost Routing (MMBCR) model treats the nodes more fairly from the standpoint of their remaining battery capacities. The nodes with the least remaining battery capacity and the nodes with highest residual-battery capacities are chosen as a path (Singh, Woo & Raghavendra, 1998; Gobriel, Mosse & Melhem, 2006; Harous, Aldubai & Nasir, 2008).

$$C_i(t)=1/B_i(t)$$

The path cost is measured as follows:

$$R(L_e) = \underset{n_i \in L_*}{Max}\, C_i(t) \tag{6}$$

$$R(L_o) = \underset{L_e \in L_*}{Min}\, R(L_e) \tag{7}$$

In Equation 7, the MMBCR model selects a path with minimum cost among all. However, there is no guarantee that the total transmission power is minimized (Wu, Tseng, Lin & Sheu, 2002).

2.6. Maximum Residual Packet Capacity Battery Cost Routing

Maximum Residual Packet Capacity Battery Cost Routing (MRPC) model was presented in Misra and Banerjee (2002). It works like a MMBCR model, but it recognizes the ability of a node not just by the residual battery capacity. It is also anticipating the energy spent in routing a packet over the connection. In the MRPC model, the nodes can change their transmission powers energetically based on the distance between the nodes. It is also integrating the effect of link layer error rates and packet retransmissions. The node lifetime is measured as follows:

$$N_i(t) = \frac{RB_i(t)}{TP_i(t)} \tag{8}$$

In Equation 8, RB_i is the residual battery capacity of the node i and TP_i is transmission energy required by the nodes i to j. The RB_i is based on the transmission power of the node *i* and is measured as follows:

$$RB_i(t) = RB_i(o) - \int_0^t TP_i(t)dt$$

$$V_{ij} = {RB_i(t)} \Big/ {TP_{ij}(t)} \quad (9)$$

The link $i,j \in V$ and the transmission power is $TP_{ii}=d_{ij}^{\theta}$. Here, *d* is the distance between the nodes *i* and *j*. The θ value lies in between 2 and 4.

$$P_j = Min \sum_{i,j=0} V_{ij} \quad (10)$$

Power aware routing algorithms must consider metrics like residual battery energy of the node and channel characteristics of the link to forward the data packets (Misra & Banerjee, 2002). These metrics increase the network lifetime and network throughput. The MRPC model chooses a path with the largest packet capacity at the critical nodes, which have the smallest residual packet transmission capacity (Sankara, Chbeir & Krishnamurthi, 2008).

2.7. Conditional Max-Min Battery Capacity Routing

Conditional Max-Min Battery Capacity Routing (CMMBCR) model takes into account the residual battery capacity of the node and total transmission power consumed while selecting a path (Toh, 2001). The CMMBCR is a hybrid protocol that attempts to arbitrate between the MTPR model and MMBCR models. When all the nodes in some possible paths have sufficient battery capacities, a path with the minimum total transmission power among all the paths is chosen. In order to maximize the lifetime of the network, the power consumption rate of each node must be evenly distributed. However, if all the nodes in a given path have higher remaining battery capacity(threshold value), then it chooses a path using the MTPR model, otherwise is selects the path(L_o)with the maximum remaining battery capacity by using the MMBCR model.

$$R(L_e) \geq \theta, \text{ for any path } L_{e \in L_*} \quad (11)$$

$$R(L_o) \geq \underset{L_e \in L_*}{Min}\, R(L_e) \quad (12)$$

The drawback of this model is that there is no guarantee to provide higher throughput (Balaswamy & Soundararajan, 2008; Ahmad S., Awan, Waqqas & Ahmad B., 2008). It does not consider the network coverage and network partition.

2.8. Power Aware Source Routing

Power Aware Source Routing (PSR) model was developed by Maleki, Dantu and Pedram (2002) to increase the lifetime of the network. The PSR model is used by a source initiated routing algorithm for the MANETs. The PSR model is obtained from the DSR model. The difference between the DSR and PSR models is that in the DSR model, the packets are transmitted along the shortest path in terms of the minimum number of hops. Node mobility and the energy depletion of nodes may cause a path to become an invalid path in the PSR model.

The PSR model is highly desirable in the MANET, since death of certain nodes leads to possible network partitioning, thus rendering other live nodes unreachable. The PSR model finds a path during the route discovery time(*t*), which is measured as follows:

$$Min(P_{j,t}) = \sum_{k \in AP} C_k(t) \quad (13)$$

$$C_k(t) = {(TP_k * FB_k)}/{(RB_k)} \quad (14)$$

Where TP_k is the transmission power of node k, FB_k is the fully charged battery capacity of node k and RB_k is the remaining battery capacity of node k at time t. The drawback of this model is that the destination node has to wait for some time after the arrival of the first RREQ packet to receive more than one possible path and then select a path with the minimum cost.

2.9. Minimum Drain Rate Routing

Minimum Drain Rate Routing (MDRR) model was proposed by Kim, Garcia-Luna-Aceves, Obraczka, Cano and Manzoni (2002). The MDRR model includes the drain rate metric in the routing process. The MDRR model behaves like power aware routing. It can be applied into one of the MANET routing protocols while finding a path from the source to destination. The MDRR model provides 2 objectives: extending the lifetime of each node and making the energy expenditure is evenly distributing among all the nodes. It avoids the over-dissipation of specific nodes by taking the current traffic into account and by utilizing the drain rate of the node's residual battery capacity. The main aim of the MDRR model is not just to extend the lifetime of each node more than that of MMBCR model, but to avoid the over-dissipation of energy at the critical nodes. It is good at mirroring the present dissipation of energy without considering queue length and number of connections passing through the nodes (Kim, Garcia-Luna-Aceves, Obraczka, Cano & Manzoni, 2003). The MDRR model does not guarantee that the total transmission power is minimized over the chosen path as compared to the MTPR model.

3. POWER AWARE ROUTING WITHOUT CRITICAL NODES

The existing model, similar to the MTPR model, transmits the data packets over the nodes with the least transmission power. Due to less transmission power, some of the nodes will receive more packets to forward to others. This model leads to network partition because critical nodes may die soon. In order to overcome the network partition problem, the PARWCN model uses 2 metrics namely, residual battery capacity of the node and noncritical nodes over the network. During the message transmission, the proposed model does not use critical-nodes for transmission of data packets over the network. For example, in Figure 2, the shortest path routing in terms of hops and transmission power will forward the packets for paths 1→7, 2→5 and 4→6 through node 3. The shortest path routing causes node 3 to die pretty early.

3.1. Solutions

In the MANET, one of the major concerns is to reduce the power usage or battery depletion level of each node in the network so that the overall lifetime of the network can be lengthened as much as possible. Special routing strategies are needed to minimize the battery depletion level

Figure 2. Problem with shortest path routing in term of hop/minimum power as metrics

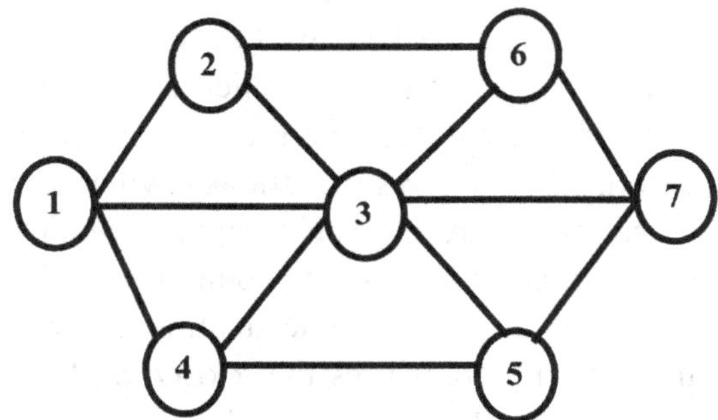

of the intermediate nodes, while at the same time forwarding data packets from the source to the destination. The battery power of each node is an important metric to determine a path. The PARWCN model addresses the problem of power aware routing algorithm, which forwards the data packets from the source to destination. The residual battery capacity and noncritical nodes are used to forward data packets from the source node to the destination.

Definition 1:

A graph $G\Xi(N,V)$ is a finite non-empty set of the nodes and collection of the links. The N is a set of nodes and V is a set of links. Each node is assigned a number(n_1,n_2, n_3,.....)∈N. But for $(x,y)\in V$, the adjacence matrix is defined as follows:

$$a = \begin{cases} 1 & if(x,y)\in V \\ 0 & \end{cases}$$

If A is 1, then the link exists between 2 nodes, else it does not exist over the network.

3.2. Route Discovery

The PARWCN model uses the DSR protocol to forward data packets from the source to the destination. The route discovery process is initiated by the source node. The source node specifies the entire path in a packet-header itself to the destination. The route discovery process allows the nodes to discover a path to the destination by using a Route Request(RREQ) packet as shown in the Table 1. In the RREQ packet, the *type* field indicates the type of packet, which is sent over the network and the *flag* field is used to make the synchronization. The *reserved* field, having value 0, is used to ignore the packet upon reception. The *hop-count* field is used to count the number of hops from the source to destination. In order to indentify a path, it uses the *RREQ_ID* field. The *originator-IP* field indicates the IP address of the source node. The *destination-IP* indicates the address of the destination node. The *originator-sequence number* field provides the current sequence number of the route entries to the source node. The *destination- sequence number* is used for the route entries pointing to the destination. The $N_i(t)$ field indicates the lifetime of the node at time t. The $V_{ij}(t)$ indicates the lifetime of a link and $NPR_{i(A\rightarrow B)}(t)$ field represents the number of possible paths.

3.3. Route Selection

Based on the RR packet, the source node uses the lifetime of the node and values of the noncritical nodes to choose a path. In order to maximize the lifetime of the network, the power consumption rate of each node must be evenly distributed. However, if all nodes with higher remaining battery capacities are above the threshold value(θ), then the PARWCN model chooses a path with the help of noncritical nodes, otherwise it selects a path with the maximum remaining battery capacity. The PARWCN model forwards the data packets as follows:

Case 1: Residual-Battery Capacity

The PARWCN model chooses a path containing the maximum remaining power of the nodes.

Table 1. RREQ packet

Type	J	R	G	U	Reserved	Hop-count
RREQ-ID						
Originator IP						
Originator-sequence number						
Destination IP						
Destination-sequence number						
$N_i(t)$						
$V_{ij}(t)$						
$NPR_{i(A\rightarrow B)}(t)$						

Definition 2:

The node lifetime is measured as follows:

$$N_i(t) = \frac{RB_i(t)}{TP_i(t)} \quad (15)$$

The residual battery capacity of the node, based on the transmission power, is measured as:

$$RB_i(t) = RB_i(0) - \int_0^t TP_i(t)dt$$

Definition 3:

The lifetime of each link is measured as:

$$V_{ij} = \frac{RB_i(t)}{TP_{ij}(t)}$$

The link $i,j \in V$ and the transmission power is $TP_{ii}=d_{ij}^{\theta}$. Where, d is the distance between the nodes i and j. The θ value lies in between 2 and 4.

$$P_j = Min\sum_{i,j=0} V_{ij}$$

Definition 4:

The lifetime of the network is defined as how long the nodes can survive in the network.

$$NET = Min\left\{\frac{RB_{i(t)}}{TP_{i(t)}}\right\}$$

$$NET = \underset{i,j \in G(v)}{Min}\left\{V_{ij}\right\} \quad (16)$$

If all the mobile nodes have higher battery power, the network lifetime will be increased.

Case 2: Noncritical Nodes

The nodes (critical nodes) connect various parts of the network and hence the survival of critical nodes is vital to maintaining the multiple paths. If the system uses the critical nodes more frequently, then there will be chance of network partition. To avoid the network partition problem, the PARWCN model uses the noncritical nodes, if they have sufficient residual battery power, the lifetime of the network increases and the chances of network partition decreases.

Let us assume that S is the source node and D is the destination node. The S wants to transmit the data to D. There will also, of course, be some intermediate nodes. If we use the critical nodes as intermediate nodes frequently, these nodes may drain-out. In order to increase the life of critical nodes, the cost of critical nodes is measured as follows:

$$C_j(P_{k,S->D})(t) = \frac{NPR_{j(S->D)}(t) - APR_{j(S->D}(t)}{NPR_{j(S->D)}(t)} \quad (17)$$

In Equation(17), $NPR_{i(S\rightarrow D)}$ indicates the number of possible paths from S to D via node i. $APR_{i(S\rightarrow D)}$ represents the number of possible paths from the S to D without going through node i. The PARWCN model assigns the weights for all the paths based on the network requirements and performance.

$$P_j = Max\sum_{l=0}^{n-1} c_l \quad (18)$$

Here, the source destination pair chooses an efficient path by using the route selection mechanism. The best path is selected using the Equations 15 and 18.

For example, in 1,000 m X 1,000 m area with 100 nodes out of which 30 nodes are considered as sources. The number of data packets sent between 5-60 packets/sec. Each node moves with the velocity of 0-20 m/sec and the simulation model was executed 25 times. Each node is initialized with 510 joules and the total simulation time was 1,000 sec. Figure 3 shows the number of surviving nodes over the network. The MTTPR model attempts to minimize the total transmission power consumed per packet, irrespective of the lifetime of a node. Therefore, there is no guarantee to extend network lifetime. The MTTPR model provides longer lifetime connections despite a shorter node lifetime because it is able to easily acquire many alternative routes. The CMMBCR model tries to evenly distribute energy consumption among all the nodes by using residual battery power. However, it allows the nodes to accept all the requests if the nodes have enough battery power, regardless of the current traffic conditions. The PARWCN model extends both the network and node lifetimes because the load is evenly distributed among all the nodes. It avoids the dissipation of nodes by taking into residual battery capacity and non-critical nodes into account. Results show that the PARWCN model keeps the nodes for a longer period of times over the network. For example, the nodes start to die at 450 sec, 501 sec, 575 sec, 600 sec for the MTTPR, CMMBCR, LPR and PARWCN models, respectively.

4. FUTURE RESEARCH

Energy consumption in a network may reveal if a topology aware protocol is practical in real life. For example, if a protocol keeps on using certain nodes in the network because they are more static, it may lead to an isolated network after these nodes deplete their power and go offline. Expanding the use of route stability metrics beyond route discovery may also yield interesting results. If the stability of each link in a path is evaluated during data communication, preemptive path failure predictions may be issued by the nodes that sense an imminent link failure. This can improve system performance in many ways. First, it reduces the delay resulting from re-establishing a valid path to the destination. Secondly, it improves energy efficiency by reducing the number of failed transmissions.

Figure 3. Number of survived nodes

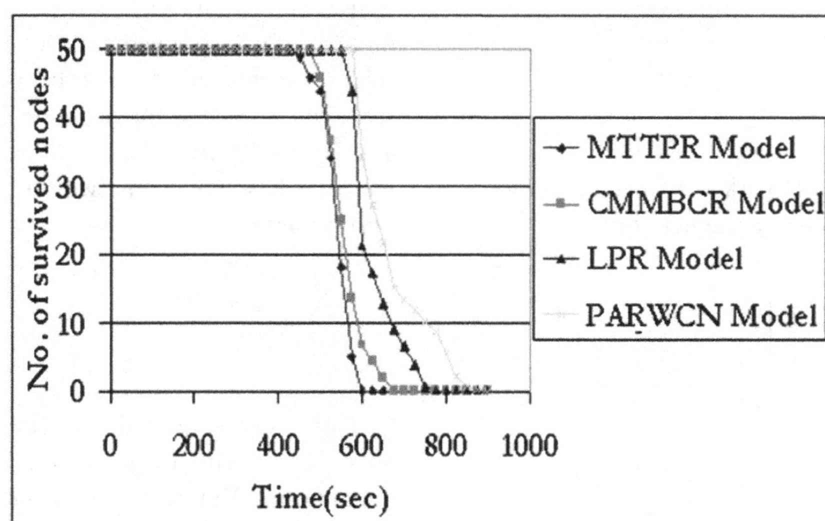

Some intuitive ideas for improving the system include:

- A better choice of paths where data packets get routed through longer paths but pass through nodes that have sufficient remaining battery capacity.
- Routing data packets through lightly loaded nodes is also energy-conserving because the contention will be lessened, resulting in fewer collisions, thus requiring less energy.

5. CONCLUSION

This chapter discussed power aware routing algorithms for the MANETs. We presented different efficient power aware routing algorithms for the MANETs by considering the total transmission power, residual battery capacity, and network connectivity. The PAMAS protocol exhibits the best performance under a light load. The MTPR model reduces power consumption among all the nodes. It fails, however, to consider the remaining battery capacity of the nodes; consequently, it may not succeed in extending the lifetime of each node in the network. In the MBCR model, a path holding the nodes with little remaining battery capacity may be still selected. The MMBCR model increases the lifetime of a node, but there is no guarantee that the system will decrease power consumption of the node. The MRPC model chooses a path, which has the largest relay capacity in terms of packets at the critical node with the smaller residual packet transmission capacity. The CMMBCR model forwards the packets from the source to destination, based on the threshold value. If a node has sufficient battery power, then the system uses the MTPR model to forward the packets. The PSR model is derived from the DSR model. In the PSR model, the destination node has to wait for some time after the first RREQ packet to the source node. The main objective of the MDRR model is to increase the lifetime of a network as compared to the MMBCR model. It avoids the over-dissipation of energy at the critical nodes. The PARRWNN model forwards the data packets based on residual battery capacity and noncritical nodes. This increases the lifetime of the network and throughput.

ACKNOWLEDGMENT

We want to express our gratitude towards the IGI Publications for giving us the opportunity to write this topic. Many thanks to our Colleagues at the Department of Computer Science and Engineering, BMS College of Engineering, Bangalore, India to support me for writing this book.

Several people helped us during the course of writing this book. We would like to specially thank all colleagues at B.M.S. College of Engineering, Bangalore and Dr. RSD. Wahidabanu, Professor and Head of the department of Electronics and Communication Engineering, Government College of Engineering, Salem, India.

The main bulk of the work was carried out by my students, namely Siva Kumar, Siva Murthy, Siva Shankar, Lashmi Kantha H.A., Manjula M., C. Y. Latha, and C. Y. Sai Rakesh Yadav. Secondly, we express our gratitude to them.

Thirdly, I want to thank Dr. S. R. Krishana Murthy, Dr. M. K. Venkatesha, Prof. K. Girish and Prof. Basavara Jakkali for their constant encouragements to do this work.

Finally, our thanks go to our family members for their supports and encouragement throughout this work.

6. REFERENCES

Ahmad, S., Awan, I., Waqqas, A., & Ahmad, B. (2008). Performance analysis of DSR and extended DSR protocols. In *Proceedings of the International Conference on Modeling and Simulation* (pp.191-196).

Balaswamy, C., & Soundararajan, K. (2008). An efficient route discovery mechanism for mobile ad hoc networks. *International Journal of Computer Science and Network Security*, *8*(10), 25–51.

Chao, C. M., Sheu, J. P., & Chou, I. C. (2006). An adaptive quorum-based energy conserving protocol for IEEE 802.11 ad hoc networks. *IEEE Transactions on Mobile Computing*, *5*(5), 166–170.

De Moraes, R. M., Sadjadpour, H. R., & Garcia-Luna-Aceves, J. J. (2006). Mobility-capacity-delay trade-off in wireless ad hoc networks. *Ad Hoc Networks*, *4*(5), 607–620. doi:10.1016/j.adhoc.2005.06.005

Gobriel, S., Mosse, D., & Melhem, R. (2006). Mitigating the flooding waves problem in energy-efficient routing for MANETs. In *Proceedings of the IEEE Conference on Distributed Computing Systems* (pp. 47-47). New York: IEEE.

Harous, S., Aldubai, M., & Nasir, Q. (2008). An energy aware multi-path routing algorithm for mobile ad hoc networks. *International Journal of Business Data Communications and Networking*, *4*(2), 58–75.

Kim, D., Garcia-Luna-Aceves, J. J., Obraczka, K., Cano, J., & Manzoni, P. (2002). Power-aware routing based on the energy drain rate for mobile ad hoc networks. In *Proceedings of the IEEE International Conference on Computer Communication and Networks* (pp. 565-569). New York: IEEE.

Kim, D., Garcia-Luna-Aceves, J. J., Obraczka, K., Cano, J., & Manzoni, P. (2003). Routing mechanisms for mobile ad hoc networks based on the energy drain rate. *IEEE Transactions on Mobile Computing*, *2*(2), 161–173. doi:10.1109/TMC.2003.1217236

Kumar, A., & Singh, M. (n.d.). *Power-aware routing in mobile ad hoc networks* [Seminar report]. Retrieved from http://www.it.iitb.ac.in/~mukesh/mywebsite/Acads/Courses/QoS/SeminarReport.pdf

Ma, C., & Yang, Y. (2005). A prioritized battery-aware routing protocol for wireless ad hoc networks. In *Proceedings of the ACM International Symposium on Modeling, Analysis and Simulation of Wireless and Mobile Systems* (pp. 45-52). New York: ACM.

Maleki, M., Dantu, K., & Pedram, M. (2002). Power-aware source routing protocol for mobile ad hoc networks. In *Proceedings of the ISLPED*, (pp. 72-75).

Misra, A., & Banerjee, S. (2002). MRPC: Maximizing network lifetime for reliable routing in wireless environments. In []. New York: IEEE.]. *Proceedings of the IEEE Wireless Communication and Networking Conference*, *2*, 800–806.

Rappaport, T. S. (1999). *Wireless communications: Principles and practice*. Englewood Cliffs, NJ: Prentice Hall.

Sánchez, J. A., & Ruiz, P. (2006). Improving delivery ratio and power efficiency in unicast geographic routing with a realistic physical layer for wireless sensor networks. In *Proceedings of The IEEE DSD* (pp. 591-597). New York: IEEE.

Sankara, S., Chbeir, R., & Krishnamurthi, S. (2008). Efficient power aware and reputation-based routing protocol for MANET. *Journal of Digital Information Management*, *6*(1), 21–28.

Scott, K., & Bambos, N. (1996). Routing and channel assignment for low power transmission in PCS. In. *Proceedings of the International Conference on Universal Personal Communications*, *2*, 498–502. doi:10.1109/ICUPC.1996.562623

Singh, S., & Raghavendra, C. S. (1998). PAMAS: Power aware multi-access protocol with signalling for ad hoc networks. *ACM Computer Communication Review*, *28*(3), 5–26. doi:10.1145/293927.293928

Singh, S., Woo, M., & Raghavendra, C. S. (1998). Power aware routing in mobile ad hoc networks. In *Proceedings of the ACM MobiCom* (pp. 181-190). New York: ACM.

Toh, C. K. (2001). Maximum battery life routing to support ubiquitous mobile computing in wireless ad hoc networks. *IEEE Communications*, *39*(6), 138–147. doi:10.1109/35.925682

Wu, S., Tseng, Y. C., & Sheu, J. (2000). Intelligent medium access for mobile ad hoc networks with busy tones and power control. *IEEE Journal on Selected Areas in Communications*, *18*, 1647–1657. doi:10.1109/49.872953

Wu, S. L., Tseng, Y. C., Lin, C. Y., & Sheu, J. P. (2002). A multi-channel MAC protocol with power control for multi-hop mobile ad hoc networks. *The Computer Journal*, *45*(1), 101–110. doi:10.1093/comjnl/45.1.101

Chapter 9
Network Address Management in MANETs Using an Ant Colony Metaphor

Alvaro Pachón
Universidad Icesi, Colombia

Juan M. Madrid
Universidad Icesi, Colombia

ABSTRACT

Address management is a critical network process, since any node wishing to join a network must first obtain an address. Network address management in a mobile ad-hoc network (MANET) is a particular challenge due to the unique operating conditions of such networks, their dynamic topology, and the events that take place inside them. This chapter presents a proposal for solving the address management problem in a MANET by applying the self-organization and emergency principles governing the behavior of social insect colonies, particularly ant colonies.

INTRODUCTION

This chapter presents a solution to the network address management problem in a MANET.

The chapter follows this structure: First, we will identify the unique operation features of a MANET. Then, we will present several approaches that have been proposed in order to solve the network address management problem. Next, we will present and support the utilization of two key concepts in our solution, namely, the self-organization concept and the ant colony metaphor. Finally, we present the design of a self-organized network address assignment function, inspired in an ant colony behavior, and evaluation results for the proposed model.

DOI: 10.4018/978-1-60960-027-3.ch009

BACKGROUND

A MANET is defined as an autonomous system, integrated by mobile hosts using wireless links to communicate with each other (Murthy & Manoj, 2004). Such hosts constitute a temporary network without the need for centralized management, but without the normally available network support services. Network nodes may move in a random fashion and organize themselves arbitrarily. Thus, topology in a MANET may change dynamically, in a very fast and unpredictable manner. The unique features of a MANET must be taken into account as design directives, and also as performance constraints, when designing protocols for them.

Some characteristics of a MANET are:

a) Nodes generate dynamic topologies. Nodes move freely in any direction, at any speed, and require a high capability of adaptation in the network.
b) Routing works in a multi-hop fashion. Each node in the network can behave as a router, and may participate cooperatively in packet delivery through an established route.
c) Bandwidth constraints. This is due to the wireless nature of the communication channels. Constraints considered here include multiple accesses to the channel, multipath interference, noise, fading and limited available spectrum; all these constraints cause limited data transmission rates.
d) Power-restricted operation. This directly impacts proposed algorithms for this kind of network, since these algorithms must not be processor-intensive.
e) Limited physical security. Because it is decentralized, a MANET is robust because it does not have a unique point of failure. However, MANETs are also vulnerable to multiple types of attacks.
f) Scalability limitations. This point is extremely important and complex due to resource limitations.

THE NETWORK ADDRESS ASSIGNMENT PROBLEM

Every node connected to a network needs a unique ID address. This address allows the node to take part in any information exchange. For this reason, address management in a network is a critical task. Address management activities include: a) selecting, reserving and assigning a unique address to every node in the network; b) releasing/recovering the address of a node leaving the network; c) solving address conflicts, if they happen, and d) solving events that negatively impact network stability, if they occur.

Two approaches for network address assignment are used in the wired network environment: the static approach, in which the network administrator assigns a network address to each network node in a manual fashion; and the dynamic approach, which needs no intervention from the network administrator. In this approach, network address assignment is implemented as a network service through the Dynamic Host Configuration Protocol (DHCP).

Neither of these two approaches can be applied directly in a MANET, because:

- MANETs have no infrastructure, and
- Nodes are mobile and move dynamically. This may prevent the DHCP server from being permanently available. Also, other nodes might not be able to establish a communication path to such a server.

The dynamic nature of MANETs generates events that do not take place in wired networks, such as network partition and merging. A MANET is partitioned when it splits into two or more subnetworks; similarly, a merge event occurs when two or more MANETs become a single network. All of these events cause the network address assignment process in a MANET to be particularly complex.

Approaches for Network Address Assignment

This section presents the different approaches proposed to solve the network address assignment problem. This is done in order to identify the key aspects and basic features a new solution approach should take into account.

Approaches for automatic network address configuration can be classified by the following two broad criteria:

a) Presence of an address assignment table. Following this criterion, solutions can be classified as stateful or stateless.
b) The address assignment process. Following this criterion, solutions can be classified as conflict-detection based and conflict-free.

Address autoconfiguration solutions can be classified into: (Weniger & Zitterbart, 2004)

a. *Stateful solutions*. This kind of solution assumes the presence of a central entity, responsible for managing the network address assignment table. Several mechanisms exist to manage this table. From this perspective, solutions can be classified as follows:
   1. *Solutions using a central address assignment table*. In this kind of solution, only one node in the network is able to assign addresses to non-configured nodes. In order for this scheme to work, the address assignment node must be permanently reachable (which cannot be always guaranteed due to the nature of MANETs). This node must be dynamically elected, and its role can migrate from one node to another over time. When an address change is needed, all involved nodes must be notified in a trustable way, so they can re-register or acquire a new address. Examples for this kind of solution are the IP Address Configuration Algorithm for Zeroconf MANETs (Gunes & Reibel, 2002) and SAAP – Simple Address Autoconfiguration Protocol (Indrayan, 2006).
   2. *Solutions using a single distributed address assignment table*. Examples for this approach are ManetConf (Nesargi & Prakash, 2002), Boleng's Protocol and Prophet Allocation Protocol (Zhou, Ni, & Mutka, 2003).
   3. *Solutions using multiple, disjoint, distributed address assignment tables*. Examples for this approach are the Buddy protocol, and the proposals by Mohsin and Prakash (2002) and Tayal and Patanaik (2004).

The two latter kinds of solutions are referred to as distributed solutions. They require synchronization among nodes in order to avoid duplicate addresses. This synchronization needs to be efficient and reliable, both hard goals to accomplish in a MANET environment. In order to achieve this, the network must be flooded periodically with synchronization requests, which consumes bandwidth resources. When two or more MANETs merge together, they have to synchronize their address tables and identify potential conflicts produced by the merge event.

b. *Stateless solutions*. In this kind of solution, nodes do not use address assignment tables. Whenever a node needs to communicate with others (and hence, requires an address), it assigns itself an address, either at random or as a function of the network interface hardware address. Then, the address uniqueness is carried out in a distributed fashion, running a duplicate address detection (DAD) process. This process is accomplished by sending broadcast messages; however, in a MANET it is uncertain whether or not a broadcast message reaches all the nodes in the network; thus, this issue should be considered and overcome in any proposed solution. Some examples for this approach are: IP address autoconfiguration for Ad Hoc Networks (Perkins et al., 2001), PDAD-Passive Duplicate Address Detection (Weniger, 2003), Weak DAD (Vaidya, 2002), QDAD-Query Duplicate Address Detection, and the AIPAC protocol (Fazio, Villari & Pulifito, 2005).

c. *Hybrid approach.* This family of solutions combines features of the two aforementioned families. They may offer better performance, but at the cost of greater complexity and overhead. Examples for this approach are the HCQA (Hybrid Centralized Query-Based Autoconfiguration) protocol (Sun & Belding-Royer, 2003), the PACMAN (Passive Autoconfiguration for Mobile Ad Hoc Network) protocol (Weniger, 2005) and the approach described in Distributed Protocol for Dynamic Address Assignment in MANET (Thoppian & Prakash, 2006).

Self-Organization

The self-organization principle has its origins in biological systems. Living organisms are formed by cells that specialize in executing specific tasks and from their individual and local behavior. Self-organization makes it possible to generate a much more complex and sophisticated structure: a living organism.

The first articles on self-organization were written in the 1960s. Ashby, Foerster, and Zopf (1962) and Foerster (2003) pioneered the analysis of the self-organization mechanisms. Later, Eigen (1979) introduced the self-organization concepts to engineering.

In order to understand a MANET as a self-organized system, we must start with the definition of an organized system. An organized system has a structure (its composing entities have some degree of organization and interaction) and a function (it serves a purpose). Thus, in a self-organized system, its internal entities will establish an organizational structure, without the need of a central coordinator. Such entities work directly and continuously in a peer-to-peer distributed fashion, reacting to changes in their local environment. This leads to better flexibility, adaptability, scalability and fault tolerance of the system. All these features are highly desirable in a MANET.

The methods for defining and characterizing the self-organization methodologies required in MANETs can be defined using two terms (Dressler, 2006): self-organization and emergency. Self-organization is defined as a process in which a global behavior appears (emerges) in the system, as a consequence of numerous interactions among the low-level components of the system. Additionally, rules specifying interactions among the low-level components are executed using exclusively local information, without reference to a global pattern. In turn, an emergent behavior (emergency) is defined as the result of collaboration among low-level components of the system.

The following are the most salient characteristics in a self- organized system (Prehofer & Bettstetter, 2005): a) Control in a self-organized system is distributed and localized; b) Individual behavior (microscopic behavior) determines the system's resulting structure and operation (macroscopic behavior); c) Application of a simple conduct at the microscopic level causes a sophisticated system organization (emergent behavior); d) The system is able to adapt in a coordinated fashion to changes inside itself, or in the environment; e) The system tries to converge towards beneficial structures while avoiding undesirable ones; f) The system is reliable against failures as a consequence of its intrinsic adaptability and distributed nature. This reliability implies the system is able to detect and correct failures without external help, and, in case of a component failure, the system degrades slowly; and g) A self-organized system is highly scalable.

Thus, if a MANET is modeled as a self-organized system, the result will be a more scalable, flexible, failure tolerant network. At the same time, it will take less effort to manage and configure such a network, as a result of self-organization. In order to use the self-organization principle in a MANET environment, a constructive approach is used: To solve a complex connectivity problem, one must first design a set of rules and protocols governing interactions among the network nodes.

The Ant Colony Metaphor

Nature has been an inspirational source for breakthrough solutions to several problems in engineering. In Dorigo and Di Caro (1999), the swarm intelligence concept is defined as a computational and behavioral metaphor, based on the group behavior of social insects (such as termites, bees and ants) and certain animals (such as birds and fish), which exhibit several forms of "intelligence" (useful behaviors), that emerge to the colony level as a result of local interactions among the individuals making part of the colony.

In particular, we will study the behavior and the dynamics of an ant colony. Ants are social insects that work and live in colonies. As a result of the mutual cooperation happening among the colony members, the whole colony exhibits complex behavioral patterns, enabling it to carry on tasks that would be very difficult from an individual point of view. For example, when ants of some species require leaving the anthill in order to search for food, they move towards the source of food laying down a chemical substance known as a pheromone. That pheromone enables ants to communicate indirectly by modifying the perception of the physical space they are in. This way of communication is known as stigmergy. When ants find no traces of pheromone along their path, they move randomly; on the other hand, when a trace of pheromone is found, ants tend to follow that trace. Thus, we can state that ants select the path to follow by using a probabilistic decision mechanism, biased by the amount of pheromone present.

As more and more ants follow the same path, they lay down more pheromone, generating a self-reinforcement effect, ultimately marking that path as the optimal trajectory towards the food source. This effect is known as the self-catalytic effect, and it can be understood as the phenomenon of leading a higher proportion of ants to the shortest path to the food, due to the high pheromone levels. The whole process is completed by the action of the environment, which causes the evaporation of the pheromone after some time. This whole process (stigmergy, pheromone laying-down, pheromone evaporation) allows ants to find the shortest path between their anthill and the food source.

The social behavior of the individuals making part of the colony can be emulated in a computing environment to solve different kinds of problems. Features common to both environments are: a) emergent behaviors can be understood from the interactions among individuals in a distributed society (natural environment case) or from the cooperative work among a group of autonomous agents (computational environment case); b) both environments use a distributed control approach, controlling the behavior of the individuals in the colony, or the agents in the computational environment; c) communications and interactions among individuals in the colony/agents in the system are localized; d) individuals in the colony/agents take stochastic decisions, as a consequence of their partial view of the environment; e) emergent behaviors are much more complex than the individual behaviors of the colony members/agents; colony members/agents interact by following very simple rules; and g) the system's global response is robust, adaptable and scalable.

Dorigo and Di Caro (1999) identify the features a system designed observing the swarm intelligence principles should have. It is important to recognize these features in order to transfer them as design premises for a proposal for automatic configuration of network addresses in MANETs. In such an environment, individuals in the colony behave as computational agents. Features noted by the author are: a) agents in the computing environment should require assignment of simple, limited resources, due to their extremely simple behavior; b) strict, centralized control should not be applied; c) agents act in a simple, localized way; d) agents do not require knowledge about the system's global task. The global task should emerge as a consequence of local interactions among agents; and e) the system should generate useful, global behaviors through self-organization. The main goal is to generate complexity from simplicity, by using simple, robust and highly adaptable algorithms.

Application of the Ant Colony Metaphor

We will solve the network address assignment problem by using a computing and behavioral metaphor, based on the collective behavior of social insects. Our goal is to emulate nature's behavior; particularly the way ants (social insects) organize themselves to execute tasks in the colony, in a cooperative and distributed way. In nature, the identity of the colony is given by the genetic identity imposed by the queen ant to each and every one of the worker ants forming the colony. This process is centralized and the queen ant is ultimately responsible of carrying it out. In the metaphor, this justifies our decision to choose a unique node in the MANET that will be responsible for network address assignment. Thus, our proposal will have a centralized approach for address assignment, and it will be distributed and cooperative (self-organized) for event management in the MANET.

In our context, a MANET will be known as a colony. One or several colonies may exist in a determined geographical area. Each network node with a permanent network address will be known as an ant. Nodes in the MANET will have functional specialization, as in nature. The nodes may assume any of the following roles: a) Node in pre-birth status. A node will assume this role just after its initialization in the simulation scenario; b) Queen ant. A node will assume this role when it takes the responsibility of giving the colony its genetic identity and assigning network addresses. In our metaphor, the queen ant will create a new worker ant for the colony each time she assigns a new address; c) Worker ant. A node will assume this role when it receives its genetic identity (network ID and permanent address) from the queen ant.

This metaphor uses exchange of messages to broadcast information about the colony. Two kinds of messages are used in order to exchange information between the queen ant and the worker ants, and between worker ants:

- Explorer ants are used to search for information; either from a neighboring ant, a queen ant or a worker ant.
- Messenger ants are used to send information to an ant or node in pre-birth status requesting it.

We also propose using some additional messages to communicate exceptional situations happening in the colony. This might be a little unorthodox application of the self-organization paradigm, but it enhances performance and functionality of the solution.

Nodes in a MANET move randomly, generating a dynamic (time-varying) topology. However, and taking into account the role of each node and its relationships with its neighbors, a MANET has a logical tree structure, where the queen ant is the root node and the worker ants are leaf nodes.

The MANET Life Cycle

In the context of our metaphor, a MANET will come to life once its first node completes its initialization and gets a permanent network address. Colony initialization happens once the queen ant (the first ant in the colony) assumes the following responsibilities: a) Gives an identity to the colony, by selecting a network identifier (NETID), and b) assumes all the tasks of the colony. The queen ant is responsible for generating the colony's genetic identifier (the NETID) and for creating new individuals in the colony. Later, as other nodes acquire addresses and thus, are "born" in the colony, the first worker ants are born, and functional specialization begins. When reaching this stage, the queen ant's sole responsibility becomes creating new individuals. The colony then begins its growth phase, with the birth of new working ants (as network addresses are assigned) and the death of old ones (whenever a node decides to leave the network). In this phase, it's possible for the colony to undergo unstable periods, as a consequence of network merge or partition processes, or as a result of the queen ant's death. Once these events are resolved, the colony will return to the growth phase, or it will become extinct if the queen ant is dead. Each time an ant dies in the colony, it has the possibility to be reborn as a new queen ant or as a new worker ant in other colony, and repeat its lifecycle.

The Node Lifecycle

Nodes in the MANET will assume any of these three roles:

a) *Node in pre-birth status*: A node will assume this role just after its initialization, i.e. it does not have a permanent address, and it does not take part in any of the processes in the MANET.
b) *Queen ant*. A node will assume this role when it is in charge of network address assignment. In our metaphor, every time the queen ant assigns an address, it creates a new worker ant for the colony. In its normal operation status, the queen ant has the following responsibilities: Those related to being a node in the MANET (sending/receiving messages, routing) and those related to management of the network address space (leasing an address for a period of time, and recovering addresses which lease has expired).
c) *Worker ant*. A node will assume this role when it participates in the collective, distributed network address assignment process, and in the collective topology maintenance process. In its normal operation status, a worker ant will have the following responsibilities: Those related to being a node in the MANET (sending/receiving messages, routing), and those related to the address assignment process. The tasks in the latter group include serving as an intermediate node in the address assignment process and validating the existence of the queen ant in order to detect network partition and merge events.

Generally speaking, and independently of its role, a node must be able to:

a) Send requests to other nodes in the simulation scenario, i.e. "talking to the simulation scenario." These requests will allow the node to verify the presence of other nodes in the simulation scenario, in order to discover new events in the network and to ask other nodes for help in the network address management process.
b) Listen to requests from other nodes in the simulation scenario, i.e. "listening from the simulation scenario". Other nodes in the simulation scenario may send messages in order to check for their presence, and to ask it for collaboration in the network address management process.

Node Addressing

With regard to addressing, the main issue of this proposal, it is necessary to consider the following items:

a) *Static component*: Related to the network address type and structure.
b) *Dynamic component*: Related to the evolution that the address of a node belonging to the colony might have with time, and with the requirements imposed by the node status.

c) *Address assignment approach*: Related to the mechanisms allowing a node to obtain a network address
d) *Management and ownership of the address space*: Related to the way that maintenance, ownership and reuse of addresses are done.

Static component: The address structure will depend on the used addressing scheme. Two options are available for the addressing scheme:

a) IP-compatible addresses, either IPv4 or IPv6.
b) Addresses not compatible with the IP structure.

We will abide by the following design premises: a) The proposal will work independently of the chosen addressing scheme, i.e. the solution will be flexible; and b) IPv4 will be used, without losing generality.

In order to identify a MANET, a prefix will be used. Our prefix will be 10, which corresponds to the A-class private address block in IPv4 (we assume every MANET in the simulation scenario is a private IPv4 network). The prefix will be represented with 8 bits. The host identifier (HID) will also have 8 bits, which allows for 256 possible addresses in the MANET. HID 0 is the network address; HID 1 is the identifier for the queen ant, and HID 255 is the network's broadcast address. Hence, the maximum number of nodes in a MANET will be 254 (one queen ant and 253 worker ants). The NETID will have 16 bits, allowing 216=65,536 different MANETs. NETID 0 is the network identifier for temporary addresses. Hence, the maximum number of NETIDs that can be generated is 65,535.

Dynamic component: In our proposal, when a node initializes, it does not belong to any colony, and it does not know its environment; hence, it will not be able to contact a queen ant to obtain a permanent address. The node must then generate a network address that allows it to explore its environment. This address is temporary and it might be generated from the information possessed by the node (i.e. its MAC address) or at random, with the risk of generating a duplicated address. Our proposal will follow the second approach, thus requiring generating and validating the node's temporary address. Having a valid temporary address, a node in pre-birth status will be able to contact its direct neighbors belonging to an existing colony, and obtain a permanent address for it to join the colony.

From a node's point of view, the types of addresses it may be assigned, and their associated stages are:

a) *Temporary address*: The node uses this type of address to recognize its environment and to request a permanent address. Such an address goes through the following stages:
    1. *In-contest stage*: During this stage, the node might have an address conflict with other nodes. This conflict must be solved and the involved nodes should resign the conflicting address and return to pre-birth status.
    2. *Ownership status*: During this stage, the node might detect another node trying to use the same network address it has claimed for itself. It should then send a message to the offending node, telling it to resign that address.
b) *Permanent address*: Used by the node to exchange information with its peers in the network; this address is unique inside the MANET.

According to the proposed network address structure, the NETID will have 16 bits in length. Many authors suggest generating the NETID from the MAC address of the node assuming the queen ant role. If this approach is followed, an injective function mapping 48-bit MAC addresses to 16-bit NETIDs should be designed. In this scenario, and considering the cardinality of the address sets, it is not possible to design such a function. Similarly, if the function could be designed, there is no guarantee about MAC address uniqueness. If there is a duplicate MAC address, that will lead to duplicate NETIDs. We will, then, generate the NETID in a random fashion. Since NETID 0 is reserved for temporary addresses, we may pick a NETID from a space of 65,535 different addresses. If we assume a uniform distribution to pick the NETID, the probability of selecting a particular address would be:

$$P(\text{selecting an address}) = \frac{1}{65,535} = 1.52902 \times 10^{-5}$$

Now, we will calculate the probability of two different networks, A and B, coming into contact with each other and having the same NETID. Let e be the event of A and B having the same NETID. Let a be the event of network A having selected NETID x, and let b be the event of network A having selected NETID x. Since a and b are independent, the probability of e is:

$$P(e)=P(a)\cdot P(b)=2.328377492\times10^{-10}$$

We can see this event is almost improbable; thus, our proposal will not consider this situation. However, implementing conflict detection and resolution algorithms into each node can solve this issue.

Mechanism for Initial Configuration of Network Addresses

In this aspect, the proposed solution is hybrid, and will abide by the following design premises:

a) Network-wide polling will not be used.
b) The process will be distributed and cooperative as it uses a special node (the queen ant) as the address assignment agent. Neighboring nodes may act as proxies in the assignment process.
c) The process will avoid addressing conflicts.
d) The process will avoid node synchronization in order to obtain a unique image of the address space
e) A special agent, the queen ant, will have the responsibility of centralized network address assignment.
f) The process will have fault tolerance and recovery mechanisms to handle an eventual collapse of the queen ant.

Network Address Assignment Approach

In our proposal, address assignment for an ordinary node (worker ant) has two phases and a different assignment approach for each phase.

- In a first phase (pre-birth status), the node has a temporary address, used to contact neighbors and to select a proxy node. This address is randomly chosen, and this may lead to duplicated addresses. Hence, it is necessary to have a DAD mechanism.
- In a second phase (during its life as a worker ant), the node has a permanent address. This address is assigned by the queen ant and used to communicate with other nodes in the MANET. Thus, it uses a conflict-free approach and no DAD mechanism is needed.

Duplicated Address Detection Approach

According to the two phases of an address lifecycle (see last section), there are two approaches for DAD:

- In the first phase (pre-birth status), broadcast-based DAD is used. Although this is the most costly approach in terms of overhead, it is the easiest one to implement, and

its reach will be restricted to the immediate neighborhood of the node.
- In the second phase (worker ant), due to the used conflict-free approach, no DAD is needed (conflict probability is zero).

Use of a Network Address Assignment Table

Our proposal assumes a centralized scheme, in which the queen ant holds the address assignment table. However, the processes for address assignment and address table maintenance are distributed and cooperative. In nature, the queen ant is solely responsible for creating new worker ants for the colony. The worker ants are responsible for the collective and distributed execution of all the other tasks in the colony. After new worker ants are born, the queen ant will need to know about their status, in order to eventually repopulate the colony. Thus, a communication mechanism must exist between the queen ant and the worker ants.

This communication mechanism is emulated by using message passing. Stigmergy is also used to strengthen/weaken the link between each worker ant and its colony, through the processes of pheromone application and evaporation. In our proposal, the queen ant keeps an entry in its address assignment table for each one of the worker ants in the colony. Such table entry stores the amount of pheromone representing the link between the worker ant and its colony. In order to belong to a colony, the amount of pheromone related to an ant must be greater than or equal to zero.

Each worker ant periodically notifies its presence to the queen ant. Every time this happens, the queen ant increases the amount of pheromone in the address table entry by one. Similarly, after a certain period of time, the queen ant evaporates the pheromone in the active table entries, decreasing the amount by one in each entry. When the amount of pheromone in a certain table entry becomes less than zero, the queen ant declares the worker ant dead, and declares its address as available. The reasoning behind these actions is as follows: If the queen ant has not heard about certain worker ants in a significant period of time, it assumes such ants have left the colony, i.e. the nodes have left the MANET. In this case, the queen ant may safely assume the addresses of the missing worker ants are available for assignment to new ants, i.e. nodes in pre-birth status. Thus, through stigmergy, the queen ant is able to recover and reassign network addresses.

Network Event Management

One of the strengths of our proposal is the comprehensive management of network events. Our proposal considers, detects and solves all possible events that may happen as a consequence of the dynamically changing network topology. The three kinds of managed events are: Neighbor querying, network merge and network partition; they will be described in the following sections.

Neighbor Querying

Neighbor querying is a key element to our proposal. Through this event: a) A node in pre-birth status is able to find another node already configured in a MANET, which may serve as a proxy for the first node in order to obtain a permanent network address, and b) A node making part of the MANET recognizes its environment, and updates its knowledge about its neighborhood.

The Network Merge Event

Network merge involves permanent contact between two or more nodes of two or more different MANETs. This contact generates a conflict in which two or more networks fight in order to prevail. Two issues arise here:

- How to detect this event: This event will be detected through detection of a NETID different to the NETID of the colony of the

detecting node. The NETID is propagated in the neighbor query process.
- How to solve this conflict: Solving this conflict determines which network prevails. In terms of our metaphor, the network with the largest NETID will survive.

Generally speaking, in a network merge event, a node might contact: a) A node belonging to a different network; b) several nodes belonging to a unique different network; or c) several nodes belonging to different networks. Thus, it is impossible to guarantee a decision with consistent information, since it is not possible to have a unique image of the network in each and every one of its nodes. Occurrence and detection of an event takes time, and the propagation of its occurrence takes some additional time. Since it is not possible to achieve synchronization among all nodes in the network, it is likely that decisions with imprecise information will be taken. The price to pay is that it generates inconsistencies that might generate temporary instability in the merge process.

On a given instant, the scenario might evolve in one direction. For example, in a merge event, network X begins to prevail over network Y. Then, based on event occurrence, a third network Z might prevail over X and Y. These inconsistency periods should be short, and should allow for the system to evolve to a stable state in which a single network prevails and the nodes in it store consistent information.

In conclusion, a MANET address space evolves through several states:

a) Stable state, in which the same NETID is detected in the neighbor query process.
b) Unstable state, in which different NETIDs are detected in the neighbor query process and a network merge event is triggered.

According to the design premises, the mechanism to solve the network merge event:

a) Should be NETID-based
b) Should be distributed
c) Should be localized
d) Should strive to minimize resource usage
e) Should be implemented in a gradual fashion.

Management of a network merge event comprises three activities:

a) *Initial detection of a merge event.* NETIDs are propagated in neighbor query messages. When a worker ant receives this message, it first must check if another ant in its same colony generated the message. If a different NETID is detected, a merge event will be initially detected.
b) *Effective merge detection.* A merge event should be triggered only when there is a high level of certainty about it, and this is determined by the existence of a permanent link between nodes belonging to different networks. To check for this permanent link, the system must wait in order for the link to consolidate, and thus discard temporary links. A permanent link is detected when several query messages coming from ants in another colony are received.
c) *Merge management.* The node detecting the network merge event must build a table of contending neighbors. This table will allow determining which nodes should change their addresses and join a new MANET. The NETID is used for taking this decision and the colony having the largest NETID will prevail over the others.

The Network Partition Event

In our proposal, a network partition event happens when:

a) One or more worker ants detect the absence of the queen ant

b) When a queen ant becomes isolated from its colony
c) When a worker ant becomes isolated from its colony

Management of a network partition event comprises two activities:

a) *Partition event detection*: A network partition event is triggered if: 1) a worker ant for a certain colony sends several query messages to its queen ant, receiving no response; or 2) an ant receives no query messages over a certain time interval.
b) *Partition event handling*: Two scenarios might trigger the network partition event:
    1. The queen ant of a MANET dies, i.e. becomes inactivated. In this case, some nodes of the network will enter a contest in order to choose a new queen ant.
    2. A section of the network becomes isolated, or the queen ant suddenly dies (with no previous warning). When a section of the network becomes isolated, the MANET splits in two groups of nodes, one of which contains the queen ant. The group including the queen ant will survive as a colony, while the other groups must generate a new queen ant. When the queen ant dies without warning, the other nodes discover this reality in gradual fashion. Then, they proceed to choose a new queen ant. In this process, it is possible to have conflicts due to the presence of multiple queen ants in the simulation scenario.

Death of a Node in a Colony

As described before, when a network merge or partition event is triggered, the involved nodes have enough information to take an adequate decision. The nodes that should "die" as a result of isolation or losing a contest should return to pre-birth status and ask their neighbors to serve as proxies. Then, they will choose a proxy and eventually get a new permanent address.

A special consideration must be taken into account when a node dies for the colony. Such a node must change its address, but it should not consider any of its former network neighbors as a valid proxy.

When one of the nodes involved in a merge event is the queen ant, the event should be specially handled. Before dying, the queen ant should broadcast a special message announcing her death. Every worker ant receiving it should: a) block its behavior as a proxy, i.e. stop serving requests from other nodes; b) stop generating messages of every kind; c) re-broadcast the queen death message; d) die for the colony and e) return to pre-birth status.

Worker ants surviving the queen ant death might become trapped in a limbo because they are no longer able to request an address from former direct neighbors of their previous network, and they might not be yet in the range of the prevailing network. In order to solve this difficulty, worker ants knowing their queen has died must stay in a loop requesting a new address until they can find neighbors from another network that may serve as proxies; or they may postulate themselves as a queen ant for the colony.

As said before, the queen ant is responsible for managing the network address table. The address table is a matrix, where each row represents a different address. The first column in the table holds the status of the address (assigned / available). The second column stores the amount of pheromone associated with the address. Each time a worker ant sends a query message to the queen ant, the latter increases the amount of pheromone. If, during a cycle of the algorithm, the queen ant receives no notifications from a worker ant, the amount of pheromone for the address is decreased. If the pheromone level reaches zero, the queen ant concludes the ant has left the colony, and its address is now available.

EXPERIMENTAL VERIFICATION

We used the NCTUns simulation tool (Wang, 2010) to implement and validate our proposed model. This tool allows the configuration of the general features of the simulation scenario, as well as the features for each node in the simulation.

The features configured in each simulation node were:

- The trajectory to follow.
- The application to execute. In this case, this application was our address management approach, which was implemented in the C programming language.
- The velocity at which each node moved within the scenario; 10 m/s by default.

Finally, the protocol stack parameters were configured as follows:

- Physical level
  - Antenna configuration: Omni directional
  - Link bandwidth: 11 Mbit/s
  - Channel: 3
  - Bit error rate: 0.0
  - Transmission range: 250 m.
  - Interference range: 550 m.
  - Link failure pattern: None.
- MAC level
  - MAC address format: 802.11 standard
  - RTS threshold: 3000 bytes
  - Log frame statistics: On
  - Queuing discipline: FIFO
  - Maximum queue size: 50 frames

The conducted experiments were aimed to fulfill three objectives: First, to verify the model's functionality; second, to verify the efficiency of the proposed solution; and third, to quantify the impact of the solution to the performance of user applications.

The verification of the approach functionality included tests for all the basic transactions in the model: a) colony initialization; b) a node (queen or worker ant) checking for neighbor existence; c) a worker ant checking for the presence of the queen ant in the colony; d) a node in the colony detecting and managing a network merge event; e) a node in the colony detecting and managing a network partition event; f) the worker ants in the colony detecting and managing the event of the death of the queen ant; and g) the model's capability to assign a permanent address to a node striving to become a worker ant in the colony, in a cooperative and distributed fashion.

For efficiency verification, we selected two metrics: a) Latency for network address self-configuration, i.e. the average time needed by a node to obtain a unique IP address in the network; and b) The scalability of the proposed solution, i.e. the impact on the performance of user applications as the number of nodes in the network increases.

To be able to evaluate the impact of the model on a typical user application, two tasks need to be conducted: First, to establish a baseline in order to have a reference point for comparisons; and second, to quantify the impact. In order to do so, we used a typical client/server application implementing an echo service, and a set of nodes behaving according to the model. The TCP and UDP protocols were used in the transport layer, and several simulation runs were executed using different message sizes in the client/server exchanges. The sizes used were: 38 bytes (same size as the explorer ants, i.e. the messages exchanged by the nodes), 64, 128, 256, 512 and 1024 bytes. Finally, the number of nodes in the scenario also was adjusted from 2 to 100.

In order to correctly evaluate the model, its behavior should be well known. The proposed model has different behaviors in its initialization and stable states.

During the initialization phase: a) the nodes wishing to obtain a permanent network address generate a temporary address at random and verify it for uniqueness. During the verification process, each node sends broadcast messages to all its neighbors; b) once they have a temporary address, the nodes may enter a contest in order to choose the queen ant. In this contest, one of the ants will be selected as the queen, and all the others will become worker ants, and will ultimately contact the queen ant in order to get a permanent network address. The contest is conducted by means of broadcast messages among all the involved nodes, so the traffic between such nodes is comparatively high in the initialization phase of the network.

During the stable operation phase: a) the nodes, now acting as ants, make a reconnaissance sweep in their coverage range to search for neighbors. Through this process, ants are able to recognize other ants in their own colony, and ants in other colonies (which will trigger network merge events); b) the queen ant makes an inventory of the worker ants and recovers the addresses of those who have left the colony and whose pheromone level has dropped to zero (this event does not generate network traffic); and c) worker ants query the queen ant, in order to reinforce their pheromone amount, thus reaffirming their presence in the colony and detecting the presence or absence of the queen ant. When a worker ant is unable to detect the presence of the queen ant, it assumes a network partition event has occurred. Traffic in this phase is considerably smaller than in the initialization phase. Thus, we propose three verification scenarios: a) initialization phase, b) a representative operation cycle in stable state, and c) sampling in some particular time instants during the simulation run.

Summarizing, the battery of verification tests considers: a) Three variables: Information unit size, number of nodes in the simulation run, and protocol type; and b) Three different time perspectives: Initialization phase, operation in stable state, and sampling in some particular time instants during the simulation run.

The activation of a node in the simulation scenario triggers three events: Acquisition of a temporary address, election of the queen ant, and acquisition of the permanent address, once the queen ant is elected. Considering the average time taken for each one of those three events, we can calculate the time elapsed in the contest for choosing the queen ant, and the average time elapsed for assigning an address to a worker ant. Knowing these values, the network address self-configuration latency can be calculated.

Results for model behavior are shown in Figure 1. In first place, we can see the time elapsed for assignment of a temporary address grows slowly with the number of nodes. Applying a linear regression, we found that the presence of each additional node only poses a 0.61 ms overhead in the temporary address assignment process.

In second place, and considering the time elapsed for the queen ant election, we can see the relationship between the number of nodes and the time for election of the queen ant is also linear, with a slope somewhat higher than in the temporary address assignment process. The slope increases when 35 nodes or more are considered.

In third place, and considering the elapsed time for the assignment of a permanent address, the graph represents the workload of the queen ant during the massive node initialization process. This graph is very similar to the second one. However, the slope becomes even higher when 35 nodes or more are considered in the scenario.

Another aspect considered to verify the model's efficiency is the overhead on user applications. In order to measure such overhead, we propose a scenario in which two nodes exchange information units, using a set of nodes running the proposed address management scheme as a middle tier. We use a client/server application implementing an echo service. As stated before, TCP and UDP protocols are used, and several information unit sizes are tested for each protocol. Each scenario is run with an increasing number of nodes in the middle tier. The overhead verification test is run once the colony ends its initialization phase and enters its stable phase. Results for TCP are shown

Figure 1. Events in the initialization phase

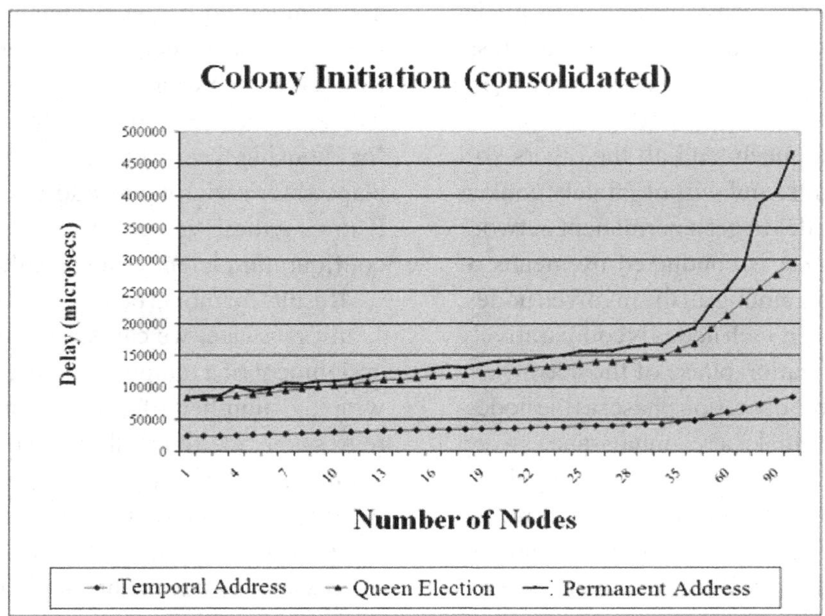

in Figure 2; similar results were obtained for the UDP protocol. The graph shows that delay remains relatively stable for a fixed message length, and it has a slight increase as the size of the information unit increases. Thus, we can conclude the overhead our solution imposes over the network is low, and it remains stable in the different tested scenarios. Since low overhead on user applications was one of the design premises of the model, we can state the model behaves as desired.

In order to appreciate the difference in traffic in the model's initialization phase and stable state, we ran a simulation scenario consisting of 50 nodes, and checked the delay in a client/server exchange, both in the initialization phase and the stable state. TCP and UDP protocols were used, and 50 samples were taken. Obtained results for TCP are shown in Figure 3; a similar behavior was observed in UDP.

The graph shows a high peak during the first instants of network operation, and then a relatively constant behavior once the stable state is reached. The undesirable overload effect of the initialization phase remains confined to a very short time interval. It is worth noting the same behavior can be observed in the worst-case scenario (simultaneous, massive initialization of all nodes in the scenario).

Results for the stable state phase (a typical operation cycle of the proposed model) are shown in Figure 4.

The graph shows there is no significant impact on the delay a user application experiences once the stable state phase of the model is reached. The delay increases slightly with the increase in the information unit size. We ran additional tests in scenarios with 80 and 100 nodes; both showed the same behavior as above.

We also tested the model's capability to return to a stable state (a state such that only one queen ant exists in each one of the colonies deployed in the simulation scenario), after a queen ant dies, or a node initializes in the vicinity of multiple networks, triggering a massive network merge event. This allows us to study convergence to a

Figure 2. Delay vs. number of nodes: TCP

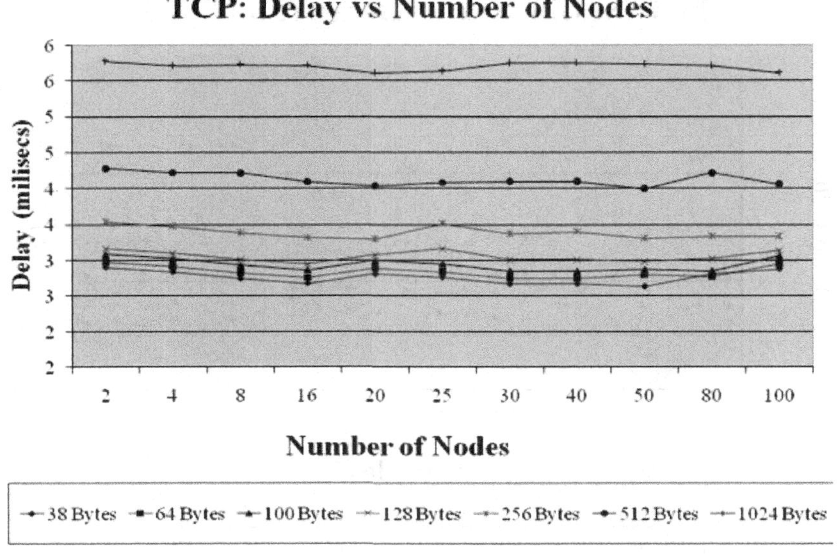

Figure 3. Delay in initialization phase: TCP

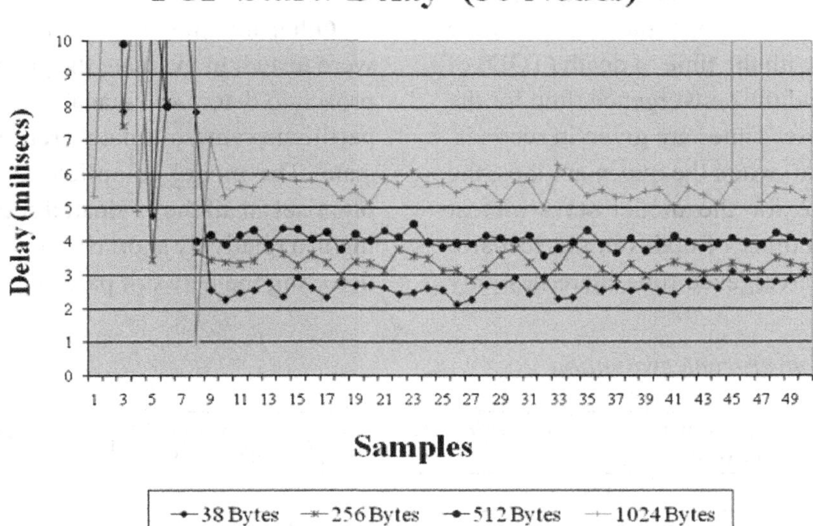

desirable situation, one of the most prized features of self-organizing systems.

We executed the proposed model in several scenarios, each one with a different node population. The event sequence that took place in all the scenarios was as follows: a) Simultaneous initialization of all the nodes; b) election of the queen ant in the colony; c) death of the queen ant (by inactivating the simulation scenario of the node in the queen ant role); d) election of a new

Figure 4. Delay in stable state: TCP

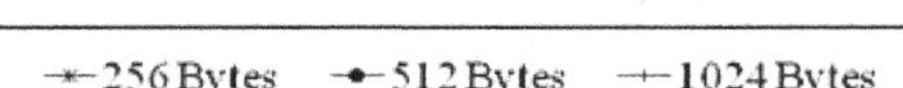

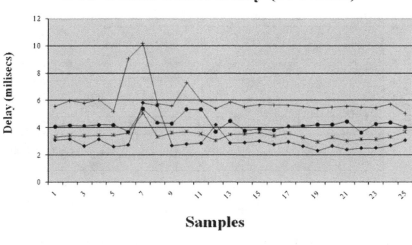

queen ant; e) operation in stable state; f) death of the queen ant; g) election of a new queen; and h) operation in stable state. Table 1 shows these scenarios, along with the time of death (TOD) of the queen ants, and the convergence time for the model, in each case. Times are given in seconds.

We can see that, when the queen ant dies, the convergence time for the model stays almost constant as the number of nodes in the scenario increases. The convergence time increases only with a significant increase in the number of nodes (from 50 to 100).

Other initialization and movement scenarios were tested, to evaluate the capability of our approach to detect and manage network merge and partition events, ultimately returning to the stable state. The model complied with all the design premises in all the evaluated scenarios, converging in a relatively short time to a stable state after detecting the network partition / merge events.

Table 1. Model convergence evaluation

Number of nodes	TOD for first queen ant	Convergence time	TOD for second queen ant	Convergence time
3	10	t<2	-	-
5	5	t<1	25	t<1
10	5	t<2	25	t<2
15	5	t<2	25	t<2
25	5	t<2	20	t<2
30	5	t<2	20	t<2
40	5	t<2	20	t<2
50	5	t<2	25	t<2
100	5	t<2	30	t<7

CONCLUSION AND FUTURE WORK

Based on the obtained experimental results, we were able to determine that our proposed model is able to identify, manage and solve all events related to management of the address space in a MANET, adequately and efficiently. Not all existing proposals do so.

It was possible to emerge (or generate) the global behavior of the system through the self-organization principle. Events partially altering colony stability were detected and solved in a localized manner, without affecting other nodes in the colony.

In each proposed verification scenario, the model was able to choose a unique queen ant for the colony, and to assign a permanent address to every node in the MANET, in a reasonable amount of time.

The proposed model was able to bring the simulation scenario to a stable state after the event with the greatest impact over the node operation (the death of the queen ant) took place. Convergence time after this event remained almost unmodified as the number of nodes in the simulation scenario was increased.

We were also able to verify that the overhead imposed by the model on user applications is low, and remains practically stable with increases in the number of nodes and the information unit size.

The proposed model may have other fields for application, which may be explored in the future. To allow a node to assume a required functionality in a spontaneous and unique fashion opens possibilities for other application scenarios, such as session key assignment and digital certificate generation for secure MANET applications.

REFERENCES

Ashby, W. R., Foerster, V., & Zopf, G. W. (1962). Principles of self-organization. *Transactions of the Univeristy of Illinois Symposium*, pp. 255-278.

Dorigo, M., & Di Caro, G. (1999). The ant-colony optimization meta-heuristic. In *New ideas in optimization*. Maidenhead, UK: McGraw-Hill.

Dressler, F. (2006). *Self-organization in ad hoc networks: Overview and classification* [Technical Report 02/06]. Erlangen, Germany: University of Erlangen, Department of Computer Sciences.

Eigen, M. (1979). *The hypercycle: A principle of natural self-organization*. Berlin: Springer-Verlag.

Fazio, M., Villari, M., & Pulifito, A. (2005). AIPAC: Automatic IP address configuration in mobile ad hoc networks. *Computer Communications*, *29*(8), 1189–1200. doi:10.1016/j.comcom.2005.07.006

Foerster, H. V. (2003). On self-organizing systems and their environments. In *Understanding essays on cybernetics and cognition* (pp. 1–19). New York: Springer.

Gunes, M., & Reibel, J. (2002). An IP address configuration algorithm for Zeroconf. In *Proceedings of International Workshop on Broadband Wireless Ad Hoc Networks and Services,* Sophia-Antipolis, France.

Indrayan, G. (2006). *Address autoconfiguration in mobile ad hoc networks*. Unpublished master's thesis, University of Colorado, Boulder, CO.

Mohsin, M., & Prakash, R. (2002). IP address assignment in a mobile ad hoc network. In *Proceedings of MILCOM 2002 Military Communications Conference,* Anaheim, CA.

Murthy, S. R., & Manoj, B. S. (2004). *Ad hoc wireless networks: Architectures and protocols*. Upper Saddle River, NJ: Prentice-Hall PTR.

Nesargi, S., & Prakash, R. (2002). MANET.conf: Configuration of hosts in a mobile ad hoc network. In *Proceedings of INFOCOM,* New York. New York: IEEE.

Perkins, C. E., Malinen, J. T., Wakikawa, R., Belding-Royer, E. M., & Sun, Y. (2001). *IP address autoconfiguration for ad hoc networks: Internet draft*. Fremont, CA: IETF. Retrieved February 12, 2010, from http://tools.ietf.org/html/draft-perkins-manet-autoconf-01

Prehofer, C., & Bettstetter, C. (2005). Self-organization in communication networks: Principles and design paradigms. *IEEE Communications Magazine*, *43*(7), 78–85. doi:10.1109/MCOM.2005.1470824

Sun, Y., & Belding-Royer, E. M. (2003). *Dynamic address configuration in mobile ad hoc networks* [Technical Report]. Santa Barbara, CA: University of California Santa Barbara, Department of Computer Science.

Tayal, A. T., & Patanaik, L. M. (2004). An address assignment for the automatic configuration of mobile ad hoc networks. *Personal and Ubiquitous Computing*, *8*(1), 47–54. doi:10.1007/s00779-003-0256-5

Thoppian, M., & Prakash, R. (2006). A distributed protocol for dynamic address assignment in mobile ad hoc networks. *IEEE Transactions on Mobile Computing*, *5*(1), 4–19. doi:10.1109/TMC.2006.2

Vaidya, N. (2002). Weak duplicate address detection in mobile ad hoc networks. In *Proceedings of ACM MobiHoc* (pp. 206-216). New York: ACM.

Wang, S. Y. (2010). NCTUns network simulator and emulator. Taiwan: NCTU Network and System Laboratory. Retrieved February 23, 2010, from http://nsl.csie.nctu.edu.tw/nctuns.html

Weniger, K. (2003). Passive duplicate address detection in mobile ad hoc networks. In *Proceedings of IEEE WCNC,* New Orleans. New York: IEEE.

Weniger, K. (2005). PACMAN: Passive autoconfiguration for mobile ad hoc networks. [JSAC]. *IEEE Journal on Selected Areas in Communications*, *23*(3), 507–519. doi:10.1109/JSAC.2004.842539

Weniger, K., & Zitterbart, M. (2004). Address autoconfiguration in mobile ad hoc networks: Current approaches and future directions. *IEEE Network*, *18*(4), 6–11. doi:10.1109/MNET.2004.1316754

Zhou, H., Ni, L., & Mutka, M. (2003). Prophet allocation for large scale MANETs. In *Proceedings of INFOCOM,* San Francisco, CA. New York: IEEE.

Chapter 10
Key Management Protocols in Mobile Ad Hoc Networks

Mohamed Elboukhari
University Mohamed I[st], Morocco

Mostafa Azizi
University Mohamed I[st], Morocco

Abdelmalek Azizi
University Mohamed I[st], Morocco & Academy Hassan II of Sciences & Technology, Morocco

ABSTRACT

Mobile ad hoc networks (MANETs) have received tremendous attention in recent years because of their self-organization and self-maintenance capabilities. MANETs are networks that do not have an underlying fixed infrastructure. However, these networks tend to be vulnerable to a number of attacks. They don't obey a centralized network management functionality; furthermore, the network topology changes dynamically. Therefore, security has become a primary concern in MANETs. The major problem in providing security services in such networks is how to manage cryptography keys, making key management a central component in MANETs. This chapter gives an overview of security in this kind of network and presents a number of MANETs key management protocols according to recent literature.

INTRODUCTION

Mobile Ad Hoc Networks

MANETs are a new paradigm of wireless communication for mobile hosts (which we call nodes). A MANET is a self-configuring and self-maintaining network composed of mobile nodes that communicate over wireless channels (Perkins, 2001). Mobile nodes communicate directly via wireless links, while those located farther apart rely on other nodes to relay messages as routers. Thus, an ad hoc network is a collection of autonomous nodes that form a dynamic, purpose-specific, and multi-hop radio network in a decentralized fashion. These networks, by definition, possess no fixed support infrastructure such as mobile switching centers, base stations, access points, and other centralized machines. Each node in such a network operates not only as a host but also as a router, forwarding packets for other mobile nodes

DOI: 10.4018/978-1-60960-027-3.ch010

in the network that may be multiple hops away from each other.

Today, the main application of ad hoc networks is in military tactical operations. Military units, equipped with wireless devices, can form an ad hoc network when they roam the battlefield. Other examples of applications include business associates sharing information during a meeting or attendees using laptop computers to participate in an interactive conference.

Security Goals

MANETs, in early research, assumed a cooperative and trusted environment, which, unfortunately, is not always true. A variety of attacks can be launched in an unfriendly environment, ranging from passive attacks to active interference. Therefore, security has become a primary concern. Ad hoc networks must meet a number of security requirements including authentication, confidentiality, integrity, authorization, non repudiation, and availability.

Authentication: enables a node to ensure the identity of the peer node with which it is communicating. We assume initially that the two legitimate parties are authentic: each is the entity it claims to be, and that third parties do not interfere by impersonating one of the two legitimate parties.

Confidentiality: ensures that certain information is never disclosed to unauthorized entities. The network transmission of sensitive information requires confidentiality, and the leakage of such information to enemies could have devastating dangerous consequences, such as revealing tactical military information or making illegal access to bank accounts.

Integrity: guarantees that an exchanged message is not altered: the received data does not contain any modification, insertion, deletion, nor replay. A message could be corrupted because of a benign failure, such as radio propagation impairments, or because of a malicious attack on the network.

Authorization: establishes a set of roles that define what each network node is or is not allowed to do. So, a user must be first identified to gain access to the resource and then the corresponding access rights are guaranteed.

No repudiation: means that the sender of a message cannot later deny sending this information, and the receiver cannot deny its reception. In the case of public key cryptography, a node *A* signs the message using its private key. Other nodes can verify the signed message by using *A*'s public key, and *A* cannot then deny the message because of its signature.

Availability: ensures the survivability of the network despite malicious incidences. For example, an attacker can use jamming to interfere with communication at the physical layer, or it can make unworkable the routing protocol at the network layer by disrupting the route discovery procedure.

Security Challenges

MANETs have specific features that pose both challenges and opportunities in achieving the security goals which are an important issue for those in security-sensitive environments.

First, the use of wireless links renders an ad hoc network accessible to both legitimate users and malicious attackers. A malicious node is susceptible to impersonation by other nodes even without gaining physical access to its victims. An eavesdropping process might give an attacker access to secret information, and violate the security goal of confidentiality. Also, an active attack might allow the adversary to delete messages, inject erroneous messages, modify messages, and so. As a result, there is no clear line of defense in MANETs from the security design perspective. The boundary that separates the inside network from the outside world becomes complex and blurred. And, therefore, there is no well-defined infrastructure where we may deploy a simple security solution.

Second, another nontrivial challenge to security is the stringent resource constraints in MANETs (such as bandwidth, memory, etc.). A transmission channel is shared among multiple networking entities, thus adding to the problem of bandwidth constraint. The computation capability of a mobile node is also constrained, and because mobile devices are typically powered by batteries, they may have very limited energy resources. Due to these resource constraints, the security mechanism for MANETs must be lightweight in terms of communication, storage and computation complexity. For MANETs, asymmetric cryptography is usually considered inappropriate and too expensive, and thus symmetric cryptography is commonly used to achieve security goals.

Third, a MANET is dynamic because of frequent changes in both its topology and its membership because nodes frequently join and leave the network and roam in the network of their own will. Therefore, frequent changes of the topology and membership tremendously raise the probability of a network being compromised. For example, each node functioning as a router and participating in forwarding packets may lead to a significant vulnerability since a malicious node can tamper and falsify the routing and data packets.

So any security solution with a static configuration will not suffice and it is desirable for any security mechanism to automatically adapt to these changes. Also, an ad hoc network may consist of more than hundreds of nodes. So, the security mechanisms should be scalable to take into account and handle any change over this kind of networks.

Cryptography and Key Management

The use of cryptography is a powerful tool for securing communications. The cryptography process changes reversibly readable data into meaningless data. Cryptography is mainly divided into two commonly known categories: symmetric key and asymmetric key approaches (Saloma, 1996). The same key is used to encrypt and decrypt messages in symmetric key cryptography, while different keys are used respectively to convert and recover data in asymmetric key cryptography. Asymmetric key cryptography can be used for authentication, integrity and privacy. It is also more suitable for key distribution than symmetric key cryptography. Symmetric key cryptography algorithms are generally more computation-efficient than those of asymmetric key cryptography.

Another cryptographic tool is threshold cryptography that is different from asymmetric key and symmetric key cryptography. For example in Shamir's (k,n) secret sharing scheme, secret information is divided into n pieces, according to a random polynomial process, and the secret can be recovered by combining any threshold k pieces based on Lagrange interpolation. These cryptographic algorithms are widely used in wired and wireless networks. They can also be used in MANETs to achieve security goals.

Although cryptography is an important tool for securing information, most cryptographic systems rely on efficient, secure and robust key management subsystems. Key management deals with key generation, key storage, distribution, updating, revocation, deleting, archiving and using keying materials in accordance with security strategies. If the key management is weak, all cryptography techniques will be ineffective. So, key management is a central part of MANET security.

The computation and complexity of key management in MANETs depend on the node's available resources and the dynamic nature of the network topology. To design schemes for key management in MANETs, some asymmetric and symmetric key management schemes have been proposed.

In this chapter, we provide a survey of recent research on key management protocols in MANETs. The chapter is organized as follows: the introduction gives a description of MANETs and the goals and challenges of security in such networks. In the key management section, we describe traditional solutions of key management, discuss the desired key management features of in MANETs and we present a classification of key management. In the section surveying key management protocols, we introduce key management protocols t that can be applied to MANETs in greater detail.

KEY MANAGEMENT PROTOCOLS IN MOBILE AD HOC NETWORKS

Traditional Solutions of Key Management

In wired networks, the standard approach to key management is based on trusted third parties (TTPs) (Kaufmanet, Perlman, & Speciner, 2002; Menezes et al., 1996). TTP is trusted by all users of the system. We distinguish three types of TTPs: in-line TTP, on-line TTP, and off-line TTP.

An in-line TTP is an active participant in the communication path between users. An on-line TTP participates actively but only for the purpose of deciding the keying material. Once the keying material is negotiated, the on-line TTP no longer participates in the data communication between the users. An off-line TTP participates with users before establishing communication links, and it remains off-line during the network operation. Key distribution center (KDC) and certificate authorities (CA) are examples of TTPs. CA is typically associated with systems that depend on asymmetric key cryptography, and is similar to an off-line TTP. KDC is typically used in systems that depend on symmetric key cryptography and functions more like an on-line TTP.

The role of TTP is mainly to simplify the key management process. TTPs have been integrated with both symmetric and asymmetric key management systems. Each user is supposed to share a secret with TTP in the case of symmetric key-based systems. Formally, the key number N depends on the user number n, as shown by the following formula: $N = \frac{n(n-1)}{2}$. KDC and key translation centers (KTC) (Oppliger, 1998) are TTPs in symmetric key management. Figure 1 describes the implementation of KDC or KTC.

1. Alice wants to share a secret key with Bob. If TTP is KDC, it creates a key. Otherwise, Alice generates it. Using the secret shared between Alice and TTP, Alice encrypts and sends the message to TTP.
2. Alice sends the encrypted session key to Bob who can decrypt it and thus use it to communicate with Alice securely.

Figure 1. Negotiation of session key using KDC or KTC

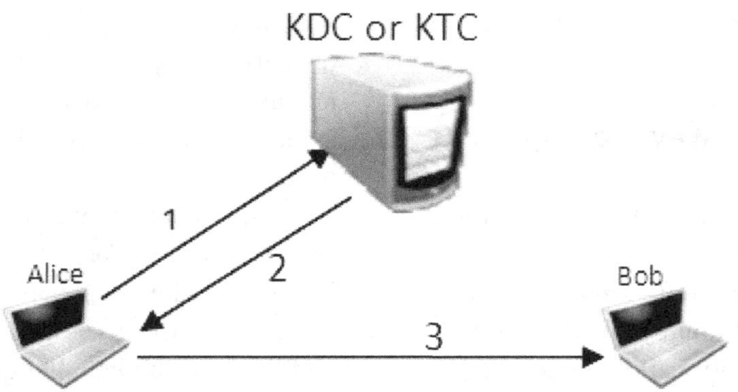

In the case of asymmetric key-based systems, each user might have access to the public key of the TTP. However, unlike the case of symmetric key-based systems, users do not need to share secret keys with each other or know the public key of each other. With the help of TTP, any user can obtain the public keys of other users. This reduces the number of keys in the system from $\frac{n(n-1)}{2}$ to n.

Since public keys do not need to be hidden, authenticity of the distribution channels is strongly demanded. The traditional approach to solving the problem of authentic distribution has been in the form of public key certificate. A certificate is a statement issued by some party, called a certification authority (CA), which guarantees that the public key indeed belongs to the claimed user. Today, there are two models of PKI (public key infrastructure) using CA: centralized and web-of-trust models (Wu et al., 2006; Yi & Kravets, 2004). In the Web-of-Trust Model, nodes can issue certificates each other and publishes the certification graph.

Classification of Key Management

Key management can be classified into two categories: contributory and distributive. In contributory key management schemes, all nodes in MANETs contribute equally in the key management process. So, every node participates in the generation and distribution of the cryptographic key and cooperates to establish a secret symmetric key (group key). This approach is not designed with ad hoc networks in mind, but the contributory solution of collaboration and self organization seems to be adequate to the nature of ad hoc networks. This solution is also suitable for a network with a small number of nodes.

Distributive schemes suppose one or more trusted entities. This approach can be centralized or decentralized. In the decentralized case, each node generates a key and tries to distribute it to the others. Centralized solutions may involve several trusted entities. Distributive key management concerns both asymmetric and symmetric key systems.

Desired Features of Key Management for MANETs

For ad hoc networks, an ideal key management scheme should be simple, never expose or distribute key materials to unauthorized nodes, and easily allow rekeying and key updates. Thus, the desired features of key management for MANETs include:

Security: Authentication is a fundamental concern to ensure no unauthorized node receives key materials and it can be later employed to prove the status of a legitimate user in the network. No user should provide private keys or issue certificates for other users unless they have been authenticated. Tolerance of intrusion means that the system's security should not succumb to one or several compromised users. The system should enable exclusion of compromised users.

Scalability: any increase in the number of nodes reduces available bandwidth. Thus, scalability of the key management protocols is crucial. Key management operations should finish in a timely accepted manner despite of the increasing number of nodes.

Applicability: applicability depends on different parameters such as network size, node mobility, and the required level of human involvement. The aim can range from group key establishment to availability of central management entities.

Robustness: key management operations should not require strict synchronization. It should survive despite of compromised or unavailable nodes. Operations in the system should be able to be completed despite of faulty nodes.

Simplicity: user-friendliness and communication overhead should be simple to the success of a key management. We believe that simplicity is crucial to the system.

SURVEY OF KEY MANAGEMENT PROTOCOLS IN MOBILE AD HOC NETWORKS

Fundamentals of Key Management

Any secure network communication requires a key management procedure between parties involved in communication as the key used by the parties might be sent through an insecure channel. Key management is the weakest part of any system's security and protocol design, and it is a fundamental part of any secure communication; therefore, any cryptosystem relies on secure, efficient, and robust key management schemes.

To design a key management scheme, a framework of trust relationships must be built for authentication of key ownerships. This framework can be distributed in some systems and it can be centralized trust third party (TTP). For example, in asymmetric cryptosystems, certification authority (CA) is the TTP. A key distribution center (KDC) is the TTP in symmetric cryptosystems, but there is no TTP in pretty good privacy (PGP).

A key exchanged during a key management scheme over an unsecure channel, suffers from being exposed to potential attacks. To avoid these attacks, we use digital signatures, hash functions, and hash function-base messages authentication code (HMAC) (Menezes et al., 1996) as techniques to assure authentication and integrity. The public key is protected by using a certificate, in which a trust party called a certification authority (CA) in public key infrastructure (PKI) vouches for the blinding of the public key with the owner's identity. Also, a cryptographic key can be compromised or discovered after a certain time; therefore, it should no longer be usable after expiration of the certificate lifetime of validity. In certain cases, the private key can be discovered during the time of validity. To address this situation, the CA needs to explicitly revoke a certificate and notify the network by publishing the certificate revocation list (CRL) in order to avoid its use.

In MANETs, limited computing resources, dynamic network topology, lack of central control facility and difficulty of network synchronization contribute to the complexity of key management protocols.

Contributory Schemes of Key Management

Contributory or group key establishment schemes are schemes in which several parties participate to create a group key to secure data exchange. Therefore, group key management is very important for communication security, and schemes in MANETs have become a field of active research. However, in large and dynamic networks, group key management is a difficult task due to scalability and security considerations (Rafaeli & Hutchison, 2003).

Regarding memberships changes, group key management must address the related security. Also, each time an old member is evicted or a new member is added to the group, the group key must be updated to ensure backward and forward security. Therefore, an efficient and scalable rekeying mechanism must be provided by the group key scheme.

Contributory schemes can be divided into three approaches: centralized, decentralized, and distributed (Rafaeli & Hutchison, 2003). In centralized group key management, a single node is used to control the whole group and is the only entity responsible for rekeying and distributing group keys to other members of the group. In decentralized approach, a set of nodes is responsible for the management of other members of the group; they participate in providing keys for other nodes. In distributed key management scheme, group members contribute to the design of group keys and are responsible equally for the rekeying and distributing group keys.

In the following subsections, we provide an overview of the protocols of contributory schemes. The 2-party Diffie hellman (DH) protocol key exchange is described first, because this protocol can be extended to a generalized version called the n-party DH key exchange model and it is used by several key management schemes. Then, we provide descriptions of the well-known key management protocols which could be utilized and adopted for MANETs, so we describe the following schemes: Ingemarsson,Tang and Wong (ING), Logical Key Hierarchy (LKH), One-Way Function Trees (OFT), Tree-Based Group Diffie-Hellmen (TGDH), Cliques (CLIQ), Burmester-Desmedt (BD) and Skinny Tree (STR).

Diffie-Hellman (DH)

Diffie-Hellman key exchange protocol (Diffie & Hellman, 1976) provides a unique symmetric key between two parties. It is based on the discrete logarithm problem (DL), which is posed as: "given g^s mod p, we obtain s"; this problem is classified to be hard. The DH protocol operates as follows: two parties A and B agree upon a large number, p, and a generator g. Each party chooses its secret, $s_A$and s_B, respectively for A and B. A sends the public value $g^{S_A} \bmod p$ to B and B sends $g^{S_B} \bmod p$ to A. Raising the received value from the other party to the power of its own secret gives a common key $g^{S_A S_B} \bmod p$. Several key management protocols are based on this protocol despite its simplicity.

Ingemarsson,Tang and Wong (ING)

The authors Ingemarsson, Tang and Wong (1982) have elaborated a contributory scheme of key management ING by extending the number of participants from 2 in the DH scheme to n participants in order to obtain a group key. Figure 2 shows how this protocol operates with four nodes arranged into a logical ring. After (n-1) rounds, the nodes can calculate the group key. Each round involves one exponentiation from every node, and every node must transmit its share to the next node in logical ring.

This protocol has several weaknesses. Importantly. it lacks authentication and is vulnerable to man-in-the middle (MIM) attacks. It also scales poorly. Finally, if the number of nodes is squared, the communicational complexity grows proportionally.

Logical Key Hierarchy (LKH)

In group key management schemes, keys can be updated by a brute force: the new group is distributed by a group manager and encrypted with an individual key for each node. The scheme logical key hierarchy (LKH) presents a way to improve the scalability of this brute force method by giving nodes additional keys and organizing the keys into a logical hierarchy. This scheme is based on a tree structure which reduces the storage space

Figure 2. ING protocol for four nodes

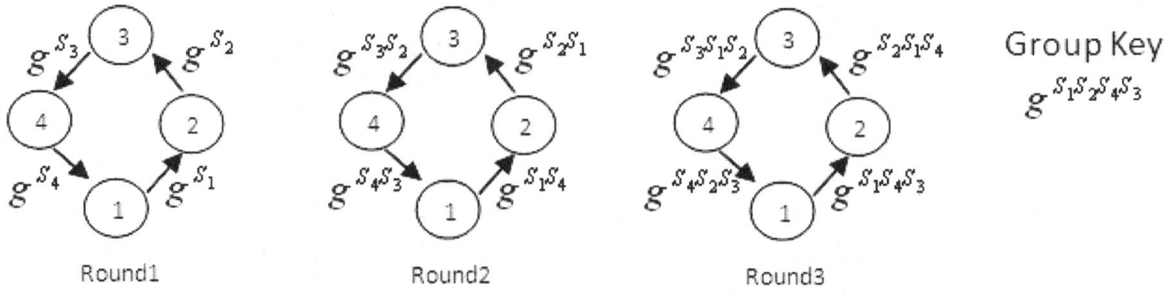

and the number of broad cost messages. LKH was proposed by Wallner, Hardere and Agee in 1998 (Wong, Gouda, & Lam, 1998). The concept of LKH is illustrated in Figure 3. The nodes (N1-N6) have the group keyK123456. The nodes (N1-N2) have the subgroup key K12 and the K34 is common to N3 and N4. K1-K6 are individual keys. If N6 is to be revoked, all keys known to N6 (K123456, K3456 and K56) should be updated. All intermediate keys from the leaf to the root are shared between N5 and N6.Therefore, N5 must receive the updated keys encrypted with its individual key. When a new node joins the group, the rekey produced follows a similar procedure. For example, if N6 is the new member, it receives a secret key *K*6 and attaches the intermediate node *N*56 logically and a rekey message is generated. The message provides the new set keys encrypted with its respective children's key.

One-Way Function Trees (OFT)

Another refinement of the basic LKH schemes focusing on communicational and computational cost has been elaborated. One-Way Function Tree (OFT) proposes a way to reduce communications, especially the size of messages (Sherman & McGrew, 2003).

The basic idea of OFT is that the keys held by node's children are blinded using a one-way hash function. Blinded keys are received by each group user from its sibling set as well as the blinded key of its own sibling. The group users can deduce each key of its ancestor set based on collected blinded keys. In LKH, the new key is encrypted with two children's key, but in OFT the blinded key is encrypted only with the key of its sibling node. Also, the message size in OFT is reduced, compared to the original LKH.

Tree-Based Group Diffie-Hellman (TGDH)

Tree-Based Group Diffie-Hellman (TGDH) is a group key agreement approaches elaborated by the authors Kim, Perrig & Tsudik (2000a, 2000b). They unified by this work two interesting trends of the group key management; To update and compute group keys, they use the concept of tree key and to achieve a provably secure and fully distributed protocol by employing Diffie-Hellman key exchange.

The description of a basic operation in this scheme is as follows: All the shares of current group contribute to generating the group key. If new members join the network, their shares are factored into the group key and the shares of old members remain unchanged. If some members are removed from the network, their shares are eliminated from the new group key and one share

Figure 3. Logical key hierarchy scheme

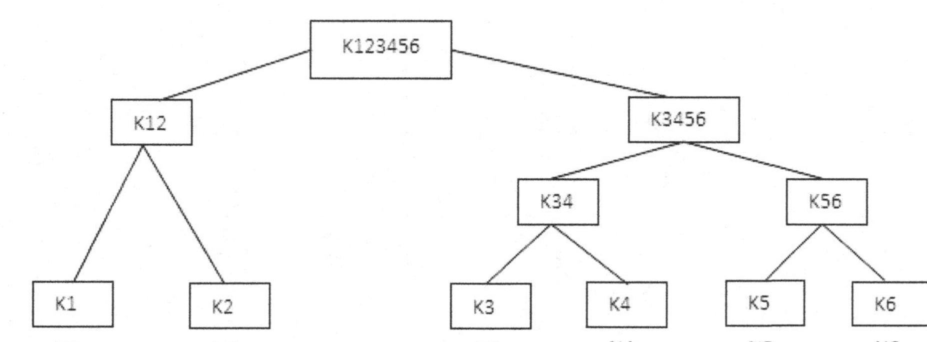

of the remaining members is changed. The RSA is used to sign messages in this scheme. Any node in the group can execute the function of computing keys and broadcast the blinded key to group members.

Figure 4 illustrates an example of member M4 joining a group. M3 takes the responsibility of a sponsor and performs the following operations. M3 renames <1,1> to <2,2> and provides a new node <1,1> as an intermediate node and another new member node <2,3>, and promotes <2,2> and <2,3> as children of <1,1>. All members know the two blinded keys BK<2,3> and BK<1,0>, so M3 can calculate the new group key K<0,0> and any member can compute the group key once M3 broadcasts the blinded key of K<1,0>.

The authors present also the operation of tree updating in leave, partition and in merge operations.

Cliques (CLIQ)

The solution of cliques (CLIQ) is described by the authors Steiner, Tsudik and Waidner (2000). Their scheme is based on multi-party extensions of the well-known Diffie-Hellman key exchange method. It achieves efficient key agreement in the context of dynamic peer groups. Also, operations of addition and deletion in this scheme can be done easily.

This protocol executes four stages. In the first stage, it collects contributions from all group members (upflow) and at the end of this stage, the user U_{n-1} possesses the number $g^{\prod\{N_k/k\in[1,n-1]\}}$. In the second stage, the user U_{n-1} publishes this value to other group members. Every user $U_i(i\neq n)$ in the third stage factors out its own exponent and transmits the result to the last user U_n. In the fourth stage, U_n raises all inputs collected from the previous stage to the power N_n and broadcasts the result of n-1values to the rest of the group. Thus, every member has a value $g^{\prod\{N_k/k\in[1,n],k\neq i\}}$ and can easily calculate the group key K_n; $K_n = g^{\prod\{N_k/k\in[1,n]\}}$.

For n=5, we provide a simple example illustrating the different steps in this scheme for a group of five members A, B, C, D, and E.

Stage 1:

$A \rightarrow B : \{g^a\}, B \rightarrow C : \{g^{ab}\}, C \rightarrow D : \{g^{abc}\}$

Stage 2:

$D \rightarrow A, B, C, E : \{g^{abcd}\}$

Stage3:

$A \rightarrow E : \{g^{bcd}\}, B \rightarrow E : \{g^{acd}\}, C \rightarrow E : \{g^{abd}\}, D \rightarrow E : \{g^{abc}\}$

Stage4:

$E \rightarrow \{A, B, C, D\} : \{g^{bcde}, g^{acde}, g^{abde}, g^{abce}\}$

Figure 4. Tree update when a new member joins the network

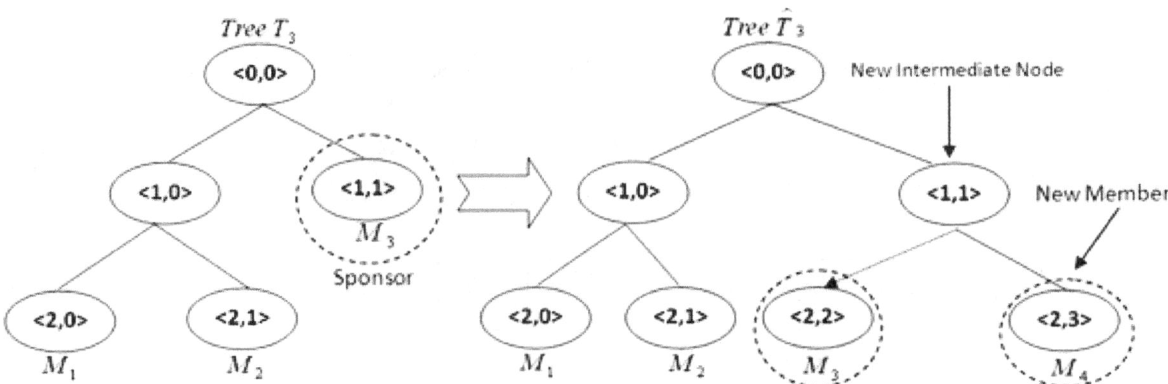

In Stage 4, each member can compute the final key (group key): $K_5=g^{abcde}$. In general, a total of $5n$-1 exponentiations is needed and the required number of messages is 2n-1.

For large groups, this scheme seems to be unsuitable because collecting contributions from all members can become very expensive.

Burmester-Desmedt (BD)

This scheme is based on the protocol of the Diffie-Hellman key distribution system. It is presented by its authors Burmester & Desmedt (1994) in their paper "A secure and efficient conference key distribution system". This protocol is described as follows:

- User $U_i(1 \le i \le n)$ generates a value of r_i, then calculates and publishes $z_i = g^{r_i} \bmod p$.
- Each user U_i computes and broadcasts the value of $X_i = (\frac{z_{i+1}}{z_{i-1}})^{r_i} \bmod p$.
- Finally, each user can discover the common key (group key) by computing the value of $k_i = (z_{i-1})^{nr_i}.X_i^{n-1}.X_{i+1}^{n-2}\ldots X_{i-2} \bmod p$. Thus, an honest user calculates the same key $K = g^{r_1r_2+r_2r_3+\ldots+r_nr_1}$. For example, in a case where $n = 5$, the users are A, B, C, D, and E. B calculates the group key by the expression: $K = \left(g^a\right)^{5b}.\left(\frac{g^{cb}}{g^{ab}}\right)^4.\left(\frac{g^{dc}}{g^{bc}}\right)^3.\left(\frac{g^{ed}}{g^{cd}}\right)^2.(\frac{g^{ae}}{g^{de}})$.

Skinny Tree (STR)

In their paper "communication-efficient Group Key Agreement," the authors Steer, Strawczynski, Diffie, and Wiener (1990) describe a group key management schemes called Skinny Tree (STR). According to the authors, this protocol trades off computation for communication efficiency. Figure 5 shows notations related to STR.

The description of this protocol is as follows. Node M_i possesses a secret r_i and the blinded

Figure 5. Different notations for STR

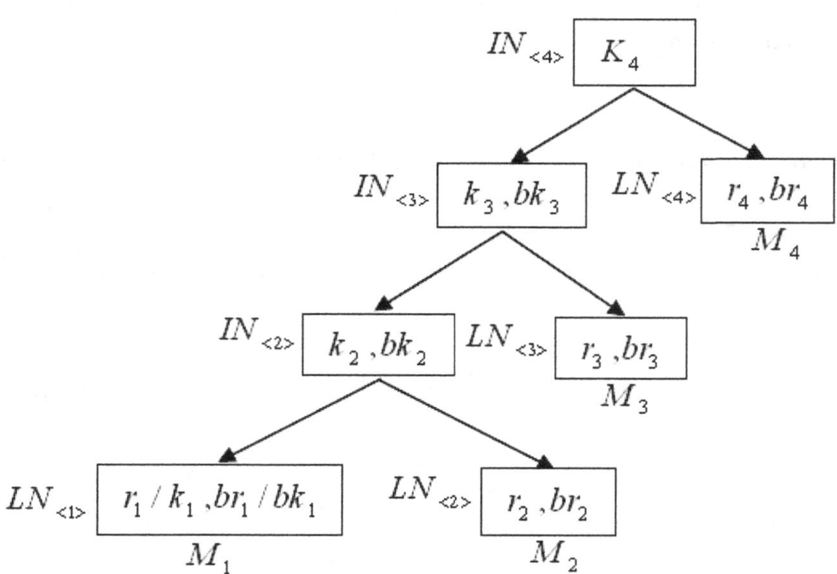

version $br_i = g^{r_i} \bmod p$. Every internal $IN_{<j>}$ has a secret k_j and the public blinded key $bk_j = g^{k_j} \bmod p$. The secret k_i (i>1) is the result of a Diffie-Hellman key agreement between the node's two children. k_i is computed recursively

$$\begin{cases} k_1 = r_1 \\ k_i = (bk_{i-1})^{r_i} \bmod p = (br_i)^{k_{i-1}} = g^{r_i k_{i-1}} \bmod p (i \geq 2) \end{cases}$$

and the group key is k_N, where N is the number of members in the network.

This protocol supposes each member knows its secret and the blinded keys of the other members, so, that M_1 and M_2 computes

$$k_2 = (br_2)^{r_1} \bmod p = (br_1)^{r_2} \bmod p = g^{r_1 r_2} \bmod p$$

$$k_3 = (br_3)^{k_2} \bmod p$$

$$k_N = (br_N)^{k_{N-1}} \bmod p$$

The group key is k_N, thus M_1 and M_2 already have the group key Next, M_1 publishes all blinded keys $bk_i = g^{k_i} \bmod p (1 \leq i \leq N-1)$. Upon receiving this message, every member can compute the group key k_n as follows. M_i(i>2) knows its secret r_i and bk_{i-1} from the message of M_1; therefore, it can drive $k_i = (bk_{i-1})^{r_i} \bmod p$. Thus, it can calculate other keys recursively up to the group key k_N.

Despite this protocol has the characteristic of communication efficiency, in large number of broadcast messages, it can be problematic in a wide ad hoc networks.

Other Contributory Schemes

There are other schemes of contributory key management which has been proposed:

Hypercube and Octopus (H&O) (Becker & Wille, 1998) is a scheme that reduces the number of rounds and exponentiations of ING from n to d ($n=2^d$), but it is vulnerable to MIM attacks and authentication is absent. Also, it scales badly.

Password Authentication Key Agreement (A-G) (Asokan & Ginzboorg, 2000) is basically H&O extended with password authentication. It doubles the number of messages and increases the computational complexity compared to H&O. It remedies H&O's vulnerability to MIM attacks, but at the price of scalability.

Other key management protocols such as MQV (Certicom Corp., 2004) are unsuitable for MANETs:

Distributive Schemes of Key Management

Public Key Schemes

Actually, several research papers propose key management schemes for MANETs. Their proposals are based on public key cryptography. The basic idea is to distribute the CA's functionality to a set of nodes. In this section, we present schemes illustrating this idea, including:

Partially Distributed Threshold CA Scheme (Z-H), Ubiquitous and Robust Access Control (URSA), Mobile Certificate Authority (MOCA), Self-Organized Key Management (PGP-A), Composite Key Management (COMP), and Secure and Efficient Key Management (SEKM).

Partially Distributed Threshold CA Scheme (Z-H)

This protocol is elaborated by Zhou and Hass (1999) in their paper entitled "Securing Ad Hoc Networks". They presented their key management scheme by using (t,n) threshold cryptography to distribute trusted keys among a set of *n* servers. The system can tolerate t-1compromised servers.

The service provided by this key management scheme has a public/private (K/S) keys pair. Each node knows exactly the public key K and trusts any certificate signed by the private key S. The public key is distributed to all nodes but the private key is split to n shares $s_1,s_2,\ldots,s_n$. Each server has one share according to a random polynomial function (Figure 6). In the system, there are three types of nodes: client, server and combiner nodes. Every node in networks possesses a public/private keys pair. The client nodes are not part of the certificate authority. The servers are special nodes who are responsible for generating partial certificates. They also store certificates in a directory structure in order to allow nodes to request certificates of other nodes. The combiner node obtains a valid certificate by combining the partial certificates.

Servers can refresh the secret shares by using the proactive secret sharing (PSS) (Herzberg, Jarecki, Krawczyk & Yung, 1995) technique or adjusting the configuration based on share redistribution techniques. Because the old shares are independent of the new ones, this decreases the success of mobile adversaries because they would have to compromise a threshold number of servers in a short time. Also, a share-refreshing to counter mobile adversaries is presented and the network nodes can use the same system public key.

This system is adequate for a small group of servers with rich connectivity is not suitable for purely ad hoc environments. Also, the system does not describe how a node can contact servers efficiently and securely in when servers are scattered across a wide area. Although the system offers a share-refreshing scheme, the problem of securely and efficiently distributing the updated shares to all nodes is not addressed.

Ubiquitous and Robust Access Control (URSA)

In the paper "URSA: Ubiquitous and Robust Access Control for Ad Hoc Networks," the URSA protocol uses threshold cryptography like Z-H. Since the nodes are capable of public key encryption, this solution is aimed towards planned long term for ad hoc networks. Some advantages of this system are efficiency and secrecy of local communications.

The capabilities of the certificate authority in URSA are distributed to all nodes in the network; therefore all nodes are capable of producing a partial certificate. Another advantage of this scheme is the system availability.

To maintain the system, every node in URSA should periodically update its certificate to protect it from being compromised. To do this, a node must have a minimum *k*one-hop neighbors and

Figure 6. Description of Z-H scheme

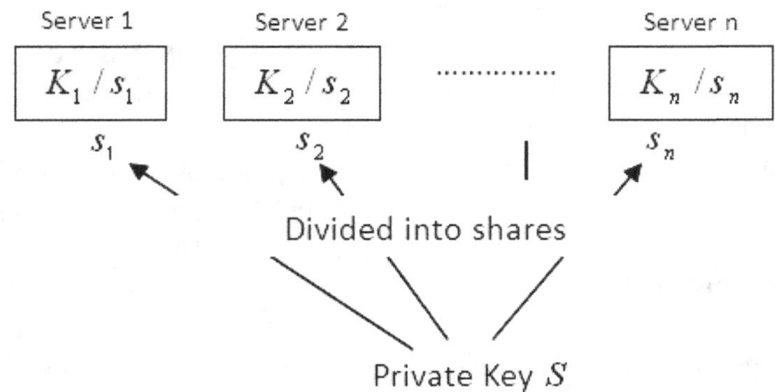

it must be given a legitimistic certificate before it can join the Ad Hoc network. The node can combine into valid certificate partial certificates.

To allow a new node to join the network, URSA provides a self-initialization phase. The new node obtains secret shares from a coalition of K neighboring nodes without supposing the existence of an online secret share dealer. In this phase, we use the extended PSS technique by shuffling the partial share and not shuffling the secret sharing polynomials; the goal of this shuffling is to prevent discovery of the original secret share by using a resulting share.

Since nodes are not well-protected because an attacker can locate a secret holder without much searching (each node has its own share), this scheme reduces security. Also, the selected parameter k may need to be larger as the attacker may be able to compromise a large number of shares between each share update. In sparse networks, if a node has a small number of neighbors and if it wants to update its certificate, the node must move around to find enough partial certificates. Also, a serious offline configuration is demanded before accessing ad hoc networks.

Mobile Certificate Authority (MOCA)

In 2002, Yi and Kravets (2002) established a scheme named Mobile Certificate Authority (MOCA). MOCA limits the candidates who hold a share of the secret key of the network; a certificate service is distributed to a set of mobile certificate authority nodes (called MOCA nodes) instead of all nodes.

If the nodes are equally equipped, the MOCA nodes are selected randomly and they are chosen according to their heterogeneity if they are computationally more powerful and physically more secure.

In this system, a node can locate $k+\alpha$ MOCA nodes randomly, based on the freshet path in its route cache, through the shortest path.

This scheme (where some nodes are computationally more powerful, physically more secure and trustworthy) is inappropriate for purely ad hoc networks. Another critical problem is how the nodes securely discover the paths of MOCA nodes and establish a key service in advance.

Self- Organized Key Management (PGP-A)

In the paper "self organized public key management for mobile ad hoc networks" (Capkun et al., 2003), the authors present a fully distributed key management scheme. Its main advantage is the configuration flexibility of the system, so this scheme does not require infrastructure, neither server, routing nor organizational/administrative.

Similar to PGP, in this system, the certificates are generated by the users themselves without the existence of any certification authority. Each user has two local certificate repositories: one updated and another non updated. The goal of maintaining a non updated certificate repository is to better estimate the certificate graph. Where

Figure 7. Illustration of a certificate chain

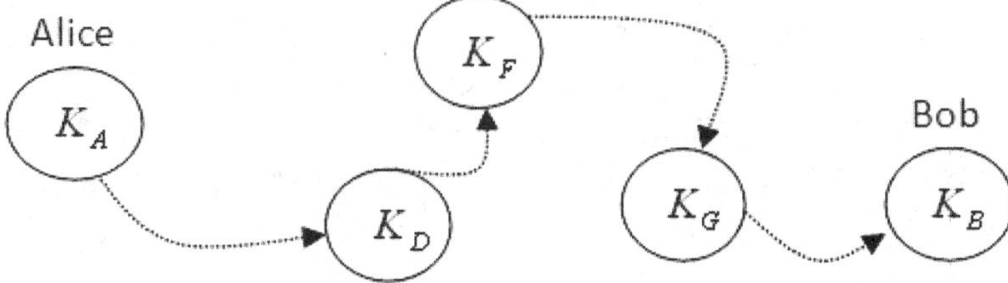

two users wish to authenticate each other's public keys, they use only the certificates stored in their combined local certificate repositories and try to find a certificate chain. An example of a chain is shown in Figure 7.

Similar to PGP, the system has problems in the initial stage before the number of generated certificates reaches a critical number; this process depends on the node's behavior and mobility. Also, this scheme is not appropriate for applications that need strong security because it lacks any trusted security anchor in a trusted structure. Each node should collect and maintain its two repositories and many certificates are needed in the system, which leads to another problem of certificates conflicting. In a purely ad hoc scenario, the certificate graph may not be strongly connected; two nodes in different components may not be able to communicate.

Composite Key Management (COMP)

In 2004, the idea of composite key management scheme was described by the authors Yi and Kravets (2004) in their paper "Composite key Management for Ad Hoc Networks." To take advantage of the positive aspects of different trusted systems, they combine centralized and fully distributed certificate chaining trust models, so that there is a compromise between security and flexibility. In their scheme, the authors incorporate a TTP into the certificate graph. TTP is the virtual Certificate Authority (CA) and it represents all nodes that comprise the virtual CA. They also introduce a confidence value as an authentication metric in order to glue two trusted systems. For example, if a node is trusted by CA, its confidence value is higher. Figure 8 gives an idea of COMP.

One problem of this scheme is that the task for assigning a confidence value to each node is a complicated and faces serious challenges.

Secure and Efficient Key Management (SEKM)

Recently, Wu et al. (2005) presented the scheme SEKM in their paper "Secure and efficient Key Management scheme in Mobile Ad Hoc Networks." This scheme is based on the technique of threshold cryptography and it represents a decentralized virtual certificate authority (CA) trusted model. The functionality of CA is distributed to a set of nodes (servers). In SEKM, a mesh-based group is formed by server nodes. All servers forming the group have a partial system private key and create a view of CA.

The problem in SEKM is that maintaining the structure server group for a large network with high mobility can be very expensive.

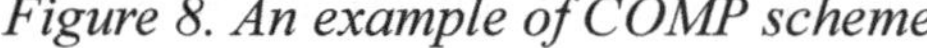
Figure 8. An example of COMP scheme

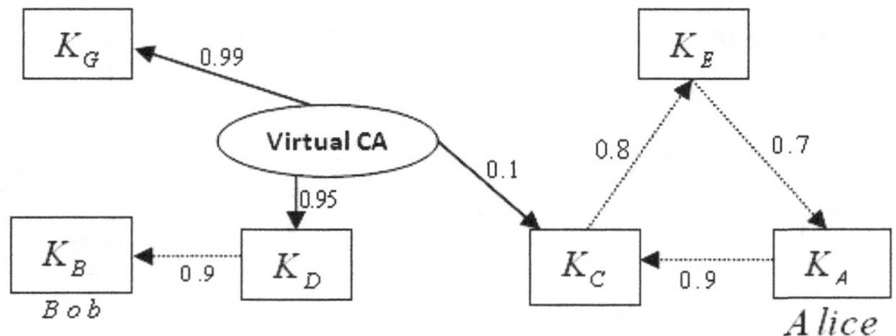

Other Public Key Schemes

Among other public key schemes, we introduce:

Ubiquitous Security Support (UBIQ) (Kong et al., 2001) is a fully distributed CA scheme. It is similar to schemes Z-H, MOCA and SEKM. In this scheme, all nodes get a share of the private CA key. UBIQ may succumb to a sybil attack (Douceur, 2002) where a single node takes more identities. Also, secure and efficient revocation is an unresolved challenge.

Autonomous Key Management (AKM) (Zhu et al., 2005) is a self-organizing and fully distribute threshold CA. Each node has a share of the private CA key. When the number of nodes increases, a hierarchy of keys is introduced. AKM increases intrusion tolerance at the price of communication and a hierarchical AKM with several regions represents a waste of bandwidth.

Mobility-Based Key Management Scheme (MOB) (Capkun et al., 2003b, 2006) is a scheme where security association is established between pairs of nodes that get close. The assumption of MOB that no one should communicate securely with parties that have not been close contradicts the evolution of PKI.

Identity-Based Public Key (IBC-K) described by Shamir in 1984, removes the need of certificates. The new cryptosystems allow user identities, e.g. email or IP addresses, to be used as public keys, and makes certificates superfluous.

Symmetric Schemes

There is some research that describe schemes based on symmetric key cryptography. Certain schemes are supposed to be incapable of performing asymmetric cryptography computation and they are appropriate to sensor nodes. In this section, we describe three schemes: Secure Pebblenets (PEBL), Distributed Key Predistribution Scheme (DKPS), and Peer Intermediaries for Key Establishment (PIKE).

Secure Pebblenets (PEBL)

The authors Basagni et al. (2001) propose a distributed key management system called PEBL in their paper "Secure Pebblenets." The word *"pebble"* is given the nodes because of their small size and large number in a large ad hoc networks, as occurs in Wireless Sensor Networks (WSNs).

In this scheme, all nodes in the ad hoc network share the secret group identity which is used in the authentication process and to generate additional keys to provide confidentiality. These keys are updated on regular intervals, while the group identity key lasts for the whole duration of the network. Protecting data is the aim of PEBL, which updates and establishes a network wide traffic encryption key, TEK. To update TEK, the network is segmented into clusters. A cluster head node is selected by each cluster. One of the cluster heads is elected as key manager. The key manager generates the traffic key TEK and distributes it to the regular nodes through the cluster heads.

Authentication is limited to group membership due to the complexity involved in key distribution. PEBL is bandwidth consuming due to the cluster formation and periodic TEK updates. Also, this solution demands an organizational/administrative infrastructure that initializes the network nodes with the shares group identity and additional parameters. Since only group authentication is supported, this solution is not suitable for ad hoc networks.

Distributed Key Pre-Distribution Scheme (DKPS)

In their paper "Distributed Symmetric Key Management for Mobile Ad Hoc Networks," the author Chan (2004) describes a distributed symmetric key management scheme. This solution overcomes the limitations of TTP and the incapability of nodes to perform computationally intensive public key algorithms.

In DKPS, each node randomly selects a set of key and satisfies the probability property of cover-free family (CFF). For each couple of two nodes, to use a shared secret key, they employ the secure shared key discovery procedure (SSD). One node performs a polynomial and sends the encrypted polynomial to another node. The sender's secret key is used to encrypt the coefficient of the polynomial. The other node multiplies the encrypted polynomial by a random value and sends back the result. Using the theory behind SSD, each node can discover the common secret key, without knowing the other non-common keys.

Peer Intermediaries for Key Establishment (PIKE)

In 2005, Chan and Perrig (2005) described a symmetric key management scheme in their paper "PIKE: Peer Intermediaries for Key Establishment in Sensor Networks." PIKE is a scheme that uses one or more sensor nodes in ad hoc networks as trusted intermediaries to perform key establishment between neighboring nodes. Every node in this scheme shares a unique secret key with a set of nodes.. The key distribution scheme can have two or more dimensions. For example, in 2-dimension, any node shares a unique secret key with each of $O(\sqrt{n})$ in the vertical and horizontal dimensions. Thus, each two nodes can have a common secret key with at least one intermediate node.

Other Symmetric Key Schemes

Below, we describe some additional protocols:

Pre-shared Group Key (PSGK) is a well-proven key management with a key distribution center redistributing a symmetric key to all members of the group. PSGK lacks intrusion tolerance and it is not elaborated for ad hoc networks.

SLiMPy (Puzar et al., 2005) is elaborated for MANETs. This scheme establishes a wide symmetric key for protection of network layer routing and application layer user data. SLiMPy adds complexity to PSGK and does not increase security.

Self-healing Session Key distribution (S-HEAL) (Staddon et al., 2002) is a scheme with revocation, designed for networks with unreliable links. The scheme demands preshared secrets and a group manager that broadcasts the current group key masked with a polynomial. Missing source authentication of the broadcasts from the group manager is a shortcoming.

Probablistic Key Predistribution (PRE) (Eschenauer & Gligor, 2002) supposes WSN nodes outfitted with a preinstalled key ring. The objective of the key ring in PRE is intrusion tolerance and the price is availability. Applicability and scalability are limited in this scheme.

Security Protocols for Sensor Networks (SPINs) (Perrig et al., 2002) supposes preinstalled individual keys between the sensor nodes and a base station. SPINs includes a scheme for authentication. This solution provides little flexibility and scales poorly.

GKMPAN (Zhu et al., 2004) supposes a pre-distributed group key with a predistributed commitment. The group key is employed to protect multicast communication. Faulty nodes may inhibit efficient exclusion and rekeying. GKMPAN increases intrusion tolerance compared to PSGK as it enables node exclusion, but at the price of reduced availability.

Key Infection (INF) (Anderson et al., 2004) is described for WSNs. INF sets up symmetric keys between the nodes and their on-hop neighbors. The security relies on the assumption that during network deployment, any attacker is only able to monitor a fixed percentage of the communication channels. INF is vulnerable to eavesdropping during key whispering and there is no authentication process.

Localized Encryption and Authentication Protocols (LEAP) (Zhu et al., 2003b) is presented for static WSNs. It requires a number of predistributed keys. Predistributed keys are used for communication between sensor nodes and the base station. This scheme does not work in a traditional ad hoc network.

CONCLUSION

In MANETs, the computation and complexity for key management is strongly subject to the restriction by the node's available resources and the dynamic nature of network topology. Therefore, key management is a hot topic in current research to design a strong scheme to overcome the challenges and vulnerabilities of MANETs.

The solutions of key management presented in this chapter differ significantly in their requirements, functionality, and complexity. However, they can be grouped into different categories depending on different criteria. Here, we have considered two categories of contributory and distributive schemes of key management. Distributive schemes themselves are divided into two categories: asymmetric and symmetric schemes.

In summary, there are several key management schemes adapted for MANETs but these schemes face various challenges and vulnerabilities. Designing and building an underlying secure, robust, and scalable key management scheme is the object of recent research which is still in its early stage.

REFERENCES

Anderson, R., Chan, H., & Perrig, A. (2004). Key infection: Smart trust for smart dust. In *Proceedings of the 12th IEEE International Conference on Network Protocols (ICNP)* (pp. 206–215). New York: IEEE.

Asokan, N., & Ginzboorg, P. (2000). Key agreement in ad-hoc networks. *Computer Communications, 23*(17), 1627–1637. doi:10.1016/S0140-3664(00)00249-8

Basagni, S., Herrin, K., Bruschi, D., & Rosti, E. (2001). Secure pebblenets. In *Proceedings of the 2nd ACM Interational Symposium on Mobile Ad Hoc Networking and Computing (MobiHoc)* (pp. 156-163). New York: ACM.

Becker, K., & Wille, U. (1998). Communication complexity of group key distribution. In *Proceedings of the 5th ACM conference on Computer and Communication Security* (pp. 1–6). New York: ACM.

Burmester, M., & Desmedt, Y. (1994). A secure and efficient conference key distribution system. In A. De Santis (Ed.), *Advances in cryptology* – EUROCRYPT '94 (Lecture Notes in Computer Science, Vol 950). Berlin: Springer.

Capkun, S., Buttya, L., & Hubaux, P. (2003). Self-organized public key management for mobile ad hoc networks. *IEEE Transactions on Mobile Computing, 2*(1), 52–64. doi:10.1109/TMC.2003.1195151

Capkun, S., Hubaux, J. P., & Buttyán, L. (2003b). Mobility helps security in ad hoc networks. Paper presented at *ACM MobiHoc*. New York: ACM.

Capkun, S., Hubaux, J. P., & Buttyán, L. (2006). Mobility helps peer-to-peer security. *IEEE Transactions on Mobile Computing, 5*(1), 43–51. doi:10.1109/TMC.2006.12

Certicom Corp. (2004). Crypto column: MQV: Efficient and authenticated key agreement. *Code & Cipher: Certicom's bulletin of security and cryptography, 1*(2).

Chan, A. (2004). Distributed symmetric key management for mobile ad hoc networks. Paper presented at *IEEE INFOCOM*. New York: IEEE.

Chan, H., & Perrig, A. (2005). PIKE: Peer intermediaries for key establishment in sensor networks. Paper presented at *IEEE INFOCOM*. New York: IEEE.

Chan, H., Perrig, A., & Song, D. (2010). (in press). Random key pre-distribution schemes for sensor networks. Paper presented at the *IEEE Security and Privacy Symposium.* New York: IEEE.

Diffie, W., & Hellman, M. E. (1976). New directions in cryptography. *IEEE Transactions on Information Theory, 22*(6), 644–654. doi:10.1109/TIT.1976.1055638

Douceur, J. R. (2002). The Sybil attack. In *Proceedings of the 1st International Workshop on Peer-to-Peer Systems (IPTPS)* (pp. 251–260).

Eschenauer, L., & Gligor, V. D. (2002). A key-management scheme for distributed sensor networks. In *Proceedings of the 9th Conference on Computer Communication Security (CCS)* (pp. 41–47).

Herzberg, A., Jarecki, S., Krawczyk, H., & Yung, H. (1995). Proactive secret sharing or: How to cope with perpetual leakage. *Lecture Notes in Computer Science, 963*, 339–352. doi:10.1007/3-540-44750-4_27

Ingemarsson, I., Tang, D., & Wong, C. (1982). A conference key distribution system. *IEEE Transactions on Information Theory, 28*(5), 714–720. doi:10.1109/TIT.1982.1056542

Kaufman, C., Perlman, R., & Speciner, M. (2002). *Network security private communication in a public world.* Upper Saddle River, NJ: Prentice Hall PTR.

Kim, Y., Perrig, A., & Tsudik, G. (2000a). *Simple and fault-tolerant key agreement for dynamic collaborative groups.* Tech. Rep. 2/USC Tech. Rep. 00-737.

Kim, Y., Perrig, A., & Tsudik, G. (2000b). Simple and fault-tolerant key agreement for dynamic collaborative groups. In *Proceedings of the 7th ACM Conference on Computer and Communications Security* (pp. 235-244). New York: ACM Press.

Kong, J., Zerfos, P., Luo, H., Lu, S., & Zhang, L. (2001). Providing robust and ubiquitous security support for mobile ad-hoc networks. In P*roceedings of the ninth International Conference on Network Protocols (ICNP)*, (pp. 251–260).

Luo, H., & Lu, S. (2004). URSA: Ubiquitous and robust access control for mobile ad hoc networks. *IEEE/ACM Transactions on Networking, 12*(6), 1049–1063. doi:10.1109/TNET.2004.838598

Luo, H., Zerfos, P., Kong, J., Lu, S., & Zhang, L. (2001). Providing robust and ubiquitous security support for mobile ad-hoc networks. Paper presented at the *9th International Conference on Network Protocols.*

Menezes, A., Oorschot, P., & Vanstone, S. (1996). *Handbook of applied cryptography*. Boca Raton, FL: CRC Press.

Oppliger, R. (1998). *Internet and intranet security*. London: Artech House.

Perkins, C. (2001). *Ad hoc networking.* Boston: Addison- Wesley.

Perrig, A., Szewczyk, R., Tygar, J. D., Wen, V., & Culler, D. (2002). SPINS: Security protocols for sensor networks. *Wireless Networks, 8*(5), 521–534. doi:10.1023/A:1016598314198

Puzar, M., Andersson, J., Plagemann, T., & Roudier, Y. (2005). SKiMPy: A simple key management protocol for MANETs in emergency and rescue operations. Paper presented at *ESAS*, Visegrad, Hungary.

Rafaeli, S., & Hutchison, D. (2003). A survey of key management for secure group communication. *ACM Computing Surveys, 35*(3), 309–329. doi:10.1145/937503.937506

Saloma, A. (1996). *Public-key cryptography.* Berlin: Springer-Verlag.

Shamir, A. (1979). How to share a secret. *Communications of the ACM, 22*(11), 612–613. doi:10.1145/359168.359176

Sherman, T., & McGrew, A. (2003). Key establishment in large dynamic groups using one-way function trees. *IEEE Transactions on Software Engineering, 29*(5), 444–458. doi:10.1109/TSE.2003.1199073

Staddon, J., Miner, S., Franklin, M., Balfanz, D., Malkin, M., & Deam, D. (2002). Self-healing key distribution with revocation. Paper presented at the *IEEE Symposium on Security and Privacy*, Oakland, CA.

Steer, D., Strawczynski, L., Diffie, W., & Wiener, M. (1990). A secure audio teleconference system. In *Advances in Cryptology*–CRYPTO '88 ([]. Berlin: Springer.]. *Lecture Notes in Computer Science, 403*, 520–528. doi:10.1007/0-387-34799-2_37

Steiner, M., Tsudik, G., & Waidner, M. (2000). Cliques: A new approach to group key agreement. In *Proceedings of the 18th International Conference on Distributed Computing Systems* (pp. 380-387). New York: IEEE.

Wong, C., Gouda, M., & Lam, S. (1998). Secure group communications using key graphs. In *Proceedings of the ACM SIGCOMM conference on Applications, Technologies, Architectures, and Protocols for Computer Communication* (pp. 68-79). New York: ACM.

Wu, B., Chen, J., Wu, J., & Cardei, M. (2006). *A survey on attacks and countermeasures in mobile ad hoc networks. Wireless/mobile network security*. Berlin: Springer.

Wu, B., Wu, J., Fernandez, E., Ilyas, M., & Magliveras, S. (2005). Secure and efficient key management scheme in mobile ad hoc networks. [JCNA]. *Journal of Network and Computer Applications, 30*(3), 937–954. doi:10.1016/j.jnca.2005.07.008

Yi, S., & Kravets, R. (2004). Composite key management for ad hoc networks. In *Proceedings of the 1st Annual International Conference on Mobile and Ubiquitous Systems: Networking and Services (MobiQuitous)* (pp. 52-61). New York: IEEE.

Yi, S., Naldurg, P., & Kravets, R. (2002). *Security aware ad hoc routing for wireless networks*. Report No. UIUCDCS-R-2002-2290. Urbana, IL: UIUC.

Zhou, L., & Haas, Z. (1999). Securing ad hoc networks. *IEEE Network Magazine, 13*(6), 24–30. doi:10.1109/65.806983

Zhu, B., Bao, F., Deng, R. H., Kankanhalli, M. S., & Wang, G. (2005). Efficient and robust key management for large mobile ad hoc networks. *Computer Networks, 48*(4), 657–682. doi:10.1016/j.comnet.2004.11.023

Zhu, S., Setia, S., & Jajodia, S. (2003b). LEAP: Efficient security mechanisms for large-scale distributed sensor networks. Paper presented at *CSS*, Washington, DC. New York: ACM.

Zhu, S., Setia, S., Xu, S., & Jajodia, S. (2004). GKMPAN: An efficient group rekeying scheme for secure multicast in ad-hoc networks. Paper presented at *Mobiquitous*, Boston.

ADDITIONAL READING

Burnett, S., & Paine, S. (2001). *RSA security's official guide to cryptography*. Emeryville, CA: RSA Press.

Chan, H., Perrig, A., & Song, D. (in press). Random key pre-distribution schemes for sensor networks. In *Proceedings of the IEEE Security and Privacy Symposium*. New York: IEEE.

Ilyas, M. (2003). *The handbook of ad hoc wireless networks*. Boca Raton, FL: CRC Press.

Karygiannis, T., & Owens, L. (2002). *Wireless network security-802.11, bluetooth and handheld devices* (pp. 800-848). Washington, DC: National Institute of Standards and Technology, Technology Administration, U.S. Department of Commerce.

Lou, W., & Fang, Y. (2003). A survey of wireless security in mobile ad hoc networks: Challenges and available solutions. In Chen, X., Huang, X., & Du, D. (Eds.), *Ad hoc wireless networks* (pp. 319–364). Dordrecht, The Netherlands: Kluwer Academic Publishers.

Murthy, C., & Manoj, B. (2005). *Ad hoc wireless networks: Architectures and protocols*. Upper Saddle River, NJ: Prentice Hall PTR.

Nichols, R., & Lekkas, P. (2002). *Wireless security models, threats, and solutions*. New York: McGraw Hill.

Ravi, S., Raghunathan, A., & Potlapally, N. (2002). Secure wireless data: System architecture challenges. Paper presented at the *International Conference on System Synthesis*, Kyoto, Japan.

Stallings, W. (2002). *Wireless communication and networks*. Upper Saddle River, NJ: Pearson Education.

Tanenbaum, A. (2002). Network security. In *Computer networks* (4th ed.). Upper Saddle River, NJ: Prentice Hall PTR.

Tanenbaum, A. (2003). *Computer networks*. Upper Saddle River, NJ: Prentice Hall PTR.

Wallner, D., Harder, E. J., & Agee, R. (1998). Key management for multicast: Issues and architectures [Internet draft, work in progress]. Fremont, CA: Internet Engineering Task Force. Retrieved from http://tools.ietf.org/html/draft-wallner-key-arch-01.txt

Wong, T., Wang, C., & Wing, J. (2002). *Verifiable secret redistribution for threshold sharing schemes* [Technical report CMU-CS-02-114-R]. Pittsburgh, PA: School of Computer Science, Carnegie Mellon University.

Wu, B., & Wu, J., & Dong, Y. (in press). An efficient group key management scheme for mobile ad hoc networks. *International Journal of Security and Networks* (*IJSN*), *3*(4).

Wu, B., Wu, J., Fernandez, E., Magliveras, S., & Ilyas, M. (2005). Secure and efficient key management in mobile ad hoc networks. In *Proceedings of the 19th IEEE International Parallel & Distributed Processing Symposium* (pp. 288.1). New York: IEEE.

Yang, H., Luo, H., Ye, F., Lu, S., & Zhang, L. (2004). Security in mobile ad hoc networks: Challenges and solutions. *IEEE Wireless Communications*, *11*(1), 38–47. doi:10.1109/MWC.2004.1269716

KEY TERMS AND DEFINITIONS

Ad Hoc Networks: Ad hoc networks are local area networks or other small networks, especially ones with wireless or temporary plug-in connections, in which some of the network devices are part of the network only for the duration of a communications session or, in the case of mobile or portable devices, while in some close proximity to the rest of the network.

Authentication: Is the process by which an entity provides its identity to another party.

Authorization: Is the process of granting access to a service or information based on a user's role in an organization.

Intrusion Tolerance: Intrusion tolerance is the ability to continue delivering a service when an intrusion occurs.

Key Management: The techniques or processes of creating, distributing, and maintaining a secret key, which will be used to protect the secrecy of communications or to ensure the original data are not maliciously altered.

Mobile Ad Hoc Network (MANET): An infrastructure- less, self-organizing network of mobile hosts connected with wireless communication channels. A MANET does not have a fixed topology because all the hosts can move freely, which results in rapid and unpredictable topology change.

Scalability: A property of a system, a network, or a process that can be modified to fit the problem area, that is, scaled to perform well with large-scale users.

Ubiquitous: Ubiquitous is being or seeming to be everywhere at the same time.

User: A user refers to a person or entity with authorized access.

Chapter 11
Connectivity and Topology Organization in Ad-Hoc Networks for Service Delivery

Cesar Vargas-Rosales
Instituto Tecnológico y de Estudios Superiores de Monterrey, Mexico

Sergio Barrientos
Instituto Tecnológico y de Estudios Superiores de Monterrey, Mexico

David Munoz
Instituto Tecnológico y de Estudios Superiores de Monterrey, Mexico

Jose R. Rodriguez
Instituto Tecnológico y de Estudios Superiores de Monterrey, Mexico

ABSTRACT

This chapter introduces the concept of connectivity and robustness of a mobile ad-hoc network as a function of the node density and coverage radius. It presents an elementary analytical model based on the spatial Poisson process to formulate the connectivity problem as the computation of the existence of wireless links forming paths obtained by Dijkstra's shortest path algorithm. It also introduces a simple clustering strategy that starts forming groups based on one-hop distance and then adjust the coverage radius of the nodes in order to decrease the interference, processing load and isolated nodes in the network. It includes results of scenarios with different robustness of origin-destination pairs and number of clusters and shows the benefits of using the introduced policies.

INTRODUCTION

Every service provider needs to deliver to its end-users the information and applications satisfying certain parameters indicating levels of quality and satisfaction. In an ad-hoc network, nodes are mobile or fixed, and have limited processing capabilities for energy, processing, memory, transmission power, etc. These limitations can produce critical scenarios for service delivery to end-users. In this chapter, we discuss important issues that a network provider must resolve in order to satisfy such quality parameters, when

DOI: 10.4018/978-1-60960-027-3.ch011

an ad-hoc network is implemented. Among these issues, we have node and network connectivity, the topology formation, the use of clusters in the topology, the network monitoring to balance traffic load, the network coverage, the wireless channel impairments, and so on.

In this chapter, we introduce a model that measures path availability that depends on user density and transmission power. The model is based on a spatial Poisson process and the coverage radius of the nodes, and it provides a measure of the *strength* of a path. The model brings together the concepts of reachability, robustness and connectivity to provide means to measure service delivery success in an ad-hoc network, and helps to make evident connectivity for service delivery by detecting trouble areas where coverage or link availability is compromised. This evidence can help service providers to determine areas where nodes can be turned on and off, depending on user density, time of day and traffic load, providing network adaptability that changes dynamically according to existing conditions of traffic, interference, and node density.

We also provide a network topology organization based on clusters that minimizes the number of disconnected nodes, and maximizes network connectivity by using paths with the minimum number of hops possible. We discuss wireless channel propagation problems in order to modify coverage of the nodes and provide a clustering organization of the nodes in the network with their decision rules and algorithms. This clustering organization is studied by varying the user density, coverage radius and mobility of nodes to provide evidence of the effects of such issues on service delivery and connectivity of the ad-hoc network.

The purpose of this chapter is to evaluate connectivity and quality as performance measures, using a connectivity method (algorithm) to find paths and clustering routines that maintain an effective topology capable of adapting to node mobility so that routing can be more responsive and optimal when mobility rates are low and more efficient when they are high.

The main ideas of a communication system are to maintain an effective topology and provide service to the users at any time. Therefore, this service needs to be fast, efficient and of quality. To maintain an effective topology, we can use a dynamic algorithm where nodes are organized into clusters where probabilistic bounds can be calculated on the availability of paths to cluster destinations over a specified interval of time. In the case of Ad-hoc networks, the main issues to be considered are mobility, interference, connectivity and quality. When some problems related to these issues appear, it is necessary to have an organization within the network, through the nodes. This organization helps to diminish the negative effects of these issues through cooperative network maintenance.

BACKGROUND

A mobile ad-hoc network, (Macker & Corson, 1998; Chakrabarti & Mishra, 2001), is defined as an autonomous system of mobile nodes connected by wireless links, where these nodes are free to move randomly and organize themselves arbitrarily, changing the wireless network topology quickly and unpredictably. It is a self-configuring network of mobile devices connected throughout wireless links. Nodes establish communication in a point to point fashion, without the need of a central unit to enable communication between nodes. Such a network may operate in a standalone fashion, or may be connected to Access Points (APs), which are larger processing units that provide communication with the rest of the public switched network.

Wireless ad-hoc networks became a popular subject for research as laptops and 802.11/Wi-Fi wireless networking became widespread in the mid to late 1990s. Many of the academic papers evaluate protocols and abilities assuming varying degrees of mobility within a bounded space, usually with all nodes within a few hops of each other, and usually with nodes sending data at a constant rate. Performance of different protocols is based on the packet drop rate, the overhead introduced by the routing protocol, and other measures.

There are two basic parts in a Wireless ad-hoc network, (Pahlavan & Krishnamurthy, 2002; Toh, 2002):

- Mobile Host (MH): A mobile host, also called mobile node, constitutes the physical interface between the mobile subscriber and other mobile hosts or other telecommunication network devices. A MH contains a control unit, a transceiver and an antenna system, and it is able to establish direct communication with any other network device in to its power transmission range.
- Wireless links: Provide high speed links that enable communication between MH's.

A wireless ad-hoc network is self-organizing and adaptive to the communication requirements of the current network conditions. Self-organizing is a fundamental characteristic of reconfigurable networks. A given node in the network has to be capable of detecting nodes that are within its transmission range, and it also must discover which other nodes can be reached through immediate connected nodes. Auto configuration is also about detecting services available in the networks. Because of this characteristic most of the protocols for traditional networks can not directly be implemented in wireless ad-hoc networks. The Network is reconfigurable upon mobility and communication needs. Contrary to cellular networks, where the communication between two cellular devices is made through a base station, wireless ad-hoc networks have a point-to-point link between nodes, which means that two nodes within their sensitivity area can communicate directly without the assistance of a base station.

The transmission range of a device in wireless ad-hoc networks can vary greatly because of the heterogeneity of the devices in the network. There are great differences among these devices, and this heterogeneity can affect communication performance, as explained in more detail in (Pahlavan & Krishnamurthy, 2002). In this chapter, these subjects are not treated in detail; instead, we work with an average transmission range of typical devices that could be in the network.

Because an ad-hoc network does not use a centralized administration, nodes can enter/leave the network as they wish. Moreover, owing to the limited transmitter range of the nodes, multiple hops may be needed to reach other nodes, so that every node in the network must act both as a host and as a router. It is important to mention that in contrast to traditional networks, an ad-hoc network could be expected to operate in an environment in which some or all the nodes are mobile. For this reason, the network functions must run in a distributed fashion, since nodes might suddenly disappear from, or show up in, the network. However, the same basic user requirements for connectivity and traffic delivery that apply to traditional networks will apply to ad-hoc networks. In general, the principal characteristics of a mobile ad-hoc network are:

- *Dynamic topology*: network topology changes rapidly owing to the free movement of the nodes.
- *Bandwidth constraint*: the bandwidth of wireless links is in general small as compared to fixed connections.
- *Energy constraint*: the set of functions offered by a node depends on its available power, so that energy conservation is important.
- *Security*: is an issue of critical importance for most networks and mobile ad-hoc networks are no exception.

- *Multiple routes*: since the topology may change rapidly, the maintenance of multiple routes may ensure continuous node reachability.

Quality of Service (QoS) can be defined as a guarantee by the network to satisfy a set of predetermined service performance constraints for the user in terms of the end-to-end delay, available bandwidth, probability of packet loss, etc., where, of course, enough network resources must be available during the service invocation to keep the guarantee. For this, the first essential task is to find a suitable path through the network, or route, between the source and destination that will have the necessary resources available to meet the QoS constraints for the desired service.

Once a route has been selected for a specific flow, the necessary resources, (bandwidth, buffer space in routers, etc.) must be reserved for the flow, which will not be available to other flows. Consequently, the amount of remaining network resources available to accommodate the QoS requests of other flows will have to be recalculated and propagated to all other pertinent nodes as part of the topology update information. QoS routing selects the path and reserves the resources in such path (Chakrabarti, & Mishra, 2001). To do this, it depends on the accurate availability of the current network state. The first is the local state information maintained at each node, which includes queueing delay and the residual CPU capacity for the node, as well as the propagation delay, bandwidth and some form of cost metric for each of its outgoing links. The totality of local state information for all nodes constitutes the global state of the network, which is also maintained at each node. While the local state information may be assumed to be always available at any particular node, the global state information is constructed by exchanging the local state information for every node among all the network nodes at appropriate moments. The process of updating the global state information is also loosely called topology updates. This process significantly affects the QoS performance of the network, since updates consume network bandwidth, and the frequent routing changes increase delay jitter experienced by users.

To determine an optimal path satisfying the QoS constraints, three distinct route finding techniques are used, which are source routing, destination routing, and hierarchical routing. In source routing, a feasible path is locally computed at the source node using the locally stored global state information and then all other nodes along this feasible path are notified by the source of their adjacent preceding and successor nodes. In distributed or hop-by-hop routing, the source as well as other nodes is involved in path computation by identifying the adjacent router to which the source must forward the packet associated with the flow. Hierarchical routing uses the aggregated partial global state information to determine a feasible path using source routing where the intermediate nodes are actually logical nodes representing a cluster.

With the rising number of network services, automatic service discovery will be a very important feature in future network scenarios, because devices may automatically discover network services, including their properties and services may advertise their existence in a dynamic way. Service Discovery Protocol (SDP) enable users of a communication network to find services, applications and devices that are available in the network, as its purpose is to allow nodes on an infrastructureless wireless network to find services offered by other nodes in the network that fulfill a certain task. This feature is especially useful for mobile users in a foreign network and for groups of users that form a spontaneous (ad-hoc) wireless network.

SDP for wireless ad-hoc networks are classified in two categories: proactive (or push-based) and reactive (or pull-based) SDPs. Proactive SDP uses a broadcast mechanism, where each node unsolicitly advertises the services it can offer to the rest of the nodes in the network. In the case of reactive SDPs, each node queries other nodes for the services it requires. It is important to mention that a problem with proactive SDPs is large bandwidth requirement for message broadcasts; in addition, there is a potential for long latency in discovering services, especially when nodes take turns in sending broadcast messages. On the other hand, reactive SDPs suffer from bandwidth overhead (but less than that for proactive SDPs) and long latency (longer than that for proactive SDPs) to find the required services. Finally, both the proactive and reactive SDPs consume the limited battery power of the network nodes.

A variety of service discovery protocols are currently under development, (Choonhwa & Sumi, 2002; Garcia, 2005). The most well known are:

- Service Location Protocol (SLP) developed by the IETF.
- Jini, which is Sun's Java-based approach to service discovery.
- Salutation.
- Microsoft's Universal Plug and Play (UPnP).
- Bluetooth Service Discovery Protocol (SDP).

Nowadays, in Ad-hoc network research, scientists have found methods to improve communications in this area. Clustering is one of these methods, which presents stable and unstable behavior. One of these is the Distributed Dynamic Clustering Algorithm (DDCA), (Toh, 2002). To find the paths in the network, one can use the Bellman Ford, Kruskal, Dijkstra, and Trellis methods. We consider Dijkstra's algorithm to find connectivity and quality, easily, in the network, (Nikolopoulos & Pitsillides, 1997). We also generate a stable Ad-hoc network in a short period of time and obtain performance measures, including connectivity and quality in the network.

A great number of studies concerning network connectivity modeling and analysis of a particular mobile ad-hoc network have been reported in recent technical literature. This problem has been tackled in many works by choosing appropriate models to describe the network and deriving results analytically from these models. Typically, the maximum transmission range has been assumed to be constant, implying that all nodes have equal transmission and reception capabilities and that the radio environment determining the attenuation of transmissions is homogenous throughout the network.

(Foh, Liu, Lee, Seet, Wong & Fu, 2005; Foh & Lee, 2004) analyze network connectivity for a one dimensional ad hoc network, but this type of mobile ad-hoc network does not appear in the majority of real-world network applications, since the spatial distribution of the nodes is quite different. The most popular model is the two-dimensional homogenous Poisson point process, characterized by the node density.

(Franceschetti, Booth, Cook, Meester & Bruck, 2004) have applied the theory of percolation in their study of connectivity, where they showed that real networks can exploit the presence of unreliable connections and anisotropic radiation patterns to achieve connectivity more easily, if they can maintain an average number of functioning connections. But (Dousse, Thiran & Hasler, 2002), demonstrated that the appearance of an unbounded cluster at a finite intensity, i.e., percolation, requires the domain to be infinite in two dimensions. Then again, in two dimensions, an infinite cluster forming is a weaker condition than full connectivity. (Philips, Panwar & Tantawi, 1989) explained that with the model of a two-dimensional Poisson point process, a larger area always requires either a longer transmission range or a greater node density, since the greater the area, the more likely a region with sparsely located nodes. This renders the connectivity of random networks in the infinite plane with limited transmission range impossible.

(Bettstetter, 2002a, 2002b), derived an analytical expression in an attempt to bind together the transmission range and the node density needed to obtain almost surely a *k*-connected network. The expression was derived starting from the probability of not having nodes in a circle of radius *r* of a random node, with transmission range *r* and generated from a Poisson process with a density, being out of range from all other nodes. With the simplifying assumption of this event being independent for all *n* nodes in the network, the probability of no node being isolated was estimated to be $\left(1 - e^{-\pi\lambda r^2}\right)^n$. Problems were encountered when trying to verify this expression with simulations of 500 nodes scattered in a square-shaped area: with a fixed range, the proportion of connected realizations turned out to be significantly less than predicted. This resulted from the fact that the simulations were carried out on a bounded area, whereas the analytical expression was derived for an infinite area. In the bounded square, nodes located near the edges of the area are likely to have fewer connections than those located in the middle. This border effect was eliminated by using a toroidal distance metric, i.e., assuming that nodes at the edge were considered close to nodes at the opposite edge, this provided more satisfactory agreement with the analytical expression, although the probability of connectivity was still overestimated and the applicability of the derived analytical expression remained ambiguous, since the domain of any real-life ad hoc network is bound to have edges anyway.

In (Bettstetter, 2002), the theoretical problem of determining the minimum number of neighbors for full connectivity in spatially uniform ad hoc wireless networks has been considered. Peer-to-peer multi-hop reservation-based communication with disjointed routes is considered, i.e., a node cannot serve as a relay in more than one route. It can be argued that even the service suppliers cannot control the number of nodes in a determined zone to obtain full connectivity, and that in a real mobile network the uniform distribution is not the most optimal, since the nodes move randomly in the scenario. Moreover, a node can be used in more than one path since the same node can form different links with different nodes. The method that we propose studies the end-to-end connectivity in a more general fashion than the method of interconnectivity of (Stine & de Veciana, 2004; Michel, 2005).

CONNECTIVITY IN AD-HOC NETWORKS

Connectivity is a widely studied problem in the field of mobile ad-hoc networks, where a fundamental property is that every node in the network should be able to communicate with every other node. The establishment of connections defines a level of connectivity of the node, and at the same time the network topology. However, in a given network, a mobile node becomes disconnected with the rest of the network simply because it has wandered off too far from a neighbor's coverage area, or because its energy reserve has dropped below a critical threshold that does not allow the node to increase transmission power, or by the influence of certain phenomena in the radio channel such as fading or shadowing, reducing its coverage area and probably affecting links to other nodes of the network. In contrast, a mobile node in a network can gain connectivity if it approaches close enough to the rest of the network, or because it increases its coverage area (as a result of a reload of its power reserve, or by the influence of constructive multi-path effects), creating new links with the other nodes. In both cases, the connectivity of the nodes and, therefore, the network topology is affected.

We begin the discussion of service delivery by introducing the procedures of neighbor discovery and address assignment that must be carried out by every node that needs services from the network provider. These procedures determine, in part, the node connectivity and the topology formation

Figure 1. Four-node ad-hoc network

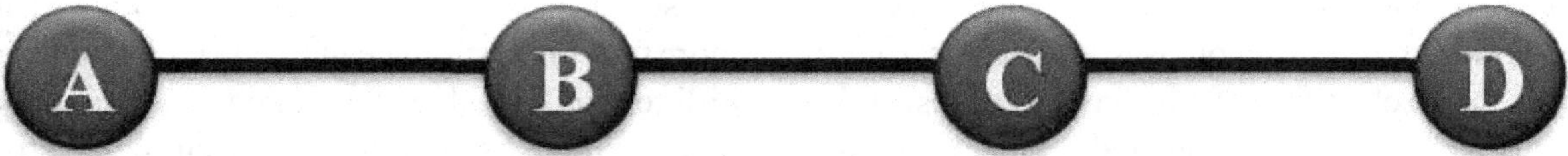

that help a network provider find out the degree to which mobility and channel impairments can be supported. New links will be established and some links will fail due to node mobility and the interference levels. This link-changing scenario determines strategies for network coverage and service delivery, since the network must have a well-established topology with maintenance algorithms and routing protocols that adapt to these changes.

We introduce the concepts of reachability and connectivity. In Figure 1, we can see an ad-hoc network with four nodes in a linear topological scenario. Assume that the nodes have carried out the procedures of neighbor discovery and address assignment and the linear topology shown is also determined by the current wireless channel conditions that fix coverage. Now, we can consider as a measure within the topology of the ad-hoc network the concept of reachability as the percentage of nodes in the network that can be reached from a specific node, considering wireless coverage. We can see that such a network in Figure 1 has 100% reachability, since every node can be reached from every other node using a path within the topology.

In contrast, in Figure 2, where we have four nodes with a different topology from that shown previously in Figure 1, we can also calculate the reachability and conclude that since every node reaches all the other nodes in the network, the reachability is also 100%. One of the main differences that we can see in the scenario in Figure 2 from that of the network in Figure 1 is that if one link fails, the network does not become disconnected as it would occur in the network of Figure 1. For example, in the network in Figure 2 we can see that several links need to fail in order to disconnect the nodes. This example tells us that reachability is not the only measure to indicate the capability of node discovery and service delivery; communication to and from every node forming an origin-destination pair reaching one another is also a measure. We can see that a node in the network in Figure 2 has more options to communicate with other nodes, i.e., the number of paths connecting every pair of nodes is more than one, giving a sense of a more robust network; hence, a concept of robustness needs to be defined and measured in ad-hoc networks.

When one node communicates with another node, a path can be created and registered in their corresponding routing tables. Up to this point, we can say that nodes communicate. Note that the incoming and outgoing paths used to communicate every pair of nodes need not be the same path. With the concepts of reachability and robustness, we can define a measure of connectivity, where the base would be the percentage of network nodes that can communicate with a specific node. Take,

Figure 2. Four-node ad-hoc network with robust topology

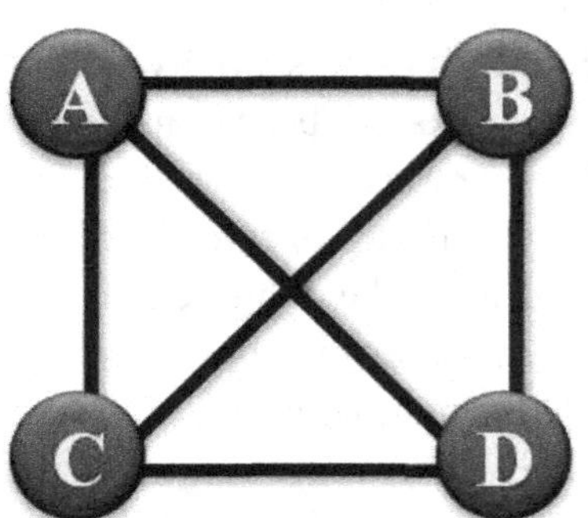

for example, node A in Figure 1. We can see that it reaches all the nodes in the network, that it also has a path to each and every node in the network, which gives the node 100% reachability and 100% communication and connectivity. However, we can also see that the connectivity point of view of node A is very different from that of node B, which has two links connecting it to the rest of the network. In Figure 2, we can see that the same nodes have a very different point of view of the network from that of Figure 1. This simple example also provides an important point to see that connectivity has a local meaning or its view is from a local position within the network, but the consequences of such reachability and connectivity are of global repercussions. We can also note that since connectivity depends on link availability, which is a physical layer issue, we need to deal with cross-layering to solve the different situations presented in the network.

Communication of Two Nodes

We see the performance of the basic case considered when two communicating nodes i and j, separated by distance t from each other, want to communicate over a two-hop path, when their coverage radius is equal (Michel, 2005). Given nodes i and j, with coverage areas $\mathcal{O}_i$ and $\mathcal{O}_i$, respectively, and the radius of coverage r, we recognize three subcases depicted in Figure 3 and described as follows:

$0<t\leq r$, in this instance, both nodes form a direct link because each node is within the coverage zone of the other node, implying that there exists direct connectivity and reachability from both communicating nodes, that is, there is bidirectional connectivity, see Figure 3(a).

$r<t\leq 2r$, in this event, at least a third node (called relay node) must lie within the intersection zone $\eth_{ij}$. This third node allows the connection by a route of two hops, providing direct connectivity and reachability in both directions; see Figure 3(b).

- $t > 2r$, in this case, there is neither a direct link nor a path of two hops between i and j, so, both nodes are disconnected, in spite of the existence of other nodes placed in the network (see Figure 3(c)). Otherwise, these nodes would act as reachable relay nodes in order to connect nodes i and j. Along these lines, this case would form a multi-hop path, specifically of more than two hops, being left out of this classification.

Special Situations

It is important to analyze some significant situations concerned with the first two sub cases, which are illustrated in a pair of details in Figures 4(a) and 4(b), respectively. As observed in Figure 4(a), where $0<t\leq r$ a direct link between nodes i and j is established regardless of the existence of relay nodes in $\eth_{ij}$. Therefore, the existence of

Figure 3. Two nodes with coverage r want to communicate to each other

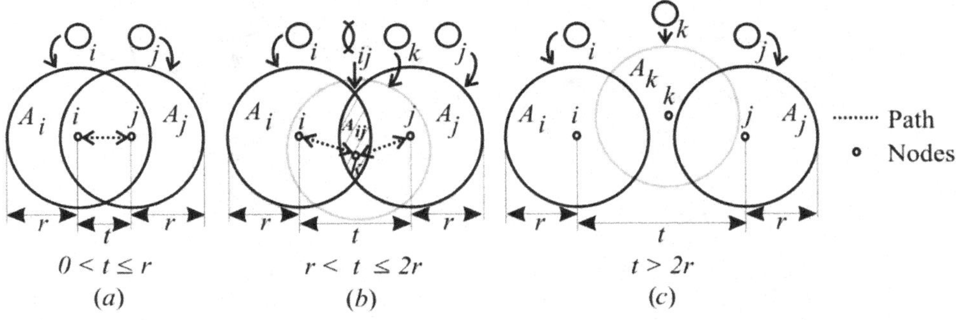

relay nodes in $\lozenge_{ij}$ between a pair of nodes i and j when $0<t\leq r$, is not essential for the connectivity between these two nodes, since they can form a direct path without the necessity of relay nodes.

Consider Figure 4(b), where the separation distance between nodes i and j is designated as t_1 and between the same node i and node l is designated as t_2. The coverage radius of the nodes r satisfies the following conditions $r\leq t_1\leq 2r$, $r\leq t_2\leq 2r$. There are no relay nodes in the area $\lozenge_{il}$, causing no connection between nodes i and l. It can also be appreciated that between nodes i and j, node k exists as a relay node in $\lozenge_{ij}$. Thus, the existence of $\lozenge_{ij}$ between a pair of nodes separated $r\leq t\leq 2r$, does not imply necessarily that there is connectivity since a relay node it is essential in the intersection zone.

The BLOC: Building-Block of Connectivity

The first step in this study is to establish a basic model called the Building-bLock Of Connectivity (BLOC), (Michel, 2005), whose formulation would allow the measurement in a concise manner of the connectivity of the more simple case in a mobile ad-hoc network, that is, between two nodes located randomly in the network. Once defined, the BLOC can be used as a brick for the construction of an analysis method versatile enough to assemble paths in any part of the network, creating a framework for connectivity, and potentially applicable to other tasks such as routing, end-to-end sessions, multi-path analysis, etc.

Measuring Connectivity with the BLOC

We obtain a measure of connectivity defined as the probability of existence of the path between an origin and a destination node, or seen in another way; it is the likelihood of the path to exist. To illustrate the definition of connectivity, we can start by showing the case when two nodes i and j are in the coverage zone of each other (A_i is the coverage area of node i) as depicted in Figure 5. The nodes establish a direct link (determined as ij) between themselves, establishing a probability of connectivity between these nodes defined as P_{cij} equal to unity, due to the existence of link ij.

Figure 4. Special situations in the two-hop case

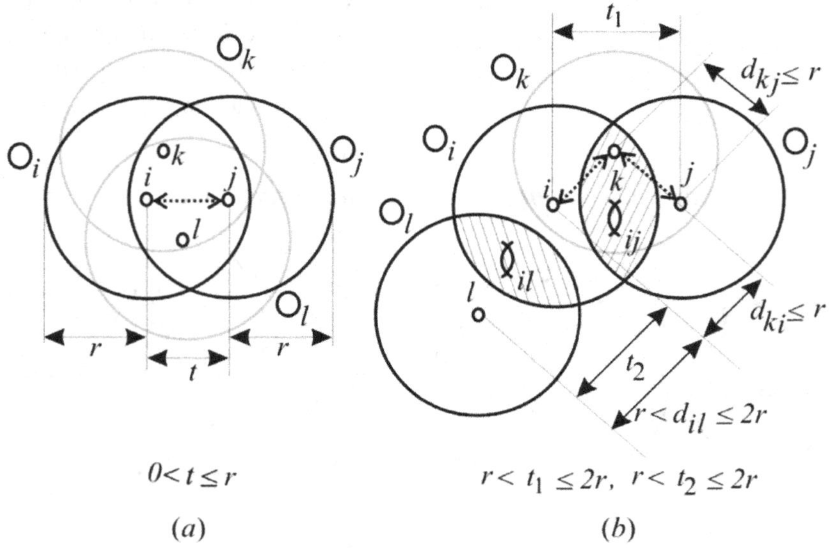

Figure 5. Two communicating nodes i and j linked by a direct path

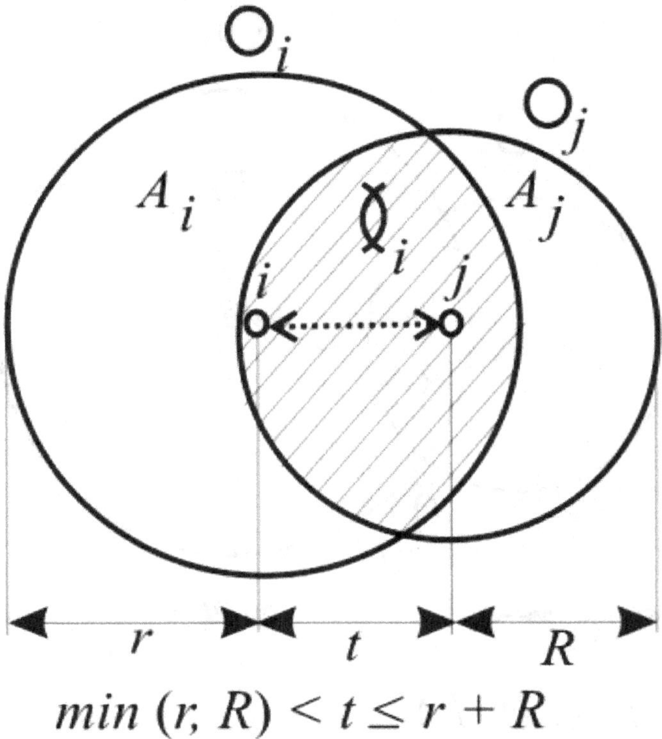

Thus, for the case of Figure 5, the probability of connectivity P_{cij} between an origin node *i* and a destination node *j*, whenever the link exist, is given by

$P_{cij}=1$ if $\exists ij$, $0<t<min\ (r,R)$, $\forall r$, R.

Now, the more interesting case to develop corresponds to the situation when a relay node *k* between *i* and *j* needs to be used, which is represented in Figure 6.

As can be seen, node *k* belongs to area A_{ij} that can be calculated using the definition given in D. Stoyan and H. Stoyan (2004). Assuming equal coverage radius for all the nodes, the probability of connectivity between nodes *i* and *j* when A_{ij} is not empty is given by

$$P_{cij} = 1 - e^{-\lambda A_{ij}},$$

where λ is the node density in nodes per square meter. In order to measure connectivity in paths, what we do is to carry out the concatenation of a number of BLOCs to form the desired path, and depending on the size of the intersection areas, the path will have a tendency to be more robust as these areas increase.

Basic Multi-Path Topologies

These topologies refer to the existence of different routes between two communicating nodes. These routes can share part of the paths used or can be two completely different paths in the network (Michel, 2005). It is important to notice that when these kinds of topologies are studied, multi-hop paths may be included, since one of the routes can be formed with various hops.

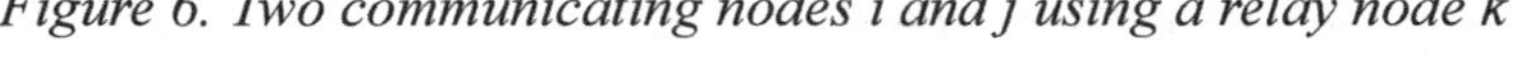

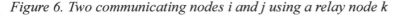

Figure 6. Two communicating nodes i and j using a relay node k

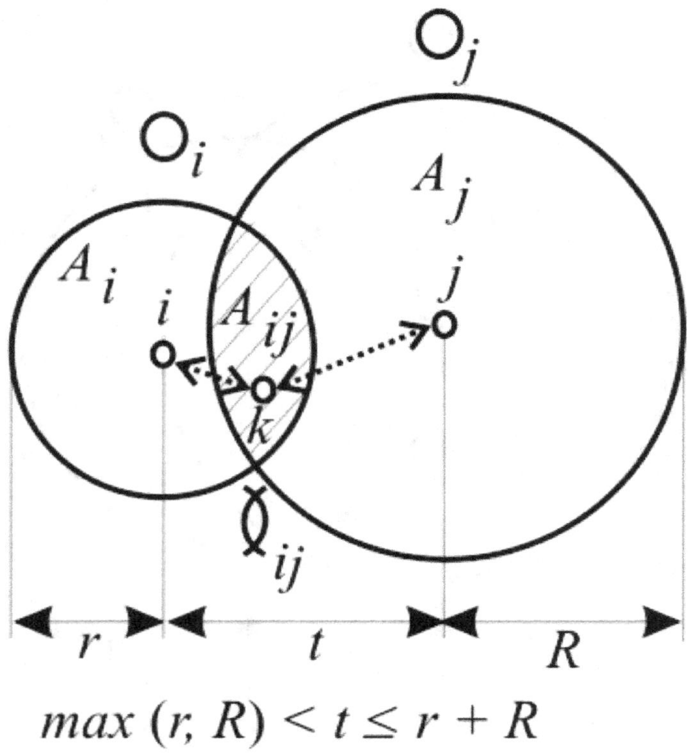

Two Nodes Connected with Disjoint Paths

With the purpose of establishing the definition of connectivity between two nodes *i* and *j* under the circumstance of having no shared paths, we present Figure 7, where we can see that the probability of connectivity between nodes *i* and *j* involves two disjoint paths. The first one is the path *i, l, m, n, j*, designated as *ij*1, and the second one is the path *i, k, j*, named as *ij*2.

While the probability of connectivity of *ij*2, P_{cij2}, is the probability of connectivity of a single BLOC, the probability that at least one path exists between *i* and *j* is given by the complement of the product of the nonexistence of such links, assuming that each path is independent. Therefore, the probability of connectivity of nodes *i* and *j*, determined as P_{cij}, is given by the event that at least one of the paths is available, i. e.,

$$P_{cij}=1-(1-P_{cij1})(1-P_{cij2}).$$

Along the previous lines, we can obtain a generalized expression for the measure of the connectivity between two nodes *i* and *j*, with previous knowledge that there are in the network *n* disjoint paths that connect them, as follows

$$P_{cij} = 1 - \prod_{k}^{n}\left(1 - P_{cijk}\right).$$

Results for this model together with clustering results are presented later in this section.

Clustering Techniques

Clustering is the process of organizing the nodes within a network so that the topology has a structure that can result in a better connectivity and an

Figure 7. A multi-path case with disjoint paths

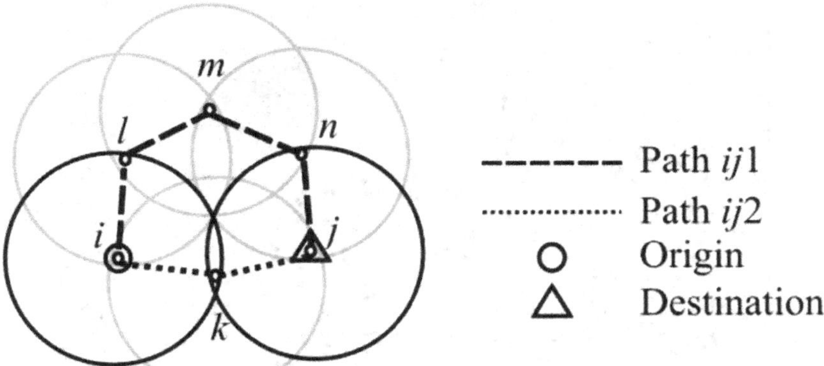

improvement in its robustness to link failures. Clustering is widely made based on separation distance of the nodes, but other variables could be included in order to give the sense of belonging to different groups. Among these variables could be remaining energy, processing speed, location, number of neighbors, transmission power, etc.

Clustering also provides the means to communicate important control functions in the network or announcements such as those needed to propagate news of a link failure or new neighboring nodes. We have a clustering algorithm that considers distance and coverage radius depending on transmission power and connectivity range.

The main scenario is a mobile ad-hoc network within a square area with a node density of λ nodes per square meter. We start by generating randomly the position of the nodes according to a Poisson spatial process. After the generation of the nodes, the node with the most neighboring nodes, defined by the number of nodes within its coverage radius, is chosen as a cluster head. The cluster head is in charge of communication control within the cluster. We need to have a manageable number of nodes within a cluster. In order to limit the number of nodes within a cluster, we define a threshold number, and whenever this threshold number is reached within a cluster, no new node can be accepted as a member of the cluster. The new node must look for another cluster to be added or in case of no connectivity; it will form its own cluster by naming itself as cluster head.

Considering the first cluster head node, if the number of neighboring nodes within its coverage radius is greater than the cluster limit fixed, the cluster head can reduce its transmission power to adjust to such limit. In Figure 8 we can see an example where a network has been generated and a cluster head has been chosen and connectivity to its one-hop neighbors is shown.

Cluster Establishment and Maintenance

In order to carry out the establishment of the clusters, we need four simple rules:

- Determine the nodes with the greatest number of neighbors at one-hop distances
- Label the nodes by the sum of the one-hop distances to those neighbors
- Consider such one-hop distances as random variables, calculate their variance.
- Assign the next cluster head as that node with the minimum variance.

These rules are used to choose the cluster heads, but they do not guarantee 100% connectivity; this is where changes as maintenance tasks must be performed. We consider the changes as follows

Figure 8. Connectivity of first cluster head in network

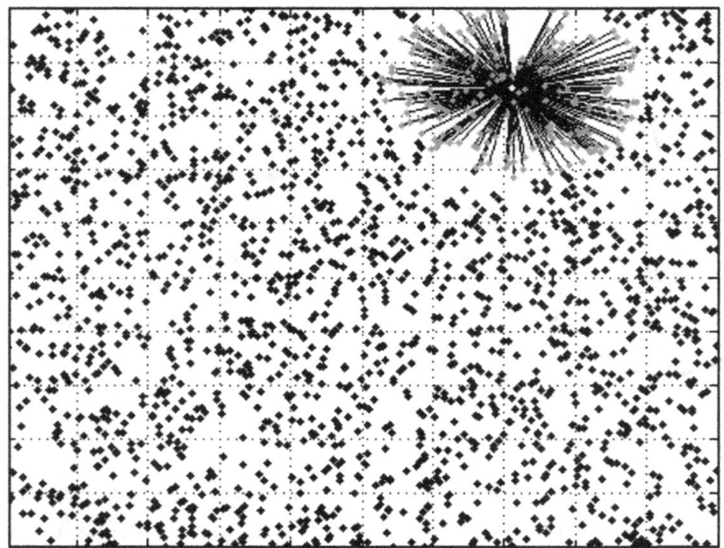

- Adjustment of the coverage radius
- Application of the variance as in the previous rules
- Extension of connectivity to use two-hop or longer paths to a cluster head.

Numerical Results

Evaluating a system performance via a model consists of defining the system model, and solving it using analytical and/or simulation techniques, but, constructing a real ad hoc network testbed for a given scenario is typically expensive and remains limited in terms of working scenarios, mobility models, etc. Furthermore, measurements are generally non-repeatable. Using a simulation or analytic model, on the other hand, permits the study of system behavior by varying all its parameters, and considering a large spectrum of network scenarios.

We generate randomly distributed nodes (called the network nodes) within a squared limited area using a two dimensional homogeneous Poisson point process. The locations of the network nodes are maintained along the duration of the simulation. The links established among the network nodes are based on the considered coverage radius, (Savvides, Park & Srivastava, 2003). For each simulation, we determine the connectivity analytically and empirically, this last is done by relative frequency computation with multiple generating processes of nodes with homogeneous Poisson processes again (referred as empirical nodes), within a squared limited area, (Michel, 2005). Finally both results, analytical and empirical, are compared and discussed to evaluate the performance of the proposed model.

We use one user density in two rectangular areas for the generation of the empirical and network nodes, respectively. The number of nodes in each case is proportional to the total area, and the network nodes must cover the empirical nodes inside the same area as shown in Figure 9(b). By allowing network nodes only within the smaller rectangle, edge effects are eliminated as depicted in Figure 9(a).

It is important to mention that the connectivity calculated depends on the routing technique utilized, and it is from the local vision of a node selected as the origin. It is also temporal since it is calculated at a specific moment in time in which the network nodes would be considered static or

Figure 9. Scenario with the dimensions for the areas

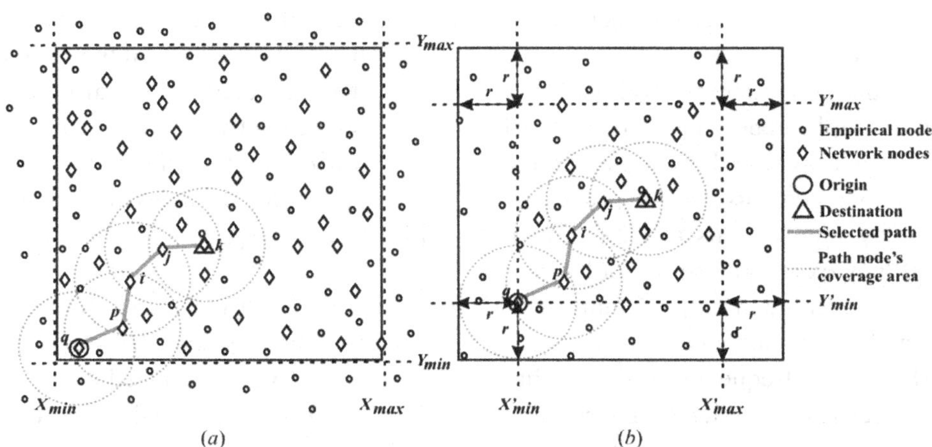

without movement. In a Poisson point process, if we select a point and look around the nodes generated, it continues to be a Poisson process, even if it does or does not coincide with a network node.

In addition, the routes have a lifetime and the topology changes by the time the routes can be updated; this implies that our study is done considering a static network.

We employ a node density of 0.0002 nodes per square meter, in a square area of 1,000 by 1,000 meters with a coverage radius for each node of r=150 meters. At first, only the distance is considered for the link formation to one-hop neighbors. The simulation was performed 5,000 times in order to obtain results to be statistically analyzed.

Results of Simulation for Connectivity

The procedure that summarizes the process of computation of the connectivity of an origin node to every destination node is established by the following steps.

1. Generate the network nodes within the squared limited area with a homogeneous Poisson point process.
2. Establish the links among the network nodes according to the distance and coverage radius.
3. Choose one origin node randomly from the network nodes.
4. Identify its neighbors up to h = 10 hops. Each node is reachable from the origin at its shortest path. Recall that the study of the model is focused on the paths with a number of hops starting from h = 3, since the BLOC already has two hops, corresponding to the first basic multi-hop topology introduced.
5. Select randomly one of the neighboring nodes as the destination node.
6. Search by the Dijkstra algorithm the different disjoint paths between the origin and destination nodes, beginning with the shortest one, and for the subsequent searches ignoring the links used by past selected paths, this process could give us equal or longer paths than the original shortest one at h hops, initially.
7. Calculate the reductions, compensations and connectivity by intersections and half moon zones (if they exist) between the origin and destination nodes analytically by applying the corresponding formulas to each case studied.

8. Compute the analytical value of connectivity by multiplying the obtained connectivity by intersections.
9. Calculate the connectivity empirically by making multiple generating processes of empirical nodes within the squared limited area with homogeneous Poisson processes, counting by intersections and half moon zones (if they exist reduced or not by their neighbors' coverage circle) the number of times a node is inside them.
10. Obtain by relative frequency the probability of having zero nodes fallen by intersection and half moon zones (if they exist), and then calculate the complement of this results to compute the probability of having at least one node in the required intersecting zones to maintain the current fixed topology constructed with the selected path formed with its former network nodes.
11. Multiply the obtained relative frequencies by intersection to calculate the empirical result of connectivity.
12. Calculate the total error percentage (percent of difference of the analytical and empirical models) from the analytical and empirical results, if it is lower than 10%, it is considered as an acceptable result.
13. Display the graphics by each simulation, e.g., of the original network nodes with their formed links, of the selected path with the generated empirical nodes, and of the representative squares of the network nodes utilized in the reduction and compensation factors for the analytical calculus.
14. Repeat steps 1 to 5 for each disjoint path.

In Figures 10 and 11, we show a simulation of a network and present the topology established by the coverage radius and the one-hop distances. Also, there is an origin-destination pair chosen and two corresponding and different four-hop routes joining such nodes that were obtained by applying the Dijkstra's shortest path algorithm.

Once we calculate the analytical and empirical probabilities of connectivity, as well as the corresponding error percentage of both results for all the routes to the destination node 19, the same procedure is applied for all the network nodes located likewise at $h = 3$ hops at their shortest paths. In the case any other node is not found, we proceed to carry out the analysis for the network nodes located at $h = 4, 5, 6, 7, 8, 9$ or 10 hops at their shortest route, registering the results of the probabilities of connectivity and errors in databases.

Figure 10. Selected path to node 19

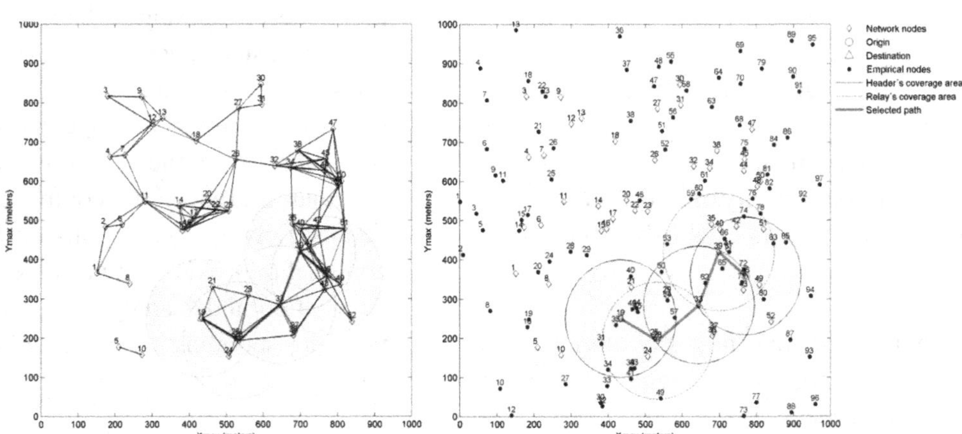

Figure 11. Second selected path to node 19

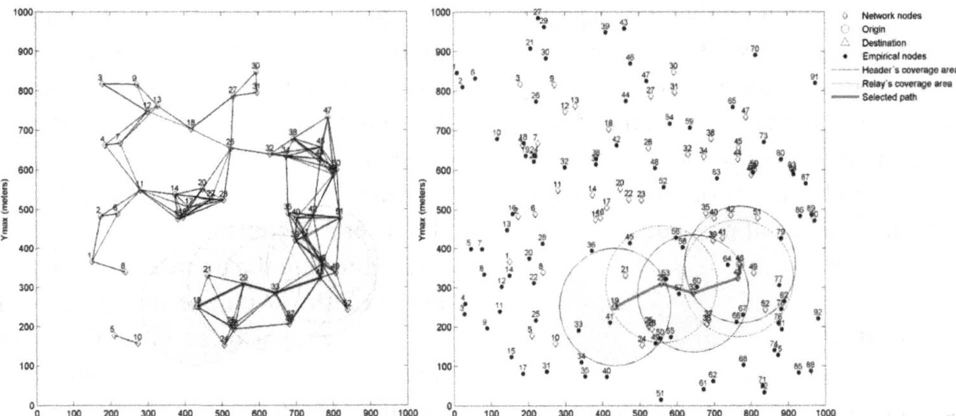

We calculate the probability of connectivity from the origin to a specific destination network node considering all the analytical results of its disjoint paths registered. The results are obtained and it is observed that the closer the values to unity of connectivity probability correspond to the destination nodes with the maximum number of disjoint paths to the origin node. In this case, all the nodes located at $h = 3$ hops at their shortest paths have more than one disjoint route, where nodes 34, 38 and 45 present the best results since each one has 7 disjoint paths to the origin node 42. In other words, these nodes offer at least one disjoint path to the origin node with high probability since they have various alternative routes, it is important to notice that these routes are not necessarily of h hops. We can analyze the probabilities of connectivity in progression for these nodes located at $h = 3$ hops, see Figure 12.

As observed in Figure 12, node 34 has the greatest value of connectivity at its shortest path, while nodes 19, 21 and 24 have the smaller values of connectivity at their shortest path. All the curves increase, with values of probability limited within zero and one. Nodes 34, 38 and 35 with the maximum number of disjoint paths have a

Figure 12. Progressive probabilities of connectivity to one destination at h = 3 hops

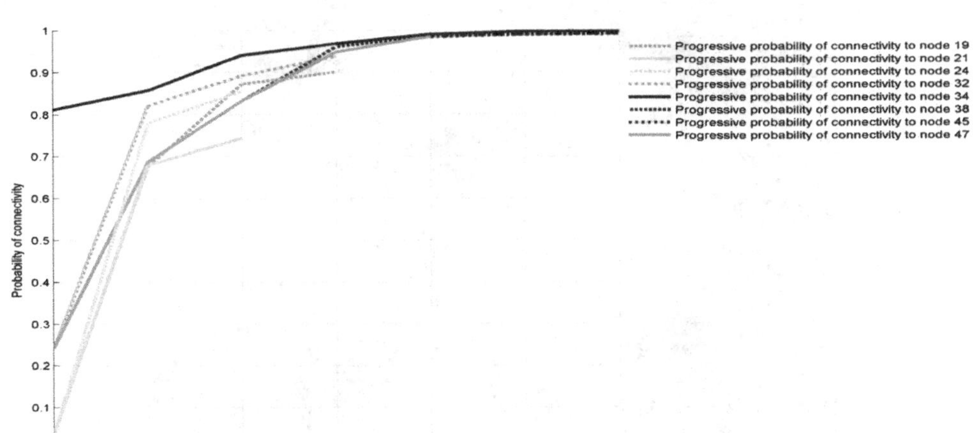

final probability of connectivity closer to unity. With these results, we can infer that with a larger value of node density, there will be a larger number of network nodes in the window, creating more available paths between an origin and destination nodes. This allows larger paths with more hops and a larger number of disjoint paths, which would approximate values of probability of connectivity closer to one.

Results for Clustering

Once we generate the nodes in a mobile ad-hoc network using the Poisson process, we proceed with the clustering rules as explained previously in this section, i.e., we select the cluster nodes in order and start making the one-hop neighboring nodes part of their clusters. This procedure considering only the distance within the coverage radius is shown in Figure 13.

We can see in Figure 13 that the cluster heads have formed clusters that have a large number of nodes, especially those clusters formed at the beginning where the cluster head tries to group as many nodes as possible. Thus, clusters formed later in the process have a smaller number of one-hop nodes. The problem in this situation is that those cluster heads at the beginning will have to process larger routing tables and transmit larger amounts of information, which could be a limiting factor due to the processing capabilities of the nodes.

Now, using the same network, but applying the criteria of adjusting the coverage radius of the nodes limiting the number of one-hop neighbors in the cluster, we have in Figure 14 the results. We can see that more clusters are formed, but that each one has a smaller number of one-hop neighbors than the first cluster formed in Figure 13. We can see that since fewer one-hop neighbors are considered as part of a cluster, more cluster heads need to be generated in the clustering process, thus more clusters will be formed compared to those in Figure 13.

Now, since the load that should be handled by the cluster heads in the network of Figure 14 is still large, we apply a reduction of coverage radius to decrease the number of one-hop neighbors. This reduction will make more nodes appear disconnected or without a cluster. Instead of creating more one-hop clusters, we generate two-hop routes to the cluster heads as shown in Figure 15.

Figure 13. One-hop cluster formation

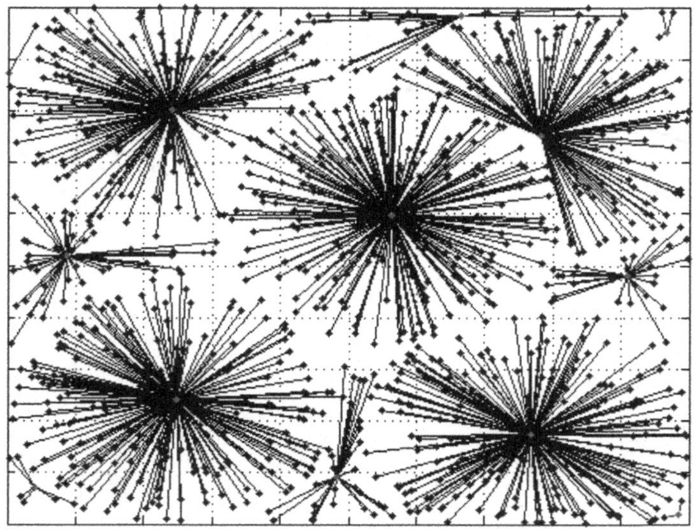

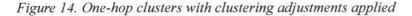

Figure 14. One-hop clusters with clustering adjustments applied

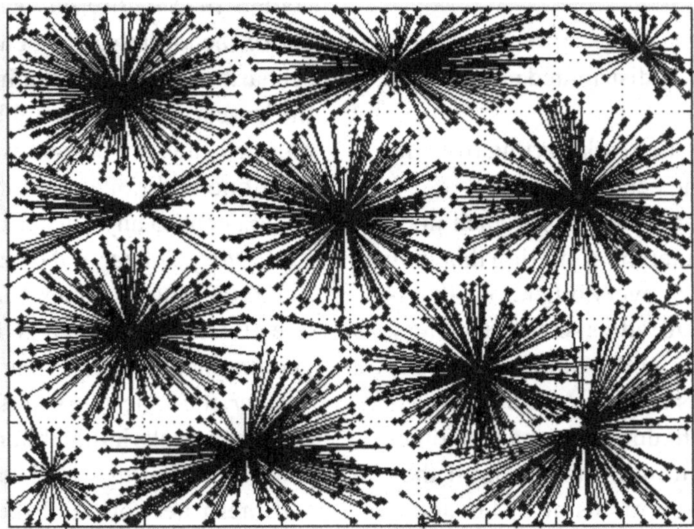

Figure 15. Two-hop clustering scenario

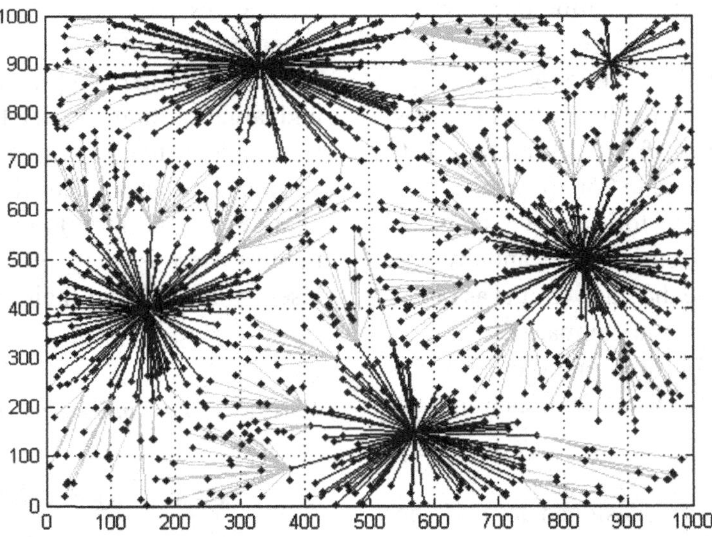

As seen in Figures 12 through 15, we find some advantages of clustering in ad hoc networks, and the dynamics that this kind of organization can achieve in different scenarios. In the previous results, we presented the traditional organization of a network topology based on neighboring distance to determine clusters and cluster heads. Now, we present a different comparison of topology organization, based on the size of the table that contains neighbor hop distances and hop count information within a cluster. We compare these results obtained to those of the scenario with no clustering in a full mesh network.

The procedure that summarizes the process of the scenario creation and computation of the connectivity of a source node or central node to every destination node is established by the following steps.

1. Generate uniformly distributed nodes in the area of interest.
2. Create a full mesh network starting from the source node or the central node.
3. Generate a neighbor's table for each node in the network under the condition that they can only connect to every other node that is within the coverage radius set to 100 meters.
4. If there are orphan nodes after a hop count of 15, these nodes can increase their coverage radius by 50 m until they reach another node associated to a cluster, or until they reach the maximum radius of 250 meters.
5. Calculate with Dijkstra's algorithm the hop distance between the two nodes that have the longest Euclidean distance in the scenario, i.e., the nodes that define the *diameter* of the network.
6. Compare the number of hops and the number of nodes connected for different values of coverage radius, from 100 meters, 150 meters, 200 meters and 250 meters.
7. Repeat this process for a cluster network initiated by the source node and by the central node. Save the same results as in the full mesh network and compare them.
8. Do the process for different node densities so that the number of nodes varies from 100 nodes to 1000 nodes.

Four algorithms were designed to find the results we mentioned before. These algorithms are called: *m x n-Cluster Head, Center-Cluster, Corner-Cluster and Density-FollowerHC.*

m x n-Cluster Head and *Density-FollowerHC* algorithms work by choosing the number of cluster heads that we would like to use in the simulation. In this particular case, we use 16 cluster heads. *m x n-Cluster Head* divides the space into 16 squares with equal areas each. The node that is closest to the center of each of these squares is chosen as the initial cluster head and topology discovery is started. In *Density-FollowerHC,* cluster heads are chosen according to the density of the nodes in the scenario. The first cluster head is the one that has the largest number of neighbors and the following cluster heads are chosen with the same rule, but with one additional condition: the node cannot be adjacent to any cluster head already chosen.

Center-Cluster and *Corner-Cluster* work like a tree topology. *Center-Cluster* starts with only one cluster head which is the node closest to the geographical center of the scenario. In *Corner-Cluster*, the node who wants to send information is the one that asks its neighbors to start the discovery process. In Figures 16 through 20, we can see a full mesh network and the different topologies that these algorithms build with the same node distribution.

In Figure 16 it is evident that a full mesh network gives us more redundancy than a cluster organization, but this redundancy comes with a price, including energy consumption, overhead, and larger routing and neighbor tables. In a cluster topology network, nodes try to keep things simple and organized when major topology changes occur. In this topology organization, our main concern is energy efficiency and overhead. Users want to keep their connection or battery

Figure 16. Full mesh network

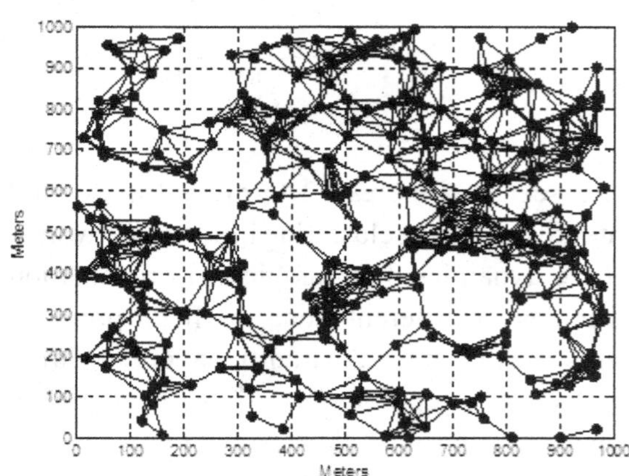

Figure 17. Density-follower head cluster topology

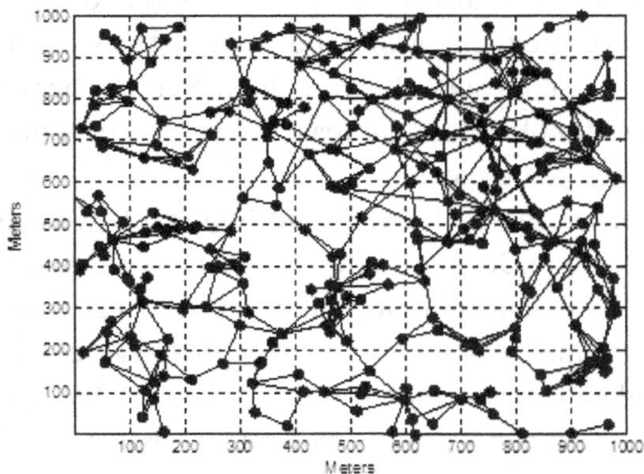

Figure 18. m x n head cluster topology

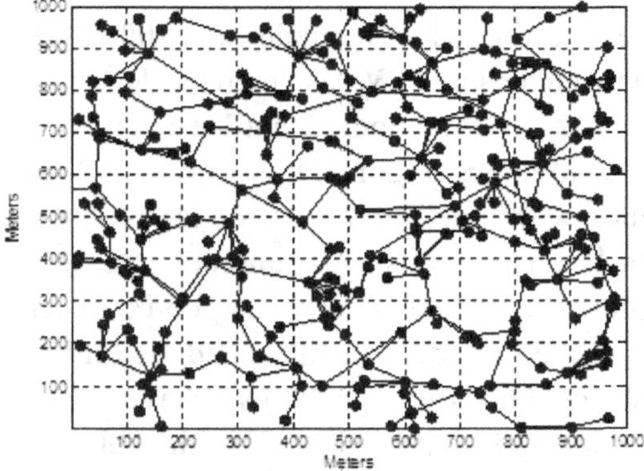

Figure 19. Corner head cluster topology

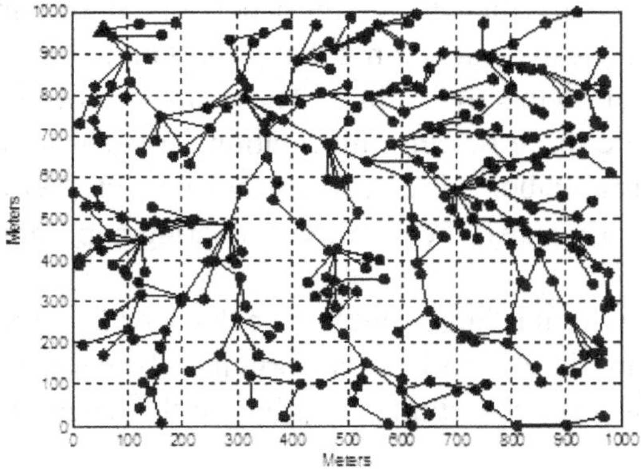

Figure 20. Center head cluster topology

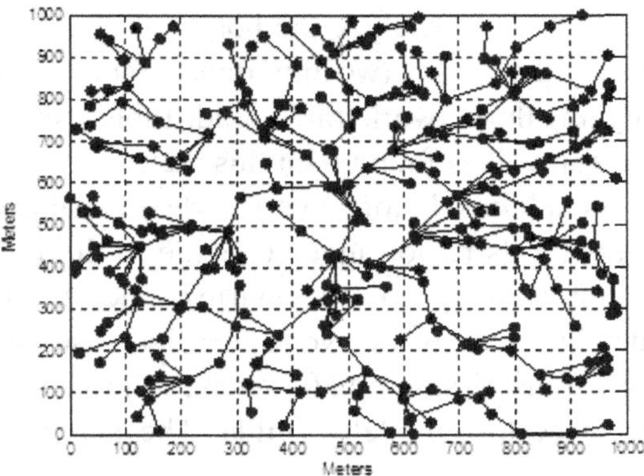

alive as long as possible, and by having this kind of organization, we increase our service time and keep our users connected as long as possible.

Also, it is important to mention that when an orphan node increases its coverage distance, it can reach more than one node. If this is the case, that orphan node creates links to all nodes that are in its range if and only if it is under a full mesh organization. However, if we are using a cluster organization, this orphan node will create a connection link to the first node who answers its petition. If within this new coverage radius it can reach more than one node, it connects to all of these nodes and increases the interference (Full Mesh Network Behavior).

In the following figures, we show the results that were found with the four algorithms and the full mesh network algorithm. We concentrate the analysis on four important issues: hop count to get to the destination, Euclidean distances and hop distances for the five cases, number of orphan nodes before coverage range is modified, and the number of connected nodes after increasing the range of nodes.

Figure 21 shows the distance hop count found with the five algorithms. The objective of the four algorithms explained before is to approximate their hop count value as much as possible to the Euclidean Distance and Full Mesh Hop Distance Calculation between the two farthest nodes in the scenario. In all the following figures, results were found by simulating the five algorithms 100 times, starting with 100 nodes in a 1000 by 1000 square meter space. We also increased the number of nodes by one hundred until we reached one thousand nodes. Figure 21 shows high Distance values when the number of nodes is less than 300, but as soon as this number increases and approaches 1000, we have a very good approximation of the Euclidean distance and the Full Mesh Distance. Our four algorithms behave well with high densities, but if we analyze the behavior of Center Cluster and Corner Cluster algorithms for a moment, we see that they do not behave well in low density scenarios. Density Follower Algorithm behaves better than *m x n* algorithm, but we still need to analyze the hop count behavior and neighbor tables, two important parameters for analyzing the network traffic load. Table 1 shows the mean values found with this metric

As explained before, every node is capable of increasing its radio range coverage to diminish the number of orphan nodes and to connect border nodes in the network. Nodes can increase their power transmission by 50 meters, following the free space loss model formula. The maximum distance the nodes can cover is 250 meters. Table 2 shows the results of the 5 algorithms, the columns provide the number of nodes used in the simulation and the rows illustrate the mean number of nodes that kept and increased their power transmission to connect.

From Tables 1 and 2, and Figure 21, we can see that the Density Follower (DF) algorithm has a better balanced performance than the rest of the algorithms. Another parameter that was calculated with this method was the hop-count. We also take the mean values to evaluate the behavior of the algorithms and compare them against each other. In Figure 22, we can appreciate some interesting results; as we can see, our four algorithms present a fewer number of hops to arrive to the destination than the full mesh network algorithm. This means that it is not that important to have a lot of connectivity lines. These lines, however, create more routing information, larger routing and neighbor tables and do not provide better performance (when we are evaluating hop-count values).

Also, it is important to note that Corner Algorithm shows the best performance because the connections are built according to the origin de-

Figure 21. Mean values of hop-distance calculations

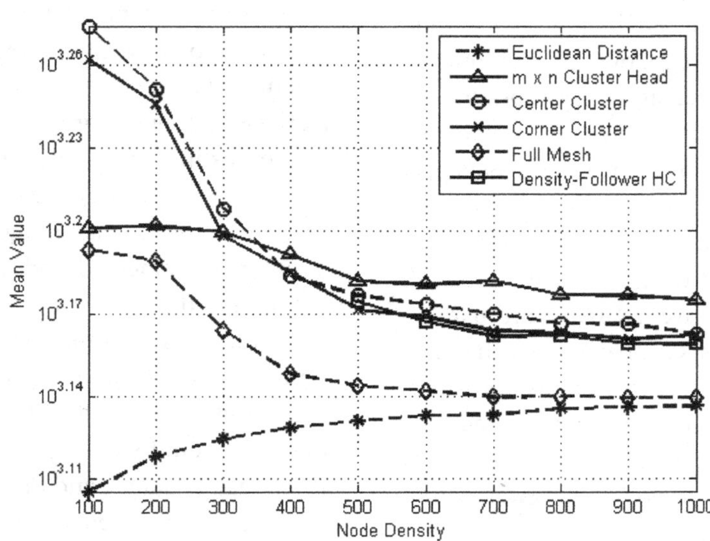

Table 1. Mean values of hop-distance calculations

Nodes Distance	100	200	300	400	500	600	700	800	900	1000
Euclidean Distance	1275	1310	1336	1344	1354	1358	1363	1364	1367	1369
m x n Cluster Head	1584	1617	1584	1543	1521	1523	1518	1503	1499	1506
Center Cluster Head	1880	1774	1597	1539	1504	1491	1477	1472	1467	1467
Corner Cluster Head	1869	1772	1573	1511	1490	1475	1467	1460	1454	1455
Full Mesh Network	1525	1556	1454	1413	1393	1386	1383	1379	1379	1380
Density Follower Head Cluster	1565	1562	1521	1502	1482	1465	1459	1451	1447	1439

Table 2. Radio range mean value

Nodes Cover	100	200	300	400	500	600	700	800	900	1000
m x n 100	47.40	156.28	265.50	367.82	469.19	568.27	668.66	767.99	867.08	967.42
m x n 150	21.38	18.70	12.68	9.64	8.72	7.97	6.78	6.57	6.02	5.09
m x n 200	21.88	14	8.90	7.51	6.18	5.14	5.11	3.84	3.89	4.28
m x n 250	9.28	10.90	12.79	14.99	15.91	18.61	19.44	21.60	23.01	23.21
Corner CH 100	48.52	190.24	298.97	399.82	500	599.96	699.96	800	900	1000
Corner CH 150	22.03	9.36	0.90	0.14	0	0.03	0.03	0	0	0
Corner CH 200	26.86	0.25	0	0	0	0	0	0	0	0
Corner CH 250	2.44	0	0	0	0	0	0	0	0	0
Center CH 100	44.51	165.33	295.48	398.88	500	599.96	698.76	800	900	1000
Center CH 150	12.21	18.75	3.59	1.03	0	0.03	1.22	0	0	0
Center CH 200	30.43	15.16	0.81	0.06	0	0	0	0	0	0
Center CH 250	18.44	0.62	0	0	0	0	0	0	0	0
Full Mesh 100	29.50	173.62	294.67	399.41	500	599.84	699.82	800	900	1000
Full Mesh 150	62.02	26.18	5.33	0.59	0	0.16	0.18	0	0	0
Full Mesh 200	10.40	0.20	0	0	0	0	0	0	0	0
Full Mesh 250	0.500	0	0	0	0	0	0	0	0	0
DF Clusterhead 100	42.14	150.65	264.80	372.30	478.41	583.95	688.67	794.18	896.55	997.70
DF Clusterhead 150	34.65	29.86	15.38	11.68	9.98	6.86	4.67	3	1.84	1.13
DF Clusterhead 200	13.63	9.56	9.88	8.40	6.36	5.17	4.21	1.75	1.02	0.81
DF Clusterhead 250	9.580	9.93	9.94	7.62	5.25	4.02	2.45	1.07	0.59	0.36

mand; this node is the one that starts the discovery and the maintenance of the network, and then initiates sending the packet to the node for which its path is the longest in the network. The origin node can repeat this process with any other node in the network. Multiple cluster heads phase 1

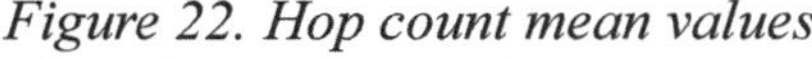

Figure 22. Hop count mean values

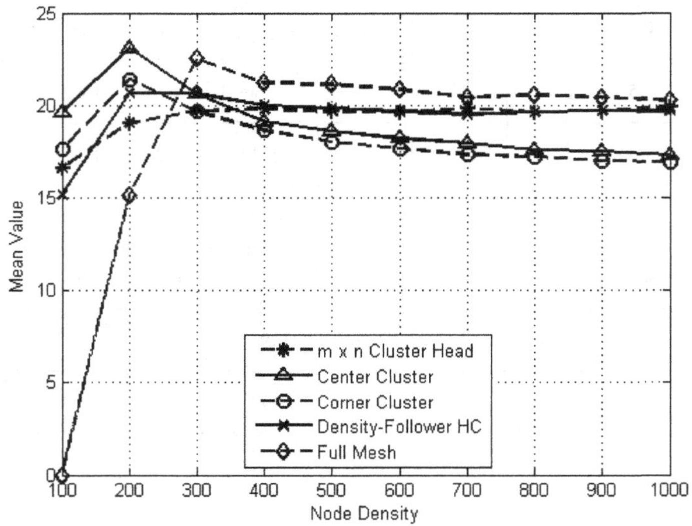

algorithms also behave better than the full mesh algorithm. These algorithms, in general, show better performance in low and high density networks and their behavior is almost constant in all the cases.

The final parameter that we calculate with these algorithms is the average number of neighboring nodes that need to be recorded in a *neighbor's* table that we denote as Neighbors Mean Values. As we can see in Table 4, we have a large number of records in the Neighbors' Tables for the Full Mesh Algorithm while in our four algorithms that number is reduced significantly. The first pattern that we see is that when the node density increases, the differences between the Full Mesh Algorithm and our 4 algorithms grow really fast. The second pattern is that when we increase the node density, Corner and Center Algorithm always have the same number of Neighbor Table records. We particularly checked this case several times and we found that this behavior continues when the density is increased.

It is important to mention that the algorithm be adaptable to any threshold desirable; by using

Table 3. Hop count mean values

Nodes Cover	100	200	300	400	500	600	700	800	900	1000
m x n Cluster Head	16.46	19.42	19.83	19.63	19.47	19.46	19.84	19.90	19.59	19.43
Center Cluster Head	19.97	22.82	20.40	19.42	18.55	18.24	17.95	17.73	17.59	17.41
Corner Cluster Head	18.08	21.21	19.63	18.65	18.02	17.73	17.39	17.20	17.11	17
Density Follower Head Cluster	14.89	20.55	20.52	20.17	19.74	19.86	19.73	19.70	19.75	19.64
Full Mesh Network	16.28	18.88	19.82	20.03	20.44	20.22	20.41	20.29	20.54	20.28

Table 4. Neighbor tables mean value

Nodes Cover	100	200	300	400	500	600	700	800	900	1000
m x n Cluster Head	243	459	665	870	1072	1276	1477	1679	1881	2082
Center Cluster Head	198	398	598	798	998	1198	1398	1598	1798	1998
Corner Cluster Head	370	398	598	798	998	1198	1398	1598	1798	1998
Full Mesh Network	486	1221	2584	4616	7191	10346	14080	18444	23294	28771
Density Follower Head Cluster	265	607	1119	1814	2684	3720	4941	6378	7961	9750

Figure 23. Neighbors table mean values

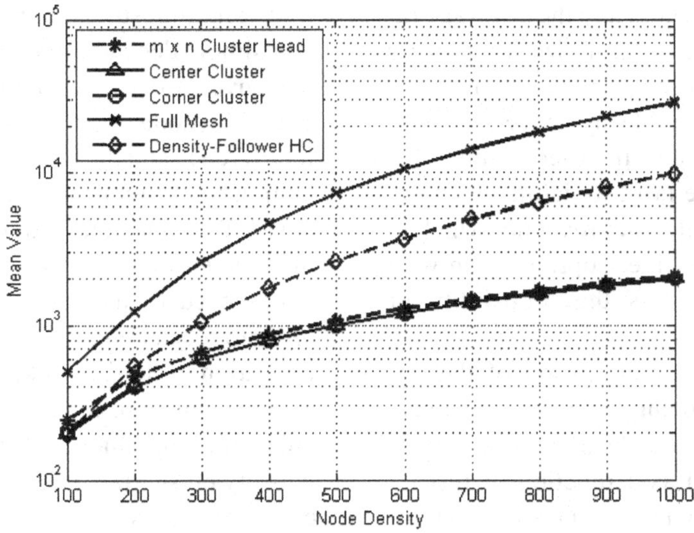

a flag in the process of building the table, we can increase the threshold to any number we want. In this chapter, we let the ordinary nodes have only one record in their tables, this number can be increased if we are looking for more redundancy.

FUTURE RESEARCH DIRECTIONS

This work presents the design of a theoretical framework for the study of connectivity, robustness and reachability in ad hoc networks; it can be extended and improved by:

- Constructing the model of connectivity using branching processes, percolation, random graphs, diffusion or clustering and migration processes.
- Generalizing the model to include heterogeneous nodes, which have different coverage radii, and other channel phenomena.
- Formulating power control rules for transmission and extend the model to evaluate interference.
- Creating a more exact method to calculate the areas of reduced intersecting zones by using points located in the contour of these

rather than making the ratio of their representative squared areas.

- Extending the model to study clustering. This would allow the study of node connectivity as a manageable process at different hierarchies of the network.
- Making area reductions in the BLOC algorithm considering nodes that are more than two-hops of distance.
- Developing the model by improving the case where a relay or orphan node causes a total reduction to the closer intersecting zone by choosing an alternative disjoint path.
- Defining control variables as the intensity of the Poisson process and the coverage radius to introduce an optimization process of the three proposed performance metrics, which are measurable by other proposed observable variables. In order to apply this methodology, we need to define an objective function, called net revenue, which is a function of non linear optimization with implicit functions as the probability of node connectivity.
- Considering the maximization of the objective function being the network net revenue (and therefore the maximization of the connectivity) as a function of restrictions concerned with the energy consumption of the nodes (where the decision variable is their range of power transmission), and with the capacity of the network for a fixed r (with decision variable as the new users generation rate), then formulate the optimization problem.
- Applying the BLOC for an analysis of connectivity with a time-varying model to study the evolution in time of the state of the network, such that the number of neighbors at time t, defined as $n(t)$, is a function of control variables such as the intensity of the Poisson process, the coverage radius, and the node's power consumption. This definition could be used to apply the theory of dynamic programming to solve the connectivity problem.
- Extending routing algorithms by using the cost of a BLOC instead of the cost of a link to obtain shortest path routes.
- Extending the model to incorporate measures of QoS such as robustness for the decision-making process of tasks such as routing and end-to-end session establishment.

CONCLUSION

We have introduced a method to measure connectivity and robustness in mobile ad-hoc networks and simple decision rules for cluster formations that have the objective of minimizing the number of orphan nodes, as well as decrease the network interference and the network processing of information by cluster head nodes. Also, strategies for cluster formation that provide 100% connectivity of the nodes were introduced. The resulting orphan nodes need to increase transmission power in order to reach nodes already within the topology formation of the network.

In conclusion, we can see that in order to decrease the large amount of information processing done by cluster head nodes, we need to decrease coverage radius and start increasing the number of hops in the paths. This decrement in coverage also helps to decrease interference since we are using less transmission power in the nodes. Once we can decide the clustering among the nodes, we can determine the interconnectivity of the clusters by using *satellite* nodes, i.e., nodes that are at the edges of the clusters and could be at a distance from other cluster head. With the network connected in this manner, we can proceed to determine an origin-destination pair of interest and the different ways to interconnect them, i.e., the number of different disjoint and joint paths that connect the origin with the destination of interest. With this information, we can proceed to calculate the connectivity probability provided by the procedure discussed. This connectivity result will provide means to choose origin-destination pairs that are more robust and hence more suitable to be used as transport of information nodes.

The results we found with the algorithms that were evaluated against a full mesh network are that with our cluster algorithms we achieved connectivity with smaller Neighbor Tables and with shorter hop counts than a Full Mesh Network. In the simulation, we show that our algorithms have a better performance when the density is higher. All these results are shown in Tables 1 through 4. These results are really important because we demonstrated that reducing the hops and the size of the tables does not necessarily mean that we reduce the connectivity in the network. In sum, we may have reduced the redundancy, but this variable can be easily adapted in the algorithm according to the needs of any specific analysis.

REFERENCES

Bettstetter, C. (2002a). On the minimum node degree and connectivity of a wireless multihop network. In *Proceedings of the ACM International Symposium on Mobile Ad Hoc Networking and Computing (MobiHoc)*, Lausanne, Switzerland (pp. 80-91). New York, ACM.

Bettstetter, C. (2002b). On the connectivity of wireless multi-hop networks with homogeneous and inhomogeneous range assignment. In *Proceedings of the IEEE Vehicular Technology Conference (VTC)*, Vancouver, Canada (pp. 1706-1710).

Chakrabarti, S., & Mishra, A. (2001). QoS Issues in ad hoc wireless networks. *IEEE Communications Magazine*, *39*(2), 142–148. doi:10.1109/35.900643

Choonhwa, C. L., & Sumi, H. (2002). Protocols for service discovery in dynamic and mobile networks. *International Journal of Computer Research*, *11*(1), 1–12.

Dousse, O., Thiran, P., & Hasler, M. (2002). Connectivity in ad-hoc and hybrid networks. In *Proceedings of 21st Annual Joint Conference of the IEEE Computer and Communications Societies (INFOCOM)* (pp. 1079-1088). New York: IEEE.

Foh, C. H., & Lee, B. S. (2004). A closed form network connectivity formula for one dimensional MANETs. In *Proceedings of the International Conference on Communications (ICC)*, Paris, France (pp. 3739-3742).

Foh, C. H., Liu, G., Lee, B. S., Seet, B. C., Wong, K. J., & Fu, C. P. (2005). Network connectivity of one-dimensional MANETs with random waypoint movement. *IEEE Communications Letters*, *9*(1), 31–33.

Franceschetti, M., Booth, L., Cook, M., Meester, M., & Bruck, J. (2004). Percolation in wireless multi-hop networks. *Journal of Statistical Physics*.

Franceschetti, M., Booth, L., Cook, M., Meester, R., & Bruck, J. (2004). Continuum percolation with unreliable and spread out connections. In *Proceedings of the ICMS Workshop on Spatial Stochastic Modeling with Applications to Communications Networks*, Edinburgh, Scotland.

Garcia, T. C. C. (2005). *Discovery service in ad hoc networks using ants.* Unpublished master's thesis, ITESM-Monterrey, Mexico.

Macker, J. P., & Corson, M. S. (1998). Mobile Ad hoc Networking and the IEFT. *ACM Mobile Computing and Communications Review*, *2*(1), 9–14. doi:10.1145/584007.584015

Michel, Z. A. E. (2005). *A theoretical framework for the evaluation of connectivity, robustness and reachability in wireless ad-hoc networks.* Unpublished master's thesis, ITESM-Monterrey, Mexico.

Nikolopoulos, S. D., Pitsillides, A., & Tipper, D. (1997). Addressing network survivability issues by finding the K-best paths through a trellis graph. In *Proceedings of the IEEE INFOCOM* (pp. 370-377). New York: IEEE.

Pahlavan, K., & Krishnamurthy, P. (2002). *Principles of wireless networks: A unified approach.* Upper Saddle River, NJ: Prentice Hall PTR.

Philips, T. K., Panwar, S. S., & Tantawi, A. N. (1989). Connectivity properties of a packet radio network model. *IEEE Transactions on Information Theory, 35*(5), 1044–1047. doi:10.1109/18.42219

Savvides, A., Park, H., & Srivastava, M. B. (2003). The n-hop multilateration primitive for node localization problems. In *Proceedings of Mobile Networks and Applications* (pp. 443-451).

Stine, J. A., & de Veciana, G. (2004). A paradigm for quality-of-service in wireless ad hoc networks using synchronous signaling and node states. *IEEE Journal on Selected Areas in Communications, 22*(7), 1301–1321. doi:10.1109/JSAC.2004.829347

Stoyan, D., & Stoyan, H. (2004). *Fractals, random shapes and point fields: Methods of geometrical statistics*. Chichester, UK: John Wiley & Sons.

Toh, C. K. (2002). *Ad hoc mobile wireless networks: Protocols and systems*. Upper Saddle River, NJ: Prentice Hall PTR.

KEY TERMS AND DEFINITIONS

Ad-Hoc Network: Autonomous system of mobile nodes connected by wireless links, where these nodes are free to move randomly and organize themselves arbitrarily changing the wireless network topology quickly and unpredictably. Communication within the network does not depend on physical fixed infrastructure.

Cluster Head: Node in charge of the management tasks within a cluster.

Clustering: The process of forming groups or clusters in a network to organize the topology.

Connectivity: Percentage of nodes communicated in both directions in a network.

Coverage Area: Area where the signal of the transmitting node is received.

Node Density: The number of nodes per square area in the network.

Reachability: Percentage of nodes that can be reached in at least one direction in the network.

Chapter 12
Location Acquisition and Applications in Mobile and Ad-Hoc Environments

David Muñoz Rodriguez
Instituto Tecnológico y de Estudios Superiores de Monterrey, Mexico

José Ramón Rodríguez Cruz
Instituto Tecnológico y de Estudios Superiores de Monterrey, Mexico

Cesar Vargas Rosales
Instituto Tecnológico y de Estudios Superiores de Monterrey, Mexico

Daniel Elias Muñoz Jimenez
Instituto Tecnológico y de Estudios Superiores de Monterrey, Mexico

ABSTRACT

This chapter addresses the relevance of location information as an important resource that supports other applications. This information is important for better network planning, development of new location-based services, fast deployment of assistance services, and support of surveillance and safety regulations, among others. Accuracy of location acquisition processes is an important factor because the potential for multiple new location-based services depends on it. However, noise is always present at least in two forms. Measurements taken with electronic instruments are inherently noisy and estimation algorithms introduce noise of their own in the assumption process. For this reason, this chapter explores several methods and techniques. A well- balanced solution should take into account the compromise between accuracy and delay and/or complexity. Many solutions have been proposed for new needs and new applications which demand more timely and accurate position locations of users or objects.

INTRODUCTION

Currently, wireless communications have modified our daily lives where people not only communicate among themselves but also access diverse ways to entertain, exchange data and trigger emergency and safety alarms, to mention just a few examples.

DOI: 10.4018/978-1-60960-027-3.ch012

The fundamental problem of position location (PL) can be formulated as that of finding or estimating the location of a device in a multidimensional space. The space dimensions will be determined by the applicability scenarios as well as the available technologies for the particular solution.

New technologies are used in the communications industry to create new services and cover new needs in the market. Wireless technologies experience continuously increasing growth, where cellular networks, Wimax, WiFi, and Bluetooth, are presently among the most common. However, new technological and market trends will foster the appearance of new applications and services.

Mobile Ad-Hoc Networks (MANETs) are based on prior technologies in hardware, but they work differently. One big difference is that communication between two terminals is not always direct. Links can be re-engineered in a cooperative manner so that all users can help locate a specific mobile in the network, depending on neighbors' information and capabilities.

This cooperative way of working enables the development of new services based on the interaction among users in the area. This can be exploited to create new working scenarios to satisfy new customers as well and providers' needs to development new services, based on location information, named Location-Based Services (LBS). This location information can be obtained by employing different PL techniques. It is worth mentioning that location information requires the presence of processing units in order to make it available to users and providers. These entities are known as LBS platforms.

This chapter addresses the relevance of location information as an important resource that supports other applications. This information is important for better network planning, development of new location-based services, fast deployment of assistance services, and support of surveillance and safety regulations. The accuracy of location acquisition processes is important because the potential for multiple new location-based services depends on it.

Following these objectives, the chapter is organized in six sections. The first section describes location information, in general. What is it? Where is it used? How it is acquired? What are the technical challenges? The second section briefly describes Internet Protocol (IP) based location. A third section is dedicated to comprehensively review PL techniques, discussing the advantages and disadvantages of each. MANETs are described and location strategies for these networks are mentioned in the fourth section of this chapter. The fifth section is dedicated to Location Based Services. This section includes the description, technological components, feasibility and accuracy and platforms in MANETs. Finally, some conclusions are presented in a sixth section.

LOCATION INFORMATION

Location information can be referred to as the knowledge of the place where a person or device is. This information is crucial for any service or application that provides site-dependent solutions. There will always be location uncertainties due to impairments caused by the environment or any other interfering element. However, the need to more for more accurately estimate position has motivated the invention of more accurate PL methods, because the applications depend on the accuracy of the location process.

Measurements and estimations for certain kinds of services demand accuracy (i.e. emergency services). PL methods can be used to provide navigation and geographical information, emergency location, movement tracing and tracking, selection of geographical coverage of communication areas and sensor measurements based on position and location patterns and the improvement of network system operations, among others. Location information data can include spatial distribution of users and assets, finding people or places of interest and certain other information, depending on the application requirements.

Location information can be obtained by using different methods that are classified into three basic groups: network-based, mobile-based and mobile-assisted methods. All three groups can be used in many different ways, and their utilization varies according to the available technology and the application scenario.

Location information will prevail as a piece of crucial information for decision-making processes. However, location monitoring and traceability are also important issues to be considered. Most of the treatments and algorithms for PL focus on scenarios where networks are static; that is, algorithm parameters are assumed not to change during the location acquisition process. Some proposals have suggested using the algorithm repeatedly over a discrete-time definition of the events in the network, allowing for information updates that are useful for the location process, such as the location of neighboring nodes, link-hop distance, and the distance toward landmarks or reference nodes. Even if the algorithm were repeated over a discrete-time evolution in a heterogeneous network, one could not ensure that information was updated properly in order to perform positioning. Factors such as processing delays and transmission power measurement could affect the accuracy of the parameter's refreshment during algorithm repetitions.

When nodes are mobile, updates are triggered, often due to topology changes and received-signal strength decays. Thus, even if a node is able to obtain the processing power needed to carry out updates, the parameters involved in such updates might be compromised due to wireless channel and propagation impairments.

A kind of location method for which performance is not strictly dependent on the environment but on the information managed by the network is described in the next section. The accuracy and technical challenges of this technique differ considerably from those mentioned above.

IP LOCATION

Internet Protocol (IP) address is an important resource used to determine the location of a user. It relies on databases to contact and register IP resources. Accuracy varies widely, depending on the number of different addresses associated with a single access point and its coverage area.

One of these databases is named ARIN, or "American Registry for Internet Numbers." ARIN contains routing-policy information for network operators within its region of service, helping them improve their ability to configure and manage their networks. ARIN allows operator submission, maintenance and retrieval of routing policy information by using its own registry information to configure routing software and hardware. ARIN uses the RPSL (Routing Policy Specification Language) which generates router configurations from the data contained within its objects. ARIN is located in a system named WHOIS, a network protocol and client-server system used on the internet to look up the names, IP addresses, and owners of server computers. This database stores the IP address of every Internet Service Provider (ISP) and its country, and it can even contain the complete registry of the distribution of the IP addresses that the ISP uses in every part of the country, providing limited geographic information.

IP2Location is another service available which works as follows: First, it retrieves the IP address from the networking protocol or server-side variable of the web server. Then, it translates the IP address to an IP number in decimal format in order to speed up the database query. Lastly, it reverse looks up the IP number from the IP2Location database to pinpoint the exact geographical location.

Another way to get location information using only the IP address is reverse Domain Name System (DNS) to obtain the hostname of the IP address. This method is based on the fact that DNS must be correctly configured, and it is not very reliable or accurate because certain domains such as.com, and.org are used in many countries. A similar process to reverse DNS is done using on-line Wi-Fi hot-spots databases where hot-spots are listed worldwide with their address information and their (Service Set Identifier) SSID included.

The next section describes PL techniques, most of which are based on processing measurement information acquired from the mobile device or node in multiple access points in the networks' fixed infrastructure and combined in order to build an estimator for the position of the device relative to the access points.

PL TECHNIQUES

PL techniques or methods are algorithms designed to obtain the coordinates or the position of a user in the network. Criteria in the algorithm design includes the PL information requirements and achievable goals (e.g., accuracy, cost, processing load, implementation times).

According to the service of interest, a PL technique must be selected. Some methods offer a very accurate result of a few feet but at the cost of expensive equipment. This, in turn, leads to high service prices to recover the investment. On the other hand, there are more economical PL techniques, but with reduced accuracy. Accuracy is also related to the measuring process, the impairments calculation and the processing load. When algorithms are more robust, results are treated in a certain way to offer more trustworthy position estimation. These algorithms, when they produce accurate results, create high-level equations to obtain the position of the user of interest, so devices in charge these calculations must have high processing capabilities in order to respond not only to one request at a time, but they must cope with hundreds or even thousands of requests that might take place in a fairly short amount of time.

Another aspect that must be considered is that highly accurate results take time to achieve. The probability of a user remaining stationary the time necessary to obtain the requested service is very low. For this reason, services must be processed and delivered just right after the PL information is obtained.

Environmental conditions are also factors that affect the accuracy of results. Some techniques are affected in crowded environments with many obstacles because signals can reflect and produce misleading data that must be discarded before processing only the information considered useful. Even climatic conditions such as rain can alter signal propagation, upsetting the algorithm's accuracy.

The ideal goal of PL techniques is to determine the exact position of a device of interest. However, it is recognized that this objective cannot be achieved due to cost constraints and, above all, intrinsic limitations. Another source of imprecision is instrument errors. Resolution can be referred to as the ability to discriminate among a group of locations in close proximity. Resolution requirements depend on the application and on the coarseness of a land quantization scheme, as well as on other error sources associated with parameter acquisition and measurement procedures. In radio PL systems, major sources of error are related to signal-propagation phenomena.

Angelides (2000) mentions that the performance of wireless location technologies must be evaluated in terms of their accuracy and yield. Accuracy relates to the ability of location technologies to pinpoint a caller or location device (usually an average measurement in meters), while yield is a measurement of the technologies to actually calculate a location (usually measured as a percentage of successful locations per hundred). The yield is equally valued in the commercial services world, because the ability to process a location is of critical importance for a large percentage of applications, such as medical emergency notification and stolen vehicle recovery.

Wireless providers use different techniques to locate and establish the position of their users. It is important to note that these techniques offer different levels of accuracy and that their usage depends on the situations and accuracy requirements of the specific application involved. Not only that, some technologies are deployed for specific wireless technologies that comply with standards associated to these technologies.

As mentioned before, PL techniques can be classified in three main categories: network-based, mobile-based and mobile-assisted techniques.=

Network-Based Techniques

Network-based techniques are location algorithms that calculate position coordinates on core devices in the infrastructure of the communications networks. These techniques have been favored in many cases where the number of nodes to be located is high and centralized processing represents a financial advantage.

These kinds of techniques are also widely used in the wireless market because of their scalability and because their implementations are compliant with standard trends. In comparison to other techniques such as mobile-based or mobile-assisted methods, these techniques rely entirely on functioning entities and do not require additional changes in mobile devices, software or hardware. Mobile-assisted or mobile-based methods require these additions not only for mobiles, but often for wireless network infrastructures.

A major characteristic of these techniques is that they do not depend on global positioning devices, which in most cases, results in other costs, specialized radio frequency (RF) hardware, and a lack of connectivity within indoor environments. In network-based implementations, one or more base stations (BSs) make the necessary measurements and send the results to a location-processing center where the position and coordinates are calculated.

In order to understand the location acquisition process, we will briefly review different network-based location methods.

Network-based techniques include those that use signal strength, angle of arrival (AOA), or time of arrival (TOA), as well as their combinations and improved variations.

Angle of Arrival (AOA) Method

AOA techniques estimate the location of a radio source by using antenna arrays able to spot the angular orientation of an incoming ray (Steiniger, 2006). These techniques offer advantages over the signal strength technique. However, signals can suffer scattering that observed angles differ from the actual angular location. In fact, precision depends on the propagation conditions. In the event of a lack of line of sight, the antenna array may use the strongest arriving path as the indicator of the source location.=

Multipath phenomenon is always a concern, even when line of sight is optimal. It is worthwhile mentioning that the accuracy obtained by this technique depends on the mobile stations (MS) to BS distance (Caffery, 1998). A general functioning procedure is depicted in Figure 1, above. Angular information allows straight-line tracing and the intersection of two lines, which is sufficient to determine MS location. Nevertheless, a third observation point makes it possible to improve location estimation and to overcome indetermination when the MS is on the segment linking two base stations.

Chalamalasetti (2003) points out that the angle resolution is limited by the size of the array and the limitations of the processing algorithm. Many implementations of this method are very slow. Resolution depends on the antenna beam width, which in turn depends on antenna size in terms of wavelength. Antenna front to back ratio will also limit the dynamic range of the measurement.

Time-Based Methods

These techniques can be grouped into two methods. Caffery (1998) mentions that according to

Figure 1. Angle of arrival method

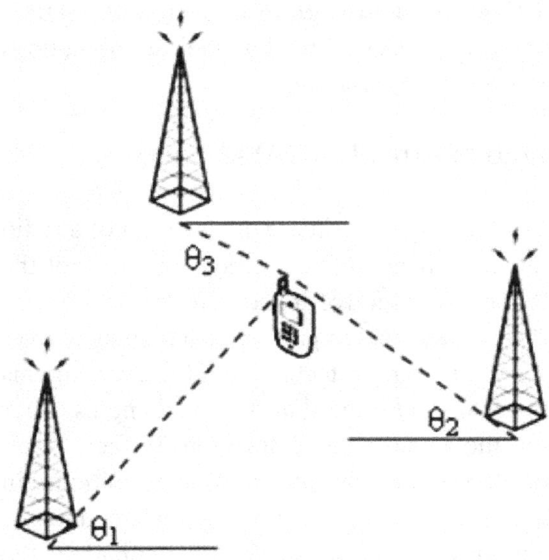

different features, these methods can be grouped by the estimation of time of arrival (TOA) of a signal transmitted between an MS and one or several BSs, and the time difference of arrival (TDOA) of a signal received at multiple BSs.

In TOA measurements, the distances between the MS and the BSs are measured by detecting the propagation time between a mobile and the BSs (Reza, 2000). As travel time is associated with distance, these measurements enable triangulation using the three circles with their respective BSs at the center of each circle. Once the three transmission ranges are determined, the intersection of the three circles will be taken as the searched location (see Figure 2). In contrast, TDOA measurements utilize differences in TOA. Note that these time differences are used to calculate the position of the mobile by creating hyperbolae, which are curves of constant TDOA for at least two BSs that are considered foci and the searched location will be placed where two hyperbolae intercept. Both time-based techniques require high-resolution timing measurements.

TOA Method

Reza (2000) and Woodacre (2003) state the TOA methodology advantages include:

Figure 2. Time of arrival method

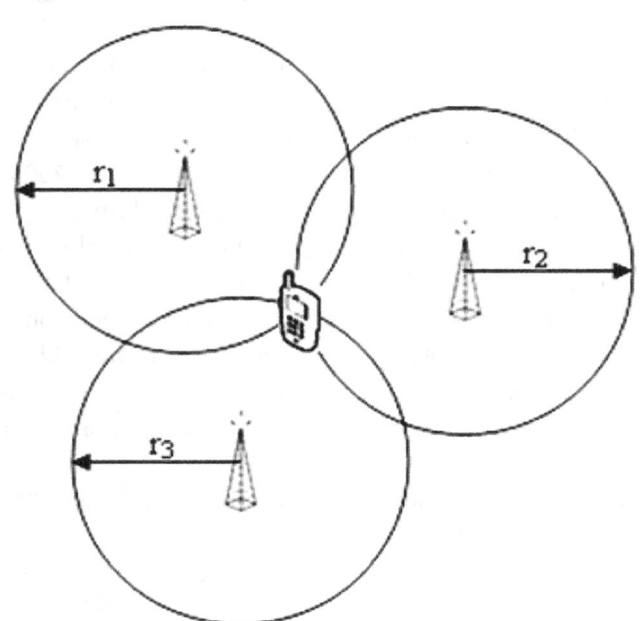

1. Synchronization with transmitter is not needed;
2. Only inter-RN synchronization is needed;
3. A very simple technology;
4. An infrastructure independent of the MSs
5. Low-power consumption.

TDOA Method

The TDOA method involves two stages in the mobile location calculation. First, the time delay difference of the signal propagated from the mobile to pairs of base stations is measured (Reza, 2000). These measurements are used to calculate the relative distance to the BSs and define a hyperbolic locus. Afterwards, the location is calculated by solving a set of conic equations.

Calculations of TDOA can be highly affected by multipath phenomena (Murphy, 2007). A signal from an MS to the BSs may be reflected on obstacles several times before reaching its destination. This reflection can increase delay, especially in urban scenarios where there are significant groups of buildings. The difference in heights between a tower and the handset also translates into inaccuracies, because the model is 2D.

This technique uses any signal transmitted by MSs; there is no need for special burst signals to operate and locate mobile users. This feature allows the TDOA method to be used on any current mobile handset with no additional software or hardware. All changes take place only in BSs when the TDOA is upgraded to the system. Murphy (2007) mentions that TDOA can also provide better reception in low-signal environments, because received signals are much more powerful than those found in an indoor GPS (Global Positioning System). In-building location is difficult with any system, because there is no direct line of sight to the transmitter, but a TDOA unit is more likely to receive a signal than a GPS unit.

U-TDOA Method

This is one of the most common location technologies on the market for two main reasons: First, U-TDOA (Uplink Time Difference of Arrival) is the most commonly used in the Global System for Mobile Communications (GSM) market, and second, it can be adapted to other kinds of wireless networks for location purposes. Unlike mobile-based technologies or mobile-assisted technologies, U-TDOA relies entirely on equipment placed within the wireless network to calculate direction. Because of this, this network technology is not limited by the low-processing capacity of the MS or the handset. Equipment located on the network infrastructure has greater processing power for calculation purposes, providing extremely high performance, even under difficult radio environments in dense urban areas and inside buildings. These enhancements offer different levels of performance and service, depending on market or application requirements.

U-TDOA can be considered compatible with other PL technologies such as cell ID, or even with those with more accurate position calculation results such as E-OTD or A-GPS. This compatibility increases its market penetration and maximizes the LBS revenue opportunity by combining all of them to produce more accurate results as well.

This network-based technology, similar to others, has the advantage of being automatically scalable with time. It is able to locate all current and future MSs added to the network by users. This is because U-TDOA does not need any substantial modification of hardware or software, allowing users to preserve their current devices.

The U-TDOA method employs a process similar to radio-signal triangulation used in TOA and TDOA methods: it calculates the location of a transmitting mobile phone by measuring the difference in time of arrival of signals at different receiver sites (called Location Measurement Units, or LMUs). When the mobile phone transmits, antennas at a number of different BSs receive the signal. The time that an individual LMU detects is a function of the distance of the transmission path between the mobile phone and each LMU antenna. The U-TDOA method uses digital-signal processing to match up the signals at pairs of LMU receivers and determine the difference in reception time. The U-TDOA equipment then computes the latitude and longitude of the handset, based on these differences (Angelides, 2000). This is shown on Figure 3.

The triangulation implemented by U-TDOA produces very accurate measurements, typically in the range of ±50 meters. U-TDOA technology can achieve these results in situations where GPS (and even A-GPS) simply fails to function, particularly in indoor environments or in dense urban environments. Also, with U-TDOA, accuracy can be scaled by adjusting the number of LMUs in the network. The latency of a U-TDOA system is about 10 seconds from the initiation of the call to the delivery of requests. This PL technology is flexible, can be implemented in many different environments, and scaled according to the necessities and demands from the operator of the network or an increasing demand of services.

Cell Identification Methods

Cell ID methods can be considered to be the predecessor to all PL technologies. They were the first kind to be developed and implemented at the same time as wireless cellular technology. In its origin, its goal was to reduce the number of paging signals in a cellular system, but precise location was not a requirement. In this case, the subscriber identified a cell color code and notified the corresponding code to a central site. In this way, the system knew which cells were able to reach a subscriber. The coarseness of this technique depended on the number of BSs associated with a single color code. The operation of TDMA demanded synchronization reception of this structure of the frames. Thus, delayed transmission was introduced, and associated delays could be used for range estimation within a cell.

There are three different cell identification methods present in the market, even though all of them can be considered as one, because two

Figure 3. Uplink time difference of arrival method

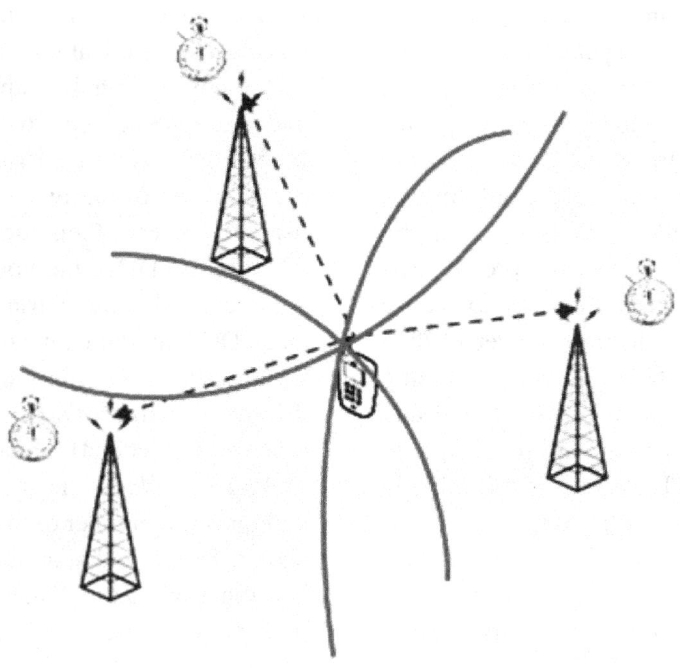

of them are improvements of the initial Cell-ID method. As we have mentioned, the following technologies are part of this technological family (Davies, 2004): Cell Identity (CI), C-ID+TA or "Cell-ID + Timing Advance (TA)", and Strength of Signals received by the handset (RXLEVs).

Cell-ID (C-ID) Identification

C-ID method is a PL technology limited by the coverage area of each BS as well as the entire wireless network of each provider. It is mostly used in networks that are divided into service areas known as cells. C-ID determines to which network cell of the network every user is connected to receive service, thus giving the simplest PL information of any technology (Laitinen, 2001). In this case, the C-ID-based location estimate is at the serving cell antenna it coordinates. For a sector cell, the C-ID method can be configured to calculate the location estimate by taking into account the antenna's azimuth, as well as the size of the cell (refer to Figure 4). Nevertheless, accuracy is very low, and it depends on the size of the cell and its radius, which can range from some hundred meters to a few kilometers, depending on the environmental conditions. When C-ID is used, wireless providers install more cells in urban areas than in rural areas. The increased number of cells increases accuracy because of the smaller cell radii of micro-cells and pico-cells.

Figure 4. Cell identification method and sectorization method

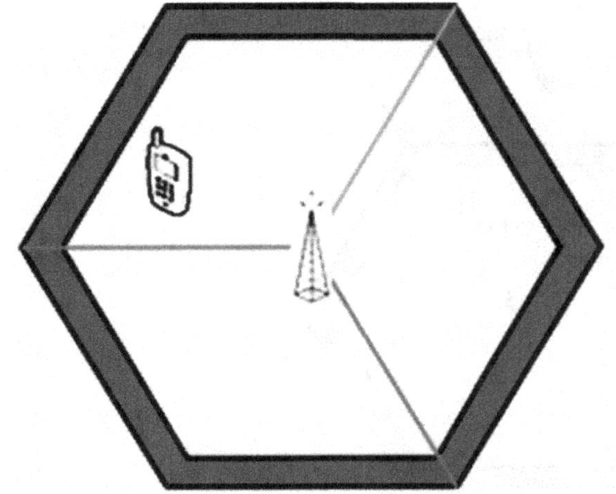

This technology, according to Davies (2004), offers the following advantages: 1) low deployment and operation costs and 2) it is inherent to all cellular based systems and it requires minimal modifications to existing systems 3) it can be implemented across the whole population of users as it can be supported by all MSs 4) Cell-ID based location is fast as no calculations are required to obtain location information, making it suitable for applications requiring high capacity, low accuracy of position and massive applications

C-ID & TA o "Cell ID & Timing Advance"

C-ID, as mentioned before, can be used along with some enhancements called "Timing Advance." TA is an integer number ranging from 0 to 63 that is introduced in the GSM system to avoid overlapping of bursts at the BTS side, and it is proportional to the distance between MS and serving BTS estimated by the system (Spirito, 2001).

This method is used in cellular networks such as GSM and it has been included in the standard. It is specified that GSM use CI and TA to define a circle (in a 2-dimensional scenario) whose center is the serving BS on which the MS location is estimated. In the case of an omni-directional serving cell, the CI & TA location estimate is at the serving cell's antenna coordinates. If the cell is a sector cell, the CI & TA method determines the location estimate in the direction of the serving cell's antenna azimuth, at a distance previously estimated by the TA capabilities (Spirito, 2001). For further graphical explanation, refer to Figure 5.

Cell ID by Signal Strength

This member of this technological family is named C-ID+TA+RXLEV, or "Cell Identification and Timing Advanced and RELEVs." It is more complex than any other member of this family for many reasons, but it also has many advantages. Its

Figure 5. Cell identification + time advanced method

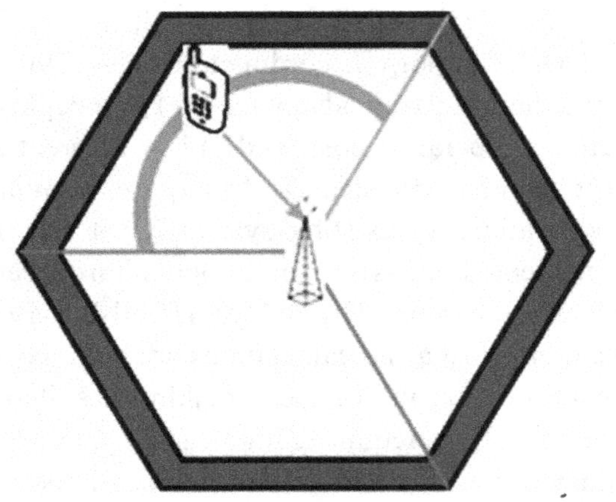

accuracy is better, but the infrastructure is more complex and it depends on the MSs (see Figure 6).

Cell ID by Signal Strength uses a mathematical model that describes path-loss attenuation with distance. This gives a signal strength measurement that provides a distance estimate between the MSs and BSs, where the MS must lie on a circle centered at the BS. By using multiple BSs, the location of the MS can be determined.

The CI & TA & RXLEV method estimates the MS's coordinates by combining C-ID, TA, and RXLEV information. RXLEVs are measurements of the strength of signals received by the MS from the serving cell and from up to six of the strongest nearest cells. The level of a signal received by an MS, or more precisely, the attenuation the signal has experienced, depends on the reciprocal position of the MS and the BTS from which the signal was transmitted. Attenuation values from multiple neighbor cells are modeled by the C-ID & TA & RXLEV location method through basic propagation models, and used to estimate the location of the MS. Optionally, the method can use propagation models tuned to best fit the propagation phenomena in specific environments, and it can be left with the possibility of using only a subset of the information available (e.g., TA only or RXLEVs only) to estimate the handset's coordinates (Spirito, 2001).

Figure 6. Cell ID & TA & RXLEV method

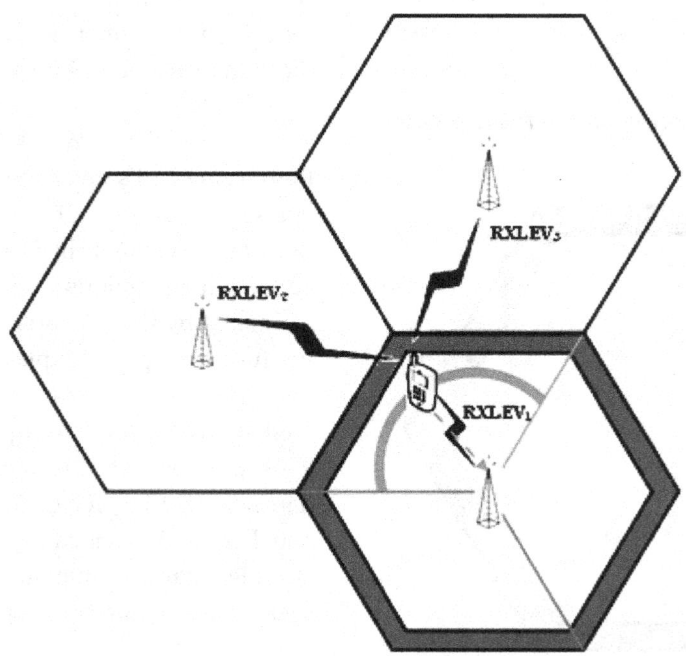

Mobile-Based Techniques

Unlike previous methods, mobile-based technologies offer certain advantages. The one and most important advantage is that network-based technologies do not very accurately estimate user location, so when designing a LBS, we need to consider which is the tolerable user position error.

In a mobile-based implementation, the MS takes measurements and estimates positions. This allows positioning, even in idle mode, by measuring control channels which are continuously transmitting. Some additional information such as BSs coordinates might be needed from the network to enable location determination in the MS. The two main methods found on the market are the E-OTD (Enhanced Observed Time Difference) and OTDOA (Observed Time Difference of Arrival), which are based on TOA and TDOA calculations, with the difference being that they are done in the MSs. Therefore, they are considered the mobile versions of these methods. These methods require changes in the mobiles and special calculation units inside the devices.

E-OTD requires the installation of devices that receive the measurements carried out by the mobile. Networks also require units specialized in sending a continuous signal to the mobile to allow the telephone software to carry out calculations.

Enhanced Observed Time Difference (E-OTD)

E-OTD is a mobile-based technology implemented mostly in GSM devices where some TDOA measurements take place. These measurements are taken from the radio signals received on the Broadcast Control Channel (BCCH) from at least two of the neighboring BSs close to the terminal. By knowing the coordinates of the closest sites and the transmission offset time between their BCCHs, the system observes the time difference measurements (OTDs) and estimates its coordinates.

Like any PL method, some factors affect E-OTD's performance and its accuracy in the estimated OTD. For instance, the multipath present in the environment and the topological characteristics are among the most important issues. For OTD estimates, this method uses LMUs dispersed in the network, the number of which per area unit will determine the accuracy of the system. That is why carriers install one LMU for every two BSs. This is done in order to increase accuracy and at the same time reduce the high costs of implementation.

An E-OTD disadvantage is that BSs must be synchronized. Therefore, the Relative Time Difference (RTD) must be calculated. In order to increase accuracy, OTD and RTD measurements must be obtained from three BSs pairs. The OTD measurements are done by the mobile. The BSs deliver coordinates and RTD values. This information allows the mobile to calculate its position. Otherwise, the mobile measures the OTD and delivers it to the network that calculates the position of the mobile user in the network (Wylie-Green, 2001).

The MSs are E-OTD-enabled software entities and they periodically measure the signals from three or more BSs. The time differences of the signal arrival to the two points (LMU and mobile) are combined to produce hyperbolic lines that intercept at the mobile. This procedure offers a two-dimensional location method. In the case of E-OTD, the mobile measures the time difference of arrival of the bursts of two close BSs. This is known as Observed Time Difference (OTD) measurements. This is shown in Figure 7.

Observed Time Difference of Arrival (OTDOA)

The OTDOA is mostly used in UMTS networks and is very similar to the E-OTD method in calculations but uses a different air interface, the Uu deployed exclusively for UMTS. It is based on measurements in the difference in time of arrival

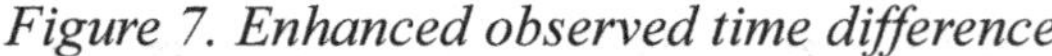

Figure 7. Enhanced observed time difference

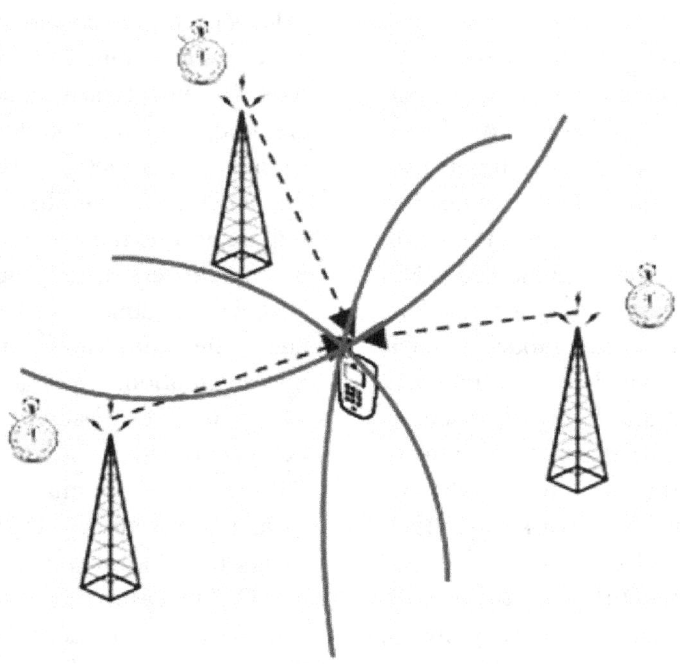

of the downlink signals received at the MS. This technique depends on the position calculating capabilities of the mobile station and the operator, such as BS position information and Relative Time Differences (RTDs) that have to be sent to the mobile station periodically (Davies, 2004).

This positioning method is based on the observation of time differences between the mobile phone and the nearest BSs. The MS knows the coordinates of the BSs in advanced. With this information and the proper algorithm, the MS is able to determine its own position by triangulating the location based on the known references. The accuracy of the OTDOA positioning method varies depending on the current location of the MS within the cell. Specially, if an MS is close to one of the BSs, it could result difficult to hear the two other BSs needed for the triangulation.

Mobile-Assisted Technologies

These technologies are a complement to those mentioned above. Location methods include solutions where the MS makes measurements and sends the results to a location center in the network for further processing. A clear example of this procedure is what we know as Assisted Global Positioning System (A-GPS), which continuously sends measurements reports to a processing unit in cellular networks in order to estimate its position by making calculations with data obtained from mobiles and network infrastructure.

A-GPS

This technology is entirely based on a former technology named GPS (Global Positioning System). A-GPS is a hybrid technology that utilizes GPS satellites in conjunction with cellular-network infrastructures to improve position-determination calculations. This technology requires mobile stations with partial GPS receivers, which introduce additional circuitry although the size, weight, memory, and power requirements are significantly less than for full GPS receivers.

The GPS is a constellation of 24 satellites that orbit the earth in 6 orbital planes (at 10,600 miles above the earth) of four satellites each. It offers location accuracy from 10 to 100 m; however, in some cases, GPS can provide accuracy to within a meter. This is achieved by using a GPS-enabled terminal and ground stations in conjunction with satellites, creating a multilateration calculation to determine positioning. GPS satellites cover the entire earth, except for the Arctic and Antarctic areas. Its main errors are caused by atmospheric conditions, mostly in the ionosphere and troposphere. Other sources of errors may be environmental, or due to obstacles located around the receiver that produce multi-path delays (Williams, 2005).

This method bases its calculations on measurements received through the GPS satellite system. An A-GPS enabled device is a GPS receiver that calculates distances by using the propagation time from satellite to receiver. Consequently, it is important to maintain a relatively strong received satellite signal. This is achieved by allowing reception of GPS satellite data at signal levels below known thresholds and, in some cases, location estimation can be also obtained when indoors.

First, the network coarsely locates the mobile terminal (MT) by using a cell-based technique. This location, combined with the GPS signals at the transmitter, reduces the search space for the GPS triangulation calculations by predicting the received signals, thus saving time. Then, the MT itself has a partial GPS receiver that clocks onto a satellite and transmits the received data back to the ground station for processing. Since a scaled-down GPS receiver is used, the size, weight, memory, and power requirements are much less. This hybrid solution can have an accuracy of about 15meters, only slightly worse than a full-scale GPS. Normal GPS fails when the satellite signals become blocked, but A-GPS survives at a lower resolution since it has network methods to fall back on (Dibdin, 2001). This is shown in Figure 8.

Traditionally, the A-GPS measurement can be done by using a location server where measurements from the networks and the satellites are

Figure 8. Assisted GPS method

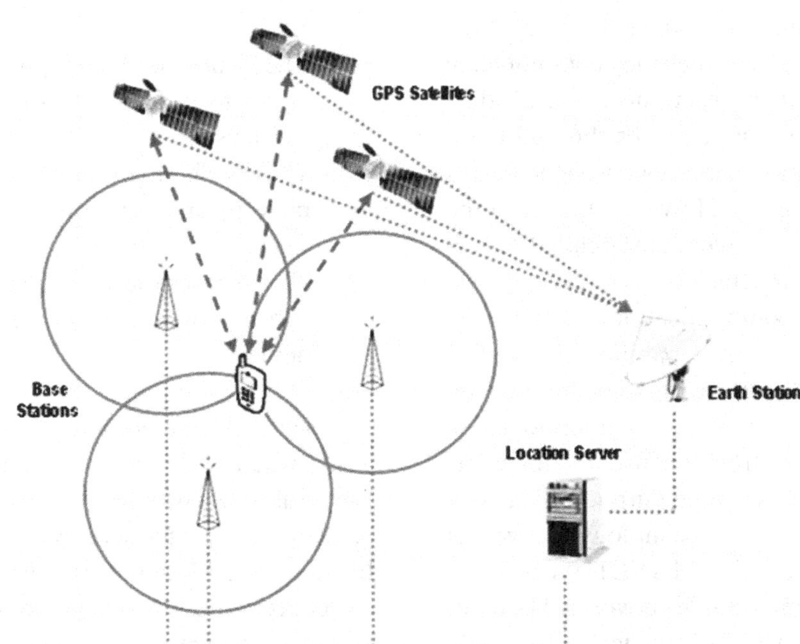

used to find users; other alternatives lie absolutely in the mobiles. In some cases, the A-GPS considers the existence of other positioning methods to make the measurements more accurate. Sometimes, the GPS and the Advanced Forward Link Trilateration (AFLT) methods are used together. The AFLT method consists of measuring the down-link signal to mobiles where a client resides and calculates its position. It requires changes in the mobile to be able to make calculations in CDMA (Code Division Multiple Access, an American standard for mobile communications) networks. Similar solutions exist for GMS-based networks.

The previous technologies rely on a fixed infrastructure of access points which are utilized as geographical references for locating mobile devices. The following section explores reconfigurable infrastructure networks that lack fixed reference points of access.

MOBILE AD-HOC NETWORKS

Most wireless communications depend on infrastructure elements from diverse networks to reach and establish communication, such as hot-spots in Wi-Fi networks. Even when they communicate with other users of the same network, all data and information exchange passes through these devices which, in most cases, can produce delays in worst case scenarios. However, this is in the process of evolving into what can be called "direct wireless communications."

Direct wireless communications among users can be understood as the capability to establish communications directly with someone else by using mobile devices, with no intermediaries or wired-fixed infrastructure, usually for communication or data exchange purposes. This can be achieved by using a technology known as Mobile Ad-hoc Networks (MANETs), which are stand-alone self-configurable networks. The main characteristic of MANETs is the lack of physical infrastructure. MANET's members may continuously join and leave the network in order to move towards a new, different one at will. Or simply leave the network because their battery charge is over and they disappear. This configuration supports multi-hop communications with changeable conditions of multi-path fading, collisions, and shadowing interference.

MANETs are groups of nodes sharing resources among all nearby mobile devices at the same physical level with the purpose of establishing short-elapsed communications to ease instant networking capabilities (Kozat et al., 2003). These nodes do not necessarily know the identities or the resources of all the other nodes around them. These resources or capabilities may vary from the support of multiple physical interfaces or processing power to multimedia libraries and higher resources. Sharing resources increases the chances of different functionalities and services all across the group of mobile users.

MANET networks present two common usages in industry: geographic-location information of nodes and the localization of contents. Both kinds of services share common characteristics that we can describe below:

- They utilize geographical position of nodes to implement different value-added services;
- They are highly sensible to user movement patterns and have the capacity to respond to these patterns; and,
- They posses routing capabilities that establish a geographic route to reach MANET devices.

Each MANET node needs routing functionalities when no direct-link condition is available. This is used when a node needs to reach a desirable device by using intermediary nodes between them. In this case, MANETs require node discovery protocols to know their neighbors. However, these protocols require a special server for this purpose.

These servers, or "directory agents," act as known, logical entities and respond by using a determined interface or port to request messages from MANET nodes when trying to obtain neighbor information. In order to create the directory service, these servers require the registration acknowledgements from MANET clients sent by broadcasting multicasting capabilities of the network clients. However, these functionalities must be added in two different ways: statically to the nodes chosen for this purposes, or dynamically to a group of nodes of the same network. However, functioning statically goes against the nature of MANET networks and functioning dynamically requires more resources from the network because of the continuous changes of members present in the network. This requires continuously informing clients of those in charge of neighbor discovery and changes in the topology of the current nodes. A directory service enables scalability in the network through the growth of the network, considerably shorter location-service times, less load on individual servers, and improvement in service performance.

There are several discovery service protocols. One of these protocols is named GCLP, or "Geographic-based Content Location Protocol." GCLP's functionalities involve the propagation of the contents and resource advertisement and queries in cross-shaped trajectories to guarantee two intersections where nodes answer. These announcements allow nodes to follow each other based on the proximity of the servers.

Another example is a non-geographic service discovery protocol named "Centralized Service Discovery," which relies on a central directory server with information about services available in the network to allow remote discovery and invocation. Flooding-based and DNS-based Service Discovery is a protocol where service providers and clients discover each other by multicast messages or advertisements. These can be aided by the following: a) SLP (Service Location Protocol) which announces services available in the network for all users by using short messages with URLs); b) UPnP (Universal Plug and Play) which is supported by Microsoft and uses the Simple Service Discovery Protocol (SSDP) for discovery on IP-based networks, where broadcast advertisements notify all the nodes in the networks about its services. These advertisements' URL direct users to the service automatically (Friedman et al, 2006).

Acording to Jeong, et al. (2005), MANETs can work by basing their functioning on Zone-Based Services. These services work only within specific, delimited areas of coverage, whose services are delivered by a number of providers who can offer different services at the same time without interfering with each other. This provides clients the advantage and possibility of choosing which available service to request. This area has minimum infrastructure, but requires the profile of each user for identification, service definition and location in each zone of service. Other MANETs can receive services by using sensors or other wireless devices or technologies. For example, RFID transponders attached to mobile devices can be detected by RFID readers. This can trigger a series of services delivered by using other technologies such as Wi-Fi covering indoor environments.

So far, we have reviewed some of the PL techniques for different scenarios. Advantages and disadvantages of these techniques have been mentioned and technical challenges have been explored. In the next part of the chapter, we focus on applications related to location of users of communication networks.

LOCATION-BASED SERVICES

Location information becomes relevant in relation to solutions and applications that can be developed and deployed. Positioning of customers allows for better planning and optimization of service-provider operation. Regulations provisioning for better safety and security demand location-information availability. PLs have also acted as enablers for new market opportunities for service providers and customers. A number of PL techniques have been described. However, PL services require specific architectures that should provide (Agre, 2001):

- user location determination with a minimum number of inputs,
- multiple ways to obtain location information must be combined to increase accuracy,
- the capability to be used in indoor and outdoor scenarios with no interference when moving transitioning from indoor to outdoors, or vice versa,
- continuous cooperation with neighboring nodes to determine position and thereby increase accuracy levels, depending on the requirements of the application, and
- the ability to easily integrate new emerging technologies.

Even though LBS seem new to the industry, this is not true. LBS first appeared when wireless technologies began being merchandized and, even today, some traditional technologies depend on LBS to function. The first location methods, known as Cell ID (of the network-based technologies), determines where in the network a user receives service coverage and provides basic network management over the entire network. Gradually, new methods were deployed on the field of wireless communications.

One reason for searching for newer, highly-accurate techniques is the demand for better emergency services, such as "911" in the United States and Canada and "112" in the European Union. Governments demand an accuracy of between 50 and 100 meters when someone calls emergency services. One organism that tries to regulate these technologies is the Location Interoperability Forum (LIF), which focuses on mobile devices, especially cellular networks.

LBS can be divided into three major groups, according to their usage: military and government industries, emergency services, and commercial. Military and government use includes all the applications employed by the US military or any other US government security agency. Many of these services can interact with sensors to respond to contingencies where human lives are at risk. Finally, the commercial applications include notification, orientation and decision-making for certain users that want to locate a place find, locate a product, or access information.

The LBS, in general terms, can be developed to satisfy specific services that respond special criteria. These criteria are associated with certain actions such as orientation and localization, navigation, search, identification and event check, to name just a few examples. When LBS are developed, designers must focus on what the users may demand, meaning what problems customers would like to have solved when they face a location or position problem. We have to emphasize that LBS are very useful, not only in one's hometown, but they are really important when one needs information about unknown places, or simply to help moving faster when traffic conditions become difficult.

Depending on the request, certain specific operations are required and every request is different, because the problem that needs to be solved often has very specific characteristics. Some of these requests only require a few operations because accessing an information database may be enough to satisfy what the client has requested. However, other requests require significantly more resources to deliver the necessary information (even on the mobile). An example of this may be navigation services, when real-time information and interactive applications on mobiles are required to provide a service. Most LBS can help people:

- Orient and locate people, places, or assets.
- Navigate in city and highway situations.
- Identify current location.

- Receive announcements of special events, including the place where events are to occur.

Despite their actions, LBS can be grouped in families according to their nature and orientation, which may require different levels of accuracy depending on the service provided. Those that focus on finding, tracking, and tracing routes demand special levels of accuracy because they are used for safety and security situations, or simply because the assets whose location is intended have important value for the owners.

In any case, this is something that LBS providers have to deal with, especially when they do not own the technologies for discovering, locating and calculating the position of users. They have to be conscious of what kind of service they want to deploy and with whom they have agreements. Service provisioning depends to a great degree on the carriers' network resources and how willing they are to improve them gradually.

Table 1 lists different families of LBS that are actually offered by communications companies. Every family has its own common characteristics and offers similar services with variances for specialized usage. The demand for accuracy is one of the most important issue LBS consider in order to deliver a proper service.

Table 1. Examples of LBS applications

Service Family	Application	Accuracy
Information and Entertainment	Traffic Information	Medium
	Driving Conditions	Medium
	Traffic Information	High
	Road Maps	High
	Gaming and Gambling	Low
	Closest POI	Medium
	Time Zone Determination	Low
	Advertisement	Low
	Information Broadcasting and News	Medium
Tracking and Tracing	Allocation Management	High
	Personnel Location	High
	Inventory Tracking	High
	Car Fee Payment and Control	High
	Insurance Assistance	Medium
	Fleet Management	Medium
	Restricted Area Determination	Low
Call Routing	Tracing Calls	High
	Mobile Communication Stablishment	Low
	Call Fee Charging	Low
	Service Provider Selection	Low
Safety Security	Personnel Monitoring	High
	Emergency Movement Monitoring	High
	Intruder Detection	High
	Emergency Service	High

Location information applications will certainly require regulations to promote and limit their use for commercial and advertising practices as well as for crime prevention and surveillance services. A number of other applications can be envisioned with wireless, network–based, position–estimation schemes such as the following (Steiniger, 2006): a) Real-time display of self-location information. (For example, a user walking across a university or company campus holding a pocket PC that provides a campus map and the real-time position of the user on the map); b) Real-time inventory systems where expensive assets can be counted automatically and localized; c) Monitoring of position-sensitive environmental variables; c) Monitoring and mapping of potentially hazardous zones in disaster areas by deploying unmanned sensing vehicles prior to the entrance of rescue teams; d) Intelligent warehouse systems to optimize stock product flow and logistics; e) Patient locators in mental healthcare institutions, newborn locators in maternity rooms and child locators in amusement parks or shopping malls; f) Real-time shopping mall guides where users with a personal digital assistant (PDA) or pocket PC can read about sales and featured products of the stores they are approaching while walking through the mall; g) Real-time amusement park, museum and tourist guides that display information about attractions, artwork, or city landmarks, according to user location; h) Mobile yellow pages; Mobile databases where information retrieval and file accessibility depend on the geographic location of a user; i) Location-aware gaming systems; j) Location-sensitive billing in cellular systems; k) Location-aware marketing systems that can track location and density of potential clients within a specified area; l) Location-aware wireless access security systems where files, information, or system access may or may not be available to a user depending on that person's current geographic position; m) In the area of communication systems, applications that include location-aware routing in reconfigurable networks, spatial diversity techniques, knowledgebase systems, distributed learning, cognitive radio, as well as user density and mobility detection used in real-time network reconfiguration and planning.

Technological Components of LBS

All LBS require platforms to deliver information regarding the coordinates of a mobile user. Different components interact to function and collaborate in order to deliver results, and these are given as follows m:

- Mobile Devices – handsets or mobile equipment necessary not only to generate requests, but also to receive information that results from these requests.
- Communications Network – this is a union of devices used to transfer information from one extreme of the communication network to the other.
- Positioning Component – hardware in charge of calculating the position after making measurements and processing them with PL methods such AOA, TDOA or A-GPS.
- Application Providers – they offer different services and develop technological platforms to deliver value-added information after processing the location information taken from calculations of the positioning components.
- Content providers – they maintain additional information that can be used by application providers to enrich the service delivered.

The components mentioned above can be considered the columns that support the platform because they are absolutely necessary, although not necessarily integrated/operated by the same owner. The relationship mentioned above means that most of the time network providers are inde-

Figure 9. Components of an LBS platform

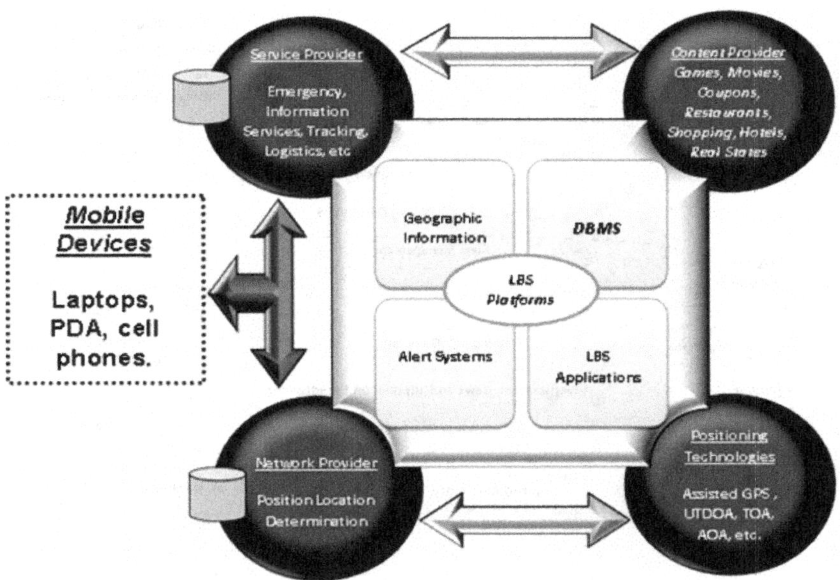

pendent of the application or LBS platform. They only share information when required and they own all data about user's location and obviously, all the devices to received it.

On the other hand, we have two more actors known as the application provider and the content provider. The first is responsible for application development, maintenance, and establishing agreements with wireless providers. The second, the content provider, owns every piece of data pertaining to places and for the information and data that helps increase the value of the services. These two actors can be together as one single entity, or only exchange data and be relatively independent.

Feasibility and Accuracy

When designing an LBS platform, we have to take into account accuracy and feasibility, which are considered the most important aspects in making a recommendation on service providers; accuracy is related to the type of service being offered, and a decision has to be made regarding the level of accuracy required by the service and if the network has the capacity to offer it; and feasibility is related to the degree of uncertainty of the real position in relation to the results calculated by the location algorithm or technology used to establish the coordinates of the user. Accuracy and feasibility varies from LBS to LBS and from technology to technology. LBS can be classified into four families. Every family requires a different range of accuracy as seen below:

The families are (Faggion, 2005): Call Routing, Safety and Security, Tracking and Tracing, and Information and Entertainment. The "Call Routing" family refers to basic services such as call set up, call fee charging and provider selection when turning on cell phones. This family requires less accuracy, except for tracing call services, which can also be associated with security in some specific cases.

A second family, "Safety and Security" is considered the most demanding family with respect to accuracy. These kinds of services require very accurate measurement results because they focus on people and their integrity which, in

Figure 10. Accuracy requirement and LBS families

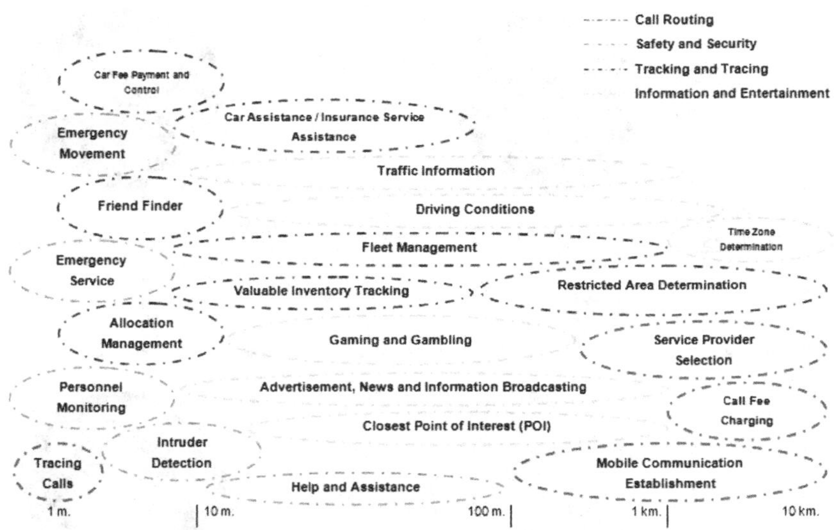

many cases, involve life or death situations. We can find services such as Personnel Monitoring, Emergency Movement Monitoring, Emergency Services and others. Telemedicine services, including emergency response can be considered as part of this family.

The "Tracking and Tracing" family includes location services to finding assets, such as cars, containers, or traffic control through automatic fee payment. This can be considered a "balanced family" because not all of the services need to be as accurate as those belonging to safety and security family. This is why these services are used for controlling entertainment devices (e.g., appointments or finding a friend), and are not considered extremely important because they do not place users at risk.

Last but not least in importance is the "Information and Entertainment" family. This family is very similar to the "Tracking and Tracing" family, with respect to accuracy requirements. Accuracy is not a strong requirement to satisfy. Even a few kilometers are acceptable when designing a LBS system for this family of services. Gaming and Gambling, Time Zone Determination, and Traffic information are examples of this LBS family.

After describing LBS families, let us compare technologies available on the market. The technologies in the following graphic can be found in current wireless technologies.

LBS Platforms in MANETs

Development in wireless networks can be increased by adding services that satisfy client needs and add value to wireless networks. Location-based services are the most common services offered for wireless users as we mentioned before. However, LBS cannot be offered without a technological platform and information from users to personalize, process data, and send back a requested service. Only after users receive the information they request can location-based services be classified as Value-Added Services (VAS).

Value-Added Services is a term used in to classify service offered to users that increase the perceived value delivered to users of a communications network. VAS require platforms that focus on remotely processing user information (especially location information), background and preferences. VAS add worth to the total service available in the coverage area. It stands alone

Figure 11. Feasibility of technologies

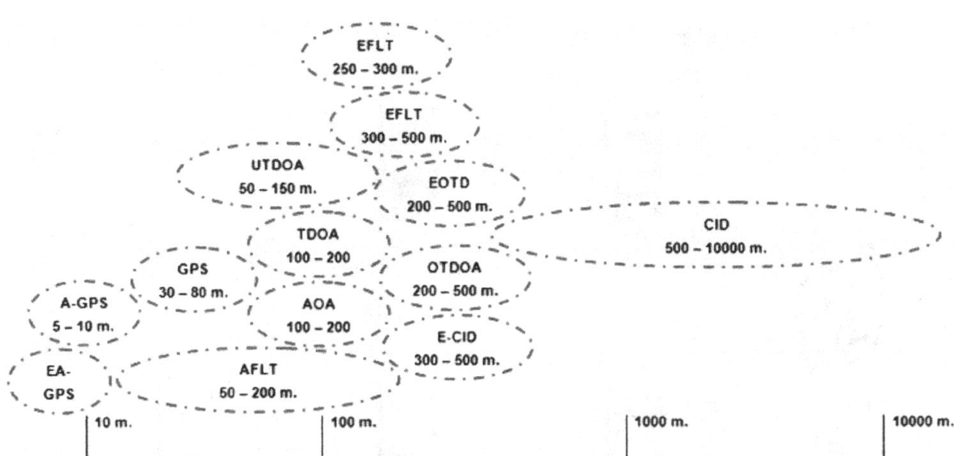

operationally and functionally and allows users to interact with different services at the same time without interference, which can be offered as a basic or premium service.

The development of VAS platforms is possible because of the increasing development of the Internet on the one hand, and the increased effort of institutions such as OGC (Open GIS Consortium), LIF (Location Interoperability Forum) and OMA (Open Mobile Alliance) to deploy them on the other. These organizations write standards and make recommendations that providers must pay attention to in order to develop platforms that are useful and compatible with the networks and technologies on the current market.

Because of the nature of ad-hoc networks and their users, a good way to offer location-based services when using this reconfigurable structure is to create a technological platform that informs and notifies users about the resources available for different services. Afterwards, users have the freedom to choose what, when and where to request a service, according to the user's specific needs or desires.

A LBS platform is basically formed by an application server which can be implemented with an inner GIS (Geographic Information Server) that processes, translates and interprets location information to generate a service response. However, this can be changed into a more complex platform with the server preserved as a core functioning entity interacting with more specialized entities to increase processing capabilities. After surveying wireless technologies, we have found five key elements to consider when developing a platform (Coulouris, 2002): Database Management Server (DBMS), Application Server, Content Provider Server(s), and Geographic Information System Server (GIS). In order to increase efficiency and control, an additional server with managing functionalities such as a Management and Control Server (MCS) could help to increase reliability of the platform. This structure is depicted in Figure 12.

Zhang (2005) remarks that application server is the core element. This entity is in charge of receiving and responding to any request from the outside. It also has two direct interactions with the MCS and the GIS. The application server is where all logical processes reside and where all results after requests are processed and obtained. Developers create servers that are capable of delivering information after requesting a service and receiving location information from users. This is achieved and aided by the MCS and the GIS. It should be mentioned here that a LBS

Figure 12. LBS platform

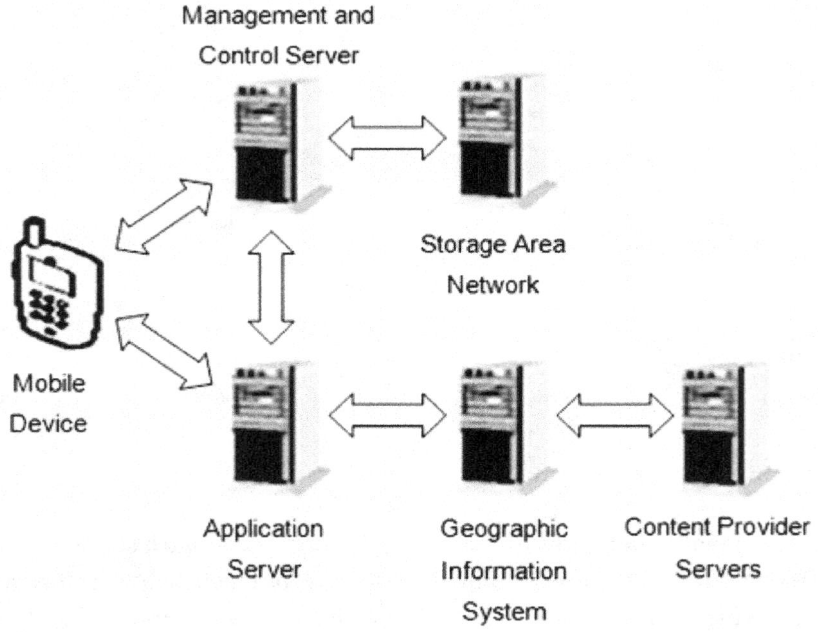

platform ought to be capable of receiving and responding to different requests from different sources due to the diversity of wireless devices and user interfaces. These sources can have different formats, such as HTTP or WAP for wireless users of laptops, PDAs, and/or cell phones. In addition, the applications have to focus on determining position and location, which comes from the measurements that mobiles can achieve internally by inner-position calculation hardware, or aided by neighbors in the same network.

A GIS (Dao, 2002) is a computer-based capability that manipulates geographical data. Some geographical data include: acquisition, compilation, storage, update, management, retrieval, presentation and analysis of data. In some cases, maps or images can also be stored in the GIS. In order to improve the resources and allow specialization of the GIS, content servers are added to give useful information by means of an object-relational database that establishes relationships between data and multimedia objects.

Another element, the DBMS, it is defined by Blazewicz (2003) as a specialized software-enabled server for data management. This data is stored in the server and can be accessed by requests named "queries," with the specific syntax related to the chosen DBMS, be it Oracle, SQL Server, MySQL, etc. A content server is similar to a single DBMS. In fact, they both require software for data management, but the main differences concern the kind of information they each store. In an LBS platform, a DBMS is used to store user profiles, preferences, and any other kind of information coming from user service requests. On the other hand, a content-provider server stores geographic-related information, from data to images and any other multimedia resource that can be used to provide services. Both entities, similar in core functioning, should be separated in order to establish a difference in the information, and to avoid confusion and loss of integrity of the information stored.

SAN, or Storage Area Networks, are used when the quantity of information is huge and, in this case, we recommended that all data reside in separated servers from the one that manages queries. The SAN is, as its name implies, a junction of servers that store data information to be accessed by using a DBMS server that, through queries sent from the application server, gathers the information and delivers it to the application server.

In the case of MANETs, the MCS is an important element. This entity ought to be server capable to keep an order of certain information for the platform. It has separate capabilities from the application server because it is in charge of generating the messages that interest users interested in accessing a service. These messages can be used for locating potential clients and responding to users who accept the service using location and position information that can be managed by this server. This functionality, instead of sending messages directly to users in the network, interacts with special servers named "UDDI." These servers are used to advertise resources online which users can access through a simple WAP portal or internet browser, where they can view all the services available and listed on a website and have access by clicking the service link for the service in which they are interested (Friedman et al., 2006). Then, the MCS announces the services of its platform and keeps it listed for future access by new customers in any part of the world).

Profiling is another capability that has to be considered for UDDI servers, which use DBMS to store and manipulate data. In this case, the MCS can register any record of data from users that access the service. This information can be used to personalize services by knowing device resources, preferences, past services, likes and dislikes, concurrence to certain services, authentication of users, and so on. In the case of WAP users, there exists a profile named UAProf that is defined by the WAP Forum. The "User Agent Profile" is used to describe the capability of the handsets and enable the end-to-end flow between handsets and platforms. This profile describes the hardware, software, application, and network features that allow the platform to deliver appropriate services to terminals. A disadvantage of the AUProf is the network hardware needed to store the information of every mobile terminal where the platform can request the information required to provide the requested service.

CONCLUSION

Location information acquisition techniques vary widely, depending on the deployed infrastructure and subjacent technologies. Cellular-based systems adopt location techniques according to the applicable air interface and applicable standard. New technologies like WiMax and LTE (Long-Term Evolution) have standardization groups who are currently reviewing the feasibility of already deployed location strategies which also take advantage of new technological features not available in previous systems. Specific location technologies like GPS provide more accuracy. However, their available coverage is not universal and hybrid solutions are common in order to offer an adequate solution, depending on the prevailing subscriber conditions.

IP (Internet Protocol) technology has become pervasive; it also exhibits great potential. For instance, location information in MANETs offers a big opportunity for LBS in large markets. Nevertheless, we have to remark that accurate and feasible location determination in these kinds of networks is hard to obtain because of the lack of a fixed infrastructure, when compared with other wireless technologies with fixed base stations or antennas. However, this lack of infrastructure does not mean it is impossible to get an accurate location.

MANETs certainly have mobile-based location methods to calculate and determine their position when necessary. This is because most of the infrastructure nodes present in the network are other mobiles, and these have to be capable enough not to depend entirely on infrastructure to make their calculations for them. This means that they have to be software-or hardware-enabled devices to process this information, aided by their neighbors and a minimum number of reference stations in the coverage area. MANET requires minimally wired infrastructure for internet access and other resources not available with other mobile devices.

LBS can be offered in MANETs, but two aspects have to be considered when choosing what service to deploy in this kind of network. First, we must consider what kind of service we want to deliver to clients or users of a MANET and, according to the specific kind of service, what level of accuracy and feasibility of calculation results we need to have in order to offer it. We mention this because services related to security and safety present tremendous risks in the case of application failure. Therefore, they require higher levels of accuracy and feasibility. In other words, we are mostly speaking of saving human lives. Because of this, the PL method must be chosen after taking into consideration whether current devices support or require changes and the cost of them not impacting users, causing them to refuse these services.

LBS platforms for MANET users have to be capable of working independently of any carrier network and reaching users automatically by giving them the chance to choose the service of their preference. These platforms must be capable of serving users from different sources, whether in WAP or in HTTP. They also have to respond in the same manner despite the capabilities or resources available in the source device. In the same way, LBS platforms must be capable not only of processing location information, but also of storing data after requesting information from users, and be capable of processing user profiles to enhance service and offer a value-added service that can be easily perceived by the LBS user.

REFERENCES

Agre, J., Akinyemi, A., Lusheng, J., Masuoka, R., & Thakkar, P. (2001). A layered architecture for location-based services in wireless ad hoc networks. In *Aerospace Conference Proceedings*. New York: IEEE.

Angelides, J. (2000). The benefits of U-TDOA. Wireless Business and Technology [Web site]. Retrieved 2009, from http://wbt.sys-con.com/read/41067.htm

Blazewicz, J. (2003). *Handbook on data management in information systems*. Berlin: Springer.

Caffery, J. (1998, April). Overview of radiolocation in CDMA cellular systems. *IEEE Communications Magazine*.

Chalamalasetti, M. (2003). The shifting landscape of wireless communications. New Delhi: Bharat Sanchar Nigam Limited. Retrieved 2009, from http://portal.bsnl.in/Knowledgebase.asp?intNewsId=8525&strNewsMore=more

Coulouris, G. (2002). *Distributed systems concepts and design*. London: Addison Wesley.

Dao, D. (2002). *Location-based services: Technical and business issues.* Sydney, Australia: Satellite Navigation and Positioning Lab, University of New South Wales. Retrieved 2007, from http://www.gmat.unsw.edu.au/snap/about/publications_year.htm

Davies, R. (2004). Development of a mobile network simulation and visualisation application. Edinburgh, UK.

Friedman, R., & Kliot, G. (2006). Location services in wireless ad hoc and hybrid networks: A survey. Haifa, Israel: Technion – Israel Institute of Technology. Retrieved 2009, from www.cs.technion.ac.il/users/wwwb/cgi-bin/tr.../CS-2006-10.pdf

Jeong, I. (2006). Zone-based service architecture for wireless ad-hoc networks. In *Proceedings of the International Conference on Networking, International Conference on Systems and International Conference on Mobile Communications and Learning Technologies.* New York: ACM Portal.

Kozat, U., & Tassiulas, L. (2003). Network layer support for service discovery in mobile ad-hoc networks. In *INFOCOM 2003: Twenty-Second Annual Joint Conference of the IEEE Computer and Communications*. New York: IEEE.

Laitinen, H. (2001). Cellular network optimisation based on mobile location. *EC GI & GIS Portal* [Web site]. Retrieved 2009, from http://www.ec-gis.org/project.cfm?id=306&db=project

Spirito, M. A. (2001). On the accuracy of cellular mobile station location. *IEEE Transactions on Vehicular Technology*, *50*(3), 674–685. doi:10.1109/25.933304

Steiniger, S. (2006). Foundations of location based services. Zürich, Switzerland: Department of Geography, University of Zürich. Retrieved 2009, from http://www.geo.unizh.ch/~sstein/

Williams, D. H. (2005). *The definitive guide to mobile positioning and location management.* New York: Mind Commerce.

Woodacre, B. (2003). TDOA positioning algorithms: Evaluation and implementation. Worcester, MA: Worcester Polytechnic Institute. Retrieved 2009, from http://www.ece.wpi.edu/Research/PPL/Publications/

Zhang, H. (2003). Extensible platform for location-based services. In *2nd International Conference on Mobile Technology, Applications and Systems*. New York: IEEE.

KEY TERMS AND DEFINITIONS

Ad-Hoc Networks: Reconfigurable networks which topology changes constantly due to the mobility of the devices forming the network.

Angle of Arrival (AOA): Technique consists on estimating the direction of arrival of a wave by measuring the electric field intensity with directional antennas.

IP Location: Localization of the device by using the IP address assigned to it for connecting to the network and the access points managing such address.

Location Based Services: Collection of applications and special information offered to customers which is pertinent due to their position and time of the day.

Position Location: Localization of a device relative to a fixed reference or coordinates within a known area.

Time Difference of Arrival (TDOA): Measures the time difference between to base stations in order to calculate the distance traveled by the signal.

Time of Arrival (TOA): Technique consists on estimating the distance of a source by calculating the time it took for propagation using time synchronization of transmitter and receiver.

Chapter 13
Quality of Service in Wireless Ad Hoc Networks and New Trends

Sudhir K. Routray
Eritrea Institute of Technology, Eritrea

ABSTRACT

This chapter introduces basic needs of quality of service (QoS) of RF ad hoc networks (mainly wireless), presents the main metrics of quality of service and the QoS effects on overall performance, and briefly discusses quality of service of wireless systems with respect to the upcoming new technologies like 3GPP LTE and the role of WLAN, while representing network QoS improvement and optimization tools and their successful applications in performance analysis. The chapter focuses on IEEE 802.11e, the main revision of the 802.11 for better QoS provisioning, as well as the coordination between planning and the performance of systems for better QoS. Additionally, it addresses the current and new trends of QoS stuff for different cellular networks and their impact on the QoS of ad-hoc networks. The chapter also explores new trends of QoS of emerging networks like the WiMAX and 4G and looks to the probable hybrid networks of the future and their QoS aspects.

1. INTRODUCTION

Ad hoc networks are ubiquitous these days. Be it commercial communication related applications or security related monitoring or the location determination, in every area the importance of wireless ad hoc networks are increasing day by day. The commercial applications are the main field where the investors see the potential for big businesses. With the growth of the wireless ad hoc networks, the competition is also growing at high speed. In the competition arena every service provider wants to give better service than its own rivals. This makes a set of criteria according to which a service can be said better or not with respect to another service. Of course in engineering these performance related parameters and performances can be measured. These measurements of the different aspects of the services are collectively known as the quality of service.

DOI: 10.4018/978-1-60960-027-3.ch013

In the beginning of the wireless communication, there was no big requirement of quality of service. Because there were no competitions among the service providers or whatever were there almost negligible. But with the improvement of the technology, the requirements and demands of the customers changed. The personal communication systems became popular in the nineties due to the PDC, TDMA and GSM (European TDMA) systems. Then the CDMA and some other systems brought the real competition between the service providers. The so called 2G system started to provide some minimum possible qualities. For voice communication the minimum bandwidth which can give uninterrupted service was set to be 16 KBPS. But this was not enough. On the GSM systems the GPRS services were started. It was a collection of non-voice services like SMS on the GSM infrastructure. The bandwidth required was more for GPRS. Since then continuously efforts are made to provide better services. Of course the ad hoc networks of the WLANs were popular before the cellular networks. Since the invention of the internet in 1989 the popularities of WLAN networks are increasing very fast. Broadband services on the WLAN have become very popular for business organizations and universities.

Ad hoc networks are difficult to manage and control. There are many important issues which comes into picture while trying to manage them properly. These issues have been addressed in the following sections. In this section some of the properties of the ad hoc networks have been given. Some common types of ad hoc networks (Perkins, 2001) have been looked at.

Normally the common understanding says that ad hoc network means wireless LAN or the WLAN. WLANs are basically of two types according to the IEEE WLAN standards. They are IEEE 802.11a (Wireless HIPERLAN) and IEEE 802.11b (well known as HIPERLAN type 2). The most popular version of ad hoc network is the WiFi or the wireless fidelity. The standards behind WiFi are the IEEE 802.11a/g/n (Perkins, 2001; Ahmad, 2005). It can provide higher data rates and better quality of service than the cellular networks like 3G with moderate mobility and limited coverage area.

Now the meaning of ad hoc networks is something different due to their use in different fields. The ad hoc networks can also be divided in to WSN (Wireless Sensor Networks) and MANET (Mobile Ad hoc NETwork). In this broad sense the meaning of ad hoc network is very different. It includes almost all kinds of sensor and mobile networks having ad hoc infrastructure. In this chapter the quality of service of all these networks have been considered as the advanced methods of the UMTS, LTE and WiMAX helps in the improvement of the quality of service of ad hoc networks. The reason why we need to consider the UMTS, LTE and WiMAX like system is that many trends of these systems are borrowed for the ad hoc networks. It is also true that sometimes the mobile networks like UMTS work like the ad hoc networks and thus can be treated as semi-ad hoc networks. So in this chapter the ad hoc network does not mean IEEE 802.11 WLAN rather all other similar networks which show similar behavior like the ad hoc networks, whether it is cellular network or WiMAX like networks. Of course it is very common now to have hybrid networks having both the cellular as well as the ad hoc characteristics. Again the QoS support is important in both of them and thus the QoS schemes are becoming hybrid as well where it is needed.

2. WHY QUALITY OF SERVICE IS IMPORTANT?

The term quality of service means the physical parameters and settings which ensure the good quality of service. In this electronic age who does not want better quality of service in their systems. Starting from real-time communications to general services like e-mail or MMS everywhere good quality is demanded. The data contents are also increasing tremendously. Video streaming and news casting like things are readily available on the hand held mobile devices. At the same time there is no monopoly of any one vendor for any aspects of these services. Competition is fierce. Those win who can fulfill the demand of the customer. Then what is the biggest demand of the customers? Definitely the first demand is good quality of service and the second is the price for these services. Both these demands can be provided with a proper quality of service support framework. There are many issues related to the good quality of service. From the basics of communication it is clear that a system having better resources provides better service. But the communication systems of this era are very complex. There are many requirements for good quality of service (Shenker et. al., 1997).

Quality of service is important from many aspects. The customer wants the best service at the minimum price and the service provider wants the maximum return by having the biggest possible customer base. These things are all surrounded about the quality of service. By systematizing these two basic needs, the motivation for QoS can be summarized in two points as given below.

- The service provider wants to provide a set of service experiences to the costumers that meet their minimum expectations (often better than other service providers) so that they would like to retain the service and hopes that they would recommend it to others they know.
- The service provider also wants to get optimum results from the available resources while getting the maximum return as well as satisfying the customers for a long time.

Ad hoc networks are the networks built for some special purpose. Of course the ad hoc networks are very common these days and many organizations are having their own ad hoc networks for their day-to-day uses. There are of course many types of ad hoc networks. Some of them are ad hoc in nature but used for a long time. Some others are only for a small time. Some of them are vehicular or mobile in nature etc. So first of all let us see the ad hoc networks and their functions. Ad hoc networks are nothing but the self organizing sensor networks having mobile nodes and variable infrastructure. That means ad hoc networks are the organized networks having sensors and a proper arrangement for the function of those sensors which work for some specific functions.

In case of the ad hoc networks the provision of the quality of service is more important. Most of the ad hoc networks have variable topologies and thus the primary resources for communication keep on varying. The wireless channels are also very much unpredictable and there characteristics change very frequently. In this variable environment it is very difficult to provide the services having some minimum threshold levels. Ad hoc networks also deal with challenging scenarios. For example the broadcasting of a horse race or a festival at a remote place needs ad hoc network. In the horse race as the horses run and the sensors and cameras have to be relocated to cover the whole scene properly. This is handled through some vehicular ad hoc network which has a link with a mother network responsible for the broadcasting. There are many such challenging and difficult situations handled through the ad hoc networks.

2.1. QoS Metrics

We have seen in the above section that quality of service plays very important role in the overall performance of a system and determines the business potential of a service provider. Here the question is that can we measure and tell whether the quality of service is good or bad or of what level? The quality of service of any network at any point or node or at any point of a link can be measured.

There are now some well defined parameters and their measurement methods to check the quality of service. Broadly the important metrics which are measured for the estimation of the QoS in the end-to-end services are: bandwidth, delay and jitter. These three parameters are measured (either directly or indirectly) to check the quality of service. Bandwidth width is concerned with the data rate and the speed of service. Delay is the time delay for a packet between the source and destination. Bigger delay may not create big problem. The problem arises when there are non-uniform delays for different packets. Jitter is the variance of the time delay. Larger is the jitter; poorer would be the quality of service. In addition to these three main metrics the probability of packet loss and the packet contention also have main roles in the quality of service.

However the actual quality of service is determined through the overall performance. In fact the quality of service is considered from the weakest service level of the system. That means the overall performance is dependent on the biggest drawback (or the weakest point which degrades the quality to the largest extent) of the network through which the traffic pass through. So the service provider has to check what is the weakest link and how can that be brought to a better level. These issues will be clear in the coming sections.

3. DIFFERENT SIGNIFICANT RESOURCES OF WIRELESS AD HOC NETWORKS

Like all communications, there are some resources needed for the wireless communications. Normally there are two primary resources needed for the communication. They are transmitted power and bandwidth. Transmit power is the power associated with the signals which carry information from the source to the destination. Similarly bandwidth is the collection or bunch of frequencies used for the communication. Every user is associated with a certain band and there are two paths (up link and down link) and they use different frequencies. There is another important resource known as the infrastructure or the hardware facilities for the transmission and reception. In case of ad hoc networks it is known as the topology. The topology or the infrastructure of an ad hoc network is not a constant; rather is keeps on changing with the requirements of different source and destination nodes. That means the topology can be managed and controlled.

As far as the quality of services of ad hoc networks are concerned, these three resources play important roles for better quality provisioning. Transmit power is the power which determines the area of coverage. Large is the amount of transmit power large is the area of coverage. Bandwidth takes care of the data rate or the speed at which the information can reach the destination. There are different kinds of services and some of the services are real time like the speech conversation and video conferencing etc. For these services the minimum threshold bandwidth should be available all the time. The provisioning of the bandwidth is thus very important for the real time services. Topology or the infrastructure also plays very important roles in the quality of services. These three resources are also inter-related. Large is the bandwidth means higher is the transmit power and vice versa. Large topology means normally larger coverage or larger customer base. Larger is the topology; larger power is required for the proper coverage. The number of hops in a network determines the delay of a communication. Larger is the topology, larger is the number of hops needed to reach the destination. Of course this is completely dependent on the location of the source and destination nodes. In an ad hoc network the control of the topology is very important and depending on the positions of the source and destination the topology can be controlled through some proper mechanism.

4. QUALITY OF SERVICE IN WIRELESS COMMUNICATION NETWORKS

Wireless networks are ubiquitous these days. Be it mobile communication network or satellite based communication network; it is found in almost all over the world. The pervasive communication and computing are found in the real applications around the world due to the wireless networks. It is clear from this spread that how important is the role of the wireless communication networks for our day to day life processes. There are also a large number of service providers vying for their business shares. From this neck to neck competition it is clear what the customers want and what the service providers are going to do.

Quality is definitely the foremost things when there is a tough competition. Customers want best possible services at the least possible cost. Customer satisfaction is the main aim of the investor to get their business going. Quality can be measured from different aspects. As we have seen in the previous sections the service quality in case of wireless communication can be judged from three main aspects. They are: the bandwidth or the data rate, the delay between the node to node transmission, and finally the jitter. Of course the other parameters which can play the role in quality of service provisioning are the buffer arrangement, probability of packet loss, flow control mechanisms etc.

Wireless networks are of various types. We can separate them on many bases. They can be permanent or temporary, fixed or ad hoc, multi-hop or single hop etc. Depending on the type the QoS provisioning are different. In case of the ad hoc networks we find much such diversity. Most of the ad hoc networks are temporary, many of them are having multi-hops, need proper routing to connect the source with the destination. That makes the ad hoc networks quite different in the family of wireless communication networks. The QoS aspects are also very much different and challenging in case of ad hoc networks (Borbash & Jennings, 2002).

Overall performance of any wireless network whether it is fixed or ad hoc, depends on a set of factors. Some of those factors have been presented below:

Radio Network Performance: The overall performance is totally dependent on the performance of the radio network. If there are there a lot of errors and mismatches on the radio interfaces then definitely the overall performance would degrade significantly.

Network Capacity or Channel Bandwidth: Network capacity is the ability of the network to handle a certain amount of data for their transfer. Of course the total capacity is divided into the individual channels for the transmission from node to node. So there should be sufficient capacity of the network to deliver a good service. In other words each channel should have minimum amount of bandwidth to handle the tasks of data communication.

Network Design: The network is designed as per the traffic statistics and load demand. The design engineers should make sure that the delay in the WLAN must not be above a certain tolerable level. If there is too much delay in the system for some specific paths; then those paths would provide bad quality of service.

Network Architecture and Protocol Design: The design of different layers of the network is very important for proper coordination between interfaces. The protocols and their operations and signaling should be properly designed. For mobile environment the accuracy of the designs matter a lot.

Service Support: Service supports are provided through many specific designs and protocols. But the service enhancement technologies must be correctly configured to harness the results. Improper deployment does not provide good quality of service.

Here in this chapter the main orientation for better service is mainly on the last one. The service support or the QoS plays the main role if the network resources are constant. So when the network operates at its optimum load or above the optimum load then QoS support is the only solution for providing better qualities.

5. QoS OF TRADITIONAL WIRELESS AD HOC NETWORKS

Ad hoc networks have a different standing in the wireless communication family. The QoS related issues are different from the other fixed and cellular networks. Due to the ad hoc nature there are many challenges in the processes concerned with the QoS provisioning. In this section the existing issues of the legacy ad hoc networks have been addressed.

5.1. Challenges of QoS Provisioning in Ad Hoc Networks

There are many challenges in the QoS provisioning[10] in the ad hoc networks. Starting from the channel assignment and bandwidth allotment to combating the multipath degradation and topology management there are so many difficult tasks. They have been represented briefly here.

The Channel: In most of the cases the ad hoc networks are wireless or at least partially wireless. The wireless channel has many random characteristics. It keeps on changing very frequently and thus there cannot be any one specific model for them. The multipath fading is a common problem for the wireless channels. There should be some arrangement to combat the multipath fading for good quality of service.

The Interferences: The amount of interferences is more in wireless networks than the wired networks. The noise distribution statistics and noise pattern do not follow a single distribution. The randomness increases in the urban areas due to the geography and industrial contribution to the noise.

Variable Topology: The topology or the nodes and links of an ad hoc network are not fixed. Depending on the demand and situation the topology keeps on changing. Changing topology poses different challenges which cannot be handled with the normal networking tools. Variable topology means variable traffic, changing throughput, changing links or paths for the packets, difficult routing and channel assignment.

Packet Contention: In wireless digital communication systems the data is sent in the form of packets. The node and other resources are shared in ad hoc networks. So there are contentions between packets of the same stream at different nodes. Due to this, the QoS metrics of a connection is affected to a large extent. The main reason behind contention is the sharing of wireless channel by different nodes in the vicinity. For proper QoS provisioning, packet contention has to be kept under control.

5.2. Support for QoS in Traditional IEEE 802.11 Ad Hoc Networks

The legacy IEEE 802.11 system has some support for QoS. But it is mainly for the wired LAN. In case of the wireless LANs there are many changes in the Physical layer and few changes in other layers. The CSMA/CA based physical layer and MAC layer is the technology available for QoS in IEEE 802.11. CSMA/CA is effective in collision avoidance, which reduces the probability of packet loss. The available bandwidth can also be used effectively through the CSMA framework. However the delay, scalability and jitter etc. cannot be controlled through the CSMA mechanism. So the CSMA/CA is not effective in improving the end-to-end QoS. WLAN technologies aim to provide connectivity and wireless access at a high bandwidth and data rate to IP-based networks in a similar way or better than the wired connections. In order to provide better QoS and higher data rates the standards of IEEE 802.11 have been upgraded to different versions given below. In the new versions the bandwidth and data rates have increased significantly. Similarly the end-to-end QoS provisioning has been evolved and better methods have been adopted which are much effective than the CSMA/CA.

WLAN Standard Versions: There are many amendments of the original WLAN standards which were first published in 1997 as the IEEE 802.11. Due to the high demand of the WLAN standards in all its application domains, there are needs of the optimization and improved performances. Gradually new improvement aspects are getting added to this wonderful technology. Altogether there are more than 30 amendments of this technology. Of course some of the amendments have been withdrawn. Here the main accepted versions have been mentioned briefly.

IEEE 802.11: This is the standard for WLAN operations at data rates up to 2Mbps in the 2.4GHz ISM (Industrial, Scientific and Medical) band. This the traditional LAN standard.

IEEE 802.11a: This is the standard for WLAN operations at data rates up to 54Mbps in the 5GHz Unlicensed National Information Infrastructure (UNII) band.

IEEE 802.11b: This is the standard for WLAN operations at data rates up to 11 Mbps in the 2.4GHz ISM band.

IEEE 802.11g: High-rate extension to 802.11b allowing for data rates up to 54Mbps in the 2.4 GHz ISM band. This is used mainly for WiFi.

IEEE 802.11e: This is the amended version of the WLAN standards for effective QoS provisioning. This is implemented in all new WLANs.

IEEE 802.11n: This is the extension in physical layer and MAC layer characteristics for the WiFi. This standard has plans for higher bandwidth and data rates. OFDM based physical layer is one of the highlights of this version. It has better QoS support.

It is difficult for the ad-hoc networks, to provide any definite hard QoS guarantees because of the changes and fluctuations in the wireless channel and interference from non-neighboring nodes. It is therefore easier to design solutions where QoS support from the network is in the form of soft-assurances rather than hard guarantees. For the same reasons, relative assurances are more common than absolute assurances. Most of this chapter refers to soft-assurances for QoS metrics, unless stated otherwise.

5.3. Distributed Coordination Function

The distributed coordination function or the DCF is a mechanism for QoS provisioning. The quality of service is provided through the DCF protocol. In fact DCF protocol attempts to provide equal access (in terms of number of packets) to all packets at all nodes that share a channel. This scheme has both advantages and disadvantages. It is some kind of first come first served like process. The main aim is to reduce the average delivery time for each packet. But this equal treatment degrades the quality for the real-time and other low delay tolerant services.

The actual network performance through the DCF can be estimated by the queuing theory. During the low load conditions when the network is working below its optimum capacity there is not much problem in the QoS provisioning. However if the load goes beyond the capacity, the DCF does not give good QoS. In any ad-hoc network the throughput that a node obtains using DCF is a function of the number of neighbors that it has (the number connected neighbors) and the state of their queues and the buffer arrangements. The throughputs of the neighbors also depend on their neighbors. So, overall throughput determination becomes a global problem for the network instead of being a local one. From this it is clear that the DCF cannot handle the difficult situations properly.

5.3.1. Point Coordination Function

IEEE 802.11 has another alternative for DCF which can handle some of the performance and QoS related aspects in a better way. Point coordination function or the PCF is normally used in fixed infrastructure networks. It takes care of some of the difficulties of the DCF. In the infrastructure mode in which PCF works properly, the stations are connected to the network through some access points (APs). Access points send some regulating pulses known as beacon frames for the better QoS provisioning. Between the beacon frames, PCF defines two periods known as, the Contention Free Period (CFP) and the Contention Period (CP). In case of CP, the DCF is used, because it can handle the QoS issues of the packets. But for CFP, the AP sends Contention Free-Poll (CF-Poll) packets to each station, one at a time, to give them the right to send a packet. The AP works as the coordinator. This allows the PCF for better management of the overall QoS. PCF is used in the Wi-Fi networks and the access points (APs) are known as Wi-Fi adapters in the Wi-Fi networks. So the PCF has some arrangements for the reduction of the inter-frame delay time. The contention periods are also handled in efficient ways.

Some researchers have proposed a dual queue mechanism to provide better quality of service in adhoc networks. That means in the MAC layer there will be two queues. One queue is for the real-time traffic and the other for the non-real-time traffic. So it is some kind of prioritized mechanism. In some other WLANs the DCF and PCF mechanisms are provide as alternatives of each other. But still it is not enough for the optimum load conditions. The new standards for the QoS enhancement have been presented in the coming sections.

Application wise also the quality of service of wireless ad hoc networks can be divided in to some important categories. Of course the applications themselves are functions of the different quality of service constraints. Some of the important classifications have been presented below.

5.4. QoS for Real-Time Applications

There are many real-time applications on the ad hoc networks. The communication networks were invented for the real time communications. That need is still there today and it will remain forever. The most commonly used real-time communications are voice conversations. Now there are many new additions to that. They are real time chatting, voice streaming (online songs, news etc.), video streaming, real time broadcasting and multicasting etc. All these applications need real-time bandwidth. There should be minimum delay, well within a certain threshold.

For proper quality of service in the real-time applications the bandwidth has to be wide enough for proper transmission of packets. There should be no bottlenecks anywhere. The delay should be the minimum or at least below the threshold level.

5.5. QoS for Multicasting

Multicasting is an effective method of data transmission to a group of users from a single source in ad hoc networks. It saves a lot of resources and delivers huge amount of data to a large number of users in a short time. These days the data rates in both the wired and wireless networks have increased dramatically. It helps in the delivery of data with rich contents. The availability of the advanced versions of the internet protocol (IPv6) and the streaming technologies it is possible to deliver TV programs and live music on the mobile and other handheld devices. Multicasting has now all the technical support from the servers and networks. The protocols for the multicasting process are evolving with the increase in the speed of data rates. Similarly the advantages from the economics points of view are also very encouraging. The amount of power and bandwidth required for multicasting is much lower than the cumulative transfer of data in a one-to-one mode or unicasting.

Having this huge demand of multicasting, the quality of service aspects of multicasting becomes very important in the ad hoc networks. The issues of quality of service of wireless ad hoc networks for the multicasting processes are largely dependent on the support for streaming of packets. If the bandwidth is good then the streaming is good and vice versa. Similarly the channel interferences and multipath like situations can play the role in reducing the qualities. It can be improved by proper arrangements in the physical layer.

5.6. QoS of Non-Real Time and Background Traffic

This is the traffic class which does not need the immediate QoS during the transmission of packets. Rather the delay is admissible but not the loss of packets. Of course there are mechanisms for the retransmission of the lost packets for this class. On the internet most of the services provided are of this class except for the VoIP and the video streaming like things.

6. QUALITY OF SERVICE ASPECTS IN UMTS AND LTE WHICH AFFECT THE QoS OF WLAN

The cellular networks are used for ubiquitous communication. But the high data rates and the service management of the cellular networks are not robust like the WLANs. Again the true ubiquitous communication is impossible without the presence of ad hoc networks. In addition to this there are some special attractions of WLANs which incorporates them as an integral part of the cellular networks. These days the integrated versions of the WLAN and the cellular networks are very popular. In order to provide better QoS, the WLAN QoS provisioning has been enhanced significantly by the standardization organizations. IETF and other standard making organizations have supported the UMTS and LTE like QoS mechanisms (3rd Generation Partnership Project, 2004; Wroclawski, 1997) in the WLAN. The traffic classification and priorities for different types of traffic are in place for WLAN. All these issues have been presented in the following sections.

Now both the 3GPP LTE and the 3GPP2 LTE have included WLAN as the integral part of their future networks. Of course the detailed description of the architecture of the 3GPP-WLAN and the 3GPP2-WLAN is not possible here. But some of the features have been included in the following sections. These are definitely the new trends of the integrated networks which have multiple features but similar QoS mechanisms.

7. IMPROVEMENT OF QoS OF AD HOC NETWORKS: IEEE 802.11E

The popularity of the ad hoc networks is due to the higher speed than the other comparable wireless services like the different cellular networks. However the wired broadband services are still better than the wireless ad hoc networks in terms of the quality of services, security and connectivity etc. Thus there is a basic need of improvement of the quality of service of the traditional WLANs. All the standardization bodies as well as the business groups realize these needs.

The QoS support starts from the very beginning of the data transfer just when the information leaves the source as shown in Figure 1. Then it is provided till the very end until the data reaches the destination. If it is a single hop system then there is only one link the information has to cover. But if it is a multi-hop network the information has to travel through several links and routers to reach the destination. Depending on the number of links the routing network is designed.

Thus the proper QoS mechanism takes care of the data from the source to the destination. The intermediate links, routers and other components

Figure 1.

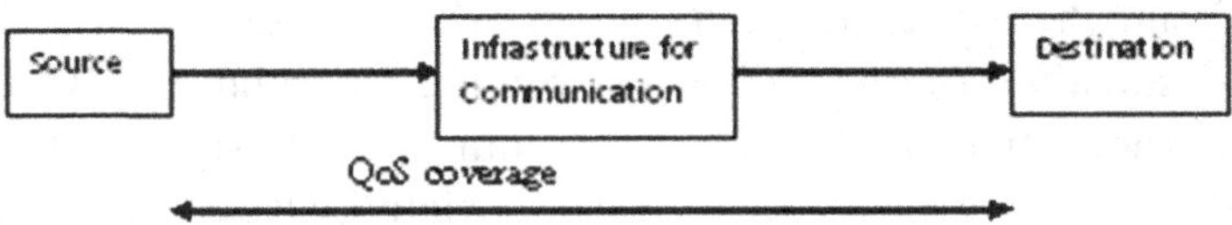

Figure 2.

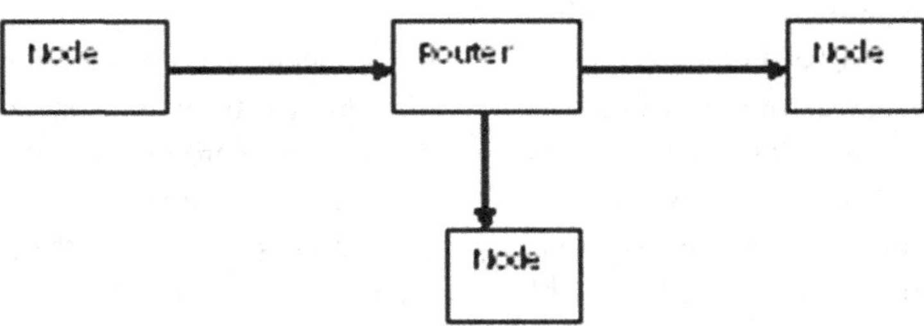

are also kept well equipped to handle the QoS of each and every packet (Gu & Zhang, 2003).

7.1. QoS Routing

For better quality of service the role of routing is very important. Routing layer determines the path of different datagram. The overall path determination and the efficiency of routing are finalized through different processes. Outing is the process, which deals with the path of the packets. The packets having same source and destination can have different paths, which packet will follow which path is determined by the routing schemes. There are many routing schemes and they work according to some algorithm. The main aim of the algorithm is to optimize some of the characteristics. In case of the shortest path routing, the selected path is the shortest one among many possible options. This is how the delay can also be minimized through a minimum delay path. But it is not true always. For a busy network the shortest path is not necessarily the best path in terms of the time delay. So for the best QoS there are some logics according to which some of the main parameters are compromised. Such routing schemes which provide best possible QoS between the source and destination are known as the QoS routing.

The Routing layer is above the MAC layer. Whatever path related decisions are made in the routing layer; it is transferred to the MAC layer for the execution. The routers are provided at some nodes. Of course in practical WLAN all the nodes are not routers. Rather routing related data may be provided to all the nodes; but only the routers decide path for different packets. The main challenges of the multi-hop networks, as described before are the changing dynamics (variable topology, multipath fade, unexpected interferences etc.). It has been shown below (Figure 3) that the nodes 1, 2, 3 are fixed nodes (solid circles) and the nodes 1' and 2' are ad hoc nodes. So in the

Figure 3. Variable and fixed nodes of WLAN

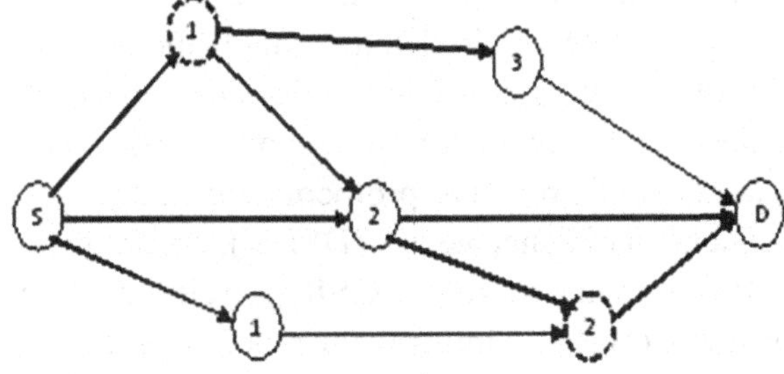

presence of the ad hoc nodes there are more options for the source to route the packets through different paths to the destination. But when the ad hoc nodes are absent (not active or alive) the number of options reduce.

The QoS routing can be of different types. Some of them have been presented in the routing layer description in the layer wise role for QoS. They are: distributed routing, multipath routing, token based routing etc. In distributed routing the routing information and infrastructure are distributed. It is found in the newly designed WLANs. Similarly multipath routing has its own advantages. Token based routing is optimal for small number of nodes. But the optimality reduces with the enlargement of the network.

7.1.1. Routing Protocols

The routing information, strategies and processes are generated, transferred and executed through the routing protocols (Ergen et. al., 2003). The ad hoc network routing protocols can be divided in to two categories, as proactive and reactive. The proactive protocols are the protocols which gather the network information and keep the routing data updated. The routing tables are updated though these protocols and thus these protocols are known as table driven routing protocols. Table driven routing protocols attempt to maintain consistent, up-to-date routing information from each node to every other node in the network. These protocols require each node to maintain one or more tables to store routing information, and they respond to changes in network topology by propagating updates throughout the network for maintaining a consistent network statistics. The roles reactive protocols are initiated through the source. These protocols come into existence if there is a demand for them for some source tasks. The examples of proactive protocols are destination sequenced distance vector (DSDV), cluster head gateway switch routing (CGSR), wireless routing protocol (WRP). Similarly the reactive protocols are ad hoc on-demand distance vector (AODV), dynamic source routing (DSR), temporally ordered routing algorithm (TORA), lightweight mobile routing (LMR), signal stability routing (SSR) and associativity based routing (ABR) etc.

7.2. Classification of Traffic (Packets) for QoS

It has been found from the previous sections that the classification or prioritizing the traffic for the QoS purpose provides a better result. According to this scheme some types of the traffic get priority over others. Of course, the priority levels can be made fixed or variable according to the engineers who monitor the QoS aspects. The classification scheme started in the internet and then the cellular networks adopted it. It is also promising for the ad hoc networks. The well known mechanism based on the classified traffic is the DiffServ (Aad & Castelluccia, 2001).

7.3. Energy Efficient QoS Routing

In case of QoS routing there are instances where the energy spent is bit high. High energy consumption in case of busy networks generates a big energy bill. In order to control this there are some energy efficient methods.

Energy in communication networks are spent in two major ways. One is the transmission of information and the second is the switching. There are almost all operation steps and the roles of protocols are activated or realized through the switching. Start or termination of some communication is executed through switching. The switching are controlled through the sensors. Good energy sensitive sensors can make the routing energy efficient.

Energy efficiency can be increased through topology control. Using a controlled topology the path length along the different links can be reduced. The throughput to certain parts of the network can be increased significantly. The channel capacity and the routing efficiency (in terms of time delay) can be increased as well. The price for topology control is paid in terms of the complex protocols. Of course with proper topology planning the complexities can be reduced to a large extent. In case of multicasting and broadcasting also the controlled topology saves a lot of energy. The topology control can be done through some intermediate layer between the routing layer and MAC layer. It has been depicted below in the block diagram. More on this can be found in (Ergen et. al.,2003; 3rd Generation Partnership Project, 2004).

7.4. New Initiatives for the Enhancement of QoS of Ad Hoc Networks

Looking at the increasing demand of the WLAN standards and the IEEE 802.11 based ad hoc networks, IEEE, IETF and the other business groups are planning to enhance the support for QoS in these networks. As a result a new standard for the WLAN has been proposed. It is IEEE 802.11e which has many provisions to enhance the quality of service of ad hoc networks. IEEE 802.11e was first approved in March 2000. Its main aim was to enhance the security, to improve the efficiency and to provide the support for QoS. However the security enhancement related provisions went out

Figure 4.

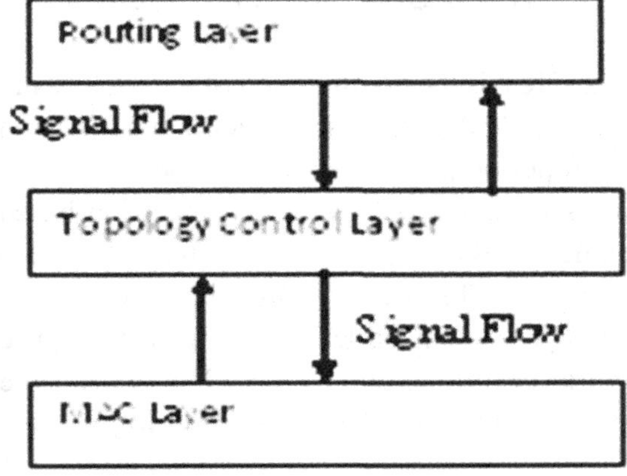

of order and thus it was taken out of the IEEE 802.11e standard and for the security provisioning a new version was proposed(i.e., IEEE 802.11i). After many rounds of discussion at the experts' level the final version of IEEE 802.11e was approved in 2005 and its main function was to provide QoS support to the adhoc networks. Since that time IEEE 802.11e is regarded as the QoS component of the WLAN standards.

7.5. IEEE 802.11e

Looking at the increasing demand of the quality of services of the ad hoc networks some advanced provisions have been made for the new standard IEEE 802.11e (Garg et.al., 2003). This standard borrows some advanced ideas from other IEEE standards for cellular networks and WMAN. It has a mechanism for service differentiation on the basis of priorities for different kind of traffics. Some of the packets get priority for processing over others depending on their status. The differentiation is done through some algorithms. In addition to the priority some other parameters like the inter-frame space, contention window dimension etc are processed. The distributed coordination function (DCF) of the IEEE 802.11 is modified to an extended version known as the enhanced distributed coordination function or EDCF.

The new MAC layer protocol of IEEE 802.11e (Gu & Zhang, 2003) is known as the hybrid coordination function or HCF. This HCF contains a contention-based channel access mechanism, commonly known as enhanced distributed channel access or EDCF, which is an enhanced version of the legacy DCF, for a prioritized QoS support. In the new mechanism through the EDCA, a single MAC contains multiple queues with different priorities that access different channels independently in parallel. Frames in each queue are transmitted using different channel access parameters and different flow controls. Here the different advanced features of IEEE 802.11e have been discussed.

7.5.1. Enhanced Distributed Channel Access

The hybrid coordination function or the HCF provides the distributed channel access through the EDCA. The IEEE 802.11 legacy MAC does not support the mechanism of differentiating packets with different priorities. Basically, the DCF is supposed to provide a channel access with equal probabilities to all stations contending for the channel access in a distributed manner. However, equal access probabilities are not desirable among stations with different priority packets. The QoS-aware MAC should be able to treat frames with different priority or QoS requirements differently. The EDCA is designed to provide differentiated and distributed channel accesses for packets with eight different priorities (from 0 to 7) by enhancing the DCF. There are different access categories depending on the priorities. Of course the priorities and the access categories have been done as per the traffic nature. So from the higher layer itself the packets come to the MAC with some priorities and MAC assigns them the access category.

In EDCA, high priority traffic has a higher chance of being sent than low priority traffic or in other words the traffic with high priority is sent before the low priority traffic (Fernandez, & Montes, 2002). Similarly, a station with high priority traffic waits less than the station having low priority traffic. But the main feature in EDCA is that, each priority level is assigned a Transmit Opportunity or TXOP. Actually, TXOP is a bounded time interval during which a station can send as many frames as possible (as long as the duration of the transmissions does not extend beyond the maximum duration of the TXOP). Sometimes the frames are too large to be transmitted in a single TXOP; in that case, they are fragmented into smaller frames and sent sequentially. Through the TXOPs the problem of low rate stations gaining an inordinate amount of channel time in the legacy IEEE 802.11 DCF MAC are reduced significantly. It is an appreciable enhancement in the QoS provisioning.

EDCA also provides contention based admission control. Admission control is a good scheme for regulating the amount of data contending for the medium, that is, the amount of data input into the base station in order to protect the existing traffic streams (TSs). Without good admission control mechanism and proper protection mechanism, the incoming and outgoing real-time traffic cannot be protected and QoS fed away from the target. Contention-based admission control schemes also heal the problem for the EDCA. The EDCA tends to experience severe performance degradation when a network is overloaded because of its contention based channel access nature. In this condition, the contention window becomes large, and more and more time is spent in back-off and collision resolution rather than sending data. This may create some degradation in the QoS. This difficulty is easily over come through the contention based admission control. EDCA has been made much adaptable than the DCF. The purpose of EDCA is to protect high priority data from low priority data. But there are cases in which the data needs to be protected from the data of same priority. The Admission Control in EDCA addresses this kind of issues. The AP publishes the available bandwidth in beacons. The clients can check the available bandwidth before adding more traffic in the network that cannot be entertained.

7.5.2. Hybrid Coordination Function

In fact HCF is the combination of the HCCA and EDCA. EDCA period is a contention period and HCCA period is a contention free period. As we have seen above EDCA is a contention-based channel access. But HCCA is a controlled channel access which has been discussed below.

EDCF (Enhanced DCF) is effective because it works according to the HCF. HCF extends the EDCF access rules in many different ways. Actu-

Figure 5. Hybrid coordination function

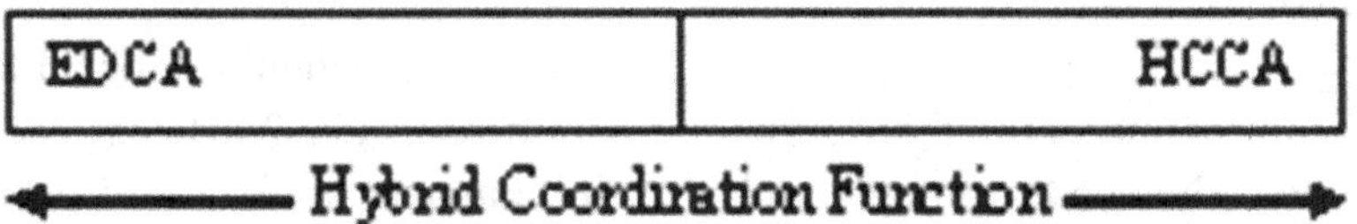

ally, HCF is the combination of DCF and PCF along with some extensions. The function of HCF is similar to that of PCF; but it uses more steps for proper coordination through the hybrid coordinators. The HC (Hybrid Coordinator) may allocate TXOPs to itself to initiate MSDU (MAC Service Data Unit) deliveries whenever it wants. But the condition is that it has to detect the channel as being idle for PIFS (PCF Inter-Frame Space), which is normally shorter than DIFS (DCF Inter-Frame Space). In order to give priority to HC over the EDCF, AIFS (Arbitration Inter-Frame Space) must be longer than PIFS. Otherwise the priority cannot be provided to the HC.

In HCF, TXOP limit specifies the maximum duration station can transmit and is specified per the access categories. There are also provisions that TXOP limit can be used to ensure that high bandwidth traffic gets greater and longer access to the medium. TXOP limit also makes the channel access protocol significantly more efficient which is not there in either PCF or DCF.

Similarly the AIFS or Arbitration Inter-Frame Space used in HCF specifies the time interval between the wireless medium becoming idle and the start of channel-access negotiation. Each access category is assigned a different AIFS, based on the priority of the traffic classes.

7.5.3. HCCA [HCF (Hybrid Coordination Function) Controlled Channel Access]

The HCCA (HCF Controlled Channel Access) works similar to the Point Coordination Function. But there are some differences and extensions of PCF in HCCA. HCCA allows the CFPs which are initiated at almost any time during a CP. This CFP is known as Controlled Access Phase (CAP) in 802.11e. CAP is initiated by the AP, whenever it wants to send a frame to a station, or receive a frame from a station, in a contention free manner. Actually, the CFP is also a CAP. All stations work in the EDCA mode during the contention period. The access of the medium is controlled by the hybrid coordinator (of course it is the AP). HCCA works as per a priority according to the classification of the traffic. In other words, the HC is not limited to certain station traffic queuing rather it can handle the traffic of multiple stations as per the traffic priority. The HC can coordinate the traffic streams or traffic sessions in any fashion according the algorithm set in HCCA. In most of the cases, stations give information about the lengths of their queues for each Traffic Class, which is executed in the HC. This information reduces the processing time in the HC. In HCCA, different stations are assigned TXOPs for the sequence of packet transfer. However during the CP, the HC allows stations to send data by sending CF-Poll frames. Through these extensions the packet priority is maintained properly and thus the QoS is maintained for the sensitive traffic classes.

HCCA is generally considered the most advanced (and complex) coordination function. With the HCCA, QoS can be configured with great precision. QoS-enabled stations have the ability to request specific transmission parameters (data rate, jitter, etc.) which should allow advanced applications like VoIP and video streaming to work more effectively on a Wi-Fi network.

7.5.4. Other Important Specifications of IEEE 802.11e

Not only the above features enrich IEEE 802.11e; it has also many other advanced protocols and specifications which make it a better standard. DLS (Direct Link Set up), APSD (Automatic Power Save Delivery), BA (Block Acknowledgement) and NoACK (No Acknowledgement) etc are some advanced specifications of IEEE 802.11e. DLS or Direct Link Setup allows direct station-to-station frame transfer within a well-defined service set. This facilitates better QoS for station-to-station transfer, which is commonly used by some consumers. APSD or Automatic Power Save Delivery is a more efficient power management method than legacy IEEE 802.11 Power Save Polling. APSD plays important roles in real-time and VoIP services, in which data rates are roughly same in both directions. NoACK is used to avoid retransmission of highly time-critical data. So the congestion can be avoided in the routers and bottlenecks. Similarly, BA or Block Acknowledgments allow an entire TXOP to be acknowledged in a single frame. This normally provides less protocol overhead when longer TXOPs are specified.

7.5.5. Amendments of IEEE 802.11e

IEEE 802.11e is not the final standard for the QoS provisioning of the adhoc networks. The amendments are accommodated to improve the overall QoS of networks. Through the advanced mechanisms of EDCF, EDCA, HCF, HCCA and other supporting provisions, IEEE 802.11e is able to provide much better QoS than the legacy IEEE 802.11. To a some extent, the QoS of WLAN can be guaranteed through IEEE 802.11e. But it is still far behind the QoS of the contemporary standards like the WiMAX. IEEE 802.11e TGe and some other such amendments are in place for even better QoS.

7.6. Differentiated Services

DiffServ mechanism for ad hoc networks (Aad & Castelluccia, 2001) has been adopted from the cellular networks. The differentiations in services are done as per some kind of packet classification. The different classes have different priorities and according to those priorities they are processed at different nodes, which is very similar in case of the 3G cellular network. This is the new approval of IETF for a better quality of service for the real-time data. Like 3G here also the real time traffic gets the priority over the non-real time traffic. Differentiated services are provided through DiffServ routing mechanism. It has been shown in the following diagram. The traffic classifier separates the incoming data stream into different categories. The traffic marker provides DSCP to each IP packets according to their classes. Traffic meter monitors the traffic flow and other aspects of the flow. Traffic shaper at the end of the DiffServ checks the QoS requirements and QoS levels.

Packet Classifier: The incoming data stream are classified into different categories in this section. It has the arrangement of identifying and classifying the different incoming flows to the ad hoc network.

Traffic Marker: This section is in charge of providing DSCP to all incoming IP packets according to their assigned classes. The following sections of traffic marker treat the packets according to their DSCP.

Traffic Meter: It measures the different delay and flow related characteristics. Actually it takes the charge of monitoring traffic flow of different nodes.

Traffic Shaper: This block assigns the access category for the prioritized data. So traffic shaper is in charge of creation of different classes ready for the processing at the next stage.

The input data is normal; but the output data is prioritized having different status for processing.

Figure 6. DiffServ routing mechanism

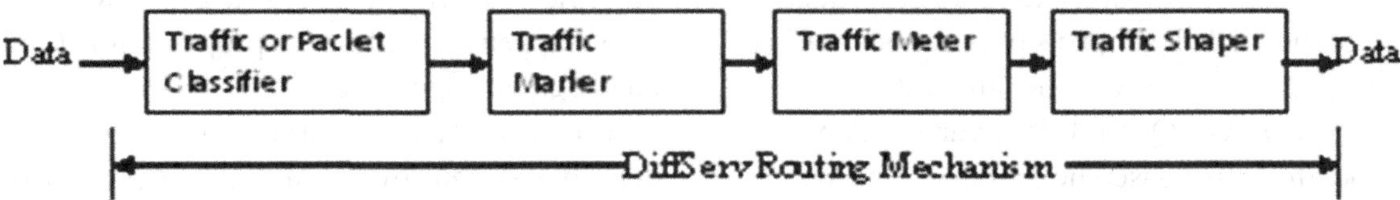

7.6.1. Traffic Classes

The classification of traffic for the DiffServ of ad hoc network is same as that of the UMTS. Different traffic classes in ad hoc network DiffServ are as follows:

Conversational: This class is the real-time communication between the source and destination. The examples are voice conversation, VoIP, video conferencing etc.

Streaming: It is also a real-time application. However the amount of data is more and thus streaming technologies are used for the transmission. The examples are inline music and video. Delay only plays a role when interacting with the server, e.g. for starting or stopping the service. However, services in this class need a guaranteed bit rate.

Interactive (Higher Priority): Interactive web browsing or instant updating applications like the running commentary or stock updates etc. These are interactive services; however their real-time requirements are not like the conversation or streaming classes.

Interactive (Lower Priority): Web browsing or gaming like applications come in this category. These are interactive services; however their real-time requirements are usually limited. They do not need a guaranteed bit rate.

Background: This traffic does not need any QoS guarantee. The examples of this class are email and file download.

The effect of DiffServ on the QoS is positive. The overall qualities of different services get better. The compromise between different services for quality improvement is impressive. But some of its secondary effects are negative. The net throughput reduces when the system operates at its optimum or beyond the optimum level. Some of the important services get delayed due to the prioritization. For example at some instant, if the real-time traffic gets huge, the important non-real time services get delayed by a large extent, which may not happen without the prioritization. But from the experiments and real observations it has been found that the end-to-end customer experiences get better through DiffServ.

8. QoS AT DIFFERENT LAYERS OF AD HOC NETWORKS

In fact the support for the QoS of any system is not concentrated in one layer. Rather there are different arrangements in different layers to ensure the proper overall quality of service. In this section these QoS related arrangements at different layers of ad hoc networks have been presented.

The IEEE 802.11 standard defines the medium access control (MAC) layer and the physical (PHY) layer specifications for LAN. Of course in case of the WLAN these things are little bit different. The physical layer is wireless, and this makes the difference in IEEE 802.11a and IEEE 802.11b. The mandatory part of the IEEE 802.11 MAC is known as the distributed coordination function or DCF, which has been described in the previous section. This DCF is based on carrier sense multiple access with collision avoidance (CSMA/CA). In the present applications most of the 802.11 devices implement only the DCF. Because of the contention-based channel access nature of the DCF, it supports only the best-effort service. However there is no guarantee of any quality of service (QoS). In the current applications like the all-IP based networks, the needs for real-time services such as Voice over IP (VoIP) and audio/video streaming over the WLANs have been increasing very fast (Yu, Choi, & Lee, 2004). But the legacy systems based on the IEEE 802.11 devices are not capable of supporting the real-time services properly and the quality degrades significantly. It is mainly due to the delay in the channel and the loss of packets. Of course IEEE 802.11e can handle these issues adroitly.

8.1. QoS Related Issues of Physical Layer

The physical layer plays vital role in the quality of service provisioning. The signal starts from the source and after the basic processing in the upper layers; it is pushed into the physical layer. Till the destination the most critical things are associated with the physical layer. Of course in the physical layer the routing is provided (Mangold, 2001; Hwang & Varshney, 2003). But that is not included in QoS issues of the physical layer.

The wireless channel is not a static channel rather its dynamics is time varying. Due to the time varying nature there are provisions of multiple data rate in the IEEE 802.11a and IEEE 802.11b standards. Depending on the channel characteristics the data rates are changed form high to low or low to high. The IEEE 802.11a standard operates in the 5.7 GHz band and supports data rates of 6, 9, 12, 18, 24, 36, 48 and 54 Mbps in the physical layer. The peak rates are available in the WiFi (IEEE 802.11 a/g/n) systems having some limitations (like low speed mobility and small coverage area). Similarly, the 802.11b standard operates in the 2.4 GHz band which supports 1, 2, 5.5 and 11 Mbps. But there is no provision in the standards to specify or to provide any mechanisms to discover the highest possible rate on a link. The changes in the data rates happen through some proper algorithm in a feedback arrangement.

For efficient use of a multi-rate physical layer, there have been several algorithms proposed for the physical layer. Some of these algorithms are closely tied to the MAC layer as well. They impact the observed throughput on a link and the end-to-end throughput of a multi-hop connection. The QoS requirements of upper layers may affect the design of this algorithm. However, most of the proposals are based only on improving the link utilization, although they may be modified to implement QoS requirements of higher layers. Some of the examples of these algorithms are the auto-rate fall back and opportunistic auto rate algorithm etc.

By reducing the data rate in the adverse conditions, the probability of packet loss is reduced. Similarly the bottleneck conditions due to the low bandwidth are also overcome and the delay is also reduced. This data rate reduction mechanism is provided through some feed back arrangements like the ARQ (Automatic Repeat reQuest). There are some effective algorithms for the enhancement of the quality of services through the step-wise reduction of data rates.

The multipath fading handling is a big challenge in IEEE 802.11 WLAN system. Now there are some good tools. The varying nature of the channel and the multipath fading can be handled properly through some multi carrier modulation schemes. OFDM or the orthogonal frequency division multiplexing is one such scheme. Using OFDM and MIMO (Gesbert, 2003) the qualities of services can also be enhanced significantly. Here some of the main features of OFDM have been presented.

8.1.1. OFDM Based Physical Layer

Provision of high speed wireless broadband services is the main aim of WLAN technologies today. Again places like airport lounge, Coffee Café, Railway stations, conference arenas etc are required to have high speed internet services, where the WLAN plays an important role. But there are many difficulties in providing high speed wireless internet services in these environments. Multipath fading and the inter-symbol interferences degrade the QoS significantly. OFDM (Ergen et. al., 2003) is chosen to be the technology to handle these drawbacks.

8.1.2. Inter-Symbol Interference Due to Time Delay

In a multipath environment, the signals and their delayed versions arrive at different times. When the time delay between the different delayed signals is a large enough fraction of the transmitted signal's symbol period (actual time allotted for one symbol transmission), a transmitted symbol may arrive at the receiver during the next symbol period. This is well known as inter-symbol interference (or ISI). At higher data rates, the symbol period or duration is shorter; hence, it takes only a small time delay to introduce ISI. In case of broadband wireless ISI is a big problem and reduces the quality of service significantly. In the conventional situations, statistical equalization is the method for dealing with ISI but at high data rates it is quite complex and requires considerable amount of processing power. OFDM appears as a better solution for controlling ISI in broadband systems like WLAN, WiMAX and 4G.

OFDM does it in a quite smart way. A guard interval is introduced before each OFDM symbol. That means the guard interval is nothing but the duration in which no information is transmitted. Digitally they are nothing but a certain number of zeros transmitted between each couple of symbols. Whatever signal comes during that interval is discarded by the receiver. But if the guard interval is properly chosen, then the OFDM signal can be kept undistorted.

8.1.3. Effective use of Bandwidth through OFDM

OFDM can reduce the extraneous bandwidths in the form of guard bands. With proper implementation the guard bands can be reduced to zero. Due to the orthogonal nature of the carriers used for different channels, it is also possible to overlap the bands on each other and still they can be recovered back in the receiver without losing the quality. Thus saving of bandwidth is very much effective in OFDM. In low bandwidth systems, where the demand for spectrum is very high OFDM comes naturally as the first choice. The bandwidth saving has been shown below.

Besides the above advantages OFDM based systems provide other advantages for digitalization and protocol supports. The process like error correction and interleaving etc. are easily supported by OFDM.

8.2. QoS of MAC Layer

MAC layer is the most important layer for the QoS related operations. Of course in any network MAC layer plays the important issues related to

Figure 7. Guard-bands

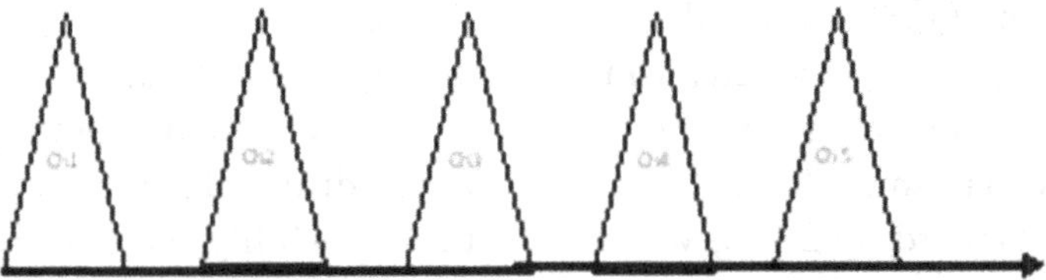

Figure 8. Overlapped bands in OFDM

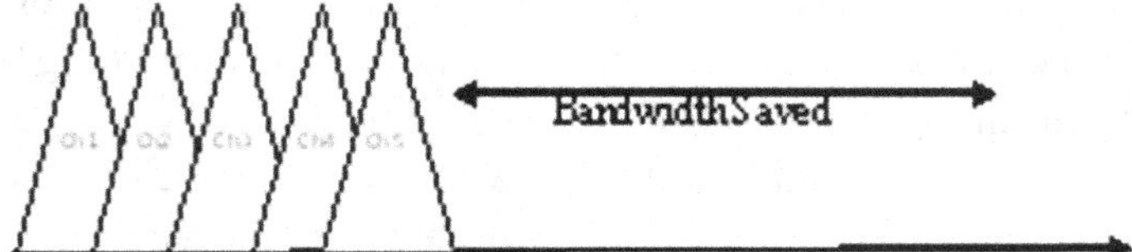

the control and quality of services. The original IEEE 802.11 specifies the details of the physical and the MAC layers (Garg et.al., 2003). But the 802.11a and 802.11b versions have been modified to change the data rates of the two standards and the physical layer has been changed to wireless channel.

The most important QoS related processes are executed in the MAC layer. The DCF, PCF processes all are MAC layer operations. In the enhanced DCF of IEEE 802.11e also takes the information from the routing layer and executes in the MAC layer (Habetha et. al., 2001). Of course the legacy CSMA/CA is also in the MAC layer and it avoids the loss of packets. The modification in the traditional DCF to the dual-queue [14] scheme as proposed by some of the researchers increased the functional utilities of the MAC layers. The ad hoc network DiffServ classifications are done through the routing layer algorithms, but the real function comes into picture through the MAC layer. Admission control, contention window size variation, bandwidth control and channel assignment all are handled through the MAC layer.

8.3. WLAN Link Layer QoS

In IEEE 802.11e, the link layer QoS has been provided. Of course, it only describes link-layer mechanisms for providing QoS on the radio interface. For end-to-end QoS, these mechanisms must be combined with the IP-based QoS signaling and provisioning mechanisms. The upcoming update to the WLAN standard, 802.11n, which also promises a major increase in bandwidth, integrates QoS support from the start. The link layer has an extended role in this new version. The challenge in providing QoS for WLAN technology lies in the fact that the radio interface is a shared medium. Access to the radio resource is not coordinated centrally.

8.4. QoS in Routing Layer

QoS routing and its related steps originate from the routing layer. The routing layer is above the MAC layer and takes care of the routing related functions. The change of topology and the optimum QoS for different paths are estimated and updated each time through some effective algorithms. When the transmission starts these algorithms play important roles in providing the QoS. Routing information are collected and updated in the TCP and other transport layers which determine the actual packet movement. But for ad hoc networks the routing layer means the layers which take care of the routing through the information from MAC layer. Of course there are some QoS routing related operations which are executed through both the routing and MAC layers. These issues have been presented in the next sub-sections.

8.4.1. Multipath Routing

This is a routing scheme that uses multiple paths simultaneously by splitting the information between different available paths, so as to increase the probability that the essential portion of the information is received at the destination without incurring excessive delay is referred to as multipath routing. Such a scheme is needed to mitigate the instability of the topology (e.g. failure of links) in an ad hoc network due to nodal mobility and changes in wireless propagation conditions (Carneiro et. al., 2004). The scheme works by adding an overhead to each packet, and good for reducing the average datagram delay for every packet. But in the changing topology sometimes it becomes too difficult to provide optimal path and QoS.

8.4.2. Distributed QoS Routing

Distributed QoS routing schemes are the optimal routing schemes for the best possible QoS. Of course there are two types of distributed QoS routing. The first one gives better bandwidth for QoS and the second one gives better delay characteristics. These two differently oriented routing schemes operate through different algorithms. With a hybrid mechanism the advantages of the two performance parameters can be realized.

8.5. QoS in the Upper Layers

QoS related actions are taken in the upper layers as well. As the TCP has the responsibility of transporting the packets safely to the destination it can play some role in the QoS. However the TCP information (Assaad & Djamal, 2006) is executed through the routing and MAC layers. The need for QoS also arises at the application layer. The application layer requests the transport layer to provide QoS services. The transport layer must request the routing layer to compute routes satisfying the QoS requirements. This request may need to travel all the way down to the physical layer. Each layer receiving a QoS request from the above layer needs to take some appropriate actions like checking and executing the updated algorithms etc.

8.6. IMS and the QoS

IMS or the IP Multimedia Subsystem is an integral part of the all-IP network systems (AIPN). In all-IP based systems the issues are quite different from the other systems. Now the most popular services like the multimedia streaming and voice over the IP are supported through the wireless ad hoc networks. So it has now more importance in the ad hoc environments.

The role of IMS for the QoS provisioning is quite significant. The importance of IMS has increased further due to the increase of AIPN networks. This enables to expand operators' service revenues and offerings. Now the IP core is common to the cellular networks as well as the WLANs and wired LANs. There are also other issues where the IMS emerged as a part of QoS infrastructure. There was a clear problem from the users' perspective in the end-to-end service provisioning, mainly related to the service QoS and service control. Service operators could guarantee certain QoS up to their service bearer, but the external IP network is out of their control and being typically pure Internet, no QoS can be guaranteed. However, QoS management and control of the different services provided by IMS enable to:

- Deliver different IP-based multimedia information between end-to-end and person-to-person or person-to-machine communication.
- It also enables different services and applications to interact in both real-time and non-real time.

Function wise the IMS layer can be separated into three main layers. They are the connectivity layer, control layer and the service layer. Connectivity layer is formed basically by the IP backbone of the system. Control layer is formed by the session control entities like PDF (Policy

Decision Function), P-CSCF(Packet Call Serving Control Protocol), S-CSCF(Switched Call Serving Control Protocol), etc., which are mainly responsible for controlling and authorizing the resources requested by a particular service (among other tasks). Similarly, service layer is the layer containing the application servers (PoC or Push-to-Talk over Cellular server, instant messaging server, streaming server, etc.), the end-users are accessing to. IMS layer is not well defined in the old systems. But in the all-IP networks (Akyildiz, Xie, & Mohanty, 2004) IMS layer has many functions and it has a great ability for enhancing the quality of services.

9. DIFFERENT PARAMETER SETTINGS AND OPTIMIZATION FOR QoS IMPROVEMENT

In every network optimization is a basic need. For quality of service the network operator spend some sizeable amount and thus there is a requirement of proper optimization. Quality f service itself is the optimization of the qualities of different services. However the process of optimization of QoS and its related operations are very complex processes. QoS provisioning itself is a difficult arrangement at different levels and layers. There are many protocols and sensors used for maintaining the quality of services at certain levels. Of course with proper pre-deployment and post deployment plans the optimization can be achieved. But the complexities can be reduced through the division of QoS in different layers. So here the optimization task has been provided in a divide and conquer principle.

9.1. QoS Optimization

QoS optimization is an advanced culture in modern data communication technology. QoS itself is an optimization of the services from the quality points of views. But QoS optimization is the judicious and efficient use of resources which support and provide better QoS at the cost of minimum spending and complexities. The optimization of QoS can be provided at different levels. These levels are can be the traffic level or the network management level, or the network management level. Optimization can be of two types from the QoS points of view. One is the optimization of the services and the other is the optimization of the resources.

The optimization of the overall QoS is done at all the QoS concerned layers. In the TCP or the transport layer there are some common processes for the optimization of services. They are, TCP tunneling (data tunneling for better performance, also similar to TCP encapsulation), adjustment of TCP parameters, connection multiplexing, RTT (real-time traffic) adjustment etc. Each process has some significance in the service optimization.

At the application layer also some arrangements give better performance. For example the rich contents when compressed, become less in amount and thus can be transferred easily.

Some other processes at this layer are server caching, content optimization and compression etc.

IP layer and the new IMS layer of the IP-based systems can manage the packets and traffic for optimal performance (Heegard et. al., 2001). Proper session control and connectivity related aspects can be optimized significantly through the IMS.

Normally the physical and MAC layers are always optimized for QoS. However, the data rate variation scalable bandwidth assignment and robust physical layers can give better QoS. Similarly the energy and bandwidth efficient routing schemes can save the resources directly.

10. OVERALL QoS MANAGEMENT AND NEW TRENDS FOR AD HOC NETWORKS

Due to the rapid growth of the WLAN, WiFi and other ad hoc networks there are new trends coming for the QoS provisioning and QoS management. In all the concerned layers, the QoS related support infrastructures are provided. For overall management of QoS there are new protocols being provided and feedback arrangements are put in place. These new trends are bringing new dimension of quality of service for the ad hoc networks.

10.1. QoS Evaluation

Quality of service is not a constant and it keeps on changing with time depending on the basic characteristics of the channel and other settings. In order to have a proper quality of service all the time, it is better to have a feedback from the end-to-end terminals. Depending on those feedbacks some precautionary steps are taken and new settings are provided for better quality of service. These collections of feedbacks and any other methods which can provide the performance of the quality of service are known as QoS evaluation. All service providers, who want to provide proper qualities in their services, do the evaluations in regular intervals.

The evaluations are done with respect to one or more QoS performance metrics. If it is with respect to bandwidth then, the QoS vs. bandwidth analysis is the main evaluation subject. Similarly, in many cases the delay, probability of packet loss and jitter characteristics are evaluated for QoS performance

From the evaluation, the service provider finds the QoS related performance detail and take some new decisions accordingly. The evaluation results are analyzed and the available alternatives are considered for implementation. These decisions are made a system known as the QoS policy management system. For big networks the role of policy management system is very crucial to provide the QoS guarantee.

10.2. QoS Policy Management System

QoS policy management is needed for the proper monitoring and management of the QoS aspects across the whole ad hoc network. Any updating in the QoS policies or the effectiveness of the new policies are evaluated and implementation decisions are taken by the policy management system. Of course QoS policy management is going to mandatory for all wireless service providers. The architecture for the policy management system can be as shown below. Here in the ad hoc network has N nodes. The service management provides the policies for the QoS management through some policy decision point or station. Through the policy decision point the policies are provided to the nodes where it would function. In the following diagram the policy updates are provided to all the nodes involved in communication.

The IEEE 802.11e proposals are going to be implemented very soon in all WLAN around the world where the QoS is important (Buddhikot, et. al., 2003). The hybrid nature of the wireless networks would increase. The better technology will replace the mediocre ones. The service of the wireless networks will be good enough and may be even very close to the wired medium communications. Hybrid schemes for the support of QoS are becoming very attractive due to the better technologies like WiMAX and 4G which are ready to incorporate WLAN as their parts.

10.3. Quality of Service in WiMAX

Quality of service in case of WiMAX is a bit different. WiMAX systems are of two types: fixed WiMAX and mobile WiMAX. In case of the fixed WiMAX the topology is almost fixed. So it is not very difficult to set the QoS parameters and protocols. The real challenge comes in case of

Figure 9.

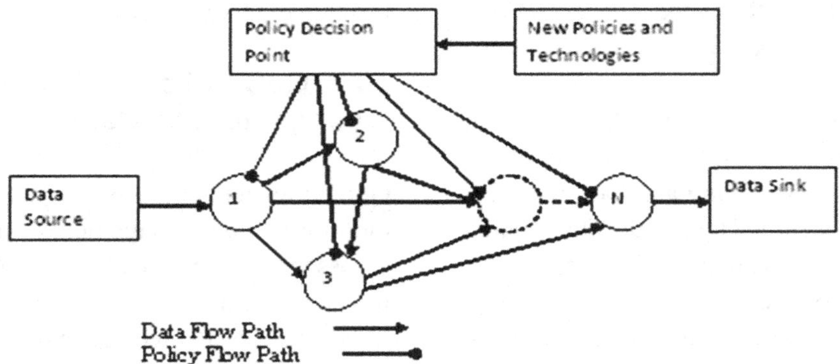

the mobile WiMAX where the topologies change and the ad hoc network like cases are found. In fact IEEE started a new standard for the larger networks which can cover a larger geography. WiMAX is based on the standard IEEE 802.16. There was no legacy system, which the WiMAX would have followed. Rather, WiMAX is the standard for WLAN for larger networks or exactly the WMAN (Wireless Metropolitan Area Network) or WAN (Wide area Network). Sometimes it is thought that WiFi can be considered as the legacy system of WiMAX. But it is not true. That consideration is due to the similarity between the IEEE 802.11 and IEEE 802.16 standards. In case of WiFi the standards we use are same as that of WLAN. Wireless fidelity is a case of wireless LAN. But the IEEE 802.16 standards are for the larger networks.

As the size of the coverage area of the wireless networks are increasing, the WiMAX standards can be used for large ad hoc networks. WiMAX has well defined support for QoS. In the future ad hoc networks, definitely the WiMAX frameworks will be helpful to provide the QoS. In WiMAX, the three basic IP QoS (integrated services or IntServ, differentiated services or DiffServ, and multiprotocol level switching, MPLS) service aspects are present. Its traffic classes are much similar to the UMTS traffic classes for DiffServ. Its QoS signaling is also advanced. The TDD (Time Division Duplex) and FDD (Frequency Division Duplex) presence makes the signaling flexible. The IMS layer of the WiMAX also supports the QoS mechanisms. WiMAX has a very well organized QoS policy management system in place. So, WiMAX unlike WLAN provides the QoS guarantee. It is a good thing for the WLAN to work out on a WiMAX like QoS support structure.

10.4. Quality of Service of 4G Networks

4G system is the next evolved version of the 3G system. In 4G the legacy systems will play main role in the different aspects of the operation, control and management. However some of the fundamental ideas of the ad hoc networks will also be used. Both the 3GPP and 3GPP2 research groups plan to provide the ad hoc network freedom to the 4G systems. Here some of the QoS aspects of the 4G networks have been discussed. 4G is an advanced technology like the WiMAX but it has got a strong legacy from the UMTS and GSM (Holma & Toskala, 2006) systems. 4G is different in many aspects. It is an LTE technology. It as many advanced features due to which the quality of service would be definitely good. Some of the example features are the presence of software defined radio; OFDM based physical layer, advanced protocols etc.

The QoS framework for the 4G would be a unified all-IPv6 architecture including the WCDMA, WLAN and other wireless features. There will be support for seamless handover and mobility enabled QoS. Mobility, QoS and AAAC (Auditing, Authentication, Authorization and Charging mechanisms) will be integrated (Ping et. al., 2005). Good policy management, DiffServ and advanced signaling will be found in 4G. However the role of WLANs would remain important in the hybrid 4G networks.

10.5. Hybrid Networks

As we have discussed before the wireless networks are becoming hybrid these days. The cellular systems have WLANS as their parts (Berkwist & Eriksson, 2006) at many places. This trend is increasing very fast and the thus the heterogeneity (Gao, Wu, & Miki, 2004) is increasing. The cellular technologies and the WLANs are now complementary to each other. In the following diagram it has been shown how the UMTS Cellular network and the WLAN co-exist and work for each other through a common IP core. This has pushed the designer for a common QoS support (Ahmavaara et. al., 2003) for both the cellular networks as well as the WLANs. Of course the whole QoS architecture for such unified network having both ad hoc and non-ad hoc parts has not been very much in applications till today. But the improvement in the QoS would give rise to such a common framework around the world.

In the future many standards and technologies are going to be unified. The WiMAX, 4G and the ad hoc networks may be the part of a common parent network having both fixed and ad hoc sections. The hybrid and heterogeneous networks would be ubiquitous. The QoS provision would also be common to all and the standards may be borrowed by each other.

Figure 10.

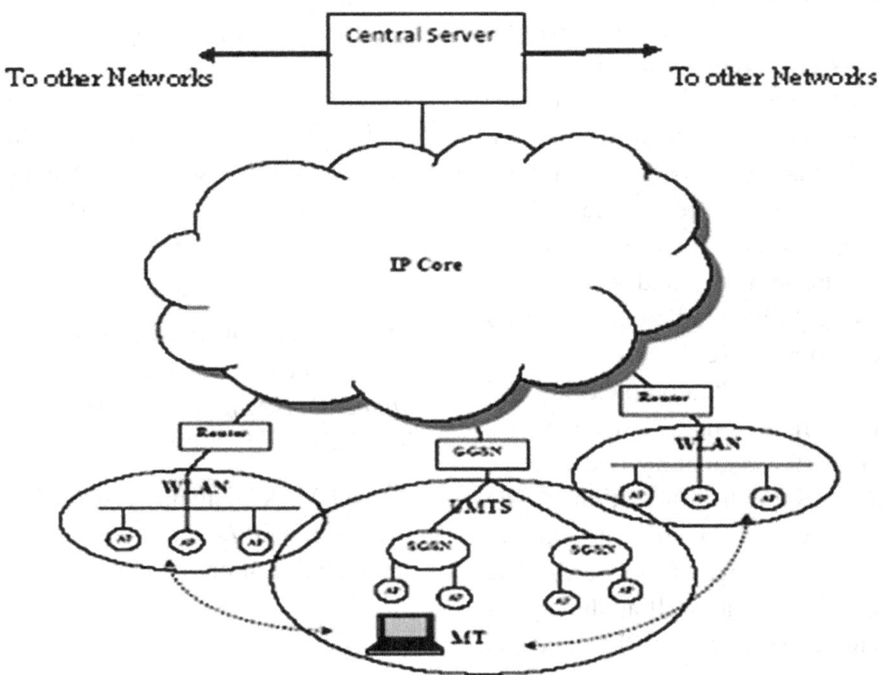

11. CONCLUSION

Quality of service provisioning is a fundamental need in the network performances. It will stay for all the ad hoc networks and its improvements will keep on happening. The new trends and protocols are coming for the optimization gradually. The IEEE 802.11e is the indication of the importance of the new tools in the quality of service enhancement. IETF is also taking many important steps for the QoS improvement in all kind of wireless networks. It is clear from the adaptation of the DiffServ mechanism in WLAN.

In the future the network topologies and the architecture will be unified. That means depending on the situation the better technology will be used. The cellular networks and the ad hoc technologies will work together as complementary solutions of each other. The standards will be also unified. The better part of each standard will stay and the awkward parts will be replaced by other standards of other rival systems and technologies. For example the WLANs will replace the cellular networks in the urban areas and in the rural and less dense areas cellular networks will prevail. But both the technologies will stay as parts of a wider unified network. Due to the wide use of all-IP systems the IMS layer will have more roles in the QoS provisioning. The physical layer can have multiple options. For example the uplink will have certain modulation technique and the downlink will have another. The use of software will increase to ensure both faster and better quality of service. Software defined radio has been tried for some WLANs to increase the QoS.

In the future networks the complexities will increase. The use of radiations will also increase at a high rate. Then the regulatory bodies have to take new actions to control these things. The radiation emissions can be taken in the quality of service aspects by the regulatory boards. The network service providers as well as the equipment designers have to take care of the radiation details and it has to be well below the danger level. Even now the equipment manufacturers and the service providers have started addressing the issues. The radiation levels are minimized with their joint collaboration and planning. Both the FCC and the European safety regulatory board have their specifications.

The new initiatives for the QoS support improvement are very promising. However there are a lot of things yet to come for better QoS provisioning. The energy efficiency as well as the overall effectiveness has to increase a lot. The need for a common framework for QoS support for IP traffic over both cellular networks and WLANs is increasing dramatically. Overall the future trends for QoS provisioning are bright and attractive.

REFERENCES

Aad, I., & Castelluccia, C. (2001). Differentiation mechanisms for IEEE 802.11. In *Proceedings of IEEE InfoCom*, Anchorage, AK. New York: IEEE.

Ahmad, A. (2005). *Wireless and mobile data networks*. Hoboken, NJ: Wiley Interscience. doi:10.1002/0471729221

Ahmavaara, K., Haverinen, H., & Pichna, R. (2003, November). Interworking architecture between 3GPP and WLAN systems. *IEEE Communications Magazine*, *41*(11). doi:10.1109/MCOM.2003.1244926

Akyildiz, I., Xie, J., & Mohanty, S. (2004, April). A survey of mobility management in next-generation all-IP based wireless systems. *IEEE Wireless Communications Magazine*, *11*(4), 16–28. doi:10.1109/MWC.2004.1325888

Assaad, M., & Djamal, Z. (2006). *TCP performance over UMTS/HSDPA systems*. Boca Raton, FL: Auerbach Publications. doi:10.1201/9781420013320

Berkwist, J., & Eriksson, E. (2006). *WLAN as a complement to UMTS*. Unpublished master's thesis. Retrieved from http://www.s3.kth.se/~matthias/current/ Ericsson.pdf

Borbash, S., & Jennings, E. (2002). Distributed topology control algorithm for multi-hop wireless networks. *Proceedings of IEEE International Joint Conference on Neural Networks*, Honolulu, HI (pp. 355–360). New York: IEEE.

Buddhikot, M., Chandranmenon, G., Han, S., Lee, Y. W., Miller, S., & Salgarelli, L. (2003, November). Design and implementation of a WLAN/CDMA2000 interworking architecture. *IEEE Communications Magazine*, *41*(11). doi:10.1109/MCOM.2003.1244928

Carneiro, G., Ruela, J., & Ricardo, M. (2004, April). Cross-layer design in 4G wireless terminals. *IEEE Wireless Communications*, *11*(2), 7–13. doi:10.1109/MWC.2004.1295732

Ergen, M., Coleri, S., & Varaiya, P. (2003, December). QoS aware adaptive resource allocation techniques for fair scheduling in OFDMA based broadband wireless access systems. *IEEE Transactions on Broadcasting*, *40*(4).

Fernandez, D., & Montes, H. (2002). Enhanced quality of service method for guaranteed bit rate services over shared channels in EGPRS systems. *Proceedings of IEEE Vehicular Technology Conference*, Birmingham, NY. New York: IEEE.

Gao, X., Wu, G., & Miki, T. (2004, June). End-to-end QoS provisioning in mobile heterogeneous networks. *IEEE Wireless Communications*, pp. 24–34. New York: IEEE.

Garg, P., Doshi, R., Greene, R., Baker, M., Malek, M., & Cheng, X. (2003). Using IEEE 802.11e MAC for QoS over wireless. In *Proceedings of IPCCC*, Phoenix, AZ.

Gesbert, D., Shafi, M., Shiu, D., Smith, P., & Naguib, A. (2003, March). From theory to practice: An overview of MIMO space-time coded wireless systems. *IEEE Journal on Selected Areas in Communications*, *21*(3), 281–302. doi:10.1109/JSAC.2003.809458

Gu, D., & Zhang, J. (2003, June). QoS enhancement in IEEE 802.11 wireless local area networks. *IEEE Communications Magazine*, *41*(6), 120–124. doi:10.1109/MCOM.2003.1204758

Habetha, J., Mangold, S., & Wiegert, J. (2001). 802.11 versus HiperLAN/2: A comparison of decentralized and centralized MAC protocols for multihop ad hoc radio networks. In *Proceedings of 5th World Multiconference on Systemics, Cybernetics and Informatics (SCI)*, Orlando, FL.

Heegard, C., Coffey, J., Gummadi, S., Murphy, P. A., Provencio, R., & Rossin, E. J. (2001, November). High-performance wireless ethernet. *IEEE Communications Magazine*, *39*(11). doi:10.1109/35.965361

Holma, H., & Toskala, A. (2006). *HSDPA/HSUPA for UMTS*. Hoboken, NJ: John Wiley & Sons. doi:10.1002/0470032634

Hwang, Y., & Varshney, P. (2003). An adaptive QoS routing protocol with dispersity for ad-hoc networks. In *Proceedings of the 36th Annual Hawaii International Conference on System Sciences* (pp. 302–311). New York: IEEE.

Mangold, S., Choi, S., & Esseling, N. (2001, September). An error model for radio transmissions of wireless LANs at 5GHz. In *Proceedings of Aachen Symposium'2001,* Aachen, Germany, (pp. 209-214).

McNair, J., & Zhu, F. (2004, June). Vertical handoffs in fourth-generation multi-network environments. *IEEE Wireless Communications*, pp. 8–15.

Perkins, C. E. (2001). *Ad hoc networking*. Reading, MA: Addison-Wesley.

Ping, Z., Xiaofeng, T., Jianhua, Z., Ying, W., Lihua, L., & Yong, W. (2005, January). A vision from the future: Beyond 3G TDD. *IEEE Communications Magazine*, *43*(1), 38–44. doi:10.1109/MCOM.2005.1381873

3rd Generation Partnership Project. (2004). 3GPP TS 23.207 V6.3.0: End-to-end quality of service (QoS) concept and architecture.

3rd Generation Partnership Project. (2006). 3GPP TS 23.207 V5.8.0: *Universal mobile telecommunication system (UMTS): End-to-end QoS concept and architecture.* Retrieved from http://www.3gpp.org

Shenker, S., Partridge, C., & Guerin, R. (1997, September). Specification of guaranteed quality of service, RFC 2212.

Wroclawski, J. (1997). The use of RSVP with IETF Integrated Services, RFC2210.

Yu, J., Choi, S., & Lee, J. (2004). Enhancement of VoIP over IEEE 802.11 WLAN via dual queue Strategy. In *Proceedings of IEEE ICC*, Paris. New York: IEEE.

ADDITIONAL READING

IEEE Draft Std 802.11e. (2001). Medium access control (MAC) enhancements for quality of service (QoS), D2.0a.

Gomez, G., & Sanchez, R. (2005). *End-to-end quality of service over cellular networks.* Chichester, UK: John Wiley & Sons Ltd. doi:10.1002/047001587X

Hewlett Packard. (2006). *Planning a wireless network, ProCurve networking.* Palo Alto, CA: Hewlett Packard Development Company.

Hiertz, G. R., Denteneer, D., Stibor, L., Zang, Y., Costa, X. P., & Walke, B. (2009). The IEEE 802.11 Universe. *IEEE Communications Magazine*, *48*(1), 62–70. doi:10.1109/MCOM.2010.5394032

Internet Engineering Task Force. (n.d.). Mobile ad hoc network (MANET) working group. Retrieved from http://www.ietf.org/html.charters/manet-charter.html

Kappler, C. (2009). *UMTS networks and beyond.* Chichester, UK: John Wiley & Sons, Ltd. doi:10.1002/9780470682029

Mohapatra, P., & Krishnamurthy, S. (2005). *Ad hoc networks: Technologies and protocols.* Berlin: Springer.

Motorola Good Technology Group. (2007). *A guide for creating effective enterprise wireless strategies.* Redwood City, CA: Motorola Good Technology.

O'Hara, B., & Patrick, A. (2005). *The IEEE 802.11 handbook: A designer's companion* (2nd ed.). New York: IEEE Press.

3rd Generation Partnership Project. (2002). Wireless IP Network Standard. 3GPP2 P.S0001, Release 4.

3rd Generation Partnership Project. (2004). Support for End-to-End QoS. 3GPP2 S.R0079-0, Release 6.

Rypinski, C. (2006). Retrospective on development of radio and wireless data communication. IEEE 802.15 Wireless next Generation Task Group, Submission 06-0107.

Sorey, R., Ananda, A., Chan, M. C., & Ooi, W. T. (2006). *Mobile, wireless, and sensor networks: Technology, applications, and future directions.* Hoboken, NJ: John Wiley & Sons, Inc.

Std, I. E. E. E. 802.11. (1999). Wireless LAN medium access control (MAC) and physical layer (PHY) specifications. Retrieved from http://www.ieee802.org/11

Yang, X., & Vaidya, N. H. (2005). On the physical carrier sense in wireless ad hoc networks. In *Proceedings of IEEE Infocom.* New York: IEEE.

Section 3
Hybrid Networks

Chapter 14
Challenges of Emerging Technologies in Transportation Systems

Antonio Guerrero-Ibáñez
University of Colima, México

Pedro Damián-Reyes
University of Colima, México

ABSTRACT

Nowadays, the number of vehicles and the need for transportation is growing quickly. There are more vehicles on the roads driving more kilometers. The road networks in major cities are not sufficient to cater for the current traffic demands due to the size of roads available. As a result, the modern society is facing more traffic jams, higher fuel bills and the increase of CO_2 emissions. It is imperative to improve the safety and efficiency of transportation. Developing a sustainable transportation system requires a better use of existing infrastructure and the application of emerging technologies. This chapter gives the readers a global vision of the traffic and transportation issues and how emerging technologies such as wireless, sensing, cellular and computing technologies contribute to the solution of transportation problems in all cities of the world.

INTRODUCTION

Modern society depends on mobility, which provides personal freedom and access to services for business and pleasure. The amount of time to travel from one location to another can vary significantly based on the current traffic conditions. The growing volume of traffic has adverse effects on the environment, public health and especially in accidents that cause fatalities, injuries and material damages. Vehicular traffic is one of the most critical concerns for a modern society where cities are ever-growing. It is of paramount importance to improve the safety and efficiency of transportation. In order to solve these serious transportation problems, the proposed solutions must be based on intelligent mechanisms and the application of emerging technologies to make traffic control and management more efficient and safety. Several research groups focus their attention on the emerging technologies as a feasible alternative to solve the transportation problems

DOI: 10.4018/978-1-60960-027-3.ch014

(Chatzigiannakis, Grammatikou & Papavassiliou, 2007; Qing, Mak, Jeff & Sengupta, 2007).

Technological advances in communications, electronics, and computing capabilities are contributing to improve the transportation systems, creating the vision towards more intelligent transportation systems. These systems, which are known as *Intelligent Transportation Systems* (ITS), attempt to apply information and communications technologies to vehicles and transportation infrastructure to manage items that are typically independent of each other, such as vehicles, loads, and routes. The final goal is to improve safety and reduce vehicle wear, transportation times, and fuel consumption. ITS can contribute to the transportation solution applying the latest information and communication technologies, such as wireless, sensing, cellular, mesh, and computing technologies to transportation systems. However, the intelligent level depends on technological integration level and the technologies used or applied (Figure 1). When integrated into the transportation system's infrastructure, and in vehicles themselves, these technologies relieve congestion, improve safety and enhance productivity. The main challenge will be to integrate all technologies within a complementary and cooperative environment that solves the transportation problems. The proposal of a new cooperative environment composed by different network technologies and integrated applications will focus on creating safer roads, more efficient mobility and minimizing the environmental impact. Additionally, the development of predictive techniques and algorithms will allow transportation systems to increase their grade of intelligence by means of advanced modeling and comparison of historical baseline.

It will be necessary to accelerate and coordinate the deployment and use of *ITS* applications and services for road transport and their connections with other modes of transport, to ensure seamless access and continuity of services. In this sense, EU has proposed an action plan that includes specific measures in these areas (Mobility and Transport, 2009):

- Optimal use of road and traffic data.
- Traffic and freight management.
- Road safety and security.
- Integrating ITS applications in the vehicle.
- Data protection and liability.

The direct benefit will be a faster, better coordinated and more harmonized use of intelligent

Figure 1. Vision of the future of intelligent transportation systems

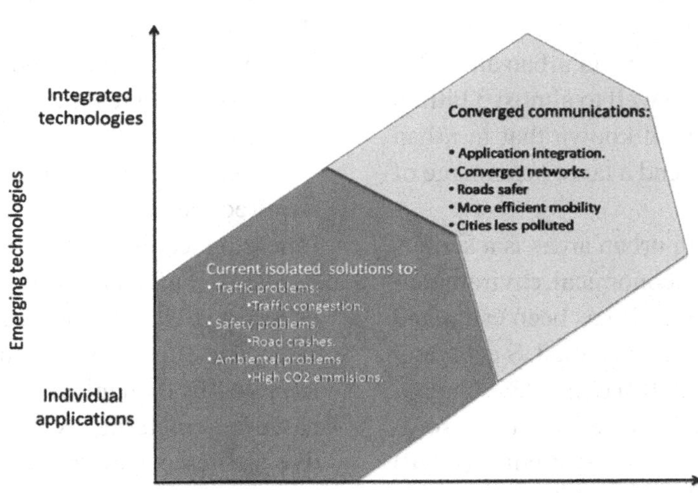

transport systems and services, which in turn will contribute to more efficient, cleaner and safer transportation systems.

This chapter gives the readers a global vision of the traffic and transportation issues, the efforts of development about standards for transportation management, and how the application of emerging technologies might contribute or are contributing to the solution of transportation challenges. The chapter is organized as follows: the first part of the chapter provides an overall view of the fundamental concepts, definitions, defined *ITS* architectures and the standards development. Some of the constituent technologies typically implemented in *ITS* are described in the second part of the chapter. Third part of the chapter presents several applications and developing projects of different countries and regions where emerging technologies are (or will be) applied. Finally, the last part of the chapter presents the conclusions of the work.

BACKGROUND

People is facing more traffic jams, higher fuel bills and the increase of CO_2 emissions due to the lack of control of the growth of vehicles in the urban zones. The technical report of the United Nations Population Fund showed that for the first time, more than half of the world's population, around 3.3 billion people, live in urban areas. By 2030, this is expected to swell to almost 5 billion (UNFPA, 2007). It is well known that in urban areas commuters can spend a large percentage of their day stuck in traffic.

Traffic congestion in urban areas is a serious problem that has a huge economical, environmental and road safety impact. It has been estimated that traffic congestion will cost the US economy over $90bn per year by 2009 (Lomax & Schrank, 2005) and the European Union economy approximately 1% of its Gross Domestic Product (GDP) by 2010 (EEA, 2006). However, traffic congestion problems cannot be solved by building additional or extended roads due to the high costs, as well as environmental and geographical limitations.

There is also an environmental cost. The technical report of the European Environment Agency (EEA) revealed that in 2004, European Union road transport accounted for 26% of greenhouse gas emissions (EEA, 2006). Even though the economic costs are significant, the human cost of vehicular accidents is astonishing. According to Commission for Global road Safety road crashes kill at least 1.3 million people each year and injure 50 million. 90% of these road casualties occur in low and middle income countries. Each year 260,000 children die on the road and another million are seriously injured, often permanently disabled. By 2015 road crashes are predicted to be the leading cause of premature death and disability for five-year-old children and above (Safety, 2009). This hidden road injury epidemic is a crisis for public health and a major contributor to the causes of poverty. Yet aid agencies, development NGOs, philanthropic foundations and key international institutions continue to neglect or ignore this rapidly growing problem. Road transport is a necessity for our mobility; however, new measures are required to make it safer and more efficient.

Based on the aforementioned, emerging technologies should be established as basic elements of transportation systems. Increasing capacity and flexibility of emerging technologies together with decreasing investment and operation costs could make possible a real development of cooperative systems.

Emerging technologies should guarantee the required demands of transportation systems. Emerging communications technologies could be used to build a network transportation system to improve safety and reduce congestion. The safety and efficiency of roads can be substantially improved by the deployment of intelligent systems based on emerging technologies, such as adaptive traffic control and management systems in cities, and traffic control and incidents detection systems on the highways. These systems will be able, for example, to improve road safety above all in the pre-crash phase when the accident can still be avoided or at least its severity significantly reduced. Each vehicle could be equipped with a wireless radio and numerous roadside units would be installed, so that vehicles and the roadside would be linked into a widespread, high-speed, and low-latency network. These roadside units would be part of a large computer network to service both public and private sector applications. Research groups are focusing their efforts on defining and prototyping communications systems and sets of standards that would use wireless technologies to enable vehicle-to-infrastructure and vehicle-to-vehicle communications and also provide a land-based network system that would support public and private sector applications. These applications would have access to selected data from all vehicles and would have the ability to communicate to vehicles.

CONCEPTS, DEFINITIONS AND CHALLENGES

Advanced technologies have been applied to assist in the management of traffic flow; it has been common for nearly 70 years with the first attempts at traffic signal control of intersections and railway crossings in the United States of America and Europe. Most of these systems have been 'internal' self contained systems, systems that operate on their own, or within a closed system environment. But as we move into the 21st century, we have an increasing need for these systems to interoperate, and to communicate with each other, in order to provide a better and safer travelling experience. Advanced technologies are applied to the dissemination of information and management of transport networks. On the whole, the application of communication, electronic and computer technologies are known as Intelligent Transportation Systems (ITS).

Each region and country has its own vision and definition of *ITS*. Some of these definitions are:

- ERTICO – *ITS* Europe defines *ITS* as *the new application that information and communications technologies are finding in urban transport and is also called "Transport Telematics"* (ERTICO-a, 1998).
- ITS America defines *ITS* as *a broad range of diverse technologies, which holds the answer to many of transportation problems. ITS is comprised of a number of technologies, including information processing, communications, control, and electronics. Joining these technologies to our transportation system will save lives, save time, and save money* (ITS America) (America, 2009).
- ITS Australia defines *ITS* as *a broad-based term which used to describe developments in communication and computing technologies applied to transport services generally* (ITS Australia).
- ITS Japan specify that *ITS offers a fundamental solution to various issues concerning transportation, which include traffic accidents, congestion and environmental pollution. ITS deals with these issues through the most advanced communications and control technologies* (ITS Japan).
- Finally, ITS Canada defines *ITS* as *the application of advanced and emerging technologies (computers, sensors, control, communications, and electronic devices) in transportation to save lives, time, money, energy and the environment* (Canada, 2009).

As read, all different regions of the world have a similar vision of *ITS*, the use of emerging technologies to solve the various issues concerning transportation.

With this in mind, in the last years the vision of the automobile industry has shown an interest in the future of vehicular communications, mainly for safety, entertainment and traffic information broadcasting applications. This vision has generated the concept of vehicular networks. Vehicular networks, also known as *VANETs*, can be considered as a subset or special case of Mobile Ad Hoc Networks (MANETs) which have been studied extensively in the literature. However, *VANETs* are distinguished from *MANETs* by their hybrid network architectures, node movement characteristics, and new application scenarios.

Vehicles can use different network technologies (such as Wi-Fi, cellular networks, WiMAX, among others) to communicate with other vehicles or with roadside base stations. System architectures can be divided into different categories according to different perspective in VANETs. From the vehicular communication perspective, VANETs can be categorized into V2V (Vehicle-to-Vehicle) and V2I (Vehicle-to-Infrastructure) (Figure 2). On the one hand, V2V refers to the Inter-Vehicle Communication (IVC), in which vehicles communicate with each other via wireless technology, commonly this kind of communication is known as V2V (vehicle to vehicle). On the other hand, V2I refers to Vehicle-to-Infrastructure Communication where vehicles communicate with roadside base stations via sensor and wireless networks, which is also called V2R (vehicle to roadside).

VANETs indicate their potential with regard to safety, traffic efficiency, and comfort. The prospective applications of VANETs are categorized into three groups which are entertainment, data collection and safety applications. Entertainment applications focus on connecting the vehicles to entertainment and comfort services using roadside stations and inter-vehicles communications. These applications support, e.g., content sharing (Nandan, Das, Pau, Gerla, & Sanadidi, 2005), advertisements, and peer-to-peer (P2P) marketing (Lee, Park, Amir, & Gerla, 2006). Safety applications focus on enabling the delivery of messages to the target receivers with acceptable performances. These applications require the network protocols to forward messages from a sender to only vehicles based on the location and driving direction. This kind of services are applied where emergency information is diffused to neighbor vehicles, and real-time response is required to avoid accidents (Xu, Mak, Ko, & Sengupta, 2004). Finally, distributed data collection applications

Figure 2. Vehicular networks scenario representation

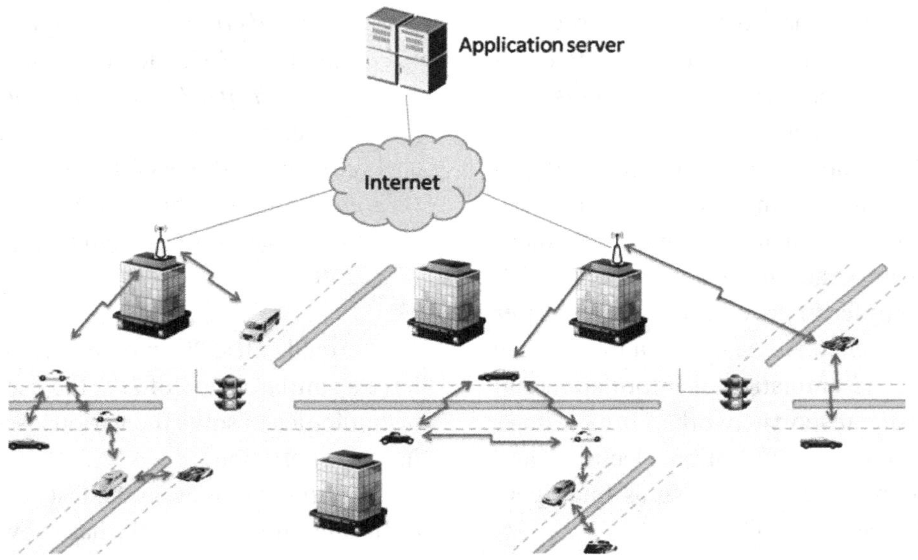

are focused on collection and spreading of traffic status and location information, e.g., parking lot and traffic congestion information (Sormani, Turconi, Costa, Frey, Migliavacca, & Mottola, 2006).

Research Challenges of Vehicular Networks

As previously mentioned, emerging technologies applied to transportation systems face several challenges. Development of intelligent transportation systems brings new challenges to vehicle driving, controlling and monitoring. In this sense, emerging technologies vision is focused on four fundamental principles: Sustainability, integration, safety, and responsiveness. These fundamental principles will be the base to achieve the main objectives previously mentioned (Figure 3)

Emerging technologies will play a major role in promoting and ensuring the sustainability of transport infrastructure. Through a range of means emerging technologies can facilitate the efficient use of existing infrastructure, regulate and control demand, encourage and facilitate the use of alternative modes, and manage congestion and its effects.

Management tools such as electronic tolling, traveler information and access control are all based on *ITS*, and are at the core of the demand management solutions that support transport infrastructure sustainability. Moreover, through a more efficient management of traffic on existing roads, *ITS* facilities can delay or deny the need of new infrastructure adding to the sustainability of all transportation infrastructures.

However, the current challenge is not to use the emerging technologies, but developing mechanisms and protocols that allow a complete integration of the different technologies to provide a seamless mechanism to disseminate and access the accurate information, facilitating the management of transportation systems and solving the issues of transportation. In this sense, the typical *ITS* based on discrete and self contained systems will have been evolved towards systems based on heterogeneous technologies.

Figure 3. Principles and objectives of emerging technologies in transportation area

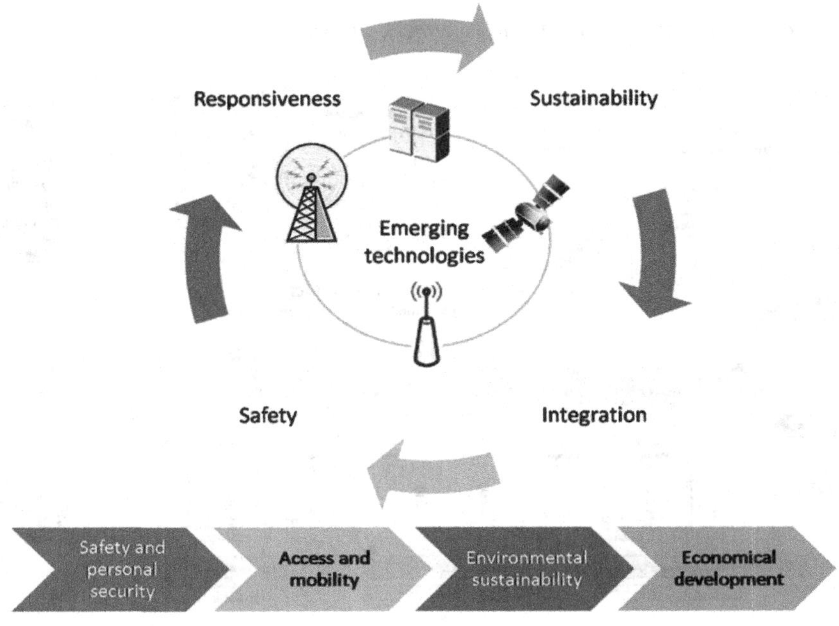

Nevertheless, one of the main challenges of *ITS* is the compatibility and portability of the developed systems. For example, a collision avoidance system is of limited use if it cannot successfully communicate due to the differences of technological development. Standards are clearly necessary to achieve these objectives.

In the last years, main efforts have been focused on developing international standards in isolate areas such as architectures design; Database Technology; Automatic Vehicle and Equipment Identification; Fee and Toll Collection; General Fleet Management and Commercial-Freight, Public Transport-Emergency; Integrated Transport Information, Management, Control; Traveler Information Systems; Route Guidance and Navigation Systems; Vehicle-Roadway Warning and Control Systems; Dedicated Short Range Communications; and Wide Area Communications-Protocols and Interfaces (Williams, 2008). ISO (*International Organization for Standardization*) has been developing *ITS* standards since 1994 (ISO TC 204, 2006), and the European Committee for Standardization (CEN) since 1991 (CEN, 2005). The main focus of new developments is the integration of emerging technologies and their generic communications standards such as 2G, 3G, Wi-Fi, Bluetooth and WiMAX in order to create the new generation of Standards that allow vehicle-vehicle (V2V) / vehicle-infrastructure (V2I) systems to operate within a heterogeneous communication environment, integrating most of the major vehicle manufacturers, transport management system providers and operators, and highway infrastructure operators.

In this sense, ISO has been developing a new communication framework, which is known as "CALM" (Communications Access for Land Mobiles) initiative (Figure 4). CALM is *the ISO approved framework for heterogeneous packet-switched communication in mobile environments* which is focused on providing a layered solution that enables continuous or quasi continuous communications between vehicles and the infrastructure, or between vehicles, using such wireless telecommunications media that are available in any particular location, and have the ability to migrate to a different available media where it is required (Evensen, 2006).

ISO TC204 Work Group 16 is developing a family of International Standards based on the CALM concept. This family of standards specifies

Figure 4. CALM architecture representation (Evensen, 2006)

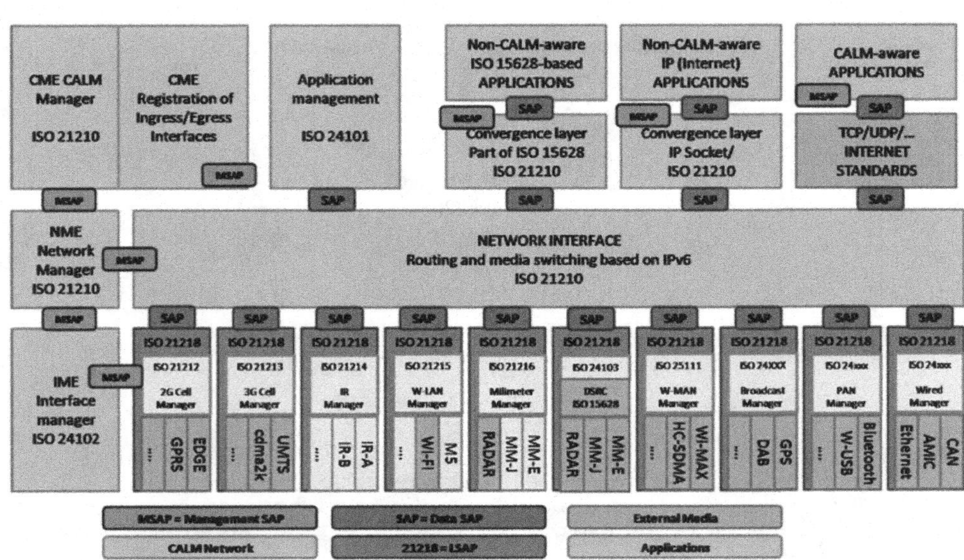

a common architecture, network protocols and communication interface definitions for wired and wireless communications using various access technologies including cellular 2nd generation, cellular 3rd generation, satellite, infra-red, 5 GHz micro-wave, 60 GHz millimetre-wave, and mobile wireless broadband. These and other access technologies that can be incorporated are designed to provide broadcast, unicast and multicast communications between mobile stations, between mobile and fixed stations and between fixed stations in the "Intelligent Transportation Systems" (ITS) sector (ISO TC204, 2008).

ISO 21217 describes the common architectural framework around which CALM-compliant communication entities called ITS stations are instantiated, and provide the architectural reference for use by the CALM family of International Standards including the lower layer service access point specifications described in, network protocol specifications (IPv6 networking) and (non-IP networking), and the ITS station management specifications.

ISO 24101 specifies structures and methods for application management, including means for installing, uninstalling and updating applications on on-board equipment (OBE) and wireless access equipment (WAE) deployed in a CALM network in a reliable and secure manner. ISO 24210 describes and specifies the network protocols and media switching based on IPv6.

A fundamental advantage of the CALM concept over traditional systems is that applications are abstracted from the access technologies that provide the wireless connectivity and the networks that transport the information from the source to the destination(s). One of the essential features of the CALM concept is the ability to support heterogeneous handover between all access technologies supported by ITS stations. With this flexibility, CALM-complaint systems provide the ability to use the most appropriate access technology for information exchange. Selection rules are supported to include user preferences and access technology capabilities to make decisions as to which access technology to use for a particular session, and when to handover between access technologies or between service providers on the same access technology. However, this feature is one of the main problems of this architecture due to the media selection at the discretion of user determined parameters. It is necessary the development of intelligent mechanisms that select the most suitable media to disseminate the information that is important for the control and management of transport systems.

The separation of application services and the communication technologies over which the service is provided will allow the equipment installed in any vehicle to be able to communicate over any medium/media that is available locally. As CALM is based on IPv6 (Internet Protocol Version 6), it will provide a full compatibility with current and new Internet services. In the next section of this chapter we will explain how the emerging technologies have been or will be applied in the transportation systems.

EMERGING TECHNOLOGIES APPLIED TO TRANSPORTATION

Emerging technologies can be applied in several ways into vehicular networks. In general the aim is to provide a set of air interface protocols and parameters for high speed vehicular communication using one or more of several available media. The range of technologies involved includes sensor and control technologies, communication and computer informatics and a tight relation between several disciplines such as computer science, engineering, telecommunications and automobile manufacturing. Although emerging technologies involve computing, electronic and communication technologies, our work will be focused on communication technologies, but we will briefly mention the other ones, too.

Computational Technologies

Recent advances in vehicle electronics through the design and implementation of embedded systems, join together to the computational techniques that are being developed have led to think in the implementation of intelligent systems on vehicles. In the beginning of the 21st century, there were individual programmable, logic controller modules with non-real-time operating systems, but nowadays there is a trend though microprocessor modules with hardware memory management and Real-Time Operating Systems. These systems will allow more sophisticated software applications to be implemented on vehicles in order to provide a high level of intelligence.

Therefore, computer technologies have been considered as the foundation of the development of applications based on algorithms, and the ones that put new intelligent techniques and methods in practice to control transport systems and to gather traffic information data. However, computer technologies face several important challenges. If the algorithms and protocols are not very efficient, problems such as latency will be huge causing the system to appear useless. Even though there are not acceptable latency amounts because this is based on the user perception; it is necessary to keep values according to the application used, for example less than 150 milliseconds for real-time applications and services.

Predictive techniques are being developed by several research groups. Artificial systems based on artificial societies and agent-modeling technology, are effective tools for this purpose (Wang & Lsansing, 2004). In this sense, artificial intelligence (Aguirre & Domínguez, 2007), neural networks (Wang, Chao, & Lee, 2008), fuzzy logic (Kulkarni & Waingankar, 2007), among others, have been applied to control and management of traffic lights in order to provide a high intelligent level.

Wireless Communications

As previously mentioned, there are several wireless access technologies that could be used as a base for vehicular networks connectivity. Recent advances in Wireless Communication technologies are likely to make significant inroads in the evolution of *ITS*. A great variety of wireless communications technologies have been proposed for intelligent transportation systems. Vehicular networks consider the use of both infrared and radio waves. VHF (*Very High Frequency*) and microwaves are a type of broadcast communication while infrared and millimeter waves are a type of directional communication. According to Hubaux, microwaves are used more frequently (Hubaux, 2004). Wireless communication can be further classified into wide-area and short-range communication systems. Short-range communication systems have two subdivisions: dedicated short-range (formerly vehicle-to-roadside) and vehicle-to-vehicle communications (Lockheed Martin Federal Systems, 1997).

The short-range communication, also known as DSRC (*Dedicated Short Range Communication*), represents one-way or two-way short- to medium-range wireless communication channels specifically designed for automotive use and a corresponding set of protocols and standards. On the one hand, the *Federal Communications Commission* (FCC) allocated the 75MHz of spectrum in the 5.9GHz band for DSRC to be used by *ITS*. On the other hand, in Europe in August 2008 the *European Telecommunications Standards Institute (*ETSI) allocated 30 MHz of spectrum in the 5.9GHz band. In the recent years, there has been considerable interest in wireless mesh networks and their deployment in metropolitan areas as a viable technology that can complement the "last-mile" connectivity solutions to the public and can extend the range of DSRC technologies.

Wide-area communications have been proposed using infrastructure networks. Unlike the short-range communications, wide-area communications require extensive and very expensive infrastructure deployment. There is lack of consensus as to what business model should support this infrastructure. Candidate wireless access technologies include 3G (3GPP, 2009), and WiMAX (IEEE 802.16) (Forum, 2009). In the rest of this section we will describe some of the emerging technologies that can be applied in *ITS*.

Wireless LAN Networks

The popularity of nowadays wireless local area networks (*WLAN*) has inspired researchers and developers to find the wide application perspectives in vehicular environments, which spawns a new type of vehicular network: wireless access for vehicular environment (WAVE) system. WAVE system defines a physical platform for both ITS and vehicular infrastructure integration (VII) allowing drivers and passengers on board accessing to real-time messages related to safety, traffic and data services. WAVE system could provide drivers with warning messages when possible accidence exists.

Some researchers and designers have several developed dedicated short range communications (DSRC) prototypes by adopting existing indoor wireless technologies, such as Wi-Fi, to a vehicular environment. Industry is calling for a new and dedicated standard for DSRC. Currently, the IEEE 802.11p workgroup is dedicated itself to the development of the physical (PHY) and *Media Access Control* (MAC) protocols for WAVE. The group is working variation of 802.11 standard that would be applied to support communication between vehicles and the roadside, or, alternatively, among vehicles themselves, operating at speeds up to 200 km/h, handling communication ranges as high as 1,000 meters. PHY and MAC layers are based on IEEE 802.11a, shifted to the 5.9 GHz band (5.850-5.925 GHz within US). The technology is promoted by the car industry both in Europe (Car2Car CC) and US (VSCC, VII). IEEE 1609 is a higher layer standard on which IEEE 802.11p is based (Department of Transportation, 2006). According to the official IEEE 802.11 Work Plan predictions the standard will be published in November 2010 (McCann, 2009).

Wireless Mesh networks

Wireless Mesh Networks (WMNs) are poised to be a key infrastructure for enabling new applications such as in public safety and entertainment. WMNs can augment computing devices with spatial and contextual characteristics of surrounding environments in addition to seamless mobility and economical broadband connectivity. Wireless mesh networks are dynamically self-organized and self-configured systems. WMN consist of a set of self-configuring mesh routers that form and maintain a wireless infrastructure. They are typically deployed in a quasi-stationary manner, where some mesh routers are fixed; creating a central infrastructure that is used as a base of the communication. This wireless infrastructure enables routing of information in a multi-hop manner.

A typical WMN comprises mesh clients and mesh routers. Mesh clients can be desktops, laptops, cellular phones, as well as *On Board Units* (OBU). Mesh routers, also known as WMN Access Points (WMN-AP), can self-configure themselves to automatically build the wireless infrastructure that establishes and maintains mesh connectivity. Mesh routers typically provide access to a fixed structure network or to the Internet. Each mesh router has a domain of wireless coverage. An OBU is associated with one AP at a time, as long as it is in the router coverage domain. WMN allows OBUs to move freely and associate themselves with different mesh routers. However, WMN does not provide guarantees on maintaining communication sessions between an OBU and the WMN.

Although WMN can be used for a large number of applications, a number of general requirements and characteristics are shared among most of these applications. These characteristics include geographic coverage, cost-effectiveness, mobility management, scalability, fault resilience, privacy and security (Lee, Jianliang, Young-Bae, & Shrestha, 2006).

Most of the research on mesh networks has been on maximizing the throughput provided to end-nodes (Ganguly et al., 2006). However the main challenge is the solution of aspects like reliability and latency, which are important issues if mesh networks are to be considered as an alternative solution of mission-critical infrastructure. These solutions require distributing content (e.g., route guidance maps) to vehicles travelling on city streets and highways. In this sense, some works like the propose by Lan et al. study the feasibility of using wireless mesh networking for traffic control (Lan, Wang, Berriman, Moors, & Hassan, 2007).

WiMAX (IEEE 802.16e)

WiMAX is a point-to-multipoint (PMP) technology that operates in the 10 to 66GHz and sub11GHz wavelengths. It can provide service over distances up to 30 miles. The IEEE 802.16e version is an extension of the IEEE 802.16 standard that was drafted specifically to deal with mobility. It is backward compatible with all IEEE 802.16 standards. And while IEEE 802.16 was conceived as a back-end technology, IEEE 802.16e has the capacity to be adapted for individual computers, and has the quality of service features to support voice. It provides connectivity for high-speed data in both stationary and mobile situations. It will enable mobile users to maintain their network connection while moving at speeds up to between 75-93 miles per hour. The upper speed limit depends on the distance of the access point from the base station as well as other transmission quality issues, i.e., air density, solar flares, electromagnetic radiation, etc. The most typical WiMAX-based architecture includes a base station mounted on a building and shall be responsible for communicating on a point to multi-point basis with subscriber stations located in automobiles.

Wireless Sensor Networks

Wireless Sensor Networks (WSNs) are suggested as a viable technology for traffic monitoring applications into the traffic systems. WSN is a low-cost, low-consumption technology characterized by self-configuration and self-healing features that make it very attractive for reducing installation and maintenance costs. Moreover, multi-hop communication allows extending arbitrarily the monitored area, thus overcoming the constraints set to the one-hop radio range by the very limited node transmission power (Akyildiz, Su, Sankarasubramaniam, & Cayirci, 2002).

Sensor systems for ITS are network systems based on vehicle and infrastructure, e.g., Intelligent vehicle technologies. Infrastructure sensors are indestructible (such as in-road reflectors) devices that are installed or embedded on the road, or surrounding the road (buildings, posts, and signs for example) as required and may be manually disseminated during preventive road construction maintenance or by sensor injection machinery for rapid deployment of the embedded radio frequency powered in-ground road sensors (Qi, 2008). Vehicle-sensing systems include deployment of infrastructure-to-vehicle and vehicle-to-infrastructure electronic beacons for identification communications

Sensing technologies like RFID (*Radio Frequency Identification)* can be used as a complementary tool for the image tracking systems. The image tracking systems have been employed for real-time traffic flow monitoring. However this kind of systems involves several limitations such as the *False Acceptable Rate* (FAR) and *False Rejection Rate* (FRR) (Tseng & Song, 2002). In this sense, a set of RFID readers can be mounted in the vicinity of the traffic signal, which communicates with a central processor and interrogates an RFID tag on each RFID-tagged vehicle at the roadway intersection. The RFID reader in combination with the control systems count the number of RFID-tagged vehicles present in each traffic flow direction at the roadway intersection. With the application of intelligent algorithms the traffic congestion level can be reduced through the dynamic manipulation of the cycle times for the different traffic lights present in the intersection (Wen, 2008; Al-Khateeb & Johari, 2008). Other interesting application is the instantaneous information recovery, driving aid, navigation safety to increase sustained monitoring of suspect vehicles operating in critical zones (Lee, Chiang, Perng, Jiang, & Wu, 2009).

Another application of sensor networks is in the loop roads. Sensors even more sophisticated have been used to replace simpler detectors placed in the roadbed, which only count the number of vehicles crossing during a unit time over the loop. The new sensors allow control systems to estimate additional information parameters (such as speed, length, and weight of vehicles and the distance between them, among others).

Cellular Networks

At present, cellular communication systems are widely used, and network coverage is nearly universal. The cellular network is reliable and will continue to evolve and mature. In addition to being popular and stable, the benefit of cellular networks is that the infrastructure is already in place. In this sense, the application of cellular networks in the transportation systems is related in the way to solve transportation problems. GPRS (*General Packet Radio Service*) infrastructure can be applied as a way to avoid the risks or congestion situations for a great number of users (Andrisano, Verdone, & Makagawa, 2000). Its radio coverage is present in most countries allowing a not complex or expensive set up of the infrastructure. Other applications of GPRS technology on the transportation systems, which has been proposed in the literature, have been focused on providing inter-vehicles communication for driver assistance.

Cellular networks have been considered due to the reliability with respect to other technologies. Cellular Infrastructure has a higher guarantee level in the propagation of the alerting messages. Since Cellular network provides a radio infrastructure, it allows the possibility to rapidly transmit the alerting message through a centralized unit, also providing different traffic information.

Overall Comparison of the Emerging Technologies

After we have presented a review of the emerging technologies that could be used as a base for vehicular networks connectivity, it is necessary to analyze the pros and cons of the different approaches presented. As can be seen, two emerging technologies are the main candidates to be used for vehicular networks communication: cellular networks, IEEE 802.11p and WiMAX.

On the one hand, the main advantages of cellular technology are coverage and reliable security, besides the infrastructure is already in place. Several countries have been using cellular networks for development of Intelligent Transportation projects. However, the main disadvantage of the cellular networks technology is the relatively high cost, together with limited bandwidth and latency make it impossible to use as a main means of communication.

On the other hand, although the fundamental technology is the same for IEEE 802.11p and WiMAX, the biggest difference between them is in coverage area. This translates into more base stations required for 802.11, which means the cost of deployment of the vehicular network infrastructure is increased in a considerable way. 802.11p base stations cannot support as many users as WiMAX base stations. In general, 802.11p was only designed to support a few users per base station (around ten) with a fixed channel size of 20 MHz per base station. WiMAX was designed to support one to no more than five hundred users per base station, each with a variable channel size from 1.5 MHz to 20 MHz (Vaughan-Nichols, 2004). There are also frequency band differences. WiMAX uses licensed spectrum whereas 802.11p uses unlicensed spectrum. WiMAX uses one of the unlicensed frequencies, but also supports two other frequencies that are licensed. What that means is that WiMAX technology includes many advantages, such as robust security features, good quality of service, and mesh and smart antenna technology that will allow better utilization of the spectrum resources.

As can be seen, the problem cannot be solved by a single technology, it is necessary to combine different emerging technologies for a complete solution of transportation systems. Using all emerging technologies in a single, uniform system would result in increased flexibility and redundancy, thus improving applications' performance. The follow section presents how the emerging technologies are being applied by the countries and regions of the world in the area of transportation systems in order to solve the problems that they face in their big cities.

INTELLIGENT TRANSPORT APPLICATIONS

Nowadays there is a variety of private and government initiatives that focus on developing and deploying applications for the control of transportation systems, among which are:

- the U.S. Department of Transportation (DOT) (http://www.rita.dot.gov/),
- the Intelligent Transportation Society of America (http://www.itsa.org/),
- the ERTICO project of the European Union (http://www.ertico.com/),
- the European Council for Automotive R&D (http://www.eucar.be/),
- the European Automobile Manufacturers' Association (http://www.acea.be/) and
- the Ministry of Land, Infrastructure, Transport and Tourism of Japan (http://www.mlit.go.jp/index_e.html).

As previously mentioned, *ITS* covers broad development fields, and is or will be implemented in various schemes, but the fields of *ITS* can be identified by user services, which represent what the system will do from the perspective of the user. Some user services can be grouped on:

- *Travel and traffic management.* This service group includes the planning travel information, drivers on route information, guides of route, ridematching and reservation, traveler services information, traffic control, incident management, travel demand management, emissions testing and mitigation and highway-rail intersection.
- *Public transportation management.* Here are included public transportation management, en-route transit information, personalized public transit and public travel security.
- *Emergency management.* This group includes emergency notification, personal security, and emergency vehicle management.
- *Advanced vehicle safety systems.* It brings together services to support the driver in order to improve safety on the road, such as, longitudinal collision avoidance, lateral collision avoidance, intersection collision avoidance, vision enhancement for crash avoidance, safety readiness, pre-crash restraint deployment and automated vehicle operation.

The rest of the section shows some of the most important projects in the transportation area that are being developed in the different regions of the world.

RITA Project: Research and Innovative Technology Administration

RITA project (http://www.rita.dot.gov/) is an initiative of The U.S. Department of Transportation's ITS program. This program is based on the fundamental principle of intelligent vehicles and intelligent infrastructure and the creation of an intelligent transportation system through integration within and between these two components.

Some of the main projects included in RITA are:

- *Intelligent infrastructure.* Focused on creating the necessary infrastructure for the intelligent transportation system establishment. This project impulses ten big developments:
  - *Freeway Management.* There are six major ITS functions that make up freeway management systems:
    - Traffic surveillance systems use detectors and video equipment to support the most advanced freeway management applications.
    - Traffic control measures on freeway entrance ramps, such as ramp meters, can use sensor data to optimize freeway travel speeds and ramp meter wait times.
    - Lane management applications can address the effective capacity of freeways and promote the use of high-occupancy commute modes.
    - Special event transportation management systems can help control the impact of congestion at stadiums or convention centers. In areas with frequent events, large changeable destination signs or other lane control equipment can be installed. In areas with occasional or one-time events, portable equipment can help smooth traffic flow.
    - Advanced communications have improved the dissemination of information to the traveling public.
    - Motorists are now able to receive relevant information on location specific traffic conditions in a number of ways, including dynamic message signs, highway advisory radio, in-vehicle signing, or specialized information transmitted only to a specific set of vehicles.
  - *Arterial management.* Arterial management systems manage traffic along arterial roadways, employing traffic detectors, traffic signals, and various means of communicating information to travelers. These systems make use of information collected by traffic surveillance devices to smooth the flow of traffic along travel corridors. They also disseminate important information about travel conditions to travelers via technologies such as dynamic message signs (DMS) or highway advisory radio (HAR).
  - *Crash prevention and safety systems.* These systems detect unsafe conditions and provide warnings to travelers to take action to avoid crashes. These systems provide alerts for traffic approaching at dangerous curves, off ramps, restricted overpasses, highway-rail crossings, high-volume intersections, and also provide warnings of the presence of pedestrians, and bicyclists, and even animals on the roadway. Crash prevention and safety systems typically employ sen-

sors to monitor the speed and characteristics of approaching vehicles and frequently also include environmental sensors to monitor roadway conditions and visibility. These systems may be either permanent or temporary. Some systems provide a general warning of the recommended speed for prevailing roadway conditions. Other systems provide a specific warning by taking into account the particular vehicle's characteristics (truck or car) and a calculation of the recommended speed for the particular vehicle based on conditions. In some cases, manual systems are employed, for example where pedestrians or bicyclists manually set the system to provide warnings of their presence to travelers.

- *Road weather management activities*. This development includes road weather information systems (RWIS), winter maintenance technologies, and coordination of operations within and between state departments of transportation. ITS applications assist with the monitoring and forecasting of roadway and atmospheric conditions, dissemination of weather-related information to travelers, weather-related traffic control measures such as variable speed limits, and both fixed and mobile winter maintenance activities.
- *Electronic payment systems* employ various communication and electronic technologies to facilitate commerce between travelers and transportation agencies, typically for the purpose of paying tolls and transit fares. Pricing refers to charging motorists a fee or toll that varies with the level of demand or within the time of the day.
- *Traveler information applications* use a variety of technologies, including Internet websites, telephone hotlines, as well as television and radio, to allow users to make more informed decisions regarding trip departures, routes, and mode of travel. Ongoing implementation of the designated 511 telephone number will improve access to traveler information across the country.
- *Incident management systems* can reduce the effects of incident-related congestion by decreasing the time to detect incidents, the time for responding vehicles to arrive, and the time required for traffic to return to normal conditions. Incident management systems make use of a variety of surveillance technologies, often shared with freeway and arterial management systems, as well as enhanced communications and other technologies that facilitate coordinated response to incidents.
- *ITS applications in emergency management* include hazardous materials management, the deployment of emergency medical services, and large and small-scale emergency response and evacuation operations.
- *ITS applications for commercial vehicle operations* are designed to enhance communication between motor carriers and regulatory agencies. Examples include electronic registration and permitting programs, electronic exchange of inspection data between regulating agencies for better inspection targeting, electronic screening systems, and several applications to assist operators with fleet operations and security.

    - *ITS can facilitate the safe, efficient, secure, and seamless movement of freight*. Applications being deployed provide for tracking of freight and carrier assets such as containers and chassis, and improve the efficiency of freight terminal processes, drayage operations, and international border crossings.
- Intelligent vehicles. Focused on creating intelligent vehicle systems for the intelligent transportation system establishment.
    - To improve the ability of drivers to avoid accidents, vehicle-mounted collision warning systems (CWS) continue to be tested and deployed. These applications use a variety of sensors to monitor the vehicle's surroundings and alert the driver of conditions that could lead to a collision. Examples include forward collision warning, obstacle detection systems, and road departure warning systems.
    - Numerous intelligent vehicle technologies exist to assist the driver in operating the vehicle safely. Systems are available to aid with navigation, while others, such as vision enhancement and speed control systems, are intended to facilitate safe driving during adverse conditions. Other systems assist with difficult driving tasks such as transit and commercial vehicle docking.
    - In an effort to improve response times and save lives, collision notification systems have been designed to detect and report the location and severity of incidents to agencies and services responsible for coordinating appropriate emergency response actions. These systems can be activated manually (Mayday), or automatically with automatic collision notification (ACN), and advanced systems may transmit information on the type of crash, number of passengers, and the likelihood of injuries.

ERTICO: ITS Europe

ERTICO–ITS Europe was founded at the initiative of leading members of the European Commission, Ministries of Transport and the European Industry. ERTICO is the network of Intelligent Transport Systems and Services stakeholders in Europe. ERTICO works on a portfolio of activities to accelerate the development and deployment of ITS across Europe and beyond. Some of the main projects included in ERTICO are:

The Cooperative Vehicle-Infrastructure Systems (CVIS) Project

CVIS project (http://www.cvisproject.org/) defines intelligent co-operative systems that are based on vehicle-to-vehicle and Vehicle to Infrastructure communications. These systems hold the promise of great improvements both in the efficiency of the transport systems and in the safety of all road users (Figure 5). Indeed intelligent Co-operative Systems increase the "time horizon", the quality and reliability of information available to the drivers about their immediate environment, the other vehicles and road users, enabling improved driving conditions leading to enhanced safety and mobility efficiency. Similarly, Co-operative Systems offer increased information about the vehicles, their location and the road conditions to the road operators and infrastructure, allowing optimized and safer use of the available road network, and better response to incidents and hazards. Intelligent Co-operative Systems will build and expand on the functionality of the autonomous and stand-alone in-vehicle and infrastructure-based systems, such as Intelligent Vehicle Safety Systems (eSafety systems),

Figure 5. The cooperative vehicle-infrastructure systems (taken by http://www.cvisproject.org/)

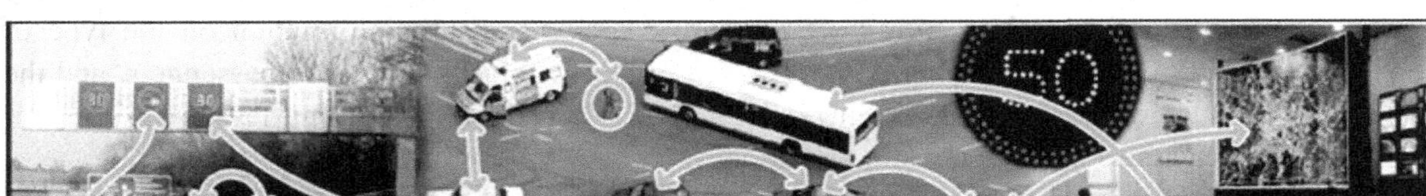

including Advanced Driver Assistance Systems (ADAS), traffic control and management systems and motorway management systems.

Among the applications that compose this initiative we can mention:

- **In-Vehicle Map updates.** To receive map updates and live traffic or road infrastructure reports, along with other relevant local information views in cars.
- **In-Vehicle Internet/Mobile Office.** To provide Internet services on board that can be used by the driver when the car is stopped or by the passengers with the car on the move.
- **Obstacle Warning.** To increase driver's awareness of obstacles by receiving live information (e.g. video) from other vehicles or roadside units.
- **Road Status Report.** To alert other drivers (and infrastructure) about road conditions / incidents (e.g. by image sharing and possibly by store and forward).
- **Flexible Lane Allocation.** To increase the capacity on certain road sections in and around towns by allowing the use of bus lanes, without causing any disturbance to the public transport.
- **Area Routing and Control** To offer alternative routes in towns in the event of an accident or incident.
- **Cooperative Traveler Assistance (CTA).** To give support to drivers by planning a personalized route to follow, and to help the roadside manager to predict traffic congestions and delays as well.
- **Personalized route planning based on expected travel times.** To provide drivers with a personalized route to follow and to help the roadside manager to predict traffic congestions and delays.
- **Urban Parking Zones.** To allow advanced booking of urban parking lots (to professional and particular drivers).

eCall Driving Group Project

eCall project (http://www.esafetysupport.org/en/ecall_toolbox/driving_group_ecall/) is an initiative giving automatic and prompt notification to the emergency services of vehicles involved in a crash situation (Figure 6). This in-vehicle emergency call service is designed to speed up emergency response to road accidents, with benefits for both casualties and other road users. The emergency call can either be made manually by vehicle occupants or automatically when in-vehicle sensors, such as when airbag deployment is activated. The process is described below:

1. The eCall Generator initiate the eCall by sensors triggered and/or manually, send the in-vehicle triggered eCall to a Public Safety Answering Point (PSAP). The eCall consists of two elements: a pure voice (audio) telephone call based on 112 and the minimum set of data (MSD).

Figure 6. The e-Call architecture (taken by http://www.esafetysupport.org/en/ecall_toolbox/)

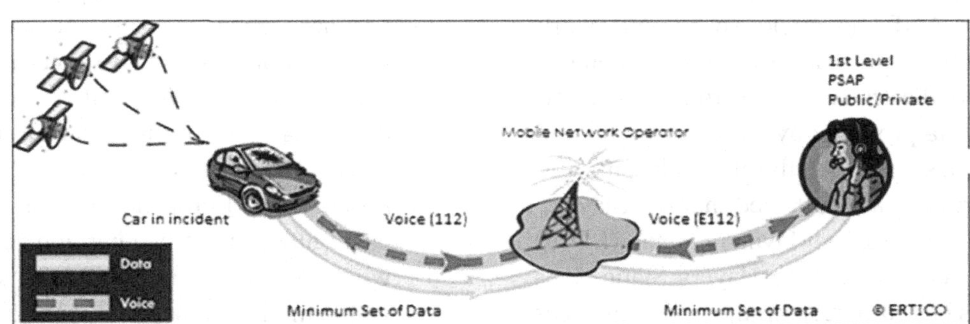

2. The eCall (data + voice) carried through the mobile network, is recognized by the mobile network operator (MNO) as a 112 emergency call, and is first handled by the MNO. Based on the 112 handling the MNO enrich the call with the CLI (caller line identification), and at the same time, according to the Universal Service Directive (USD), and the E112 recommendation, add the best location available (based on the best effort principle). After the 112 handling, the telecom operator delivers the 112-voice together with the CLI, mobile location and the **eCall MSD** to the appropriate PSAP.
3. The PSAP transmits an acknowledgement to the eCall Generator specifying that the MSD has been properly received.
4. After acquiring the accident information from the eCall generator, the PSAP can then deploy ambulance and hospital preparation more efficiently.

The SISTER: "Satcoms in Support of Transport on European Roads"

The SISTER Project (http://www.sister-project.org/) will promote the integration of satellite and terrestrial communications with GALILEO to enable mass-market take-up by road transport applications. SISTER will establish how satellite communications can be used as part of the operational implementation of ITS applications.

The GALILEO programme is Europe's initiative to develop a civil global navigation satellite system that provides highly accurate and reliable positioning, navigation and timing services. GALILEO will be compatible and interoperable with GPS and GLONASS, offering multiple civil frequencies. GALILEO will also provide instantaneous positioning services at the meter level as a result of improved orbits, better clocks, dual frequency and enhanced navigation algorithms. GALILEO will also offer guarantees on service availability and will inform users within 6 seconds of a failure of any satellite. This will allow the system to be used in safety-critical, mission-critical and business-dependent applications. The combined use of GALILEO, GPS and GLONASS systems will offer a very high level of performances for user communities and businesses.

SAFESPOT Project: Cooperative Systems for Road Safety

The SAFESPOT system (http://www.safespot-eu.org/) is aimed at improving road safety using cooperative applications based on data exchange among vehicles and among vehicles and infrastructure through an ad-hoc network.

The system is composed of a set of "nodes" (in other words SAFESPOT equipped vehicles or Road Side Units), which are able to exchange information with the other nodes through short range wireless communication (IEEE802.11p*) called the VANET (Vehicle Ad-hoc NETwork) and to use this information in order to generate messages for the drivers. A node runs applications using the data provided by the other nodes and/or by its own sensors. All the available data, after a fusion process, are collected in a multilayered Data Base named Local Dynamic Map (LDM). LDM consists of four different layers: Static Maps, Landmarks (fixed objects in the road, e.g. trees, buildings, road signs), Temporary Objects (e.g. fog area, road works), Dynamic Objects.

EasyWay Project

EasyWay (http://www.easyway-its.eu/1/) is a project for Europe-wide ITS deployment on main Trans European Road Network (TERN) corridors driven by national road authorities and operators with associated partners including the automotive industry, telecom operators and public transport stakeholders. It sets clear targets, identifies the set of necessary ITS European services to deploy (Traveller Information, Traffic Management and Freight and Logistic Services) and is an efficient platform that allows the European mobility stakeholders to achieve a coordinated and combined deployment of these pan-European services (taken from http://www.easyway-its.eu/1/).

To achieve a really good grip on the effects of ITS, it is necessary to put the European road user at the center of the perspective. The White Paper, to which the EasyWayProgramme is linked, sets targets for 2020 to make a positive impact on traffic flow, traffic safety and the environment. From analysis of the current effects and estimates of the potential of ITS, the following main objectives of the EasyWayProgramme have been established: Traffic safety improvement, Traffic flow/reduction of congestions, Better environment.

The main activities in EasyWay project are:

- *Europe-Wide Traveller Information Services.* This activity provides the European user with comprehensive local and peri-urban, regional and cross-border travel information with a co-modal perspective allowing for well-informed travel decisions, both pre-trip and on-trip, to be taken. The objective of this service is to provide the European traveler with relevant information in a harmonized manner which is easy to understand. This includes viable mode alternatives, such as bus, train and ferry, as well as road traffic status.
- *Europe-Wide Traffic Management Services.* This provides guidance to the European traveler and hauler on the condition of the road network. They detect incidents and emergencies implementing response strategies to ensure safe and efficient use of the road network and optimize the existing infrastructure for all transport, including across borders.
- *Freight and Logistics Services.* Freight and Logistics services provide comprehensive, seamless, accurate and dynamic information about road conditions and accompany many traffic management measures to improve road network performance. Such information enables informed route choices, thus improving transport efficiency. Cross-border network management, proper monitoring, handling of dangerous and oversized goods transport and easily understandable advice to all drivers will increase traffic safety on the TERN. The provision of relevant information about national regulations and restrictions as well as designated routes and administrative handling are important issues for future "e-commerce" services for freight. The proposed services will accommodate the growing flow of Heavy Goods Vehicles (HGV) on the TERN through capacity management and rerouting advice. This includes supporting the transfer of goods transport from road to other modes through

> integrated information services and physical transfer hubs. Co-modality can be achieved by facilitating the shift from one transport mode to another via the harmonization of standards and the integration of the various transport modes into efficient logistics chains.

EasyWay projects will enhance access to modal and intermodal exchange points for the European freight community.

The Large-Scale European Field Operational Test on Active Safety Systems (euroFOT)

Vehicle manufacturers, automotive suppliers, institutes and other stakeholders have joined forces in a "smart drive" to test various intelligent in-vehicle systems across Europe, with the aim of making our road transport safer, more efficient, and more comfortable.

euroFOT (http://www.eurofot-ip.eu/*)* is establishing a comprehensive, technical, and socio/economic assessment programme for evaluating the impact of intelligent vehicle systems on safety, the environment, and driver efficiency. The project is assessing several technically mature systems using vehicles that include both passenger cars and trucks across Europe.

The results of euroFOT are expected to be a major contributor to the processes of deploying ICT systems for transport across Europe. The insights gained during the project will help policymakers decide on the right policy framework, and business leaders to make informed decisions on the best way to bring these technologies to the market.

Some developed technologies are explained as follow (Figure 7):

a) Adaptive Cruise Control (ACC) uses headway sensors to continuously measure the distance to other vehicles, automatically adjusting the speed to ensure the vehicle does not get too close to the one in front. The driver activates the cruise control by setting the desired maximum speed and then

Figure 7. Some examples of the intelligent in-vehicle systems developed at "Smart-Drive"

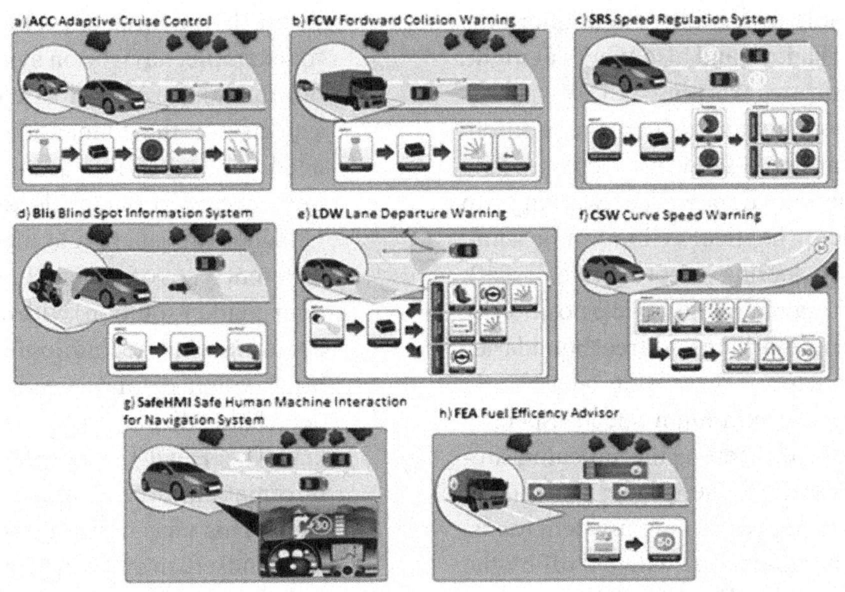

selecting the time gap to the vehicles in front. ACC then adjusts the vehicle's speed to match that of preceding vehicle as necessary.

b) Forward Collision Warning (FCW) can help avoid rear-end impacts or minimize the effects of these type of collisions. A radar installation continuously scans the area in front of a vehicle. If it then approaches too close to another vehicle, then the driver is alerted via sound and light signals. If the risk of a collision increases despite the warnings, the brakes are pre-charged to prepare for efficient braking by the driver. When a collision is imminent and the driver does not react, the car automatically brakes to reduce the impact of the accident. There are variations in the level of implementation of brake support in different models.

c) Speed Regulation System help to maintain the speed limit according to the road where a vehicle is.

d) Blind Spot Information System uses small cameras in each side mirror to detect when a car or motorcycle has entered the driver's blind spot. A warning light then indicates that another vehicle is in that position. The system is able to recognize and ignore the car's own shadow, and also works at night.

e) Lane Departure Warning (LDW) assists the driver to maintain his/her lane position, giving a warning if the vehicle crosses lane markings unintentionally. The warning can be acoustic or haptical (vibration or small torque on the steering wheel or driver's seat). The system maintains the vehicle position by detecting lane markings or street boundaries via a video sensor. A warning occurs only above a certain minimum speed. Specific driver actions, e.g. setting the indicator, suppress the warning. The system is intended to operate on highways or equivalent roads, and can if necessary be switched off by the driver. Impairment Warning (IW) alerts tired and distracted drivers. A camera monitors the car's movements between the lane markings and calculates the risk of the driver losing control of the vehicle. A message in the display advises the driver if it is time to take a break.

f) Curve-speed warning (CSW) technology has been developed to help drivers identify potentially dangerous situations if a bend in the road is taken too fast, and warn the driver in advance allowing him time to react properly. The information about such bends is drawn from pre-existing digital maps of the road and analysis of the geometric characteristics of the bend. By combining this information with external factors such as weather conditions and estimates of road friction, the maximum recommended speed for the bend is estimated. If the vehicle is approaching at a speed higher than the recommended value, the system can warn the driver of the potential hazard, prepare the safety systems in the vehicle, or actively inhibit further acceleration of the vehicle.

g) Safe Human Machine Interaction – Navigation. For all in-vehicle information and communication systems intended for use by the driver while the vehicle is in motion, for example, navigation systems and traffic information, essential safe design and use aspects for the human/machine interface need to be taken into account. The navigation system provides location and route guidance information to the driver. Several different types of system (e.g. OEM fitment, after-market solution) with different display positions and technologies (e.g. central information display, head-up, or separate detachable display) are already on the market. The Head-Up Display puts selected information directly in the driver's line of sight. This virtual display is projected onto the windscreen and can be easily seen in all light conditions. The driver, by avoiding the need to refocus from long distance to close up, can take in information such as speed or route directions far more quickly.

h) Fuel efficiency adviser (FEA): Dynafleet, a transport information system from Volvo Trucks provides in real time the current location of vehicles, their fuel consumption, messages, driver times, service intervals and much more. Fuel-efficient driving, or eco-driving, is supported through on-board functions for the driver as well as follow-up reports in the back-office system Dynafleet Online.

As we can see, there is a great effort in different regions of the world in order to solve the traffic problems that they are facing. We can observe that each responsible actor is trying to contribute to solve the transportation problems. However, now the main challenge will be the integration of all works into a one solution that will help to make more efficient and safer the transportation systems.

CONCLUSION

The modern society demands safe and efficient transportation systems. One of the main priorities of different countries of the world is to improve safety, reliability, adaptability and quality of transport services. There is a high effort in research and development of those intelligent transportation systems that can meet increasing traffic requirements, reduce negative effects on environment and ensure safety of road traffic participants. Recent Technical development has made possible the creation and usage of integrated intelligent systems.

The chapter has presented how the different emerging technologies could be applied to the creation of transportation systems in order to solve the problems that the modern society is facing. Main efforts have been focused into two development areas; the first one is the creation and implementation of intelligent infrastructures, based on emerging telecommunication technologies, in places where transport system users transit, such as roads, freeways, or streets. The second area is related to the creation of intelligent vehicles by means of the implementation of several technologies inside vehicles that allow them to communicate and take advantage of intelligent infrastructure, but, at the same time, they should be self-government vehicles in order to provide drivers the support at anytime.

The chapter presented some of the main projects that are being developed by the different regions of the world in order to achieve the creation of an intelligent transportation system that would really benefit the citizens that make use of the different means of transportation.

However, it was determined that no single technology can provide a complete solution for the creation of a vehicular network. In fact, the most feasible wireless solution shall use a combination of technologies to enable spreading valuable information that allows the transportation systems to increase their safety and efficiency. The solution consists of a combination of different emerging technologies. This allows the network to use aspects from all available network infrastructures. Essentially, each technology will have to be applied in a complement way, not compete with it. The devices that are integrated into the vehicles must support multiple technologies and provide seamless handovers. The future work will have to be focused to the management of the new integrated environment and the development of intelligent algorithms that allow providing the service and information to end-users based on the current environment.

In this chapter the advances that have been reached in the establishment of intelligent transportation systems have been demonstrated as well as the engagement that government and private initiative have established with the citizens to offer safer, more efficient in addition to more reliable means of transportation and communication routes. However, there is a lot of work to make. It is necessary to carry out studies of usability, acceptation of the technology, and several kinds of proofs related with the users in order to analyze if the goals have been fulfilled.

One of the main essentials to success or fail in technology is the users′ approval, so that all efforts to apply new technologies in the transport system should be supported by extensive research on needs of users, otherwise all objectives to achieve an intelligent transportation system may never be realized.

REFERENCES

Aguirre, J. L., & Domínguez, J. H. (2007). Traffic light control through agent-based coordination. In *IASTED international conference on artificial intelligence and applications, Innsbruck, Austria* (pp. 145–150). Calgary, Canada: ACTA Press.

Akyildiz, I. F., Su, W., Sankarasubramaniam, Y., & Cayirci, E. (2002). A survey on sensor networks. *IEEE Communications Magazine*, 102–114. doi:10.1109/MCOM.2002.1024422

Al-Khateeb, K., & Johari, J. A. (2008). Intelligent dynamic traffic light sequence using RFID. *International Conference on Computer and Communication Engineering, (ICCCE)*, Kuala, Lumpur (pp. 1367-1372). New York: IEEE.

Andrisano, O., Verdone, R., & Makagawa, M. (2000). Intelligent transportation system: The role of third-generation mobile radio networks. *IEEE Communications Magazine*, 144–151. doi:10.1109/35.868154

CEN. (2005). *TS 17261: Intelligent transport systems - Automatic vehicle and equipment identification - Intermodal good transport architecture and terminology*. Brussels: Comité Européen de Normalisation.

Chatzigiannakis, V., Grammatikou, M., & Papavassiliou, S. (2007). Extending driver's horizon through comprehensive incident detection in vehicular networks. *IEEE Transactions on Vehicular Technology*, 3256–3265. doi:10.1109/TVT.2007.906410

Commission for Global Road Safety. (2009). *Make roads safe, a decade of action for road safety*. London: Commission for Global Road Safety.

DOT. (2006). *IEEE 1609 - Family of standards for wireless access in vehicular environments (WAVE)*. Washington, DC: U.S. Department of Transportation, Research and Innovative Technology Administration.

EEA. (2006). *Greenhouse gas emission trends and projections in Europe 2006*. Copenhagen: European Environment Agency.

EEA. (2006). *Technical report 9: Urban sprawl in Europe - the ignored challenge*. Copenhagen: European Environmental Agency.

ERTICO-a. (1998). *Intelligent city transport: A guidebook to intelligent transport systems*. Brussels: ITS City Pioneers Consortium.

ERTICO-b. (1998). *Intelligent city transport: ITS planning handbook*. Brussels: ITS City Pioneers Consortium.

ERTICO-c. (1998). *Intelligent city transport: ITS toolbox*. Brussels: ITS City Pioneers Consortium.

Evensen, K. (2006). *CALM architecture and CALM M5 convenor*. Dallas, TX: Q-Free.

Ganguly, S., Navda, V., Kim, K., Kashyap, A., Niculescu, D., & Izmailov, R. …Das, S. (2006). *Performance optimizations for deploying VoIP services in mesh networks*. Retrieved from http://www.wings.cs.sunysb.edu/~anand/paper/jsac06.pdf

3GPP. (2009). *3GPP - 3rd Generation Partnership Project*. Retrieved from http://www.3gpp.org

Hubaux, J. P. (2004). *Technical report IC/2004/24 a survey of inter-vehicle communication.* Lausanne, Switzerland: School of Computer and Communication Sciences.

Intelligent Transportation Society of America. (2009). *ITS America*. Retrieved from http://www.itsa.org/

Intelligent Transportation Society of Australia. (2009). *ITS Australia*. Retrieved from http://www.its-australia.com.au

Intelligent Transportation Systems Society of Canada. (2009). *ITS Canada*. Retrieved from http://www.itscanada.ca

ISO TC204. W. G. (2008). *ISO TC204 WG16 CALM*. Retrieved 2009, from http://www.calm.hu/

ISO TC 204, W. 1. (2006). *Intelligent transport systems — System architecture, taxonomy and terminology — Procedures for developing ITS deployment plans utilising ITS system architecture.*

Japan, I. T. S. (2009). *ITS Japan*. Retrieved from http://www.its-jp.org/english/

Kulkarni, G. H., & Waingankar, P. G. (2007). Fuzzy logic based traffic light controller. *International Conference on Industrial and Information Systems (ICIIS)*, Penadeniya, Sri Lanka (pp. 107-110). New York: IEEE.

Lan, K. C., Wang, Z., Berriman, R., Moors, T., & Hassan, M. (2007). Implementation of a wireless mesh network testbed for traffic control. *Proceedings of 16th International Conference on Computer Communications and Networks (ICCCN)*, Honolulu, HI (pp. 1022-1027). New York: IEEE.

Lee, M., Jianliang, Z., Young-Bae, K., & Shrestha, D. (2006). *Emerging standards for wireless mesh technology* (pp. 56–63). IEEE Wireless Communications.

Lee, T., Chiang, H., Perng, J., Jiang, J., & Wu, B. (2009). Multi-sensor information integration on DSP platform for vehicle navigation safety and driving aid. In *Proceedings of the 2009 IEEE International Conference on Networking, Sensing and Control*, Okayama, Japan (pp. 653-658). New York: IEEE.

Lee, U., Park, J. S., Amir, E., & Gerla, M. (2006). FleaNet: A virtual market place on vehicular networks. In *IEEE V2VCOM,* San Francisco (pp. 1-8). New York: IEEE.

Lockheed Martin Federal Systems. (1997). *ITS communications document.* Washington, DC: Federal Highway Administration, US Department of Transportation.

Lomax, T., & Schrank, D. (2005). *Urban mobility study*. College Station, TX: Texas Transportation Institute.

McCann, S. (2009, September 14). *Official IEEE 802.11 Working Group Project timelines*. Retrieved September 30, 2009, from http://grouper.ieee.org/groups/802/11/Reports/802.11_Timelines.htm

Mobility and Transport. Directorate General. (2009). *Intelligent transport system: A smart move for Europe.* Brussels: European Communities.

Nandan, A., Das, S., Pau, G., Gerla, M., & Sanadidi, M. (2005). *Co-operative downloading in vehicular ad-hoc wireless networks. IEEE WONS, Switzerland* (pp. 32–41). New York: IEEE.

Qi, L. (2008). Research on intelligent transportation system technologies and applications. In *Workshop on Power Electronics and Intelligent Transportation System*, (pp. 529-531).

Qing, X., Mak, T., Jeff, K., & Sengupta, R. (2007). Medium access control protocol design for vehicle–vehicle safety messages. In *IEEE Transaction on Vehicular Technology* (pp. 499–518). New York: IEEE.

Sormani, D., Turconi, G., Costa, P., Frey, D., Migliavacca, M., & Mottola, L. (2006). Towards lightweight information dissemination in intervehicular networks. In *ACM VANETS, Los Angeles, CA* (pp. 20–29). New York: ACM.

Tseng, S. T., & Song, K. T. (2002). Real-time image tracking for traffic monitoring. In *The IEEE 5th International Conference on Intelligent Transportation Systems*, (pp. 1-6). New York: IEEE.

UNFPA. (2007). *Technical report: State of world population 2007: Unleashing the potential of urban growth*. New York: United Nations Population Fund.

Vaughan-Nichols, S. (2004). *Achieving wireless broadband with WiMAX* (pp. 10–13). IEEE Computer.

Wang, F. Y., & Lsansing, S. J. (2004). From artificial life to artificial societies: New methods in studying social complex systems. *Journal of Complex Systems and Complexity Science*, pp. 33-41.

Wang, M. H., Chao, K. H., & Lee, R. H. (2008). An intelligent traffic light control based on extension neural network. In *Knowledge-based intelligent information and engineering systems* (pp. 17–24). Berlin: Springer.

Wen, W. (2008). A dynamic and automatic traffic light control expert system for solving the road congestion problem. *Expert Systems with Applications: An International Journal*, pp. 2370-2381.

Williams, B. (2008). *Intelligent transport systems standards*. Norwood, MA: Artech House Publishers.

WiMAX Forum. (2009). *WiMAX forum*. Retrieved from http://www.wimaxforum.org/home/

Xu, Q., Mak, T., Ko, J., & Sengupta, R. (2004). *Vehicle-to-vehicle safety messaging in DSRC. ACM VANET, Philadelphia, PA* (pp. 19–28). New York: ACM.

APPENDIX

Table of acronyms

ACN	Automatic Collision Notification.
ADAS	Advanced Driver Assistance Systems.
CALM	Communications Access for Land Mobiles.
CTA	Cooperative Traveler Assistance.
CVIS	Cooperative Vehicle-Infrastructure Systems.
CWS	Collision Warning Systems.
DMS	Dynamic Message Signs.
DOT	Department of Transportation.
DSRC	Dedicated Short Range Communication.
EEA	European Environment Agency.
ETSI	European Telecommunications Standards Institute.
FAR	False Acceptable Rate.
FCC	Federal Communications Commission.
FRR	False Rejection Rate.
GDP	Gross Domestic Product.
GPRS	General Packet Radio Service.
HAR	Highway Advisory Radio.
HGV	Heavy Goods Vehicle.
IPv6	Internet Protocol version 6.
ISO	International Organization for Standardization.
ITS	Intelligent Transportation Systems.
IVC	Inter-Vehicular Communication.
LDM	Local Dynamic Map.
MAC	Media Access Control.
MANET	Mobile Ad Hoc Networks.
OBE	On-Board Equipment.
OBU	On-Board Units.
OEM	Original Equipment Manufacturer.
PMP	Point-to-MultiPoint.
PSAP	Public Safety Answering Point.
P2P	Peer-to-Peer.
RFID	Radio Frequency IDentification.
RITA	Research and Innovative Technology Administration.
RWIS	Road Weather Information Systems.
TERN	Trans European Road Network.
VANET	Vehicle Ad-hoc NETwork.
VHF	Very High Frequency.

continues on following page

Table of acronyms continued

VII	Vehicular Infrastructure Integration.
V2I	Vehicle-to-Infrastructure.
V2R	Vehicle to Roadside.
V2V	Vehicle-to-Vehicle.
WAE	Wireless Access Equipment.
WAVE	Wireless Access for Vehicular Environment.
WLAN	Wireless Local Area Network.
WMN	Wireless Mesh Network.
WMN-AP	Wireless Mesh Network Access Point.
WSN	Wireless Sensor Network.

Chapter 15
IP Mobility Support in Hybrid Wired–Mobile Ad Hoc Networks

Luis Armando Villaseñor-González
CICESE Research Center, Mexico

ABSTRACT

Mobile ad hoc networks (MANETs) make use of a distributed routing mechanism to support connectivity between nodes within the ad hoc network. A wireless ad hoc network can be deployed for multiple applications, such as extending the coverage of wire based networks, where interworking is achieved via wireless access routers. However, the implementation of a hybrid (i.e. wired and wireless) network is not straightforward and several issues must be solved for these types of deployments to become a reality. One concern is related to terminal mobility while preserving ongoing communication sessions over IP networks; as a mobile node moves from one subnetwork to a new subnetwork, a mobility protocol (e.g. Mobile IP) is required for the mobile node to preserve a communication session without having to reestablish the session with a correspondent node. This issue is more complex in a hybrid network where the wireless domain is composed of a mobile ad hoc network (MANET). For instance, MANET routing protocols usually do not account for the connectivity toward a wired network, such as the Internet, via a single or multiple access routers. As a result, there are multiple routing issues that must be taken into consideration to support interconnectivity between nodes located in a hybrid network topology. The main contribution of this work is to present a review on the state of the art of IP mobility support for hybrid wired–MANETs and discuss some of the relevant issues in this area. In addition, two case studies are presented where macromobility (e.g. Mobile IP) and micromobility (Mobile-IP – HAWAII) protocols are implemented to support IP mobility on hybrid networks.

DOI: 10.4018/978-1-60960-027-3.ch015

INTRODUCTION

During the last decade there has been a tremendous growth in the implementation and deployment of wireless local area networks (WLANs), in particular those based on the IEEE 802.11 standard. A wireless network can be classified either as a wireless infrastructure network, or as a wireless ad hoc network. A wireless infrastructure network is characterized by the use of a central coordination device (e.g. an access point or a base station), whereas in a wireless ad hoc network there is no central coordination device and the wireless nodes must implement a distributed coordination mechanism (i.e. routing protocol) to enable communication between them. Experts believe that wireless networks will not replace the wired infrastructure, but instead they will provide additional capabilities, such as extending the coverage of service provided by a wired network like the Internet. An additional benefit of wireless networks is the support of mobility as the user is no longer constrained to a physical connection within a building.

A mobile ad hoc network (MANET) is defined as an autonomous network where there is no single point of coordination and it is formed by a collection of mobile nodes which communicate using the wireless medium. These types of networks are characterized by dynamic topologies and limited bandwidth. Usually, mobile nodes have limited resources, such as batteries. In a MANET, each mobile node (MN) can transmit information using a direct link or a multi-hop link to propagate packets to a destination node; as a result, all the mobile nodes in a MANET must implement the routing functionality (Benzaid, Minet, & Agha, 2004). Furthermore, the design of fast and efficient routing protocols is essential in the performance of mobile ad hoc networks.

The mobile nodes in a MANET do not require implementing a specific hierarchical subnetwork addressing scheme, as opposed to wired networks, where a node is usually assigned a single IP address which belongs to a specific subnetwork. As a result, there are different routing issues related to the support of connectivity between mobile nodes in a MANET and a wired network, such as the Internet, which is based on a hierarchical addressing scheme. On the other hand, routing protocols for MANETs generally provide a node with routing information allowing the forwarding of packets to other nodes inside the MANET, and there is usually no implicit support for the routing of packets toward a wired network via a single or multiple access routers.

There is currently an intrinsic problem related to mobility in computer data networks which implement the IP network protocol stack; this issue is related to the fact that IP addresses are commonly used as both an identifier and a locator of a node within a subnetwork (Wisely, Eardley, & Burness, 2002). When a node changes its point of attachment to the network (e.g. the MN moves to a different subnetwork or access router) the assigned IP address can no longer be used as a locator for the node in the new subnetwork. To address this issue, there have been different proposals like Mobile IP, which is a well- known and accepted approach to support macromobility (i.e. mobility between different administrative domains). On the other hand, mobility inside a single administrative domain is called micromobility; micromobility protocols try to reduce the overhead, packet loss and path reestablishment latency which is commonly experienced by macromobility protocols during handoff. The most common micromobility protocols are HAWAII, Cellular IP and Hierarchical Mobile IP (Campbell, Gomez & Kim, 2002).

A hybrid network (i.e. wired and wireless) introduces additional challenges; one concern is related to terminal mobility while preserving ongoing communication sessions during a layer 3 handoff procedure. As a MN moves from one subnetwork to a new subnetwork, a mobility protocol is required to allow the MN to preserve a communication session without having to reestablish the session with a correspondent node; this issue

Figure 1. Hybrid (i.e. wired-wireless) network topology

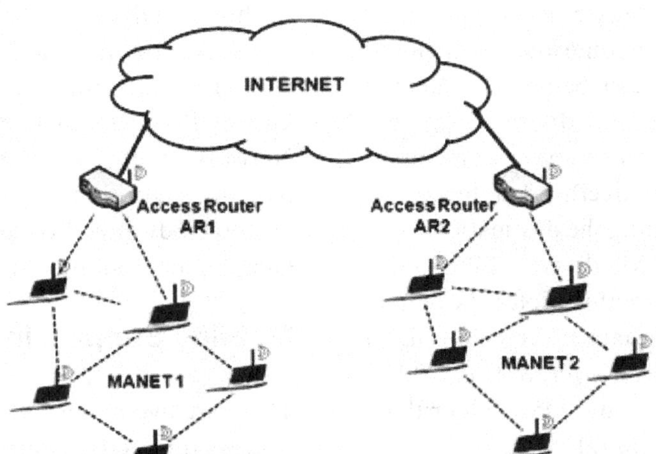

becomes more complex in a hybrid network where the wireless domain is composed by a MANET. For instance, MANET routing protocols usually do not account for the connectivity toward a wired network, such as the Internet. As a result, there are multiple routing issues that must be taken into consideration for the support of interworking between nodes located in a hybrid network. Figure 1 illustrates a hybrid network topology where the wireless domains are composed by MANETs.

This chapter provides a review on the state of the art of IP mobility support for hybrid wired and wireless ad hoc networks. The chapter is then complemented with two case studies where the author has analyzed the support of the Mobile IP protocol for macromobility, and the HAWAII protocol for micromobility over hybrid networks.

WIRELESS AD HOC NETWORKS AND MOBILE IP

MANET routing algorithms can be classified into two different categories: non-positional algorithms and positional algorithms. Non-positional algorithms can be further classified as proactive (table-driven), reactive (on-demand), or hybrid. Proactive, or table-driven algorithms, periodically propagate control messages to update the network topology, making routes immediately available when they are needed. The disadvantage of these algorithms, however, is that they require additional bandwidth to periodically transmit topology traffic, resulting in significant network congestion because each individual node must maintain the necessary routing information and is responsible for propagating topology updates in response to instantaneous changes in network connectivity (Perkins, 2000). Important examples of proactive protocols include Optimized Link State Routing (OLSR) (Clausen & Jacquet, 2003) and Topology Dissemination Based on Reverse Path Forwarding (TBRPF) (Ogier, Lewis, & Templin, 2004). These two protocols record the routes for all of the destinations in the ad hoc network, resulting in minimal initial delay (latency) when communicating with arbitrary destinations. The proactive protocols store route information before it is actually needed and are table driven because the information is available in well-maintained tables.

On the other hand, on-demand, or reactive protocols, acquire routing information only as needed. Consequently, reactive routing protocols often use less bandwidth for maintaining route tables. The disadvantage of these protocols, however, is that the Route Discovery (RD) latency for many applications can substantially increase. Most applications may suffer delay when they start because a destination route must be acquired before communication can begin. On-demand protocols make use of a route discovery process before the first data packet can be sent, resulting in reduced control traffic overhead at the cost of increased latency in finding the destination route (Zou, Ramamurthy, & Magliveras, 2002). Examples of these types of routing protocols include Ad hoc On-Demand Distance Vector (AODV) routing (Perkins, Belding-Royer, & Das, 2003), and Dynamic source Routing (DSR) algorithms (Johnson, Maltz, & Hu, 2007).

A routing protocol that combines both proactive and reactive approaches is called a hybrid routing protocol. The most popular protocol in this category is the Zone Routing Protocol (ZRP) (Schaumann, 2002). In ZRP, the network is divided into overlapping routing zones that can use independent protocols within and between each zone. ZRP is considered a hybrid routing protocol because it combines proactive and reactive approaches to maintain valid routing tables without causing excessive overhead. Communication within a specific zone is realized by the Intrazone Routing Protocol (IARP), which provides effective direct neighbor discovery (proactive routing). On the other hand, communication between different zones is realized by the Interzone Routing Protocol (IERP), which provides routing capabilities among nodes that must communicate between zones (reactive routing).

Scalability represents the principal disadvantage of purely proactive and reactive routing algorithms in highly mobile environments. A second disadvantage is their very low communication throughput, which sometimes results from a potentially large number of retransmissions (Mauve, Widmer, & Hartenstein, 2001). To overcome these limitations, however, several new types of routing algorithms that employ geographic position information have been developed, including: Location-Aided Routing (LAR) (Ko & Vaidya, 1998), Distance Routing Effect Algorithm for Mobility (DREAM) (Basagni, Chalamtac, & Syrotiuk., 1998), Grid Location Service (GLS) (Li, Jannotti, Couto, Karger, & Morris, 2000), Greedy Perimeter Stateless Routing for Wireless Networks (GPSR) (Karp & Kung, 2000), Location Routing Algorithm with Cluster-Based Flooding (Santos, Edwards, Edwards, & Seed, 2005), and Geographic Routing Protocols (Zollinger, 2005).

Mobility Support in IP

There are two major functions assigned to the IP address of a node within a specific subnetwork. The IP address can be used to identify a particular host in the whole network, and it can also be used to find a route between endpoints. In this way, the packets addressed to a specific destination are routed via intermediate router nodes according to the IP address of the destination endpoint. Consequently, a MN requires an IP address to provide identification to the terminal, and may require a temporary IP address while it is located in a foreign network. The Mobile IP protocol extends the functionality of IP by supporting these two different functionalities of an IP address, one which is used for identification and the second one which is used for localization (Wisely, Eardley, & Burness, 2002).

The mobility support at the network layer has the advantage of being independent from the link layer. Mobile IP allows terminal mobility while preserving ongoing communication sessions; this is achieved by means of preserving the session identifier, associated to the mobile node's IP address, which is denoted as the home address. As the mobile node moves outside of its home IP subnetwork a new localization identifier is generated; this new localization identifier is denoted as the care-of-address (CoA) and indicates the current mobile node localization in the network. There are currently two versions for the support of terminal mobility, one defined for IPv4 and a second one defined for the IPv6 network protocol stack, namely Mobile IPv4 (MIPv4) (Perkins, 2002) and Mobile IPv6 (MIPv6) (Johnson, Perkins, & Arkko, 2004). It should be noted that the IPv6 protocol stack implements the support for mobility, but this mechanism is only effective in wireless networks where the mobile nodes are one-hop away from the access router (Lamont, Wang, Villasenor, Randhawa, & Hardy, 2003).

Some of the general terminology employed in Mobile IP includes the following terms:

- *Correspondent Node* (CN): A node that communicates with a MN. It can be mobile or stationary and may be located anywhere in the Internet.
- *Home Address*: An IP address that is assigned for an extended period of time to a MN and is usually employed as part of the session identifier by the application.
- *Care-of-Address* (CoA): An address associated with the MN when located in a foreign network.
- *Home Agent* (HA): A router located at the mobile node's home network; this device keeps a record of the mobile node's CoA when the MN is located in a foreign network.
- *Foreign Agent* (FA): A router on a mobile node's visited network. A foreign agent is not required in IPv6 as its functionality has been incorporated as part of the router services.
- *Encapsulation*: Consists in adding a new IP header to an IP packet, as a result the original IP packet becomes part of the payload in a new IP packet.
- *Tunnel*: A delivery path between two nodes where the IP packets are encapsulated.

Figure 2 illustrates the Mobile IP architecture and describes the procedure employed as part of the mobility protocol:

- The mobile agents advertise their presence via Agent Advertisement messages. A MN may optionally solicit an Agent Advertisement message.
- A MN receives these Agent Advertisements and determines whether it is on its home network or on a foreign network.
- When a MN moves away from its home network, it gets a CoA from the foreign network, either by request or by listening to an agent advertisement. While the MN is located away from its home network, the MN registers every new CoA with its HA.
- A packet addressed toward the mobile node arrives to the home network via standard IP routing (Step 1 in Figure 2).

Figure 2. Mobile IP network architecture

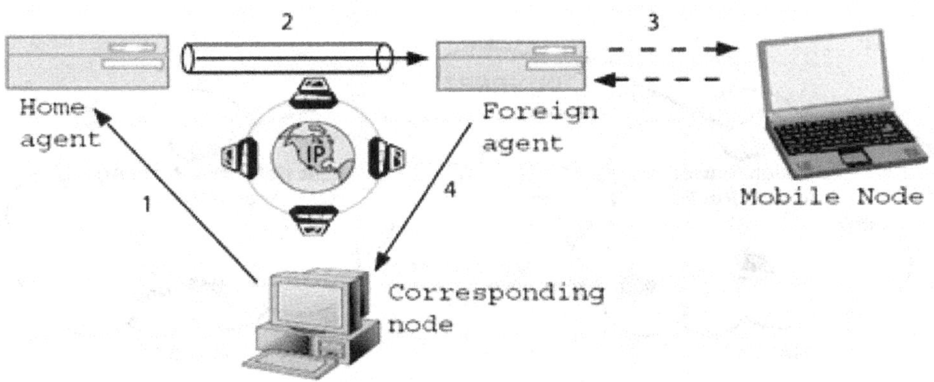

- The packet is intercepted and encapsulated by the HA; the encapsulated packet is tunneled by the HA to the MN by employing the mobile's CoA (Step 2 in Figure 2).
- The packet is taken off the tunnel by the FA and sent to the MN (Step 3 in Figure 2).
- The packets sent by the MN to the correspondent node are directly handled by means of standard IP routing (Step 4 in Figure 2).
- In the reverse direction, packets sent by the MN are generally delivered to their destination using standard IP routing mechanisms, not necessarily passing through the home agent.

Figure 2 shows that messages are triangulated as the CN's messages are first sent to the HA, then these messages are encapsulated and sent from the HA to the MN, finally messages from the MN to the CN are sent using a direct route. To avoid this triangulation, a known procedure is to implement the route optimization mechanism; the idea is that the correspondent node will be able to directly send encapsulated packets to the mobile node by employing the mobile's CoA. The route optimization procedure requires an update on the CN's protocol stack to support the Mobile IP protocol.

CASE STUDY I: MOBILE IPV6 AND OLSR

The case study presented in this section is based on a previous work by the author published in (Villasenor-Gonzalez, Gonzalez-Sanchez, Sanchez-Garcia, & Aquino-Santos, 2008). This case study is concerned with the implementation of the MIPv6 protocol.

In Mobile IP, a MN is always identified by its home address regardless of its current point of attachment in the Internet (Wisely, Eardley, & Burness, 2002). When the MN moves to a foreign network, the home address can no longer be used as a localizer of the MN; in this case, MIPv6 relies on the use of a temporary address denominated the CoA address which will be used for localization purposes. Once a MN has acquired a CoA in a foreign network, the MN will register this address with the home agent via a Binding Update (BU) message; next, the home agent transmits a Binding Update Acknowledgment which is transmitted back to the MN; this process is illustrated in Figure 3.

The Optimized Link State Routing (OLSR) Protocol

The OLSR is defined as a proactive routing mechanism for mobile ad hoc networks (Clausen

Figure 3. Mobile IPv6 handoff procedure

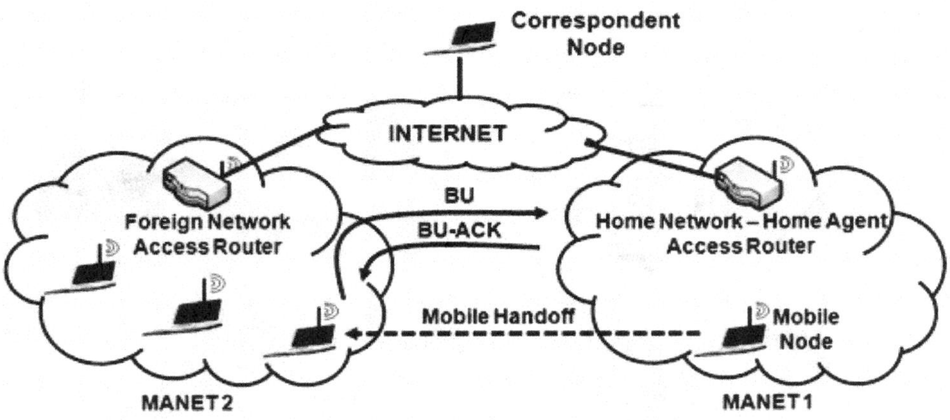

& Jacquet, 2003). It optimizes the pure link state protocol by propagating the topology information via selected nodes, which are called multi-point relays (MPRs). In the OLSR protocol, the algorithm relies on the transmission of two control messages to propagate topology information: the HELLO message and the Topology Control (TC) message. Each node in the MANET will periodically transmit a HELLO message to identify itself to any one-hop neighbor node; in addition, the HELLO message includes information regarding the one-hop neighbors of the node transmitting the HELLO message. As the MN receives the HELLO messages, it can create a one-hop neighbors list, as well as a two-hop neighbors list. By employing the OLSR topology lists, a MN can proceed to select a subset of one-hop neighbor nodes which will become MPR nodes. The selection of MPR nodes follows a heuristic algorithm, where the main objective is to create a subset of one-hop neighbor nodes which can provide connectivity (i.e. routing) to the complete set of two-hop neighbor nodes. A description of the MPR selection algorithm can be consulted in (Clausen & Jacquet, 2003).

MIPv6 and OLSR Interoperability Issues

This case study is related with the interoperability issues that arise during the integration of wired networks implementing the MIPv6 protocol and mobile ad hoc networks implementing the OLSR routing protocol.

In most cases, the routing protocol supports the discovery of routes among the member nodes of the ad hoc network and does not provide routing support toward nodes in the wired network via an access router. In (Ruiz, Ros, & Gomez-Skarmeta, 2005) the authors describe a list of interoperability issues between Mobile IP and routing protocols for MANETS, some of these issues include:

- *Discovering Internet Gateways*: The mobile nodes in the MANET should be able to discover the Internet Gateway (i.e. access router) to support connectivity toward the wired network.
- *Address Auto-configuration*: This refers to the process by which a MN, in a MANET located in a foreign network, obtains and configures an IP address.
- *Reaching a Destination*: The routing mechanism for the MANET should be able to provide route discovery support toward nodes in the wired and wireless ad hoc networks.
- *Duplicate Address Detection*: The mobile nodes should acquire a unique IP address within the foreign network and must avoid two nodes to end up with the same IP address.
- *Name Resolution*: A name resolution service might be required by the mobile nodes when joining a foreign network, in addition to the auto-configuration mechanism for the IP address.

Mobile IPv6 Support for OLSR

This section presents a proposal for the interoperability between OLSR and MIPv6; this work was initiated as part of a research project at the Communications Research Centre in Ottawa Canada, where a testbed was developed and a couple of articles were published as part of this work (Lamont, Wang, Villasenor, Randhawa, & Hardy, 2003; Lamont, Wang, Villasenor, Randhawa, Hardy, & McConnel, 2002). Later, this work was extended as part of a master's degree thesis developed at the CICESE Research Center (Gonzalez-Sanchez, 2005), where the interoperability issues are analyzed under a controlled simulation scenario, as opposed to a testbed scenario; two different approaches to support such interoperability are described to support the discovery of the access router in a foreign network by the mobile node (MN):

1. The mobile nodes discover the access router via the Host Network Association (HNA) OLSR message.
2. The mobile nodes discover the access router via an upgraded HELLO message.

Interoperability via the HNA Message

In this approach, the access router will broadcast and inform about its existence to other nodes in the MANET via the HNA message, which is a supported OLSR message (Clausen & Jacquet, 2003). It should be noted that HNA messages are designed to support the discovery of access routers in a MANET; consequently, the use of the HNA messages can be considered to be the preferred way of providing the interoperability with MIPv6, as in the implementations presented in (Lamont, Wang, Villasenor, Randhawa, & Hardy, 2003) and (Benzaid, Minet, & Agha, 2004). The HNA message includes the following information: the Internet Gateway IPv6 address and the network address prefix. By means of the HNA message, a MN can discover if it is located in a foreign network, in such case it will proceed to auto-configure an IP address to be used as a CoA address; similarly, the MN will discover the IPv6 address of the access router and define this to be a default route in the routing table. It should be noted that the OLSR protocol does not define a specific mechanism for the auto-configuration procedure of MIPv6 via the HNA messages.

In the proposal presented in this case study, the MIPv6 stateless auto-configuration process at the MN is triggered by a self-sent Router Advertisement (RA) message which is created by the MN once the HNA message has been received. In this way, the Mobile IPv6 protocol will assume it has received a standard RA message from an access router and will proceed to calculate a CoA in exactly the same way as if the MN had been located one-hop away from the real access router. To support this approach, the OLSR protocol has been modified to implement the creation of a router advertisement message which is similar to the one used in MIPv6. In addition, the Mobile IPv6 protocol requires the implementation of a primitive (i.e. to communicate between protocols) to support the registration of the IPv6 CoA address into the OLSR agent space. This last requirement is essential for the MN to inform other nodes in the MANET of its new CoA address via the OLSR HELLO message.

Interoperability via an Upgraded HELLO Message

The second approach makes use of the OLSR HELLO messages. Each MN periodically transmits a HELLO message toward the one-hop neighbors (i.e. the time-to-live parameter in the HELLO packet is set to 1). In this proposal, the OLSR packets are modified to include a new message, which we denote as the Access Router Information (ARI) message; the ARI message is transmitted along with the HELLO messages. This new message includes the same information as in the HNA message, that is, the access router's IPv6 address and the network address prefix; in addition, a hop-count field is included. The resulting ARI message format is 36 bytes long, as illustrated in Figure 4.

The access router includes the required information in the ARI message, which is broadcasted along with the HELLO messages; when the one-hop neighbor nodes receive the HELLO messages and discover the existence of the access router (via the ARI message), they locally register the access router information and proceed to generate an ARI message which will be transmitted along with their own broadcasted HELLO messages. The hop count field in the ARI message is increased by one as soon as new mobile nodes learn of the existence of the access router and begin to transmit their own ARI message. In this

Figure 4. ARI message format

0 1 2 3
0 1 2 3 4 5 6 7 8 9 0 1 2 3 4 5 6 7 8 9 0 1 2 3 4 5 6 7 8 9 0 1

AR Hop Count	Reserved	Checksum
Access Router IPv6 Address (16 bytes)		
Network Address Prefix (16 bytes)		

way, the multi-hop MANET nodes will eventually discover the existence of the access router including the hop distance toward it. It should be noted that ARI messages are only transmitted by the nodes that have discovered an access router.

Once the access router has been discovered by a MN, via the ARI messages, the OLSR agent proceeds to create and transmit a MIPv6 RA message which will be sent to itself (i.e. source and destination addresses are the same). In this way, the RA message will be received by the mobile's MIPv6 process thus allowing the MN to compute a CoA.

Reducing Layer 3 Mobile Handoff Latency

During preliminary tests, it was discovered early that the performance of the integrated MIPv6 and OLSR processes was greatly dependent on the capability of the MN to discover a route to the access router. The latency associated to the discovery of routes in OLSR is highly related to the transmission cycle of the OLSR TC messages, which are transmitted every 5 seconds, as suggested in (Clausen & Jacquet, 2003). In other words, the layer 3 mobile handoff procedure depends on the time required by the MN to find a route to the access router in addition to the time required by the MN to acquire a CoA. Furthermore, once the MN has acquired a CoA and a route to the access router is available, the binding update procedure with the home agent cannot be successfully executed until the access router, in the foreign network, has discovered a route toward the mobile's CoA address. That is, even if the MN has a CoA and the capability to transmit packets to the home agent, the home agent cannot successfully communicate with the MN until the access router in the foreign network discovers a route toward the MN identified by its CoA in the MANET. As a result, the MN will not be able to receive the Binding Update Acknowledgement message from the home agent if no route has been established from the access router toward the MN using the MN's CoA address. In addition, it is not possible to forward data packets from the home agent toward the MN, as the forwarded packets make use of the CoA address for delivery. To solve this issue, a mechanism is proposed to help reduce the layer 3 mobile handoff latency; the proposal is based on allowing the MN to generate an OLSR TC message. This TC message is generated once a CoA address has been acquired by the MN; it should be noted that this is a special TC message as the MN does not need to be a multi-point relay node to transmit it. Recall from the OLSR description, that TC messages are only transmitted by the MPR nodes and they are used to inform other nodes that they are the last hop toward the multi-point relay selectors. In this way, as the mobile nodes receive a TC message, they can proceed to update their routing tables and establish a route, via the multi-point relay nodes, toward the multi-point relay selectors. In our case, the special TC message is used to inform other nodes in the MANET that the

MN (which is currently identified in the foreign network with the home address) is the last hop to the node with the CoA address, which in this case is the MN itself. This special TC message only includes the CoA address of the MN.

Description of the Simulation Scenario

The simulation scenario is composed of two networks, a home network and a foreign network, which are both connected to the Internet. Figure 5 illustrates the scenario used to evaluate the layer 3 handoff latency of the proposed mobility mechanism. In the illustrated scenario, the mobile node (MN) begins at its home network and is located at a two-hop distance from its access router, which implements the functionality of the home agent. Different topologies are evaluated by increasing the hop distance of the MN toward the access router in the foreign network. It should be noted that the mobile nodes in the foreign network are assumed to be static; this is important for the derivation of the handoff latency results in terms of the mobility protocol while avoiding any additional topology issues, such as, outdated routes (due to mobility) within the MANET. Consequently, the performance results will provide an upper bound for the layer 3 handoff latency during a handoff procedure. It should be noted that the layer 3 handoff latency will suffer in a real network scenario with mobile nodes, as the handoff latency becomes a function of the specific mobility parameters of a given scenario. In summary, the simulation results presented in this work can be used as a benchmark (i.e. upper bound) to evaluate other proposals that involve the implementation of MIPv6 and OLSR.

The following group of delay metrics is used to evaluate the performance of the proposed implementations for the integration of MIPv6 and the OLSR protocol:

- T_{TC1}: is defined as the time it takes the MN to receive the first TC message from the multi-point relay node selected by the access router in the foreign network; in Figure 5, this node is denoted as MPR_{FN-AR}. This metric is important as it provides a measure of the time required by the MN to discover a route to the access router. This metric is evaluated as, $T_{TC1} = t_{TC1} - t_h$, where t_{TC1} is the time when the MN received the first TC message from the MPR_{FN-AR} node

Figure 5. Simulation scenario

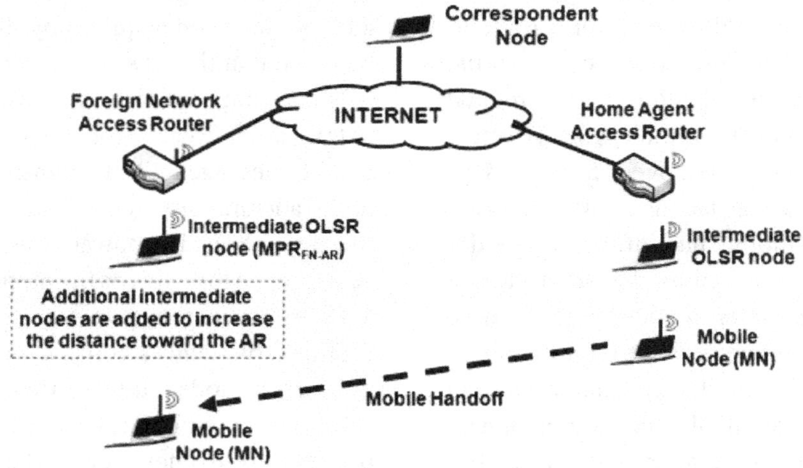

and t_h is the time when the MN received the first HELLO in the foreign network.

- $T_{COA\text{-}TC1}$: is defined as the time it takes the MN to acquire a CoA after the node has received the first TC message from the $MPR_{FN\text{-}AR}$. This metric is evaluated as $T_{COA\text{-}TC1} = t_{COA} - t_{TC1}$, where t_{COA} is the time when the MN acquired the CoA.
- T_{COA}: is defined as the time it takes the MN to acquire a CoA after it has arrived in the foreign network. This metric is evaluated as $T_{COA} = t_{COA} - t_h$.
- T_{Data}: is defined as the time it takes the MN to start receiving data traffic once the layer 3 mobile handoff process has finalized.

As part of the simulation, a correspondent node transmits CBR traffic to the MN to trigger the tunneling functionality of the Mobile IPv6 protocol (i.e. packets are forwarded from the home agent to the MN). The simulation results were gathered using the NS-2 simulation tool (The Network Simulator - ns-2, 2009). The NS-2 tool is a discrete event simulation tool and was developed for research related to computer networks and network protocols. The wireless interfaces of the mobile nodes implement the IEEE 802.11b standard and are configured in NS-2 with a coverage range of 200 meters. The CBR packet size is 1000 bytes and they are generated every 50 ms. Table 1 shows the default configuration parameters for the OLSR protocol (Clausen & Jacquet, 2003).

The simulated scenarios implement different approaches to discover the access router. The scenarios using the HNA message are denoted by HNA-N (i.e. normal implementation) and HNA-T (i.e. improved implementation). Similarly, the scenarios implementing the enhanced HELLO message functionality are denoted as HEL-N (i.e. normal implementation) and HEL-T (i.e. improved implementation). It should be noted that the improved implementation scenarios are related with the transmission of the TC message by the MN once it has acquired a CoA. The numerical results were derived by calculating the average result of 1000 simulations for each specific scenario.

Table 1. OLSR configuration parameters

HELLO Interval	2 sec.
TC Interval	5 sec.
HNA Interval	5 sec.

Performance Results

Figure 6 shows the average time $T_{AVG\text{-}TC1}$ required by the MN to receive the first TC message from $MPR_{FN\text{-}AR}$; these results include scenarios where the MN arrives at the foreign network and is located at a different hop distance from the access router. From the $T_{AVG\text{-}TC1}$ results, it is clear that the MN learns of the last-hop toward the access router (i.e. the multi-point relay node of the access router) sooner if it is located at 2-hops from the access router. On the contrary, if the MN is located at 3 or more hops from the access router, $T_{AVG\text{-}TC1}$ increases and stabilizes around 5.8 – 5.9 seconds. This is explained by the fact that at a 2-hop distance the $MPR_{FN\text{-}AR}$ node is the neighbor of the MN. Once the MN selects $MPR_{FN\text{-}AR}$ as its own multi-point relay node, the TC message is immediately broadcast by $MPR_{FN\text{-}AR}$. For hop distances greater than 2, the MN cannot receive the TC messages from $MPR_{FN\text{-}AR}$ until the MN has selected a multi-point relay node (i.e. from the 1-hop neighbor set of nodes) which can forward the TC messages generated by $MPR_{FN\text{-}AR}$. Hence, the $T_{AVG\text{-}TC1}$ increases for these scenarios, as the MN has to select one neighbor node to act as a multi-point relay node and then it has to wait for the $MPR_{FN\text{-}AR}$ to generate a new TC message.

Figure 7 shows the average time $T_{AVG\text{-}COA\text{-}TC1}$ required by the MN to acquire a CoA once it has received the first TC from $MPR_{FN\text{-}AR}$. It can be observed that the implementation of the enhanced HELLO message reduces the latency associated with the MN acquiring a CoA. This can be ex-

Figure 6. Average time the MN receives the first TC message from the $MPR_{FN\text{-}AR}$

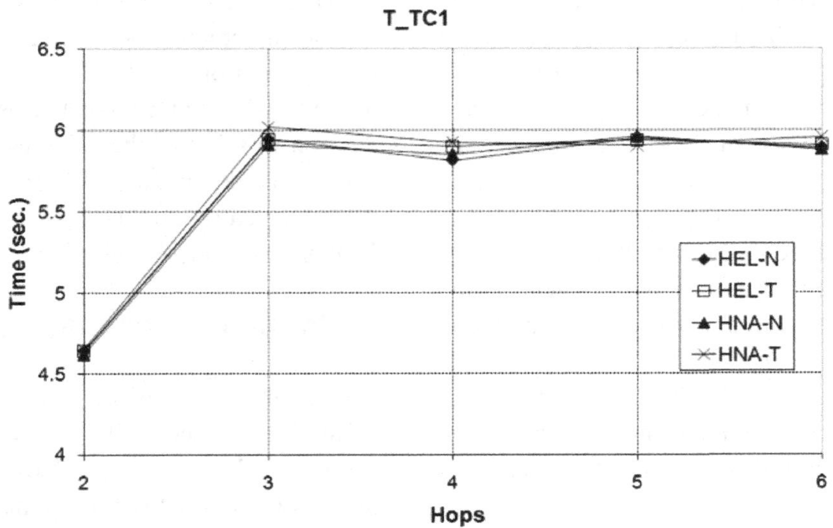

plained by the fact that HELLO messages are transmitted every 2 seconds, as opposed to the HNA messages which are transmitted every 5 seconds. It should be noticed that the mechanism employed to reduce the layer 3 mobile handoff latency (i.e. the MN transmits a TC message as soon as it gets a CoA) does not provide an additional performance improvement for the $T_{AVG\text{-}COA\text{-}TC1}$ metric in any of the simulated scenarios. This last observation is explained by the fact that $T_{COA\text{-}TC1}$ is a random variable which depends on the transmission process of the TC and HNA messages (or the enhanced HELLO messages). On the other hand, the transmission of the

Figure 7. Average time required by the MN to acquire the CoA after T_{TC1}

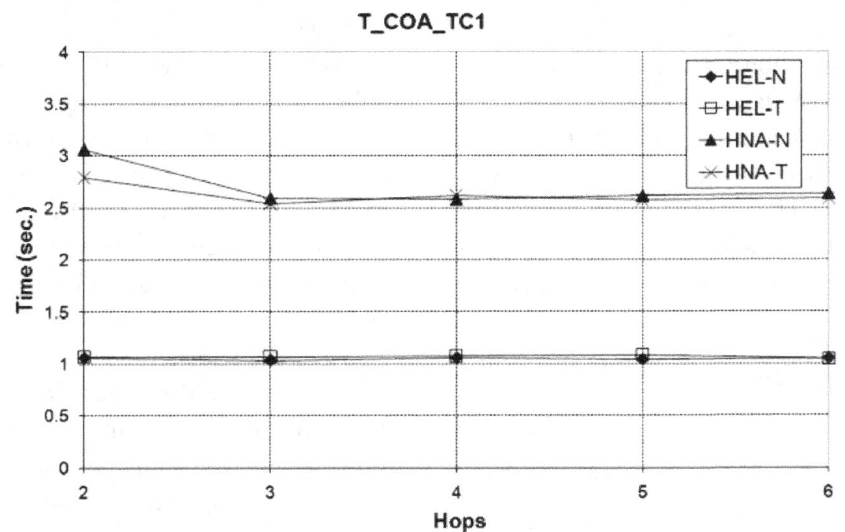

special TC message (i.e. employed to reduce the layer 3 mobile handoff latency) is only executed after the CoA address has been configured, so it is not related to the $T_{AVG\text{-}COA\text{-}TC1}$ metric.

Figure 8 shows the average time $T_{AVG\text{-}COA}$ required by the MN to acquire a CoA in the foreign network. It is observed that the scenarios implementing the enhanced HELLO functionality provide an improved performance, as opposed to those making use of the HNA functionality; this is a direct consequence of the performance results observed in Figure 7. Also, from Figure 8 it can be observed that in general $T_{AVG\text{-}COA}$ increases as the hop distance to the access router increases. This would seem to be inconsistent with the results from the $T_{AVG\text{-}TC1}$ and $T_{AVG\text{-}COA\text{-}TC1}$ metrics, illustrated in Figure 6 and Figure 7, which present constant results regardless of the hop distance toward the access router. In other words, one might be compelled to consider that $T_{COA} = T_{TC1} + T_{COA\text{-}TC1}$, but this is not true as the metric T_{TC1} does not represent the actual time at which the MN has acquired a route toward the access router. Recall that TC messages only provide information regarding the last hop (i.e. the multi-point relay node) toward a group of nodes (i.e. the multi-point relay selectors); as a result, the MN cannot establish a route to the access router until it has received and processed TC messages from the intermediate multi-point relay nodes (i.e. between the access router and the MN). Then, as the hop distance between the access router and the MN increases, the number of cycles to receive the TC messages from the intermediate multi-point relay nodes also increases.

Figure 9 shows the average time, $T_{AVG\text{-}DATA}$, required by the MN to start receiving data in the foreign network; this metric provides a good measure of the layer 3 handoff latency. It is clear that scenarios implementing the enhanced HELLO functionality provide an improved performance than those relying on the HNA messages functionality to trigger the stateless auto-configuration of MIPv6. Furthermore, it can be observed that the mechanism employed to reduce the layer 3 handoff latency by means of transmitting a TC message once the node has learned of his CoA does reduce handoff latency. The normal operation of the integrated mechanism in OLSR-MIPv6 shows higher handoff latency as the access

Figure 8. Average time required by the MN to acquire the CoA in the foreign network

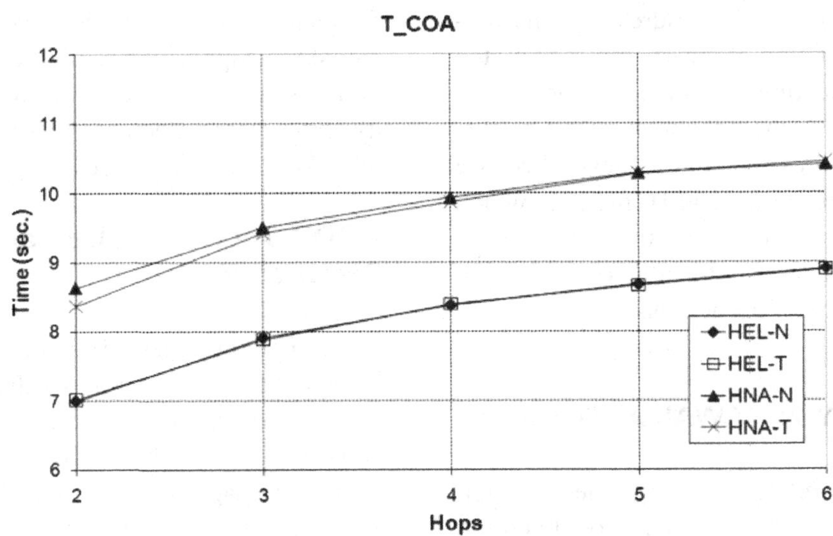

Figure 9. Average time required by the MN to start receiving data in the foreign network

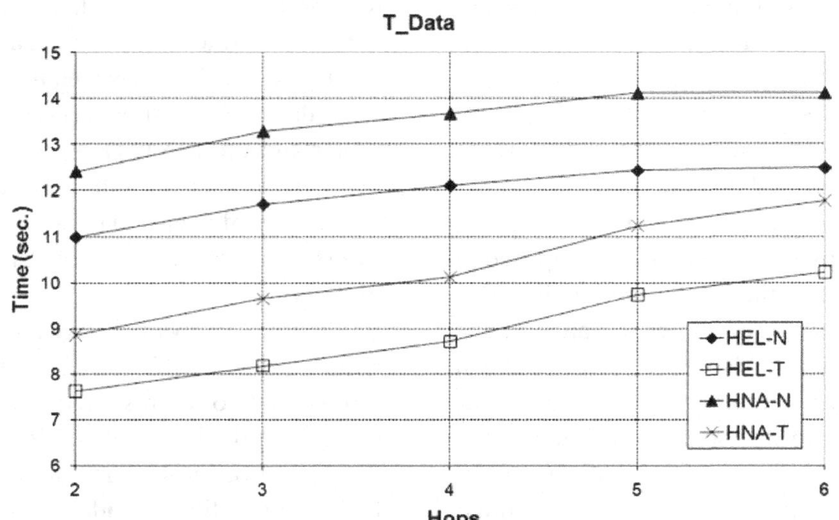

router, in the foreign network, takes too long to learn the CoA address of the MN in the foreign network. That is, the access router in the foreign network will not learn of the existence of the MN with its CoA address until a neighbor of the MN recognizes the MN with its new address (i.e. CoA) and becomes a multi-point relay node of the MN; only then this multi-point relay node can transmit a TC message to inform other nodes in the MANET of the existence of a node (i.e. the MN in the foreign network) with CoA address. On the contrary, the transmission of the TC message by the MN reduces the time required by the access router to discover the MN with its CoA; this performance improvement is achieved because the MN can transmit a special TC message which includes the CoA acquired by the MN, thus allowing other nodes in the MANET to learn sooner of the MN's CoA address.

CASE STUDY 2: HAWAII AND AODV

This case study is related with the implementation of the HAWAII micromobility protocol and the AODV MANET routing protocol and is based on the research by (Ramirez-Mondragón, 2007). Figure 10 illustrates the network architecture considered for this scenario.

The domain root router (DRR) is the gateway of the local administrative domain and provides connectivity to the Internet. Within the local administrative domain, the network is composed of routers and access routers (AR) that provide connectivity between the wired and wireless ad hoc domains. The AODV routing mechanism is implemented to support the routing of packets within the ad hoc network, and the HAWAII micromobility protocol is implemented to support the routing of packets within the wired infrastructure network.

AODV: Ad Hoc on Demand Distance Vector

The Ad hoc On-demand Distance Vector (AODV) is a reactive routing protocol that uses different topology control messages to support communication between the mobile nodes. The main topology control messages used in AODV include: Route Request (RREQ), Route Reply (RREP), Route

Figure 10. Hybrid wireless network scenario

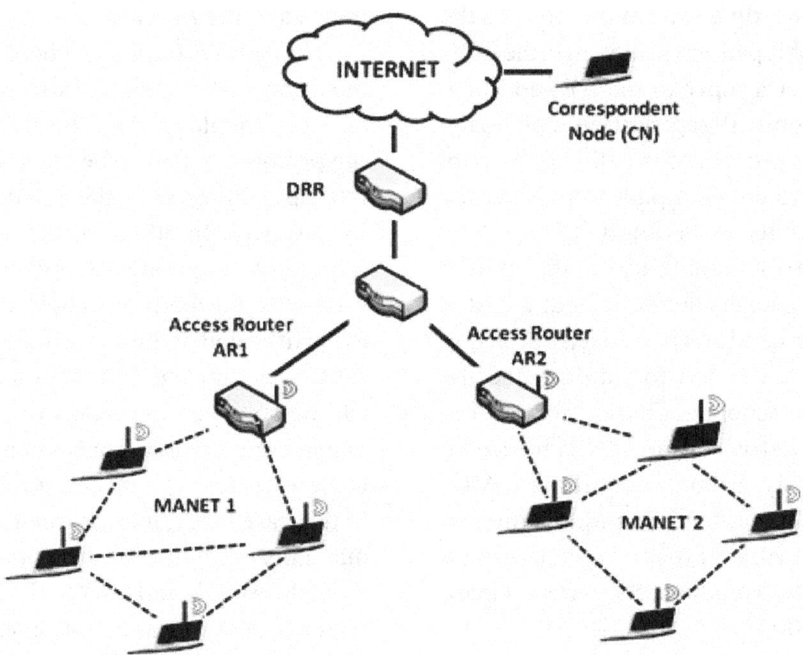

Error (RERR) and HELLO message. The AODV routing protocol tries to find the shortest route possible using the hop count metric (Perkins, Belding-Royer, & Das, 2003).

When a mobile node wants to communicate with another node and does not already have a valid route to that node, it initiates a route discovery process to locate it. The route discovery process begins with the source node broadcasting a RREQ packet to its neighbors to find a route, and these neighbor nodes rebroadcast the RREQ packet to their neighbors. This process continues until a RREQ packet finds a destination node or an intermediate node with a valid route to the destination. During the flooding of the RREQ message a reverse path (i.e. toward the sender node) is created. When the RREQ message reaches a destination node, a unicast RREP message is sent back to the source node; the RREP message uses the reverse path to reach the source node. As the RREP message travels back to the source node, a forward route is created along the intermediate nodes which propagate the RREP message. Upon receiving the RREP message, the source node can begin to send data to the destination node using the path that has been setup during the route discovery process. AODV also relies on the RERR message to report any problem along an established and active route. A source node must discover a new route upon receiving a RERR message.

Micromobility and HAWAII

The HAWAII (Handoff-Aware Wireless Access Internet Infrastructure) micromobility protocol proposes dividing the network into a hierarchy of domains. The gateway node within each domain is called the domain root router (DRR) and each mobile node has an IP address and a home domain. As the mobile node moves within a single domain, the mobile node's IP address is conserved. When a mobile node enters for the first time into a HAWAII domain, the MN sends a Mobile IP registration request to the nearest access router (AR). Next, the AR sends a HAWAII path setup message to the DRR. The routers along the path between the

AR and the DRR establish a forwarding entry to enable packet forwarding toward the MN. As the DRR receives the AR path setup message, the DRR proceeds to deliver a reply to the AR, and then the AR sends a Mobile IP registration reply to the mobile node. This procedure is called power up, and is employed to create a path to provide the MN with connectivity to the Internet.

Depending on the capability of the mobile host and the way packets are delivered, two different schemes for handoffs have been defined in HAWAII, these are the non-forwarding and the forwarding handoff schemes. The non-forwarding scheme is employed when the MN can receive data simultaneously from two different ARs, while the forwarding scheme is employed when the MN is only capable of receiving data from a single AR (Ramjee, Varadhan, Salgarelli, Thuel, Wang, & Porta, 2002).

AODV and HAWAII Interoperability

The proposed interoperable routing protocol for hybrid networks integrates the functionalities of the AODV routing protocol and the HAWAII micromobility protocol. The main objective is to be able to provide the best routing path for data to be transmitted along wired and/or wireless network segments within a single administrative domain. The case study presented herein considers two approaches for the selection of an access router by the MN. The selection criteria are made in terms of: a) the Euclidean distance between the MN and the AR; b) the number of hops between the MN and the AR.

The AODV routing protocol is used to provide routing support to the mobile nodes within the wireless domain, i.e. when a communication session is initiated and the sender and the receiver nodes are both located in the wireless segment of the hybrid network. On the other hand, the HAWAII micromobility protocol is used to control the local mobility handoffs of the mobile nodes within the hybrid network; in this way, it is possible to provide connectivity between the mobile nodes and the Internet.

The AODV routing protocol does not consider the support for packet forwarding in a hybrid network topology. As a result, the AODV routing protocols needs to be extended to support the interoperability with the HAWAII micromobility protocol. In addition, the access routers are required to implement the AODV and HAWAII protocols. Furthermore, each access router needs to be informed of the existence of the other access routers within the administrative domain. This can be achieved by means of a hybrid network management protocol or by manual configuration at the access routers in the administrative domain. In this case study, it is assumed access routers are manually configured to support the interoperability of the AODV and HAWAII protocols. It should be noted that this assumption can be considered realistic as the administrative domain is considered to be owned by a single operator which has the centralized control of the hybrid network.

The mobile nodes implement the AODV routing protocol and are required to exchange Mobile IP control messages with the access routers; however, they are not required to support HAWAII control messages. As a result of the hybrid network environment, the AODV protocol needs to be extended as the mobile nodes must be capable of identifying the access router within the administrative domain. In addition, the mobile nodes need to able to identify which node is the domain router DRR.

Within the wireless domain, the mobile nodes will receive and process AODV control messages (e.g. RREQ, RREP, RERR); in addition, as part of the HAWAII interoperability support, the mobile nodes are required to receive and process the router advertisement messages sent by the access routers. In the case of the access routers, they are also required to receive and process MIP registration requests.

When a mobile node receives a router advertisement message, it will proceed to transmit a

MIP registration request message which is sent to the node that generated the router advertisement message. Two possible scenarios may arise: a) when the mobile node receives the router advertisement from an access router located at a one-hop distance, the mobile node proceeds to transmit a MIP registration request message and the next-hop field is set to the access router's IP address; b) the mobile node receives a router advertisement message from an intermediate node (i.e. the access router is 2 or more hops away). In this last case, if the mobile node does not have a cached route toward the access router, it triggers a route discovery process to find a route toward the access router.

As part of the MIP implementation, the access routers periodically transmit router advertisement messages toward the mobile nodes in the wireless domain. However Mobile IP specifies that router advertisement messages should be transmitted with a time-to-live (TTL) set to 1; consequently, router advertisement messages are only received by the access router's 1-hop neighbor set. To address this issue, the mobile nodes are configured to forward the router advertisement messages. In this way, mobile nodes located far from the access routers are able to receive the router advertisement messages.

When a mobile node receives a router advertisement for the first time (i.e. it is not associate to any other access router), it proceeds to register with this access router regardless of the distance between the mobile node and the access router. The following procedure describes the association process: (1) the mobile node receives a router advertisement message, (2) the mobile node proceeds to transmit a MIP registration request and it is sent to the access router, (3) when the access router receives the MIP registration request it proceeds to transmit a HAWAII route update message to the domain router, (4) the HAWAII route update message is routed toward the domain router through intermediate routing nodes, (5) the domain router proceeds to transmit a HAWAII acknowledgement message to the access router, (6) finally, the access router proceeds to transmit a MIP registration acknowledgement message to the mobile. When the mobile node associates with the access router, it proceeds to register the newly discovered access router in a local agent list. The cached information includes the time to live, the expiry time of the router advertisement and the distance toward the access router. Once a mobile node is associated with an access router, the mobile node is enabled to forward the router advertisement message generated by its associated access router node.

To reduce the overhead related to the forwarding of router advertisement messages in the wireless domain, the mobile nodes are required to discard any router advertisement messages sent by an access router different to the currently associated one. Similarly, mobile nodes discard any duplicated router advertisement messages sent by the currently associated access router which have already been processed by the mobile node.

Description of the Simulation Scenario

The proposed interoperable routing mechanism for hybrid networks was implemented in the NS-2 package. Figure 11, illustrates the topology employed during simulation. The simulation scenario considers a single administrative domain composed by a wired backbone and several wireless access routers. In addition a MANET overlaps the coverage area of the multiple wireless access routers.

The simulation results include performance metrics related to the packet loss, packet delay, delay jitter, throughput and the number of handoffs; the Random Waypoint model is employed as the node's mobility model (Johnson & Maltz, 1996). Table 2 presents a summary of the simulation parameters used in NS-2.

The simulation results consider two scenarios which are evaluated in terms of the traffic load.

Figure 11. Simulated network topology

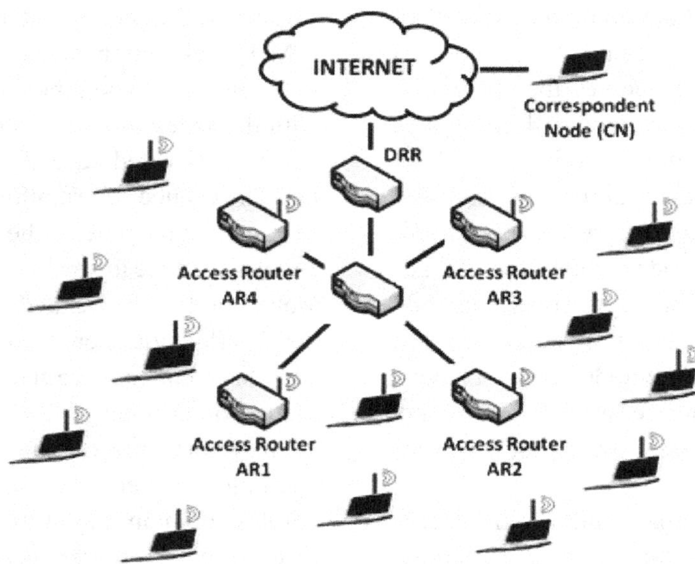

Table 2. Simulation parameters

Number of nodes	30
Average node speed	1, 2 and 4 m/s
Pause time	0 sec.
Simulation Area	1000 x 1000 m.
Simulation time	600 secs.

The first scenario considers a low traffic environment where 10% of the mobile nodes generate traffic which is sent toward other nodes in the MANET. The second scenario considers a high traffic environment where 80% of the mobile nodes generate traffic toward other nodes in the MANET. The simulation results consider three different implementations of AODV and HAWAII:

- The aodv+Hawaii implementation considers the MN will associate with any access router and will not consider any special criteria for this selection.
- The aodv+Hawaii+distance implementation considers the MN will associate with the closest distance-wise (i.e. in terms of the Euclidean distance) access router.
- The aodv+Hawaii+hops implementation considers the MN will associate with the closest hop-wise (i.e. in terms of the number of hops between the MN and the AR) access router.

Low Traffic Simulation Results

This scenario considers that 10% of the mobile nodes will establish a communication session with other nodes in the MANET. Figure 12, shows the packet loss rate as a function of the average mobile node speed. From the results it can be observed that the packet loss rate increases slightly as the mobile node increases its average speed. Furthermore, the aodv+Hawaii and aodv+Hawaii+distance show the best performance results as opposed to the aodv+Hawaii+hops implementation.

Figure 13 shows the average throughput as a function of the average mobile node speed. These results are closely related to the packet delivery rate results and clearly show that the aodv+Hawaii and aodv+Hawaii+distance provide a higher

Figure 12. Average packet loss rate results

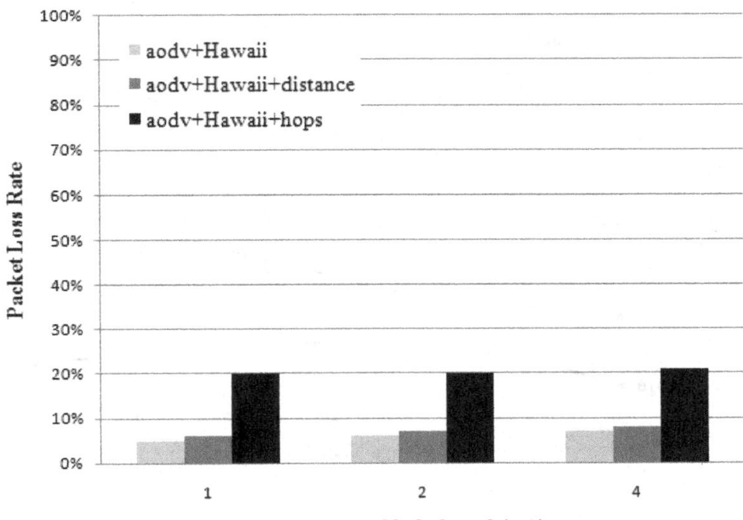

throughput as opposed to the aodv+Hawaii+hops implementation which experiences a higher packet loss rate.

Figure 14 and Figure 15 show the average jitter and the average delay, respectively, as a function of the average mobile node speed. From these results, it is clear that the aodv+Hawaii performs better than any of the other two possible implementations. Regarding the aodv+Hawaii+distance and the aodv+Hawaii+hops implementations, the simulations results indicate that the hop count criterion performs worst when compared with the distance selection criterion employed by the mobile nodes to select the access router.

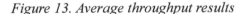

Figure 13. Average throughput results

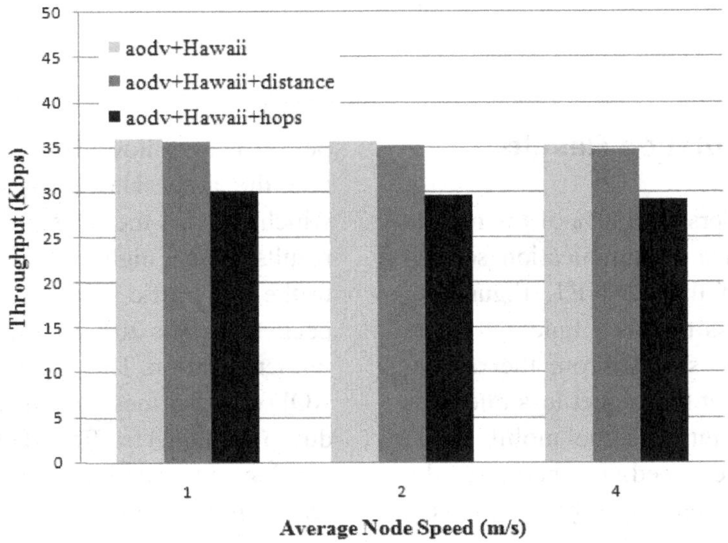

Figure 14. Average jitter results

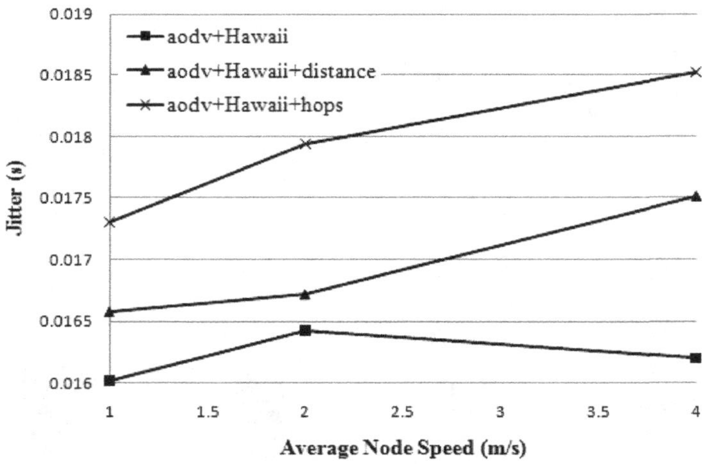

Figure 15. Average delay results

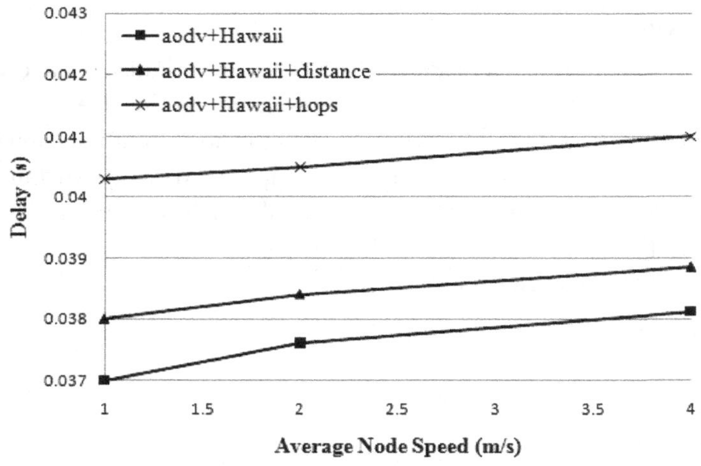

High Traffic Simulation Results

This scenario considers that 80% of the mobile nodes will establish a communication session with other nodes in the MANET. Figure 16, shows the packet loss rate as a function of the average mobile node speed. From the results, it can be observed that the packet loss rate does not change significantly as the mobile node increases its average speed. Furthermore, the aodv+Hawaii implementation shows the best performance followed by aodv+Hawaii+distance and the aodv+Hawaii+hops implementation, which delivers the worst packet loss rate. These results show a higher packet loss rate compared to the low traffic scenario where the maximum packet loss was 20% for the aodv+Hawaii+hops implementation. This is explained by the fact the AODV control messages are exposed to collisions due to the higher traffic in the network. As a result, topology information becomes unreliable, thus resulting in a higher loss rate.

Figure 16. Average packet loss rate results

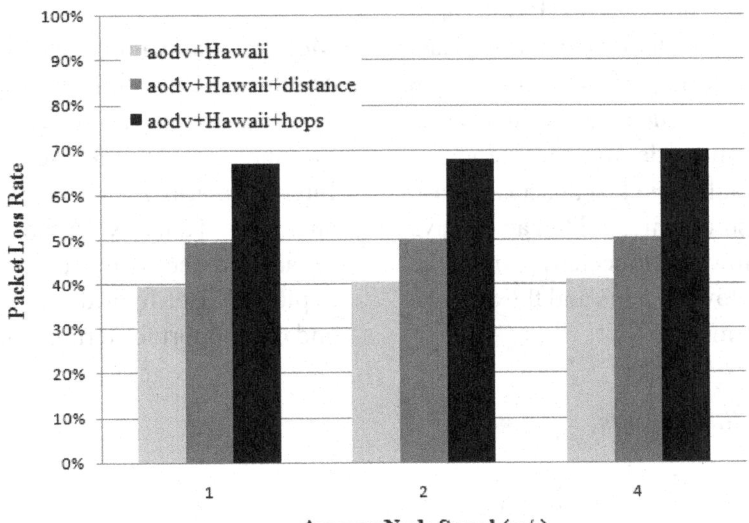

Figure 17 shows the average throughput as a function of the average mobile node speed. These results are closely related to the packet delivery rate results and clearly show that the aodv+Hawaii achieves the highest throughput followed by aodv+Hawaii+distance and finally by the aodv+Hawaii+hops implementation, which delivers the lowest throughput as a result of the higher packet loss rate.

Figure 18 and Figure 19 show the average jitter and the average delay, respectively, as a function of the average mobile node speed. From these results, it is clear that the aodv+Hawaii performs better than any of the other two possible

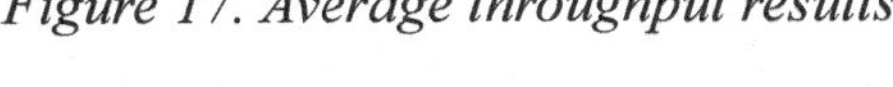
Figure 17. Average throughput results

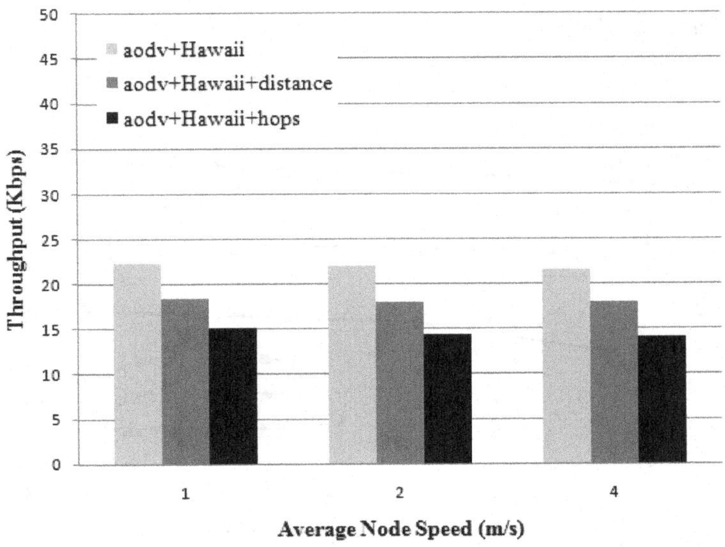

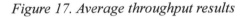

implementations. Regarding the aodv+Hawaii+distance and the aodv+Hawaii+hops implementations, the simulations results indicate that the hop count criteria performs worst when compared with the distance selection criteria employed by the mobile nodes to select the access router. From these results it is clear that an increase of network traffic results in higher jitter and delays as compared to the low traffic scenario where the jitter results were below 18.5 ms and the average delay was below 41 ms.

Figure 18. Average jitter results

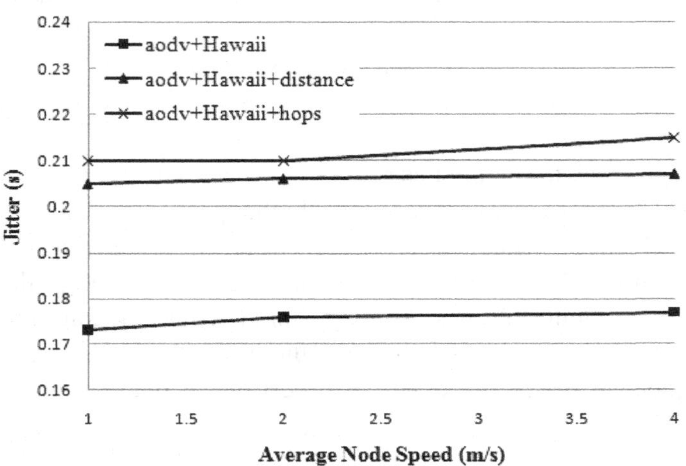

Figure 19. Average delay results

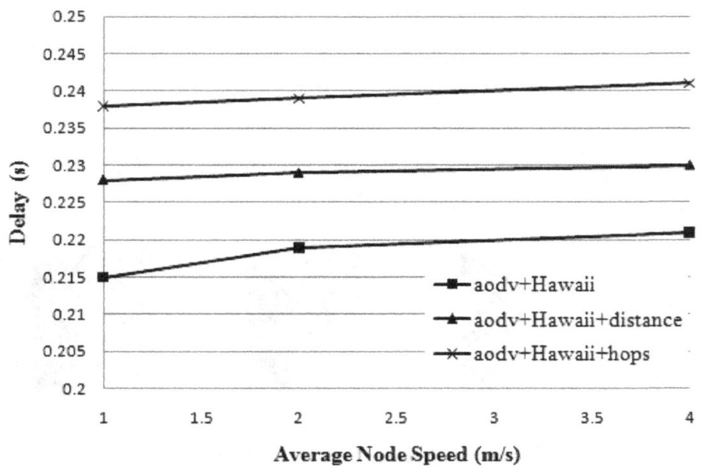

FUTURE RESEARCH DIRECTIONS

Mobile broadband is rapidly becoming a reality and there are currently new wireless technologies which are being proposed to provide this kind of support to mobile users such as Worldwide Interoperability for Microwave Access (WiMAX) and Long Term Evolution (LTE). This type of broadband access technologies will support the deployment of hybrid wired-wireless networks, and the support for terminal mobility will need to be addressed as part of the deployment of these new emerging wireless networking technologies.

The WiMAX standard is going to provide support for terminal mobility based on the IEEE 802.16e standard and further relaying capabilities are being incorporated in the IEEE802.16j standard. As a result, a new array of challenges will need to be addressed, including the interoperability and Mobile IP services with existing wireless technologies such as 802.11 (Li, Qin, Low, & Gwee, 2007) and (Pontes, Silva, José Jailton, Otavio Rodrigues, & Dias, 2008). Similarly, LTE considers the integration with non-3GPP access technologies, such as Wi-Fi, using client as well as network based mobile IP. Consequently the interoperability issues between hybrid wired and wireless networks, where the wireless segment is composed by a MANET, and the proposals to solve some of these issues (as described in this chapter) can be extended to the new emerging wireless broadband access technologies.

CONCLUSION

Terminal mobility is related with the support of a handoff operation when the mobile user changes its point of attachment to the network. One particular aspect of terminal mobility is related with the capability to continue ongoing communication sessions during the handoff operation without having to reestablish the communication session. Terminal mobility protocols can be classified in macromobility and micromobility protocols. A macromobility protocol is employed when a mobile terminal changes its point of attachment in the network from one administrative domain to a different administrative domain. On the other hand, micromobility protocols are employed when terminal mobility happens within a single administrative domain.

This chapter presented the support of terminal mobility in a WLAN hybrid networking environment and two case studies were discussed which integrated Mobile IP and HAWAII with the OLSR and the AODV MANET routing protocols, respectively.

In the case of OLSR and MIPv6, some approaches have been described to address the interoperability issues. These proposals do not rely on the modification of any ICMPv6 messages and are based on extending the functionality of some specific OLSR message types such as the HNA and HELLO messages. The numerical results have shown that several factors affect the layer 3 mobile handoff latency. One of these factors is related to the delay during the discovery of a route toward the access router, which is partly related to the T_{TC1} metric. Another factor is the time required by the mobile node (MN) to acquire the CoA, denoted in this work as T_{COA}. The route discovery process is related to the transmission cycle of the TC messages, which are used by the OLSR protocol for topology control. On the other hand, the T_{COA} metric is affected by both the route discovery of the access router, and the reception cycle of the OLSR messages required to identify the access router, which in this work are handled by the HNA and enhanced HELLO messages (i.e. using ARI messages). From the performance results, one can conclude that the use of enhanced HELLO messages reduces the layer 3 mobile handoff latency, as opposed to the use of the HNA messages which are defined in OLSR to discover access routers in a MANET. It should be noticed that this increase in performance comes at the expense of a slight increase of control overhead due to the larger OLSR packets used to carry the ARI message along with the HELLO messages; however, this may not be a critical factor as the ARI message size is equal to 36 bytes, which is comparable to a HELLO message reporting information of two neighbors. The interoperability between OLSR and MIPv6 also introduced an improved mechanism to reduce the layer 3 mobile handoff latency. The proposal is based on the transmission of a self-generated TC message which is broadcasted by the MN immediately after the CoA has been auto-configured. This approach improves the handoff latency by reducing the time required to create a reverse route from the access router to the MN, thus lowering the time required by the MN to start receiving data packets in the foreign network.

With respect to the interoperability between AODV and the HAWAII micromobility protocol, a hybrid network architecture was introduced. The proposal considered three different implementations of AODV and HAWAII.

The simulation results show that the basic aodv+Hawaii implementation provides an improved performance as compared to the aodv+Hawaii+distance and aodv+Hawaii+hops approaches. Nevertheless in (Ramirez-Mondragón, 2007) it was shown that aodv+Hawaii provides the worst performance results as compared to aodv+Hawaii+distance and aodv+Hawaii+hops under a sparce (i.e. low density) scenario composed of a relatively small number of mobile nodes. Thus, the implementation of any of the previous three approaches must take into consideration the specific characteristics of the network under operation, especially in terms of the density of mobile nodes.

ACKNOWLEDGMENT

This work was sponsored in part by the Mexican Council for Science and Technology (CONACYT) under project grant J48391-Y.

REFERENCES

Basagni, S., Chalamtac, I., & Syrotiuk, V. R. (1998). A distance routing effect algorithm for mobility (DREAM). In P*roceedings of MOBICOM*, (pp. 76-84). New York: ACM.

Benzaid, M., Minet, P., & Agha, K. A. (2004). Integrating fast mobility in the OLSR routing protocol. In *Proceedings of the 4th International Workshop on Mobile and Wireless Communications Network*, (pp. 217-221). New York: IEEE.

Benzaid, M., Minet, P., & Agha, K. A. (2004). Performance evaluation of the implementation integrating mobile-IP and OLSR in full-IP networks. In *IEEE Wireless Communications and Networking Conference* (pp. 1697-1702). New York: IEEE.

Campbell, A. T., Gomez, J., & Kim, S. (2002). Comparison of IP micromobility protocols. *IEEE Wireless Communications*, *9*(1), 72–82. doi:10.1109/MWC.2002.986462

Clausen, T., & Jacquet, P. (2003, October). *Optimized link state routing protocol.* Fremont, CA: The Internet Engineering Task Force (IETF). Retrieved September 17, 2009, from http://www.ietf.org/rfc/rfc3626.txt

Gonzalez-Sanchez, A. L. (2005). *Mobility support between MANETs and the internet, using IPv6 and the OLSR Routing Protocol.* Master thesis, CICESE Research Center, Mexico.

Johnson, D., & Maltz, D. (1996). Dynamic source routing in ad hoc wireless networks. *Mobile Computing, 353*, 153-181. Dordrecht, The Netherlands: Kluwer Academic Publishers.

Johnson, D., Perkins, C. E., & Arkko, J. (2004). *Mobility support in IPv6.* Fremont, CA: The Internet Engineering Task Force (IETF). Retrieved September 17, 2009, from http://www.ietf.org/rfc/rfc3775.txt

Johnson, D. B., Maltz, D. A., & Hu, Y. C. (2007). *The dynamic source routing protocol for mobile ad hoc networks (DSR)*. Retrieved October 1, 2009, from http://www.ietf.org/rfc/rfc4728.txt

Karp, B., & Kung, H. T. (2000). GPSR: Greedy perimeter stateless routing for wireless networks. In *Proceedings of the 6th Annual ACM/IEEE International Conference on Mobile Computing and Networking (MobiCom)* (pp. 243-254). New York: ACM.

Ko, Y., & Vaidya, N. H. (1998). Location-aided routing (LAR) in mobile ad hoc networks. In *Proceedings of IEEE/ACM Mobicom* (pp. 66-75). New York: IEEE.

Lamont, L., Wang, M., Villasenor, L., Randhawa, T., Hardy, R., & McConnel, P. (2002). An IPv6 and OLSR based architecture for integrating WLANs and MANETs to the internet. In *Proceedings of the International Symposium on Wireless Personal Multimedia* (pp. 816-820).

Lamont, L., Wang, M., Villasenor, L., Randhawa, T., & Hardy, S. (2003). Integrating WLANs & MANETs to the IPv6 based internet. In *Proceedings of the IEEE International Conference on Communications* (pp. 1090-1095). New York: IEEE.

Li, B., Qin, Y., Low, C. P., & Gwee, C. L. (2007). A survey on mobile WiMAX. *IEEE Communications Magazine*, *45*(12), 70–75. doi:10.1109/MCOM.2007.4395368

Li, J., Jannotti, J., Couto, D. S., Karger, D. R., & Morris, R. (2000). A scalable location service for geographic ad hoc routing. In *Proceedings of ACM Mobicom* (pp. 120-130). New York: ACM.

Mauve, M., Widmer, J., & Hartenstein, H. (2001). A survey on position-based routing in mobile ad-hoc networks. *IEEE Network Magazine*, *15*(6), 30–39. doi:10.1109/65.967595

Ogier, R. G., Lewis, M. G., & Templin, F. L. (2004). *Topology dissemination based on reverse-path forwarding (TBRPF)*. Retrieved October 1, 2009, from http://www.ietf.org/rfc/rfc3684.txt

Perkins, C., Belding-Royer, E., & Das, S. (2003). *Ad hoc on-demand distance vector (AODV) routing*. Retrieved September 30, 2009, from http://www.ietf.org/rfc/rfc3561.txt

Perkins, C. E. (2000). *Ad hoc networking*. Reading, MA: Addison Wesley.

Perkins, C. E. (2002). *Mobility Support for IPv4*. Fremont, CA: The Internet Engineering Task Force (IETF). Retrieved September 17, 2009, from http://www.ietf.org/rfc/rfc3344.txt

Pontes, A. B., Silva, D. D., José Jailton, J., Otavio Rodrigues, J., & Dias, K. L. (2008). Handover management in integrated WLAN and mobile WiMax networks. *IEEE Wireless Communications*, *15*(5), 86–95. doi:10.1109/MWC.2008.4653137

Ramirez-Mondragón, E. (2007). *Routing mechanism for hybrid wireless networks (Infrastructure-Ad Hoc)*. Master's thesis, CICESE Research Center, Ensenada, Mexico.

Ramjee, R., Varadhan, K., Salgarelli, L., Thuel, S. R., Wang, S. Y., & Porta, T. L. (2002). HAWAII: A domain-based approach for supporting mobility in wide-area wireless networks. *IEEE/ACM Transactions on Networking*, *10*(3), 396–410. doi:10.1109/TNET.2002.1012370

Ruiz, P. M., Ros, F. J., & Gomez-Skarmeta, A. (2005). Internet connectivity for mobile ad hoc networks: Solutions and challenges. *IEEE Communications Magazine*, *43*(10), 118–125. doi:10.1109/MCOM.2005.1522134

Santos, R. A., Edwards, A., Edwards, R. M., & Seed, N. L. (2005). Performance evaluation of routing protocols in vehicular ad-hoc networks. *International Journal of Ad Hoc and Ubiquitous Computing*, *1*(1/2), 80–91. doi:10.1504/IJAHUC.2005.008022

Schaumann, J. (2002). *Analysis of the zone routing protocol*. Retrieved October 1, 2009, from http://www.netmeister.org/misc/zrp/zrp.pdf

TheNetwork Simulator: ns-2. (2009). Retrieved September 30, 2009, from http://www.isi.edu/nsnam/ns/

Villasenor-Gonzalez, L. A., Gonzalez-Sanchez, A. L., Sanchez-Garcia, J., & Aquino-Santos, R. (2008). Macromobility support for mobile ad hoc networks using IPv6 and the OLSR routing protocol. *Computer Communications*, *31*(14), 3137–3144. doi:10.1016/j.comcom.2008.04.015

Wisely, D., Eardley, P., & Burness, L. (2002). *IP for 3G networking technologies for mobile communications*. Hoboken, NJ: John Wiley & Sons, Ltd.

Zollinger, A. (2005). *Networking unleashed: Geographic routing and topology control in ad hoc and sensor networks.* Unpublsihed doctoral dissertation, Swiss Federal Institute ofTechnology Zurich, Switzerland.

Zou, X., Ramamurthy, B., & Magliveras, S. (2002). Routing techniques in wireless ad hoc networks: Classification and comparison. In *Proceedings ot the Sixth World Multiconference on Systemics* (pp. 1–6). Cybernetics and Informatics.

Chapter 16
Game Theory for Resource Allocation in Wireless Networks

Danda B. Rawat
Old Dominion University, USA

Chandra Bajracharya
Old Dominion University, USA

Gongjun Yan
Old Dominion University, USA

ABSTRACT

Wireless technologies and devices are becoming increasingly ubiquitous in modern society. Wireless resources are natural and fixed, whereas wireless technologies and devices are increasing day-by-day, resulting in spectrum scarcity. As a consequence, efficient use of limited wireless resources has become an issue of vital importance in wireless systems. As demand increases, management of limited wireless resources for optimal allocation becomes crucial. Optimal allocation of limited wireless resources results in quick and reliable dissemination of information to larger service areas. Recently, game theory has emerged as an efficient tool to help optimally allocate wireless resources. Game theory is an optimization technique based on strategic situations and decision-making, and has found its application in numerous fields. The first part of this chapter presents a review of game theory and its application in resource allocation at different layers of the protocol stack of the network model. As shown by a recent study, static assignment of frequency spectrum by governmental bodies, such as FCC (Federal Communications Commission) in the United States, is inefficient since the licensed systems do not always fully utilize their frequency bands. In such a scenario, unlicensed secondary (cognitive radio) users can identify the idle spectrum bands and use them opportunistically. In order to access the licensed spectrum dynamically and opportunistically, the dynamic spectrum access functionality needs to be incorporated in the next generation (XG) wireless networks. Different game theory approaches for dynamic spectrum access are discussed in the second part of the chapter.

DOI: 10.4018/978-1-60960-027-3.ch016

I. INTRODUCTION

Wireless networks, in general, refer to communication networks where the interconnection between users is achieved without the use of wires. Wireless communication systems and networks are regarded as the tools for "anytime-anywhere connection." Wireless communications and networks have experienced booming growth in past few decades with billions of new wireless devices coming into use each year. With more wireless devices being used for different purposes and application scenarios, wireless technologies and devices are becoming more ubiquitous. But wireless resources (e.g. bandwidth) are natural and limited. Therefore, it is important to make efficient use of the limited wireless resources available. Optimal allocation of resources in wireless systems can thus, be thought as in terms of active management of wireless resources. Efficient allocation of resources in the wireless system results in fast and reliable dissemination of information to the destination region. In general, resource allocation in centralized systems, such as centralized cellular system and infrastructure-based ad-hoc networks, is somewhat easy and optimal. However, allocation is difficult and might not always be optimal in decentralized systems such as ad-hoc networks.

Government bodies, such as Federal Communications Commission (FCC) in the United States, assign a fixed RF spectrum to be used by service providers for a fixed duration over a specified geographic region. The fixed frequency allocation strategy has been one of the main techniques to mitigate the interference among adjacent spectrum-band users in conventional wireless systems. With the rapid spread and advancement of wireless technologies and increasing number of devices, there has been an increasing concern over the issue of spectrum scarcity. One of the common ways to solve the problem of spectrum scarcity in conventional wireless systems is to increase the system throughput or goodput (bits/second) in the given RF band by using optimization approaches. Researchers have used a variety of techniques for system optimization and this subject matter is still drawing a lot of research interest and effort from all over the world. Various factors causing spectrum scarcity have also been presented and discussed in the literature (Akyildiz, Lee, Vuran, & Mohanty, 2006; Haykin, 2005). One of them is the legacy *command-and-control* regulation, which limits the dynamic spectrum access users. While almost the entire RF spectrum has already been allocated to different service providers, the fact remains that the allocated spectrum is not being fully utilized at all time and in all spaces. This indicates that spectrum scarcity is not due to the actual lack of RF spectrum, but because of the wasteful static allocation to the service providers. Thus, with the rising concern over spectrum scarcity, dynamic spectrum access in wireless communications has recently become the focus of research in academia as well as in industries all over the world (Akyildiz, Lee, Vuran, & Mohanty, 2006). The primary objective of *dynamic spectrum access* is to utilize the frequency band dynamically and/or opportunistically without creating harmful interference to the primary users. There are numerous techniques proposed in the literature for optimal allocation of wireless resources in legacy systems as well as in dynamic spectrum access environments.

Recently, game theory has emerged as a viable tool for obtaining a socially optimal resource allocation in distributed ad-hoc networking (MacKenzie & Dasilva, 2005). This chapter will focus first of all on the basics of game theory, and then go on to explain frequently occurring terminologies and definitions in game theory approaches for resource allocation. The chapter will then present game theoretic approaches for resource allocation in different layers of the protocol stack of the network model, followed by game theoretic approaches for dynamic spectrum access (DSA) in cognitive radio networks (de Figueiredo, 2009; Haykin, 2005; Mitola & Maguire, 1999). It is important to note that dynamic spectrum access in *Cognitive radio* networks increases spectral efficiency (Haykin, 2005; Mitola & Maguire, 1999). Basically, cognitive radios can operate in a spectrum overlay or underlay approach (Zhao & Swami, 2007). In a spectrum overlay approach, cognitive radio users are required to sense the spectrum to find idle bands and use those bands opportunistically and optimally. It is worth mentioning that spectrum sensing is the fundamental step in cognitive radio systems. For spectrum sensing, cognitive radios can use suitable signal processing technique as mentioned in (Rawat & Yan, 2009) to identify the idle band in the targeted range of frequency. In the spectrum underlay approach, cognitive radio users are allowed to coexist with primary users and transmit simultaneously along with the primary users, but have severe power constraints imposed upon them so as not to cause any harmful interference to the primary users. In this method, a cognitive radio system does not have to sense for idle spectrum band, which could be regarded as its advantage. However, cognitive radio users in the spectrum underlay approach are not allowed to transmit with high power even if the primary users are not using their spectrum because the primary users might use their assigned spectrum at any time. It should be noted that cognitive radio users are not allowed to create harmful interference to *active* primary users in either approach. This chapter deals with the spectrum overlay approach, and more specifically, *dynamic spectrum access* functionality where cognitive radio users compete for resources without creating harmful interference to legacy primary users. For dynamic spectrum access, the state of the art research results of several game-theoretic models for dynamic spectrum applications such as iterative water-filling game, potential game, Stackelberg game, non-cooperative game, super-modular game, bargaining, and auction are also presented.

The rest of the chapter is organized as follows: Section II describes game theory and its different terminologies. Section III presents the system model and application of game theory in wireless systems for dynamic resource allocation as well as dynamic spectrum access in cognitive radio system in distributed scenarios. Section III also describes the advantages of game theoretic approaches for resource allocation and Section IV summarizes the book chapter.

II. BACKGROUND OF GAME THEORY

Game theory is basically the study of mathematical models of conflicts and cooperation among intelligent and rational agents. The term "intelligent" implies that the individual agents understand the structure of the operating situation, and "rational" means that the individual agents are interested in increasing their corresponding payoffs or utilities. Game theory utilizes mathematical models in formulating, analyzing and understanding strategic scenarios and decision making. Game theory has important applications in numerous fields such as political science, economic, psychology, biology and so on. This section presents a review of game theory, in general, and presents the game theoretic approaches for resource allocation in wireless networks.

A) History of Game Theory

The idea behind game theory is not new, and the basics of modern game theory can be regarded to be a result of few seminal ideas. The work performed by Augustin Cournot in 1838 is regarded as the earliest example of formal game-theoretic analysis. In 1881, Fransis Ysidro Edgeworth showed the two-person economy game. In 1920's, the mathematician Emile Borel suggested a formal theory of games. There are numerous contributors in the development of game theory. However, it is widely known that John von Neumann and Oskar Morgenstern established game theory after the publication of *Theory of Games and Economic Behavior* in 1940's.

Based on his previous publications, John Nash analytically demonstrated in his work (Nash, 1950) that finite games always have equilibrium points. Then, game theory broadened to different areas including operation research, political science, economics, biology and so on. After the Nobel Prize was awarded to John C. Harsanyi, John F. Nash Jr. and Reinhard Selten in 1994, game theory received special attention. Recently, game theory has also found its application in the field of wireless communications and networking for resource allocation (MacKenzie & Dasilva, 2005; Nash, 1950).

B) Definition of Games and Game Theory

A *game* is a formal description of strategic situations and game theory is the formal study of decision-making where each player must make choices that potentially affect the interests of the other players. Game theory aims at modeling and understanding conflicts and cooperation among rational agents/players and can be applied whenever the actions of several agents are interdependent. In this regard, game theory provides a way of formulating, analyzing and understanding the strategic scenarios. It is worth mentioning that the agents/players in a game can be individuals, groups, firms, or any combination of these.

A game has three basic elements:

- **Set of players, which are the active agents in the system**. A player is an agent who makes decisions in a game and a player is said to be rational if he/she seeks to play in a manner that maximizes his/her own payoff. It is often assumed that the rationality of all players is common knowledge.
- **Set of strategies or strategic actions available to players**. A strategy is one of the possible actions of a player. In an extensive game, a strategy is a complete plan of choices, one for each decision point of the player.
- **Player's payoff function that maps the strategies or their preferences**. A payoff is a number, also called utility, which reflects the desirability of an outcome to a player, for whatever reason. When the outcome is random, payoffs are usually weighted with their probabilities. The expected payoff incorporates the player's attitude towards risk.

Games can be described formally at various levels of detail. In particular, games can be represented and categorized into different forms according to the characteristics and properties taken into considerations.

C) Classification of Games

A game with only one player is usually called a *decision problem,* however, in general, there are many players involved in a game. Fundamentally, games can be split into two branches as follows:

Cooperative **and** ***Non-cooperative*****:** A *cooperative* game, also known as a *coalitional game,* is a high-level description where the payoff is obtained through the cooperation of its members and the payoff is based on a joint decision made by each potential group or coalition. Political science can be considered as an example of a cooperative game. The different parties in parliament can be treated as the players of the game. The strength of a party in the parliament can be determined according to the number of seats of elected party members. Interest of a game is to describe which cooperation or coalition or joint decision of parties in a parliament can form a majority. Therefore, it is important to note that the cooperative game depends on the relative amounts of power held by various players in the game. In cooperative game theory, the details of individual players' choices are not crucial to determining the outcome of the game.

A *non-cooperative* game, in contrast, is closely connected to minimax optimization (Kassam & Poor, 1983) and is concerned with the analysis of strategic choices. The players in the game are assumed to be *rational.* In *non-cooperative* game theory, players make choices out of their own interest without interaction with others. However, cooperation can arise in non-cooperative games, when players find it in their own best interests. Furthermore, the *non-cooperative* game is called *separable* if its payoff function is separable into two independent or separable parameters.

The basic difference between these two games – cooperative and non-cooperative – is whether or not the players in the game make a joint decision with the choice of available strategies.

***Static* and *dynamic games*:** A *static game* is also known as a *one-shot* game. Players choose their strategies only once and simultaneously in a static game. Whereas in *dynamic game,* also known as a *repeated game*, individual players choose their strategies either asynchronously or alternately and/or more than once. The Bertrand model (Bertrand, 1883) of oligopoly competition is an example of a static game, while the Stackelberg model (He, Prasad, Sethi, & Gutierrez, 2007) is an example of a dynamic game. Moreover, dynamic game theory can be viewed as a combination of game theory and optimal control since optimal control is performed on the fly alternately and more than once.

Symmetric* and *asymmetric games: This type of distinction can be made based on whether the players have identical strategy sets or not. That is, a symmetric game will have identical strategies for individual players, and an asymmetric game will not have identical strategy sets for all players. The prisoner's dilemma (presented in next section) is symmetric game since each player has identical options to choose.

Simultaneous* and *sequential games: In *simultaneous game*, individual players choose their strategies simultaneously without knowing the actions of others. Whereas, in *sequential game*, players have some knowledge about earlier actions of other players and they choose their strategies based on the partial knowledge.

Perfect information* and *imperfect information games: In perfect information game, each player has knowledge about previously chosen strategies (or moves) by all other players. In imperfect information game, individual players might have partial knowledge about other players' moves. Most of the games studied in game theory are imperfect-information games.

Discrete and continuous games: A game, which deals with a finite number of players, moves, events, outcomes, etc, can be called discrete game. In continuous game, players choose their strategies from a continuous strategy set.

Zero-sum and non-zero-sum games*:* A game is said to be *zero-sum* (Dutta, 1999) if for any outcome, the sum of the payoffs to all players is zero. In a two-player zero-sum game, one player's gain is the other player's loss, so their interests are diametrically opposed. A game, which does not satisfy zero-sum criteria, is called *non-zero-sum* game.

A game can be repeated and can consist *of finite* or *infinite* repetitions of a given one-shot game in sequence, and therefore this type of game is called repeated or super game. Moreover, a game can be repeated with some probability and the strategy in this context can be dependent on other players' previous choices.

D) Representation of Games

A game can be represented in different forms. Most non-cooperative games are presented in the normal and the extensive forms, while the characteristic function form is used to define cooperative games.

i. Normal Form

A game can be represented in the *Normal form,* also known as *strategic form*, in which the system cannot be rewritten any further once it is written properly (as shown in Tables 1 and 2), and the game is represented in a matrix. The *normal form* is the basic type of game studied in non-cooperative game theory where each player's strategies and the outcomes that result from each possible combination of choices are generally put in a matrix form.

ii. Extensive Form

The other form of game representation is *extensive form* (also known as *game tree*) in which the game is represented as a tree. In contrast to normal form, *extensive form* consists of a complete description of how the game is played over time in a tree form that includes the order in which players take actions, the information that players have at the time, and the uncertainty resolution time. It is worth mentioning that a game in extensive form can be either analyzed directly or converted into an equivalent normal form.

iii. Characteristic function form:

In this form, a *characteristic function* determines the payoff of each partnership in a game. It is important to point out that the standard assumption for empty coalition obtains a payoff of zero. Moreover, the characteristic function form neglects the details of individual players (instead takes the outcome of coalition). When a payoff of a coalition depends on both members and the way of partitioning of players, the game is called partitioned function form.

Table 1. Hoping to meet each other

		Ana	
		Home	Downtown
John	Home	(J, A) = (0,0)	(J, A) = (0,1)
	Downtown	(J, A) = (1,0)	*(J, A) = (2,2)*

Table 2. Prisoner's dilemma

		Prisoner B	
		Stays Silent	Betrays
Prisoner A	Stays Silent	*(A, B)=(1 year, 1year)*	*(A, B)=(10 years, 0 years)*
	Betrays	*(A, B)=(0 years, 10 years)*	*(A, B)=(5 years, 5 years)*

E) Strategies of Game Theory

A game consists of strategies chosen by the players and the players determine their outcomes. Basically, the strategies can be *pure* or *mixed.*

Pure strategy: A *pure strategy* is predetermined plan covering all possible situations in a game and not involving the use of randomness or probability. Furthermore, a player's strategy set is the set of pure strategies available to that player.

Mixed strategy: In contrast to pure strategy, *mixed strategy* involves an assignment of a probability to each pure strategy and thus a player selects an action from pure strategy set randomly (with some probability). A *strategic-form* game might not always have a Nash equilibrium for which the choice of strategy is performed deterministically. In such cases, individual players may randomly choose their strategies among those *pure* strategies with certain probabilities. This scheme of randomizing the choice by selecting from pure strategies with certain probability is called a *mixed* strategy. Nash (1950) showed that any finite strategic-form game has equilibrium provided that mixed strategies are allowed in the game. As before, an equilibrium point is a situation where no player can improve *on average* (i.e., expected value in randomized game) payoffs by unilateral deviation. It is also worth mentioning that there are infinitely mixed strategies available to a player even if his/her strategy set is finite since probabilities are continuous. One can regard pure strategy as a special case of a mixed strategy, in which that particular pure strategy is selected with probability 1.

Dominance strategy: As mentioned above, players in a game are assumed to be rational and choose the most convenient outcome. Among many choices, one outcome will be best among others, and the strategy that results in the best outcome is referred to as the *dominance* strategy. A rational player will never choose to play a dominated strategy (or under other's preference). A strategy dominates another strategy of a player if it always gives a better payoff to that player, regardless of what the other players are doing. It weakly dominates the other strategy if it is always at least as good. This idea is illustrated with the help of the well-known example of the Prisoner's Dilemma in the next section.

Nash equilibrium: In some games, there are no dominated strategies, and therefore it is hard to provide more specific advice on how to play the game. Therefore, the concept of *Nash equilibrium* (Nash, 1950) is important to find social/collective optimal outcomes. Note that the Nash equilibrium recommends a strategy to each player that the player cannot improve upon *unilaterally* given that the opponents follow the recommendation. It is reasonable for each player to expect his opponents also to follow the recommendation since the other players are also rational in the game. In other words, Nash equilibrium (also known as strategic equilibrium) is a list of strategies for individual players in which no player can unilaterally change his/her strategy and get a better payoff. Moreover, it might be possible that some Nash equilibra are not acceptable in a dynamic game because one or more players in the game may want to avoid those outcomes. Therefore, at each stage of the game, the *sub-game perfection* criterion requires that the strategy followed be still *social* optimal at that point and onwards.

F) Examples

This section deals with some examples, which will help to understand the basic concept of game theory.

Example 1 - Hoping to meet each other:

We consider two people, John and Ana, as players of the game "hoping to meet each other" as in Carlisle (2009). Both of them have two choices: the first is to *stay at home ("no meet" or 0)* where they would not meet each other and the second is to *go to the downtown ("meet" or 1)* where they could meet each other. Furthermore, both of them enjoy meeting each other. However, both of them are not allowed to communicate with each other before deciding whether to *stay at home* or to *go to the downtown*. Each of them prefers going downtown hoping to meet each other since they enjoy each-other's company. Formally, the following normal or matrix form in Table 1 represents the game.

Both players have a set of strategies {Home, Downtown}. The notation (J, A) represents an outcome because of choice of strategy for John and Ana, where J is the utility corresponding to player John and A is utility corresponding to Ana. If both players are maximizing their individual utilities, each will go to the downtown no matter what the other player does. Therefore, going downtown is the dominant strategy in this example. So {Downtown, Downtown} is a Nash equilibrium point for this game. Therefore, John and Ana, if they are rational, do not need to make an agreement (or cooperate) ahead of time. They can choose their best option without cooperation, and the best outcome will occur for both of them.

Example 2: Prisoner's Dilemma:

Merrill Flood and Melvin Dresher framed this concept originally in 1950 and Albert W. Tucker formally set the game with prison sentence payoffs and named it the "prisoner's dilemma" (Poundstone, 1992). In this game, the police arrest two suspects but do not have sufficient evidence to convict them. The police decide to separate the prisoners and separately offer them the same deal: if one testifies (defeat from the other) for the prosecution against the other and the other remains silent (cooperates with the other), the betrayer goes free and the silent accomplice receives the full 10-year sentence. If both remain silent, both prisoners are sentenced to only one year in jail for a minor charge. If each betrays the other, each receives a five-year sentence. Each prisoner must choose to betray the other or to remain silent. Each one is assured that the other would not know about the betrayal before the end of the investigation. How should the prisoners act?

It is noted that the Prisoner's Dilemma is a game in normal/strategic form between two players. Each player has two strategies: "Stay Silent" and "Betray". Formally, the game with possible outcomes is summarized as in Table 2.

As seen from Table 2, regardless of what the opponent chooses, each player always receives a higher payoff (lesser sentence) by betraying, and betraying is the strictly dominant strategy in this game. For a prisoner, no matter what opponent prisoner chooses, it is better to betray than to stay silent. (Since, betraying can result either 5 years or 1 year, whereas sitting silent can result either 10 years or free from charge.) If both players act similarly, both betray, and both get a lower payoff than they would get by staying silent. Based on rational players' choices (the cost of staying longer in jail because of their choices), the game appears to be a dilemma. Therefore, it is important to point out that in a non-zero-sum game, Nash equilibrium does not need to be an *optimal* but is called a *socially optimal*. By observing Table 2, for one-shot game, Nash equilibrium is (Betrays, Betrays).

III. APPLICATION OF GAME THEORY IN WIRELESS NETWORKS

This section introduces a system model for resource allocation in ad hoc networks and presents the applications of game theory in wireless systems for resource allocation. This section also discusses game theoretic approaches for dynamic spectrum access applicable to cognitive radio networks.

A) System Model

This section presents the system model applicable for game theoretic approaches for resource allocation in wireless networks. The system model consists of K peer-to-peer links with transmitter-receiver pairs as shown in Figure 1.

The received signal at the receiver of kth link is

$$\mathbf{r}_{k} = \underbrace{\mathbf{H}_{kk}\mathbf{x}_{k}}_{\text{desired-signal}} + \sum_{j=1,j\neq k}^{K} \mathbf{H}_{kj}\mathbf{x}_{j} + \mathbf{n}_{k} \qquad (1)$$

where $\mathbf{H}_{kj}$ is an $N x N$ channel matrix from transmitter j to receiver k (i.e., the channel $\mathbf{H}_{kk}$ is the channel matrix between k-transmitter and k-receiver), $\boldsymbol{x}_k$ is the N-dimensional transmitted signal vector from transmitter k, and $\mathbf{n}_{k} = [n_1^k, \ldots . n_n^k, \ldots ., n_N^k]^{T}$ is the N-dimensional additive white noise vector. Where N is the number of sub-channels (sub-carriers) in orthogonal frequency division multiplexing (OFDM) or processing gain (signal space dimension) in code division multiple access (CDMA) systems. The transmit signal can be expressed as $\mathbf{x}_k = \mathbf{P}_k \mathbf{S}_k \mathbf{b}_k$ *with* transmit power $\mathbf{P}_{k} = \text{diag}\{p_k^1, p_k^2, \ldots ., p_k^N\}$, transmit waveform (or codeword) $\mathbf{S}_k$ and information symbol $\boldsymbol{b}_k$. The diagonal element of all channel matrices consists of sub-channel gains, that is, $\mathbf{H}_{kk} = \text{diag}\{h_{kk}^1, h_{kk}^2\ h_{kk}^n, \ldots ., h_{kk}^N\}$, $\forall k,j$. It is worth noting that the system model in (1) is general in the sense than it can be used for both OFDM and CDMA systems, which will include almost all wireless standards. The first term in Equation (1) is the desired signal for k^{th} link, the second term is interference for k^{th} link from all other active users and the last term is additive noise for k^{th} link. The signal-to-interference-plus-noise

Figure 1. Ad hoc wireless network with peer-to-peer transmissions

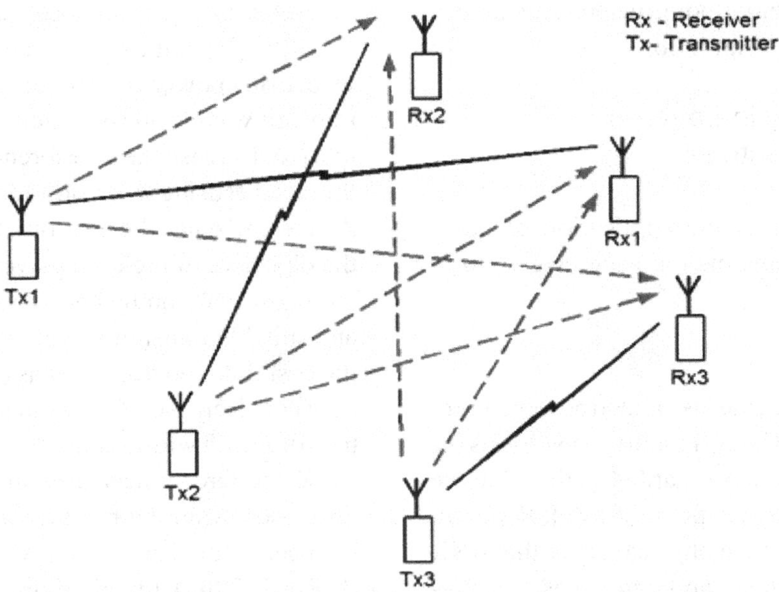

ratio (SINR) for user k in sub-channel n can be written as

$$\gamma_k^n = \frac{h_{kk}^n p_k^n}{n_n^k + \sum_{j \neq k} h_{kj}^n p_j^n} \tag{2}$$

where p_k^n is transmit power of user *k* in sub-channel *n*. In order to have successful transmission of information from the transmitter to the intended receiver, the quality-of-service (QoS) requirement can be defined as $\gamma_k^n \geq \gamma_k^{n*}$, where γ_k^{n*} is the minimum SINR required to meet outage probability. It is important to note that the bit error rate (BER) and minimum SINR matching criteria have a one-to-one relationship. That is, $BER_k^n \leq \varepsilon_k^n \Leftrightarrow \gamma_k^n \geq \gamma_k^{n*}$, and can be used alternatively.

B) Game Theory for Wireless Resource Allocation

This section deals with game theoretic approaches for resource allocation in wireless networks. Formally, a game is presented with its specific components followed by its applications for resource allocation.

i. Game Formulation

As mentioned previously, a game consists of three components: players, payoffs and preferences. Formally, the resource allocation game (RAG) in a wireless network can be defined as

$$RAG = \langle \check{s}, \{A_k\}_{k \in K}, \{U_k\}_{k \in K} \rangle \tag{3}$$

where the players are the active links *K*= {1, 2, ..., ***K***} in the system with strategies A_k and the payoffs $u_k \in U_k$ for *k=1, 2, 3, ..., K*. Individual players compete against each other by choosing their strategies to maximize their own utilities subject to some QoS constraints. Since players do not cooperate with each other in the non-cooperative game, the only reasonable outcome of the resource allocation game is a Nash Equilibrium (Nash, 1950) of the conflict. As mentioned previously, it must be pointed out that the Nash equilibrium is not necessarily an optimal outcome. However, it is a socially optimal point where a game can have an optimal configuration.

ii. Game Theory in Layered Protocol Perspectives

This section presents the application of game theory to ad hoc networks at each layer of protocol stack.

a. Physical Layer

At the physical layer, the distributed power control and selection of optimal signaling waveforms (or codeword) by a node is regarded as the resource allocation procedure (Popescu, Rawat, Popescu, & Saquib, 2009). At the physical layer, the SINR at the node of interest can be taken as a performance function. Equivalently, the rate function, which is a function of SINR, can also be taken as a function for performance measure. In the game theoretic approach, the performance function can be regarded as the payoff (utility or cost) function.

Separable Non-Cooperative Game For Power and Waveform Adaptation

The non-cooperative game can be formulated as the resource allocation in single cell of the CDMA cellular system (Popescu, et al., 2009) for a single codeword/waveform per user. In the proposed game the payoff function for an individual player is defined as the product of it transmit power p_k and interference i_k experienced by that user (i.e., $C_k = p_k . i_k$). Therefore, the payoff function of a player in this game is referred to as a cost function. Formally the non-cooperative game is defined as

$$NPCG = \left\langle \check{s}\ , \{A_k\}_{k\in K}, \{C_k\}_{k\in K} \right\rangle \qquad (4)$$

The interference experienced by a user k does not depend on its own power p_k, therefore the cost function is separable in terms of transmit power and interference function. So the game is modeled as separable non-cooperative game. The action of user k, A_k, is to choose feasible power $\{p_k: p_k \in (0,P_{\max}]\ \}$ with P_{max} as the maximum power level using power control sub-game, and suitable transmit waveform (or codeword in CDMA system) to decrease the interference experienced by the receiver using waveform adaptation sub-game. As the game has the cost function for each user, the objective of the each player is to decrease its own cost function by choosing minimum power and suitable transmit waveform. In other words, the cost function decreases as the transmit power of user k decreases. Consequently, each user will try to transmit with minimum power. Additionally, as the interference decreases, the cost function also decreases. A similar resource allocation problem has been studied in (Menon, Mackenzie, Buehrer, & Reed, 2009) for distributed receivers using potential games. This problem will be revisited in the next section.

b. Medium Access Control (MAC) Layer

In the MAC layer, multiple users contend among each other to gain access to the medium. This contention itself forms a game, and the system can be formulated using a game theoretic approach. Formally, the game can be defined as

$$MACG = \left\langle \check{s}\ , \{A_k\}_{k\in K}, \{u_k\}_{k\in K} \right\rangle \qquad (5)$$

The nodes in the network are rational players K=1, ..., $\boldsymbol{K}$, and the channel access time is the utility/payoff function u_k of individual players. The objective of the game will be to maximize the channel access time by choosing a proper back-off period (which will be A_k in the game). Alternatively, the Medium Access Control Game (MACG) can be defined as "setting of the probability of packet transmission" as an action of the player, and 'maximizing individual throughput' as the utility. It should be noted that the unfair share of medium (channel) by any user decreases the chances for others. Therefore, the game theoretic approach for the MAC layer is essential for a fair allocation (Srivastava, et al., 2005; Zou & Chigan, 2008).

c. Network Layer

The main function of the network layer is to route and forward packets in the network. As the network topology changes due to the mobility or ON/OFF behaviors of nodes, the routing path in the network might also change. Zakiuddina et al. (2005) have proposed the game theoretic routing in ad hoc networking. The game is modeled as a zero-sum game between two players – the network itself and the set of routers. The network overhead and the performance metrics (such as delay, routing time and so on) are taken as the utility functions for the game. The effectiveness of three ad hoc routing techniques (link state routing, distance vector routing and multicast routing) in frequently changing network topologies has been observed. The utility function can be considered in terms of correctness of routing, routing time (i.e., convergence), and network overhead.

d. Transport Layer

The transport layer is responsible for encapsulating application data blocks into data units (segments) suitable for transfer to the network infrastructure for transmission to the destination host, or performing the reverse operation on datagrams obtained from network layers and delivering its payload to an application layer. At the transport layer, the game theoretic approach can be applied for rational nodes in the network to analyze the robustness of the congestion control methods. Specifically, nodes can be considered as players, congestion control as strategies and maximizing throughput as utility functions. Akella et al. (2002) have formulated the congestion control game with maximizing of throughput as a payoff. It is important to note that the game theoretic approach is socially optimal whenever the nodes involved in the game are rational.

C) Game Theory for Dynamic Spectrum Access

This Section describes the applications of game theory for dynamic spectrum access in wireless networks. As described in previous sections, several researches for resource allocation in statically allocated spectrum are still ongoing around the globe. However, in the present scenario of almost all the RF spectrum already allocated to the service providers and yet, the spectrum not being fully utilized (Akyildiz, Lee, Vuran, & Mohanty, 2006), there needs to be some mechanism to access the under-utilized spectrum opportunistically and dynamically without creating harmful interference to the licensed users. Such a technique of dynamic spectrum access will help to reduce the spectrum scarcity problem, thereby increasing the spectral efficiency. Cognitive radio (Haykin, 2005) technology is one approach for dynamic spectrum access to increase the spectral efficiency. Basically, a cognitive radio senses the spectrum band over a wide range of frequency bands using suitable sensing methods as mentioned in (Rawat and Yan, 2009) and exploits this information in a dynamic and opportunistic manner, without generating harmful interference to incumbent licensed users. Dynamic spectrum access with optimal resource allocation has been a major research problem and has been discussed in the literature (Attar, Nakhai, & Aghvami, 2009; Etkin, Parekh, & Tse, 2007; Maskery, Krishnamurthy, & Zhao, 2009; van der Schaar & Fu, 2009). This section deals with several game theoretic models for dynamic spectrum applications e.g. iterative water filling, potential game, Stackelberg game, super-modular game, bargaining, and auction.

i. Iterative Water-Filling Game

The iterative water-filling game is a type of non-cooperative game in which players perform resource allocation for one user treating the signal from others as a noise, and repeating the procedure to all other users iteratively. In interference channels, efficient power allocation in individual channels is necessary to increase the spectral efficiency and especially increase throughput and decrease the interference to other sub-channels or users. A centralized approach can achieve an optimal solution, but with very high communication overhead and complexity. In dynamic spectrum access environments for distributed systems, a low complexity but feasible solution can be achieved by iterative water-filling game. Using the SINR for link k in sub-channel n in Equation (2), the rate (in bits/sec/Hz) for user k in sub-channel n can be defined as

$$R_k^n = \log_2(1 + \gamma_k^n) \tag{6}$$

The overall rate for link k can be calculated as $R_k = \sum_{n=1}^{N} R_k^n$. A non-cooperative game can be formulated using SINR expressed as a utility function where individual users/links try to increase their SINR. Equivalently, the problem can also be formulated as the rate maximization problem since the increase in SINR increases the rate. Formally, the non-cooperative rate maximization game (NCG) can be expressed as

$$NCG = \left\langle \check{s}\ , \{A_k\}_{k\in K}, \{R_k\}_{k\in K} \right\rangle \tag{7}$$

where A_k={$\boldsymbol{p}_k$: $p_k^n \geq 0, \sum_n p_k^n \leq p_{\max}$ } with p_k={ $p_k^n, \forall n$ }. In this game, the individual links increase the rates given that the total transmit power of individual users does not exceed $p_{max.}$ This game has Nash equilibrium which can be found by iterative water-filling (Yu, Ginis, & Cioffi, 2002). Because a user does not know the distribution of other users' transmitted signals, the user assumes the interference as a noise, and applies the single user water-filling algorithm. The same procedure is used iteratively for all users, i.e. every user assumes interference from other users as noise and applies the water-filling algorithm. This algorithm is efficient for distributed resource allocation using local information in the interference systems. However, the convergence speed of the algorithm can be very slow when the interference to the link is high. Furthermore, the Nash equilibrium might not be optimal from the perspective of system design. Han et al. (2007) have shown that the referee-based game can improve the shortcomings of iterative water-filling game in multi-cell OFDM networks to achieve optimal resource allocation. In the referee-based non-cooperative game, a referee is introduced that will take care of all the players not to fall in undesirable conditions, the referee intervenes only when it is necessary, otherwise the game will be like the conventional non-cooperative game. It is also important to point out that the non-cooperative game can have multiple Nash equilibra with different initialization of algorithms.

ii. Potential Game

In *potential game*, the players work in a non-cooperative manner. However, their strategy implicitly leads to a common system goal. Therefore, this type of game is regarded as the bridge between the non-cooperative and cooperative behaviors of players. One of the nice characteristics of this type of game is the convergence property to the Nash equilibrium. The potential game has been used in the study of interference avoidance (Menon, Mackenzie, Buehrer, et al., 2009; Menon, Mackenzie, Hicks, Buehrer, & Reed, 2009).

In potential game, any changes in the utility function of a player/user due to a unilateral deviation by the player are reflected in a global function known as the potential function, and therefore the game is a *normal form game* (Monderer & Shapley, 1996). The potential game can be defined as exact potential game (EPG) which satisfies the exact potential function as below

$$EPG = \left\langle \check{s}\ ,\{A_k\}_{k\in K},\{u_k\}_{k\in K} \right\rangle \qquad (8)$$

If there exists $V: A \rightarrow R$, known as the exact potential function which satisfies $u_k(a, a_{-k}) - u_{-k}(\check{a}, a_{-k}) = V(a, a_{-k}) - V(\check{a}, a_{-k})\ \forall k \in K, a \in A, \tilde{a} \in A$ with a new strategy $\check{a}$. The potential function (utility function in potential game) is a sum of the inverse SINR (ISINR) function as given in (Menon, Mackenzie, Buehrer, et al., 2009). The main goal of this game is to minimize ISINR (i.e., equivalent to maximization of sum of SINRs) of the network with minimum transmit power and optimal waveform strategies. Menon et al., (2009) have shown that potential game has Nash equilibrium.

iii. Stackelberg Game

Stackelberg game is a non-cooperative two-stage game which consists of a leader and its followers (Basar & Olsder, 1999; He, et al., 2007). This two-stage leader-followers game in a wireless network consists of a network that functions as a leader that announces its decision to the other players (followers of the leaders). Then the followers take the announced decision into account when adapting their strategies from a feasible set of the strategies. Formally the Stackelberg Power control Game (SPG) can be expressed as

$$SPG = \left\langle \check{s}\ ,\{A_k\}_{k\in K},\{u_k\}_{k\in K} \right\rangle \qquad (9)$$

The network working as a leader announces the minimum SINR needed not to exceed outage probability (i.e., u_k) for all the players, and individual followers/users allocate the optimal transmit power (i.e., A_k) to meet the announced QoS in terms of SINR. In this game, individual followers will transmit with minimum power but will meet the minimum SINR requirement, which was announced by the network leader to meet the overall system performance. Saraydar, Mandayam, and Goodman (2002) have shown that Stackelberg game has Nash equilibrium.

iv. Super-Modular Game

In the Super-modular game, when a player chooses higher action to maximize his/her utility, the others want to do the same thing. This feature of the super modular game is referred to as "*strategic complementarities.*" The details of the super modular game (SMG) can be found in (Topkis, 1998). The function is said to be super modular in $\boldsymbol{x}=\{x_1, \ldots\ x_i,\ x_j \ldots\ x_K\}$ if the twice differential function f has increasing difference in variables (x_i, x_j) if $\partial^2 f\ /\ \partial x_i \partial x_j \geq 0$ for any feasible x_i and x_j, and for $i \neq j$. The game $SMG = \left\langle \check{s}\ ,\{A_k\}_{k\in K},\{s_k\}_{k\in K} \right\rangle$ is said to be super modular if for each player k

- the strategy space is non-empty and compact sub-lattice
- the utility function (payoff function) s_k is continuous in all the players' strategies and is super modular in player k's strategy

The utility function in the super modular game can be taken as the logarithmic of SINR as mentioned in (Huang, Berry, & Honig, 2006b). That is, $u_k=\theta_i \log(\gamma_k)$ for high SINR regime and, $u_k=\theta_i \log(1+\gamma_k)$ for low SINR regime, or general case. Here θ_i is the user dependent priority parameter. The authors have proposed an efficient algorithm called Asynchronous Distributed Pricing (ADP) to solve the maximization of $\sum_{k=1}^{K} u_k$ with feasible power allocation, and shown that the game has Nash equilibrium.

v. Bargaining Game

Bargaining, also known as haggling, is a type of negotiation between two parties that eventually come to an agreement. In the bargaining game, the resources are allocated according to the players' agreement through a bargaining process. Individual player interest is to maximize personal interests; however, players have to follow the bargaining agreement. As in (Owen, 2001; Yaiche, Mazumdar, & Rosenberg, 2000), the bargaining game can be studied using cooperative game theory. In cooperative game theory, individual players need minimum payoffs as a benefit of cooperation. Otherwise, players will not cooperate. In a dynamic spectrum access environment, the licensed system may not give access to its spectrum to other secondary users unless they reach an agreement in which licensed system will receive payoffs and the secondary user will get access to other spectra with the cost determined by the cooperative or bargaining agreement. Formally, the bargaining game can be defined as

$$BG = \left\langle \check{s}\ , \{A_k\}_{k \in K}, \{B_k\}_{k \in K} \right\rangle \tag{10}$$

where $B_k = \sum_{k=1}^{K} (u_k - u_k^b)$ is the bargaining game utility function with $u_k = \theta_i \log(1+\gamma_k)$ or $u_k = \theta_i \log(\gamma_k)$ and $u_k^b, \forall k$, as the minimum payoff that the player k will expect or he/she will not cooperate. It is important to point out that the B_k becomes $\sum_{k=1}^{K} u_k$ when we set $u_k^b = 0, \forall k$, and the problem is converted into a rate maximization problem. Peng et al. (2006) and Suris et al. (2007) have used bargaining games extensively for distributed spectrum sharing. It is also worth mentioning that the bargaining game helps to reduce the interference and work for global optimization.

vi. Auction

This type of game is suitable when two players (e.g., seller and buyer) have asymmetric information. Huang et al (2006a) have studied the auction mechanisms for sharing spectrum among a group of users. The utility function used is a function of the received signal-to-interference plus noise ratio. The authors have proposed two types of auctions, which are shown to be socially optimal and the algorithms converge globally to the Nash equilibra.

D) Advantages of Game Theoretic Approaches

There are many advantages of game theoretic approaches for resource allocation in wireless networks. Especially in decentralized networks, the optimization problem could be NP-hard and an exact solution might not be possible. The game theory can be used to solve the problem by providing a socially optimal Nash equilibrium. The following sub-section consists of major advantages of game theoretic approaches.

i. Game Theory and Wireless Self-Organization

Wireless networks are becoming increasingly popular and are gaining new interests in the field of sensor networks and ad hoc networks, where self-organization is very important to facilitate large-scale and rapid deployment and eventually reduce costs. Game theory can facilitate the self-organization in ad hoc networks by using proper strategies to obtain optimal payoffs for random access with a proper power control mechanism.

ii. Game Theory and Large Scale Network

One can model the resource allocation using game theory for small-scale networks. Often, 2- or 3-player games that are easy to describe, such as the prisoner's dilemma, help one better understand the subtleties regarding basic issues such as rationality. Finding the efficient techniques for describing and analyzing a game such as Nash equilibrium becomes easy for such small games. Once everything is set up for small-scale network, one can apply such a resource allocation model in large-scale networks, which will have

Nash equilibrium similar to small-scale network. Therefore, game theory is considered an important tool to determine the scalability of wireless networks. For instance, one can use an analogous example to address this issue when one needs 2^n-1 numbers to describe a probability distribution on a space for n binary random variables. For a large n (=500 say) it is almost impossible to write down the probability distribution. One can write down the probability distribution for a smaller n (*e.g.* n=3), and can generalize for higher values of n. Therefore, it can be concluded that similar approaches can be used in game theoretic approaches.

iii. Game Theory and Performance Evaluation

Game theory has been recently regarded as a tool to evaluate the performance of wireless networks through payoff functions. The number of steps needed to reach the game at Nash equilibrium, which is regarded as a socially optimal point of resource allocation, can determine the speed of the algorithm.

iv. Learning in Games

There has been a great deal of work in game theoretic approach on learning to play well in different settings. Learning to play optimally in a reinforcement learning setting, where an agent interacts with an unknown (but fixed) environment, is one of the greatest advantages of game theoretic approach. After few steps, the player faces a tradeoff between exploration and exploitation. The question is how many steps it takes to learn to play well enough to reach the optimal point.

All in all, game theory is an emerging tool for optimal resource allocation in wireless networks to increase spectral efficiency and measure network performance.

IV. CONCLUSION

In this chapter, we presented game theory and its application to resource allocation in conventional wireless networks and dynamic spectrum access in cognitive radio-based wireless networks.

Use of game theory is exciting because of its relevance to a wide number of applications, although the principles are simple. Self interest and interdependent decisions are everywhere, and thus game theory is emerging as a new technique for scenarios where self-interested agents cooperate and/or compete. Perhaps the most interesting application of game theory involves wireless communications. The ideas and game theoretic approaches for wireless networks described in this chapter should be viewed as starting points. Aside from resource allocation and the spectrum sharing approaches presented here, one can apply game theory in other fields of wireless networks such as wireless network security and spectrum sensing. And there are still many other avenues to apply game theoretic approaches.

REFERENCES

Akella, A., Seshan, S., Karp, R., Shenker, S., & Papadimitriou, C. (2002). Selfish behavior and stability of the internet: A game-theoretic analysis of TCP. *ACM SIGCOMM SIGCOMM Computer Communication Rev*, *32*(4), 117–130. doi:10.1145/964725.633037

Akyildiz, I. F., Lee, W.-Y., Vuran, M. C., & Mohanty, S. (2006). NeXt generation/dynamic spectrum access/cognitive radio wireless networks: A survey. *Computer Networks*, *50*(13), 2127–2159. doi:10.1016/j.comnet.2006.05.001

Attar, A., Nakhai, M., & Aghvami, A. (2009). Cognitive radio game for secondary spectrum access problem. *IEEE Transactions on Wireless Communications*, *8*(4), 2121–2131. doi:10.1109/TWC.2009.080884

Basar, T., & Olsder, G. (1999). *Dynamic noncooperative game theory*. Philadelphia, PA: Society for Industrial and Applied Mathematics.

Bertrand, J. (1883). Book review of theorie mathematique de la richesse sociale and of recherches sur les principles mathematiques de la theorie des richesses. *Journal de Savants*, *67*, 499–508.

de Figueiredo, R. J. P. (2009). Cognitive signal processing: an emerging technology for the prediction of behavior of complex human/machine systems. In *Proceedings of the International Conference on Communications, Circuits and Systems (ICCCAS)* (pp. 1-2). New York: IEEE.

Dutta, P. K. (1999). *Strategies and games: Theory and practice*. Cambridge, MA: MIT Press.

Etkin, R., Parekh, A., & Tse, D. (2007). Spectrum sharing for unlicensed bands. *IEEE Journal on Selected Areas in Communications*, *25*(3), 517. doi:10.1109/JSAC.2007.070402

Han, Z., Ji, Z., & Ray Liu, K. J. (2007). Non-cooperative resource competition game by virtual referee in multi-cell OFDMA networks. *IEEE Journal on Selected Areas in Communications*, *25*(6), 1079–1090. doi:10.1109/JSAC.2007.070803

Haykin, S. (2005). Cognitive radio: Brain-empowered wireless communications. *IEEE Journal on Selected Areas in Communications*, *23*(2), 201–220. doi:10.1109/JSAC.2004.839380

He, X., Prasad, A., Sethi, S. P., & Gutierrez, G. (2007). A survey of Stackelberg differential game models in supply and marketing channels. [JSSSE]. *Journal of Systems Science and Systems Engineering*, *16*(4), 385–413. doi:10.1007/s11518-007-5058-2

Huang, J., Berry, R., & Honig, M. L. (2006a). Auction-based spectrum sharing. *ACM Mobile Networks and Applications Journal*, *11*(3), 405–418. doi:10.1007/s11036-006-5192-y

Huang, J., Berry, R., & Honig, M. L. (2006b). Distributed interference compensation for wireless networks. *IEEE Journal on Selected Areas in Communications*, *24*(5), 1074–1084. doi:10.1109/JSAC.2006.872889

Kassam, S., & Poor, H. (1983). Robust signal processing for communication systems. *IEEE Communications Magazine*, *21*(1), 20–28. doi:10.1109/MCOM.1983.1091322

MacKenzie, A. B., & Dasilva, L. A. (2005). Game theory for wireless engineers. *Synthesis Lectures on Communications*, *1*, 1–86. doi:10.2200/S00014ED1V01Y200508COM001

Maskery, M., Krishnamurthy, V., & Zhao, Q. (2009). Decentralized dynamic spectrum access for cognitive radios: Cooperative design of a non-cooperative game. *IEEE Transactions on Communications*, *57*(2), 459. doi:10.1109/TCOMM.2009.02.070158

Menon, R., Mackenzie, A., Buehrer, R., & Reed, J. (2009). Interference avoidance in networks with distributed receivers. *IEEE Transactions on Communications*, *57*(10), 3078–3309. doi:10.1109/TCOMM.2009.10.070362

Menon, R., Mackenzie, A., Hicks, J., Buehrer, R., & Reed, J. (2009). A game-theoretic framework for interference avoidance. *IEEE Transactions on Communications*, *57*(4), 1087–1098. doi:10.1109/TCOMM.2009.04.070192

Mitola, J., & Maguire, G. Q. (1999). Cognitive radio: Making software radios more personal. *IEEE Personal Communications, 6*(4), 13-18. doi: citeulike-article-id:167416

Monderer, D., & Shapley, L. (1996). Potential games. *Journal of Games and Economic Behavior*, *14*(44), 124–143. doi:10.1006/game.1996.0044

Nash, J. (1950). Equillibrium points in n-person games. *Proceedings of the National Academy of Sciences of the United States of America, 36*, 48–49. doi:10.1073/pnas.36.1.48

Owen, G. (2001). *Game theory* (3rd ed.). New York: Academic Press.

Peng, C., Zheng, H., & Zhao, B. Y. (2006). Utilization and fairness in spectrum assignment for opportunistic spectrum access. *ACM Mobile Network Applications*, *11*(4), 555–576. doi:10.1007/s11036-006-7322-y

Popescu, D. C., Rawat, D. B., Popescu, O., & Saquib, M. (2010). Game theoretic approach to joint transmitter adaptation and power control in wireless systems. *IEEE Transactions on Systems, Man, and Cybernetics, Part B: Cybernetics. Special Issue Game Theory*, *40*(3), 675–682.

Poundstone, W. (1992). *Prisoner's dilemma*. New York: Doubleday.

Rawat, D. B., & Yan, G. (2009). Signal processing techniques for spectrum sensing in cognitive radio systems: Challenges and perspectives. Paper presented at the *IEEE/IFIP Asian Himalayas International Conference on Internet (AH-ICI)*.

Saraydar, C. U., Mandayam, N. B., & Goodman, D. J. (2002). Efficient power control via pricing in wireless data networks. *IEEE Transactions on Communications*, *50*(2), 291–303. doi:10.1109/26.983324

Srivastava, V., Neel, J., Mackenzie, A. B., Menon, R., Dasilva, L. A., & Hicks, J. E. (2005). Using game theory to analyze wireless ad hoc networks. *IEEE Communications Surveys & Tutorials*, *7*(4), 46–56. doi:10.1109/COMST.2005.1593279

Suris, J. E., DaSilva, L., Han, Z., & MacKenzie, A. (2007). Cooperative game theory approach for distributed spectrum sharing. Paper presented at the *IEEE International Conference on Communications*, Glasgow, Scotland.

Topkis, D. M. (1998). *Supermodularity and complementarity*. Princeton, NJ: Princeton University Press.

van der Schaar, M., & Fu, F. (2009). Spectrum access games and strategic learning in cognitive radio networks for delay-critical applications. *Proceedings of the IEEE, 97*(4), 720–740. doi:10.1109/JPROC.2009.2013036

Yaiche, H., Mazumdar, R. R., & Rosenberg, C. (2000). A game theoretic framework for bandwidth allocation and pricing in broadband networks. *IEEE/ACM Transactions on Networking, 8*(6), 667–678. doi:10.1109/90.879352

Yu, W., Ginis, G., & Cioffi, J. M. (2002). Distributed multiuser power control for digital subscriber lines. *IEEE Journal on Selected Areas in Communications*, *20*(5), 1105–1116. doi:10.1109/JSAC.2002.1007390

Zakiuddin, I., Hawkins, T., & Moffat, N. (2005). Towards a game theoretic understanding of adhoc routing. *Electronic Notes in Theoretical Computer Science*, *119*(1), 67–92. doi:10.1016/j.entcs.2004.07.009

Zhao, Q., & Swami, A. (2007). A survey of dynamic spectrum access: Signal processing and networking perspectives. In *Proceedings of the IEEE International Conference on Acoustics, Speech and Signal Processing (ICASSP)* (Vol. 4, pp. 349-1352).

Zou, C., & Chigan, C. (2008). A game theoretic DSA-driven MAC framework for cognitive radio networks. Paper presented at the *IEEE International Conference on Communications* (ICC).

KEY TERMS AND DEFINITIONS

Cognitive Radio: Technology is one approach for dynamic spectrum access to increase the spectral efficiency.

Dynamic Spectrum Access: Is to utilize the frequency band dynamically and opportunistically.

Game: Is a formal description of strategic situations.

Mixed Strategy: Is an assignment of a probability to each pure strategy.

Nash Equilibrium: Is important to find social/collective optimal outcomes.

Pure Strategy: Is predetermined plan covering all possible situations in a game.

Stackelberg Game: Is a non-cooperative two-stage game that consists of a leader and its followers.

Wireless Resource Allocation: Resources such as bandwidth or power are utilized as optimally as possible.

Zero-Sum: If for any outcome, the sum of the payoffs to all players is zero.

Compilation of References

Aad, I., & Castelluccia, C. (2001). Differentiation mechanisms for IEEE 802.11. In *Proceedings of IEEE InfoCom*, Anchorage, AK. New York: IEEE.

Acaccia, G., Michelini, R., Molfino, R., & Razzoli, R. (2003). Mobile robots in greenhouse cultivation: Inspection and treatment of plants. Paper presented at the *1st International Workshop on Advances in Service Robotics,* Bardolino, Italia.

Acevedo, O. C., Ortega-Farías, S., Hidalgo, A. C., Moreno, S. Y., & Cordova, A. F. (2005). Efecto de Diferentes Niveles de Agua Aplicada en Post-Cuaja y en Post-Pinta Sobre la Calidad del Vino cv. Cabernet Sauvignon. *Agricultura Técnica, 65*(4). doi:.doi:10.4067/S0365-28072005000400006

Adamchuk, V. I., Hummel, J. W., Morgan, M. T., & Upadhyaya, S. K. (2004). On-the-go soil sensors for precision agriculture. *Computers and Electronics in Agriculture, 44*(1), 71–91. .doi:10.1016/j.compag.2004.03.002

Adee, S. (2010, February). Wireless sensors that live forever. *IEEE Spectrum*, 14. doi:10.1109/MSPEC.2010.5397767

Agre, J., Akinyemi, A., Lusheng, J., Masuoka, R., & Thakkar, P. (2001). A layered architecture for location-based services in wireless ad hoc networks. In *Aerospace Conference Proceedings*. New York: IEEE.

Aguirre, J. L., & Domínguez, J. H. (2007). Traffic light control through agent-based coordination. In *IASTED international conference on artificial intelligence and applications, Innsbruck, Austria* (pp. 145–150). Calgary, Canada: ACTA Press.

Ahmad, A. (2005). *Wireless and mobile data networks.* Hoboken, NJ: Wiley Interscience. doi:10.1002/0471729221

Ahmavaara, K., Haverinen, H., & Pichna, R. (2003, November). Interworking architecture between 3GPP and WLAN systems. *IEEE Communications Magazine, 41*(11). doi:10.1109/MCOM.2003.1244926

Ahmed, A. A., Shi, H., & Shang, Y. (2003). A survey on network protocols for wireless sensor. In *Proceedings of the International Conference on Information Technology: Research and Education (ITRE'03)* (pp. 301-305). New York: IEEE Computer Society.

Akella, A., Seshan, S., Karp, R., Shenker, S., & Papadimitriou, C. (2002). Selfish behavior and stability of the internet: A game-theoretic analysis of TCP. *ACM SIGCOMM SIGCOMM Computer Communication Rev, 32*(4), 117–130. doi:10.1145/964725.633037

Akyidiz, I. F., Su, W., Sankarasubramaniam, Y., & Cayirci, E. (2002). A survey on sensor networks. *IEEE Communications Magazine, 40*(8), 102–116. doi:10.1109/MCOM.2002.1024422

Akyildiz, I., & Kasimoglu, I. (2004). Wireless sensor and actor networks: Research challenges. *Ad Hoc Networks, 2*(4), 351–367. .doi:10.1016/j.adhoc.2004.04.003

Akyildiz, I., Su, W., Sankarasubramaniam, Y., & Cayirci, E. (2002). Wireless sensor networks: A survey. *Computer Networks, 38*(4), 393–422. doi:10.1016/S1389-1286(01)00302-4

Akyildiz, I., Xie, J., & Mohanty, S. (2004, April). A survey of mobility management in next-generation all-IP based wireless systems. *IEEE Wireless Communications Magazine, 11*(4), 16–28. doi:10.1109/MWC.2004.1325888

Akyildiz, I. F., Lee, W.-Y., Vuran, M. C., & Mohanty, S. (2006). NeXt generation/dynamic spectrum access/cognitive radio wireless networks: A survey. *Computer Networks*, *50*(13), 2127–2159. doi:10.1016/j.comnet.2006.05.001

Akyildiz, I. F., Vuran, M. C., & Akan, O. B. (2006). A Cross-Layer Protocol for Wireless Sensor Networks. *Conference on Information Sciences and Systems (CISS)*. Princeton, NJ.

Alippi, C., Anastasi, G., Galperti, C., Mancini, F., & Roveri, M. (2007). Adaptive sampling for energy conservation in wireless sensor networks for snow monitoring applications. In *Proceedings of the IEEE International Conference on Mobile Adhoc and Sensor Systems*, (pp. 1-6).

Al-Khateeb, K., & Johari, J. A. (2008). Intelligent dynamic traffic light sequence using RFID. *International Conference on Computer and Communication Engineering, (ICCCE)*, Kuala, Lumpur (pp. 1367-1372). New York: IEEE.

Alvarado, P., González, A., & Villaseñor, L. (2009). *D2ARS*. Retrieved September 2009, from www.d2ars.org/d2ars/system/files/paper2.pdf

Alzaid, H., Park, D., Nieto, J. G., Boyd, C., & Foo, E. (2009). A forward and backward secure key management in wireless sensor networks for PCS/SCADA. In *Proceedings of the first ICST International Conference on Sensor Systems and Software (SCUBE)* (Vol. 24, pp. 66-82).

Anderson, R., Chan, H., & Perrig, A. (2004). Key infection: Smart trust for smart dust. In *Proceedings of the 12th IEEE International Conference on Network Protocols (ICNP)* (pp. 206–215). New York: IEEE.

Andrisano, O., Verdone, R., & Makagawa, M. (2000). Intelligent transportation system: The role of third-generation mobile radio networks. *IEEE Communications Magazine*, 144–151. doi:10.1109/35.868154

Angelides, J. (2000). The benefits of U-TDOA. Wireless Business and Technology [Web site]. Retrieved 2009, from http://wbt.sys-con.com/read/41067.htm

Anliker, U., Ward, J. A., Lukowicz, P., Tröster, G., Dolveck, F., & Baer, M. (2004, December). AMON: A Wearable Multiparameter Medical Monitoring and Alert System. *IEEE Transactions on Information Technology in Biomedicine*, *8*(4), 415–427. doi:10.1109/TITB.2004.837888

Ashby, W. R., Foerster, V., & Zopf, G. W. (1962). Principles of self-organization. *Transactions of the Univeristy of Illinois Symposium*, pp. 255-278.

Asokan, N., & Ginzboorg, P. (2000). Key agreement in ad-hoc networks. *Computer Communications*, *23*(17), 1627–1637. doi:10.1016/S0140-3664(00)00249-8

Aspnes, J., Goldenberg, B., & Yang, R. Y. (2004). On the computational complexity of sensor network localization. In A. Nikoletseas & J. Rolim (Eds.), In *Proceedings of First International Workshop on Algorithmic Aspects of Wireless Sensor Networks (ALGOSENSORS 2004)* (pp. 32-44). New York: Springer-Verlag.

Assaad, M., & Djamal, Z. (2006). *TCP performance over UMTS/HSDPA systems*. Boca Raton, FL: Auerbach Publications. doi:10.1201/9781420013320

Attar, A., Nakhai, M., & Aghvami, A. (2009). Cognitive radio game for secondary spectrum access problem. *IEEE Transactions on Wireless Communications*, *8*(4), 2121–2131. doi:10.1109/TWC.2009.080884

Aviles Garcia, J. A. (2008). Una técnica para la caracterización de nodos en Redes de Sensores Inalámbricas. Unpublsihed doctoral thesis (pp. 1-146). Cartagena, Spain: Universidad Politécnica de Cartagena.

Awerbuch, B. (1985). Complexity of network synchronization. [JACM]. *Journal of the ACM*, *32*(4), 804–823. doi:10.1145/4221.4227

Bahl, P., & Padmanabhan, V. N. (2000). RADAR: An in-building RF-based user location and tracking system. In *Proceedings of the Nineteenth Annual Joint Conference of the IEEE Computer and Communications Societies, INFOCOMM 2000* (pp. 775-784).

Basagni, S., Chalamtac, I., & Syrotiuk, V. R. (1998). A distance routing effect algorithm for mobility (DREAM). In P*roceedings of MOBICOM*, (pp. 76-84). New York: ACM.

Basagni, S., Herrin, K., Bruschi, D., & Rosti, E. (2001). Secure pebblenets. In *Proceedings of the 2nd ACM Interational Symposium on Mobile Ad Hoc Networking and Computing (MobiHoc)* (pp. 156-163). New York: ACM.

Basar, T., & Olsder, G. (1999). *Dynamic noncooperative game theory*. Philadelphia, PA: Society for Industrial and Applied Mathematics.

Beaver, C., Gallup, D., Neumann, W., & Torgerson, M. (2002). *Key management for SCADA* (Report No. SAND2001-3252). Albuquerque, NM: Sandia National Laboratories, the Center for SCADA Security, Cryptography and Information Systems Surety Department. Retrieved October 13, 2009, from http://www.sandia.gov/scada/documents/013252.pdf

Becker, K., & Wille, U. (1998). Communication complexity of group key distribution. In *Proceedings of the 5th ACM conference on Computer and Communication Security* (pp. 1–6). New York: ACM.

Beckwith, R., Teibel, D., & Bowen, P. (2004). Report from the field: Results from an agricultural wireless sensor network. In *Proceedings of the 29th Annual IEEE International Conference on Local Computer Networks (LCN)* (pp. 471-478). New York: IEEE.

Bell, K. L., Steinberg, Y., Ephraim, Y., & Van Trees, H. L. (1997). Extended Ziv-Zakai lower bound for vector parameter estimation. *IEEE Transactions on Information Theory*, *43*(2), 624–637. doi:10.1109/18.556118

Bell, G. (2007). *Bell's Law for the birth and death of computer classes: A theory of the computer's evolution* [Technical report MSR-TR-2007-146]. San Francisco, CA: Microsoft Research, Silicon Valley, Microsoft Corporation.

Benzaid, M., Minet, P., & Agha, K. A. (2004). Integrating fast mobility in the OLSR routing protocol. In *Proceedings of the 4th International Workshop on Mobile and Wireless Communications Network*, (pp. 217-221). New York: IEEE.

Benzaid, M., Minet, P., & Agha, K. A. (2004). Performance evaluation of the implementation integrating mobile-IP and OLSR in full-IP networks. In *IEEE Wireless Communications and Networking Conference* (pp. 1697-1702). New York: IEEE.

Berkwist, J., & Eriksson, E. (2006). *WLAN as a complement to UMTS*. Unpublished master's thesis. Retrieved from http://www.s3.kth.se/~matthias/current/ Ericsson.pdf

Bertrand, J. (1883). Book review of theorie mathematique de la richesse sociale and of recherches sur les principles mathematiques de la theorie des richesses. *Journal de Savants*, *67*, 499–508.

Bettstetter, C. (2002a). On the minimum node degree and connectivity of a wireless multihop network. In *Proceedings of the ACM International Symposium on Mobile Ad Hoc Networking and Computing (MobiHoc)*, Lausanne, Switzerland (pp. 80-91). New York, ACM.

Bettstetter, C. (2002b). On the connectivity of wireless multi-hop networks with homogeneous and inhomogeneous range assignment. In *Proceedings of the IEEE Vehicular Technology Conference (VTC)*, Vancouver, Canada (pp. 1706-1710).

Biswas, P., Lian, T., Wang, T., & Ye, Y. (2006). Semidefinite programming based algorithms for sensor network localization. [TOSN]. *ACM Transactions on Sensor Networks*, *2*(2), 188–220. doi:10.1145/1149283.1149286

Blazewicz, J. (2003). *Handbook on data management in information systems*. Berlin: Springer.

Bogart, K. (2006). *Three most common methods - Measuring vine water status*. Practical Winery & Vineyard Magazine.

Bonivento, A., Fischione, C., & Necchi, L. (2007). System Level Design for clustered wireless sensor networks. *IEEE Trans. on Industrial Informatics*, *3*(3), 204–214.

Borbash, S., & Jennings, E. (2002). Distributed topology control algorithm for multi-hop wireless networks. *Proceedings of IEEE International Joint Conference on Neural Networks*, Honolulu, HI (pp. 355–360). New York: IEEE.

Boulis, A., Ganeriwal, S., & Srivastava, M. B. (2003). Aggregation in sensor networks: an energy-accuracy trade-off. In *Proceedings of the IEEE International Workshop on Sensor Network Protocols and Applications*, (pp. 128-138).

Buddhikot, M., Chandranmenon, G., Han, S., Lee, Y. W., Miller, S., & Salgarelli, L. (2003, November). Design and implementation of a WLAN/CDMA2000 interworking architecture. *IEEE Communications Magazine*, *41*(11). doi:10.1109/MCOM.2003.1244928

Bullock, D. S., Kitchen, N., & Bullock, D. G. (2007, October). Multidisciplinary teams: A necessity for research in precision agriculture systems. *Crop Science*, *47*, 1765–1769. .doi:10.2135/cropsci2007.05.0280

Bulusu, N., Heidemann, J., & Estrin, D. (2000). GPS-less low-cost outdoor localization for very small devices. *IEEE Personal Communications*, *7*(5), 28–34. doi:10.1109/98.878533

Burmester, M., & Desmedt, Y. (1994). A secure and efficient conference key distribution system. In A. De Santis (Ed.), *Advances in cryptology* – EUROCRYPT '94 (Lecture Notes in Computer Science, Vol 950). Berlin: Springer.

Burrell, J., Brooke, T., & Beckwith, R. (2004). Vineyard computing: Sensor networks in agricultural production. *IEEE Pervasive Computing / IEEE Computer Society [and] IEEE Communications Society*, *3*(1), 38–45. doi:10.1109/MPRV.2004.1269130

Caffery, J. (1998, April). Overview of radiolocation in CDMA cellular systems. *IEEE Communications Magazine*.

Cambridge. (2009). *Cambridge advanced learner's dictionary* (3rd ed.). Cambridge, UK: Cambridge. Retrieved from http://dictionary.cambridge.org/dictionary

Campanoni, S., & Fornaciari, W. (2008). Models and tradeoffs in WSN sytem-level Design. In *Proceedings of the 11th Euromicro Conference on Digital System Design*, (pp. 676-683).

Campbell, A. T., Gomez, J., & Kim, S. (2002). Comparison of IP micromobility protocols. *IEEE Wireless Communications*, *9*(1), 72–82. doi:10.1109/MWC.2002.986462

Campbell-Clause, J., & Fisher, D. (2005). *Irrigation techniques for winegrapes. Farmnote*. South Perth, Australia: Western Australian Department of Agriculture.

Capkun, S., Buttya, L., & Hubaux, P. (2003). Self-organized public key management for mobile ad hoc networks. *IEEE Transactions on Mobile Computing*, *2*(1), 52–64. doi:10.1109/TMC.2003.1195151

Capkun, S., Hubaux, J. P., & Buttyán, L. (2006). Mobility helps peer-to-peer security. *IEEE Transactions on Mobile Computing*, *5*(1), 43–51. doi:10.1109/TMC.2006.12

Čapkun, S., Hamdi, M., & Hubaux, J. (2001). GPS-free positioning in mobile ad-hoc networks. In *Proceedings of the 34th Annual Hawaii International Conference on System Sciences*, (pp. 3481–3490). Washington, DC: IEEE Computer Society.

Capkun, S., Hubaux, J. P., & Buttyán, L. (2003b). Mobility helps security in ad hoc networks. Paper presented at *ACM MobiHoc*. New York: ACM.

Carneiro, G., Ruela, J., & Ricardo, M. (2004, April). Cross-layer design in 4G wireless terminals. *IEEE Wireless Communications*, *11*(2), 7–13. doi:10.1109/MWC.2004.1295732

Castillo Luzón, C. A. (2007). *Implementación de un prototipo de red de sensores inalámbricos para invernaderos* (pp. 1–110). Quito, Ecuador: Escuela Politécnica Nacional.

Cederval, M., & Moses, R. L. (1997). Efficient maximum likelihood DOA estimation for signal with known waveforms in the presence of multipath. *IEEE Transactions on Signal Processing*, *45*(3), 808–811. doi:10.1109/78.558512

CEN. (2005). *TS 17261: Intelligent transport systems - Automatic vehicle and equipment identification - Intermodal good transport architecture and terminology*. Brussels: Comité Européen de Normalisation.

Certicom Corp. (2004). Crypto column: MQV: Efficient and authenticated key agreement. *Code & Cipher: Certicom's bulletin of security and cryptography, 1*(2).

Chakrabarti, S., & Mishra, A. (2001). QoS Issues in ad hoc wireless networks. *IEEE Communications Magazine*, *39*(2), 142–148. doi:10.1109/35.900643

Chalamalasetti, M. (2003). The shifting landscape of wireless communications. New Delhi: Bharat Sanchar Nigam Limited. Retrieved 2009, from http://portal.bsnl.in/Knowledgebase.asp?intNewsId=8525&strNewsMore=more

Chan, A. (2004). Distributed symmetric key management for mobile ad hoc networks. Paper presented at *IEEE INFOCOM*. New York: IEEE.

Chan, H., & Perrig, A. (2005). PIKE: Peer intermediaries for key establishment in sensor networks. Paper presented at *IEEE INFOCOM*. New York: IEEE.

Chan, H., Perrig, A., & Song, D. (2010). (in press). Random key pre-distribution schemes for sensor networks. Paper presented at the *IEEE Security and Privacy Symposium*. New York: IEEE.

Chang, C. C., Muftic, S., & Nagel, D. J. (2007). Measurement of energy costs of security in wireless sensor nodes. In *Proceedings of the Sixteenth International Conference on Computer Communications and Networks (ICCCN'07)* (pp. 95-102). New York: IEEE Computer Society.

Chargoy, L., Vázquez, J., Ortegón, J., & Chan, F. (2009). *Sistema de transmisión a largas distancias por radio-frecuencia.* Universidad de Quintana Roo, División de Ciencias e Ingeniería, Ingeniería en Redes. Chetumal, México: UQRoo.

Chatzigiannakis, V., Grammatikou, M., & Papavassiliou, S. (2007). Extending driver's horizon through comprehensive incident detection in vehicular networks. *IEEE Transactions on Vehicular Technology*, 3256–3265. doi:10.1109/TVT.2007.906410

Choi, S., Kim, B., Park, J., Kang, C., & Eom, D. (2004). An implementation of wireless sensor network for security system using Bluetooth. *IEEE Transactions on Consumer Electronics*, *50*(1), 236–244.

Chong, E. K. P., & Zak, S. H. (Eds.). (2008). *An introduction to optimization*. Hoboken, NJ: John Wiley and Sons.

Choonhwa, C. L., & Sumi, H. (2002). Protocols for service discovery in dynamic and mobile networks. *International Journal of Computer Research*, *11*(1), 1–12.

Clausen, T., & Jacquet, P. (2003, October). *Optimized link state routing protocol.* Fremont, CA: The Internet Engineering Task Force (IETF). Retrieved September 17, 2009, from http://www.ietf.org/rfc/rfc3626.txt

Commission for Global Road Safety. (2009). *Make roads safe, a decade of action for road safety*. London: Commission for Global Road Safety.

Coulouris, G. (2002). *Distributed systems concepts and design*. London: Addison Wesley.

Cowan, T. (2000). Precision agriculture and site-specific management: Current status and emerging policy issues. *CRS Report for Congress*, 1-26.

Cox, T., & Cox, M. (Eds.). (1994). *Monographs on Statistics and Applied Probability 59: Multidimensional Scaling*. London: Chapman and Hall.

Crossbow Technologies. (2008). *Crosbow techonologies*. Retrieved 2008, from http://www.xbow.com

Crossbow Technology Inc. (2006). Mica2 datasheet. San Jose, CA: Crossbow Technology Inc. Retrieved October 13, 2009, from http://www.xbow.com/Products/Product_pdf_files/Wireless_pdf/MICA2_Datasheet.pdf

Crossbow. (2009). *Xbow*. Retrieved December from http://www.crossbow.com

Culler, D., Estrin, D., & Srivastava, M. (2004). Guest editors' introduction: Overview of sensor networks. *Computer*, *37*(8), 41–49. .doi:10.1109/MC.2004.93

Dao, D. (2002). *Location-based services: Technical and business issues.* Sydney, Australia: Satellite Navigation and Positioning Lab, University of New South Wales. Retrieved 2007, from http://www.gmat.unsw.edu.au/snap/about/publications_year.htm

Davies, R. (2004). Development of a mobile network simulation and visualisation application. Edinburgh, UK.

Dawson, R., Boyd, C., Dawson, E., & Nieto, J. M. G. A. L. (2006). SKMA: A key management architecture for SCADA systems. In R. Buyya, T. Ma, R. Safavi-Naini, C. Steketee & W. Susilo (Eds.), *Proceedings of the Fourth Australasian Symposium on Grid Computing and e-Research (AusGrid'06) and the Fourth Australasian Information Security Workshop (Network Security) (AISW'06),* (Vol. 54, pp. 183-192). ACT, Australia: Australian Computer Society.

de Figueiredo, R. J. P. (2009). Cognitive signal processing: an emerging technology for the prediction of behavior of complex human/machine systems. In *Proceedings of the International Conference on Communications, Circuits and Systems (ICCCAS)* (pp. 1-2). New York: IEEE.

Diffie, W., & Hellman, M. E. (1976). New directions in cryptography. *IEEE Transactions on Information Theory*, *22*(6), 644–654. doi:10.1109/TIT.1976.1055638

Doherty, L., Ghaoui, L. E., & Pister, K. S. J. (2001). Convex position estimation in wireless sensor networks. [Washington, DC: IEEE Computer Society.]. *Proceedings - IEEE INFOCOM*, *2001*, 1655–1663.

Dorigo, M., & Di Caro, G. (1999). The ant-colony optimization meta-heuristic. In *New ideas in optimization.* Maidenhead, UK: McGraw-Hill.

DOT. (2006). *IEEE 1609 - Family of standards for wireless access in vehicular environments (WAVE)*. Washington, DC: U.S. Department of Transportation, Research and Innovative Technology Administration.

Douceur, J. R. (2002). The Sybil attack. In *Proceedings of the 1st International Workshop on Peer-to-Peer Systems (IPTPS)* (pp. 251–260).

Dousse, O., Thiran, P., & Hasler, M. (2002). Connectivity in ad-hoc and hybrid networks. In *Proceedings of 21st Annual Joint Conference of the IEEE Computer and Communications Societies (INFOCOM)* (pp. 1079-1088). New York: IEEE.

Dressler, F. (2006). *Self-organization in ad hoc networks: Overview and classification* [Technical Report 02/06]. Erlangen, Germany: University of Erlangen, Department of Computer Sciences.

Dutta, P. K. (1999). *Strategies and games: Theory and practice*. Cambridge, MA: MIT Press.

Edordu, C., & Sacks, L. (2006). Self organising wireless sensor networks as a land management tool in developing countries: A preliminary survey. In *London Communications Symposium* (pp. 4-7). London: University College London.

EEA. (2006). *Greenhouse gas emission trends and projections in Europe 2006*. Copenhagen: European Environment Agency.

EEA. (2006). *Technical report 9: Urban sprawl in Europe - the ignored challenge*. Copenhagen: European Environmental Agency.

Eigen, M. (1979). *The hypercycle: A principle of natural self-organization*. Berlin: Springer-Verlag.

Elbert, B. (2008). Wireless soil sensors to help farming, improve understanding of carbon, nitrogen cycles. *Biopact*. Heverlee, Belgium: Biopact. Retrieved from http://news.mongabay.com/bioenergy/

Enck, W., Ongtang, M., & McDaniel, P. (2009). Understanding android security. *IEEE Security & Privacy*, *7*(1), 50–57. doi:10.1109/MSP.2009.26

Eren, T., Goldenberg, D. K., Whitley, W., Yang, R. Y., Morse, A. S., Anderson, B. D. O., & Belhumer, P. N. (2004). Rigidity, computation, and randomization in network localization. [Washington, DC: IEEE Computer Society.]. *Proceedings - IEEE INFOCOM*, *2004*, 2673–2684.

Ergen, M., Coleri, S., & Varaiya, P. (2003, December). QoS aware adaptive resource allocation techniques for fair scheduling in OFDMA based broadband wireless access systems. *IEEE Transactions on Broadcasting*, *40*(4).

Ermis, E., & Saligrama, V. (2005). Adaptive statistical sampling methods for decentralized estimation and detection of localized phenomena. *Paper presented at the 4th international symposium on Information processing in sensor networks.*

Eroski, F. (2008). Diseñan una red de sensores inalámbricos aplicables en la agricultura de precisión. Retrieved from http://www.consumer.es/seguridad-alimentaria/2008/08/12/179220.php

ERTICO-a. (1998). *Intelligent city transport: A guidebook to intelligent transport systems*. Brussels: ITS City Pioneers Consortium.

ERTICO-b. (1998). *Intelligent city transport: ITS planning handbook*. Brussels: ITS City Pioneers Consortium.

ERTICO-c. (1998). *Intelligent city transport: ITS toolbox*. Brussels: ITS City Pioneers Consortium.

Eschenauer, L., & Gligor, V. D. (2002). A key-management scheme for distributed sensor networks. In *Proceedings of the 9th Conference on Computer Communication Security (CCS)* (pp. 41–47).

Etkin, R., Parekh, A., & Tse, D. (2007). Spectrum sharing for unlicensed bands. *IEEE Journal on Selected Areas in Communications*, *25*(3), 517. doi:10.1109/JSAC.2007.070402

Evensen, K. (2006). *CALM architecture and CALM M5 convenor*. Dallas, TX: Q-Free.

Fazio, M., Villari, M., & Pulifito, A. (2005). AIPAC: Automatic IP address configuration in mobile ad hoc networks. *Computer Communications*, *29*(8), 1189–1200. doi:10.1016/j.comcom.2005.07.006

Ferentinos, K. P., & Tsiligiridis, T. A. (2005). Heuristic design and energy conservation of wireless sensor networks for precision agriculture. Paper presented at *International Congress on Information Technologies in Agriculture, Food and Environment (ITAFE'05)*, Adana, Turkey.

Fernandez, D., & Montes, H. (2002). Enhanced quality of service method for guaranteed bit rate services over shared channels in EGPRS systems. *Proceedings of IEEE Vehicular Technology Conference*, Birmingham, NY. New York: IEEE.

Ferro, E., & Potorti, F. (2005). Bluetooth and wi-fi wireless protocols: A survey and a comparison. *IEEE Wireless Communications Magazine*, *12*(1), 12–23. doi:10.1109/MWC.2005.1404569

Flannigan, M. D., Amiro, B. D., Logan, K. A., Stocks, B. J., & Wotton, B. M. (2006). Forest fires and climate change in the 21st century. *Mitigation and Adaptation Strategies for Global Change*, *11*(4), 847–859. .doi:10.1007/s11027-005-9020-7

Foerster, H. V. (2003). On self-organizing systems and their environments. In *Understanding essays on cybernetics and cognition* (pp. 1–19). New York: Springer.

Foh, C. H., Liu, G., Lee, B. S., Seet, B. C., Wong, K. J., & Fu, C. P. (2005). Network connectivity of one-dimensional MANETs with random waypoint movement. *IEEE Communications Letters*, *9*(1), 31–33.

Foh, C. H., & Lee, B. S. (2004). A closed form network connectivity formula for one dimensional MANETs. In *Proceedings of the International Conference on Communications (ICC)*, Paris, France (pp. 3739-3742).

Franceschetti, M., Booth, L., Cook, M., Meester, M., & Bruck, J. (2004). Percolation in wireless multi-hop networks. *Journal of Statistical Physics*.

Franceschetti, M., Booth, L., Cook, M., Meester, R., & Bruck, J. (2004). Continuum percolation with unreliable and spread out connections. In *Proceedings of the ICMS Workshop on Spatial Stochastic Modeling with Applications to Communications Networks*, Edinburgh, Scotland.

Friedman, R., & Kliot, G. (2006). Location services in wireless ad hoc and hybrid networks: A survey. Haifa, Israel: Technion – Israel Institute of Technology. Retrieved 2009, from www.cs.technion.ac.il/users/wwwb/cgi-bin/tr.../CS-2006-10.pdf

Gandham, S. R., Dawande, M., Prakash, R., & Venkatesan, S. (2003). Energy efficient schemes for wireless sensor networks with multiple mobile base stations. In [GLOBECOM]. *Proceedings of the IEEE Global Telecommunications Conference*, *1*, 377–381.

Ganesan, D., Krishnamachari, B., Woo, A., Culler, D., Estrin, D., & Wicker, S. (2002). *An empirical study of epidemic algorithms in large scale multihop wireless networks* (Report No. IRB-TR-02-003). Berkeley, CA: Intel Research Berkeley.

Ganguly, S., Navda, V., Kim, K., Kashyap, A., Niculescu, D., & Izmailov, R. …Das, S. (2006). *Performance optimizations for deploying VoIP services in mesh networks.* Retrieved from http://www.wings.cs.sunysb.edu/~anand/paper/jsac06.pdf

Gao, T., Greenspan, D., Welsh, M., Juang, R., & Alm, A. (2005). Vital signs monitoring and patient tracking over a wireless network. In *Proceedings of the 27th Annual International Conference of the IEEE EMBS* (pp. 102-105). New York: IEEE.

Gao, X., Wu, G., & Miki, T. (2004, June). End-to-end QoS provisioning in mobile heterogeneous networks. *IEEE Wireless Communications*, pp. 24–34. New York: IEEE.

García, M. A., Gutiérrez, S., López, H. C., & Ruiz, A. (2007). State of the art of robot technology applied to greenhouses. *Avances en Investigación Agropecuaria*, *11*(9).

Garcia, T. C. C. (2005). *Discovery service in ad hoc networks using ants.* Unpublished master's thesis, ITESM-Monterrey, Mexico.

Garey, M. R., & Johnson, D. S. (1979). *Computers and intractability: A guide to the theory of NP-completeness*. New York: W. H. Freeman.

Garg, P., Doshi, R., Greene, R., Baker, M., Malek, M., & Cheng, X. (2003). Using IEEE 802.11e MAC for QoS over wireless. In *Proceedings of IPCCC*, Phoenix, AZ.

Gasperi, M. (2008). *LabVIEW for LEGO MINDSTORMS NXT*. Allendale, NJ: NTS Press.

Gaviria, N., Aguirre, J. A., & Aedo, J. E. (2009). Data collection and Signal Processing strategy for low power consumption in Wireless Sensor Networks Nodes. In *Proceedings of the IEEE 2009 Latincom*, (pp. 1-5).

Gesbert, D., Shafi, M., Shiu, D., Smith, P., & Naguib, A. (2003, March). From theory to practice: An overview of MIMO space-time coded wireless systems. *IEEE Journal on Selected Areas in Communications*, *21*(3), 281–302. doi:10.1109/JSAC.2003.809458

Gold, M. V. (2007). *Sustainable agriculture: Definitions and terms. Alternative Farming Systems Information Center*. Beltsville, MD: United States Department of Agriculture.

Gonzalez-Sanchez, A. L. (2005). *Mobility support between MANETs and the internet, using IPv6 and the OLSR Routing Protocol*. Master thesis, CICESE Research Center, Mexico.

GPP. (2009). *3GPP - 3rd Generation Partnership Project*. Retrieved from http://www.3gpp.org

Griffin, T. W., Lowenberg-DeBoer, J., Lambert, D. M., Peone, J., Payne, T., & Daberkow, S. G. (2004). *Adoption, profitability, and making better use of precision farming data* [Staff paper]. West Lafayette, IN: Purdue University.

Groenen, P., & Borg, I. (Eds.). (1997). *Modern multidimensional scaling, theory and applications*. New York: Springer-Verlag.

Gu, D., & Zhang, J. (2003, June). QoS enhancement in IEEE 802.11 wireless local area networks. *IEEE Communications Magazine*, *41*(6), 120–124. doi:10.1109/MCOM.2003.1204758

Gui, C., & Mohapatra, P. (2004). Power conservation and quality of Surveillance in target tracking sensor networks. In *Proceedings of ACM Mobile Computing and Networking Conference (MobiCom)*, (pp. 129-143).

Guiguere, E. (2000). *Java 2 micro edition*. Chichester, UK: John and Wiley Sons.

Gunes, M., & Reibel, J. (2002). An IP address configuration algorithm for Zeroconf. In *Proceedings of International Workshop on Broadband Wireless Ad Hoc Networks and Services,* Sophia-Antipolis, France.

Günther, C. G. (1989). An identity-based key-exchange protocol. In J. J. Quisquater & J. Vandewalle (Eds.), *Proceedings of the Workshop on the Theory and Application of Cryptographic Techniques on Advances in cryptology* (Lecture Notes in Computer Science, pp. 29-37). Berlin: Springer.

Habetha, J., Mangold, S., & Wiegert, J. (2001). 802.11 versus HiperLAN/2: A comparison of decentralized and centralized MAC protocols for multihop ad hoc radio networks. In *Proceedings of 5th World Multiconference on Systemics, Cybernetics and Informatics (SCI)*, Orlando, FL.

Han, Z., Ji, Z., & Ray Liu, K. J. (2007). Non-cooperative resource competition game by virtual referee in multi-cell OFDMA networks. *IEEE Journal on Selected Areas in Communications*, *25*(6), 1079–1090. doi:10.1109/JSAC.2007.070803

Hartung, C., Balasalle, J., & Han, R. (2005). *Node compromise in sensor networks: The need for secure systems* (Technical Report No. CU-CS-990-05). Boulder, CO: University of Colorado at Boulder, Department of Computer Science. Retrieved October 13, 2009, from http://www.cs.colorado.edu/department/publications/reports/docs/CU-CS-990-05.pdf

Hatler, M., Gurganious, D., & Ritter, M. (2008). *Perpetual power solutions for WSN*. San Diego, CA: ON World.

Hayes, M. (1996). *Statistical Digital Signal Processing and Modeling*. John Wiley & Sons.

Haykin, S. (2005). Cognitive radio: Brain-empowered wireless communications. *IEEE Journal on Selected Areas in Communications*, *23*(2), 201–220. doi:10.1109/JSAC.2004.839380

He, X., Prasad, A., Sethi, S. P., & Gutierrez, G. (2007). A survey of Stackelberg differential game models in supply and marketing channels. [JSSSE]. *Journal of Systems Science and Systems Engineering*, *16*(4), 385–413. doi:10.1007/s11518-007-5058-2

Heegard, C., Coffey, J., Gummadi, S., Murphy, P. A., Provencio, R., & Rossin, E. J. (2001, November). High-performance wireless ethernet. *IEEE Communications Magazine*, *39*(11). doi:10.1109/35.965361

Hefeeda, M., & Bagheri, M. (2007). Wireless sensor networks for early detection of forest fires. In *IEEE Internatonal Conference on Mobile Adhoc and Sensor Systems*, Pisa, Italy (pp. 1-6). New York: IEEE. doi:10.1109/MOBHOC.2007.4428702

Heidemann, J. (2003). Medium Access Control in Wireless Sensor Networks. *USC/ISI Tech. Report ISI-TR-580.*

Heinzelman, W. B., Chandrakasan, A. P., & Balakrishnan, H. (2002). An application-specific protocol architecture for wireless microsensor networks. *IEEE Transactions on Wireless Communications, 1*(4), 660–670. doi:10.1109/TWC.2002.804190

Heinzelman, W., Chandrakasan, A., & Balakrishnan, H. (2000). Energy-Efficient Communication Protocol for Wireless Microsensor Networks. *Paper presented at the 33rd Hawaii International Conference on System Sciences (HICSS).*

Heinzelman, W., Kulik, J., & Balakrishnan, H. (1999). Adaptive Protocols for Information Dissemination in Wireless Sensor Networks. In *Proceedings of the 5th ACM/IEEE Mobile Computing and Networking Conference (MobiCom)*, (pp. 174-185). Seattle.

Herzberg, A., Jarecki, S., Krawczyk, H., & Yung, H. (1995). Proactive secret sharing or: How to cope with perpetual leakage. *Lecture Notes in Computer Science, 963*, 339–352. doi:10.1007/3-540-44750-4_27

Hightower, J., & Borriello, G. (2001). Location systems for ubiquitous computing. *Computer, 34*(8), 57–66. doi:10.1109/2.940014

Hill, J. L. (2003). *System architecture for wireless sensor networks.* PhD Thesis. University of California, Berkeley.

Hill, J. L., Szewczyk, R., Woo, A., Hollar, S., Culler, D. E., & Pister, K. S. J. (2000). System architecture directions for networked sensors. In *Proceedings of the Ninth International Conference on Architectural Support for Programming Languages and Operating Systems, (ASPLOS'00)* (pp. 93-104).

Hirakawa, A., Saraiva, A., & Cugnasca, C. (2002). Wireless robust robot for agricultural applications. In *Proceedings of the World Congress of Computers in Agriculture and Natural Resources* (pp. 13-15).

Holger, K., & Willing, A. (2005). *Protocols and Architectures for Wireless Sensor Networks.* John Wiley & Sons.

Holler, M. (2009). Camalie cineyards. Retrieved from http://www.camalie.com/

Holma, H., & Toskala, A. (2006). *HSDPA/HSUPA for UMTS.* Hoboken, NJ: John Wiley & Sons. doi:10.1002/0470032634

Hong, Y., & Scaglione, A. (2006). Energy-efficient broadcasting with cooperative transmissions in wireless sensor networks. *IEEE Transactions on Wireless Communications, 5*(10), 2844–2855. doi:10.1109/TWC.2006.04608

Howard, A., Matarić, M., & Sukhatme, G. (2001). Relaxation on a mesh: A formalism for generalized localization. In *Proceedings of the IEEE/RSJ International Conference on Intelligent Robots and Systems* (pp. 1055–1060). Washington, DC: IEEE Computer Society

Hu, L., & Evans, D. (2004). Localization for mobile networks. In *Proceedings of the 10th annual international conference on Mobile Computing and Networking*, Philadelphia, PA (pp 45-57). New York: ACM.

Huang, J., Berry, R., & Honig, M. L. (2006a). Auction-based spectrum sharing. *ACM Mobile Networks and Applications Journal, 11*(3), 405–418. doi:10.1007/s11036-006-5192-y

Huang, J., Berry, R., & Honig, M. L. (2006b). Distributed interference compensation for wireless networks. *IEEE Journal on Selected Areas in Communications, 24*(5), 1074–1084. doi:10.1109/JSAC.2006.872889

Hubaux, J. P. (2004). *Technical report IC/2004/24 a survey of inter-vehicle communication.* Lausanne, Switzerland: School of Computer and Communication Sciences.

Hwang, Y., & Varshney, P. (2003). An adaptive QoS routing protocol with dispersity for ad-hoc networks. In *Proceedings of the 36th Annual Hawaii International Conference on System Sciences* (pp. 302–311). New York: IEEE.

IEEE 802.15.4. (2003, October). IEEE 802.15.4, Wireless Medium Access Control (MAC) and Physical Layer (PHY) Specications for Low-Rate Wireless Personalworks (LRWPANS) [Technical report]. New York: IEEE.

IEEE 802.15.4a. (2007, January). IEEE p802.15.4a/d7, Part 15.4: Wireless Medium Access Control (MAC) and Physical Layer (PHY) Specifications for Low-Rate Wireless Personal Area Networks (LR-WPANS): Amendment to add alternate PHY [Technical report]. New York: IEEE.

IEEE. 802.11-2007. (2007). Standard and Amendment 1 (Radio Resource Measurement). New York: IEEE.

IEEE. 802.15.6. (2009). IEEE 802.15 WPAN™ Task Group 6 (TG6) Body Area Networks. Retrieved from http://www.ieee802.org/15/pub/TG6.html

Imad, M., & Ilyas, M. (2005). *Handbook of Sensor Network: Compact Wireless and Wired Sensing Systems*. CRC Press.

Indrayan, G. (2006). *Address autoconfiguration in mobile ad hoc networks.* Unpublished master's thesis, University of Colorado, Boulder, CO.

Ingemarsson, I., Tang, D., & Wong, C. (1982). A conference key distribution system. *IEEE Transactions on Information Theory, 28*(5), 714–720. doi:10.1109/TIT.1982.1056542

Intanagonwiwat, C., Govindan, R., & Estrin, D. (2000). Directed diffusion: a scalable and robust communication paradigm for sensor networks. In *Proceedings of the ACM Mobile Computing and Networking (MobiCom)*, (pp. 56-67). Boston.

Intelligent Transportation Society of America. (2009). *ITS America*. Retrieved from http://www.itsa.org/

Intelligent Transportation Society of Australia. (2009). *ITS Australia*. Retrieved from http://www.its-australia.com.au

Intelligent Transportation Systems Society of Canada. (2009). *ITS Canada*. Retrieved from http://www.its-canada.ca

ISO TC 204, W. 1. (2006). *Intelligent transport systems — System architecture, taxonomy and terminology — Procedures for developing ITS deployment plans utilising ITS system architecture.*

ISO TC204. W. G. (2008). *ISO TC204 WG16 CALM*. Retrieved 2009, from http://www.calm.hu/

Jafari, R., & Andre, A. E. (2005). Wireless sensor networks for health monitoring. In *Proceedings of the Second Annual International Conference on Mobile and Ubiquitous Systems (MobiQuitous)* (pp. 479-481).

Japan, I. T. S. (2009). *ITS Japan*. Retrieved from http://www.its-jp.org/english/

Jeong, I. (2006). Zone-based service architecture for wireless ad-hoc networks. In *Proceedings of the International Conference on Networking, International Conference on Systems and International Conference on Mobile Communications and Learning Technologies.* New York: ACM Portal.

Jinghua, W., Huan, H., Bo, C., Yuanyuan, C., & Tingting, G. (2009). Data Aggregation and Routing in Wireless Sensor Networks Using Improved Ant Colony Algorithm. *International Forum on Computer Science-Technology and Applications, 3*, 215–218. doi:10.1109/IFCSTA.2009.292

Johnson, D. B., Maltz, D. A., & Hu, Y. C. (2007). *The dynamic source routing protocol for mobile ad hoc networks (DSR)*. Retrieved October 1, 2009, from http://www.ietf.org/rfc/rfc4728.txt

Johnson, D., & Maltz, D. (1996). Dynamic source routing in ad hoc wireless networks. *Mobile Computing, 353*, 153-181. Dordrecht, The Netherlands: Kluwer Academic Publishers.

Johnson, D., Perkins, C. E., & Arkko, J. (2004). *Mobility support in IPv6.* Fremont, CA: The Internet Engineering Task Force (IETF). Retrieved September 17, 2009, from http://www.ietf.org/rfc/rfc3775.txt

Johnson, T., & Margalho, M. (2006). Wireless sensor networks for agroclimatology monitoring in the Brazilian Amazon. In *Proceedings of the International Conference on Communication Technology,* Guilin, China (pp. 1-4).

Jones, V. Halteren van, A., Widya, I., Dokovski, N., Koprinkov, G., Bults, R., Konstantas, D., & Herzog, R. (2006). MobiHealth: Mobile health services based on body area networks. In S. L. Robert & H. Istepanian, *M-Health: Emerging mobile health systems* (p. 624). Berlin: Springer.

Jorstad, I., Dustdar, S., & Van Do, T. (2005). An analysis of current mobile services and enabling technologies. *International Journal of Ad Hoc and Ubiquitous Computing, 1*(1-2).

Jurdak, R., Baldi, P., & Videira Lopes, C. (2007). Adaptive Low Power Listening for Wireless Sensor Networks. *IEEE Transactions on Mobile Computing, 6*(8), 988–1004. doi:10.1109/TMC.2007.1037

Kaiser, W., & Rundel, P. (2008). *Researchers use NI LabVIEW and NI CompactRIO to perform environmental monitoring in the Costa Rican rain orest.* Austin, TX: National Instruments. Retrieved September 2009, from http://sine.ni.com/cs/app/doc/p/id/cs-11143

Kannan, A. A., Mao, G., & Vucetic, B. (2006). Simulated annealing based wireless sensor network localization. *Journal of Computers, 1*(2), 15–22. doi:10.4304/jcp.1.2.15-22

Karaca, O., & Sokullu, R. (2009). Comparative Study of Cross Layer Frameworks for Wireless Sensor Networks. In *Proceedings of the Wireless Communication Society, Vehicular Technology, Information Theory and Aerospace & Electronics Systems Technology (Wireless VITAE)*, (pp. 896-900). Denmark.

Karl, H., & Willig, A. (Eds.). (2005). *Protocols and architectures for wireless sensor networks.* Chichester, UK: John Wiley & Sons. doi:10.1002/0470095121

Karlof, C., & Wagner, D. (2003). Secure routing in wireless sensor networks: Attacks and countermeasures. *Ad Hoc Networks, 1*(2-3), 293–315. doi:10.1016/S1570-8705(03)00008-8

Karp, B., & Kung, H. T. (2000). GPSR: Greedy perimeter stateless routing for wireless networks. In *Proceedings of the 6th Annual ACM/IEEE International Conference on Mobile Computing and Networking (MobiCom)* (pp. 243-254). New York: ACM.

Kassam, S., & Poor, H. (1983). Robust signal processing for communication systems. *IEEE Communications Magazine, 21*(1), 20–28. doi:10.1109/MCOM.1983.1091322

Kaufman, C., Perlman, R., & Speciner, M. (2002). *Network security private communication in a public world.* Upper Saddle River, NJ: Prentice Hall PTR.

Kho, J., Rogers, A., & Jennings, N. R. (2007). Decentralised adaptive sampling of wireless sensor networks. In *Proceedings of the First International Workshop on Agent Technology for Sensor Networks, a workshop of the 6th International Joint Conference on Autonomous Agents and Multiagent Systems (AAMAS-07)*, (pp. 55-62).

Kim, D., Lee, S., Hwang, T., Won, K., & Chung, D. (2006). A wireless sensor node processor with digital baseband based on adaptive threshold adjustment for emotional lighting system. *IEEE Transactions on Consumer Electronics, 52*(4), 1362–1367. doi:10.1109/TCE.2006.273157

Kim, Y., Perrig, A., & Tsudik, G. (2000b). Simple and fault-tolerant key agreement for dynamic collaborative groups. In *Proceedings of the 7th ACM Conference on Computer and Communications Security* (pp. 235-244). New York: ACM Press.

Kinney, P. (2003). ZigBee technology: Wireless control that simply works. In *Communications Design Conference*, San Jose, CA (pp. 1-20).

Kitchen, N. R. (2008). Emerging technologies for real-time and integrated agriculture decisions. *Computers and Electronics in Agriculture, 61*(1), 1–3. .doi:10.1016/j.compag.2007.06.007

Klonowski, M., Kutylowski, M., Ren, M., & Rybarczyk, K. (2007). *Forward-secure key evolution in wireless sensor networks.* In F. Bao, S. Ling, T. Okamoto, H. Wang & C. Xing (Eds.), *Proceedings of the Sixth International Conference on Cryptology and Network Security (CANS'07)* (Lecture Notes in Computer Science, Vol. 4856, pp. 102-120). Berlin: Springer.

Ko, Y., & Vaidya, N. H. (1998). Location-aided routing (LAR) in mobile ad hoc networks. In *Proceedings of IEEE/ACM Mobicom* (pp. 66-75). New York: IEEE.

Kong, J., Zerfos, P., Luo, H., Lu, S., & Zhang, L. (2001). Providing robust and ubiquitous security support for mobile ad-hoc networks. In P*roceedings of the ninth International Conference on Network Protocols (ICNP)*, (pp. 251–260).

Kotamäki, N., Thessler, S., Koskiaho, J., Hannukkala, A. O., Huitu, H., & Huttula, T. (2009). Wireless in-situ Sensor Network for Agriculture and Water Monitoring on a River Basin Scale in Southern Finland: Evaluation from a Data User's Perspective. *Sensors (Basel, Switzerland), 9*(4), 2862–2883. .doi:10.3390/s90402862

Kozat, U., & Tassiulas, L. (2003). Network layer support for service discovery in mobile ad-hoc networks. In *INFOCOM 2003: Twenty-Second Annual Joint Conference of the IEEE Computer and Communications.* New York: IEEE.

Krim, H., & Viberg, M. (1996). Two decades of array signal processing research: The parametric approach. *IEEE Signal Processing Magazine*, *13*, 67–94. doi:10.1109/79.526899

Krishnamachari, B., Estrin, E., & Wicker, S. (2002). Impact of data aggregation in wireless sensor networks. *Paper presented at the 22nd International Conference on Distributed Computing Systems.*

Kröller, A., Fekete, S., Pfisterer, D., & Fischer, S. (2006). Deterministic boundary recognition and topology extraction for large sensor networks. In *Proceedings of the seventeenth annual ACM-SIAM Symposium on Discrete Algorithms (SODA)* (pp. 1000-1009). New York: ACM press.

Kruskal, J. B., & Wish, M. (1978). Multidimensional scaling. In Uslaner, E. (Ed.), *Sage university papers: Quantitative applications in the social sciences*. Newbury Park, CA: Sage Publications.

Kulkarni, G. H., & Waingankar, P. G. (2007). Fuzzy logic based traffic light controller. *International Conference on Industrial and Information Systems (ICIIS)*, Penadeniya, Sri Lanka (pp. 107-110). New York: IEEE.

Laifenfeld, M., & Trachtenberg, A. (2008). Identifying codes and covering problems. *IEEE Transactions on Information Theory*, *54*(9), 3929–3950. doi:10.1109/TIT.2008.928263

Laitinen, H. (2001). Cellular network optimisation based on mobile location. *EC GI & GIS Portal* [Web site]. Retrieved 2009, from http://www.ec-gis.org/project.cfm?id=306&db=project

Lamont, L., Wang, M., Villasenor, L., Randhawa, T., Hardy, R., & McConnel, P. (2002). An IPv6 and OLSR based architecture for integrating WLANs and MANETs to the internet. In *Proceedings of the International Symposium on Wireless Personal Multimedia* (pp. 816-820).

Lamont, L., Wang, M., Villasenor, L., Randhawa, T., & Hardy, S. (2003). Integrating WLANs & MANETs to the IPv6 based internet. In *Proceedings of the IEEE International Conference on Communications* (pp. 1090-1095). New York: IEEE.

Lamport, L. (1981). Password authentification with insecure communication. *Communications of the ACM*, *24*(11), 770–772. doi:10.1145/358790.358797

Lan, K. C., Wang, Z., Berriman, R., Moors, T., & Hassan, M. (2007). Implementation of a wireless mesh network testbed for traffic control. *Proceedings of 16th International Conference on Computer Communications and Networks (ICCCN)*, Honolulu, HI (pp. 1022-1027). New York: IEEE.

Langendoen, K., & Reijers, N. (2003). Distributed localization in wireless sensor networks: a quantitative comparison. *Computer Networks: The International Journal of Computer and Telecommunications Networking*, *43*(4), 499–518.

Langendoen, K. (2005). *The MAC alphabet soup*. Retrieved October 2009, from https://apstwo.st.ewi.tudelft.nl/~koen/MACsoup

Le Borgne, Y., Santini, S., & Bontempi, G. (2007). Adaptive model selection for time series prediction in wireless sensor networks. *Signal Processing*, *87*(12), 3010–3020. doi:10.1016/j.sigpro.2007.05.015

Lecture Notes of the Institute for Computer Sciences. Social Informatics and Telecommunications Engineering, Springer. Retrieved October 13, 2009, from http://eprints.qut.edu.au/27605/1/c27605.pdf

Lee, M., Jianliang, Z., Young-Bae, K., & Shrestha, D. (2006). *Emerging standards for wireless mesh technology* (pp. 56–63). IEEE Wireless Communications.

Lee, T., Chiang, H., Perng, J., Jiang, J., & Wu, B. (2009). Multi-sensor information integration on DSP platform for vehicle navigation safety and driving aid. In *Proceedings of the 2009 IEEE International Conference on Networking, Sensing and Control*, Okayama, Japan (pp. 653-658). New York: IEEE.

Lee, U., Park, J. S., Amir, E., & Gerla, M. (2006). FleaNet: A virtual market place on vehicular networks. In *IEEE V2VCOM,* San Francisco (pp. 1-8). New York: IEEE.

Li, X., & Pahlavan, K. (2004). Super-resolution TOA estimation with diversity for indoor geolocation. *IEEE Transactions on Wireless Communications*, *3*(1), 224–234. doi:10.1109/TWC.2003.819035

Li, B., Qin, Y., Low, C. P., & Gwee, C. L. (2007). A survey on mobile WiMAX. *IEEE Communications Magazine*, *45*(12), 70–75. doi:10.1109/MCOM.2007.4395368

Li, J., Jannotti, J., Couto, D. S., Karger, D. R., & Morris, R. (2000). A scalable location service for geographic ad hoc routing. In *Proceedings of ACM Mobicom* (pp. 120-130). New York: ACM.

Lo, B. (2005). Body Sensor Network-Wireless Sensor Platform for Pervasive Healthcare Monitor. *Paper presented at the 3rd International conference on Pervasive Computing (PERVASIVE).*

Lockheed Martin Federal Systems. (1997). *ITS communications document.* Washington, DC: Federal Highway Administration, US Department of Transportation.

Lomax, T., & Schrank, D. (2005). *Urban mobility study.* College Station, TX: Texas Transportation Institute.

López Riquelme, J., Soto, F., Suardíaz, J., & Iborra, A. (2004). Red de Sensores Inalámbrica para Agricultura de Precisión. In *II Teleco-Forum* (pp. 3–4). Cartagena, Spain: Universidad Politécnica de Cartagena.

Luo, H., & Lu, S. (2004). URSA: Ubiquitous and robust access control for mobile ad hoc networks. *IEEE/ACM Transactions on Networking*, *12*(6), 1049–1063. doi:10.1109/TNET.2004.838598

Luo, H., Zerfos, P., Kong, J., Lu, S., & Zhang, L. (2001). Providing robust and ubiquitous security support for mobile ad-hoc networks. Paper presented at the *9th International Conference on Network Protocols.*

MacKenzie, A. B., & Dasilva, L. A. (2005). Game theory for wireless engineers. *Synthesis Lectures on Communications*, *1*, 1–86. doi:10.2200/S00014ED1V01Y200508COM001

Macker, J. P., & Corson, M. S. (1998). Mobile Ad hoc Networking and the IEFT. *ACM Mobile Computing and Communications Review*, *2*(1), 9–14. doi:10.1145/584007.584015

Madden, S., Franklin, M., Hellertein, J., & Hong, W. (2005). TinyDB: and acquisitional query processing system for sensor networks. *ACM Transactions on Database Systems*, *30*(1), 122–173. doi:10.1145/1061318.1061322

Malan, D., Fulford-jones, T., Welsh, M., & Moulton, S. (2004). CodeBlue: An ad hoc sensor network infrastructure for emergency medical care. Paper presented in *MobiSys Workshop on Applications of Mobile Embedded Systems (WAMES 2004).*

Malvick, K. (1995). Corn stalk rots. [Department of Crop Sciences, University of Illinois at Urbana-Champaign.]. *Urbana (Caracas, Venezuela)*, IL.

Mangold, S., Choi, S., & Esseling, N. (2001, September). An error model for radio transmissions of wireless LANs at 5GHz. In *Proceedings of Aachen Symposium'2001,* Aachen, Germany, (pp. 209-214).

Mao, G., & Fidan, B. (Eds.). (2009). *Localization algorithms and strategies for wireless sensor networks.* Hershey, PA: Information Science Reference.

Mao, G., Fidan, B., & Anderson, B. D. O. (2007). Localization. In Mahalik, N. P. (Ed.), *Sensor networks configuration: Fundamentals, standards, platforms and applications* (pp. 281–315). New York: Springer-Verlag.

Marcelín-Jiménez, R. (2007). Locally-constructed trees for ad-hoc routing. *Telecommunication Systems*, *36*(1-3), 39–48. doi:10.1007/s11235-007-9055-z

Marrón, P. J., Lachenmann, A., & Minder, D. (2005). TinyCubus: A Flexible and Adaptive Framework for Sensor Networks. In *Proceedings of the 2nd European Workshop on Wireless Sensor Networks*, (pp. 278-289).

Maskery, M., Krishnamurthy, V., & Zhao, Q. (2009). Decentralized dynamic spectrum access for cognitive radios: Cooperative design of a non-cooperative game. *IEEE Transactions on Communications*, *57*(2), 459. doi:10.1109/TCOMM.2009.02.070158

Mauve, M., Widmer, J., & Hartenstein, H. (2001). A survey on position-based routing in mobile ad-hoc networks. *IEEE Network Magazine*, *15*(6), 30–39. doi:10.1109/65.967595

Mauw, S., van Vessem, I., & Bos, B. (2006). Forward secure communication in wireless sensor networks. In J. A. Clark, R. F. Paige, F. Polack & P. J. Brooke (Eds.), *Proceedings of the Third International Conference on Security in Pervasive Computing (SPC '06)* (Lecture Notes in Computer Science, Vol. 3934, pp. 32-42). Berlin: Springer.

McCann, S. (2009, September 14). *Official IEEE 802.11 Working Group Project timelines*. Retrieved September 30, 2009, from http://grouper.ieee.org/groups/802/11/Reports/802.11_Timelines.htm

McClanahan, R. (2003). SCADA and IP: Is network convergence really here? *Industry Applications Magazine, IEEE, 9*(2), 29–36. doi:10.1109/MIA.2003.1180947

McGraw-Hill. (2005). Forest fire. In *Encyclopedia of science and technology*. New York: McGraw-Hill Professional Publishing.

McGuire, M., Plataniotis, K. N., & Venetsanopoulos, A. N. (2003). Location of mobile terminals using time measurements and survey points. *IEEE Transactions on Vehicular Technology, 52*(4), 999–1011. doi:10.1109/TVT.2003.814222

McNair, J., & Zhu, F. (2004, June). Vertical handoffs in fourth-generation multi-network environments. *IEEE Wireless Communications*, pp. 8–15.

Meier, R. (2009). *Professional Android application development*. Indianapolis, IN: Wiley Publishing, Inc.

Melodia, T., Vuran, M. C., & Pompili, D. (2006). The state-of-the-art in cross-layer design for wireless sensor networks. In *Proceedings of the EuroNGI Workshops on Wireless and Mobility*, Springer Lecture Notes on Computer Science (LNCS), Vol. 388, (pp. 78-92).

Menezes, A., Oorschot, P., & Vanstone, S. (1996). *Handbook of applied cryptography*. Boca Raton, FL: CRC Press.

Menon, R., Mackenzie, A., Buehrer, R., & Reed, J. (2009). Interference avoidance in networks with distributed receivers. *IEEE Transactions on Communications, 57*(10), 3078–3309. doi:10.1109/TCOMM.2009.10.070362

Menon, R., Mackenzie, A., Hicks, J., Buehrer, R., & Reed, J. (2009). A game-theoretic framework for interference avoidance. *IEEE Transactions on Communications, 57*(4), 1087–1098. doi:10.1109/TCOMM.2009.04.070192

Meulenaer, G. D., Gosset, F., Standaert, F. X., & Pereira, O. (2008). On the energy cost of communication and cryptography in wireless sensor networks. In *Proceedings of the Fourth IEEE International Conference on Wireless & Mobile Computing, Networking & Communication, (WIMOB '08)* (pp. 580-585). New York: IEEE Computer Society.

Michel, Z. A. E. (2005). *A theoretical framework for the evaluation of connectivity, robustness and reachability in wireless ad-hoc networks.* Unpublished master's thesis, ITESM-Monterrey, Mexico.

Mitola, J., & Maguire, G. Q. (1999). Cognitive radio: Making software radios more personal. *IEEE Personal Communications, 6*(4), 13-18. doi: citeulike-article-id:167416

Mobility and Transport. Directorate General. (2009). *Intelligent transport system: A smart move for Europe.* Brussels: European Communities.

Mohsin, M., & Prakash, R. (2002). IP address assignment in a mobile ad hoc network. In *Proceedings of MILCOM 2002 Military Communications Conference,* Anaheim, CA.

Monderer, D., & Shapley, L. (1996). Potential games. *Journal of Games and Economic Behavior, 14*(44), 124–143. doi:10.1006/game.1996.0044

Montero, F., Brasa, A., Montero-Garcia, F., & Orozco, L. (2007). Redes de Sensores Inalámbricas para Viticultura de Precisión en Castilla-La Mancha. In *Proceedings of the XI Congreso SECH. Actas de Horticultura, 48*(1), 158-160. Albacete, Spain: Sociedad Española de Ciencias Hortícolas.

Moore, D., Leonard, J., Rus, D., & Teller, S. (2004). Robust distributed network localization with noisy range measurements. In J. A. Stankovic (Ed.), *Proceedings of the 2nd International Conference on Embedded Networked Sensor Systems* (pp. 50-61). New York: ACM Press.

Mostofi, Y., Chung, T. H., Murray, R. M., & Burdick, J. W. (2005). Communication and sensing trade-offs in decentralized mobile sensor networks: a cross-layer design approach. In *Proceedings of the 4th international symposium on information processing in sensor networks*, (pp. 118 – 125).

Murthy, S. R., & Manoj, B. S. (2004). *Ad hoc wireless networks: Architectures and protocols*. Upper Saddle River, NJ: Prentice-Hall PTR.

Nandan, A., Das, S., Pau, G., Gerla, M., & Sanadidi, M. (2005). *Co-operative downloading in vehicular ad-hoc wireless networks. IEEE WONS, Switzerland* (pp. 32–41). New York: IEEE.

Nash, J. (1950). Equillibrium points in n-person games. *Proceedings of the National Academy of Sciences of the United States of America, 36*, 48–49. doi:10.1073/pnas.36.1.48

National Institute of Standards and Technology. (2001). *FISP 197: Advanced Encryption Standard (AES), Federal Information Processing Standards Publication 197*. Gaithersburg, MD: U.S. Department ofCommerce/NIST.

National Instruments. (2009). *NI Wi-Fi Data Acquisition*. Austin, TX: National Instruments. Retrieved September 2009, from http://www.ni.com/dataacquisition/wifi/

Naumowicz, T. (2007). Enabling wireless sensor networks: Integration of WSNs into development environments. Paper presented at *Microsoft Research Summer School 2007*, Cambridge, UK.

Naushad, H. (2006). *A survey on energy-efficient MAC protocols for wireless sensor networks* [Mid-term project report]. Lahore, Pakistan: Lahore University of Management Sciences, Wireless Communications and Computer Networks.

Navarro, J. L., Azevedo, A., & Vera, J. (2006). *Redes inalámbricas de sensores para la vigilancia no invasiva de espacios naturales*. VECTOR PLUS.

Nerguizian, C., Despins, C., & Affes, S. (2006). Geolocation in mines with an impulse fingerprinting technique and neural networks. *IEEE Transactions on Wireless Communications, 5*(3), 603–611. doi:10.1109/TWC.2006.1611090

Nesargi, S., & Prakash, R. (2002). MANET.conf: Configuration of hosts in a mobile ad hoc network. In *Proceedings of INFOCOM,* New York. New York: IEEE.

Ni, Y., Kremer, U., Stere, A., & Iftode, L. (2005). Programming ad-hoc networks of mobile and resource-constrained devices. In *Proceedings of the 2005 ACM SIGPLAN Conference on Programming Language Desing and Implementation* (pp. 249-260). New York: ACM.

Niculescu, D., & Nath, B. (2003). DV Based positioning in ad hoc networks. *Kluwer Journal of Telecommunications Systems, 4*(1-4), 267–280. doi:10.1023/A:1023403323460

Niculescu, D., & Nath, B. (2003, March). *Ad hoc positioning system using AoA*. Paper presented at the IEEE Twenty-Second Annual Joint Conference of the IEEE Computer and Communications Societies, San Francisco, CA.

Niculescu, D., & Nath, B. (2004). Error characteristics of ad hoc positioning systems. In J. Murai (Ed.), *Proceedings of the 5th ACM International Symposium on Mobile ad hoc Networking and Computing* (pp. 20-30). New York: ACM press.

Nikolopoulos, S. D., Pitsillides, A., & Tipper, D. (1997). Addressing network survivability issues by finding the K-best paths through a trellis graph. In *Proceedings of the IEEE INFOCOM* (pp. 370-377). New York: IEEE.

Nilsson, D. K., Roosta, T., Lindqvist, U., & Valdes, A. (2008). Key management and secure software updates in wireless process control environments. In V. D. Gligor, J. P. Hubaux, & R. Poovendran (Eds.), *Proceedings of the first ACM conference on Wireless Network Security (WISEC'08)* (pp. 100-108). New York: ACM.

Ogier, R. G., Lewis, M. G., & Templin, F. L. (2004). *Topology dissemination based on reverse-path forwarding (TBRPF)*. Retrieved October 1, 2009, from http://www.ietf.org/rfc/rfc3684.txt

Ohkubo, M., Suzuki, K., & Kinoshita, S. (2003). Cryptographic approach to privacy-friendly tags. In *Proceedings of the Workshop on RFID Privacy.* Cambridge, MA: MIT Press.

Oppliger, R. (1998). *Internet and intranet security*. London: Artech House.

O'Reilly, F., & Connolly, M. (2005). Sensor networks and the food industry. In *Workshop on Real-World Wireless Sensor Networks (REALWSN'05)*, Stockholm, Sweden (pp. 1-23). Kista, Sweden: SICS.

Otto, C., Milenković, A., Sanders, C., & Jovanow, E. (2006). System architecture of a wireless body area sensor network for ubiquitous health monitoring. *Journal of Mobile Multimedia, 1*(4), 307–326.

Pahlavan, K., & Krishnamurthy, P. (2002). *Principles of wireless networks: A unified approach*. Upper Saddle River, NJ: Prentice Hall PTR.

Palomino, M., Ortegón, J., Vázquez, J., & Chan, F. (2009). Sistemas de adquisición de datos para el estado de Quintana Roo. In *Congreso Nacional de Ingeniería Eléctrica y Electrónica del Mayab,* Instituto Tecnológico de Mérida, Mexico (pp. 325-333).

Paradiso, J. (2005). Energy scavenging for mobile and wireless electronics. *IEEE Pervasive Computing Journal*, *4*(1), 18–27. doi:10.1109/MPRV.2005.9

Park, S., & Sivakumar, R. (2008). Energy Efficient Correlated Data Aggregation for Wireless Sensor Networks. *International Journal of Distributed Sensor Networks*, *4*(1), 13–27. doi:10.1080/15501320701774592

Paschalidis, I. C., & Guo, D. (2007). Robust and distributed localization in sensor networks. In *Proceedings of the 46th IEEE Conference on Decision and Control*, New Orleans, LA (pp. 933-938). New York: IEEE Computer Society.

Patwari, N. (2005). *Location estimation in sensor networks*. Unpublished doctoral dissertation, University of Michigan, Ann Arbor, MI.

Patwari, N., & Hero, A. O., III. (2003). Using proximity and quantized RSS for sensor localization in wireless networks. In C. S. Raghavendra, & K. Sivalingam (Eds.), *Proceedings of the 2nd ACM international conference on Wireless sensor networks and applications* (pp. 20-29). New York: ACM press.

Peleg, D. (Ed.). (2000). *Distributed computing: A locality-sensitive approach*. Philadelphia, PA: Society for Industrial and Applied Mathematics.

Peng, C., Zheng, H., & Zhao, B. Y. (2006). Utilization and fairness in spectrum assignment for opportunistic spectrum access. *ACM Mobile Network Applications*, *11*(4), 555–576. doi:10.1007/s11036-006-7322-y

Perkins, C. E. (2002). *Mobility Support for IPv4.* Fremont, CA: The Internet Engineering Task Force (IETF). Retrieved September 17, 2009, from http://www.ietf.org/rfc/rfc3344.txt

Perkins, C. E., Malinen, J. T., Wakikawa, R., Belding-Royer, E. M., & Sun, Y. (2001). *IP address autoconfiguration for ad hoc networks: Internet draft*. Fremont, CA: IETF. Retrieved February 12, 2010, from http://tools.ietf.org/html/draft-perkins-manet-autoconf-01

Perkins, C., Belding-Royer, E., & Das, S. (2003). *Ad hoc on-demand distance vector (AODV) routing*. Retrieved September 30, 2009, from http://www.ietf.org/rfc/rfc3561.txt

Perrig, A., Szewczyk, R., Tygar, J. D., Wen, V., & Culler, D. (2002). SPINS: Security protocols for sensor networks. *Wireless Networks*, *8*(5), 521–534. doi:10.1023/A:1016598314198

Pestana-Leao, L. M., & Rodríguez-Peralta, L. M. (2007, October). *Collaborative localization in wireless sensor networks.* Paper presented at the Conference on Sensor Technologies and Applications (SENSORCOMM 2007), Valencia, Spain.

Philips, T. K., Panwar, S. S., & Tantawi, A. N. (1989). Connectivity properties of a packet radio network model. *IEEE Transactions on Information Theory*, *35*(5), 1044–1047. doi:10.1109/18.42219

Pietre-Cambacedes, L., & Sitbon, P. (2008). Cryptographic key management for SCADA systems-issues and perspectives. *International Journal of Security and its Applications,* *2*(3), 31-40.

Ping, Z., Xiaofeng, T., Jianhua, Z., Ying, W., Lihua, L., & Yong, W. (2005, January). A vision from the future: Beyond 3G TDD. *IEEE Communications Magazine*, *43*(1), 38–44. doi:10.1109/MCOM.2005.1381873

Polastre, J., Hill, J., & Culler, D. (2004). Versatile Low Power Media Access for Wireless Sensor Networks. *Paper presented at the 2nd ACM Conference on Embedded Networked Sensor Systems.* Baltimore.

Ponce, P. (2008). *Developing a novel, portable intelligent greenhouse using graphical system design*. Austin, TX: National Instruments. Retrieved September 2009, from http://sine.ni.com/cs/app/doc/p/id/cs-12081

Pontes, A. B., Silva, D. D., José Jailton, J., Otavio Rodrigues, J., & Dias, K. L. (2008). Handover management in integrated WLAN and mobile WiMax networks. *IEEE Wireless Communications*, *15*(5), 86–95. doi:10.1109/MWC.2008.4653137

Popescu, D. C., Rawat, D. B., Popescu, O., & Saquib, M. (2010). Game theoretic approach to joint transmitter adaptation and power control in wireless systems. *IEEE Transactions on Systems, Man, and Cybernetics, Part B: Cybernetics. Special Issue Game Theory*, *40*(3), 675–682.

Prehofer, C., & Bettstetter, C. (2005). Self-organization in communication networks: Principles and design paradigms. *IEEE Communications Magazine*, *43*(7), 78–85. doi:10.1109/MCOM.2005.1470824

Priyantha, N. B., Miu, A. K. L., Balakrishnan, H., & Teller, S. (2001). The cricket compass for context-aware mobile applications. In C. Rose (Ed.), *Proceedings of the 7th annual international conference on Mobile computing and networking* (pp. 1-14). New York: ACM Press.

Puzar, M., Andersson, J., Plagemann, T., & Roudier, Y. (2005). SKiMPy: A simple key management protocol for MANETs in emergency and rescue operations. Paper presented at *ESAS*, Visegrad, Hungary.

Qi, L. (2008). Research on intelligent transportation system technologies and applications. In *Workshop on Power Electronics and Intelligent Transportation System*, (pp. 529-531).

Qing, X., Mak, T., Jeff, K., & Sengupta, R. (2007). Medium access control protocol design for vehicle–vehicle safety messages. In *IEEE Transaction on Vehicular Technology* (pp. 499–518). New York: IEEE.

Rafaeli, S., & Hutchison, D. (2003). A survey of key management for secure group communication. *ACM Computing Surveys*, *35*(3), 309–329. doi:10.1145/937503.937506

Raghunathan, V., Schurgers, C., Park, S., & Srivastava, M. (2002). Energy aware wireless sensor networks. *IEEE Signal Processing Magazine*, *19*(2), 40–50. doi:10.1109/79.985679

Ramirez-Mondragón, E. (2007). *Routing mechanism for hybrid wireless networks (Infrastructure-Ad Hoc).* Master's thesis, CICESE Research Center, Ensenada, Mexico.

Ramjee, R., Varadhan, K., Salgarelli, L., Thuel, S. R., Wang, S. Y., & Porta, T. L. (2002). HAWAII: A domain-based approach for supporting mobility in wide-area wireless networks. *IEEE/ACM Transactions on Networking*, *10*(3), 396–410. doi:10.1109/TNET.2002.1012370

Ramos Pascual, F. (2009). Redes de sensores inalámbricos. Retrieved from http://www.radioptica.com/sensores/

Rawat, D. B., & Yan, G. (2009). Signal processing techniques for spectrum sensing in cognitive radio systems: Challenges and perspectives. Paper presented at the *IEEE/IFIP Asian Himalayas International Conference on Internet (AH-ICI).*

rd Generation Partnership Project. (2004). 3GPPTS 23.207 V6.3.0: End-to-end quality of service (QoS) concept and architecture.

rd Generation Partnership Project. (2006). 3GPPTS 23.207 V5.8.0: *Universal mobile telecommunication system (UMTS): End-to-end QoS concept and architecture.* Retrieved from http://www.3gpp.org

Ren, M., Das, T. K., & Zhou, J. (2006). Diverging keys in wireless sensor networks. In S. K. Katsikas, J. Lopez, M. Backes, S. Gritzalis, & B. Preneel (Eds.), *Proceedings of the Ninth conference on Information Security (ISC '06)* (Lecture Notes in Computer Science, Vol. 4176, pp. 257-269). Berlin: Springer.

Rendl, W. F. (2005). Semidefinite programming and integer programming. In Aardal, K., Nemhauser, G., & Weismantel, R. (Eds.), *Handbook on discrete optimization* (pp. 393–514). Amsterdam: Elsevier.

Richtel, M. (2009, May 27). Google: Expect 18 Android phones by year's end. *The New York Times*.

Rizvi, S., & Riasat, A. (2007). Use of self-adaptive methodology in wireless sensor networks for reducing energy consumption. In *Proceedings of the International Conference on Information and Emerging Technologies*. (pp. 1-7).

Rodríguez, F., & Berenguel, M. (2004). *Control y Robótica en Agricultura.* España: Universidad de Almería.

Roman, R., Alcaraz, C., & Lopez, J. (2007). The role of wireless sensor networks in the area of critical information infrastructure protection. *Information Security Technical Report*, *12*(1), 24–31. doi:10.1016/j.istr.2007.02.003

Römer, K., & Santini, S. (2006). An Adaptive Strategy for Quality-Based Data Reduction in Wireless Sensor Networks. In *Proceedings of the 3rd International Conference on Networked Sensing Systems* (INSS), (pp. 29-36).

Roy, R., & Kailath, T. (1989). ESPRIT – Estimation of signal parameters via rotational invariance techniques. *IEEE Transactions on Signal Processing*, *37*(7), 984–995. doi:10.1109/29.32276

Ruiz, P. M., Ros, F. J., & Gomez-Skarmeta, A. (2005). Internet connectivity for mobile ad hoc networks: Solutions and challenges. *IEEE Communications Magazine*, *43*(10), 118–125. doi:10.1109/MCOM.2005.1522134

Ruíz Ibarra, E. C. (2006). *Protocolo de enrutamiento para redes de sensores y actuadores inalámbricos*. Ensenada, México: CICESE.

Ruiz-Garcia, L., Lunadei, L., Barreiro, P., & Robla, J. I. (2009). A review of wireless sensor technologies and applications in agriculture and food industry: State of the art and current trends. *Sensors (Basel, Switzerland)*, *9*(6), 4728–4750. .doi:10.3390/s90604728

Sammons, P. J., & Furukawa, T. A. (2005). Autonomous pesticide spraying robot for use in a greenhouse. In *Proceedings of the Australasian Conference on Robotics and Automation* (pp. 1-9). Sydney, Australia: ACRA.

Sangiovanni-Vincentelli, A. (2008). Is a Unified Methodology for System-Level Design Possible? Special Issue on Design in the Late and Post-Silicon Era. *IEEE Design & Test of Computers*, *25*(4), 346–358. doi:10.1109/MDT.2008.104

Santini, S. (2006). Towards adaptive wireless sensor networks. *Paper presented at the 3rd European Workshop on Wireless Sensor Networks*.

Santos, R. A., Edwards, A., Edwards, R. M., & Seed, N. L. (2005). Performance evaluation of routing protocols in vehicular ad-hoc networks. *International Journal of Ad Hoc and Ubiquitous Computing*, *1*(1/2), 80–91. doi:10.1504/IJAHUC.2005.008022

Saraydar, C. U., Mandayam, N. B., & Goodman, D. J. (2002). Efficient power control via pricing in wireless data networks. *IEEE Transactions on Communications*, *50*(2), 291–303. doi:10.1109/26.983324

Savarese, C., Rabaey, J. M., & Langendoen, K. (2002). Robust positioning algorithms for distributed ad hoc wireless sensor networks. In C. S. Schlatter (Ed.). *Proceedings of the General Track: 2002 USENIX Annual Technical Conference* (pp. 317-327). Berkeley, CA: USENIX Association

Savvides, A., Garber, W. L., Adlakha, S., Moses, R. L., & Srivastava, M. B. (2003). On the error characteristics of multihop node localization in ad-hoc sensor networks. In F. Zhao, L. J. Guibas (Eds.), *Proceedings of the Second International Workshop IPSN 2003* (pp. 317-332). New York: Springer.

Savvides, A., Han, C. C., & Srivastava, M. B. (2001). Dynamic fine-grained localization in ad hoc networks of sensors. In C. Rose (Ed.), *Proceedings of the 7th annual international conference on Mobile computing and networking* (pp. 166–179). New York: ACM press.

Savvides, A., Park, H., & Srivastava, M. B. (2002). The bits and flops of the n-hop multilateration primitive for node localization problems. In C. S. Raghavendra, & K. M. Sivalingam (Ed.), *Proceedings of the 1st ACM International Workshop on Wireless Sensor Networks and Applications* (pp. 112–121). New York: ACM Press.

Savvides, A., Park, H., & Srivastava, M. B. (2003). The n-hop multilateration primitive for node localization problems. In *Proceedings of Mobile Networks and Applications* (pp. 443-451).

Schaumann, J. (2002). *Analysis of the zone routing protocol*. Retrieved October 1, 2009, from http://www.netmeister.org/misc/zrp/zrp.pdf

Shakshuki, E., & Malik, H. (2007). Agent Based Approach to Minimize Energy Consumption for Border Nodes in Wireless Sensor Network. In *Proceedings of the 21st International Conference on Advanced Networking and Applications*. (pp. 134-141).

Shamir, A. (1979). How to share a secret. *Communications of the ACM*, *22*(11), 612–613. doi:10.1145/359168.359176

Shang, Y., Ruml, W., Zhang, Y., & Fromherz, M. P. J. (2004). Localization from connectivity in sensor networks. *IEEE Transactions on Parallel and Distributed Systems*, *15*(11), 961–964. doi:10.1109/TPDS.2004.67

Shang, Y., Ruml, W., Zhang, Y., & Fromherz, M. P. J. (2003). Localization from mere connectivity. In M. Gerla (Ed.), *Proceedings of the 4th ACM International Symposium on Mobile Ad Hoc Networking & Computing* (pp. 201-212). New York: ACM press.

Shebli, F., Dayoub, I., Rouvaen, J. M., & Zaouche, A. (2007). A new optimization approach for energy consumption within wireless sensor networks. In *Proceedings of the Third Advanced International Conference on Telecommunications (AICT)*, (pp. 14-20).

Shenker, S., Partridge, C., & Guerin, R. (1997, September). Specification of guaranteed quality of service, RFC 2212.

Sherman, T., & McGrew, A. (2003). Key establishment in large dynamic groups using one-way function trees. *IEEE Transactions on Software Engineering*, *29*(5), 444–458. doi:10.1109/TSE.2003.1199073

Sims, J. (2009). Rapidly serving imagery. *Imaging Notes*, *24*(1), 30–33.

Sinopoli, B., Sharp, C., Schenato, L., Schaffert, S., & Sastry, S. S. (2003). Distributed control applications within sensor networks. *IEEE Proceedings*, *91*(8), 1235–1246. doi:10.1109/JPROC.2003.814926

Slama, I. Jouaber, B., & Zeghlache, D. (2007). Optimal Power management scheme for Heterogeneous Wireless Sensor Networks: Lifetime Maximization under QoS and Energy Constraints. In *Proceedings of the Third International Conference on Networking and Services.* (pp. 66-75).

Sohraby, K., Minoli, D., & Znati, T. (2007). *Wireless Sensor Networks: Technology, Protocols, and Applications*. Wiley & Son. doi:10.1002/047011276X

Sormani, D., Turconi, G., Costa, P., Frey, D., Migliavacca, M., & Mottola, L. (2006). Towards lightweight information dissemination in intervehicular networks. In *ACM VANETS, Los Angeles, CA* (pp. 20–29). New York: ACM.

Spirito, M. A. (2001). On the accuracy of cellular mobile station location. *IEEE Transactions on Vehicular Technology*, *50*(3), 674–685. doi:10.1109/25.933304

Sreenath, K. (2007). *Adaptive sampling with mobile WSN.* Msc. Thesis, University Of Texas At Arlington.

Srinivasan, A., & Wu, J. (2006). A survey on secure localization in wireless sensor networks. In Furht, B. (Ed.), *Encyclopedia of wireless and mobile communications*. Boca Raton, FL: CRC Press, Taylor and Francis Group.

Srivastava, V., & Motani, M. (2005). Cross-Layer Design: A Survey and the Road Ahead. *IEEE Communications Magazine*, *43*(12), 112–119. doi:10.1109/MCOM.2005.1561928

Srivastava, V., Neel, J., Mackenzie, A. B., Menon, R., Dasilva, L. A., & Hicks, J. E. (2005). Using game theory to analyze wireless ad hoc networks. *IEEE Communications Surveys & Tutorials*, *7*(4), 46–56. doi:10.1109/COMST.2005.1593279

Staddon, J., Miner, S., Franklin, M., Balfanz, D., Malkin, M., & Deam, D. (2002). Self-healing key distribution with revocation. Paper presented at the *IEEE Symposium on Security and Privacy*, Oakland, CA.

Steer, D., Strawczynski, L., Diffie, W., & Wiener, M. (1990). A secure audio teleconference system. In *Advances in Cryptology* – CRYPTO '88 ([). Berlin: Springer.]. *Lecture Notes in Computer Science*, *403*, 520–528. doi:10.1007/0-387-34799-2_37

Steiner, M., Tsudik, G., & Waidner, M. (2000). Cliques: A new approach to group key agreement. In *Proceedings of the 18th International Conference on Distributed Computing Systems* (pp. 380-387). New York: IEEE.

Steiniger, S. (2006). Foundations of location based services. Zürich, Switzerland: Department of Geography, University of Zürich. Retrieved 2009, from http://www.geo.unizh.ch/~sstein/

Stine, J. A., & de Veciana, G. (2004). A paradigm for quality-of-service in wireless ad hoc networks using synchronous signaling and node states. *IEEE Journal on Selected Areas in Communications*, *22*(7), 1301–1321. doi:10.1109/JSAC.2004.829347

Stockwell, W. (2007). Wireless sensor networks for precision agriculture. In *EU-US Workshop on Wirelessly Networked Embedded Systems*. Edinburgh, Scotland: University of Edinburgh.

Stoyan, D., & Stoyan, H. (2004). *Fractals, random shapes and point fields: Methods of geometrical statistics*. Chichester, UK: John Wiley & Sons.

Su, W., & Lim, T. L. (2006). Cross-Layer Design and Optimization for Wireless Sensor Networks. *Paper presented at the Seventh ACIS International Conference on Software Engineering, Artificial Intelligence, Networking, and Parallel/Distributed Computing (SNPD).* Las Vegas.

Sun, Y., & Belding-Royer, E. M. (2003). *Dynamic address configuration in mobile ad hoc networks* [Technical Report]. Santa Barbara, CA: University of California Santa Barbara, Department of Computer Science.

Suris, J. E., DaSilva, L., Han, Z., & MacKenzie, A. (2007). Cooperative game theory approach for distributed spectrum sharing. Paper presented at the *IEEE International Conference on Communications*, Glasgow, Scotland.

Szczechowiak, P., Oliveira, L. B., Scott, M., Collier, M., & Dahab, R. (2008). NanoECC: Testing the limits of elliptic curve cryptography in sensor networks. In *Proceedings of the Fifth European Conference (EWSN'08)* ([]. Berlin: Springer.]. *Lecture Notes in Computer Science, 4913*, 305–320. doi:10.1007/978-3-540-77690-1_19

Tang, Q., Yang, L., Giannakis, G. B., & Qin, T. (2007). Battery power efficiency of PPM and FSK in wireless sensor networks. *IEEE Transactions on Wireless Communications, 6*(4), 1308–1319. doi:10.1109/TWC.2007.348327

Tayal, A. T., & Patanaik, L. M. (2004). An address assignment for the automatic configuration of mobile ad hoc networks. *Personal and Ubiquitous Computing, 8*(1), 47–54. doi:10.1007/s00779-003-0256-5

Teemu Ahonen, R. V. (2008). Network, greenhouse monitoring with wireless sensor netword. In *Proceedings of the IEEE/ASME International Conference on Mechatronic and Embedded Systems and Applications,* Beijing (pp. 403-408). New York: IEEE.

The Bluetooth Special Interest Group. (2009). BT Core v3.0. Retrieved from http://www.bluetooth.com

The Network Simulator: ns-2. (2009). Retrieved September 30, 2009, from http://www.isi.edu/nsnam/ns/

Thoppian, M., & Prakash, R. (2006). A distributed protocol for dynamic address assignment in mobile ad hoc networks. *IEEE Transactions on Mobile Computing, 5*(1), 4–19. doi:10.1109/TMC.2006.2

Timmons, W., & Scanlon, N. F. (2004). *Analysis of the performance of IEEE 802.15.4 for medical sensor body area networking. Paper presented in.* IEEE Sensor and Ad Hoc Communications and Networks.

Toh, C. K. (2002). *Ad hoc mobile wireless networks: Protocols and systems*. Upper Saddle River, NJ: Prentice Hall PTR.

Topkis, D. M. (1998). *Supermodularity and complementarity*. Princeton, NJ: Princeton University Press.

Tors, F., Sanders, S., Winters, C., Brebels, S., & Van Hoof, C. (2004). Wireless network of autonomous environmental sensors. *Proceedings of IEEE Sensors, 2*, 923–926. doi:10.1109/ICSENS.2004.1426322

Tran, D. A., & Nguyen, T. (2006). Localization in wireless sensor networks based on support vector machines. *IEEE Transactions on Parallel and Distributed Systems, 19*(7), 981–994. doi:10.1109/TPDS.2007.70800

Tseng, S. T., & Song, K. T. (2002). Real-time image tracking for traffic monitoring. In *The IEEE 5th International Conference on Intelligent Transportation Systems*, (pp. 1-6). New York: IEEE.

Turner, N. C. (1988). Measurement of plant water status by the pressure chamber technique. *Irrigation Science, 9*(4), 289–308. .doi:10.1007/BF00296704

UNFPA. (2007). *Technical report: State of world population 2007: Unleashing the potential of urban growth.* New York: United Nations Population Fund.

Vaidya, N. (2002). Weak duplicate address detection in mobile ad hoc networks. In *Proceedings of ACM MobiHoc* (pp. 206-216). New York: ACM.

Van Cutsem, T., Mostinckx, S., Boix, E., Dedecker, J., & De Meuter, W. (2007). AmbientTalk: Objetc-oriented Event-driven Programming in Mobile Ad hoc Networks. In *Proceedings of the XXVI International Conference of the Chilean Society of Computer Sciencie* (pp. 3-12). Washington, DC: IEEE.

Van Dam, T., & Langendoen, K. (2003). An adaptive energy-efficient MAC protocol for wireless sensor networks. In *Proceedings of the first international conference on Embedded networked sensor systems – (SenSys '03)* (pp. 171-180). New York: ACM Press. doi: 10.1145/958491.958512

van der Schaar, M., & Fu, F. (2009). Spectrum access games and strategic learning in cognitive radio networks for delay-critical applications. *Proceedings of the IEEE, 97*(4), 720–740. doi:10.1109/JPROC.2009.2013036

Van der Werff, T. J. (2003, February). 10 emerging technologies that will change the world. *MIT's Technology Review*.

Van Hoesel, L. F., & Havinga, P. J. (2004). A Lightweight Medium Access Protocol (LMAC) for Wireless Sensor Networks: Reducing Preamble Transmissions and Transceiver State Switches. *Paper presented at the 1st International Workshop on Networked Sensing Systems (INSS).* Tokio, Japan.

Vandenberghe, L., & Boyd, S. (1996). Semidefinite programming. *SIAM Review*, *38*(1), 49–95. doi:10.1137/1038003

Varga, A. (2009). *OMNeT++ Community Site*. Retrieved November 2009, from http://www.omnetpp.org/

Vass, D., Vincze, Z., Vida, R., & Vidács, A. (2006). *Energy Effiency in Wireless Sensor Networks Using Mobile Base Station.* In book: EUNICE 2005: Networks and Applications Towards a Ubiquitously Connected, 196, 173-186. Boston:Springer.

Vaughan-Nichols, S. (2004). *Achieving wireless broadband with WiMAX* (pp. 10–13). IEEE Computer.

Vellidis, G., Garrick, V., Pocknee, S., Perry, C., Kvien, C., & Tucker, M. (2007). How wireless will change agriculture. In J. Stafford, *Precision Agriculture*, Skiathos, Greece (pp. 57-67). Wageningen, The Netherlands: Wageningen Academic Publishers.

Venugopalan, R., Ganesan, P., Peddabachagari, P., Dean, A., Mueller, F., & Sichitiu, M. (2003). Encryption overhead in embedded systems and sensor network nodes: Modeling and analysis. In J. H. Moreno, P. K. Murthy, T. M. Conte & P. Faraboschi (Eds.), *Proceedings of the International Conference on Compilers, architecture, and synthesis for embedded systems (CASES'03)* (pp. 188-197). New York: ACM.

Verkasalo, H. (2006). Empirical observations on the emergence of mobile multimedia services an applications in the U.S. and Europe. In *Proceedings of the 5th International Conference on Mobile and Ubiquitous Multimedia,* Stanford, CA. Ng, J. W. P., Lo, B. P., Wells, O., Sloman, M., Peters, N., Darzi, A.,... Yang, G. Z. (2004). Ubiquitous monitoring environment for wearable and implantable sensors. Paper presented at *International Conference on Ubiquitous Computing (Ubicomp).*

Vertoda. (2009). *Wireless sensor networks & agriculture* (pp. 1-16). Ballincolling, Ireland: Sykoinia Limited.

Vicaire, P. A., & Stankovic, J. A. (2004). *Elastic localization: Improvements on distributed, range free localization for wireless sensor networks* (Report No. CS-2004-35). Charlottesville, VA: University of Virginia.

Vieira, M. A. M., Coelho, C. N., Jr., da Silva, D. C., Jr., & da Mata, J. M. (2003). Survey on wireless sensor network devices. In *Proceedings of the Ninth IEEE International conference on Emerging Technologies and Factory Automation (ETFA'03)* (Vol. 1, pp. 537-544). New York: IEEE Computer Society.

Villasenor-Gonzalez, L. A., Gonzalez-Sanchez, A. L., Sanchez-Garcia, J., & Aquino-Santos, R. (2008). Macromobility support for mobile ad hoc networks using IPv6 and the OLSR routing protocol. *Computer Communications*, *31*(14), 3137–3144. doi:10.1016/j.comcom.2008.04.015

Walker, K., Kabashi, A., Abdelnour, J., Ngugi, K., Underwood, J., Elmirghani, J., & Prodanovic, M. (2008). Interaction design for rural agricultural sensor networks. Paper presented at the *International Congress on Environmental Modelling and Software,* Catalonia, Barcelona.

Walters, J. P., Liang, Z., Shi, W., & Chaudhary, V. (2006). Wireless sensor network security: A survey. In Y. Xiao (Ed.), *Security in distributed, grid, and pervasive computing* (pp. 367-410). Boca Raton, FL: Auerbach Publications, CRC Press.

Wander, A., Gura, N., Eberle, H., Gupta, V., & Shantz, S. C. (2005). Energy analysis of public key cryptography for wireless sensor networks. In *Proceedings of the Third IEEE International Conference on Pervasive Computing and Communications (PerCom'05)* (pp.324-328). New York: IEEE Computer Society.

Wang, L., & Xiao, Y. (2006). A survey of Energy-Efficient Scheduling Mechanism in Sensor Netwoks. *Mobile Networks and Applications*, *11*(5), 723–740. doi:10.1007/s11036-006-7798-5

Wang, Q., Fan, Y., Dong, Ya., & Duan, S. (2005). Power auto-adaptive wireless sensor network and application. In. *Proceedings of the IEEE International Symposium on Communications and Information Technology*, *1*, 391–395.

Wang, X., Ma, J., Wang, S., & Bi, D. (2007). Time series forecasting for energy-effcient organization of wireless sensor networks. *Sensors (Basel, Switzerland)*, *7*, 1766–1792. doi:10.3390/s7091766

Wang, N., Zhang, N., & Wang, M. (2006). Wireless sensors in agriculture and food industry: Recent development and future perspective. *Computers and Electronics in Agriculture*, *50*(1), 1–14. doi:10.1016/j.compag.2005.09.003

Wang, M. H., Chao, K. H., & Lee, R. H. (2008). An intelligent traffic light control based on extension neural network. In *Knowledge-based intelligent information and engineering systems* (pp. 17–24). Berlin: Springer.

Wang, F. Y., & Lsansing, S. J. (2004). From artificial life to artificial societies: New methods in studying social complex systems. *Journal of Complex Systems and Complexity Science*, pp. 33-41.

Wang, S. Y. (2010). NCTUns network simulator and emulator. Taiwan: NCTU Network and System Laboratory. Retrieved February 23, 2010, from http://nsl.csie.nctu.edu.tw/nctuns.html

Weber, V. (2009). Smart sensor networks: Technologies and applications for green growth. In *ICTs, the environment and climate change*, Helsingør, Denmark (pp. 1-48). Paris: Organisation for Economic Co-operation and Development.

Weinstein, E., & Weiss, A. J. (1988). A general class of lower bounds in parameter estimation. *IEEE Transactions on Information Theory*, *34*(2), 338–342. doi:10.1109/18.2647

Wen, W. (2008). A dynamic and automatic traffic light control expert system for solving the road congestion problem. *Expert Systems with Applications: An International Journal*, pp. 2370-2381.

Weniger, K. (2005). PACMAN: Passive autoconfiguration for mobile ad hoc networks. [JSAC]. *IEEE Journal on Selected Areas in Communications*, *23*(3), 507–519. doi:10.1109/JSAC.2004.842539

Weniger, K., & Zitterbart, M. (2004). Address autoconfiguration in mobile ad hoc networks: Current approaches and future directions. *IEEE Network*, *18*(4), 6–11. doi:10.1109/MNET.2004.1316754

Weniger, K. (2003). Passive duplicate address detection in mobile ad hoc networks. In *Proceedings of IEEE WCNC*, New Orleans. New York: IEEE.

Wen-Tzu, C., & Chih-Nan, H. (2008). Entering the mobile service market via mobile platforms: Qualcomm's Brew Platform and Nokia's Preminent Platform. *Telecommunications Policy*, *32*(6), 399–411. doi:10.1016/j.telpol.2008.04.004

Williams, D. H. (2005). *The definitive guide to mobile positioning and location management*. New York: Mind Commerce.

Williams, B. (2008). *Intelligent transport systems standards*. Norwood, MA: Artech House Publishers.

WiMAX Forum. (2009). *WiMAX forum*. Retrieved from http://www.wimaxforum.org/home/

Wisely, D., Eardley, P., & Burness, L. (2002). *IP for 3G networking technologies for mobile communications*. Hoboken, NJ: John Wiley & Sons, Ltd.

Wong, C., Gouda, M., & Lam, S. (1998). Secure group communications using key graphs. In *Proceedings of the ACM SIGCOMM conference on Applications, Technologies, Architectures, and Protocols for Computer Communication* (pp. 68-79). New York: ACM.

Woo, A., Tong, T., & Culler, D. (2003). Taming the Underlying Challenges of Reliable Multihop Routing in sensors networks. In *Proceeding of ACM SenSys*, (pp. 14-27).

Wood, G. V. (2006). *ALARM-NET: Wireless sensor networks for assisted-living and residential monitoring* [Technical Report CS-2006-11]. Charlottesville, VA: Department of Computer Science, University of Virginia.

Woodacre, B. (2003). TDOA positioning algorithms: Evaluation and implementation. Worcester, MA: Worcester Polytechnic Institute. Retrieved 2009, from http://www.ece.wpi.edu/Research/PPL/Publications/

Wroclawski, J. (1997). The use of RSVP with IETF Integrated Services, RFC2210.

WSNIndia. (2009). Agriculture and environmental applications. *Search*. Retrieved from http://www.wsnindia.com

Wu, B., Chen, J., Wu, J., & Cardei, M. (2006). *A survey on attacks and countermeasures in mobile ad hoc networks. Wireless/mobile network security*. Berlin: Springer.

Wu, B., Wu, J., Fernandez, E., Ilyas, M., & Magliveras, S. (2005). Secure and efficient key management scheme in mobile ad hoc networks. [JCNA]. *Journal of Network and Computer Applications*, *30*(3), 937–954. doi:10.1016/j.jnca.2005.07.008

Xu, Q., Mak, T., Ko, J., & Sengupta, R. (2004). *Vehicle-to-vehicle safety messaging in DSRC. ACM VANET, Philadelphia, PA* (pp. 19–28). New York: ACM.

Yaiche, H., Mazumdar, R. R., & Rosenberg, C. (2000). A game theoretic framework for bandwidth allocation and pricing in broadband networks. *IEEE/ACM Transactions on Networking*, *8*(6), 667–678. doi:10.1109/90.879352

Ye, F., Zhong, G., Cheng, L., & Zhang, L. (2003). PEAS: A robust energy conserving protocols for long-lived sensor network. In *Proceeding of the 23rd International Conference on Distributed Computing Systems*, (pp. 28-37).

Ye, W., Heidemann, J., & Estrin, D. (2002). An energy-efficient MAC protocol for wireless sensor networks. In *Proceeding of the 21st Conference of the IEEE Computer and Communications Societies (INFOCOM)*, (pp. 1567–1576). New York.

Yi, S., & Kravets, R. (2004). Composite key management for ad hoc networks. In *Proceedings of the 1st Annual International Conference on Mobile and Ubiquitous Systems: Networking and Services (MobiQuitous)* (pp. 52-61). New York: IEEE.

Yi, S., Naldurg, P., & Kravets, R. (2002). *Security aware ad hoc routing for wireless networks*. Report No. UIUCDCS-R-2002-2290. Urbana, IL: UIUC.

Yick, J., Mukherjee, B., & Ghosal, D. (2008). Wireless sensor network survey. *Computer Networks*, *52*(12), 2292–2330. doi:10.1016/j.comnet.2008.04.002

Yu, Y., Estrin, D., & Govindan, R. (2001). *Geographical and Energy-Aware Routing: A Recursive Data Dissemination Protocol for Wireless Sensor Networks. Technical Report*. UCLA Computer Science Department.

Yu, W., Ginis, G., & Cioffi, J. M. (2002). Distributed multiuser power control for digital subscriber lines. *IEEE Journal on Selected Areas in Communications*, *20*(5), 1105–1116. doi:10.1109/JSAC.2002.1007390

Yu, J., Choi, S., & Lee, J. (2004). Enhancement of VoIP over IEEE 802.11 WLAN via dual queue Strategy. In *Proceedings of IEEE ICC*, Paris. New York: IEEE.

Zakiuddin, I., Hawkins, T., & Moffat, N. (2005). Towards a game theoretic understanding of ad-hoc routing. *Electronic Notes in Theoretical Computer Science*, *119*(1), 67–92. doi:10.1016/j.entcs.2004.07.009

Zhang, H. (2003). Extensible platform for location-based services. In *2nd International Conference on Mobile Technology, Applications and Systems*. New York: IEEE.

Zhang, W., & Liang, Z. Hou., Z, & Tan., M. (2007). A Power Efficient Routing Protocol for Wireless Sensor Network. Networking, Sensing and Control. In *Proceeding of the IEEE International Conference on Networking, Sensing and Control*, (pp. 20-25).

Zhang, Z. (2004). Investigation of wireless sensor networks for precision agriculture. In *ASABE Annual Meeting*. St. Joseph, MI: American Society of Agricultural and Biological Engineers.

Zhao, F., & Guibas, L. (Eds.). (2004). *Wireless sensor networks, an information processing approach*. San Francisco: Morgan Kaufmann.

Zhao, A., Yu, J., & Li, Z. (2009). A Data Aggregation Scheme in Wireless Sensor Networks for Structure Monitoring. In *Proceeding of the International Conference on Information Management, Innovation Management and Industrial Engineering*, Vol. 4, (pp. 623-626).

Zhao, Q., & Swami, A. (2007). A survey of dynamic spectrum access: Signal processing and networking perspectives. In *Proceedings of the IEEE International Conference on Acoustics, Speech and Signal Processing (ICASSP)* (Vol. 4, pp. 349-1352).

Zhou, L., & Haas, Z. (1999). Securing ad hoc networks. *IEEE Network Magazine*, *13*(6), 24–30. doi:10.1109/65.806983

Zhou, H., Ni, L., & Mutka, M. (2003). Prophet allocation for large scale MANETs. In *Proceedings of INFOCOM*, San Francisco, CA. New York: IEEE.

Zhu, B., Bao, F., Deng, R. H., Kankanhalli, M. S., & Wang, G. (2005). Efficient and robust key management for large mobile ad hoc networks. *Computer Networks*, *48*(4), 657–682. doi:10.1016/j.comnet.2004.11.023

Zhu, S., Setia, S., & Jajodia, S. (2003b). LEAP: Efficient security mechanisms for large-scale distributed sensor networks. Paper presented at *CSS*, Washington, DC. New York: ACM.

Zhu, S., Setia, S., Xu, S., & Jajodia, S. (2004). GKMPAN: An efficient group rekeying scheme for secure multicast in ad-hoc networks. Paper presented at *Mobiquitous*, Boston.

Zollinger, A. (2005). *Networking unleashed: Geographic routing and topology control in ad hoc and sensor networks.* Unpublsihed doctoral dissertation, Swiss Federal Institute of Technology Zurich, Switzerland.

Zou, X., Ramamurthy, B., & Magliveras, S. (2002). Routing techniques in wireless ad hoc networks: Classification and comparison. In *Proceedings ot the Sixth World Multiconference on Systemics* (pp. 1–6). Cybernetics and Informatics.

Zou, C., & Chigan, C. (2008). A game theoretic DSA-driven MAC framework for cognitive radio networks. Paper presented at the *IEEE International Conference on Communications* (ICC).

About the Contributors

Raúl Aquino Santos graduated from the University of Colima with a BE in Electrical Engineering, received his MS degree in Telecommunications from the Centre for Scientific Research and Higher Education in Ensenada, Mexico in 1990. He holds a PhD from the Department of Electrical and Electronic Engineering of the University of Sheffield, England. Since 2005, he has been with the College of Telematics, at the University of Colima, where he is currently a Research-Professor in telecommunications networks. His current research interests include wireless and sensor networks.

Victor Rangel Licea received the B.Eng (Hons) degree in Computer Engineering in the Engineering Faculty from the National Autonomous University of Mexico (UNAM) in 1996, the M.Sc in Telematics at from the University of Sheffield, UK in 1998, and the PhD in performance analysis and traffic scheduling in cable networks in 2002, from the University of Sheffield. Since 2002, he has been with the School of Engineering, UNAM, where he is currently a Research-Professor in telecommunications networks. His research focuses on fixed, mesh and mobile broadband wireless access networks, QoS over IP, traffic shaping and scheduling.

Arthur Edwards Block received his masters degree in Education from the University of Houston in 1985. He has been a researcher-professor at the University of Colima since 1985, where he has served in various capacities. He has been with the School of Telematics since 1998. His primary areas of research are Computer Assisted Language Learning (CALL), distance learning, collaborative learning, multimodal leaning and mobile learning. The primary focus of his research is presently in the area of mobile collaborative learning.

* * *

José Edinson Aedo is an Associate Professor in the Department of Electronics Engineering at the Antioquia University and director of the Control and Microelectronic research Group. Aedo's current research interest is oriented towards system integration by providing "off-the-shelf" hardware/software solutions to industrial application in the areas of Digital Signal Processing, Communications, Industrial Controls, Microelectronics and Multimedia Solutions including Distance Learning Solutions. His research interests include embedded system design, ASIC design and intelligent systems, including neuronal networks and fuzzy systems.

Johnny Aguirre Morales was born in Medellin, Colombia. He received his BSc in Electronics Engineering from the University of Antioquia, where he worked in a system for computational intelligence algorithms implementation in 8-bit microcontrollers. In 2005 he joined the microelectronics and control research group at the same university. There he obtained an MSc degree. In his MSc thesis, he proposed a strategy to reduce power consumption in the wireless sensor network nodes using filters predictors to reduce transmissions made by the node. He did a research internship at the University of South Florida (USF) in 2007, where he worked on signal processing algorithms implementation in systems with low computational power. He is currently working as a lecturer at the University of Antioquia, where he has taught courses in digital signal processing, circuits, programming languages and microcontroller's architectures.

Hani Alzaid received his BS in Computer Engineering from King Saud University in Riyadh, KSA in 2000. He received his MS degree in Computer Science and Engineering from University of New South Wales in Sydney, Australia in 2005. He is currently working towards his PhD in Computer Science. His broader research interests are in Wireless Sensor Network Security domain. Specifically he is interested in reputation-based solutions for securing data aggregation in WSNs, and security aspects of the integration between WSNs and SCADA systems.

Abdelmalek Azizi obtained his first Doctorate degree in Number Theory in 1985 at Mohammed V University. He then obtained a PhD at Laval University (Canada) in April 1993 in the same speciality. Since this date, he supervises the organization of the doctorates studies in class field theory and its applications in Cryptography at Mohammed First University, Oujda, Morocco. Currently, he directs the Laboratory of "Arithmetic, Scientific computation and Applications" at Mohammed First University, Oujda, Morocco. He is interested in research in several fields such the history of mathematics and cryptography in Morocco, the class field theory and its applications to cryptography and the Mathematical didactic.

Mostafa Azizi received the diploma of engineer in automatic and computer industry in 1993 from school Mohammadia of engineers, Rabat, Morocco and he received the PhD in computer science in 2001 from the university Montreal, Canada. He is currently professor at university of Mohamed first, Oujda, Morocco. His main interests include aspect of real time, embedded system, security and communication and management of the computer systems in relation with process industry.

Chandra Bajracharya received her Bachelor's Degree in Electrical Engineering in 2002 from Tribhuvan University, Kathmandu, Nepal and Master's Degree in Power System Engineering in 2007 form Norwegian University of Science and Technology, Norway. She worked as an assistant lecturer in Institute of Engineering, Tribhuvan University from 2002 to 2006. She is currently working toward the PhD at the Department of Electrical and Computer Engineering, Old Dominion University, Norfolk, VA, USA. Her research interests are in the areas of RF communications, optimization in power systems, digital signal and image processing.

Sergio Mauricio Barrientos Velasco received his bachelor's degree in Telecommunications Engineering from Universidad Catolica San Pablo La Paz in November 2007 and his master's degree from ITESM-Monterrey in December 2009. He was with the Centre for Electronics and Telecommunications from January 2008 until December 2009 as a Research and Teaching Assistant. He has experience with wireless ad hoc networks in routing, VoIP and signal processing. His interests include wireless networks, fixed routing protocols, optimization of algorithm and traffic analysis.

Leonardo Betancur was born in Manizales, Colombia in 1980. He has received his BE in Electronic Engineering from National University of Colombia in 2003; He is working towards his PhD degree in Telecommunications Engineering at Pontificia Bolivariana University, where he is currently a Professor in the Department of Computer and Telecommunications Engineering. His research interests include capacity, channel modeling and channel estimation in Ultra Wide Band systems, OFDM and physical issues in wireless networks sensors and body area networks.

Colin Boyd received the PhD in Mathematics from the University of Warwick in 1985. He worked for five years for British Telecom Research Laboratories as a research engineer and was Lecturer at University of Manchester between 1989 and 1995. He joined Queensland University of Technology in 1995 and was promoted to full professor in 2005. He is currently Research Director of QUT's Information Security Institute. His main research interests are in cryptographic protocols. He has published over 140 fully refereed publications including a well known book on Protocols for Authentication and Key Establishment. Google Scholar reports more than 2000 citations of his research.

Alejandro Arturo Castillo Atoche obtained his Masters Degree on Electric Engineering by the Center of Research and Advanced Studies of IPN (Cinvestav Guadalajara), at Guadalajara, Mexico in 2002. He gained an Electronic Engineering on Digital Systems by the Technological Institute of Merida, Mexico in 2000. Currently he is professor at the Autonomous University of Yucatan and Technological Institute of Merida; he is pursuing his PhD at Cinvestav Guadalajara. His research interests are telecommunications devices design, digital microelectronics design and digital signal processing.

Humberto Cervantes De Ávila was born in Zacatecas, Zacatecas (México) in 1965. He received his B. Eng. Degree in Electronics and Communications from University of Zacatecas, México in 1989 and the MS degree in Applied Physics from the Scientific Research and Higher Education Center of Ensenada (CICESE- by its initials in Spanish-) Ensenada, México, in 1992. Since 1990 he has worked as Professor at the Engineer School of University of Baja California, Ensenada, México. He is currently a PhD student in computer engineering at the University of Baja California, Ensenada, México. His research interests include wireless sensor networks in general and specifically wireless body area networks.

Freddy Chan Puc obtained his PhD on Electronic Engineering by the National Center of Research and Technological Development (Cenidet), at Cuernavaca, Mexico in 2008, and his Masters Degree on Electronic Engineering by the same center in 1999. He gained an Electronic Engineering by the Technological Institute of Merida, Mexico in 1997. Currently he is professor at the University of Quintana Roo. His research interests are: power electronics devices, renewable energies, reliability of electronic devices and automation.

Pedro Damián-Reyes is a professor of computer science at the School of Telematics in University of Colima; he leads the Multimedia Laboratory. His research interests include ubiquitous computing, context-aware computing and software development. He holds a BSc from the Instituto Tecnológico de Colima and MSc from the University of Colima and Phd from Student at the Centro de Investigación Científica y de Educación Superior de Ensenada (CICESE) in Baja California, México.

Mohamed Elboukhari received the DESA (diploma of high study) degree in numerical analysis, computer science and treatment of signal in 2005 from the University of Science, Oujda, Morocco. He is currently a PhD student in the University of Oujda in the field of computer science. His research interests include cryptography, quantum cryptography and wireless network security.

Ernest Foo is a senior lecturer in Computer Science at Queensland University for Technology. He received his PhD from QUT in the area of computer security. The main contribution was the development of secure electronic payment protocols. His current research interests include wireless sensor network security protocols but he is also interested in identity management, RFID security and electronic commerce protocols for electronic tendering, contracting and billing.

Natalia Gaviria is an Assistant Professor in the Department of Electronics Engineering at the Antioquia University and director of the Research Group in Applied Telecommunications. Her research interest is oriented towards QoS provision in wireless networks, based on traffic models, His research interests include wireless mesh networks, wireless sensor networks and computational intelligence applied to admission and congestion control in wireless networks.

Jose R. Gallardo received a BSc degree in Physics and Mathematics from the National Polytechnic Institute in Mexico City, a M.Sc. degree in Electrical Engineering from CICESE Research and Graduate Education Center in Ensenada, Mexico, and a DSc degree in Electrical Engineering from the George Washington University, in Washington, DC. From December 2000 to July 2008 Gallardo held a tenured position as a full professor at the Electronics and Telecommunications Department of CICESE Research Center. From August 2007 to July 2008 he was a visiting professor at the University of Western Ontario, in London, Ontario, Canada. He is currently a Research Associate at the Broadband Wireless and Internetworking Research Laboratory of the University of Ottawa. His main areas of interest are medium-access control and routing protocols, call admission control, service differentiation, resource sharing, quality of service, traffic modeling, as well as performance evaluation of communications networks through mathematical modeling and simulation with recent emphasis on wireless local- area, mesh and sensor networks.

Juan Gonzalez Nieto is a Senior Research Fellow at the Information Security Institute, Queensland University of Technology. He obtained his doctorate in the field of cryptographic protocols in 2002. Much of his research has been centred on protocols for authentication and key establishment and on public-key primitives. He has authored over 50 international journal and conference papers. As a member of the Information Security Institute, he has worked on numerous contract research and consultancy projects for the industry and government sectors in a variety of information security areas, including security management, e-commerce applications and communications security.

Antonio Guerrero-Ibáñez is a professor of telecommunications and networks at the School of Telematics in University of Colima, Colima, Mexico; he leads the research group *computer networks* at School of Telematics. His research interests include the areas of intelligent transportation systems for vehicular traffic control, wireless sensor networks and heterogeneous wireless networks with particular emphasis on the services and network management based on quality of service. He holds a BSc in Computer Systems Engineering (1996) and MSc in Telematics area (1999) from University of Colima,

Colima, Mexico, and PhD in Telematics Engineering (2008) from Technical University of Catalonia (UPC), Barcelona, Spain.

Mauricio López-Villaseñor graduated in 1983 at the Metropolitan Autonomous University Unit Iztapalapa (UAM-I) as Electronic engineer with the main subject in Communications. At the end of the 1980's, he studied for the Master degree at the Division for Postgraduate Studies at the Engineering Faculty of the National Mexican Autonomous University. The subjects of his interest are the wireless networks, digital signal processing and basic systems in microcontrollers. He has published two books as co_author: Practice Manual for Electronic laboratory II (Basic Analog Electronics) and Problems of Spectral Analysis, both published by UAM. He also has served in other positions: Coordinator for the electronic engineering degree (UAM-I), Head of the Electronic Engineering, Head of Communication Networks and Interconnectivity. He is currently Head of Networks and Telecommunications of the Department of Electrical Engineering, for both the Division of Basic Sciences and Engineering at the Metropolitan Autonomous University Unit Iztapalapa. He also has taken part in several academic commissions.

Juan Manuel Madrid has a BS in Computer Science and a specialization degree in IT Management from Universidad Icesi (Cali, Colombia). He worked for the Information and Telecommunication Technology Center (ITTC) at the University of Kansas (USA), in research projects involving fiber optics and information retrieval. Currently he's pursuing a MSc degree in Information Security from Nova Southeastern University (USA). He works as an associate professor and chair of the ICT Engineering undergraduate program at Universidad Icesi. His research interests include information security and multimedia networks.

Ricardo Marcelín-Jiménez received his BSc in Electronics Engineering from the Metropolitan Autonomous University (UAM, Mexico City) in 1987, the MSc in Computer Eng. from the National Polytechnic Institute (CINVESTAV-IPN) in 1992 and the PhD degree in Computer Science from the National Autonomous University of Mexico (UNAM) in 2004. He is a full professor with tenure at the Department of Electrical Engineering at the UAM - Iztapalapa. His research interests are in the theory and practice of distributed computing, specially issues related to coordination and fault-tolerance. Marcelín-Jiménez is a SNI member, level I.

Carlos Moreno-Escobar received his BSc in Electronics Engineering from the Metropolitan Autonomous University (UAM, Mexico City) in 2008. Currently, he is in the MSc program on Sciences and Information Technologies, at the UAM. His research interests are localization, energy consumption and routing of wireless sensor networks.

Miguel E. Martínez-Rosas was born in Méxcio City, he received a BS in Electronic Engineering from the National Polytechnic Institute, Mexico, in 1988 and the MS and PhD both from CICESE Research Center, Mexico in 1993 and 2000 respectively. He is a staff member at the Faculty of Engineering in the University of Baja California, Mexico since 1997. From 2001 to 2003 was postdoctoral fellow at the University of Bordeaux and from 2003 to 2004 was postdoctoral fellow in the Physics Department of Trinity College Dublin. Currently he leads the "Communications and Electronic Instrumentation" group, his main research topics are optical sensors, and WSN applied to agriculture.

Danny Alexandro Múnera Ramírez received his BSc in Electronics Engineering from the University of Antioquia, Medellín, Colombia, in 2007 whit a thesis on support vector machines applied to voice recognition. Currently, he is working on his MSc in engineering focusing in Wireless Sensor Networks protocol's architecture whit the support of the investigation group GITA at the Faculty of Engineering in the University of Antioquia. He is currently a researcher in the *Alianza regional en TICs Aplicadas* (ARTICA). His research focuses on Cross-Layer Protocols and new simulation frameworks for Wireless Sensor Networks, telemedicine applications with WSN, operative systems for embedded systems and computational intelligence.

Daniel Elias Muñoz-Jimenez was born on July 6th, 1983 in the city of Veracruz, Veracruz, México. From August 2001 to December 2005, he studied at the Universidad Cristóbal Colón (UCC) of Veracruz City, bachelor degree in Telecommunications Engineering, in April, 2006. In December 2008 he obtained his MSc degree in Telecommunications Management from the Instituto Tecnológico y de Estudios Superiores de Monterey (ITESM). Currently he is with Axtel.

David Muñoz Rodríguez received the BS, MS, and PhD degrees in electrical engineering from the Universidad de Guadalajara, Guadalajara, México, Cinvestav México City, México, and University of Essex, Colchester, England, in 1972, 1976 and 1979, respectively. He has been Chairman of the Communication Department and Electrical Engineering Department at Cinvestav, IPN. In 1992, he joined the Centro de Electrónica y Telecomunicaciones, Instituto Tecnológico y de Estudios Superiores de Monterrey, Monterrey, México, where he is the Director. His research interests include transmission and personal communication systems.

Andres Navarro was born in Medellín, Colombia in 1969. He has obtained the Electronic Engineer degree in 1993 and a Master on Technology Management in 1999, both from Universidad Pontificia Bolivariana in Medellín. He received the Doctor Ingeniero en Telecomunicación degree from Universidad Politecnica de Valencia, Spain in 2003. He is full professor at Universidad Icesi in Cali, Colombia and the leader of i2T Research Group. Professor Navarro has been advisor of the National Science and Technology System in Colombia (Colciencias) and participates in Cost 2100 Action. His research interests are wireless systems, planning and optimization of wireless systems and propagation models in the Andean and rainforest regions.

Juan Ivan Nieto Hipólito received his MSc degree in Electronics and Telecommunications from CICESE Research Center, México in 1994. From August 1994 to February 2001 he was a full-time associate professor at the Autonomous University of Baja California (UABC), México. From February 2001 to July 2005 he was a PhD student at the Computer Architecture Department of the Polytechnic University of Catalonia (UPC) in Spain. He received the Laurea (cum Laude) PhD from UPC in Computer and Networks Technologies in July 2005. Since July 2005 he is full professor at the Autonomous University of Baja California (UABC), México. Currently, he is the Coordinator Program of Master and Doctorate degrees at the Engineering Faculty of the UABC-Ensenada, and he leads the "TELEMATIC" research group. His scientific interests are in wireless networks performance, and mac and routing protocols.

Jaime Silverio Ortegón Aguilar obtained his PhD on Electric Engineering by the Center of Research and Advanced Studies of IPN (Cinvestav Guadalajara), at Guadalajara, Mexico in 2007, and his Masters Degree on Electric Engineering by the same center in 2002. He gained a Licentiate on Computer Science by the Autonomous University of Yucatan (2000). Currently he is professor at the University of Quintana Roo. His research interests are computer vision, digital image processing, and telecommunications devices design.

Alvaro Pachón has a BS in Computer Science from Universidad Icesi (Cali, Colombia), a specialization degree in Computer Networks from Universidad del Valle (Cali, Colombia), and a DEA in Information Technologies from Universidad de Vigo (Spain). He's currently pursuing a PhD in ICT Engineering from Universidad de Vigo. He currently works as professor and chair of the ICT Department of Universidad Icesi. His research interests include ad-hoc networks, optimization, and 4G communication systems.

Mayra Palomino Cardeña obtained her Network Engineering Degree from University of Quintana Roo at Chetumal, Mexico in 2009. Currently she works for Quintana Roo's State Government. Her research interests are telecommunications devices and automation.

Dong Gook Park received his BS in electronics from Kyungpook National University in 1986, an MS in electronics from the Korea Advanced Institute of Science and Technology (KAIST) in 1989, and a PhD in 2001 from Queensland University of Technology (QUT) in Brisbane, Australia. From 1989 to 2004, he was with Korea Telecom (KT), where he worked on security issues in digital cellular networks, WLANs. Working on his PhD degree, he was involved in an international collaborative research project between KT and QUT for future mobile network security. In 2004, he joined the School of Information Technology, SunChon National University, Korea. His research interest includes modeling and analysis of authentication and key establishment protocols.

Víctor Ramos received the BSc degree in Electronics Engineering (1995) from the Metropolitan Autonomous University, Mexico, the M.Sc. degree in Networks and Distributed Systems (2000) and the Ph.D. degree in Computer Science (Networking, 2004), both from the University of Nice-Sophia Antipolis, France. He did his PhD in the Rodeo research team at INRIA Sophia Antipolis, France. From august to december 2004 he was a visiting doctoral member at INRIA/IRISA Rennes, France, with the Armor group (now Dionysos). He serves and has served as reviewer for several international conferences and journals as Infocom, Globecom, PAM, ICN, IEEE ToN, IEEE JSAC, IEEE Transactions on Wireless Communications, IEEE Transactions on Automatic Control and IEEE Transactions on Neural Networks. He is currently the Head of the Electrical Engineering Department of the Metropolitan Autonomous University in Mexico City. His main research interests include voice over IP, performance evaluation of computer protocols and pricing wireless networks.

Danda B. Rawat received his Bachelor's Degree in Computer Engineering in 2002 and the Master's Degree in Information and Communication Engineering in 2005 from Tribhuvan University, Kathmandu, Nepal. He worked as an assistant lecturer in Institute of Engineering, Tribhuvan University from 2002 to 2006 and as a Network Engineer at Center for Information Technology from 2003 to 2004. He also worked as an ICT Officer for Government of Nepal from January 2004 to December 2006. He is currently PhD Candidate with the Department of Electrical and Computer Engineering, Old Dominion University, Norfolk, VA, USA. He has authored and co-authored more than 20 journal papers, book chapters, and conference papers. He has served as technical program committee (TPC) member and committee member for several workshops and conferences. He also served as a reviewer for several IEEE Transactions/Journals and conferences. His research interests are in the areas of wireless communications, wireless cellular/ad-hoc networks, computer networks, cognitive radio networks, wireless security, vehicular communications and intelligent transportation systems. He is the recipient of Outstanding PhD Researcher Award 2009 given by Department of Electrical and Computer Engineering, Old Dominion University, Norfolk, VA, USA.

José Ramón Rodríguez Cruz received his PhD in electrical Engineering from CINVESTAV-IPN Zacatenco in August 2000. Thereafter he joined the Center for Electronics and Telecommunications at Instituto Tecnológico y de Estudios Superiores de Monterrey (ITESM), Campus Monterrey, Mexico. He was a member of SNI for 8 years. He participated in several Government projects involving security and RF systems implementation. His line of research is Joint Source and Channel Coding, RF propagation channel modeling among others.

César Rosado Villanueva obtained his Network Engineering Degree from University of Quintana Roo at Chetumal, Mexico in 2010. Currently he works for Quintana Roo's State Government. His research interests are telecommunications devices and automation.

Sudhir K. Routray works as an Assistant Professor in the department of Electrical Engineering of Eritrea Institute of Technology, Mai Nefhi, Asmara, Eritrea since February, 2009. Eritrea Institute of technology employs international faculty as per the UNDP funded higher education projects. Prior to this he used to tech in different colleges of Biju Pattnaik University of Technology, Rourkela, India for four years. Before that he worked in the UK as a lecturer and also for the RM group. He is in the editorial board of two international journals. He got his degrees from Utkal University (India) and The University of Sheffield (UK). He has authored two books in the areas of popular science.

Miguel Ángel Ruiz-Sánchez graduated in electronic engineering from the Universidad Autónoma Metropolitana, Mexico City. He received his PhD in computer science from the University of Nice Sophia Antipolis, France, in 2003 for his thesis on Optimization of Packet Forwarding in Best-effort Routers. During his PhD studies, he was with the Planete team at INRIA Sophia-Antipolis, France. In 1995 he joined the Electrical Engineering Department of the Universidad Autónoma Metropolitana-Iztapalapa in Mexico City, where he is currently professor. His courses include "Computer Networks", "Computer Architecture and Organization" and "Computer Performance Evaluation". His current research interests include forwarding in IP routers and protocols for Wireless Sensor Networks.

Manuel Ruiz-Sandoval received his BSc in Civil Engineering from the Universidad Autónoma Metropolitana (UAM, Mexico City) in 1993, the M.Sc. in Civil Eng. from the Universidad Nacional Autónoma de México (UNAM) in 1999 and the PhD in Civil Eng. from University of Notre Dame, USA, in 2004. He is a full professor at the Materials Department in UAM – Azcapotzalco. His research focus is in smart sensors.

Oleg Yu Sergiyenko received the BS and MS degrees in Kharkiv National University of Automobiles and Highways, Kharkiv, Ukraine, in 1991, 1993, respectively. He received the PhD degree in Kharkiv National Polytechnic University on specialty "Tools and methods of non-destructive control" in 1997.

In March 1997, he joined the Kharkiv National University of Automobiles and Highways. He has written 47 papers and holds 1 patent of Ukraine. In December 2004 was invited by Engineering Institute of Baja California Autonomous University for researcher position. He is currently Head of Applied Physics Department of Engineering Institute of Baja California Autonomous University, Mexico. His scientific interests are in automated metrology & smart sensors, control systems, robot navigation, 3D coordinates measurement.

César Vargas Rosales received a PhD in electrical engineering from Louisiana State University in 1996. Thereafter, he joined the Center for Electronics and Telecommunications at Instituto Tecnológico y de Estudios Superiores de Monterrey (ITESM), Campus Monterrey, Mexico. He is currently the Telecommunications and Microelectronics program Director at ITESM. Vargas is a member of the Sistema Nacional de Investigadores (SNI) since 1997, and is the coauthor of the book Position Location Techniques and Applications. He has carried out research in the area of personal communication systems on CDMA, smart antennas, adaptive resource sharing, location information processing, and multimedia services. His research interests are personal communications networks, position location, mobility and traffic modeling, intrusion detection, and routing in reconfigurable networks. Vargas is the IEEE Communications Society Monterrey Chapter Head and has been a Senior Member of the IEEE since 2001.

G. Varaprasad was born in Kamalapadu village(near Guntakal, Andhra Pradesh, India) and obtained B.Tech Degree in Computer Science & Engineering from Sri Venkateswara University, Tirupati in 1999, where he was awarded Rotary Merit Scholarship from the Rotary Club, New Delhi. He received M.Tech Degree in Computer Science & Engineering from Visvesvaraya Technological University, Belguam in 2001 and then obtained PhD Degree in Computer Science & Engineering from Anna University, Chennai, in 2004 under the guidance of Dr. R.S.D. Wahidabanu. His PhD work was supported by the University Grants Commission, New Delhi, Government of India. He worked as a Junior Research Fellow at GCE Campus, Anna University for over 3 years. During this period, he worked on the routing algorithms for mesh network and mobile ad hoc networks. In 2004, he joined with Protocol Engineering Technology (PET) Lab, Department of Electrical Communication Engineering, Indian Institute of Science, Bangalore as a Post-doctoral fellow under the guidance of Dr. P. Venkataram. Since 2005, he has been with B.M.S. College of Engineering, Bangalore in the Department of Computer Science and Engineering, where he is now Assistant Professor under M.Tech course.

Mabel Vázquez Biseño, received her MSc degree in Electronics and Telecommunications from CICESE Research Center, México in 2001. In 2008 she received her PhD degree in Computers and Networks from INT and Paris 6 University. She has been a lecturer of several BSc and MSc computers and networks courses at the Autonomous University of Baja California (UABC), México, since 2002. Her research interests include computer networks, mobile computing, m-health and software for Internet.

Javier Vázquez Castillo obtained his Masters Degree on Electric Engineering by the Center of Research and Advanced Studies of IPN (Cinvestav Guadalajara), at Guadalajara, Mexico in 2002. He gained an Electronic Engineering on Digital Systems by the Technological Institute of Merida, Mexico in 2000. Currently he is professor at the University of Quintana Roo and PhD student at Cinvestav Guadalajara. His research interests are telecommunications devices design, digital microelectronics design and digital signal processing.

Luis Armando Villaseñor-Gonzalez is a faculty member at the Department of Electronics and Telecommunications in CICESE and is a member of the Advanced Mobile Wireless Communications research group (CIMA). Villaseñor obtained his PhD in Electrical Enginnering from the University of Ottawa in Canada and his master's degree at CICESE in Mexico. He collaborated as a Network Research Engineer at the Communications Research Centre (CRC) in Ottawa, Canada. At CRC he was involved in a variety of research activities in network technologies for the Government of Canada between 1999 and 2003. He is currently a member of the IEEE. His research interests include medium access control and routing protocols for wireless ad hoc and sensor networks, wireless personal area networks (WPAN), wireless local area networks (WLAN) and wireless wide area networks (WWAN).

Gongjun Yan received a BS in Mechanic Engineering from the Sichuan Institute of Technology in China in 1999 and began his MS in Computer Science at the University of Electronics Science and Technology of China in 2001. In 2005, Yan began work on his PhD at Old Dominion University in Computer Science. He has been working on the issues surrounding Vehicular Ad-Hoc Networks and Wireless Communication. He has published about 30 papers and book chapters, entitled with 3 patents, acted as conference chairs/co-chairs for 6 conferences and reviewed about 50 papers and manuscripts. Recently Gongjun received the Best Student Paper Award at the 9th IEEE Conference on Service Operations, Logistics and Informatics (SOLI) held in Chicago in July 2009. He also received a travel grant from U.S National Research Foundation for the sixth IEEE International Conference on Mobile Ad-hoc and Sensor Systems (IEEE MASS 2009).

Index

C

D

H

I

J

K

L

M

N

O

P

Q

R

S

T

Z